D0171837

EUROPEAN LANGUAGES

A ROUGH GUIDE DICTIONARY PHRASEBOOK

Compiled by

LEXUS

Credits

Compiled by Lexus with Václav Řeřicha, Nadine Mongeard
Morandi, Horst Kopleck, Costas Panayotakis, Michela
Masci, Norma de Oliveira Tait, Fernando León Solís
Lexus Series Editors: Sally Davies, Peter Terrell
Rough Guides Phrase Book Editor: Jonathan Buckley
Rough Guides Series Editor: Mark Ellingham

This first edition published in 1999 by Rough Guides Ltd, 62–70
Shorts Gardens, London WC2H 9AB.
Reprinted April 2000.

Distributed by the Penguin Group.

Penguin Books Ltd, 27 Wrights Lane, London W8 5TZ
Penguin Books USA Inc., 375 Hudson Street, New York 10014, USA
Penguin Books Australia Ltd, 487 Maroondah Highway,
PO Box 257, Ringwood, Victoria 3134, Australia
Penguin Books Canada Ltd, Alcorn Avenue,
Toronto, Ontario, Canada M4V 1E4
Penguin Books (NZ) Ltd, 182–190 Wairau Road,
Auckland 10, New Zealand

Typeset in Bembo and Helvetica to an original design by Henry Iles.
Printed in Spain by Graphy Cems.

No part of this book may be reproduced in any form without permission from
the publisher except for the quotation of brief passages in reviews.

© Lexus Ltd 1999
512pp.

British Library Cataloguing in Publication Data
A catalogue for this book is available from the British Library.

ISBN 1-85828-466-X

Help us get it right

Lexus and Rough Guides have made great efforts to be accurate and
informative in this Rough Guide European phrasebook. However, if you
feel we have overlooked a useful word or phrase, or have any other
comments to make about the book, please let us know. All contributors
will be acknowledged and the best letters will be rewarded with a free
Rough Guide phrasebook of your choice. Please write to 'European
Phrasebook Update', at either Shorts Gardens (London) or Hudson Street
(New York) – for full addresses see above. Alternatively you can email us at
mail@roughguides.co.uk

Online information about Rough Guides can be found at our Web site
www.roughguides.com

CONTENTS

Introduction   5
Abbreviations & Notes   6

Czech

Pronunciation 8; language notes 9; days,
months, time, numbers 10-12
English-Czech   15
Czech-English   57
food   71
drink   77

French

Pronunciation 80; language notes 81; days,
months, time, numbers 82-84
English-French   87
French-English   129
food   143
drink   149

German

Pronunciation 152; language notes 153; days,
months, time, numbers 154-156
English-German   159
German-English   203
food   217
drink   223

Greek

Pronunciation 226; language notes 227; days, months, time, numbers 228-230

English-Greek	233
Greek alphabet	268
Greek-English	269
food	285
drink	293

Italian

Pronunciation 296; language notes 297; days, months, time, numbers 298-300

English-Italian	303
Italian-English	345
food	359
drink	365

Portuguese

Pronunciation 368; language notes 368-369; days, months, time, numbers 370-372

English-Portuguese	375
Portuguese-English	419
food	433
drink	439

Spanish

Pronunciation 442; language notes 442-443; days, months, time, numbers 444-446

English-Spanish	449
Spanish-English	491
food	505
drink	511

Introduction

The Rough Guide European phrasebook is a highly practical basic introduction to seven contemporary European languages: **Czech, French, German, Greek, Italian, Portuguese** and **Spanish**. Laid out in clear A-Z style, each section uses key-word referencing to lead you straight to the words and phrases you want – so if you need to book a room, just look up 'room'. The Rough Guide gets straight to the point in every situation, in bars and shops, on trains and buses, and in hotels and banks.

The main part of each language section in the Rough Guide is a double dictionary: English into each of the seven languages then each of the seven languages into English. Before that, there's a page explaining the pronunciation system we've used, then a section giving some very basic features of each language as well as other essentials like numbers, days, months and telling the time.

The section that goes from English into each of the foreign languages gives easy-to-use transliterations of the foreign words wherever pronunciation might be a problem, and to get you involved quickly in two-way communication, the Rough Guide includes dialogues featuring typical responses on key topics – such as finding a room and asking directions.

In the Czech/French/German/Greek/Italian/Portuguese/Spanish-English dictionaries, we've given some basic words and phrases you're likely to hear as well as signs, labels, instructions and other words you might come across in print or in public places.

Finally each section in the Rough Guide rounds off with a Menu Reader, giving a run-down of food and drink terms that you'll find indispensable whether you're eating out, stopping for a quick drink, or browsing through a local food market.

Have a good trip!

Abbreviations

adj	adjective
f	feminine
fam	familiar usage
fpl	feminine plural
m	masculine
mpl	masculine plural
n	neuter
npl	neuter plural
pl	plural
pol	polite usage
sing	singular
US	American English

Notes

When two forms of a verb are given in phrases such as:

can you ...? est-ce que tu peux/vous pouvez ...?
would you like a drink? vuoi/vuole qualcosa da bere?

the first is the familiar form and the second the polite form (see the entry for **you**).

When two translations are given as in the following examples:

doctor o médico, a médica
lawyer o/i thikigoros
friend der Freund/die Freundin
the white one el blanco, la blanca

the first is masculine and the second is feminine.

Language Notes

There are no articles in Czech, no words for 'a' or 'the'. So, for example, **okno** can mean 'window', 'a window' or 'the window', depending on context.

Czech has a complex system of seven different case endings, which means that some words given in this phrasebook may often occur in a modified form. For example:

kostel	**proti kostelu**
church	opposite the church
oběd	**po obědě**
lunch	after lunch

Czech words for 'I', 'you', 'he' etc are often omitted as subjects unless special emphasis is necessary. For example:

nevím	**jsem unavený**
I don't know	I'm tired
já nevím	**já jsem unavený**
I don't know	I am tired
(but she might)	(even if you're not)

Here is a useful verb – 'to be':

jsem [sem] I am **jste** [steh] you are (plural or polite form)
jsi [si] you are (familiar form) **jsme** [smeh] we are
je [yeh] he/she/it is **jsou** [soh] they are

The familiar form is used to speak to people you are on friendly terms with.

Most Czech verbs have two forms, shown in this book as, for example:

buy kupovat [koopovut]/koupit [kohpit]

In general the first of these two forms (**kupovat**) is used to talk about the present as well as about continuing or repeated activity in the past or future. The second form (**koupit**) is used to talk about completed events in the past.

Days

Monday pondělí [pondyelee]
Tuesday úterý [00teree]
Wednesday středa [strJeda]
Thursday čtvrtek [chutvurtek]
Friday pátek [pahtek]
Saturday sobota
Sunday neděle [nedyeleh]

Months

January leden
February únor [00nor]
March březen [brJezen]
April duben [dooben]
May květen [kvyeten]
June červen [cherven]
July červenec [chervenets]
August srpen [surpen]
September září [zarJee]
October říjen [rJee-yen]
November listopad [listoput]
December prosinec [prosinets]

Time

what time is it? kolik je
hodin? [kolik yeh ho-dyin]
one o'clock jedna hodina
[yedna ho-dyina]
two/three/four o'clock
dvě/tři/čtyri hodiny
[dvyeh/trJi/chutirJi ho-dyini]
five o'clock[1] pět hodin [pyet
ho-dyin]
it's one o'clock je jedna

hodina [yeh yedna ho-dyina]
it's two/three/four o'clock jsou
dvě/tři/čtyři hodiny [soh
dvyeh/trJi/chutirJi ho-dyini]
it's five o'clock[1] je pět hodin
[yeh pyet ho-dyin]
five past one jedna hodina a
pět minut [yedna ho-dyina a
pyet minoot]
ten past two dvě hodiny a
deset minut [dvyeh ho-dyini a
deset minoot]
quarter past one[2] čtvrt na
dvě [chutvurt na dv-yeh]
quarter past two čtvrt na tři
[chutvurt na trJi]
half past one půl druhé [pool
drooheh]
half past ten půl jedenácté
[pool yedenahtsteh]
twenty to ten za dvacet
minut deset [za dvutset minoot
deset]
quarter to two tři čtvrtě na
dvě [trJi chutvurtyeh na dvyeh]
quarter to ten tři čtvrtě na
deset [trJi chutvurtyeh na deset]
at one o'clock v jednu
hodinu [vyednoo ho-dyinoo]
at two/three/four o'clock ve
dvě/tři/čtyři hodiny [veh
dvyeh/trJi/chutirJi ho-dyini]
at five o'clock1 v pět hodin
[fpyet ho-dyin]
at half past four v půl páté
[fpool pahteh]
14.00 čtrnáct hodin
[chuturnahtst ho-dyin]

17.30 sedmnáct třicet [sedumnahtst trJitset]
noon poledne [poledneh]
midnight půlnoc [poolnots]

a.m. (12 p.m. to 5 a.m.) v noci [vnotsi]
a.m. (5 to 9 a.m.) ráno [rahno]
a.m. (9 to 12 a.m.) dopoledne [dopoledneh]
p.m. (12 to 5 p.m.) odpoledne [otpoledneh]
p.m. (5 to 10 p.m.) večer [vetcher]
p.m. (10 to 12p.m.) v noci [vnotsi]

hour hodina [ho-dyina]
minute minuta [minoota]
second sekunda [sekonda]
quarter of an hour čtvrt hodiny [chutvurt ho-dyini]
half an hour půl hodiny [pool ho-dyini]
three quarters of an hour tři čtvrtě hodiny [trJi chutvurtyeh ho-dyini]

[1] for numbers from five to twelve use **hodin**

[2] when expressing time past the hour, always refer to the next hour

Numbers

0	nula [noola]
1	jeden/jedna/jedno [yeden/yedna/yedno]
2	dva/dvě [dva/dvyeh]
3	tři [trJi]
4	čtyři [chutirJi]
5	pět [pyet]
6	šest [shest]
7	sedm [sedum]
8	osm [osum]
9	devět [devyet]
10	deset [deset]
11	jedenáct [yedenahtst]
12	dvanáct [dvunahtst]
13	třináct [trJinahtst]
14	čtrnáct [chuturnahtst]
15	patnáct [putnahtst]
16	šestnáct [shestnahtst]
17	sedmnáct [sedumnahtst]
18	osmnáct [osumnahtst]
19	devatenáct [devutenahtst]
20	dvacet [dvutset]
21	dvacet jeden/jedna/jedno [dvutset yeden/yedna/yedno]
22	dvacet dva/dvě [dvutset dva/dvyeh]
23	dvacet tři [dvutset trJi]
30	třicet [trJitset]
31	třicet jeden/jedna/jedno [trJitset yeden/yedna/yedno]
32	třicet dva/dvě [trJitset dva/dvyeh]
33	třicet tři [trJitset trJi]
40	čtyřicet [chutirJitset]

50	padesát [pudesaht]
60	šedesát [shedesaht]
70	sedmdesát [sedumdesaht]
80	osmdesát [osumdesaht]
90	devadesát [devudesaht]
100	sto [sto]
101	sto jeden/jedna/jedno [sto yeden/yedna/yedno]
102	sto dva/dvě [sto dva/dvyeh]
200	dvě stě [dvyeh styeh]
300	tři sta [trJi sta]
400	čtyři sta [chutirJi stah]
500	pět set [pyet set]
600	šest set [shest set]
700	sedm set [sedum set]
800	osm set [osum set]
900	devět set [devyet set]
1,000	tisíc [tyiseets]
2,000	dva tisíce [dva tyiseetseh]
3,000	tři tisíce [trJi tyiseetseh]
4,000	čtyři tisíce [chutirJi tyiseetseh]
5,000*	pět tisíc [pyet tyiseets]
1,000,000	milión [mili-yawn]

* for 5,000 or more use **tisíc**

English

→

Czech

A

a, an no words in Czech
about (roughly) asi [usi]
 a film about Moravia film o
 Moravě
above nad [nut]
abroad v zahraničí
 [zuhrunyitchee]
accept přijmout [prJeemoht]
accident nehoda
across: across the road přes
 cestu [prJes tsestoo]
adapter (for voltage) adaptér
 [udupter]
 (plug) rozdvojka [rozdvoyka]
address adresa [udresa]
adult (man/woman) dospělý
 [dos-pyelee]/dospělá
advance: in advance předem
 [prJedem]
after po
afternoon odpoledne
 [otpoledneh]
aftersun cream krém po
 opalování [opalavah-nyee]
afterwards potom
again znovu [znovoo]
against proti [protyi]
ago: a week ago před týdnem
 [prJet]
Aids Aids
air vzduch [vzdooH]
 by air letadlem [letudlem]
air-conditioning klimatizace
 [klimutizatseh]
airmail: by airmail letecky
 [letetski]

airport letiště [letyish-tyeh]
airport bus autobus na letiště
 [owtoboos]
alcohol alkohol [ulkohol]
all všichni [fshiHnyi]
 that's all, thanks to je
 všechno, děkuji [yeh – dyekoo-
 yi]
allergic alergický [alergitskee]
all right dobře [dobrJeh]
 I'm all right jsem v pořádku
 [sem fporJahtkoo]
 are you all right? (fam) jsi v
 pořádku? [si]
 (pol) jste v pořádku? [steh]
almost skoro
alone sám m [sahm], sama f
 [suma]
already už [oosh]
also také [tukeh]
altogether celkem [tselkem]
always vždy [vuJdi]
ambulance sanitka [sunitka]
America Amerika [umerika]
American americký
 [umeritskee]
and a
angry rozzlobený [rozlobenee]
animal zvíře [zveerJeh]
annoying nepříjemný [neprJee-
 yemnee]
another (different) jiný [yinee]
 (one more) ještě jeden [yeshtyeh
 yeden]
 another beer, please ještě
 jedno pivo [yedno]
antiseptic antiseptikum [unti–]
any: I don't have any nemám
 [nemahm]

apartment byt [bit]
apple jablko [yabluko]
apricot meruňka [meroon^{yeh}ka]
arm paže [puJeh]
arrival příjezd [p^rJee-yest]
arrive přijet [prJi-yet]
art gallery galerie [guleri-eh]
as: as big as velký jako [velkee yuko]
ashtray popelník [popel-nyeek]
ask žádat [Jahdut]/požádat
  I didn't ask for this (said by man/woman) to jsem nechtěl/nechtěla [sem neHutyel]
aspirin aspirin [uspirin]
at: at the hotel v hotelu
  at the station na nádraží
  at six o'clock v šest hodin
  at Jan's u Jana [oo yuna]
aunt teta
Australia Austrálie [owstrahli-eh]
Australian australský [owstrulskee]
autumn podzim
away: go away! jděte pryč! [yudyeteh pritch]
  is it far away? je to daleko? [yeh to duleko]
awful hrozný [hroznee]

B

baby děťátko [dyetyahtko]
back (of body) záda [zahda]
  (back part) zadní část [zudnyee chahst]
  at the back vzadu [vzudoo]
  I'll be back soon brzy budu zpátky [burzi boodoo spahtki]
bad špatný [shputnee]
badly špatně [shput-nyeh]
bag taška [tushka]
  (handbag) kabelka [kubelka]
baggage zavazadla [zuvuzudla]
baggage checkroom úschovna zavazadel [00sHovna zuvuzudel]
bakery pekárna
balcony balkón [bulkawn]
ball (large) balón [balawn]
  (small) míček [meetchek]
banana banán [banahn]
band (musical) skupina [skoopina]
bandage obvaz [obvus]
Bandaids® náplasti [nahplustyi]
bank (money) banka [bunka]
bar bar
barber's holičství [holitchstvee]
basket koš [kosh]
  (in shop) košík [kosheek]
bath koupel [kohpel]
bathroom koupelna [kohpelna]
battery baterie [bateri-eh]
be být [beet]
beans fazole [fuzoleh]
beautiful krásný [krahsnee]
because protože [protoJeh]
  because of ... kvůli ... [kv00li]
bed postel
  I'm going to bed now jdu spát [doo spaht]
bed and breakfast nocleh se

snídaní [notsleн seh snyeedun-yee]

bedroom ložnice [loJ-nyitseh]

beef hovězí [hovyezee]

beer pivo

before před [prJet]

begin: when does it begin?
 kdy to začíná? [gudi to zutcheenah]

behind za

below pod [pot]

belt pásek [pahsek]

beside: beside the ... vedle... [vedleh]

best nejlepší [naylepshee]

better lepší

between mezi

beyond za

bicycle kolo

big velký [velkee]

bikini bikiny [bikini]

bill účet [ootchet]
 (US) bankovka [bunkovka]

could I have the bill, please?
 mohu dostat účet, prosím?
 [mohoo dostut]

bin popelnice [popel-nyitseh]

bird pták [ptahk]

birthday narozeniny [narozenyini]

happy birthday! všechno
 nejlepší k narozeninám!
 [fsheнno naylepshee]

biscuit sušenka [sooshenka]

bit: a little bit trochu [troнoo]
 a big bit velký kus [velkee koos]
 a bit of ... kousek ... [kohsek]
 a bit expensive trochu drahé

[draheh]

bite (noun: by insect) štípnutí [shtyeepnoo-tee]

black černý [chernee]

blanket deka

blind slepý [slepee]

blinds okenice [okenitseh]

block of flats činžovní dům [chinJov-nyee doom]

blond (adj) světlovlasý [svyetlovlusee]

blood krev [kref]

blouse halenka [hulenka]

blow-dry foukaná [fohkunah]

blue modrý [modree]

boat (small) člun [chloon]
 (for passengers) loď [lod^{yeh}]

body tělo [tyelo]

boiler bojler [boyler]

bone kost

book (noun) kniha [kunyiha]
 (verb) rezervovat [reservovut]

bookshop, bookstore
 knihkupectví [kuniн-koopets-tvee]

boot (footwear) bota

border (of country) hranice [hrunyitseh]

borrow půjčit si [poo-ichit]

both oba

bottle láhev [lah-hef]

bottle-opener otvírák [otveerahk]

bottom (of person) zadek [zudek]

at the bottom of ... (road etc)
 na konci ... [kontsi]
 (hill) na úpatí ... [oopatyee]

box krabice [krubitseh]

boy chlapec [Hlupets]
boyfriend přítel [prJeetel]
bra podprsenka [potprsenka]
bracelet náramek [narumek]
brake brzda [burzda]
brandy koňak [konyuk]
bread chléb [Hlep]
break (something) rozbít
[rozbeet]
(arm etc) zlomit
breakfast snídaně
[snyeedunyeh]
breast prs [purs]
bridge (over river) most [mosst]
bring přinést [prJinest]
I'll bring it back later přinesu
to zpět později [prJinesoo to
spyet pozdyay-yi]
Britain Velká Británie [velkah
britahni-eh]
British britský [britskee]
brochure brožura [broJoora]
broken rozbitý [rozbitee]
(bone) zlomený [zlomenee]
brother bratr [brutr]
brown hnědý [hnyedee]
brush (for hair, cleaning) kartáč
[kurtahtch]
building budova [boodova]
bulb (light bulb) žárovka
[Jarofka]
bunk lůžko [lOOshko]
burn (noun) spálenina
[spahlenyina]
burst: a burst pipe prasklá
trubka [prusklah troopka]
bus autobus [owtoboos]
what number bus is it to ...?
který autobus jede do ...?

[kuteree – yedeh]

dialogue

does this bus go to ...?
jede tento autobus do ...?
no, you need a number ...
ne, musíte jet autobusem
číslo ... [neh mooseeteh yet –
cheeslo]

bus station autobusové
nádraží [owtoboosoveh
nahdraJee]
bus stop autobusová zastávka
[–ovah zustahfka]
busy (restaurant etc) rušný
[rooshnee]
but ale [aleh]
butcher's řeznictví [rJez-nyits-
tvee]
butter máslo [mahslo]
button knoflík [kunofleek]
buy kupovat [koopovut]/koupit
[kohpit]
by: by bus/car
autobusem/autem
by the window u okna [oo]
by Thursday do čtvrtka

C

cabbage zelí [zelee]
cable car lanovka [lunofka]
café kavárna [kuvarna]
cake dort
call říkat [rJeekut]/říct [rJeetst]
(phone) telefonovat

[telefonovut]
what's it called? jak se tomu říká? [yuk seh tomoo rJeekah]
he/she is called ... jmenuje se ... [yumenoo-yeh seh]
camera fotoaparát [foto-upuraht]
camp kempovat [kempovut]
camping gas butan [bootun]
campsite tábořiště [tahborJish-tyeh]
(more luxurious) autokempink [owto–]
can konzerva
can: can you ...? můžeš ...? [moozhesh]
can I have ...? mohu dostat ...? [mohoo dostut]
I can't ... nemohu ...
Canada Kanada [kunuda]
Canadian kanadský [kunutskee]
cancel rušit [rooshit]/zrušit
candies bonbóny [bonbawni]
candle svíčka [sveetchka]
can-opener otvírák konzerv [otveerahk konzerf]
car auto [owto]
card (birthday etc) blahopřání [bluhoprJah-nyee]
(business) navštívenka [nufsh-tyeevenka]
cardphone telefon na kartu [kurtoo]
car hire pronájem automobilů [pronï-em owtomobiloo]
car park parkoviště [purkovish-tyeh]
carpet koberec [koberets]

carrot mrkev [murkef]
carry nést
cash hotové peníze [hotoveh penyeezeh]
cash desk pokladna [pokludna]
cash dispenser bankovní automat [bunkov-nyee owtomut]
castle zámek [zahmek]
cat kočka [kotchka]
cathedral katedrála [kutedrahla]
cave jeskyně [yeski-nyeh]
ceiling strop
cellar (for wine) vinný sklep [vinee]
centimetre centimetr [tsentimetr]
centre střed [strJet]
certainly určitě [oortchi-tyeh]
chair židle [Jidleh]
champagne šampaňské [shumpan^yeh'skeh]
change (noun: money) drobné [drobneh]
(verb: money) proměnit [pro-mnyenyit]
(trains) přesedat [prJesedat]
(clothes) převlékat se [prJevlekut seh]/převléknout se [prJevleknoht]

dialogue

do we have to change (trains)? musíme přesedat? [mooseemeh prJesedut]
yes, change at Brno/no, it's a direct train ano, přesedáte v Brně/ne, je to přímý spoj [uno

prJesedahteh v brunyeh/neh yeh
to prJeemee spoy]

cheap levný [levnee]
check (US: noun) šek [shek]
(US: bill) účet [ootcnet]
(verb) kontrolovat
[kontrolovut]/zkontrolovat
checkbook šeková knížka
[shekovah kunyeeJka]
cheers! (toast) na zdraví!
[zdruvee]
cheese sýr [seer]
chemist's lékárna
cheque šek [shek]
cheque card bankovní
průkaz majitele konta
[bunkov-nyee prookas muh-yiteleh]
chest (body) hruď [hroot^yeh]
chewing gum žvýkačka
[Jveekutchka]
chicken (meat) kuřecí maso
[koorJetsee muso]
child dítě [dyeetyeh]
chips hranolky [hrunolki]
(US) lupínky [loopeenki]
chocolate čokoláda
[chokolahda]
a hot chocolate (horká)
čokoláda
Christmas Vánoce [vahnotseh]
Christmas Eve Štědrý večer
[shtyedree vetcher]
merry Christmas! Veselé
Vánoce! [veseleh]
church kostel
cider kvašený jablečný mošt
[kvushenee yubletchnee mosht]
cigar doutník [doht-nyeek]

cigarette cigareta [tsigureta]
cinema kino
city město [mnyesto]
city centre střed města [strJet
mnyesta]
clean (adj) čistý [chistee]
can you clean these for me?
můžete mi to vyčistit?
[mooJeteh – vitchis-tyit]
clever chytrý [Hitree]
climbing horolezectví
[horolezets-tvee]
clock hodiny [ho-dyini]
close (verb) zavírat
[zuveerut]/zavřít [zuvurJeet]
closed zavřeno [zavurJeno]
clothes šaty [shuti]
clothes peg kolík na prádlo
[koleek]
cloudy zamračeno
[zamrutcheno]
coach (bus) autobus [owtoboos]
(on train) vagón [vagawn]
coach station autobusové
nádraží [owtoboosoveh
nahdruJee]
coach trip výlet autobusem
[veelet]
coat (long coat) kabát [kubaht]
(jacket) bunda [boonda]
coathanger ramínko na šaty
[rumeenko na shuti]
code (when dialling) směrové
číslo [smnyeroveh cheeslo]
coffee káva [kahva]
coin mince [mintseh]
Coke® kokakola
cold studený [stoodenee]
I'm cold je mi zima [yeh]

I have a cold jsem nachlazený [sem nuh-Hluzenee]

collar límec [leemets]

collect call hovor na účet volaného [00tchet]

colour barva [burva]

comb (noun) hřeben [hrɹeben]

come přijít [prɹi-yeet]

come back vrátit se [vrahtit seh]

come in vstoupit [fstohpit]

comfortable pohodlný [pohodlnee]

complaint stížnost [styeeɹnost]

completely úplně [00pul-nyeh]

computer počítač [potcheetutch]

concert koncert [kontsert]

conditioner (for hair) vlasový regenerátor [vlusovee regenerahtor]

condom prezervativ [–vutif], kondom

congratulations! blahopřeji! [bluhoprɹay-i]

connection spoj [spoy]

constipation zácpa [zahtspa]

consulate konzulát [konzoolaht]

contact kontaktovat [kontuktovut]

contact lenses kontaktní čočky [kontaktnyee chotchki]

cooker vařič [vurɹitch]

cookie sušenka [sooshenka]

corkscrew vývrtka [veevurtka]

correct (right) správný [sprahvnee]

cost stát [staht]

cotton bavlna [buvulna]

cotton wool vata [vuta]

couchette lehátkový vůz [lehahtkovee v00s]

cough (noun) kašel [kushel]

cough medicine lék na kašel

could: could you ...? (to man/woman) mohl/mohla byste ...? [mohul/mo-hla bisteh]

could I have ...? (said by man/woman) mohl/mohla bych dostat ...? [biH dostut]

I couldn't ... (said by man/woman) nemohl/nemohla bych ...

country (nation) země [zemnyeh]
(countryside) venkov [venkof]

couple (two people) pár, dvojice [dvo-yitseh]

a couple of ... několik ... [nyekolik]

courier kurýr [kooreer]

course (main course etc) chod [Hot]

of course samozřejmě [sumozrɹay-mnyeh]

cousin (male/female) bratranec [brutrunets]/sestřenice [sestrɹenyitseh]

crazy bláznivý [blahz-nyivee]

cream (on milk, in cake) smetana [smetuna]
(lotion) krém

credit card platební karta [plutebnyee]

dialogue

can I pay by credit card?
mohu platit platební
kartou? [mohoo plutyit
plutebnyee kartoh]
**which card do you want to
use?** kterou kartou
chcete platit? [kuteroh kartoh
Hutseteh]
yes, sir ano, pane [uno
puneh]
what's the number? jaké
máte číslo? [yakeh mahteh
cheeslo]
and the expiry date? do
kdy platí? [dog-di plutyee]

crisps lupínky [loopeenki]
crossroads křižovatka
[krJiJovutka]
crowded plný lidí [pulnee
lidyee]
cry plakat [plukut]
crystal křišťálové sklo [krJisht-
tyahloveh]
cup šálek [shahlek]
cupboard skříň s policemi
[skrJeen^yeh s politsemi]
curtains (at window) záclona
[zahtslona]
cushion polštář [polshtarJ]
Customs clo [tslo]
cyclist (man/woman) cyklista/
cyklistka
Czech (adj) český [cheskee]
(language) čeština [chesh-tyina]
(man) Čech [cheH]
(woman) Češka [cheshka]

the Czechs Češi [cheshi]
Czech Republic Česká
republika [cheskah]

D

dad tatínek [tutyeenek]
damage (verb) poškodit
[poshkodyit]
damn! hrome! [hromeh]
damp vlhký [vulH-kee]
dance (noun) tanec [tunets]
(verb) tancovat [tuntsovat]
dangerous nebezpečný
[nebespetchnee]
dark (adj: colour) tmavý [tmuvee]
(hair) tmavovlasý [tmuvovlasee]
date: what's the date today?
kolikátého je dnes?
[kolikahteho yeh]
daughter dcera [dutsera]
day den
the day after den poté [poteh]
the day before den předtím
[prJet-tyeem]
dead mrtvý [murtvee]
deaf hluchý [hlooHee]
decaffeinated coffee bez
kofeinu [bes kofaynoo]
decide rozhodnout se
[rozhodnoht seh]
deckchair lodní lehátko [lod-
nyee lehahtko]
deep hluboký [hloobokee]
definitely určitě [oorchityeh]
delay (noun) zpoždění [spoJ-
dyenyee]
delicatessen lahůdky [lah-

hootki]

delicious lahodný [lahodnee]

dentist (man/woman) zubní lékař [zoob-nyee lekurJ]/zubní lékařka

deodorant deodorant [deh-odorunt]

department store obchodní dům [opHod-nyee doom]

departure odjezd [od-yest]

depend: it depends to záleží [zahleJee]

dessert dezert

destination cíl [tseel]

develop rozvinout [rozvinoht]

dialling code směrové číslo [smneyroveh cheeslo]

diarrhoea průjem [proo-yem]

diesel (fuel) motorová nafta [–ovah nufta]

difference rozdíl [rozdyeel]

different jiný [yinee]

difficult obtížný [op-tyeeJnee]

dining room jídelna [yeedelna]

dinner večeře [vetcherJeh]

direct (adj) přímý [prJeemee]

direction směr [smnyer]

directory enquiries telefonní informace [telefon-nyee informatseh]

dirty špinavý [shpinavee]

disco diskotéka

disgusting nechutný [neHootnee]

district obvod [obvot]

divorced rozvedený [rozvedenee]

do dělat [dyelut]/udělat [oodyelut]

what shall we do? co budeme dělat? [tso boodemeh]

doctor (man/woman) doktor/doktorka

dog pes

don't: don't do that! nedělejte to! [neh-dyelayteh]

door dveře [dverJeh]

double dvojitý [dvo-yitee]

double bed manželská postel [munJelskah]

double room pokoj pro dvě osoby [pokoy pro dvyeh osobi]

down dolů [doloo]

down here tady [tudi]

downstairs v přízemí [fprJeezemee]

dozen tucet [tootset]

draught beer točené pivo [totcheneh]

dress (noun) šaty [shuti]

drink (noun) nápoj [nahpoy] (verb) pít [peet]/napít

what would you like to drink? co si dáte? [tso si dahteh]

drinking water pitná voda [pitnah]

drive řídit [rJeedyit]

driver (man/woman) řidič [rJidyitch]/řidička

driving licence řidičský průkaz [rJiditch-skee prookus]

drug lék

drugs (narcotics) droga

drunk (adj) opilý [opilee]

dry suchý [sooHee]

dry-cleaner chemická čistírna [Hemitskah chis-tyeerna]

during během [byehem]

dustbin popelnice [popel-nyitseh]

duvet peřina [perJina]

E

each každý [kuJdee]

ear ucho [oo-нo]

early časně [chusnyeh]

earring náušnice [nah-oosh-nyitseh]

east východ [veeнod]

Easter Velikonoce [velikonotseh]

easy snadrý [snudnee]

eat jíst [yeest]

economy class turistickou třídou [tooreestitskoh trJeedoh]

egg vejce [vaytseh]

either: either ... or ... buď ... nebo ... [boot^yeh]

elbow loket

electric elektrický [elektritskee]

electricity elektřina [elektrJina]

elevator výtah [veetuн]

else: something else něco jiného [nyetso yineho]

somewhere else někde jinde [nyegdeh yindeh]

embassy ambasáda [umbusahda], velvyslanectví [velvislunetstvee]

emergency naléhavý případ [nulehavee prJeepat]

empty prázdný [prahzdnee]

end (noun) konec [konets]

(verb) končit/ukončit [ookontchit]

at the end of the street na konci ulice [nah kontsi oolitseh]

engaged (toilet, telephone) obsazeno [opsuzeno]

(to be married) zasnoubený [zusnohbenee]

England Anglie [ungli-eh]

English anglický [unglitskee]

enjoy: to enjoy oneself bavit se [buvit seh]

enormous obrovský [obrofskee]

enough dost

it's not big enough není to dost velké [nenyee – velkeh]

that's enough to stačí [to stutchee]

entrance vchod [fhot]

envelope obálka [obahlka]

equipment vybavení [vibuvenyee]

especially zejména [zaymena]

euro Euro [ehooroh]

Eurocheque eurošek [eh-oorooshek]

Europe Evropa

evening večer [vetcher]

good evening dobrý večer [dobree]

this evening dnes večer

eventually nakonec [nakonets]

ever vždy [vuJdi]

every každý [kuJdee]

everyone každý člověk [chlo-vyek]

everything všechno [fsheHno]

everywhere všude [fshoodeh]

exactly! přesně! [prJes-nyeh]

excellent skvělý [skvyelee]

excellent! skvělé! [skvyeleh]

except kromě [kromnyeh]
exchange rate devizový kurz
[devizovee koors]
exciting vzrušující [vuzrooshoo-
yeetsee]
excuse me (to get past) s
dovolením [sdovoleh-nyeem]
(to get attention/say sorry)
promiňte! [promin^{yeh}teh]
exhibition výstava [veestuva]
exit východ [veeHot]
expensive drahý [drahee]
eye oko
eyeglasses brýle [breeleh]

F

face tvář [tvarj]
faint (verb) omdlívat
[omdleevut]/omdlít
fair (funfair) pouť [poht^{yeh}]
(trade) veletrh [veleturH]
(adj) spravedlivý [spruvedlivee]
fairly docela [dotsela]
fall upadnout [oopudnoht]
(US: autumn) podzim
family rodina [ro-dyina]
fantastic fantastický
[fantastitskee]
far daleko [duleko]

dialogue

is it far from here? je to
odsud daleko? [yeh to
otsoot]
no, not very far ne, není to
daleko [neh nenyee]

it's about 20 kilometres je
to asi 20 kilometrů [yeh to
usi dvutset kilometroo]

farm statek [stutek]
fashionable módní [mawdnyee]
fast rychlý [riHlee]
fat (person) tlustý [tloostee]
father otec [otets]
faucet kohoutek [kohohtek]
fault: sorry, it was my fault
promiňte, to byla moje
chyba [promin^{yeh}teh to bila mo-yeh
Hiba]
favourite oblíbený [obleebenee]
fax (noun) fax [fuks]
feel cítit [tsee-tyit]
I feel unwell necítím se
dobře [netsee-tyeem]
felt-tip (pen) fix
ferry trajekt [tra-yekt]
(small) přívoz [prjeevos]
fetch sehnat [sehunut]
I'll fetch him seženu ho
[seJenoo]
few: a few několik [nyekolik]
a few days několik dní
few tourists málo turistů
[mahlo]
fiancé snoubenec [snohbenets]
fiancée snoubenka [snohbenka]
field pole [poleh]
fight (noun) rvačka [rvutchka]
filling (in tooth) plomba
film film
find najít [na-yeet]
find out zjistit [zyis-tyit]
fine (weather) pěkný [pyeknee]
(punishment) pokuta [pokoota]

finger prst [purst]
finish končit [kontchit]
fire hoří [horJee]
fire brigade požární sbor
first první [purvnyee]
  at first napřed [nuprJet]
first aid kit lékarnička [lekar-
  nyitchka]
first class (travel etc) první
  třídou [purvnyee trJeedoh]
first floor první poschodí
  [posHodyee]
  (US) přízemí [prJeezemee]
first name jméno [yumeno]
fish (noun) ryba [riba]
fit: it doesn't fit me to mně
  nesedí [mnyeh nesedyee]
fix (repair) spravit [spruvit]
  (arrange) zařídit [zarJee-dyit]
fizzy šumivý [shoomivee]
flat (noun: apartment) byt [bit]
  (adj) plochý [ploHee]
  I've got a flat tyre mám
  prázdnou pneumatiku
  [mahm prahzdnoh pneh-oomutikoo]
flavour příchut' [prJeeHoot^{yeh}]
flight let
flight number číslo letu
  [cheeslo leetoo]
floor (of room) podlaha
  [podluha]
  (storey) poschodí [posHodyee]
  on the floor na podlaze
  [podlazeh]
florist's květinářství [kuvyeh-
  tyinarJ-stvee]
flower květina [kvyetyina]
flu chřipka [HrJipka]
fluent: he speaks fluent Czech

mluví plynně česky [mloovee
  plin-nyeh cheski]
fly (noun) moucha [moh-Ha]
  (verb) letát [letaht]/letět [letyet]
food jídlo [yeedlo]
foot chodidlo [Hodidlo]
  on foot pěšky [pyeshki]
football (game) fotbal [fotbul]
  (ball) fotbalový míč [fotbulovee
  meech]
for pro
  do you have something
  for ...? (headache/diarrhoea etc)
  máte něco na ...? [mahteh
  nyetso]
foreign cizí [tsizee]
foreigner (man/woman) cizinec
  [tsizinets]/cizinka
forest les
forget zapomenout
  [zupomenoht]
  I forget zapomínám
  [zupomeenahm]
  I've forgotten (said by
  man/woman)
  zapomněl/zapomněla jsem
  [zupomnyel – sem]
fork (for eating) vidlička
  [vidlitchka]
fortnight čtrnáct dní
  [chturnahtst dunyee]
forwarding address budoucí
  adresa [boodohtsee]
fountain fontána [fontahna]
foyer (of hotel) hala [hula]
  (of theatre) foyer
France Francie [frantsi-eh]
free svobodný [svobodnee]
  (no charge) bezplatný

[besplutnee]
freeway dálnice [dahlnyitseh]
French francouzský
[fruntsohskee]
French fries hranolky
[hrunolki]
frequent častý [chustee]
fresh čerstvý [cherstvee]
fridge lednička [lednyitchka]
fried smažený [smaJenee]
friend přítel
[prJeetel]/přítelkyně
[prJeetelki-nyeh]
friendly přátelský [prJahtelskee]
from z, od [ot]
   from Monday to Friday od
   pondělí do pátku [ot pon-
   dyelee do pahtkoo]
   from next Thursday od
   příštího čtvrtka [prJeesh-
   tyeeho]
front předek [prJedek]
   in front/at the front vpředu
   [fprJedoo]
   in front of the hotel před
   hotelem
fruit ovoce [ovotseh]
fruit juice ovocný džus
[ovotsnee joos]
full plný [pulnee]
full board plná penze [pulnah
penzeh]
fun: it was fun byla to legrace
[bila to legrutseh]
funny (strange) divný [dyivnee]
   (amusing) legrační [legrutch-
nyee]
further dále [dahleh]
future: in future v

budoucnosti [boodohtsnosti]

G

game hra
garage (for fuel) čerpací
stanice [cherputseh stunyitseh]
   (for repairs) opravna
   automobilů [opruvna
   owtomobiloo]
   (for parking) garáž [garahJ]
garden zahrada [zuhruda]
garlic česnek [chesnek]
gas plyn [plin]
   (US) benzín [benzeen]
gas station benzínová stanice
[benzeenovah stunyitseh]
gate vrata [vruta]
   (at airport) východ [veeHot]
gay homosexuál
gents (toilet) páni [pahnyi],
muži [mooJi]
Germany Německo
[nyemetsko]
get (fetch) přinášet
[prJinahshet]/přinést [prJinest]
   how do I get to ...? jak se
   dostanu do ...? [yuk seh
   dostunoo]
get back (return) vrátit se [vrah-
tyit seh]
get off vystoupit [vistohpit]
   where do I get off? kde
   musím vystoupit? [gudeh
   mooseem]
get on (to train etc) nastoupit
[nustohpit]
get out (of car etc) vystoupit

[vistohpit]

get up (in the morning) vstávat
[fstahvut]/vstát [fstaht]

gift shop dárkový obchod
[darkovee opHot]

gin gin [jin]

  a gin and tonic gin a tonic

girl dívka [dyeefka]

girlfriend přítelkyně [prJeetelki-
nyeh]

give dávat [dahvut]/dát

give back vracet
[vrutset]/vrátit [vrah-tyit]

glad: I'm glad (said by
man/woman) jsem rád/ráda
[sem raht/rahda]

glass (material) sklo
(tumbler) sklenice [sklenyitseh]

  a glass of wine sklenice vína

glasses (spectacles) brýle
[breeleh]

glassware sklo

gloves rukavice [rookavitseh]

go chodit [Hodit]/jít [yeet]

  where are you going? kam
jdete? [deteh]

  where does this bus go? kam
jede tento? [kum yedeh]

  let's go! pojďme!
[poyd^{yeh}dumeh]

  she's gone (left) šla pryč [shla
pritch]

  a hamburger to go prodej
hamburgerů přes ulici
[proday – prJes oolitsi]

go away odejít [oday-eet]

  go away! jdete pryč! [dyeteh
pritch]

go back (return) vrátit se

[vrahtyit seh]

go down (the stairs etc) sejít
[seh-yeet]

go in vejít [veh-yeet]

go out (in the evening) jít ven
[yeet]

go through projít [pro-yeet]

go up (the stairs etc) jít nahoru
[yeet nahoroo]

God Bůh [booH]

gold zlato [zluto]

good dobrý [dobree]

  good! dobře! [dobrJeh]

  it's no good to není dobré
[nenyee dobreh]

goodbye nashledanou [nus-
Hledunoh]

good evening dobrý večer
[dobree vetcher]

good morning dobré ráno
[dobreh rahno]

good night dobrou noc
[dobroh nots]

got: we've got to ... musíme
... [mooseemeh]

  I've got to ... já musím [yah
mooseem]

  have you got any ...? máte...?
[mahteh]

gradually postupně [postoop-
nyeh]

gram gram [grum]

grapefruit grapefruit

grapes hrozny [hrozni]

grass tráva [trahva]

grateful vděčný [vdyetchnee]

great (excellent) skvělý
[skvyelee]

green zelený [zelenee]

greengrocer's obchod se zeleninou a ovocem [opHot seh zelenyinoh a ovotsem]

grey šedý [shedee]

grilled grilovaný [grilovanee]

grocer's obchod s potravinami [opHot spotruvinami]

ground: on the ground na zemi

ground floor přízemí [prJeezemee]

group skupina [skoopina]

guest host [hosst]

guesthouse penzión [penzi-awn]

guide (man/woman) průvodce [pr00votseh]/průvodkyně [pr00votki-nyeh]

guidebook průvodce

guided tour turistický zájezd [tooreestitskee zah-yest]

H
—

hair vlasy [vlusi]

haircut ostříhání [ostrJeehah-nyee]

hairdresser's (men's) holičství [holitch-stvee] (women's) kadeřnictví [kudairJnits-tvee]

hairdryer vysoušeč vlasů [visohshetch vlus00], fén

half půl [p00l]

half an hour půl hodiny [ho-dyini]

half a litre půl litru

half board polopenze [polopenzeh]

half price poloviční cena [tsena]

ham šunka [shoonka]

hamburger hamburger

hand ruka [rooka]

handbag kabelka [kubelka]

hand luggage příruční zavazadlo [prJeerootch-nyee zuvuzudlo]

hangover kocovina [kotsovina]

happen stát se

what has happened? co se stalo? [stulo]

happy šťastný [shtyustnee]

harbour přístav [prJeestuf]

hard tvrdý [tvurdee] (difficult) těžký [tyeshkee]

hardly těžko [tyeshko]

hardly ever skoro nikdy [nigdi]

hardware shop železářství [JelezarJstvee]

hat klobouk [klobohk]

hate nenávidět [nyenahvi-dyet]

have mít [meet]

can I have a ...? mohu dostat ...? [mohoo dostut]

do you have ...? máte ...? [mahteh]

do I have to ...? musím ...?

hayfever senná rýma [sennah reema]

he on

head hlava [hluva]

headache bolest hlavy [hluvi]

headlights přední světla [prJed-nyee svyetla]

hear slyšet/uslyšet [ooslishet]
heat horko
heater přenosná kamínka [prJenosnah kameenka]
heating topení
heavy těžký [tyeshkee]
heel (of foot) pata [puta]
　(of shoe) podpatek [potputek]
hello dobrý den [dobree]
　(on phone) haló [halaw]
help (noun) pomoc [pomots]
　(verb) pomáhat [pomah-hat]
　help! pomoc!
　can you help me? můžete mi pomoct? [mooJeteh mi pomotst]
her: I haven't seen her (said by man/woman) neviděl/neviděla jsem ji [nevidyel – sem yi]
　to her jí [yee]
　for her pro ni [pronyi]
　that's her to je ona [yeh]
　that's her towel to je její ručník [yeh-yee]
herbal tea bylinný čaj [bilinnee chI]
here zde [zdeh], tady [tudi]
　here is/are ... zde je/jsou ... [yeh/sch]
　here you are (offering) prosím [proseem]
hers její [yeh-yee]
　that's hers to je její [yeh]
hey! hej! [hay]
hi! ahoj! [uhoy]
high vysoký [visokee]
highway dálnice [dahlnitseh]
hill pahorek [puhorek]
him: I haven't seen him (said by man/woman) neviděl/neviděla

jsem ho [nevidyel – sem]
　to him jemu [yemoo]
　for him pro něho [nyeho]
　that's him to je on [yeh]
hip bok
hire (verb) pronajmout si [pronImoht]
　for hire k pronajmutí [pronImoo-tye]
his: it's his car to je jeho auto [yeh yeho]
　that's his to je jeho
hitch-hike stopovat [stopovut]
hole díra [dyeera]
holiday (work) dovolená [dovolenah]
　(school) prázdniny [prahz-nyini]
　(public) státní svátek [staht-nyee svahtek]
　on holiday na prázdninách [prahzd-nyinahH], na dovolené [dovoleneh]
home domov [domof]
　at home doma
　we go home tomorrow zítra jedeme domů [yedemeh domoo]
horrible strašný [strushnee]
horse kůň [kOOn^yeh]
hospital nemocnice [nemots-nyitseh]
hot horký [horkee]
　(spicy) pálivý [pahlivee]
　I'm hot je mi horko [yeh mi]
hotel hotel
hour hodina [ho-dyina]
house dům [dOOm]
how jak [yuk]
　how many? kolik?

how do you do? těší mě
[tyeshee mnyeh]

dialogues

how are you? jak se máte?
[yuk seh mahteh]
fine, thanks, and you?
děkuji, dobře, a vy?
[dyekoo-yi dobrJeh a vi]

how much is it? kolik to
stojí? [sto-yee]
200 crowns dvě stě korun
[koroon]
I'll take it vezmu si to
[vezmoo si to]

Hungary Maďarsko
[mudyursko]
hungry hladový [hludovee]
hurry: I'm in a hurry spěchám
[spyeHahm]
hurt: it hurts to bolí [bolee]
husband manžel [manJel]

I
■

I já [yah]
ice led [let]
ice cream zmrzlina [zmurzlina]
ice lolly nanuk [nunook]
idiot idiot
if jestli [yestli]
ill nemocný [nehmotsnee]
immediately okamžitě [okumJi-
tyeh]
important důležitý [dooleJitee]

impossible nemožný
[nehmoJnee]
in: it's in the centre je to v
centru [yeh]
in my car v mém autě
in Carlsbad v Karlových
Varech [kurloveeH vureH]
in May v květnu
in English anglicky [unglitski]
is he in? je tady? [yeh tudi]
in five minutes za pět minut
**include: does that include
meals?** jsou v tom i jídla?
[soh ftom i –yeedla]
indigestion špatné trávení
[shpatneh travenyee]
indoors vevnitř [vevnyitrJ]
information informace
[informutseh]
injured zraněný [zrunyenee]
insect hmyz [humis]
inside uvnitř [oov-nyitrJ]
  inside the hotel v hotelu
instead místo [meesto]
  instead of ... místo ...
intelligent inteligentní
[inteligent-nyee]
interesting zajímavý [zuh-
yeemavee]
international mezinárodní
[mezinarod-nyee]
interpret tlumočit [tloomotchit]
interpreter tlumočník
[tloomotch-nyeek]/tlumočnice
[tloomotch-nyitseh]
intersection křižovatka
[krJiJovutka]
into do
  I'm not into ... nezajímám se

moc o ... [neza-yeemahm seh mots]

introduce představit [prJetstuvit]

may I introduce ...? mohu vám představit ...? [mohoo vahm prJetstuvit]

invitation pozvání [pozvah-nyee]

Ireland Irsko

Irish irský [irskəe]

iron (for ironing) žehlička [Jeh-hlitchka]

island ostrov [ostrof]

it to

it is ... to je ... [yeh]

is it ...? je to ...?

where is it? kde je to? [gudeh]

it was ... to byl ... [bil]

J

jacket sako [suko]

jam džem [jem]

jeans džínsy [jeensi]

jewellery klenoty [klenoti]

job zaměstnání [zumnyestnah-nyee], práce [prahtseh]

joke (noun) žert [Jert]

journey cesta [tsesta]

have a good journey! šťastnou cestu! [shtyustnoh tsestoo]

juice šťáva [shtyahva]

jumper svetr [svetur]

just (only) jen, jenom [yen]

just two jen dva

just for me jen pro mě

[mnyeh]

just here právě tady [prahvyeh tudi]

K

Karlsbad Karlovy Vary [kurlovi vuri]

keep nechat si [neHut]

keep the change drobné si nechte [drobneh si neHuteh]

key klíč [kleetch]

kilo kilo

kilometre kilometr

kind (generous) laskavý [luskavee]

kiss (noun) polibek

(verb) líbat [leebut]/políbit

kitchen kuchyně [kooHinyeh]

knee koleno

knife nůž [noosh]

knock down srazit [sruzit]

know (somebody, a place) znát [znaht]

(something) vědět [vyedyet]

I don't know nevím [neveem]

I didn't know that (said by man/woman) nevěděl/neviděla jsem to [nevyedyel – sem]

L

ladies' room dámy [dahmi]

lady dáma [dahma]

lager ležák [leJahk]

lake jezero [yezero]

lamb (meat) jehněčí
[yehnyetchee]

lamp lampa [lumpa]

language jazyk [yuzik]

large velký [velkee]

last poslední [poslednyee]
(previous) minulý [minoolee]

last week minulý týden

last Friday minulý pátek

last night minulou noc
[minooloh nots]

late pozdě [pozdyeh]

later později [pozday-yi]
I'll come back later vrátím se
později [vrahtyeem seh
pozdyay-yi]

laugh smát se [smaht seh]

launderette, laundromat
veřejná prádelna [verJaynah
prahdelna]

laundry (clothes) prádlo
[prahdlo]

lawyer (man/woman) právník
[prahv-nyeek]/právnička
[prahv-nyitchka]

leaflet leták [letahk]

leak (of gas) únik [oonyik]
(liquid) téct [tetst]

learn učit se [oochit seh]

least: at least přinejmenším
[prji-naymensheem]

leather kůže [kooJeh]

leave odjet [odyet]
(leave behind) nechat [neHut]
I am leaving tomorrow
odjíždím zítra [odyeeJ-dyeem]
may I leave this here? mohu
to tady nechat? [mohoo to tudi
neHut]
I left my coat in the bar

nechal jsem kabát v baru
[neHul sem]

left levý [levee]

left luggage (office) úschovna
zavazadel [oosHovna zuvuzadel]

leg noha

lemon citrón [tsitrawn]

lemonade limonáda
[limonahda]

lend půjčovat [poo-
itchovut]/půjčit [poo-itchit]

less méně [menyeh]
less expensive méně drahý
[drahee]

lesson lekce [lektseh]

let off: will you let me off at ...?
necháte mě vystoupit v ...?
[neHahteh mnyeh]

letter dopis

letterbox poštovní schránka
[poshtov-nyee suHrahnka]

lettuce salát [salaht]

library knihovna [kunihovna]

licence povolení [povolenyee]

lift (in building) výtah [veetuH]
could you give me a lift?
můžete mě svézt? [mooJeteh
mnyeh svest]

light (noun) světlo [svyetlo]
(not heavy) lehký [leHkee]
do you have a light? máte
oheň? [mahteh oHen^yeh]

light bulb žárovka [Jarofka]

lighter (cigarette) zapalovač
[zupulovutch]

like: I like it líbí se mi to
I don't like it nelíbí se mi to
[neleebee]
do you like ...? líbi se

vám ...? [vahm]
would you like a drink? dáte si něco na pití? [dahteh si nyetso na pityee]
what's it like? jaké to je? [yukeh to yeh]
one like this to samé [sumeh]
line linka
lips rty [ruti]
listen poslouchat [poslohHut]
litre litr
little (adj) malý [mulee]
just a little, thanks jenom trochu, děkuji [yenom troHoo dyekoo-yi]
a little milk trochu mléka
live žít [Jeet]
loaf bochník chleba [boH-nyeek Hleba]
local místní [meestnyee]
a local wine místní víno
lock (noun) zámek [zahmek]
(verb) zamknout [zumknoht]
lock out: I've locked myself out (said by man/woman) zabouchl/zabouchla jsem si dveře [zubohHul/zubohHla sem]
locker (for luggage etc) skříňka na zavazadla [skrJeen^{yeh}ka na zuvuzudla]
London Londýn [londeen]
long dlouhý [dloh-hee]
how long does it take? jak dlouho to trvá? [turvah]
a long time dlouho
one day/two days longer o den/dva dny déle [deleh]
look dívat se [dyeevut seh]/podívat se

look out! pozor!
can I have a look? mohu se podívat? [mohoo seh po-dyeevut]
look after starat se [sturut seh]/postarat se o
look at dívat se [dyeevut seh]/podívat se na
look for hledat [hledut]
I'm looking for ... hledám ... [hledahm]
lorry nákladní auto [nahklud-nyee owto]
lose ztrácet [strahtset]/ztratit [strutyit]
I'm lost
I've lost my bag (said by man/woman) ztratil/ztratila jsem tašku [strutyil – tushkoo]
lost property (office) ztráty a nálezy [strahti ah nahlezi]
lot: a lot, lots spousta [spohsta]
a lot of people spousta lidí
not a lot moc ne [mots neh]
loud hlasitý [hlusitee]
lounge hala [hula]
love milovat [milovut]
lovely rozkošný [roskoshnee]
low nízký [nyeeskee]
luck štěstí [shtyes-tyee]
good luck! mnoho štěstí!
luggage zavazadla [zuvuzudla]
lunch oběd [obyet]

M

mad (insane) bláznivý [blahz-nyivee]
magazine časopis [chusopis]

maid (in hotel) pokojská
[pokoyskah]
mail pošta [poshta]
(verb) poslat poštou [poslut
poshtoh]
mailbox poštovní schránka
[poshtov-nyee sнrahnka]
main hlavní [hluv-nyee]
main course hlavní chod [нot]
main road (in town) hlavní
třída [trჯeeda]
(in country) hlavní silnice [sil-
nyitseh]
make dělat [dyelut]/udělat
[oodyelut]
make-up make-up
man člověk [chlo-vyek]
manager manažer [manaჯer],
vedoucí [vedohtsee]
can I see the manager?
mohu mluvit s vedoucím?
[mohoo mloovit svedohtseem]
many mnoho
map mapa [mupa]
Marienbad Mariánské Lázně
[mariahnskeh lahznyeh]
market trh [turн]
marmalade marmeláda
married: I'm married (said by
man/woman) jsem
ženatý/vdaná [sem
ჯenutee/vdunah]
mascara maskara [muskura]
match (football etc) zápas
[zahpus]
matches zápalky [zahpalki]
matter: it doesn't matter na
tom nezáleží [nezahleჯee]
what's the matter? co se

děje? [tso seh dyay-eh]
mattress matrace [mutrutseh]
may: may I see it? mohu to
vidět? [vidyet]
maybe možná [moჯnah]
mayonnaise majonéza [mī-
oneza]
me: that's for me to je pro mě
[yeh pro mnyeh]
me too já také [yah tukeh]
meal jídlo [yeedlo]
mean myslet [mislet],
znamenat [znamenut]
what does it mean? co to
znamená? [znumenah]
meat maso [muso]
medicine lék
medium (size, steak) střední
[strჯed-nyee]
medium-dry středně suché
[strჯed-nyeh sooнeh]
medium-rare středně
propečený [propetchenee]
mend opravovat
[opruvovut]/opravit [opruvit]
men's room páni [pahnyi],
muži [mooჯi]
mention: don't mention it
není zač [nenyee zutch]
menu jídelní lístek [yeedelnyee
leestek]
message vzkaz [fskus]
metre metr
midday poledne [poledneh]
middle: in the middle
uprostřed [ooprostrჯet]
midnight půlnoc [poolnots]
milk mléko
mind: never mind to nevadí

[to nevudyee]
mine: it's mine to je moje [yeh mo-yeh]
mineral water minerálka [minerahlka]
minute minuta [minoota]
just a minute okamžik, prosím [okumʒik]
mirror zrcadlo [zurtsudlo]
Miss slečna [sletchna]
(speaking to someone) slečno
missing chybí [Hibee]
there's a suitcase missing chybí kufr
mistake chyba [Hiba]
money peníze [penyeezeh]
month měsíc [mnyeseets]
moped moped
more více [veetseh]
can I have some more water, please? mohu dostat více vody, prosím? [mohoo dostut]
more expensive dražší [drushee za-yeemuh-vyayshee]
more than 50 více než padesát [nesh]
morning ráno [rahno]
this morning dnes ráno
most: most of the time většinu času [vyetshinoo chusoo]
mother matka [mutka]
motorbike motocykl [mototsikul]
motorway dálnice [dahlnitseh]
mountain hora
mouse myš [mish]
mouth ústa [oosta]
movie film
movie theater kino

Mr pan [pun]
(speaking to someone) pane [puneh]
Mrs paní [punyee]
Ms slečna [sletchna]
(speaking to someone) slečno
much mnoho
much better/worse mnohem lépe/hůře
not much moc ne [mots neh]
mum maminka [muminka]
museum muzeum [moozeh-oom]
mushrooms houby [hohbi]
music hudba [hoodba]
music festival hudební festival [hoodeb-nyee festivul]
must: I must já musím [yah mooseem]
mustard hořčice [horʒtchitseh]
my můj [moo-i], moje [mo-yeh]
myself: I'll do it myself (said by man/woman) udělám to sám/sama [oodyelahm to sahm/suma]
by myself sám/sama

N

nail (finger) nehet
name jméno [yumeno]
my name's ... jmenuji se ... [yumenoo-yi seh]
what's your name? jak se jmenujete? [yuk seh yumenoo-yeteh]
napkin ubrousek [oobrohsek]
narrow (street) úzký [ooskee]

nasty (person) zlý [zlee]
(weather, accident) ošklivý
[oshklivee]
national národní [narod-nyee]
natural (behaviour etc)
přirozený [prJirozenee]
(of nature) přírodní [prJeerod-
nyee]
near blízko [bleesko]
  where is the nearest ...? kde
  je nejbližší ...? [gudeh yeh
  nayblishee]
nearly téměř [temnyerJ]
necessary nezbytný
[nezbitnee]
neck krk [kurk]
necklace náhrdelník [nah-
hrudel-nyeek]
necktie vázanka [vahzanka],
kravata [kruvuta]
need: I need ... potřebuji ...
[potrJeboo-yi]
needle jehla [yehla]
neither ... nor ... ani ... ani ...
[unyi]
nephew synovec [sinovets]
never nikdy [nyigdi]
new nový [novee]
news (radio, TV etc) zprávy
[sprahvi]
newsagent's noviny–časopisy
[novini-chusopisi]
newspaper noviny
New Year Nový rok [novee]
  Happy New Year! šťastný
  Nový rok! [shtyustnee]
New Year's Eve Silvestr
New Zealand Nový Zéland
  [novee]

next příští [prJeesh-tyee]
  next week příští týden
  next to vedle [vedleh]
nice (food) dobrý [dobree]
  (looks, view etc) pěkný
  [pyeknee]
  (person) milý [milee]
niece neteř [neterJ]
night noc [nots]
no ne [neh]
  I've no change nemám
  drobné [nemahm drobneh]
  there's no ... left už
  žádný/žádná není ... [oosh
  Jahdnee/Jahdnah nenyee]
nobody nikdo [nyigdo]
noisy: it's too noisy je to moc
  hlučné [yeh to mots hlootchneh]
non-alcoholic nealkoholický
  [neh-ulkoholitskee]
none žádný [Jahdnee]
non-smoking compartment
  nekuřácké kupé
  [nekoorJahtskeh koopeh]
no-one nikdo [nyigdo]
nor: nor do I ani já ne [unyi yah
  neh]
normal normální [normahlnyee]
north sever
northeast severovýchod
  [–veeHot]
northwest severozápad
  [–zahput]
Northern Ireland Severní
  Irsko
nose nos
not ne [neh]
  no, I'm not hungry ne,
  nemám hlad [nemahm hlut]

37

not that one to ne
note (banknote) bankovka
[bunkofka]
nothing nic [nyits]
  nothing else nic jiného
  [yineho]
now nyní [ninyee]
number číslo [cheeslo]
nuts (food) ořechy [orJeнi]

O

o'clock: 5 o'clock pět hodin
[ho-dyin]
odd (strange) divný [dyivnee]
of z
off (lights) zhasnuto [zhusnooto]
  it's just off Malostranské
  square je to hned vedle
  Malostranského náměstí [yeh
  to hnet vedleh]
often často [chusto]
  how often are the buses? jak
  často jezdí autobusy? [yuk –
  yezdyee]
oil olej [olay]
ointment mast [must]
OK dobře [dobrJeh]
  are you OK? jsi v pořádku?
  [si fporJahtkoo]
  that's OK thanks (it doesn't
  matter) to je dobré, díky [yeh
  dobreh dyeeki]
  I'm OK (nothing for me) pro mě
  nic [mnyeh nyits]
  (I feel OK) cítím se dobře [tsee-
  tyeem seh dobrJeh]
old starý [sturee]

olives olivy [olivi]
omelette omeleta
on na
  (lights) rozsvíceno
  [rosveetseno]
  on television v televizi
  I haven't got it on me nemám
  to u sebe [nemahm to oo sebeh]
  what's on tonight? co dávají
  dnes večer? [tso dahvi-yee dnes
  vetcher]
once (one time) jednou [yednoh]
  at once (immediately)
  okamžitě [okumJi-tyeh]
one jeden [yeden], jedna,
  jedno
  the white one ten bílý
  [beelee]
one-way ticket jednou
  [yednoh]
onion cibule [tsibooleh]
only jenom [yenom]
  it's only 6 o'clock je teprve
  šest hodin [yeh tepurveh]
open (adj) otevřený
  [otevrJenee]
  (verb: door) otevřít [otevrJeet]
operator (telephone: man/woman)
  spojovatel [spo-
  yovutel]/spojovatelka
opposite proti [protyi]
  opposite my hotel proti
  mému hotelu
or nebo
orange (fruit) pomeranč
  [pomeruntch]
  (colour) oranžový [orunJovee]
orange juice pomerančová
  šťáva [pomeruntchovah shtyahva]

order: can we order now?
můžeme si objednat?
[mOOJemeh si ob-yednut]
ordinary obyčejný [obitchaynee]
other jiný [yinee]
  the other one ten druhý
  [droohee]
our/ours náš [nahsh], naše
  [nusheh]
out: she's out šla ven [shla]
outdoors venku [venkoo]
outside... před ... [prJet]
over: over here tady [tudi]
  over there tamhle [tum-hleh]
  over 500 nad pět set
overnight (travel) přes noc
  [prJes nots]
own: my own ... můj vlastní ...
  [mOO-i vlustnyee]

P

pack krabice [krubitseh]
  (verb: suitcase) balit [bulit]
package (small parcel) balík
  [buleek]
pain bolest
  I have a pain here bolí mě
  tady [bolee mnyeh tudi]
painful bolestivý [bolestyivee]
painkillers lék proti bolesti
  [protyi bolestyi]
pair: a pair of ... pár ...
panties kalhotky [kulhotki]
pants (underwear: men's) spodky
  [spotki]
  (women's) kalhotky
  (US: trousers) kalhoty

pantyhose punčocháče
  [poontchoHahtcheh]
paper papír [pupeer]
  (newspaper) noviny [novini]
parcel balík [buleek]
pardon (me)? prosím?
  [proseem]
parents: my parents moji
  rodiče [mo-yi rodyitcheh]
park (noun) park [purk]
  (verb) parkovat [purkovut]
parking parkování [purkovah-
  nyee]
parking lot parkoviště
  [parkovish-tyeh]
part (noun) část [chahst]
partner (boyfriend, girlfriend etc)
  partner [partner]
party (group) skupina [skoopina]
  (celebration) oslava [osluva],
  party
passport cestovní pas [tsestov-
  nyee pus]
**past: just past the information
  office** hned za informační
  kanceláří [hnet]
pavement chodník [Hod-nyeek]
pay (verb) platit [plutyit]
  can I pay, please? mohu
  zaplatit, prosím? [mohoo]
pay phone telefon na mince
  [mintseh]
peach broskev [broskef]
peanuts burské oříšky
  [boorskeh orJeeshki]
pear hruška [hrooshka]
peas hrášek [hrahshek]
pen pero
pencil tužka [tooshka]

people lidé [lideh]
pepper (spice) pepř [pepurJ]
  (vegetable) paprikový lusk
  [paprikovee loosk]
per: per night za noc [nots]
per cent procento [protsento]
perfume parfém [purfem]
perhaps možná [moJnah]
person osoba
petrol benzín [benzeen]
petrol station benzínová
  stanice [benzeenovah stunyitseh]
pharmacy lékárna
phone (noun) telefon
  (verb) telefonovat [telefonovut]
phone book telefonní seznam
  [telefonyee seznum]
phone box telefonní budka
  [bootka]
phonecard telefonní karta
  [kurta]
phone number telefonní číslo
  [cheeslo]
photo fotografie [fotografi-eh]
picture obraz [obrus]
piece kus [koos]
pill pilulka [piloolka]
pillow polštář [polshtarJ]
pineapple ananas [ununus]
pink růžový [rooJovee]
place (noun) místo [meesto]
  at your place (fam) u tebe [oo
  tebeh]
  (pol) u vás [vahs]
plane letadlo [letudlo]
plant rostlina
plasters náplasti [nahplustyi]
plastic bag igelitová taška
  [igelitovah tushka]

plate talíř [tuleerJ]
platform nástupiště
  [nahstoopish-tyeh]
  which platform is for Plzeň,
  please? z kterého nástupiště
  jede vlak na Plzeň? [skutereho
  – jedeh vluk na pulzen^yeh]
play (noun: in theatre) hra
  (verb) hrát [hraht]
pleasant příjemný [prJee-
  yemnee]
please prosím [proseem]
  yes, please ano, prosím [uno]
plenty: plenty of ... spousta ...
  [spohsta]
plug (electrical) zástrčka
  [zahsturtchka]
  (in sink) zátka [zahtka]
poisonous jedovatý [yedovutee]
police policie [politsi-eh]
policeman policista [politsista]
police station policejní
  stanice [politsay-nyee stunitseh]
polite zdvořilý [zdvorJilee]
polluted znečištěný [znetchish-
  tyenee]
pool (for swimming) bazén
  [buzen]
pork vepřové maso [veprJoveh
  muso]
port (for boats) přístav
  [prJeestuf]
possible možný [moJnee]
  is it possible to ...? je
  možné ...? [yeh moJneh]
  as ... as possible tak ... jak to
  jen bude možné [tuk ... yuk to
  yen boodeh moJneh]
post (noun: mail) pošta [poshta]

(verb) poslat poštou [poslut poshtoh]

postcard pohlednice [pohlednyitseh]

post office pošta [poshta]

poste restante poste restante

potato brambora [brumbora]

potato chips lupínky [loopeenki]

pound (money, weight) libra

prefer: I prefer ... preferuji ... [preferoo-yi]

pregnant těhotná [tyehotnah]

prescription recept [retsept]

present (gift) dárek

pretty pěkný [pyeknee]

price cena [tsena]

private soukromý [sohkromee]

probably asi [usi]

problem problém

no problem! to není problém! [nenyee]

pronounce: how is this pronounced? jak se to vyslovuje? [yuk seh to vislovoo-yeh]

public holiday den pracovního klidu [prutsov-nyeeho klidoo]

pull táhnout [tah-hunoht]

purple fialový [fi-alovee]

purse (for money) peněženka [penyeJenka]

(US: handbag) kabelka [kubelka]

push tlačit [tlatchit]

put položit [poloJit]

pyjamas pyžamo [piJamo]

Q

quarter čtvrt [chutvurt]

question otázka [otahska]

queue (noun) fronta

quick rychlý [riHlee]

quickly rychle [riHleh]

quiet (place, hotel) tichý [tyiHee]

quiet! ticho! [tyiHo]

quite (fairly) docela [dotsela]

(very) úplně [OOpulnyeh]

quite a lot docela hodně [hodnyeh]

R

radiator radiátor [rudi-ahtor]

radio rádio [rahdi-o]

rail: by rail vlakem [vlukem]

railway železnice [Jelez-nyitseh]

rain (noun) déšť [dehsht^yeh]

it's raining prší [purshee]

rape (noun) znásilnění [znahsil-nyenyee]

rare (steak) krvavý [kurvahvee]

raspberry malina [mulina]

rather: I'd rather ... radši bych ... [rutshi biH]

razor (dry) břitva [brJitva]

(electric) holicí strojek [holitsee stro-yek]

read číst [cheest]

ready připravený [prJipruvenee]

real skutečný [skootetchnee]

really opravdu [opruvdoo]

receipt potvrzení [potuvrzenyee]

recently v poslední době [fposled-nyee dobyeh]

reception recepce [retseptseh]

receptionist recepční [retseptch-nyee]

recommend: could you recommend ...? (to man/woman) mohl/mohla byste doporučit ...? [mohul/mo-hla bisteh doporootchit]

red červený [cherveneh]

red wine červené víno [cherveneh veeno]

refund (noun) peněžitá náhrada [penyeJitah nah-hruda]

region region [regi-on]

registered: by registered mail doporučeně [doporootchenyeh]

remember: I don't remember nepamatuji si [nepumutoo-yi]

rent (noun: for apartment etc) nájemné [nah-yemneh] (verb) najmout si [nïmoht]

repair opravovat [opruvovut]/opravit [opruvit]

repeat opakovat [opukovut]/zopakovat

reservation rezervace [rezervutseh]

reserve rezervovat [rezervovut]

dialogue

can I reserve a table for tonight? můžu si na dnes večer rezervovat stůl? [mooJoo – vetcher – stool]

yes madam, for how many people? ano, paní, pro

kolik osob? [uno punyee]

for two pro dva

and for what time? a na kolik hodin? [ho-dyin]

for eight o'clock na osm hodin

and could I have your name please? a na jaké jméno, prosím? [yukeh yumeno]

restaurant restaurace [restowratseh]

restaurant car jídelní vůz [yeedel-nyee voos]

rest room toaleta [to-uleta]

return ticket zpáteční (lístek) [spahtetchnyee leestek]

reverse charge call hovor na účet volaného [oochet voluneho]

rice rýže [reeJeh]

right (correct) správně [sprahv-nyeh] (not left) pravý [pravee]

that's right! správně! [sprahv-nyeh]

ring (on finger) prsten [prusten]

ring back zavolat zpět [zuvolut spyet]

river řeka [rJeka]

road ulice [oolitseh]

is this the road for ...? je to cesta na ...? [yeh to tsesta]

rob: I've been robbed (said by man/woman) byl/byla jsem oloupen/oloupena [bil/bila sem olohpen]

roll (bread) rohlík [ro-hleek]

roof střecha [strJeнa]
room pokoj [pokoy]

dialogue

do you have any rooms?
máte nějaký volný pokoj?
[mahteh nyeh-yukee volnee]
for how many people? pro
kolik osob?
for one/for two pro
jednoho/pro dva [yednoho]
yes, we have rooms free
ano, máme volné pokoje
[uno mahmeh volneh poko-yeh]
for how many nights will it
be? na kolik nocí? [notsee]
just for one night jen na
jednu noc [yen nah yednoo]
how much is it? kolik to
stojí? [sto-yee]
... with bathroom and ...
without bathroom ... s
koupelnou a ... bez
koupelny [skohpelnoh a ...
bes kohpelni]
can I see a room with
bathroom? mohu se
podívat na pokoj s
koupelnou? [mohoo seh
podyeevut]
OK, I'll take it dobře,
vezmu to [dobrJeh vezmoo]

room service hotelová
obsluha [hotelovah opslooha]
rosé (wine) růžové víno
[rooJoveh veeno]
round trip ticket zpáteční

[spahtetch-nyee]
route trasa [trusa]
rubbish (waste) odpadky
[otputki]
(poor quality goods) krámy
[krahmi]
rucksack ruksak [rooksuk]
rude drzý [durzee]
rum rum [room]
run (person) běhat [byehut]

S

sad smutný [smootnee]
safe (not in danger) v bezpečí
[vbespetchee]
(not dangerous) bezpečný
[bespetchnee]
salad salát [salaht]
salad dressing zálivka
[zahlifka]
sale: for sale na prodej
[proday]
salt sůl [sool]
same: the same to samé
[sumeh]
the same again, please ještě
jednou to samé, prosím
[yeshtyeh yednoh]
sand písek [peesek]
sandals sandály [sandahli]
sandwich obložený chléb
[obloJenee нlep]
sanitary napkins/towels
dámské vložky [dahmskeh
vloshki]
sauce omáčka [omahtchka]
saucepan pánev [pahnef]

sausage párek

say: how do you say ... in Czech? jak řeknete česky ...? [yuk rJekneteh cheski]

what did he say? co říkal? [tso rJeekal]

scarf (for neck) šála [shahla]

(for head) šátek [shahtek]

schedule (US) jízdní řád [yeezd-nyee rJaht]

school škola [shkola]

scissors: a pair of scissors nůžky [nOOshki]

Scotch tape® izolepa

Scotland Skotsko

Scottish skotský [skotskee]

sea moře [morJeh]

seat sedadlo [sedudlo]

is this anyone's seat? je to něčí sedadlo? [yeh to nyetchee]

second (adj) druhý [droohee]

(of time) sekunda [sekoonda], vteřina [fterJina]

second class (travel) druhou třídou [drcohoh trJeedoh]

see vidět [vidyet]/uvidět [oovidyet]

can I see? mohu se podívat? [mohoo seh po-dyeevut]

have you seen ...? (to man/woman) viděl/viděla jste ...? [vidyal – steh]

see you! nashle! [nus-Hleh]

I see (I understand) rozumím [rozoomeem]

self-catering apartment byt bez stravování [bit bes struvovah-nyee]

self-service samoobsluha [samo-opslooha]

sell prodávat [prodahvut]

Sellotape® izolepa

send posílat [poseelut]/poslat [poslut]

separated: I'm separated (from wife) nežiji s manželkou [neJi-yi s munJelkoh] (from husband) nežiji s manželem

separately (pay, travel) zvlášť [zvlahsht^yeh]

serious vážný [vahJnee]

service station autoservis [owtoservis]

serviette ubrousek [oobrohsek]

set menu menu [meni]

several několik [nyekolik]

sex sex

shade: in the shade ve stínu [veh styeenoo]

shampoo (noun) šampón [shumpawn]

share (room, table etc) dělit se [dyelit seh]/rozdělit se o

shaver holicí strojek [holitsee stro-yek]

shaving foam pěna na holení [pyena na holenyee]

she ona

sheet (for bed) prostěradlo [pros-tyerudlo]

sherry šery [sheri]

ship loď [lot^yeh]

shirt košile [koshileh]

shit! do prdele! [prudeleh]

shoe bota

shoelaces tkaničky [tku-nyitchki]

shoe polish krém na boty
shoe repairer opravář obuvi [oprvahrJ oboovi]
shop obchod [opHot]
short krátký [krahtkee]
shorts šortky [shortki]
should: what should I do? co mám dělat? [tso mahm dyelut]
shout křičet [krJitchet]
shoulder rameno [rumeno]
show (in theatre) představení [prJetstuvenyee]
  could you show me? (to man/woman) mohl/mohla byste mi to ukázat? [mohul/mo-hla bisteh – ookahzut]
shower (in bathroom) sprcha [spurHa]
shut (verb) zavírat [zuveerut]/zavřít [zuvrJeet]
  when do you shut? kdy zavíráte? [gudi zuveerahteh]
  they're shut mají zavřeno [mī-yi zuvrJeno]
  shut up! buď zticha! [boot^yeh styiHa]
shutter (on window) okenice [okenyitseh]
sick nemocný [nemotsnee]
side strana [struna]
side salad salát [salaht]
sidewalk chodník [Hod-nyeek]
sight: the sights of ... turistické atrakce ... [tooristitskeh utruktseh]
silk hedvábí [hedvahbee]
silly hloupý [hlohpee]
silver (noun) stříbro [strJeebro]
since: since yesterday od včerejška [ot fcherayshka]
sing zpívat [speevut]/zazpívat [zuspeevut]
single: a single to ... jednou do ... [yednoh]
  I'm single (said by man/woman) jsem svobodný/svobodná ... [sem svobodnee/svobodnah]
single room jednolůžkový pokoj [yednolOOshkovee pokoy]
sister sestra
sit: can I sit here? mohu se tady posadit? [mohoo seh tudi posu-dyit]
sit down posadit se [posudyit seh]
size velikost
skin kůže [kOOJeh]
skirt sukně [sook-nyeh]
sky obloha
sleep spát [spaht]
sleeping bag spací pytel [sputsee pitel]
sleeping car lůžkový vůz [lOOshkovee vOOs]
Slovak (adj) slovenský [slovenskee]
  (language) slovenština [slovensh-tyina]
  (man) Slovák [slovahk]
  (woman) Slovenka
Slovakia Slovensko
Slovak Republic Slovenská republika [slovenskah repooblika]
slow pomalý [pomulee]
  slow down! zpomal! [spomul]
slowly pomalu [pomuloo]
small malý [mulee]

smell: it smells (smells bad) smrdí to [smurdyee]

smile usmívat se [oosmeevut seh]/usmát se [oosmaht]

smoke (noun) kouř [kohrj]

do you mind if I smoke? bude vám vadit, když budu kouřit? [bodeh vahm vudyit gudij boodoo kohrjit]

I don't smoke já nekouřím [yah nekohrjeem]

snow (noun) sníh [snyeeн]

it's snowing sněží [snyeJee]

so: it's so good je to moc dobré [yeh to mots dobreh]

not so fast ne tak rychle [neh tuk riнleh]

so am I já také [yah tukeh]

so do I já také

so-so tak tak [tuk]

soap mýdlo [meedlo]

soap powder mýdlový prášek [meedlovee prahshek]

sober střízlivý [strJeezlivee]

sock ponožka [ponoshka]

soda (water) soda

soft (material etc) měkký [mnyekee]

soft drink nealkoholický nápoj [neh-ulkoholitskee nahpoy]

sole podrážka [podrahshka]

some: can I have some water/rolls? mohu dostat trochu vody/nějaké rohlíky? [mohoo dostut troнoo – nyayukeh]

somebody někdo [nyegdo]

something něco [nyetso]

sometimes někdy [nyegdi]

somewhere někde [nyegdeh]

son syn [sin]

song píseň [peesen^yeh]

soon brzy [burzi]

sore: it's sore je to bolavé [yeh to bolaveh]

sorry: (I'm) sorry promiňte [promin^yehteh]

sorry? (didn't understand) prosím? [proseem]

sort: what sort of ...? jaké ...? [yukeh]

soup polévka [polefka]

south jih [yiн]

South Africa Jižní Afrika [yiJnyee ufrika]

South African (adj) jihoafrický [yiho-ufritskee]

southeast jihovýchod [yihoveeнot]

southwest jihozápad [yihozahpat]

souvenir suvenýr [sooveneer]

speak mluvit [mloovit]

do you speak English? mluvíte anglicky? [mlooveeteh unglitski]

I don't speak ... nemluvím ... [nemlooveem]

spectacles brýle [breeleh]

spend utrácet [ootrahtset]/utratit [ootrutyit]

spoon lžíce [luJeetseh]

spring (season) jaro [yuro]

square (in town) náměstí [nahmnyes-tyee]

stairs schody [sнodi]

stamp známka [znahmka]

start začátek [zutchahtek]

(verb) začít [zutcheet]/začínat
[zutcheenut]

the car won't start auto
nestartuje [owto nestartoo-yeh]

starter (food) předkrm
[pr.Jetkurm]

starving: I'm starving umírám
hlady [oomeerahm hludi]

station nádraží [nahdruJee]

stay: where are you staying?
kde bydlíte? [gudeh bidleeteh]

I'm staying at ... bydlím v ...
[bidleem]

I'd like to stay another two
nights (said by man/woman)
rád/ráda bych zůstal/zůstala
další dvě noci [rahd/rahda biH
zoostul – dulshee dvyeh notsi]

steak biftek

steal krást [krahst]

my bag has been stolen
ukradli mi tašku [ookrudli mi
tushkoo]

steep (hill) prudký [prootkee]

still: I'm still waiting ještě
čekám [yeshtyeh chekahm]

stomach žaludek [Juloodek]

stomach ache bolest žaludku
[Julootkoo]

stone (rock) kámen [kahmen]

stop zastavovat
[zustuvovut]/zastavit [zustuvit]

please, stop here (to taxi driver
etc) zastavte tady, prosím
[zustufteh tudi proseem]

storm bouře [bohrJeh]

straight: it's straight ahead je
to přímo před vámi [yeh to
pr.Jeemo pr.Jet vahmi]

strange (odd) divný [dyivnee]

strawberry jahoda [yuhoda]

street ulice [oolitseh]

string provázek [provahzek]

strong silný [silnee]

stuck zaseklý [zusseklee]

student (male/female) student
[stoodent]/studentka

stupid hloupý [hlohpee]

suburb předměstí [prJed-
mnyestyee]

subway (US) metro

suddenly najednou [nī-yednoh]

sugar cukr [tsookr]

suit (noun) oblek

suitcase kufr [koofr]

summer léto

in the summer v létě [vletyeh]

sun slunce [sloontseh]

in the sun na slunci

sunblock krém s ochranným
faktorem [soHruneem fuktorem]

sunburn spálenina (sluncem)
[spahlenyina sloontsem]

sunglasses sluneční brýle
[sloonech-nyee breeleh]

sunstroke úpal [oopul]

suntanned opálený [opahlenee]

suntan oil olej na opalování
[olay na opulovah-nyee]

supermarket velká
samoobsluha [velkah samo-
opslooha]

supper večeře [vetcherJeh]

supplement (extra charge)
doplatek [doplutek]

sure: are you sure? (said to
man/woman) jste si tím
jistý/jistá? [stesi tyeem

yistee/yistah]
sure! jistě! [yistyeh]
surname příjmení [prJee-yumenyee]
sweater pulovr [poolovur]
sweet (taste) sladký [slutkee]
(noun: dessert) dezert [dezert], moučník [mohtch-nyeek]
sweets bonbóny [bonbawni]
swim plavat [pluvut]
I'm going for a swim jdu si zaplavat [yudoo si zupluvut]
swimming costume plavky [plufki]
swimming pool plavecký bazén [pluvetskee buzen]
swimming trunks plavky [plufki]
switch (noun) vypínač [vipeenutch]
switch off (lights) zhasnout [zhusnoht]
(TV, engine) vypnout [vipnoht]
switch on (lights) rozsvítit [rosveetyit]
(TV, engine) zapnout [zupnoht]

T

table stůl [stool]
table wine stolní víno [veeno]
take brát [braht]/vzít [vzeet]
(accept) přijmout [prJeemoht]
fine, I'll take it dobře, beru to [dobrJeh beroo turvah]
a hamburger to take away prodej hamburgerů přes

ulici [proday – prJes oolitsi]
talk (verb) mluvit [mloovit]
tall vysoký [visokee]
tampons tampóny [tumpawni]
tan (noun) opálení [opahlenyee]
tap kohoutek [kohohtek]
taste (noun) chuť [Hoot^yeh]
taxi taxi [tuksi]

dialogue

to the airport/to the Forum Hotel, please na letiště/do hotelu Forum, prosím [letyish-tyeh/do hoteloo – proseem]
how much will it be? kolik to bude stát? [boodeh staht]
... crowns ... korun [koroon]
that's fine, right here, thanks to je dobré, tady, děkuji [yeh dobreh tudi dyekoo-yi]

tea čaj [tchī]
teacher (man/woman) učitel [ootchitel]/učitelka
telephone telefon
television televize [televizeh]
tell: could you tell him ...? (to man/woman) mohl/mohla byste mu říct ...? [mohul/mohla bisteh moo rJeetst]
tennis tenis
terrible strašný [strushnee]
terrific fantastický [fantastitskee]
than než [nesh]

thank: thanks díky [dyeeki]
 thank you děkuji vám
 [dyekoo-yi vahm]
 thank you very much děkuji
 mockrát [motskraht]
 no thanks ne, díky [neh]

dialogue

> **thanks** díky
> **that's OK, don't mention it**
> to je v pořádku, není zač
> [yeh fporJahtkoo nenyee zutch]

that: that man ten muž
 that woman ta žena
 that one tamten [tumten]
 that's nice to je pěkné [yeh
 pyekneh]
 is that ...? je to ...?
 the no word in Czech
theatre divadlo [divudlo]
their/theirs jejich [yeh-yiH]
them jim [yim]
 for them pro ně [nyeh]
 who? — them kdo? – oni
 [gudo onyi]
then potom
there tam [tum]
 is there ...? je tady ...? [yeh
 tudi]
 are there ...? jsou tady ...?
 [soh tudi]
 there is/are ... tady je/jsou ...
 there you are (giving something)
 prosím [proseem]
these: these men ti muži [tyi]
 can I have these? mohu
 dostat tyto? [mohoo dostut tito]

they oni [onyi], ony [oni], ona
thick silný [silnee]
thief (man/woman) zloděj
 [zlodyay]/zlodějka
thin tenký [tenkee]
thing věc [vyets]
 my things mé věci [meh]
think myslet [mislet]
 I'll think about it budu o tom
 přemýšlet [boodoo –
 prJemeeshlet]
thirsty: I'm thirsty mám žízeň
 [mahm Jeezen^yeh]
this: this man tento muž
 this woman tato žena [tuto]
 this one tento
 is this ...? je to ...?
those ti [tyi], ty [ti] ta
thread nit [nyit]
throat hrdlo [hurdlo]
through skrz [skurs]
thumb palec [pulets]
thunderstorm bouře [bohrJeh]
ticket lístek [leestek]
 (for plane) letenka

dialogue

> **a return ticket to Tábor**
> zpáteční do Tábora
> [spahtetch-nyee]
> **coming back when?** kdy
> se vracíte? [gudi seh
> vrutseeteh]
> **today/next Tuesday**
> dnes/v úterý
> **that will be 64 crowns**
> šedesát čtyři korun
> [koroon]

tie (necktie) vázanka [vahzunka], kravata [kruvuta]
tights punčocháče [poontchoHahtcheh]
time čas [chus]
  what's the time? kolik je hodin? [yeh ho-dy'n]
  next time příště [prɹeesh-tyeh]
  four times čtyřikrát [chtirɹikraht]
timetable jízdní řád [yeezd-nyee rɹaht]
tin (can) plechovka [pleHofka]
tin opener otvírák konzerv [otveerahk konzerf]
tip (for waiter etc) spropitné [spropitneh]
tired unavený [oonuvenee]
tissues papírové kapesníky [pupeeroveh kuɒesnyeeki]
to: to Prague do Prahy [pruhi]
  to the Czech Republic do České republiky [cheskeh repoobliki]
  to the post office na poštu [poshtoo]
toast (bread) topinka
today dnes
toe palec [ɒulets]
together společně [spoletch-nyeh]
toilet toaleta [to-uleta]
toilet paper toaletní papír [to-ulet-nyee pupeer]
tomato rajčé jablko [rɹitcheh yubulko]
tomorrow zítra [zeetra]
  tomorrow morning zítra ráno [rahno]

the day after tomorrow pozítří [pozeetrɹee]
tonic (water) tonik
tonight dnes večer [vetcher]
too (excessively) příliš [prɹeelish]
  (also) také [tukeh]
  too much příliš mnoho
  me too já také [yah tukeh]
tooth zub [zoop]
toothache bolest zubu [zooboo]
toothbrush kartáček na zuby [kartahtchek na zoobi]
toothpaste pasta na zuby [pusta]
top: on top of it k tomu [tomoo]
  at the top nahoře [nuhorɹeh]
torch baterka [buterka]
tour (noun) prohlídka [prohleetka]
tourist (man/woman) turista [toorista]/turistka
tourist information office turistická informační kancelář f [tooristitskah informuchnyee kuntselarɹ]
towards směrem k [smnyerem]
towel ručník [roochnyeek]
town město [mnyesto]
  in town ve městě [veh mnyes-tyeh]
town centre střed města [strɹet mnyesta], centrum města [tsentroom]
toy hračka [hrutchka]
track (US: at station) nástupiště [nahstoopish-tyeh]
traffic lights semafor [semufor]

train vlak [vluk]
 by train vlakem
 is this the train for ...? jede to
 do ...? [yedeh]
train station železniční
 stanice [zheleznitch-nyee
 stunyitseh]
tram tramvaj [trumvī]
translate překládat
 [prJeklahdut]/přeložit [prJeloJit]
trashcan popelnice
 [popelnitseh]
travel cestovat [tsestovut]
travel agent's cestovní
 agentura [tsestov-nyee
 ugentoora]
travellers' cheque cestovní
 šek [shek]
tree strom
trip (excursion) výlet [veelet]
trousers kalhoty [kulhoti]
true skutečný [skootetchnee]
try zkusit [skoosit]
try on zkusit si
T-shirt tričko [tritchko]
tuna tuňák [toonyahk]
turn: turn left/right zabočte
 doleva/doprava [zubotchteh]
twice dvakrát [dvukraht]
twin room dvoulůžkový
 pokoj [dvohlooshkovee pokoy]
tyre pneumatika [puneh-
oomutika]

U

umbrella deštník [desht-nyeek]
uncle strýc [streets]

under pod
underground (railway) metro
underpants spodky [spotki]
understand: I understand
 rozumím [rohzoomeem]
 I don't understand
 nerozumím
university univerzita
 [ooniverzita]
unleaded petrol bezolovnatý
 benzín [bezolovnutee benzeen],
 Natural [nutoorul]
until do
up nahoře [nahorJeh]
 (upwards) nahoru [nahoroo]
 up there tam nahoře [tum
 nahorJeh]
upstairs nahoře [nahorJeh]
urgent naléhavý [nuleh-huvee]
us nás [nahs]
 for us pro nás
USA Spojené státy americké
 [spo-yeneh stahti umeritskeh]
use používat
 [pohJeevut]/použít [pohJeet]
useful užitečný [ooJitetchnee]

V

vacation (from school, university)
 prázdniny [prahzd-nyini]
 (from work) dovolená
 [dovolenah]
valid (ticket etc) platný [plutnee]
value (noun) hodnota
vanilla vanilka [vunilka]
veal telecí maso [teletsee muso]
vegetables zelenina [zelenyina]

vegetarian (noun: man/woman) vegetarián [vegeturiahn]/ vegetariánka

very velmi

I like it very much moc se mi to líbí [mots seh – leebee]

view výhled [vee-hlet]

village vesnice [ves-nyitseh]

visit (verb) navštívit [nufsh-tyeevit]/navštěvovat [nufsh-tyevovut]

vodka vodka [votka]

voice hlas [hlus]

W

waist pás [pahs]

wait čekat [chekut]/počkat [potchkut]

waiter číšník [cheesh-nyeek]

waiter! pane vrchní! [puneh vurн-nyee]

waitress číšnice [cheesh-nyitseh]

waitress! paní vrchní! [punyee vurн-nyee]

(to a younger one) slečno! [sletchno]

wake-up call buzení telefonem [boozenyee]

Wales Wales

walk: is it a long walk? je to pěšky daleko? [yeh to pyeshki duleko]

wall stěna [styena], zeď [zet^yeh]

wallet náprsní taška [nahprus-nyee tushka]

want: I want a ... chci ... [Hutsi]

I don't want any ... nechci žádný ... [neHutsi Jahdnee]

I don't want to ... nechci ...

what do you want? co chcete? [tso Hutseteh]

warm teplý [teplee]

wash mýt [meet]/umýt [oomeet]

(oneself) mýt se [seh]

washhand basin umývadlo [umeevudlo]

washing (clothes) prádlo [prahdlo]

washing machine pračka [prutchka]

washing powder prášek na praní [prahshek na prunyee]

wasp vosa

watch (wristwatch) hodinky [ho-dyinki]

water voda

way: it's this way je to tudy [yeh to toodi]

it's that way je to tamtudy [tumtoodi]

is it a long way to ...? je daleko do ...? [yeh duleko]

no way! v žádném případě! [vJahdnem prJee-pudyeh]

dialogue

could you tell me the way to ...? (to man/woman) mohl/mohla byste mi říct, kudy se jede do ...? [mohul/mo-hla bisteh mi rJeetst koodi seh yedeh]

go straight on until you

reach the traffic lights
jeďte rovně, až na
křižovatku se semaforem
[yedyeteh rovnyeh ush na
krɟiɟovutkoo seh semuforem]
turn left zabočte doleva
[zabotchteh]
take the first on the right
zabočte první doprava
[purvnyee dopruva]

we my [mi]
weather počasí [potchusee]
week týden [teeden]
 a week (from) today za týden
weekend víkend [veekend]
weight váha [vah-ha]
welcome: you're welcome
 (don't mention it) prosím
 [proseem]
well: she's not well necítí se
 dobře [netsee-tyee seh dobrɟeh]
 you speak English very well
 mluvíte moc dobře anglicky
 [mlooveeteh mots ... unglitski]
 well done! výborně! [veebor-
nyeh]
 this one as well tento také
 [tukeh]
 well-done (meat) dobře
 propečený [dobrɟeh
 propetchenee]
Welsh velšský [velshskee]
west západ [zahpat]
wet mokrý [mokree]
what? cože? [tsoɟeh]
 what's that? co je tohle? [tso
 yeh to-hleh]
wheel kolo

when? kdy? [gudi]
 when's the train? kdy jede
 vlak? [yedeh vluk]
where? kde? [gudeh]
which: which bus? který
 autobus? [kuteree owtoboos]
while: while I'm here zatímco
 jsem tady [zutyeemtso sem tudi]
whisky whisky
white bílý [beelee]
white wine bílé víno [beeleh
 veeno]
who? kdo? [gudo]
whole: the whole week celý
 týden [tselee teeden]
whose: whose is this? čí je
 to? [chee yeh]
why? proč? [protch]
 why not? proč ne? [neh]
wide široký [shirokee]
wife manželka [munɟelka]
wind (noun) vítr [veetr]
window (of house) okno
 (of shop) výklad [veeklut]
 in the window (of shop) ve
 výkladě [veh veekludyeh]
wine víno [veeno]
wine list nápojový lístek
 [nahpo-yovee leestek]
winter zima
with s
without bez
woman žena [ɟena]
wood (material) dřevo [drɟevo]
wool vlna [vulna]
word slovo
work (noun) práce [prahtseh]
 it's not working nefunguje to
 [nefoongoo-yeh]

worry: I'm worried mám
starosti [mahm sturostyi]
worse: it's worse je to horší
[yeh to horshee]
worst nejhorší [nayhorshee]
would: would you give this
to ...? (to man/woman) dal/dala
byste to ...? [dul/dula bisteh]
wrap: could you wrap it up?
(to man/woman) mchl/mohla
byste to zabalit? [mohul/mo-hla
zubulit]
wrist zápěstí [zahpyes-tye]
write psát [psaht]/napsat
[nupsut]
could you write it down? (to
man/woman) mohl/mohla
byste to napsat? [mohul/mo-hla
bisteh]
wrong: it's the wrong key to je
špatný klíč [yeh shpahtnee]
there's something wrong
with ... něco je v nepořádku
... [nyetso yeh fneporJahtkoo]
what's wrong? co se děje?
[tso seh dyay-eh]

(pl or pol) vy
this is for you to je pro
tebe/vás [yeh pro tebeh/vahs]
young mladý [mludee]
your/yours (sing, fam) tvůj
[tvoo-i], tvoje [tvo-yeh]
(pl or pol) váš [vahsh], vaše
[vahsheh]
youth hostel (turistická)
ubytovna mládeže
[tooristitskah oobitovna mlahdeJeh]

Z

zero nula [noola]
zip zip
zoo zoologická zahrada
[zo-ologitskah]

Y

year rok
yellow žlutý [Jlutee]
yes ano [uno]
yesterday včera [fchera]
the day before yesterday
předevčírem [prJedefcheerem]
yet nicméně [nitsmenyeh], už
[oosh]
you (sing, fam) ty [ti]

Czech

→

English

a [a] and
ačkoliv [utchkolif] although
advokát m [udvokaht],
  advokátka f lawyer
ahoj [uhoy] hello, hi; cheerio
ale [uleh] but
ambulance [umbooluntseh] out-
  patients' department
anglický [unglitskee] English
Anglie [ungli-eh] England
ani ... ani ... [unyi] neither ...
  nor ...
ano [uno] yes
asi [usi] about; probably
autobusová zastávka
  [owtoboosovah zustahfkah] bus
  stop
autobusové nádraží
  [owtoboosoveh nahdruJee] bus
  station

balíky parcels
barva [burva] colour
bavlna [buvulna] cotton
bazén [buzen] swimming pool
během [byeh-hem] during
benzín [benzeen] petrol,
  gasoline
bez [bes] without
bezcelný [bes-tselnee] duty-
  free
bezolovnatý [bezolovnutee]
  lead-free
bezpečný [bespetchnee] safe
bezplatný [besplutnee] free (of
  charge)
bezprostřední [besprostrJed-
  nyee] immediate
bezvízový styk [bezveezovee stik]

no visa required
bílý [beelee] white
bláznivý [blah-znyivee] mad
blízký [bleeskee] near
bohatý [bohutee] rich
bolest pain
brát/vzít [braht/vuzeet] to take
bratr [brutur] brother
broušené sklo [brohsheneh] cut
  glass
brzy [burzi] soon
buď... nebo [boot^{yeh}] either ...
  or ...
budova [boodova] building
Bůh [booH] God
bydlet [bidlet] to live; to stay
byt [bit] flat, apartment
být [beet] to be
byt a strava [bit a struva] board
  and lodging

celkový [tselkovee] complete
celnice [tsel-nyitseh] customs
celý [tselee] all; whole
cena [tsena] price
  v ceně [ftsenyeh] included
cenová: I./II./III./IV. cenová
  skupina restaurant price
  categories 1/2/3/4, 1 being
  the most expensive
cesta [tsesta] journey; road
cestovat [tsestovut] to travel
cestovní kancelář [tsestov-nyee
  kuntselarJ] travel agency
cestovní pas [tsestov-nyee pus]
  passport
cestovní šek [tsestov-nyee shek]
  travellers' cheque
cizí [tsizee] foreign; strange

cizinec **m** [tsizinets], cizinka **f**
  foreigner; stranger
clo [tslo] customs
co? [tso] what?
cože? [tsoJeh] what?
cukrárna [tsookrarna] cake
  shop; café; confectionery
  shop

čas [chus] time
časně [chus-nyeh] early
časopis [chusopis] magazine
část [chahst] part
často [chusto] often
Čechy [cheHi] Bohemia
čekárna [chekarna] waiting
  room
čekat [chekut] to wait
černý [chernee] black
čerstvě natřeno wet paint
červený [chervenee] red
Česká republika [cheskah
  repooblika] Czech Republic
Češi [cheshi] the Czechs
čeština [chesh-tyina] Czech
čí [chee] whose
číslo [cheeslo] number
ci číst [cheest] to read
čistírna [chis-tyerna] dry
  cleaner's
čistý [chistee] clean
číšnice [cheesh-nyitseh] waitress
číšník [cheesh-nyeek] waiter
člověk [chlo-vyek] man
ČR [cheh er] Czech Republic

dále! [dahleh] come in!
daleko [duleko] far (away)
dálkový spoj [dahlkovee spoy]

long-distance bus
dálnice [dahl-nyitseh]
  motorway, highway
dáma [dahma] lady
dámy [dahmi] ladies' (room)
daň [dun^yeh] tax
dárek gift
dát [daht] to give
datum narození [narozenyee]
  date of birth
dávat/dát [dahvut] to give
dcera [tsera] daughter
děkuji (vám) [dyekoo-yi (vahm)]
  thank you
dělat/udělat [oodyelut] to
  make; to do
den day
déšť [desht^yeh] rain
děti [dyetyi] children
děvče [dyeftcheh] girl
devizový kurs [devizovee koors]
  exchange rate
devizy [devizi] hard currency
díky [dyeeki] thanks
dítě [dyeetyeh] child
divadlo [dyivudlo] theatre
dívat se/podívat se [po-dyeevut
  seh] to look
dívka [dyeefka] girl
divný [dyivnee] funny; strange
dlouho [dloh-ho] a long time
dlouhý [dloh-hee] long; tall
dnes today
dnes večer [vetcher] tonight
do until; to
dobrou chuť [dobroh Hoot^yeh]
  enjoy your meal!
dobrý [dobree] good
dobrý den [den] hello

58

dobře! [dobrJeh] good!
dojet [do-yet] to arrive
doklad [doklut] document
doma home; at home
dopis letter
dospělá [dos-pyelah] adult
dost enough
dostávat/dostat
 [dostahvut/dostut] to get
doutník [doht-nyeek] cigar
dovoleno allowed
drahý [druhee] expensive
drzý [durzee] rude
dřevo [drJevo] wood
důležitý [dooleJitee] important
dům [doom] house
dveře [dverJeh] door
dvojitý [dvo-yitee] double

foukaná [fohkunah] blow-dry
fronta queue
fungovat [foongovut] to work,
 to function

garsoniéra [gurzoni-era] flatlet,
 small apartment

hala [hula] lounge; hall
halenka [hulenka] blouse
havarijní pojištění [huvahri-nyee
 po-yishtyen-nyee] car insurance
 covering accidents
hezký [heskee] handsome
hlava [hluva] head
hlavní nádraží [nahdruJee] main
 station
hledat [hledut] to look for
hnědý [hnyedee] brown
hodina [ho-dyina] hour

hodiny [ho-dyini] clock
hoch [hoH] boy
holič m [holitch], **holička f**
 men's hairdresser
hora mountain
horko heat
horký [horkee] hot
horší [horshee] worse
hoří! [horJee] fire!
hospoda pub
host m/f [hosst] guest
hostinec [hos-tyinets] pub
hotelová obsluha [–lovah op-
 slooha] room service
hotovost cash
hovořit to speak; to talk
hra game; play
hranice [hrunyitseh] border
hrát [hraht] to play
hrdlo [hurdlo] throat
hrozný [hroznee] appalling
hubený [hoobenee] thin
hudba [hoodba] music

chlapec [Hlupets] boy
chléb-pečivo [Hlep-petchivo]
 baker's shop
chodidlo [Ho-dyidlo] foot
chodit/jít [Ho-dyit/yeet] to go; to
 walk
chodník [Hod-nyeek] pavement,
 sidewalk
chudý [Hoodee] poor
chutný [Hootnee] tasty
chyba [Hiba] mistake
chytnout/chytit [Hitnoht/Hi-tyit]
 to catch
chytrý [Hitree] clever

i as well as

informace [informutseh] information; directory enquiries

já [yah] I

jak [yuk] how; what; as

jako [yuko] as, like

jaký [yukee] what; what sort

jaro [yuro] spring (season)

jazyk [yuzik] tongue; language

je [yeh] he/she/it is; it; them
to je ... it is ...
je tady ...? [tudi] is there ...?

jeden [yeden] one

jediný [yedyinee] (the) only

jedna [yedna], **jedno** [yedno] one

jednolůžkový pokoj [yednolooshkovee pokoy] single room

jednosměrná silnice [yednosmnyernah seelnyitseh] one-way street

jednou [yednoh] once

jeho [yeho] (of) him/it; his

její [yeh-yee] her(s)

jejich [yeh-yeeH] their(s)

jen [yen] just; only
jen ve všední dny on weekdays only

jestli [yestli] if

ještě [yeshtyeh] still
ještě ne [neh] not yet

jezdit/jet [yezdyit/yet] to travel; to go

jezero [yezero] lake

ji [yi] her

jídelna [yeedelna] dining room

jídelní vůz [yeedel-nyee voos] restaurant car

jídlo [yeedlo] food; meal

jih [yiH] south

jinak [yinuk] otherwise

jinde [yindeh] elsewhere

jiný [yinee] other

jíst [yeest] to eat

jistý [yistee] quite sure

jít [yeet] to go; to walk

jízdenka [yeezdenka] ticket

jízdní kolo [yeezd-nyee] bicycle

jízdní řád [rJaht] timetable, (US) schedule

jižně [yiJnyeh] south

jméno [yumeno] name

jsem [sem] I am

jsi [si] you are

jsme [smeh] we are

jsou [soh] they are
jsou tady ...? [tudi] are there ...?

jste [steh] you are

k to; towards

kabát [kubaht] coat

kabelka [kubelka] handbag, (US) purse

kadeřnictví [kuderJnyits-tvee] ladies' hairdresser's

kartáč [kurtahtch] brush

kašna [kushna] fountain

kavárna [kuvarna] coffee bar

každodenní [kuJdodenyee] every day

každý [kuJdee] every

Kč Czech Crown

kde [gudeh] where

kdo [gudo] who

kdy? [gudi] when?
když [gudiJ] when
kino cinema, movie theater
klíč [kleetch] key
klimatizace [klimutizutseh] air-conditioning
kniha [kunyiha] book
knihkupectví [kunyiнkoopetstvee] bookshop, bookstore
knihovna [kunyihovna] library
kolik? how many?; how much?
kolo bicycle; wheel
konec [konets] end
konečná [konetchnah] terminus
konečně [konetch-nyeh] at last
konto bank account
kopec [kopets] hill
kostel church
košík [kosheek] basket
koupaliště [kohpulish-tyeh] swimming pool
koupel [kohpel] bath
koupelna [kohpelna] bathroom
koupit [kohpit] to buy
kouření zakázáno no smoking
kouřit [kohrJit] to smoke
kousek [kohsek] a little bit
krabička [krubitchka] packet
král [krahl] king
královna [krahlovna] queen
krásný [krahsnee] beautiful
krást [krahst] to steal
krejčí [kraytchee] tailor
krev [kref] blood
krk [kurk] neck
kromě [kromnyeh] except
křestní jméno [krJest-nyee yumeno] Christian name
křišťálové sklo [krJish-tyahloveh] crystal
který [kuteree] that
kuchyň [kooнin^yeh] kitchen
kupovat/koupit [koopovut/kohpit] to buy
kurs [koors] exchange rate
kuřácké kupé [koorJaht-skeh koopeh] smoking compartment
kus [koos] piece
kvůli [kv00li] because of

laciný [lutsinee] cheap
láhev [lah-hef] bottle
lahodný [lah-hodnee] delicious
láska [lahska] love
lázně [lahznyeh] spa
led [let] ice
legrační [legrutch-nyee] funny
lehký [leнkee] light
lékárna pharmacy
lékař m [lekurJ], **lékařka f** doctor
lepší [lepshee] better
les wood, forest
let flight
letadlo [letudlo] plane
leták [letahk] leaflet
letecky [letetski] by air
letenka plane ticket
letět [letyet] to fly
letiště [letyish-tyeh] airport
léto summer
levný [levnee] cheap
levý [levee] left
líbit se [leebit seh] to like
libra pound

lidé [lideh] people
lístek [leestek] ticket
loď [lot^{yeh}] boat; ship
ložnice [loʒnyitseh] bedroom
lůžko [looshko] bed
lůžkový vůz [looshkovee voos] sleeping car
lyže [liʒeh] ski
lyžování [liʒovah-rryee] skiing
lžíce [luʒeetseh] spoon

má [mah] my; mine; he/she/it has
Maďarsko [mucyursko] Hungary
málo [mahlo] few
malý [mulee] small
manžel [munʒel] husband
manželka [munʒelka] wife
manželská postel [munʒelskah] double bed
máte [mahteh] you have
matka [mutka] mother
mé [meh] my; mine
mě [mnyeh] (of) me
méně [menyeh] less
měsíc [mnyeseets] month; moon
město [mnyesto] town
mezi among; between
mezinárodní [mezinarod-nyee] international
mí [mee] my; mine
milovat [milovut] to love
milý [milee] nice
miminko baby
mimo provoz out of order
místenky reservations
místo [maesto] seat; place

místo narození [nurozenyee] place of birth
mít [meet] to have
mít rád [raht] to like
mladík [mluh-dyeek] young man
mladý [mludee] young
mluvit [mloovit] to speak
mne [mneh] me; of me; to me
mnoho much; many
mnohokrát děkuji [dyekoo-yi] thank you very much
moc [mots] a lot
moci [motsi] can; to be able
modrý [modree] blue
moje [mo-yeh] my; mine
mokrý [mokree] wet
moře [morʒeh] sea
most [mohst] bridge
možná [moʒnah] maybe
možný [moʒnee] possible
mrtvý [murtvee] dead
mu [moo] him
můj [moo-i] my; mine
muset [mooset] must; to have to
muž [moosh] man
muži [mooʒi] men; gents, men's room
my [mi] we
myslet [mislet] to think
mýt/umýt [meet] to wash

na on; onto; for; to
nábytek [nahbitek] furniture
nad [nut] above; over
nádherný [nahdhernee] wonderful
nádraží [nahdruʒee] station

nafta [nufta] diesel

nahoru [nuhoroo] up

nahoře [nuhorJeh] upstairs

náhradní díly [nah-hrud-nyee dyeeli] spare parts

nahý [nuhee] naked

nacházet/najít [nuHahzet/nī-eet] to find

nájemné [nah-yemneh] rent

najímat/najmout [nī-eemut/nīmoht] to rent; to hire

najít [nī-yeet] to find

nákladní auto [nahklud-nyee] truck

nákup [nahkoop] shopping

naléhavý [nuleh-huvee] urgent

nalevo [nulevo] on/to the left

napětí voltage

napít se [nupeet seh] to have a drink

naplnit [nupulnyit] to fill

napravo [nupruvo] on/to the right

na prodej [proday] for sale

napsat [nupsut] to write

národnost nationality

narozeniny [nurozenyini] birthday

nás [nahs] (of) us

nashle [nus-Hleh] bye

nashledanou [nus-Hledunoh] goodbye

nástup [nahstoop] entrance, entry

nástupiště [nahstoopish-tyeh] platform, (US) track

náš [nash], **naše** [nusheh] our(s)

Natural [nutoorul] unleaded

petrol/gas

nazdar [nuzdur] hello; goodbye

na zdraví! [zdruvee] cheers!

ne [neh] no; not

ně [nyeh] it; them

nebezpečí [nebespetchee] danger

nebezpečný [nebespetch-nee] dangerous

nebo or

něco [nyetso] something

nedaleko [neduleko] not far

něho [nyeho] (of) him/it

nehoda accident

nějací [nyayutse] some; any

nějaká [nyayukah], **nějaké** [nyayukeh], **nějaký** [nyayukee] a; some; any

nejbližší [nay-blishee] the nearest

nejede v ... does not run on ...

nejlepší [nay-lepshee] the best

nejsem [naysem] I am not

někde [nyegdeh] somewhere

někdo [nyegdo] somebody

někdy [nyegdi] sometimes

několik [nyekolik] a few

nekuřáci [nekoorJahtsi] non-smokers

nemám ... [nemahm] I don't have ...

Německo [nyemetsko] Germany

nemoc [nemots] disease

nemocnice [nemots-nyitseh] hospital

nemocný [nemotsnee] ill

nemožný [nemoɹnee] impossible

není [nenyee] he/she/it is not; there is not

není zač [zutch] you're welcome

neparkovat no parking

nepřetržitý provoz [neprɹeturɹitee provos] 24-hour service

nestaví v ... does not stop in ...

nevím [neveem] I don't know

než [nesh] than

ni [nyi] her

nic [nyits] nothing

nikde [nyigdeh] nowhere

nikdo [nyigdo] nobody

nikdy [nyigdi] never

nízký [nyeeskeɹ] low

noc [nots] night

nocleh se snídaní [notsleH seh snyeedunyee] bed and breakfast

noha [noha] leg

nos nose

nosit/nést to carry

nouzový východ [nohzovee veeHot] emergency exit

noviny [novini] newspaper

nový [noveɹ] new

nůž [noosh] knife

nyní [ninyee] now

oba both

oběd [obɥet] lunch

obchod [opHot] business; shop

obchodní dům [opHodnyee doom] department store

obraz [obrus] picture

obrovský [obrofskee] tremendous

obsah [opsuH] contents

obtížný [op-tyeeɹnee] difficult

obvod [obvot] district

obyčejný [obitchaynee] ordinary, usual

od [ot] since

odbavení [odbuvenyee] check-in

odjet [odyet] to leave

odjezd [odyest] departure

odlety departures

odlišný [odlishnee] different

odpoledne [otpoledneh] afternoon

odpověd' [otpovyet^yeh] answer

oheň [ohen^yeh] fire

okamžitě [okumɹityeh] immediately

okno window

oko eye

olej [olay] oil

omezení rychlosti speed limit

on he; it

ona she; it; they

oni [onyi] they

ono it

ony they

opatrný [oputurnee] careful

opilý [opilee] drunk

opouštět/opustit [opohshtyet/opoostyit] to leave

opravdový [opruvdovee] true

opravit [opruvit] to repair

orloj [orloy] clock; town clock

osamělý [osumnyelee] lonely

osoba person

osobní vlak [osobnyee] local train

osobní výtah customer lift/elevator; passenger lift/elevator

ostrov island

ošklivý [oshklivee] ugly

otáčet/otočit [otahtchet/ototchit] to turn

otec [otets] father

otevírací doba [oteveerutsee] opening times

otevřeno [otevrʃeno] open

otevřít [otevrʃeet] to open

pálivý [pahlivee] hot (spicy)

pan [pun] Mr

pane [puneh] Mr; sir

panelák [punelahk] apartment block

paní [punyee] Mrs; married; madam

páni [pahnyi] gents, men's room

paragon [purugon] receipt

parkovat/zaparkovat [zupurkovut] to park

parkoviště [purkovishtyeh] car park, parking lot

patřit [putrʃit] to belong

patro [putro] floor

pekařství [pekurʃ-stvee] baker's shop

pěkný [pyeknee] beautiful; pretty; fine

peníze [penyeezeh] money

pes dog

pilný [pilnee] fast

píseň [peesenʸeh] song

pít/napít se [peet/nupeet seh] to drink

pitná voda [pitnah] drinking water

pivnice [pivnyitseh] pub

placené parkoviště paying car park/parking lot

platit/zaplatit [zuplutyit] to pay

platný [plutnee] valid

plavat [pluvut] to swim

plavecký bazén [pluvetskee buzen] swimming pool

plná penze [pulnah penzeh] full board, European plan

plný [pulnee] full

po after

počítač [potcheetutch] computer

počkat [potchkut] to wait

pod [pot] below; under

podívat se [podyeevut seh] to look

podpis signature

podzim autumn, (US) fall

pohlaví [po-Hluvee] sex, gender

pojištění [po-yishtyenyee] insurance

pokažený [pokuʃenee] faulty; broken

pokoj [pokoy] room

policejní stanice [politsaynyee stunyitseh] police station

polo- half–

polopenze [polopenzeh] half board, American plan

Polsko Poland

pomalu [pomaloo] slowly

pomoc [pomots] help

poplatek [poplutek] fee; charge

poschodí [posHodyee] floor

posílat/poslat [poseelut/poslut] to send

poslední [poslednyee] last

poslouchat [poslohHut] to listen to

postel bed

poštovní schránka [poshtovnyee sHrahnka] letterbox, mailbox

potom then

pouze pro personál staff only

pozdě [pozdyeh] late

pozítří [pozeetrJee] the day after tomorrow

pozor! attention!; look out!; caution!

práce [prahtseh] work

pracovat [prutsovut] to work

Praha [pruha] Prague

pravdivý [pruvdyivee] true

právnička f [prahv-nyitchka], právník m [prahvnyeek] lawyer

pravý [pruvee] genuine

prázdný [prahzdnee] empty; vacant

prezervativ [prezervutif] condom

pro for

proč? [protch] why?

prodat [produt] to sell

prodávat/prodat [prohdahvut] to sell

prodejna [prodayna] shop

prominňte [promin^yehteh] sorry

pronájem automobilů [proní-em owtomobiloo] car rental

pronajmutí: k pronajmutí [pronīmoo-tyee] for hire, to rent

prosím [proseem] please; here you are; you're welcome

prosím? pardon (me)?

proti [protyi] opposite; against

protože [protoJeh] as, since; because

provoz [provos] traffic

prst [purst] finger

průvodce [proovotseh] guide (man); guidebook

průvodkyně [proovotki-nyeh] guide (woman)

první [purvnyee] first

první poschodí [pos-Hodyee] first floor, (US) second floor

první třídou [purvnyee trJeedoh] first class (travel etc)

před [prJet] before; in front of

předčíslí [prJet-cheeslee] dialling code

předevčírem [prJedef-cheerem] the day before yesterday

předložte jízdenky! tickets please!

přednost v jízdě right of way

předseda vlády [prJetseda vlahdi] prime minister

překládat/přeložit [prJeklahdut/prJeloJit] to translate

přes [prJes] over; across; through

při [prJi] during, close at

přicházet/přijít [prJi-Hahzet/prJi-yeet] to come

příjemný [prJee-yemnee] pleasant

přijet [prJi-yet] to arrive

příjmení [prJee-menyee]

surname
příliš [prJeelish] too much; too
 many
přímo [prJeemo] straight on;
 directly
přímý [prJeemee] direct
přinášet/přinést
 [prJinahshet/prJinest] to bring
připravený [prJipruvenee] ready
příští [prJeeshtyee] next
přítel [prJeetel] friend;
 boyfriend
přítelkyně [prJeetelkinyeh]
 friend; girlfriend
přívoz [prJeevos] ferry
přízemí [prJeezemee] ground
 floor, (US) first floor;
 downstairs
psát/napsat [psaht/nupsut] to
 write
půjčovna aut [poo-itchovna owt]
 car rental
půl [pool] half
 půl hodiny [pool ho-dyini] half
 an hour

radnice [rudnyitseh] town
 hall
Rakousko [rukohsko] Austria
ráno [rahno] morning
rodiče [ro-dyitcheh] parents
rodina [ro-dyina] family
rok year
rovně [rovnyeh] straight on
rozkošný [roskoshnee] lovely
rozumět [rozoomnyet] to
 understand
ruka [rooka] hand
Rusko Russia

rušný [rooshnee] busy
rybí speciality [ribee]
 fishmonger's; fish dishes
rychlý [riHlee] quick

ředitel m [rJedyitel], **ředitelka f**
 manager
řeka [rJeka] river
řeznictví [rJeznits-tvee]
 butcher's
řídit [rJeedyit] to drive
říkat/říct [rJeekut/rJeetst] to say;
 to tell

s with
sám [sahm] myself; yourself;
 himself; alone
sazba [suzba] charges
sbohem [zbo-hem] goodbye
sem pull
sestra sister
sever north
schody [sHodi] stairs
schránka [sHrahnka] letterbox,
 mailbox
skoro [skoro] almost
skrz [skurs] through
skupina [skoopina] group
skvělý [skvyelee] excellent
slečna [sletchna] Miss; single
 woman
Slovensko Slovakia
slovo word
směnárna [smnyenarna] bureau
 de change
smrt [smurt] death
smutný [smootnee] sad
snadný [snudnee] easy
sněžit [snyeJit] to snow

snídaně [snyeedunyeh] breakfast

soukromý [sohkromee] private

spát [spaht] to sleep

spotřebovat do use before

spousta [spohsta] a lot (of)

sprcha [spurHa] shower

srdce [surdtseh] heart

stanice [stunyitseh] station; stop

starožitnost [sturoJitnost] antique

starý [sturee] old

stát [staht] to cost; to stand

státní svátek [svahtek] public holiday

stejný [staynee] same

strýc [streets] uncle

střed [strJet] centre

stříbro [strJeebro] silver

studený [stoodenee] cold

stůj! [stoo-i] stop!

stůl [stool] table

suchý [sooHee] dry

svá [svah] my; your; his/her/its; our; their; one's

svátek [svahtek] public holiday; name day

své [sveh], svůj [svoo-i] my; your; his/her/its; our; their; one's

syn [sin] son

šálek [shahlek] cup

šatna [shutna] cloakroom, (US) checkroom

široký [shirokee] wide

škoda [shkoda] pity

škola [shkola] school

špatný [shputnee] bad

šťastný [shtyustnee] happy

ta this (one); that (one); these; those

tábořiště [tahborJishtyeh] campsite

tady [tudi] here

tady je [yeh] here is

tahat/táhnout [tah-Hnoht] to pull

tak [tuk] so

také [tukeh] also, too

takový [tukovee] such

tam [tum] there; push

tě [tyeh] (of) you

tebe [tebeh] you; of/to you

ted' [tet^{yeh}] now

tělo [tyelo] body

téměř [teh-mnyerJ] nearly

ten this (one); that (one)

teplota temperature

těší mě! [tyeshee mnyeh] nice to meet you!

teta aunt

těžký [tyeshkee] heavy

ti [tyi] (to) you; these; those

ticho [tyiHo] silence

tlačit [tlutchit] to push

to it; this (one); that (one)

tomu [tomoo] (to) him; (to) it

trasa [trusa] route

tráva [trahva] grass

trochu [troHoo] a little bit (of); some

trosky [troski] ruins

třída [trJeeda] class; avenue; main street

turistická stezka tourist path

tvá [tvah] your(s)

tvář [tvarJ] face

tvé [tveh], **tví** [tvee], **tvoje** [tvo-yeh], **tvoji** [tvo-yi], **tvůj** [tvoo-i] your(s)

ty [ti] you; these; those

týden [teeden] week

u [oo] by; at

ubytování [oobitovah-nyee] accommodation

ubytovna mládeže [mlah-deJeh] youth hostel

účet [oochet] bill, (US) check; account

učit [oochit] to teach

učitel m [ootchitel], **učitelka f** teacher

udělat [oo-dyelut] to make; to do

údolí [oodolee] valley

ucho [ooHo] ear

ulice [oolitseh] street

umění [oo-mnyenyee] art

unavený [oonuvenee] tired

úplně [oopulnyeh] quite

úřad [oorJut] office

ústa [oosta] mouth

ústředna [oostryedna] operator

už [oosh] already

v in; at

válka [vahlka] war

valuty [valooti] foreign currency

vás [vahs] (of) you

váš [vahsh], **vaše** [vusheh], **vaši** [vushi] your(s)

vážný [vahJnee] serious

včera [ftchera] yesterday

včetně [fchetnyeh] inclusive

ve [veh] in; at

věc [vyets] thing; matter

večer [vetcher] evening

večeře [vetcherJeh] dinner

vědět [vyedyet] to know

vedle [vedleh] next to

vedoucí m/f [vedohtsee] manager; manageress

věk [vyek] age

velikost [velikost] size

velký [velkee] big; large

velmi mnoho very much

velvyslanectví [velvislunetstvee] embassy

ven out

věřit [vyerJit] to believe

vesnice [vesnyitseh] village

větší [vyetshee] bigger

většina [vyetshina] (the) most (of)

vhoďte minci insert money

vchod [fHot] way in, entrance

více [veetseh] more

vítáme vás! [veetahmeh vahs] welcome!

vjezd zakázán no entry

vlak [vluk] train

vnitrostátní linky domestic flights

voda water

volat [volut] to call

volno vacancy; free time

vpravo [fpruvo] right

vstupenka [fstoopenka] ticket

vstupte! [fstoopteh] come in!

vstup volný admission free

vstup zakázán no admittance, no entry

všední den [fshednyeə] weekday

všechno [fsheHno] everything; all

všechno nejlepší! [naylepshee] best wishes!

všichni [fshiHnyi] all

všude [fshoodeh] everywhere

vy [vi] you

výdejna jízdenek [veedayna yeezdenek] ticket office

východ [veeHot] exit; gate; east

výlet [veelet] trip

vyprodáno [viprodahno] sold out

výprodej [veeproday] sale

vysoký [visokee] high

výstup [veestoop] exit

vystupovat/vystoupit [vistoopovut/vistohpit] to get off

výtah [veetuH] lift, elevator

vytočte číslo dial number

významný [veeznumnee] important

vzdálenost [vuzdahlenost] distance

vzít [vuzeet] to take

vždy [vuJdi] always

z of; from

za behind; in; after, past the; per

začátek [zutchahtek] beginning

záda [zahda] back

zahraniční linky international flights

záchod [zahHot] toilet, restroom

zakázaný [zukahzunee] forbidden; prohibited

zákaz parkování no parking

západ [zahput] west

záruční lhůta best before; guarantee period

zastávka na znamení request stop

zavazadla [zuvuzudla] baggage

zavřeno [zuvrJeno] closed

zde [zdeh] here

zeď [zet^{yeh}] wall

zelený [zelenee] green

zima winter

zítra [zeetra] tomorrow

zlato [zluto] gold

zlomený [zlomenee] broken

zlý [zlee] bad

známka [znahmka] stamp

znovu [znovoo] again

zpoždění [spoJdyenyee] delay

zrušit [zrooshit] to cancel

ztráty a nálezy [strahti a nahlezi] lost property, lost and found

zub [zoop] tooth

žádný [Jahdnee] no ...; none

žena [Jena] woman

ženský [Jenskee] female; women's

židle [Jidleh] chair

žít [Jeet] to live

žlutý [Jlootee] yellow

MENU READER

Food: Essential terms

bread chléb [Hlep]
butter máslo [mahslo]
cup šálek [shahlek]
dessert dezert
fish ryba [riba]
fork vidlička [vidlitchka]
glass: a glass of ... sklenice
... [sklenyitseh]
knife nůž [nOOsh]
main course hlavní chod
[Hluv-nyee Hot]
meat maso [muso]
menu jídelní lístek [yeedelnyee
leestek]
pepper pepř [pepurJ]
plate talíř [tuleerJ]

salad salát [salaht]
salt sůl f [sOOl]
set menu set menu menu
[meni]
soup polévka [polefka]
spoon lžíce f [luJeetseh]
starter předkrm [prJetkurm]
table stůl [stOOl]

another ..., please ještě jedno
... [yeshtyeh yedno]
excuse me! promiňte!
[prominyehteh]
could I have the bill, please?
mohu dostat účet, prosím?
[mohoo dostut proseem]

Food: Menu Reader

ananas [ununus] pineapple
anglická slanina [unglitskah slun-yina] bacon
angrešt [ungresht] gooseberry
baklažán [bukluJahn]
aubergine, eggplant

bažant [buJunt] pheasant
bezmasá jídla [bezmusah yeedla]
meatless dishes
boršč [borshtch] Russian-style beetroot and cabbage soup

borůvky [boroofki] bilberries, blueberries

bramborové hranolky [bramboroveh hrunolki] chips, French fries

bramborové knedlíky [kunedleeki] potato dumplings

brambory [brumbori] potatoes

brokolice [brokolitseh] broccoli

broskev [broskef] peach

brukev na paprice [brookef na pupritseh] kohlrabi with red peppers

celer [tseler] celery

cibule [tsibooleh] onion

citrón [tsitrawr] lemon

cukína [tsookina] courgettes, zucchini

černý rybíz [chernee ribees] blackcurrants

čerstvý [cherstvee] fresh

červená řepa [chervenah rJepa] beetroot

červený rybíz [chervenee] red-currants

čevapčiči [chevuptchitchi] spicy meatballs

čočka [chotchka] lentils

daněk [dunyek] venison

dezert dessert

divoký kanec [dyivokee kunets] wild boar

divoký králík na česneku [krahleek na chesnekoo] wild rabbit with garlic

do krvava [kurvuva] rare

domácí [domahtsee] home-made

dort cake; gâteau

dortík [dortyeek] tart

dršťky [dursht^{yeh}ki] tripe

drůbež [droobesh] poultry

drůbky [droopki] giblets

dušené hovězí maso [doosheneh hovyezee] beef stew

dušený [dooshenee] stewed

fazole [fuzoleh] beans

fazolky [fuzolki] green beans

filé [fileh] fillet (of fish)

fritovaný [fritovunee] deep-fried

gaskoňský kotlet [guskon^{yeh}skee] pork chop with cream and mushrooms

guláš [goolahsh] goulash, meat stew with paprika

grilovaný [grilovunee] grilled

hlávkové zelí [hlahfkoveh zelee] cabbage

hlávkový salát [hlahfkovee sulaht] lettuce

hodně vypečený [hodnyeh vipetchenee] well-done

holub [holoop] pigeon

houby [hohbi] mushrooms

houskové knedlíky [hohskoveh kunedleeki] bread dumplings

hovězí [hovyezee] beef

hovězí játra na slanině [yahtra na slunyinyeh] calves' liver stewed with onions and bacon

hovězí maso [muso] beef

hovězí tokáň [tokahn^{yeh}] beef stewed in wine and tomato purée

hrachová kaše [hruHovah kusheh] boiled peas with pieces of bacon

hranolky [hrunolki] chips,
French fries

hrášek [hrahshek] peas

hroznové víno [hroznovee veeno]
grapes

hruška [hrooshka] pear

humr [humur] lobster

husa [hoosa] goose

chlebíčky [Hlebeetchkee] open
sandwiches

chlupaté knedlíky se zelím
[Hlooputeh kunedleeki seh zeleem]
Bohemian potato
dumplings with cabbage

chřest [HrJest] asparagus

jablko [yubulko] apple

jablkový závin [yubulkovee
zahvin] apple strudel

jahody [yuhodi] strawberries

játra [yahtra] liver

jazýček [yuzeetchek] tongue

jednotlivá jídla [yednotlivah yeed-
la] à la carte

jehně [yehnyeh] lamb

jelení hřbet přírodní [yelenyee
hurJbet prJeerodnyee] saddle of
venison

jelení maso [muso] venison

jelito [yelito] black pudding

jídelní lístek [yeedelnyee leestek]
menu

kadeřávek [kuderJahvek] savoy
cabbage

kachna [kuHna] duck

kančí [kuntchee] wild boar

kapr [kupur] carp

karotka [kurotka] carrots

kaše [kusheh] buckwheat
cereal; purée

kedluben [kedlooben] kohlrabi

klobása [klobahsa] smoked
sausage

kmín [kumeen] caraway seed

knedlíky [kunedleeki]
dumplings

kotleta chop

králík [krahleek] rabbit

krevety [kreveti] shrimps

krocan [krotsun] turkey

krokety [kroketi] croquettes

krupice [kroopitseh] semolina

krvavý [kurvuvee] rare

křehký koláč s jablky [krJeHkee
kolahtch s yubulki] apple pie

křenová šlehačka [krJenovah
shlehutchka] horseradish sauce

křepelčí vajíčka [krJepeltchee
vi-eetchka] quail's eggs

kukuřice [kookoorJitseh] maize;
sweet corn; corn on the
cob

kuře [koorJeh] chicken

kůzle pečené [koozleh
petcheneh] roast kid

květák [kvyetahk]
cauliflower

kynuté knedlíky [kinooteh
kunedleeki] dumplings filled
with jam or fruit

kyselé zelí [kiseleh zelee] sauerkraut

kyselý [kiselee] sour

kýta [keeta] thigh; joint;
haunch

ledvinky [ledvinki] kidneys

lívance [leevuntseh] pancakes
with jam

losos salmon

luštěninová jídla [looshtyenyino-vah yeedla] dishes containing beans or pulses

mák [mahk] poppy seeds

makrela [mukrela] mackerel

maliny [mulini] raspberries

maso [muso] meat

masová směs na roštu [musovah smnyes na roshtoo] mixed grill of beef, veal, pork, calves' or pigs' kidney, smoked sausage and ham

meruňka [meroon^{yeh}ka] apricot

míchaná vejce [meeHanah vayt-seh] scrambled eggs

moravský vrabec [morufskee vrubets] 'Moravian Sparrows' – pieces of pork sprinkled with caraway seeds and roasted

moučníky [mohtchnyeeki] desserts

mrkev [murkef] carrot

mušle [mooshleh] mussels

nadívaný [nudyeevunee] stuffed

na jehle [yenleh] on a skewer

nakládaný [nuklahdunee] pick-led

na kmíně [kumeenyeh] with caraway seeds

na roštu [roshtoo] grilled

ne moc vypečený [neh mots vipetchenee] medium-rare

noky [noki] small flour and potato dumplings

nudle [noodleh] noodles

opékané brambory [opekuneh brumbori] fried potatoes

oplatky [oplutki] waffles

ostružiny [ostrooJini] blackber-ries

ovoce [ovotseh] fruit

palačinka [pulutchinka] pancake

pálivá paprika [pahlivah puprika] hot red pepper

paprika green or red pepper

paprikový lusk [puprikovee] pepper, capsicum

párek sausage, frankfurter

párek v rohlíku [rohleekoo] hot dog

paštika [pahshtyika] pâté

pečená husa [petchenah hoosa] roast goose

pečená šunka s vejci [petchenah shoonka svaytsi] ham and eggs

pečené kuře s nádivkou [petcheneh koorJeh s nahdyifkoh] stuffed roast chicken

pečený [petchenee] roast; baked; grilled

pepř [pepurJ] pepper (spice)

plněné rajče zapečené [pulnyeneh rītcheh zupetcheneh] stuffed tomato au gratin

plzeňská pivní polévka [pulzen^{yeh}skah pivnyee polefka] Pilsen-style beer soup

pomeranč [pomeruntch] orange

pórek leek

povidla homemade thick plum jam

předkrmy [prJedkurmi] starters, appetizers

přílohy [prJeelohi] side dishes

přírodní vepřové žebírko
[prjeerodnyee veprjoveh Jebeerko]
grilled pork chop

pstruh [pustrooH] trout

ragú [rug00] stew

rajče [rītcheh] tomato

rak [ruk] crayfish

roštěná přírodní na roštu
[roshtyenah prjeerodnyee na rosh-
too] grilled sirloin steak

rožeň [roJen^yeh] spit; skewer

růžičková kapusta [r00Jitchko-
vah kupoosta] Brussels sprouts

ryba [riba] fish

rybí polévka z kapra [ribee pole-
fka skupra] carp soup

ryby [ribi] fish

rýže [reeJeh] rice

rýžový nákyp s jablky [reeJovee
nahkip syubulki] rice pudding
with apples

salám [sulahm] salami

salát [sulaht] lettuce; salad

sardinka [surdinka] sardine

segedínský guláš [segedeenskee
goolahsh] pork goulash with
sauerkraut

sekaná pečeně [sekunah
petchenyeh] meatloaf

sele [sehleh] suckling pig

skopové maso [skopoveh muso]
mutton

sladký [slutkee] sweet

slanina [slunyina] bacon

sleď [slet^yeh] herring

slepice [slepitseh] chicken

sluka [slooka] snipe

**smažené bramborové hra-
nolky** [smuJeneh brumboroveh

hrunolki] chips, French fries

smažené kuře [koorJeh] fried
chicken

smažený [smuJenee] fried (in
breadcrumbs)

smetana [smetuna] cream

srnčí [suruntchee] venison

**steak z tuňáka po provensál-
sku** [toonyahka po
provensahlskoo] tuna, tomatoes,
white wine and garlic

studené předkrmy [stoodeneh
prjetkurmi] hors d'oeuvres,
starters, appetizers

svíčková [sveetchkovah] sirloin

svíčková omáčka [omahtchka]
sour cream sauce, usually
served with fillet of beef

škubánky s mákem [shkoobahn-
ki smahkem] potato
dumplings with poppy
seeds and sugar

šlehačka [shlehutchka]
whipped cream

špekové knedlíky [shpekoveh
kunedleeki] bread and bacon
dumplings

špenát [shpenaht] spinach

štika na pivě [shtyika na pivyeh]
pike in beer

šunka [shoonka] ham

švestkové knedlíky [shvestkoveh
kunedleeki] plum dumplings

švestky [shvestki] plums

telecí [teletsee] veal

teplá šunka [teplah shoonka]
boiled ham, served hot

teplé předkrmy [tepleh prjetkur-
mi] entrées

teplý [teplee] hot; warm

těstoviny [tyestovini] noodles; pasta

topinka s česnekem [chesnekem] toasted rye bread rubbed with garlic

treska na roštu [roshtoo] grilled cod

třešně [trJeshnyeh] cherries

tuňák [toonyahk] tuna fish

tvaroh [tvuroH] cottage cheese

tykev [tikef] marrow

uherský salám [ooherskee sulahm] Hungarian spicy salami with cucumber

uzené vařené [oozeneh vurJeneh] boiled smoked meat

uzeniny [oozenyini] smoked meats

uzený [oozenee] smoked

vaječná jídla [vī-etchnah yeedla] egg dishes

vanilková zmrzlina [vunilkovah zmurzlina] vanilla ice cream

vařený [vurJenee] boiled

vejce [vaytseh] egg

veka white French-style bread

vepřová pečeně [veprJovah petchenyeh] roast pork

vepřové maso [veprJoveh muso] pork

vepřový guláš [veprJovee goolahsh] pork goulash

vepřový řízek [rJeezek] breaded pork cutlet

vídeňský telecí řízek [veeden{yeh}skee teletsee rJeezek] fried veal in breadcrumbs

višně [vishnyeh] sour cherries; morello

vlašské ořechy [vlushskeh orJeHi] walnut

zadělávaná slepice [zudyelahvunah slepitseh] chicken with white sauce

zajíc [zī-eets] hare

zákusky [zahkooski] desserts

zapečená šunka s vejci [zupetchenah shoonka zvaytsi] ham and eggs

zapečený [zupetchenee] roast; baked; grilled

zavařenina [zuvurJenyina] preserves; jam

závin [zahvin] apple strudel

zavináč [zuvinahtch] rollmop herring in vinegar

zelené fazole [zeleneh fuzoleh] green beans

zelenina [zelenyina] vegetables

zeleninová jídla [zelenyinovah yeedla] vegetable dishes

zelí [zelee] cabbage

zmrzlina [zmurzlina] ice cream

zvěřina [zuvyerJina] game

žampióny [Jumpi-awni] mushrooms

žebírko [Jebeerko] ribs

žraločí řízek [zHrulotchee rJeezek] shark fillet

Drink: Essential terms

beer pivo
bottle láhev [lah-heſ]
brandy koňak [konyuk]
coffee káva [kahva]
cup: a cup of ... šálek ...
[shahlek]
fruit juice ovocný džus [ovot-
snee joos]
gin gin [jin]
  a gin and tonic gin a tonic
glass: a glass of ... sklenice
... [sklenyitseh]
milk mléko
mineral water minerálka [min-
erahlka]
orange juice pomerančová
šťáva [pomeruntchovah shtyahva]
red wine červené víno [cher-
veneh veeno]

rosé růžové víno [rooʝoveh
veeno]
soda (water) soda
soft drink nealkoholický
nápoj [neh-ulkoholitskee nahpoy]
sugar cukr [tsookr]
tea čaj [tchī]
tonic (water) tonik
vodka vodka [votka]
water voda
whisky whisky
white wine bílé víno [beeleh
veeno]
wine víno [veeno]
wine list nápojový lístek
[nahpo-yovee leestek]

another ..., please ještě jedno
...[yeshtyeh yedno]

Drink: Menu Reader

Becherovka® [beнerofka]
  sweet herbal digestive
  liqueur
bez kofeinu [bes kofaynoo]
  decaffeinated
bílá káva [beelah kahva] white
  coffee
bílé víno [beeleh veeno] white
  wine

burčák [boortchahk] very
  young, slightly alcoholic
  wine
čaj [tchī] tea
čaj s citrónem [tsitrawnem]
  lemon tea
čaj s mlékem tea with milk
černá káva [chernah kahva]
  black coffee

77

černé pivo [cherneh] dark beer

červené víno [cherveneh veeno] red wine

čokoláda se šlehačkou [chokolahda seh shlehutchkoh] hot chocolate with whipped cream

džus [joos] juice

horké kakao [horkeh kukuh-o] hot chocolate

káva [kahva] coffee

led [let] ice

ledová káva [ledovah kahva] cold, black coffee, often served with ice cream and whipped cream

ledový čaj [ledovee chī] iced tea

ležák [leJahk] lager

minerálka [minerahlka] mineral water

mléko milk

mražená káva [mruJenah kahva] iced coffee

nealkoholický [neh-ulkoholitskee] non-alcoholic

ovocná šťáva [ovotsnah shtyahva] fruit juice

ovocný čaj [ovotsnee chī] herbal tea

pivo beer

pomerančová šťáva [pomeruntchovah shtyahva] orange juice

řezané pivo [rJezuneh] mix of light and dark beers

sladké [slutkeh] sweet

s ledem [sledem] with ice

slivovice [slivovitseh] plum brandy

suché víno [sooHeh veeno] dry wine

šampaňské [shumpun^{yeh}skeh] champagne

svařené víno [svahrJeneh] mulled wine with lemon and spices

světlé pivo [svyetleh] light, pale beer

šumivý [shoomivee] fizzy

vídeňská káva [veeden^{yeh}skah kahva] coffee with whipped cream

víno [veeno] wine

vinný střik [vinee strJik] spritzer, wine and soda water

víno [veeno] wine

voda water

FRENCH

DICTIONARY PHRASEBOOK

Pronunciation

In this phrase book, the French has been written in a system of imitated pronunciation so that it can be read as though it were English. Bear in mind the notes on pronunciation given below:

AN   a French nasal sound; say the English word 'tan' clipping off the final 'n' and you are close

ay   as in m**ay**

e   as in g**e**t

g   always hard as in **g**oat

ī   as the 'i' sound in m**i**ght

j   like the 's' sound in plea**s**ure

ñ   like the final sound in lasa**gn**e

ON   a French nasal sound; say the English word 'on' through your nose and cutting off the final 'n'

ᴏᴏ   like the 'ew' in f**ew** but without any 'y' sound

r   comes from the back of the throat

uh   like the 'e' in butt**e**r but a little longer

y   as in **y**es

Language Notes

Articles in French vary according to the gender of a noun. To say 'the', use **le** [luh] for masculine nouns (**m**) and **la** for feminine nouns (**f**). The plural of both is **les** [lay]. For example:

le café	**la difficulté**	**les enfants**
the café	the difficulty	the children

The corresponding words for 'a' are **un** [an] for masculine nouns and **une** [œn] for feminine nouns:

un café	**une difficulté**
a café	a difficulty

The **s** (or sometimes **x**) on the end of a French word in the plural is not normally pronounced **les enfants** [lay zONfON] the children.

The common words **de** [duh] (of, from) and **à** (at, in, to) change when used with **le** and **les**:

le nom du supermarché [dOO] the name of the supermarket
au supermarché [o] at/to the supermarket
le prix des chambres [day] the price of the rooms
aux filles to the girls

Adjectives agree with nouns. For example:

il est content/fou [kontON/foo] he is happy/crazy
elle est contente/folle [kontONt/fol] she is happy/crazy

Here is a useful verb – 'to be':

je suis [juh swee] I am	**nous sommes** [noo som] we are
tu es [tOO ay] you are	**vous êtes** [voo zet] you are
(familiar form)	(plural or polite singular form)
il/elle est [eel/el ay] he/she/ it is	**ils/elles sont** [eel/el son] they are (**m/f**)

The familiar form **tu** is used to speak to people you are on friendly terms with. In the English-French section, when two forms of the verb are given in phrases such as 'can you ...?' **est-ce que tu peux/vous pouvez ...?**, the first is the familiar form and the second the polite form (see the entry for you).

Days

Monday lundi [lANdee]
Tuesday mardi [mardee]
Wednesday mercredi [mairkruhdee]
Thursday jeudi [juhdee]
Friday vendredi [vONdruhdee]
Saturday samedi [samdee]
Sunday dimanche [deemONsh]

Months

January janvier [jONvee-ay]
February février [fayvree-ay]
March mars [marss]
April avril [avreel]
May mai [may]
June juin [jwAN]
July juillet [jwee-yay]
August août [oo]
September septembre [septONbr]
October octobre [oktobr]
November novembre [novONbr]
December décembre [daysONbr]

Time

a.m. du matin dOO matAN
p.m. (afternoon) de l'après-midi duh lapray-meedee (evening) du soir dOO swahr

what time is it? quelle heure est-il? [kel urr eteel]
one o'clock une heure [OOn urr]
two o'clock deux heures [duh zur]
it's one o'clock il est une heure [eel ay OOn urr]
it's two o'clock il est deux heures [eel ay duh zurr]
it's ten o'clock il est dix heures [eel ay dee zurr]
five past one une heure cinq [OOn urr sANk]
ten past two deux heures dix [duh zurr deess]
quarter past one une heure et quart [OOn urr ay kar]
quarter past two deux heures et quart [duh zurr ay kar]
half past ten dix heures et demie [dee zurr ay duhmee]
twenty to ten dix heures moins vingt [dee zurr mwAN vAN]
quarter to two deux heures moins le quart [duh zurr mwAN luh kar]
at half past four à quatre

heures et demie [a katr urr ay duhmee]

at eight o'clock à huit heures [a weet urr]

14.00 quatorze heures [katorz urr]

17.30 dix-sept heures trente [deesset urr trONt]

2 a.m. deux heures du matin [duh zurr dOO matAN]

2 p.m. deux heures de l'après-midi [duh zurr duh lapray-meedee]

6 a.m. six heures du matin [seez urr dOO matAN]

6 p.m. six heures du soir [seez urr dOO swahr]

noon midi [meedee]

midnight minuit [meenwee]

an hour une heure [OOn urr]

a minute une minute [OOn meenOOt]

two minutes deux minutes [duh meenOOt]

a second une seconde [OOn suhgONd]

a quarter of an hour un quart d'heure [AN kar durr]

half an hour une demi-heure [OOn duhmee urr]

three quarters of an hour trois quarts d'heure [trwa kar durr]

Numbers

0	zéro [zayro]
1	un [AN]
2	deux [duh]
3	trois [trwa]
4	quatre [katr]
5	cinq [sANk]
6	six [seess]
7	sept [set]
8	huit [weet]
9	neuf [nuhf]
10	dix [deess]
11	onze [ONz]
12	douze [dooz]
13	treize [trez]
14	quartorze [katorz]
15	quinze [kANz]
16	seize [sez]
17	dix-sept [deesset]
18	dix-huit [deez-weet]
19	dix-neuf [deez-nuhf]
20	vingt [vAN]
21	vingt-et-un [vANtay-AN]
22	vingt-deux [vAN-duh]
23	vingt-trois [vAN-trwa]
30	trente [trONt]
31	trente-et-un [trONtay-an]
40	quarante [karONt]
50	cinquante [sANkONt]
60	soixante [swassONt]

70	soixante–dix [swassONt-deess]
80	quatre–vingts [katr-vAN]
90	quatre–vingt–dix [katr-vAN-deess]
100	cent [sON]
110	cent dix [sON deess]
200	deux cents [duh sON]
1,000	mille [meel]
2,000	deux mille [duh meel]
5,000	cinq mille [sANk meel]
1,000,000	un million [AN meel-yON]

In French, millions are written with spaces instead of commas, e.g. 1 500 000. Thousands are written without spaces or commas, e.g. 2700. Decimals are written with a comma, e.g. 3.5 would be 3,5 in French.

Ordinals

1st	premier [pruhm-yay]
2nd	deuxième [duhz-yem]
3rd	troisième [trwaz-yem]
4th	quatrième [katree-yem]
5th	cinquième [sANk-yem]
6th	sixième [seez-yem]
7th	septième [set-yem]
8th	huitième [weet-yem]
9th	neuvième [nuhv-yem]
10th	dixième [deez-yem]

English

→

French

A

a, an un, une [AN, ᴏᴏn]
about (roughly) environ [ONveerON]
  a film about France un film sur la France [sᴏᴏr]
above au–dessus de [o-duh-sᴏᴏ duh]
abroad à l'étranger [a laytrONjay]
accept accepter [axeptay]
accident l'accident m [axeedON]
across: across the road de l'autre côté de la route [duh lohtr kohtay duh]
adapter l'adaptateur m [adaptaturr]
  (plug) la prise multiple [preez mᴏᴏlteepl]
address l'adresse f [adress]
adult l'adulte mf [adᴏᴏlt]
advance: in advance d'avance [davONss]
after après [apray]
afternoon l'après-midi m [apray-meedee]
aftersun cream la crème après-soleil [krem apray-sᴏlay]
afterwards ensuite [ONsweet]
again de nouveau [duh noovo]
against contre [kONtr]
ago: a week ago il y a une semaine [eelya]
AIDS le SIDA [seeda]
air l'air m
  by air en avion [ON avyON]

air-conditioning la climatisation [kleemateezass-yON]
airmail: by airmail par avion [avyON]
airport l'aéroport m [a-airopor]
airport bus la navette de l'aéroport [navet]
alcohol l'alcool m [alkol]
all tout [too]
  that's all, thanks c'est tout, merci [say too mairsee]
allergic allergique [alairjeek]
all right d'accord [dakor]
  I'm all right ça va [sa]
  are you all right? ça va?
almost presque [presk]
alone seul [surl]
already déjà [dayja]
also aussi [o-see]
altogether en tout [ON too]
always toujours [toojoor]
ambulance l'ambulance f [ONbᴏᴏlONss]
America l'Amérique f [amayreek]
American américain(e) [amayreekAN, -ken]
and et [ay]
angry fâché [fashay]
animal l'animal m [aneemal]
annoying ennuyeux [ONwee-uh]
another un/une autre [ohtr]
  another beer, please encore une bière, s'il vous plaît [ONkor - seel voo play]
antiseptic le désinfectant [dayzANfektON]

any: I don't have any je n'en ai pas [juh nON ay pa]

apartment l'appartement **m** [apartmON]

apple la pomme [pom]

apricot l'abricot **m** [abreeko]

arm le bras [bra]

arrival l'arrivée **f** [areevay]

arrive arriver [areevay]

art gallery le musée d'art [mOOzay]

as: as big as aussi gros que [ohsee gro kuh]

ashtray le cendrier [sONdreeay]

ask demander [duhmONday]

I didn't ask for this ce n'est pas ce que j'ai commandé [suh nay pa suh kuh jay komONday]

aspirin l'aspirine **f** [aspeereen]

at: at the hotel à l'hôtel [a]

at the station à la gare

at the café au café [o]

at six o'clock à six heures

at Paul's chez Paul [shay]

aunt la tante [tONt]

Australia l'Australie **f** [ostralee]

Australian australien(ne) [ostralee-AN, -en]

autumn l'automne **m** [oton]

away: go away! allez-vous en! [alay-voo zON]

awful affreux [afruh]

B

baby le bébé [baybay]

back (of body) le dos [doh]

(back part) l'arrière **m** [aree-air]

at the back à l'arrière

I'll be back soon je reviens bientôt [juh ruhv-yAN b-yANto]

bad mauvais [movay]

badly mal

bag le sac

(handbag) le sac à main [mAN]

baggage les bagages **mpl** [bagahj]

baggage checkroom la consigne [kONseeñ]

bakery la boulangerie [boolONjree]

balcony le balcon [balkON]

ball (large) le ballon [balON]

(small) la balle [bal]

banana la banane [banan]

band (musical) le groupe

bandage le pansement [pONsmON]

Bandaids® les pansements **mpl** [pONsmON]

bank (money) la banque [bONk]

bar le bar

barber's le coiffeur pour hommes [kwafurr poor om]

basket le panier [pan-yay]

bath le bain [bAN]

bathroom la salle de bain [sal duh bAN]

battery la pile [peel]

(for car) la batterie

be être [etr]

beach la plage [plahj]

beach umbrella le parasol

beans les haricots [areeko]

beautiful beau, **f** belle [bo, bel]

because parce que [parss-kuh]

because of ... à cause de ...

[a kohz duh]

bed le lit [lee]
 I'm going to bed je vais me
 coucher [juh vay muh kooshay]
bed and breakfast la chambre
 avec petit déjeuner [shONbr
 avek puhtee dayjuhnay]
bedroom la chambre à
 coucher [shONbr a kooshay]
beef le bœuf [burf]
beer la bière [bee-air]
before avant [avON]
begin: when does it begin? à
 quelle heure est-ce que ça
 commence? [sa kom-mONss]
behind derrière [dairyair]
Belgian belge [belj]
Belgium la Belgique [beljeek]
below sous [soo]
belt la ceinture [sANtOOr]
berth (on ship) la couchette
 [kooshet]
beside: beside the ... à côté
 du/de la ... [a kotay dOO/duh]
best le meilleur [may-yurr]
better mieux [m-yuh]
between entre [ONtr]
beyond au delà [o duhla]
bicycle le vélo [vaylo]
big grand [grON]
bikini le bikini
bill l'addition f [adeess-yON]
 (US) le billet (de banque)
 [bee-yay duh bONk]
 could I have the bill, please?
 l'addition, s'il vous plaît [seel
 voo play]
bin la poubelle [poo-bel]
bird l'oiseau m [wazo]

birthday l'anniversaire m
 [aneevairsair]
 happy birthday! bon
 anniversaire!
biscuit le biscuit [beeskwee]
bit: a little bit un peu [AN puh]
 a big bit un gros morceau
 [gro morso]
 a bit of ... un morceau de ...
 a bit expensive un peu cher
bite (by insect) la piqûre
 [peekOOr]
black noir [nwahr]
blanket la couverture
 [koovairtOOr]
blind aveugle [avurgl]
blinds (on window) les stores
 [stor]
block of flats l'immeuble m
 [eemurbl]
blond blond [blON]
blood le sang [sON]
blouse le chemisier [shuhmeez-
 yay]
blow-dry le brushing
blue bleu [bluh]
boat le bateau [bato]
body le corps [kor]
bone l'os m [oss]
book le livre [leevr]
 (verb) réserver [rayzairvay]
bookshop, bookstore la
 librairie [leebrairee]
boot (footwear) la botte [bot]
border (of country) la frontière
 [frONt-yair]
borrow emprunter [ONprANtay]
both les deux [lay duh]
bottle la bouteille [bootay]

bottle-opener l'ouvre-bouteille **m** [oovr-bootay]
bottom (of person) le derrière [dairyair]
  at the bottom of ... (hill etc) en bas de ... [ON ba duh]
box la boîte [bwat]
boy le garçon [garsON]
boyfriend le petit ami [puhtee tami]
bra le soutien-gorge [soot-yAN-gorj]
bracelet le bracelet [braslay]
brake le frein [frAN]
brandy le cognac
bread le pain [pAN]
break casser [kassay]
breakfast le petit déjeuner [ptee day-juhnay]
breast le sein [sAN]
bridge (over river) le pont [pON]
bring apporter [aportay]
  I'll bring it back later je le rapporterai plus tard [raportuhray]
Britain la Grande-Bretagne [grONd-bruhtañ]
British britannique [breetaneek]
brochure le prospectus [prospektOOss]
broken cassé [kassay]
brother le frère [frair]
brown marron [marON]
  (hair) brun [brAN]
brush (for hair) la brosse [bross]
building le bâtiment [bateemON]
bulb l'ampoule **f** [ONpool]

bunk la couchette [kooshet]
burn la brûlure [brOOlOOr]
burst: a burst pipe un tuyau crevé [twee-o kruhvay]
bus le bus [bOOss]
  what number bus is it to ...? quel bus va à ...? [kel]

dialogue

> does this bus go to ...?
> est-ce que ce bus va à ...?
> no, you need a number ...
> non, vous devez prendre le ... [prONdr]
> where does it leave from?
> où est-ce que je le prends? [weskuh juh luh prON]

bus station la gare routière [gar root-yair]
bus stop l'arrêt d'autobus **m** [aray dotobOOss]
busy (person, line) occupé [okOOpay]
but mais [may]
butcher's la boucherie [booshree]
butter le beurre [burr]
button le bouton [bootON]
buy acheter [ashtay]
by: by bus/car en bus/voiture [ON]
  by the window près de la fenêtre [pray duh]
  by Thursday pour jeudi [poor]

C

cabbage le chou [shoo]

cabin (on ship) la cabine [kabeen]

cable car le téléférique [taylayfayreek]

café le café

cake le gâteau [gato]

call appeler [aplay]
(to phone) téléphoner [taylayfonay]
what's it called? comment ça s'appelle? [komON sa sa-pel]
he/she is called ... il/elle s'appelle ...

camera l'appareil-photo **m** [aparay-]

camp camper [kONpay]

camping gas le butagaz

campsite le terrain de camping [terrAN duh kONpeeng]

can (tin) la boîte [bwat]

can: can you ...? peux-tu/pouvez-vous ...? [puh-t00/poovay-voo]
can I ...? est-ce que je peux ...? [eskuh juh puh]
I can't ... je ne peux pas ... [juh nuh puh pa]

Canada le Canada

Canadian canadien(ne) [kanadee-AN, -ee-en]

cancel annuler [an00lay]

candies les bonbons [bONbON]

candle la bougie [boo-jee]

can-opener l'ouvre-boîte **m** [oovr-bwat]

car la voiture [vwat00r]

carafe une carafe

card la carte [kart]

cardphone le téléphone à carte [taylayfon a kart]

car hire la location de voitures [lokass-yON duh vwat00r]

car park le parking [parkeeng]

carpet la moquette [moket]

carrot la carotte [karrot]

carry porter [portay]

cash l'argent liquide **m** [arjON leekeed]

cash desk la caisse [kess]

cash dispenser le distributeur automatique de billets de banque [deestreeb00turr otomateek duh bee-yay duh bONk]

castle le château [shato]

cat le chat [sha]

cathedral la cathédrale [katay-dral]

cave la grotte [grot]

ceiling le plafond [plafON]

cellar (for wine) la cave [kahv]

centimetre le centimètre [sONteemetr]

centre le centre [sONtr]

certainly certainement [sairten-mON]

chair la chaise [shez]

champagne le champagne [shONpañ]

change (coins) la monnaie [monay]
(verb) changer [shONjay]

dialogue

do we have to change
(trains)? est-ce qu'il faut
changer? [eskeel fo]
yes, change at Bordeaux
oui, il faut changer à
Bordeaux
no, it's direct non, c'est
direct [say deerekt]

Channel la Manche [mONsh]
Channel Tunnel le tunnel sous
la Manche [toonel soo la mONsh]
cheap bon marché [bON
marshay]
check (US) le chèque [shek]
(US: bill) l'addition f [adeess-yON]
(verb) vérifier [vayreef-yay]
checkbook le chéquier
[shaykee-ay]
check-in l'enregistrement des
bagages m [ONrejeestruh-mON day
bagahj]
cheers! (toast) santé! [sONtay]
cheese le fromage [fromahj]
chemist's la pharmacie
[farmassee]
cheque le chèque [shek]
cheque card la carte
d'identité bancaire [kart
deedONteetay bONkair]
chest (body) la poitrine
[pwatreen]
chewing gum le chewing-
gum [shween-gom]
chicken (meat) le poulet
[poolay]

child l'enfant mf [ON-fON]
chips les frites [freet]
(US) les chips fpl [cheeps]
chocolate le chocolat [shokola]
a hot chocolate un chocolat
chaud [sho]
Christmas Noël [no-el]
Christmas Eve la veille de
Noël [vay duh]
merry Christmas! joyeux
Noël! [jwy-uh]
church l'église f [aygleez]
cider le cidre [seedr]
cigar le cigare [see-gar]
cigarette la cigarette [see-]
cinema le cinéma [seenayma]
city la ville [veel]
city centre le centre-ville
[sONtr-veel]
clean (adj) propre [propr]
can you clean these for me?
pouvez-vous me nettoyer
ça? [poovay-voo muh net-wy-ay sa]
clever intelligent [ANtayleejON]
climbing l'escalade f
clock l'horloge f [orloj]
close (verb) fermer [fairmay]
closed fermé [fairmay]
clothes les vêtements [vetmON]
clothes peg la pince à linge
[pANss]
cloudy nuageux [noo-ahjuh]
coach (bus) le car
(on train) le wagon [vagON]
coach station la gare routière
[gar rootee-air]
coach trip l'excursion en
autocar f [exkoorss-yON ON
otokar]

coast la côte [koht]

coat (long coat) le manteau [moNto]
(jacket) la veste [vest]

coathanger le cintre [saNtr]

code (when dialling) l'indicatif **m** [aNdeekateef]

coffee le café [kafay]

coin la pièce [p-yess]

Coke® le coca-cola

cold froid [frwa]
I'm cold j'ai froid [jay]
I have a cold je me suis enrhumé [juh muh swee zoNroomay]

collar le col

collect call une communication en PCV [-kass-yoN oN pay-say-vay]

colour la couleur [koolurr]

comb le peigne [peñ]

come venir [vuhneer]

come back revenir

come in entrer [oNtray]

comfortable confortable [koNfort-abl]

complaint la réclamation [rayklamass-yoN]

completely complètement [koNpletmoN]

computer l'ordinateur **m** [ordeenaturr]

concert le concert [koNsair]

conditioner (for hair) l'après-shampoing **m** [apray-shoNpwaN]

condom le préservatif [prayzairvateef]

congratulations! félicitations! [fayleesseetass-yoN]

connection (in travelling) la correspondance

constipation la constipation [koNsteepass-yoN]

consulate le consulat [koNsoo-la]

contact contacter [koNtaktay]

contact lenses les lentilles de contact **fpl** [loNtee]

cooker la cuisinière [kweezeenyair]

cookie le biscuit [beeskwee]

corkscrew le tire-bouchon [teer-booshoN]

correct (adj) correct, exact

Corsica la Corse [kors]

cost coûter [kootay]

cotton le coton [kotoN]

cotton wool le coton hydrophile [kotoN eedrofeel]

couchette la couchette

cough la toux [too]

cough medicine le sirop contre la toux [seero koNtr]

could: could you ...? pourriez-vous ...? [pooree-ay-voo]
could I have ...? j'aimerais ... [jemray]
I couldn't ... (wasn't able to) je ne pouvais pas ... [juh nuh poovay pa]

country (nation) le pays [payee]
(countryside) la campagne [koNpañ]

couple (man and woman) le couple [koopl]
a couple of ... quelques ... [kelkuh]

courier le/la guide [geed]
course (of meal) le plat [pla]
 of course bien sûr [b-yAN sOOr]
cousin le cousin, la cousine
 [koozAN, koozeen]
crazy fou, f folle [foo, fol]
cream la crème [krem]
credit card la carte de crédit
 [kart duh kraydee]

dialogue

can I pay by credit card?
est-ce que je peux payer
par carte de crédit? [eskuh
juh puh pay-ay]
which card do you want to
use? avec quelle carte
désirez-vous payer?
yes, sir oui monsieur
what's the number? quel
est le numéro? [nOOmayro]
and the expiry date? et la
date d'expiration? [ay la dat
dexpeerass-yON]

crisps les chips fpl [cheeps]
crossroads le carrefour
 [karfoor]
crowded (streets, bars) bondé
 [bONday]
cry pleurer [plurray]
cup la tasse [tass]
cupboard l'armoire f
 [armwahr]
curtains les rideaux mpl
 [reedo]
cushion le coussin [koossAN]
Customs la douane [dwan]

cyclist le/la cycliste [seekleest]

D
—

dad le papa
damage endommager
 [ONdoma-jay]
damn! zut! [zOOt]
damp humide [OO-meed]
dance la danse [dONss]
 (verb) danser [dONsay]
dangerous dangereux [dONj-
ruh]
dark (colour) foncé [fONsay]
 (hair) brun [brAN]
date: what's the date today?
quel jour sommes-nous? [kel
joor som-noo]
daughter la fille [fee]
day le jour [joor]
 the day after le lendemain
 [lONdmAN]
 the day before la veille [vay]
dead mort [mor]
deaf sourd [soor]
decaffeinated coffee le café
décaféiné [daykafeenay]
decide décider [dayseeday]
deckchair la chaise longue
 [shez lON-g]
deep profond [profON]
definitely certainement
 [sairten-mON]
delay le retard [ruhtar]
delicatessen l'épicerie fine f
 [aypeesree feen]
delicious délicieux [dayleess-
yuh]

dentist le/la dentiste [dON-teest]

deodorant le déodorant [dayodorON]

department store le grand magasin [grON magazAN]

departure le départ [daypar]

depend: it depends ça dépend [sa daypON]

dessert le dessert [desair]

destination la destination [desteenass-yON]

develop développer [dayv-lopay]

dialling code l'indicatif **m** [ANdeekateef]

diarrhoea la diarrhée [dee-aray]

diesel (fuel) le gas-oil

difference la différence [deefayrONss]

different différent [deefayrON]

difficult difficile [deefeesseel]

dining room la salle à manger [sal a mONjay]

dinner le dîner [deenay]

direct (adj) direct [deerekt]

direction le sens [sONss]

directory enquiries les renseignements [rONsen-yuhmON]

dirty sale [sal]

disco la discothèque

disgusting dégoûtant [daygootON]

district le quartier [kart-yay]

divorced divorcé [deevorsay]

do faire [fair]

what shall we do? qu'est-ce qu'on fait? [keskON fay]

doctor le médecin [maydsAN]

dog le chien [shee-AN]

don't! non! [nON]

door (of room) la porte [port] (of train, car) la portière [port-yair]

double double [doobl]

double bed le grand lit [grON lee]

double room la chambre pour deux personnes [shONbr poor duh pairson]

down en bas [ON ba]

downstairs en bas

dozen la douzaine [doozen]

draught beer la bière pression [bee-air press-yON]

dress la robe [rob]

drink la boisson [bwassON] (verb) boire [bwahr]

what would you like to drink? qu'est-ce que tu veux/vous voulez boire? [keskuh]

drinking water l'eau potable **f** [o pot-abl]

drive conduire [kONdweer]

driver (of car) le conducteur [kONdOOkturr] (of bus) le chauffeur

driving licence le permis de conduire [pairmee duh kONdweer]

drug (medical) le médicament [maydeekamON]

drugs (narcotics) la drogue [drog]

drunk ivre [eevr]

dry sec, **f** sèche [sek, sesh]

dry-cleaner le teinturier [tANtooree-ay]
during pendant [pONdON]
dustbin la poubelle [poo-bel]
duvet la couette [kwet]

E

each (every) chaque [shak]
ear l'oreille f [oray]
early tôt [toh]
earring la boucle d'oreille [bookl doray]
east l'est m [est]
Easter Pâques [pak]
easy facile [fasseel]
eat manger [moNjay]
economy class la classe économique [klass aykonomeek]
egg l'œuf m [urf]
either: either ... or ... soit ... soit ... [swa]
elbow le coude [kood]
electric électrique [aylektreek]
electricity l'électricité f [aylektreesseetay]
elevator l'ascenseur m [asoNsurr]
else: something else autre chose [ohtr shohz]
somewhere else ailleurs [ī-yurr]
embassy l'ambassade f [oNbasad]
emergency l'urgence f [oorjONss]
empty vide [veed]

end la fin [fAN]
(verb) finir [feeneer]
at the end of the street au bout de la rue [o boo duh la roo]
engaged (toilet, telephone) occupé [okoopay]
(to be married) fiancé [f-yONsay]
England l'Angleterre f [ONgluhtair]
English anglais [ONglay]
enjoy: to enjoy oneself s'amuser [samoozay]
enormous énorme [aynorm]
enough assez [assay]
it's not big enough ce n'est pas assez grand
that's enough ça suffit [sa soofee]
entrance l'entrée f [ONtray]
envelope l'enveloppe f [ONvlop]
equipment (for climbing etc) l'équipement m [aykeepmoN]
especially spécialement [spays-yalmoN]
euro l'euro m [urro]
Eurocheque l'Eurochèque m [urroshek]
Europe l'Europe f [urrop]
evening le soir [swahr]
this evening ce soir
eventually finalement [feenalmoN]
ever jamais [jamay]
every chaque [shak]
everyone tout le monde [too luh moNd]
everything tout [too]

everywhere partout [partoo]
exactly! exactement!
[exaktuhmON]
excellent excellent [exsaylON]
  excellent! parfait! [parfay]
except sauf [sohf]
exchange rate le cours du
change [koor dœ shONj]
exciting passionnant [pass-
yonON]
excuse me pardon [par-dON]
exhibition l'exposition **f**
[expozeess-yON]
exit la sortie [sortee]
expensive cher [shair]
eye l'œil **m** [uh-ee]
eyeglasses les lunettes [lœnet]

F

face le visage [veezahj]
faint (verb) s'évanouir
[sayvanweer]
fair la foire [fwahr]
  (adj) juste [jœst]
fairly (quite) assez [assay]
fall (US) l'automne **m** [oton]
  (verb) tomber [tONbay]
family la famille [famee]
fantastic fantastique
[fONtasteek]
far loin [lwAN]

dialogue

is it far from here? c'est
loin d'ici? [say lwAN dee-see]
no, not very far non, pas

très loin
it's about 20 kilometres
c'est à vingt kilomètres
environ [ONveerON]

farm la ferme [fairm]
fashionable à la mode [mod]
fast rapide [rapeed]
fat (person) gros, **f** grosse [gro,
gross]
father le père [pair]
faucet le robinet [robeenay]
fault le défaut [dayfo]
  sorry, it was my fault désolé,
c'est de ma faute [say duh ma
foht]
favourite préféré [prayfay-ray]
fax le fax
feel sentir [sONteer]
  I feel unwell je ne me sens
pas bien [juh nuh muh sON pa b-
yAN]
felt-tip pen le stylo-feutre
[steelo-furtr]
ferry le ferry
fetch aller chercher [alay
shairshay]
  I'll fetch him j'irai le
chercher [jeeray]
few: a few quelques-uns,
quelques-unes [kelkuh-zAN,
kelkuh-zŒN]
  a few days quelques jours
fiancé le fiancé [fee-ONsay]
fiancée la fiancée [fee-ONsay]
field le champ [shON]
fight la bagarre [bagar]
filling (in tooth) le plombage
[plONbahj]

film (movie) le film [feelm]
(for camera) la pellicule
[peleekœl]
find trouver [troovay]
find out découvrir
[daykoovreer]
fine (weather) beau [bo]
(punishment) l'amende **f**
[amONd]
finger le doigt [dwa]
finish terminer [tairmeenay]
fire le feu [fuh]
fire brigade les pompiers
[pONp-yay]
first premier [pruhm-yay]
at first tout d'abord [too
dabor]
first aid kit la trousse de
premiers secours [trooss duh]
first class (compartment etc) de
première (classe) [duh pruhm-
yair klass]
first floor le premier [pruhm-
yay]
(US) le rez-de-chaussée [rayd-
shoh-say]
first name le prénom [praynON]
fish le poisson [pwassON]
fit: it doesn't fit me ce n'est
pas la bonne taille [suh nay pa
la bon tī]
fix réparer [rayparay]
fizzy gazeux [gazuh]
flat (apartment) l'appartement
m [apartmON]
(adj) plat [pla]
I've got a flat tyre j'ai un
pneu à plat [jay un pnuh]
flavour l'arôme **m** [arohm]

flight le vol
flight number le numéro de
vol [nœmay-ro]
floor (of room) le plancher
[plONshay]
(storey) l'étage **m** [aytahj]
on the floor par terre [tair]
florist le/la fleuriste [flurreest]
flower la fleur [flurr]
flu la grippe [greep]
**fluent: he speaks fluent
French** il parle couramment
le français [kooramON]
fly la mouche [moosh]
(verb) voler [volay]
we're flying home nous
repartons en avion [noo
ruhpartON ON av-yON]
food la nourriture [nooreetœr]
foot le pied [p-yay]
on foot à pied
football (game) le football
(ball) le ballon de football
[balON]
for pour [poor]
**do you have something
for ...?** (headache/diarrhoea etc)
avez-vous quelque chose
contre ...? [avay-voo kelkuh-
shohz kONtr]
foreign étranger [aytrONjay]
foreigner l'étranger **m**,
l'étrangère **f** [aytrONjay, -jair]
forest la forêt [foray]
forget oublier [ooblee-ay]
I forget, I've forgotten j'ai
oublié [jay ooblee-ay]
fork (for eating) la fourchette
[foorshet]

fortnight la quinzaine [kANzen]
forwarding address l'adresse pour faire suivre le courrier f
fountain la fontaine [foNten]
foyer (of hotel) le hall [awl]
 (of theatre) le foyer
France la France [froNss]
free libre [leebr]
 (no charge) gratuit [gratwee]
freeway l'autoroute f [otoroot]
French français, f française [froNsay, -ez]
 the French les Français
 French fries les frites **fpl** [freet]
Frenchman le Français [froNsay]
Frenchwoman la Française [froNsez]
frequent fréquent [fraykoN]
fresh frais, f fraîche [fray, fresh]
fridge le frigo [freego]
fried frit [free]
friend l'ami m, l'amie f [amee]
friendly amical [ameekal]
from de [duh]
 from Monday to Friday du lundi au vendredi [dœ ... o]
 from next Thursday à partir de jeudi prochain [a parteer]
front l'avant m [avoN]
 in front of the hotel devant l'hôtel [duhvoN]
 at the front à l'avant
fruit les fruits **mpl** [frwee]
 fruit juice le jus de fruit [jœ duh frwee]
full plein [plAN]
 full board la pension

complète [poNs-yoN koNplet]
fun: it was fun on s'est bien amusé [oN say b-yAN amœzay]
funny (strange, amusing) drôle
further plus loin [plœ lwAN]
future le futur [fœtœr]
 in future à l'avenir [a lavneer]

G

game (cards etc) le jeu [juh]
 (match) la partie [partee]
garage (for fuel) la station d'essence [stass-yoN dessoNss]
 (for repairs, parking) le garage [garahj]
garden le jardin [jardAN]
garlic l'ail m [ı]
gas le gaz
 (US) l'essence f [essoNss]
gas station la station-service [stass-yoN-sairveess]
gate le portail [port-ı]
 (at airport) la porte [port]
gay homosexuel
gents (toilet) les toilettes pour hommes [twalet poor om]
Germany l'Allemagne f [almañ]
get (fetch) obtenir [obtuhneer]
 how do I get to ...? pouvez-vous m'indiquer comment aller à ...? [poovay-voo mANdeekay komoN talay]
get back (return) rentrer [roNtray]
get off descendre [duhsoNdr]
 where do I get off? où dois-

je descendre? [oo dwaj]
get on (to train etc) monter [mONtay]
get out (of car etc) descendre [duhsONdr]
get up (in the morning, stand up) se lever [suh luhvay]
gift le cadeau [kado]
gin le gin [djeen]
 a gin and tonic un gin-tonic
girl la fille [fee]
girlfriend la petite amie [puhteet amee]
give donner [donay]
give back rendre [rONdr]
glad content [kONtON]
glass le verre [vair]
 a glass of wine un verre de vin
glasses (spectacles) les lunettes [lOOnet]
gloves les gants **mpl** [gON]
go aller [alay]
 where are you going? où vas-tu/allez-vous? [oo vatOO/alay voo]
 where does this bus go? où va ce bus?
 let's go! allons-y! [alONzee]
 she's gone (left) elle est partie [partee]
 a hamburger to go un hamburger à emporter [ONportay]
go away partir [parteer]
 go away! va t'en!/allez-vous-en! [vatON/alay-voo-zON]
go back (return) retourner [ruhtoornay]

go down descendre [duhsONdr]
go in entrer [ONtray]
go out (in the evening) sortir [sorteer]
go through traverser [travairsay]
go up monter [mONtay]
God Dieu [d-yuh]
gold l'or **m**
good bon, **f** bonne [bON, bon]
 good! bien! [b-yAN]
 it's no good ça ne va pas [sa nuh va pa]
goodbye au revoir [o ruh-vwa]
good evening bonsoir [bON-swa]
good morning bonjour [bON-joor]
good night bonne nuit [bon nwee]
got: we've got to leave il faut que nous partions [eel fo kuh]
 I've got to ... il faut que je ...
 have you got any ...? est-ce que tu as/vous avez des/du ...? [eskuh tOO a/voo zavay ...]
gradually peu à peu [puh a puh]
gram(me) le gramme
grapefruit le pamplemousse [pONpluh-mooss]
grapes le raisin [rez-AN]
grass l'herbe **f** [airb]
grateful reconnaissant [ruhkonessON]
great (excellent) fantastique [fONtasteek]
green vert [vair]
greengrocer's le marchand de

légumes [marshON duh laygOOm]
grey gris [gree]
grilled grillé [gree-yay]
grocer's l'épicerie **f** [aypeesree]
ground le sol
  on the ground par terre [tair]
ground floor le rez-de-chaussée [rayd-shoh-say]
group le groupe [groop]
guest l'invité(e) [ANveetay]
guesthouse la pension [pONs-yON]
guide le guide [geed]
guidebook le guide
guided tour la visite guidée [veezeet geeday]

H

hair les cheveux **mpl** [shuhvuh]
haircut la coupe de cheveux [koop]
hairdresser le coiffeur [kwafurr]
hairdryer le sèche-cheveux [sesh-shuhvuh]
half la moitié [mwatee-ay]
  half an hour une demi-heure [duhmee-urr]
  half a litre un demi-litre
half board la demi-pension [duhmee-pONs-yON]
half-bottle la demi bouteille [bootay]
half price moitié prix [mwatee-ay pree]
ham le jambon [jONbON]
hamburger le hamburger [ONboorgair]
hand la main [mAN]
handbag le sac à main
hand luggage les bagages à main **mpl** [bagahj]
hangover la gueule de bois [gurl duh bwa]
happen arriver [areevay]
  what has happened? qu'est-ce qui s'est passé? [say passay]
happy heureux [ur-ruh]
harbour le port [por]
hard dur [dOOr]
  (difficult) difficile [deefeesseel]
hardly à peine [a pen]
  hardly ever presque jamais [presk jamay]
hardware shop la quincaillerie [kAN-ky-ree]
hat le chapeau [shapo]
hate détester [daytestay]
have avoir [avwahr]
  can I have a ...? j'aimerais ... [jemray]
  do you have ...? avez-vous ...? [avay-voo]
  do I have to ...? est-ce que je dois ...? [eskuh]
hayfever le rhume des foins [rOOm day fwAN]
he il [eel]
head la tête [tet]
headache le mal de tête
headlights les phares **mpl** [far]
hear entendre [ONtONdr]
heat la chaleur [shalurr]
heater (in room) le radiateur [rad-yaturr]
heating le chauffage

heavy lourd [loor]

heel le talon [talON]

hello bonjour [bONjoor]
(in the evening) bonsoir
[bONswahr]
(on phone) allô

help l'aide f [ed]
(verb) aider [ayday]
help! au secours! [o suhkoor]
can you help me? est-ce que
vous pouvez m'aider? [eskuh
voo poovay]

her: I know her je la connais
to her à elle [el]
for her pour elle
that's her c'est elle [set el]
that's her towel/her bike c'est
sa serviette/son vélo [say -
sON]

herbal tea la tisane [teezahn]

here ici [ee-see]
here is/are ... voici ... [vwa-
see]
here you are (offering) voilà
[vwala]

hers: that's hers c'est à elle
[set a el]

hey! hé! [hay]

hi! salut!

high haut [o]

highway l'autoroute f [otoroot]

hill la colline [koleen]

him: I know him je le connais
to him à lui [lwee]
for him pour lui
that's him c'est lui [say]

hip la hanche [ONsh]

hire: for hire à louer [loo-ay]
(verb) louer

his: it's his car c'est sa voiture
[say]
it's his bike c'est son vélo
[say sON]
that's his c'est à lui [set a
lwee]

hitchhike faire de l'autostop
[fair duh lotostop]

hole le trou [troo]

holiday les vacances fpl
[vakONss]
on holiday en vacances
[ON]

Holland la Hollande [ollOnd]

home la maison [mezzON]
at home (in my house etc) chez
moi [shay mwa]
(in my country) dans mon pays
[dON mON payee]
we go home tomorrow nous
rentrons demain [rONtrON
duhmAN]

horrible horrible [oreebl]

horse le cheval [shuhval]

hospital l'hôpital m [opee-
tal]

hot chaud [sho]
(spicy) épicé [aypeessay]
I'm hot j'ai chaud [jay]

hotel l'hôtel m [otel]

hour l'heure f [urr]

house la maison [mezzON]

house wine la cuvée du
patron [kOOvay dOO]

how comment [komON]
how many? combien? [kONb-
yAN]
how do you do? enchanté!
[ONshONtay]

dialogues

how are you? comment vas-tu/allez-vous? [komON va-tOO/alay-voo]
fine, thanks, and you? bien, merci, et toi/vous? [b-yAN mairsee ay twa]

how much is it? c'est combien? [say kONb-yAN]
... francs ... francs [frON]
I'll take it je le prends [juh luh prON]

hungry: I'm hungry j'ai faim [jay fAN]
hurry: I'm in a hurry je suis pressé [juh swee pressay]
hurt: it hurts ça fait mal [sa fay]
husband le mari [maree]

I

I je [juh]
ice la glace [glass]
with ice avec des glaçons [glassON]
ice cream la glace [glass]
ice lolly l'esquimau **m** [eskeemo]
idiot l'idiot **m** [eedee-o]
if si [see]
ill malade [malad]
immediately tout de suite [toot sweet]
important important [ANportON]

impossible impossible [ANposs-eebl]
in: it's in the centre c'est au centre [set o sONtr]
in my car dans ma voiture [dON]
in Dijon à Dijon
in May en mai [ON]
in English en anglais
is he in? il est là? [eel ay la]
in five minutes dans cinq minutes
include: does that include meals? est-ce que les repas sont compris? [eskuh lay ruhpa sON kONpree]
indigestion l'indigestion **f** [ANdeejest-yON]
indoors à l'intérieur [lANtay-ree-urr]
information les renseignements **mpl** [rONsen-yuhmON]
injured blessé [blessay]
insect l'insecte **m** [ANsekt]
inside à l'intérieur [lANtayree-urr]
inside the hotel dans l'hôtel [dON]
instead: instead of ... au lieu de ... [o l-yuh duh]
intelligent intelligent [ANtayleejON]
interesting intéressant [ANtayressON]
international international [ANtairnass-yonal]
interpreter l'interprète **mf** [ANtairpret]

intersection le carrefour [karfoor]
into dans [dON]
  I'm not into ... je n'aime pas ... [juh nem pa]
introduce présenter [prayzONtay]
  may I introduce ...? puis-je vous présenter ...? [pweej voo]
invitation l'invitation **f** [ANveetass-yON]
Ireland l'Irlande **f** [eerlONd]
Irish irlandais [eerlONday]
iron (for ironing) le fer à repasser [fair a ruh-passay]
island l'île **f** [eel]
it ça [sa]
  it is ... c'est ... [say]
  is it ...? est-ce ...? [ess]
  where is it? où est-ce que c'est? [weskuh say]
  it was ... c'était ... [saytay]
Italy l'Italie **f** [eetalee]

J

jacket la veste [vest]
jam la confiture [kONfeetœr]
jeans le jean
jellyfish la méduse [maydœz]
jewellery les bijoux [beejoo]
job le travail [trav-I]
joke la plaisanterie [plezzONtree]
journey le voyage [vwy-ahj]
  have a good journey! bon voyage!
juice le jus [jœ]
jumper le pull [pool]

just (only) seul [surl]
  just two seulement deux [surlmON]
  just for me seulement pour moi [poor mwa]
  just here juste ici [jœst ee-see]

K

keep garder [garday]
  keep the change gardez la monnaie [garday la monay]
key la clé [klay]
kilo le kilo
kilometre le kilomètre [keelo-metr]
kind aimable [em-abl]
kiss le baiser [bezzay]
  (verb) embrasser [ONbrassay]
kitchen la cuisine [kweezeen]
knee le genou [juh-noo]
knife le couteau [kooto]
knock down renverser [rONvairsay]
know (somebody, a place) connaître [konetr]
  (something) savoir [savwahr]
  I don't know je ne sais pas [juh nuh say pa]
  I didn't know that je ne savais pas [savay]

L

ladies' room les toilettes (pour dames) [twalet poor dam]
lady la dame [dam]

lager la bière [bee-air]

lake le lac

lamb l'agneau **m** [an-yo]

lamp la lampe [lONp]

language la langue [lONg]

large grand [grON]

last dernier [dairn-yay]

  last week la semaine dernière [suhmen dairn-yair]

  last Friday vendredi dernier

  last night hier soir [yair swahr]

late tard [tar]

later plus tard [plω tar]

  I'll come back later je reviendrai plus tard [juh ruhvee-ANdray]

laugh rire [reer]

launderette, laundromat la laverie automatique [lavree otomateek]

laundry (clothes) le linge sale [lANj sal]

lawyer l'avocat **m** [avoka]

leaflet le dépliant [daypleeON]

leak la fuite [fweet]

learn apprendre [aprONdr]

least: at least au moins [o mwAN]

leather le cuir [kweer]

leave (go away) partir [parteer]

  I am leaving tomorrow je pars demain [juh par]

  may I leave this here? puis-je laisser ceci ici? [pweej lessay suhsee ee-see]

  I left my coat in the bar j'ai oublié ma veste au bar [jay ooblee-ay]

left la gauche [gohsh]

left luggage (office) la consigne [kONseeñ]

leg la jambe [jONb]

lemon le citron [seetrON]

lemonade la limonade [leemonad]

lend prêter [pretay]

less moins [mwAN]

  less expensive moins cher

lesson la leçon [luhsON]

let laisser [lessay]

let off: will you let me off at ...? pouvez-vous me laisser descendre à ..., [poovay-voo muh lessay duhsONdr a]

letter la lettre [letr]

letterbox la boîte à lettres [bwat a letr]

lettuce la laitue [letω]

library la bibliothèque [beeblee-otek]

licence le permis [pairmee]

lift (in building) l'ascenseur **m** [asONsurr]

  could you give me a lift? pouvez-vous m'emmener? [poovay-voo mONmuhnay]

light la lumière [lωm-yair] (not heavy) léger [lay-jay]

  do you have a light? avez-vous du feu? [avay-voo dω fuh]

light bulb l'ampoule **f** [ONpool]

lighter (cigarette) le briquet [breekay]

like aimer [aymay]

  I like it ça me plaît [sah muh play]

  I don't like it ça ne me plaît pas

I'd like a beer je voudrais une bière [juh voodray]

would you like a drink? veux-tu/voulez-vous boire quelque chose? [vuh-tOO/voolay-voo]

what's it like? comment est-ce? [komON ess]

one like this un comme ça [kom]

line la ligne [leeñ]

lip la lèvre [levr]

listen écouter [aykootay]

litre le litre [leetr]

little petit [puhtee]

just a little, thanks un tout petit peu, s'il vous plaît [AN too puhtee puh]

a little milk un peu de lait [duh]

live (verb) vivre [veevr]

loaf le pain [pAN]

local local

a local wine un vin de la région [duh la rayjON]

lock la serrure [sair-rOOr]
(verb) fermer à clé [fairmay a klay]

lock out: I've locked myself out je me suis enfermé dehors [juh muh swee zONfairmay]

locker (for luggage etc) le casier [kaz-yay]

London Londres [lONdr]

long long, **f** longue [lON, lON-g]

how long does it take? combien de temps est-ce que ça prend? [eskuh sa prON]

a long time longtemps [lONtON]

one day/two days longer un jour/deux jours en plus [ON plOOss]

look regarder [ruhgarday]

look out! attention! [atONs-yON]

can I have a look? puis-je regarder? [pweej]

look after garder [garday]

look at regarder [ruhgarday]

look for chercher [shairshay]

I'm looking for ... je cherche ... [juh shairsh]

lorry le camion [kam-yON]

lose perdre [pairdr]

I've lost my way je suis perdu [juh swee pairdOO]

I've lost my handbag j'ai perdu mon sac à main [jay]

lost property (office) les objets trouvés [objay troovay]

lot: a lot, lots beaucoup [bo-koo]

not a lot pas beaucoup [pa]

a lot of people beaucoup de monde

loud fort [for]

lounge le salon

love l'amour **m** [amoor]
(verb) aimer [aymay]

lovely (view, present etc) ravissant [ravee-sON]
(meal) délicieux [dayleess-yuh]
(weather) magnifique [mAN-yeefeek]

low bas [ba]

luck la chance [shONss]

good luck! bonne chance!
[bon]
luggage les bagages **mpl**
[bagahj]
lunch le déjeuner [dayjuhnay]
Luxembourg le Luxembourg
[lꝺxONboor]

M

mad (insane) fou, **f** folle [foo,
fol]
magazine le magazine
maid (in hotel) la femme de
chambre [fam duh shONbr]
mail le courrier [kooree-ay]
(verb) poster [postay]
mailbox la boîte à lettres [bwat
a letr]
main principal [prANseepal]
main course le plat principal
[pla]
main road (in town) la rue
principale [rꝺ]
(in country) la grande route
[grONd root]
make faire [fair]
make-up le maquillage
[makee-ahj]
man l'homme **m** [om]
manager le patron [pa-trON]
can I see the manager? puis-
je parler au patron? [pweej
parlay o]
many beaucoup [bo-koo]
map (of city) le plan [plON]
(road map, geographical) la carte
[kart]

market le marché [marshay]
marmalade la confiture
d'oranges [kONfeetꝺr dorONj]
married: I'm married je suis
marié [juh swee maree-ay]
mascara le mascara
match (football etc) le match
matches les allumettes **fpl**
[alꝺmet]
matter: it doesn't matter ça ne
fait rien [sa nuh fay ree-AN]
what's the matter? qu'est-ce
qu'il y a? [keskeel ya]
mattress le matelas [matla]
may: may I see it? puis-je
le/la voir?
maybe peut-être [puht-etr]
mayonnaise la mayonnaise
me moi [mwa]
that's for me c'est pour moi
[say]
me too moi aussi [o-see]
meal le repas [ruhpa]
mean (verb) signifier [seen-
yeefee-ay]
meat la viande [veeONd]
medicine le médicament
[maydeekamON]
medium (size) moyen [mwy-AN]
medium-dry (wine) demi-sec
[duhmee-sek]
medium-rare (steak) à point
[pwAN]
mend réparer [rayparay]
men's room les toilettes pour
hommes [twalet poor om]
mention: don't mention it je
vous en prie [juh voo zON pree]
menu la carte [kart]

message le message [messahj]
metre le mètre [metr]
midday midi [meedee]
middle: in the middle au milieu [o meel-yuh]
midnight minuit [meenwee]
milk le lait [lay]
mind: never mind tant pis [toN pee]
mine: it's mine c'est à moi [set a mwa]
mineral water l'eau minérale **f** [o meenayral]
minute la minute [meenoot]
just a minute un instant
mirror le miroir [meer-wahr]
Miss Mademoiselle [mad-mwazel]
miss (train, bus etc) rater
missing: to be missing manquer [moNkay]
there's a suitcase missing il manque une valise
mistake l'erreur **f** [air-rurr]
money l'argent **m** [arjoN]
month le mois [mwa]
moped la mobylette [mobeelet]
more plus [plooss]
can I have some more water, please? est-ce que je peux avoir encore un peu d'eau, s'il vous plaît? [eksuh juh puh avwahr oNkor - seel voo play]
more expensive plus cher [ploo shair]
more than 50 plus de cinquante
morning le matin [matAN]
this morning ce matin

most: most of the time la plupart du temps [plOOpar]
mother la mère [mair]
motorbike la moto
motorway l'autoroute **f** [otoroot]
mountain la montagne [moNtañ]
mouse la souris [sooree]
mouth la bouche [boosh]
movie le film [feelm]
movie theater le cinéma [seenayma]
Mr Monsieur [muhss-yuh]
Mrs Madame [ma-dam]
Ms Madame; Mademoiselle [ma-dam, mad-mwazel]
much beaucoup [bo-koo]
much better/much worse beaucoup mieux/bien pire
much hotter beaucoup plus chaud
not much pas beaucoup [pa]
mum la maman [ma-moN]
museum le musée [moozay]
mushrooms les champignons **mpl** [shoNpeen-yoN]
music la musique [moozeek]
must: I must je dois [juh dwa]
mustard la moutarde [mootard]
my mon [moN], ma; **pl** mes [may]
myself: I'll do it myself je le ferai moi-même [mwa-mem]
by myself (said by man/woman) tout seul/toute seule [too surl/toot surl]

N

nail (finger) l'ongle **m** [ONgl]
name le nom [nON]
 my name's John je m'appelle John [juh ma-pel]
 what's your name? comment tu t'appelles/vous appelez-vous? [komON too ta-pel/voo zaplay-voo]
napkin la serviette [sairv-yet]
narrow (street) étroit [aytrwa]
nasty (person, taste) désagréable [dayzagray-abl]
 (weather, accident) mauvais [mo-vay]
national national [nass-yonal]
natural naturel [natoo-rel]
near près [pray]
 where is the nearest ...? où est le/la ... le/la plus proche? [ploo prosh]
nearly presque [presk]
necessary nécessaire [naysessair]
neck le cou [koo]
necklace le collier [kol-yay]
necktie la cravate [kravat]
need: I need ... j'ai besoin de ... [jay buhzwAN duh]
needle l'aiguille **f** [aygwee]
neither ... nor ... ni ... ni ...
nephew le neveu [nuhvuh]
never jamais [jamay]
new nouveau, **f** nouvelle [noovo, noovel]
news (radio, TV etc) les informations [ANformass-yON]

newsagent's le marchand de journaux [marshON duh joorno]
newspaper le journal [joor-nal]
New Year le Nouvel An [noovel ON]
 Happy New Year! bonne année! [bon anay]
New Year's Eve la Saint-Sylvestre [sAN seelvestr]
New Zealand la Nouvelle-Zélande [noovel zaylONd]
next prochain [proshAN]
 next week la semaine prochaine
 next to à côté de [a kotay duh]
nice (food) bon [bON]
 (looks, view etc) joli [jolee]
 (person) sympathique [sANpateek]
niece la nièce [nee-ess]
night la nuit [nwee]
no non [nON]
 I've no change je n'ai pas de monnaie [juh nay pa duh]
 there's no ... left il n'y a plus de ... [eel nya ploo]
nobody personne [pairson]
noisy: it's too noisy c'est trop bruyant [say tro brwee-yON]
non-alcoholic sans alcool [sON zalkol]
none aucun [o-kAN]
non-smoking compartment le compartiment non-fumeurs [kONparteemON nON-foomurr]
no-one personne [pairson]
nor: nor do I moi non plus [mwa nON ploo]
normal normal [nor-mal]

north le nord [nor]
northeast le nord-est [nor-est]
northwest le nord-ouest [nor-west]
Northern Ireland l'Irlande du Nord f [eerlONd]
nose le nez [nay]
not pas [pa]
 no, I'm not hungry non, je n'ai pas faim [juh nay pa]
 not that one pas celui-là [suhlwee-la suhlwee-see]
note (banknote) le billet (de banque) [bee-yay (duh bONk)]
nothing rien [ree-AN]
 nothing else rien d'autre [dohtr]
now maintenant [mANtnoN]
number le numéro [nOOmayro]
nuts les noisettes fpl [nwazet]

O

o'clock: it's 10 o'clock il est dix heures [urr]
odd (strange) étrange [aytroNj]
of de [duh]
off (lights) éteint [aytAN]
 it's just off the Champs Elysées c'est tout près des Champs Elysées [say too pray day]
often souvent [soovON]
 how often are the buses? à quel intervalle les bus passent-ils? [kel ANtairval]
oil l'huile f [weel]
ointment la pommade [pomahd]

OK d'accord [dakor]
 are you OK? ça va? [sa va]
 that's OK thanks merci, ça va [mairsee]
 I'm OK (nothing for me) ça va comme ça
 (I feel OK) ça va
old vieux, f vieille [v-yuh, v-yay]
olive oil l'huile d'olive f [weel doleev]
olives les olives fpl [oleev]
omelette l'omelette f
on sur [sOOr]
 on television à la télévision
 I haven't got it on me je ne l'ai pas sur moi [juh nuh lay pa sOOr mwa]
 what's on tonight? qu'est-ce qu'il y a ce soir? [keskeel-ya suh swahr]
once une fois [OOn fwa]
 at once (immediately) tout de suite [toot sweet]
one un, une [AN, OOn]
 the white one le blanc, la blanche
one-way ticket un aller simple [alay sANpl]
onion l'oignon m [on-yON]
only seulement [surlmON]
 it's only 6 o'clock il n'est que six heures [eel nay kuh]
open (adj) ouvert [oovair]
 (verb) ouvrir [oovreer]
operator (telephone) le/la standardiste [stONdardeest]
opposite: opposite my hotel

en face de mon hôtel [ON fass duh]

or ou [OO]

orange (fruit) l'orange **f** [orONj]
(colour) orange

orange juice le jus d'orange [jOO]

order: can we order now? est-ce que nous pouvons commander? [eskuh noo poovON komONday]

ordinary ordinaire [ordeenair]

other autre [ohtr]
the other one l'autre

our notre, **pl** nos

ours le/la nôtre [nohtr]

out: he's out il est sorti [eel ay sortee]

outdoors en plein air [ON plAN air]

outside à l'extérieur de [extayree-urr duh]

over: over here par ici [ee-see]
over there là-bas [laba]
over 500 plus de cinq cents [plOO duh]

overnight (travel) de nuit [duh nwee]

own: my own ... mon propre ... [propr]

P

pack: a pack of ... un paquet de ... [pakay duh]
(verb) faire ses bagages [fair say bagahj]

package (at post office) le colis [kolee]

pain la douleur [doolurr]
I have a pain here j'ai mal ici [jay mal ee-see]

painful douloureux [doolooruh]

painkillers les analgésiques **mpl** [an-aljayzeek]

pair: a pair of ... une paire de ... [pair duh]

panties le slip [sleep]

pants (underwear) le slip
(US) le pantalon [pONtalON]

pantyhose le collant [kollON]

paper le papier [papyay]
(newspaper) le journal [joor-nal]

parcel le colis [kolee]

pardon (me)? pardon? [par-dON]

parents: my parents mes parents [parON]

park le parc
(verb) se garer [suh garay]

parking lot le parking [parkeeng]

part une partie [partee]

partner (boyfriend, girlfriend) le/la partenaire [partuhnair]

party (group) le groupe
(celebration) la fête [fet]

passport le passeport [pass-por]

past: just past the information office tout de suite après le centre d'information [toot sweet apray]

pavement le trottoir [trotwahr]

pay (verb) payer [pay-ay]
can I pay, please? l'addition, s'il vous plaît [ladeess-yON seel voo play]

pay phone la cabine téléphonique [kabeen taylayfoneek]

peach la pêche [pesh]

peanuts les cacahuètes **fpl** [kaka-wet]

pear la poire [pwahr]

peas les petits pois **mpl** [puhtee pwa]

pen le stylo [steelo]

pencil le crayon [kray-ON]

people les gens [jON]
  too many people trop de monde [tro duh mONd]

pepper (spice) le poivre [pwahvr]
  (vegetable) le poivron [pwahvrON]

per: per night par nuit
  per cent pour cent [poor sON]

perfume le parfum [parfAN]

perhaps peut-être [puht-etr]

person la personne [pairson]

petrol l'essence **f** [essONss]

petrol station la station-service [stass-yON-sairveess]

pharmacy la pharmacie [farmasee]

phone le téléphone [taylay-]
  (verb) téléphoner

phone book l'annuaire du téléphone **m** [anꝏair dꝏ taylayfon]

phone box la cabine téléphonique [kabeen taylayfoneek]

phonecard la télécarte [taylay-kart]

phone number le numéro de

téléphone [nꝏmayro]

photo la photographie [foto-grafee]

picture l'image **f** [eemahj]

piece le morceau [morso]

pill la pilule [peelꝏl]

pillow l'oreiller **m** [oray-yay]

pineapple l'ananas **m** [anana]

pink rose [roz]

place l'endroit **m** [ONdrwa]
  at your place (fam) chez toi [shay twa]
  (pol) chez vous [voo]

plane l'avion **m** [av-yON]

plant la plante [plONt]

plasters les pansements **mpl** [pONsmON]

plastic bag le sac en plastique [ON plass-teek]

plate l'assiette **f** [ass-yet]

platform le quai [kay]
  which platform is it for Paris? c'est quelle voie pour Paris? [say kel vwa]

play (verb) jouer [joo-ay]
  (in theatre) la pièce de théâtre [p-yess duh tay-atr]

pleasant agréable [agray-abl]

please s'il vous plaît [seel voo play]
  (if using 'tu' form) s'il te plaît [seel tuh]
  yes please oui, merci [wee mairsee]

plenty: plenty of ... beaucoup de ... [bo-koo duh]

plug (electrical) la prise [preez]
  (in sink) le bouchon [booshON]

poisonous toxique

police la police
policeman l'agent de police
m [ajON]
police station le commissariat
[komeessaree-a]
polite poli [polee]
polluted pollué [polœ-ay]
pool (for swimming) la piscine
[peeseen]
pork le porc [por]
port (for boats) le port [por]
possible possible [posseebl]
is it possible to ...? est-ce
qu'on peut ...? [eskON puh]
as ... as possible aussi ... que
possible [o-see]
post (mail) le courrier [kooree-
ay]
(verb) poster [poss-tay]
postcard la carte postale [kart
poss-tal]
post office la poste [posst]
poste restante la poste
restante
potato la pomme de terre
[pom duh tair]
potato chips les chips **fpl**
[cheeps]
pound (money) la livre
(sterling) [leevr (stairleeng)]
(weight) la livre
prefer: I prefer ... je préfère ...
[juh prayfair]
pregnant enceinte [ONSANt]
prescription l'ordonnance **f**
[ordonONss]
present (gift) le cadeau [kado]
pretty joli [jolee]
price le prix [pree]

private privé [preevay]
probably probablement [prob-
abluhmON]
problem le problème [prob-lem]
no problem! pas de
problème! [pa duh]
public holiday le jour férié
[joor fayree-ay]
pull tirer [teeray]
purple violet [veeolay]
purse (for money) le portemonnaie [port-monay]
(US: handbag) le sac à main
[mAN]
push pousser [poossay]
put mettre [metr]
pyjamas le pyjama [peejama]

Q

quarter le quart [kar]
question la question [kest-yON]
queue la queue [kuh]
quick rapide [rapeed]
quickly vite [veet]
quiet (place, hotel) tranquille
[trONkeel]
quiet! silence! [seelONss]
quite (fairly) assez [assay]
(very) très [tray]
quite a lot pas mal [pa]

R

radiator le radiateur [rad-yaturr]
radio la radio [ra-deeo]
rail: by rail en train [ON trAN]

railway le chemin de fer [shuhmAN duh fair]
rain la pluie [plwee]
 it's raining il pleut [eel pluh]
rape le viol [veeol]
rare (steak) saignant [sen-yON]
raspberry la framboise [frONbwahz]
rather: I'd rather ... je préfère ... [juh prayfair]
razor le rasoir [razwahr]
read lire [leer]
ready prêt [pray]
real véritable [vayreet-abl]
really vraiment [vraymON]
receipt le reçu [ruhsoo]
recently récemment [ray-samON]
reception la réception [ray-seps-yON]
receptionist le/la réceptionniste [rayseps-yoneest]
recommend: could you recommend ...? pourriez-vous me recommander ...? [pooree-ay-voo muh ruhkomONday]
red rouge [rooj]
red wine le vin rouge [VAN]
refund le remboursement [rONboorss-mON]
region la région [rayjeeON]
registered: by registered mail en recommandé [ON ruhkomONday]
remember: I don't remember je ne me souviens pas [juh nuh muh soov-yAN pa]
rent (for apartment etc) le loyer

[lwy-ay]
(verb) louer [loo-ay]
repair réparer [rayparay]
repeat répéter [raypaytay]
reservation la réservation [rayzairvass-yON]
reserve réserver [rayzairvay]

dialogue

can I reserve a table for tonight? j'aimerais réserver une table pour ce soir [jemray]
yes madam, for how many people? certainement madame, pour combien de personnes? [sairten-mON ... poor KONb-yAN duh pairson]
for two pour deux
and for what time? et pour quelle heure? [ay poor kel urr]
for eight o'clock pour huit heures
and could I have your name please? pourrais-je avoir votre nom s'il vous plaît? [poorayj avwahr votr nON seel voo play]

restaurant le restaurant [restorON]
restaurant car le wagon-restaurant [vagON]
rest room les toilettes [twalet]
return (ticket) l'aller-retour **m** [alay-ruhtoor]

reverse charge call le PCV
[pay-say-vay]
rice le riz [ree]
right (correct) juste [jœst]
 (not left) droit [drwa]
 that's right c'est juste [say
 jœst]
ring (on finger) la bague [bag]
ring back rappeler
river la rivière [reev-yair]
road la route [root]
 is this the road for ...? est-ce
 la bonne route pour aller
 à ...? [ess la bon root poor alay]
rob: I've been robbed j'ai été
 dévalisé [jay aytay dayvaleezay]
roll (bread) le petit pain [puhtee
 pAN]
roof le toit [twa]
room la chambre [shONbr]

dialogue

do you have any rooms?
est-ce que vous avez des
chambres? [eskuh voo zavay
day]
for how many people?
pour combien de
personnes? [poor kONb-yAN
duh pairson]
for one/two pour une
personne/deux personnes
yes, we have rooms free
oui, nous avons des
chambres libres [leebr]
**for how many nights will it
be?** ce serait pour
combien de nuits? [suh

suhray poor kONb-yAN duh nwee]
just for one night pour
une nuit seulement
[surlmON]
how much is it? combien
est-ce? [ess]
**400 francs with bathroom
and 350 francs without
bathroom** quatre cents
francs avec salle de bain
et trois cent cinquante
francs sans salle de bain
[frON - sal duh bAN ay]
**can I see a room with
bathroom?** est-ce que je
pourrais voir une
chambre avec salle de
bain? [eskuh juh pooray vwahr]
OK, I'll take it d'accord, je
la prends [dakor juh la prON]

room service le service en
chambre [sairveess ON
shONbr]
rosé (wine) le rosé [rozzay]
round trip ticket l'aller-retour
m [alay-ruhtoor]
route l'itinéraire **m** [eeteenay-
rair]
rubbish (waste) les ordures
[ordœr]
 (poor quality goods) la camelote
 [kamlot]
rucksack le sac à dos [do]
rude grossier [gross-yay]
rum le rhum [rum]
run (person) courir [kooreer]

sad triste [treest]

safe (not in danger) en sécurité [ON saykOOreetay]
(not dangerous) sûr [sOOr]

salad la salade [sa-lad]

salad dressing la vinaigrette

sale: for sale à vendre [vONdr]

salt le sel

same: the same le/la même [mem]
the same again, please la même chose, s'il vous plaît [shohz seel voo play]

sand le sable [sabl]

sandals les sandales **fpl** [SON-dal]

sandwich le sandwich [sONd-weetch]

sanitary napkin/towel la serviette hygiénique [eejee-ayneek]

sauce la sauce [sohss]

saucepan la casserole

sausage la saucisse [soseess]

say: how do you say ... in French? comment dit-on ... en français? [komON deet-ON]
what did he say? qu'est-ce qu'il a dit? [keskeel a dee]

scarf (for neck) l'écharpe **f** [aysharp]
(for head) le foulard [foolar]

schedule (US) l'horaire **m** [orair]

school l'école **f** [aykol]

scissors: a pair of scissors

une paire de ciseaux [seezo]

Scotch tape® le scotch

Scotland l'Écosse **f** [aykoss]

Scottish écossais [aykossay]

sea la mer [mair]
by the sea au bord de la mer [o bor]

seafood les fruits de mer [frwee duh mair]

seasick: I feel seasick j'ai le mal de mer [jay luh mal duh mair]

seat le siège [see-ej]
is this anyone's seat? est-ce que cette place est prise? [eskuh set plass ay preez]

second (adj) second [suhgON]
(of time) la seconde [suhgONd]

second class (travel) en seconde [ON suhgONd]

see voir [vwahr]
can I see? est-ce que je peux voir? [eskuh juh puh]
have you seen ...? est-ce que tu as/vous avez vu ...? [tOO a/voo zavay vOO]
see you! à bientôt! [b-yANto]
I see (I understand) je vois [juh vwa]

self-catering apartment l'appartement (de vacances) **m** [apartmON (duh vakONss)]

self-service le self-service [-sairveess]

sell vendre [vONdr]

Sellotape® le scotch

send envoyer [ONvwy-ay]

separated: I'm separated je suis séparé [juh swee sayparay]

separately (pay, travel) séparément [sayparay-mON]

serious (person, situation, problem) sérieux [sayree-uh]
(illness) grave [grahv]

service station la station-service [stass-yON sairveess]

serviette la serviette [sair-]

set menu le menu (à prix fixe) [muhnOO (a pree feex)]

several plusieurs [plOOz-yurr]

sex le sexe

shade: in the shade à l'ombre [lONbr]

shampoo le shampoing [shONpwAN]

share (room, table etc) partager [partajay]

shaver le rasoir [razwahr]

shaving foam la mousse à raser [razay]

she elle [el]

sheet (for bed) le drap [dra]

shellfish les crustacés [krOOstassay]

ship le bateau [bato]

shirt la chemise [shuhmeez]

shit! merde! [maird]

shoe la chaussure [shoshOOr]

shoelaces les lacets **mpl** [lassay]

shoe polish le cirage [seerahj]

shoe repairer le cordonnier [kordon-yay]

shop le magasin [magazAN]

short (time, journey) court [koor]
(person) petit [puhtee]

shorts le short

should: what should I do? que dois-je faire? [kuh dwaj fair]

shoulder l'épaule **f** [aypol]

show (in theatre) le spectacle [spekt-akl]
could you show me? pourrais-tu/pourriez-vous me montrer? [pooray-tOO/pooree-ay-voo muh mONtray]

shower (in bathroom) la douche [doosh]

shut (verb) fermer [fairmay]
when do you shut? à quelle heure fermez-vous? [kel urr fairmay-voo]
they're shut c'est fermé [say fairmay]
shut up! tais-toi/taisez-vous! [tay-twa/tezzay-voo]

shutter (on window) le volet [volay]

sick malade [malad]

side le côté [kotay]

side salad la salade [sa-lad]

sidewalk le trottoir [trotwahr]

sight: the sights of ... les endroits à voir à ... [lay zONdrwa a vwahr]

silk la soie [swa]

silly idiot [eed-yo]

silver l'argent **m** [arjON]

since: since yesterday depuis hier [duhp-wee]

sing chanter [shONtay]

single: a single to ... un aller simple pour ... [alay sAN-pl]
I'm single je suis célibataire [juh swee sayleebatair]

single bed le lit d'une personne [lee dOOn pairson]

single room la chambre pour une personne [shONbr poor ɔn pairson]

sister la sœur [surr]

sit: can I sit here? est-ce que je peux m'asseoir ici? [eskuh juh puh masswahr ee-see]

sit down s'asseoir

size la taille [tī]

skin la peau [po]

skirt la jupe [jɶp]

sky le ciel [s-yel]

sleep dormir [dormeer]

sleeping bag le sac de couchage [kooshahj]

sleeping car le wagon-lit [vagON-lee]

slow lent [lON]

slow down! moins vite! [mwAN veet]

slowly lentement [lONtmON]

small petit [puhtee]

smell: it smells ça sent mauvais [mo-vay]

smile sourire [sooreer]

smoke la fumée [fɶmay]

do you mind if I smoke? est-ce que ça vous dérange si je fume? [eskuh sa voo dayrONj see juh fɶm]

I don't smoke je ne fume pas

snow la neige [nej]

so: it's so good c'est tellement bien [say telmON]

not so fast pas si vite!

so am I moi aussi [mwa o-see]

so do I moi aussi

soap le savon [savON]

soap powder la lessive [lesseev]

sober sobre [sobr]

sock la chaussette [sho-set]

soda (water) le soda

soft doux, f douce [doo, dooss]

soft drink la boisson non-alcoolisée [bwassON nON-alkoleezay]

sole la semelle [suhmel]

some: can I have some water/peanuts? j'aimerais de l'eau/des cacahuètes, s'il vous plaît [jemray duh lo/day-seel voo play]

somebody quelqu'un [kel-kAN]

something quelque chose [kelkuh shohz]

sometimes parfois [parfwa]

somewhere quelque part [kelkuh par]

son le fils [feess]

song la chanson [shONsON]

soon bientôt [b-yANto]

sore: it's sore ça fait mal [sa fay mal]

sorry: (I'm) sorry je suis désolé, excusez-moi [juh swee dayzolay, eskɶzay-mwa]

sorry? (didn't understand) pardon? [par-dON]

sort: what sort of ...? quel genre de ...? [kel jONr duh]

soup le potage [potahj]

south le sud [sɶd]

South Africa l'Afrique du Sud f [afreek dɶ sɶd]

South African (adj) sud-africain [sɶd afreekAN]

southeast le sud-est [sɶd-est]

southwest le sud-ouest [sood-west]

souvenir le souvenir

Spain l'Espagne f [españ]

speak: do you speak English? parlez-vous l'anglais? [parlay-voo]

I don't speak ... je ne parle pas ... [juh nuh parl pa]

spectacles les lunettes [loonet]

spend dépenser [daypONsay]

spoon la cuillère [kwee-yair]

spring (season) le printemps [prANtoN]

square (in town) la place [plass]

stairs l'escalier m [eskal-yay]

stamp le timbre [tANbr]

start le début [dayboo]
(verb) commencer [kom-ONSsay]

the car won't start la voiture refuse de démarrer [ruhfooz duh daymaray]

starter (food) l'entrée f [ONtray]

station la gare [gar]

stay: where are you staying? où logez-vous? [oo lojay-voo]

I'm staying at ... je loge au ... [juh loj o]

I'd like to stay another two nights j'aimerais rester deux nuits de plus [jemray restay]

steak le steak

steal voler [volay]

my bag has been stolen on m'a volé mon sac [ON ma volay]

steep (hill) raide [red]

still: I'm still waiting j'attends

toujours [toojoor]

stomach le ventre, l'estomac m [vONtr, estoma]

stomach ache les maux d'estomac [mo destoma]

stone (rock) la pierre [p-yair]

stop s'arrêter [sa-retay]

to stop the car arrêter la voiture

please, stop here (to taxi driver etc) arrêtez-moi ici, s'il vous plaît [aretay-mwa ee-see seel voo play]

storm la tempête [tON-pet]

straight: it's straight ahead c'est tout droit [say too drwa]

strange (odd) bizarre, étrange [aytrONj]

strawberry la fraise [frez]

street la rue [roo]

string la ficelle [feessel]

strong fort [for]

stuck coincé [kwANsay]

student l'étudiant m, l'étudiante f [aytood-yON, -yONt]

stupid stupide [stoopeed]

suburb le faubourg [fo-boor]

subway (US) le métro [maytro]

suddenly tout d'un coup [too dAN koo]

sugar le sucre [sookr]

suit le costume

suitcase la valise [valeez]

summer l'été m [aytay]

in the summer en été

sun le soleil [solay]

in the sun au soleil [o]

sunblock l'écran total m [aykrON toh-tal]

sunburn le coup de soleil [koo duh solay]

sunglasses les lunettes de soleil [lOOnet duh solay]

sunstroke l'insolation f [ANsolass-yON]

suntanned bronzé [brONzay]

suntan oil l'huile solaire f [weel solair]

supermarket le supermarché [sOOpairmarshay]

supper le dîner [deenay]

supplement (extra charge) le supplément [sOOplaymON]

sure: are you sure? vous êtes sûr? [voo zet sOOr]

sure! d'accord! [dakor]

surname le nom de famille [nON duh famee]

sweater le pullover

sweet (taste) sucré [sOOkray]
(dessert) le dessert [dessair]

sweets les bonbons mpl [bONbON]

swim nager [nahjay]
I'm going for a swim je vais me baigner [juh vay muh benyay]

swimming costume le maillot de bain [my-o duh bAN]

swimming pool la piscine [peesseen]

swimming trunks le slip de bain [sleep duh bAN]

Swiss suisse [sweess]

switch l'interrupteur m [ANtairOOpturr]

switch off (TV, lights) éteindre [aytANdr]

switch on (TV, lights) allumer [alOOmay]

Switzerland la Suisse [sweess]

T

table la table [tahbl]

table wine le vin ordinaire [VAN ordeenair]

take prendre [prONdr]
(accept) accepter [axeptay]
fine, I'll take it d'accord, je le prends [juh luh prON]
a hamburger to take away un hamburger à emporter [ONportay]

talk parler [parlay]

tall grand [grON]

tampons les tampons mpl [tONpON]

tan le bronzage [brONzahj]

tap le robinet [robeenay]

taste le goût [goo]

taxi le taxi

dialogue

to the airport/to Hotel ... please à l'aéroport/à l'Hôtel ..., s'il vous plaît [seel voo play]

how much will it be? combien est-ce que ça me coûtera? [kONb-yAN eskuh sa muh kootuhra]

about 75 francs à peu près soixante-quinze francs [puh pray - frON]

that's fine right here thanks
vous pouvez me déposer
ici, merci [muh daypozay ee-
see mairsee]

tea (drink) le thé [tay]
teacher (junior) l'instituteur m,
l'institutrice f [ANsteetŒturr,
-treess]
(secondary) le professeur [-urr]
telephone le téléphone
[taylay-]
television la télévision
[taylayveez-yON]
tell: could you tell him ...?
pourriez-vous lui dire ...?
[pooree-ay-voo lwee deer]
tennis le tennis [teneess]
terrible épouvantable
[aypoovONt-abl]
terrific fantastique [fONtasteek]
than que [kuh]
thanks, thank you merci
[mairsee]
thank you very much merci
beaucoup [bo-koo]
no thanks non, merci

dialogue

thanks merci
that's OK, don't mention it
il n'y a pas de quoi [eel
n-ya pa duh kwa]

that: that building ce bâtiment
[suh]
that woman cette femme
[set]

that one celui-là, f celle-là
[suhlwee-la, sel-la]
that's nice c'est joli [say]
is that ...? est-ce que
c'est ...? [eskuh say]
the (singular) le, f la [luh]
(plural) les [lay]
theatre le théâtre [tay-atr]
their leur [lurr]
theirs le/la leur [luh/la lurr]
them: I know them je les
connais [juh lay konay]
for them pour eux, f pour
elles [uh, el]
who? – them qui? –
eux/elles
then (after that) alors [alor]
there là
is/are there ...? y a-t-il ...?
[yateel]
there is/are ... il y a ... [eel ya]
there you are (giving something)
voilà [vwala]
these: these ... ces ...[say]
can I have these? j'aimerais
ceux-ci/celles-ci, s'il vous
plaît [suh-see/sel-see seel voo
play]
they ils, f elles [eel, el]
thick épais [aypay]
thief le voleur, f la voleuse
[volurr, -urz]
thin mince [mANss]
thing la chose [shohz]
my things mes affaires [may
zafair]
think penser [pONsay]
I'll think about it je vais y
réfléchir [vay zee rayflesheer]

thirsty: I'm thirsty j'ai soif [jay swaf]

this: this building ce bâtiment [suh]

this woman cette femme [set]

this one celui-ci, **f** celle-ci [suhlwee-see, sel-see]

is this ...? est-ce que c'est ...? [eskuh say]

those: those ...ces ... [say]

which ones? – those lesquel(le)s? – ceux-là/celles-là [suh-la/sel-la]

thread le fil [feel]

throat la gorge [gorj]

through par

thumb le pouce [pooss]

thunderstorm l'orage **m** [orahj]

ticket (for bus, train, plane) le billet [bee-yay]

(for cinema, cloakroom) le ticket [teekay]

dialogue

a return ticket to Dijon un aller-retour pour Dijon [alay-ruhtoor]

coming back when? avec retour à quelle date? [ruhtoor]

today/next Tuesday aujourd'hui/mardi prochain

that will be 300 francs trois cents francs, s'il vous plaît [froN]

tie (necktie) la cravate [kravat]

tights le collant [kollON]

time le temps [toN]

what's the time? quelle heure est-il? [kel urr eteel]

next time la prochaine fois

four times quatre fois

timetable l'horaire **m** [orair]

tin (can) la boîte [bwat]

tin-opener l'ouvre-boîte **m** [oovr-bwat]

tip (to waiter etc) le pourboire [poorbwahr]

tired fatigué [fateegay]

tissues les kleenex® **mpl**

to: to Strasbourg/London à Strasbourg/Londres

to Brittany/England en Bretagne/Angleterre [ON]

to the post office à la poste

to the bar au bar [o]

toast (bread) le pain grillé [pAN gree-yay]

today aujourd'hui [ojoordwee]

toe l'orteil **m** [ortay]

together ensemble [ONsoNbl]

toilet les toilettes [twalet]

toilet paper le papier hygiénique [papyay eejee-ayneek]

tomato la tomate [tomat]

tomorrow demain [duhmAN]

tomorrow morning demain matin

the day after tomorrow après-demain [apray]

tonic (water) le schweppes®

tonight ce soir [suh swahr]

too (excessively) trop [tro]

(also) aussi [o-see]
too much trop
me too moi aussi [mwa]
tooth la dent [dON]
toothache le mal de dents [mal duh dON]
toothbrush la brosse à dents [bross]
toothpaste le dentifrice [dONteefreess]
top: on top of ... sur ... [sOOr]
at the top en haut [ON o]
torch la lampe de poche [lONp duh posh]
tour l'excursion **f** [exkOOrs-yON]
tourist le/la touriste [tooreest]
tourist information office le centre d'information touristique [sONtr dANformass-yON tooreesteek]
towards vers [vair]
towel la serviette [sairvee-et]
town la ville [veel]
in town en ville [ON]
town centre le centre-ville [sONtr-]
toy le jouet [joo-ay]
track (US: at station) le quai [kay]
traffic lights les feux [fuh]
train le train [trAN]
by train en train [ON]
is this the train for ...? est-ce que ce train va bien à ...? [eskuh suh trAN va b-yAN a]
train station la gare [gar]
translate traduire [tradweer]
trashcan la poubelle [poo-bel]
travel voyager [vwyahj-ay]
travel agent's l'agence de voyages **f** [ajONss duh vwyahj]
traveller's cheque le chèque de voyage [shek duh vwyahj]
tree l'arbre **m** [arbr]
trip le voyage [vwyahj]
(excursion) l'excursion **f** [exkOOrs-yON]
trousers le pantalon [pONtalON]
true vrai [vray]
try essayer [esay-ay]
try on essayer [essay-ay]
T-shirt le T-shirt
tuna le thon [tON]
turn: turn left/right tournez à gauche/droite [toornay]
twice deux fois [duh fwa]
twin room la chambre à deux lits [shONbr]
tyre le pneu [p-nuh]

U

umbrella le parapluie [paraplwee]
uncle l'oncle **m** [ONkl]
under (in position) sous [soo]
(less than) moins de [mwAN duh]
underground (railway) le métro [maytro]
underpants le slip [sleep]
understand: I understand je comprends [juh kONprON]
I don't understand je ne comprends pas [pa]
university l'université **f** [OOneevairseetay]
unleaded petrol l'essence sans plomb **f** [essONss sON plON]

until jusqu'à [jœska]
up en haut [ON o]
  up there là-haut [la-o]
upstairs en haut [ON o]
urgent urgent [œrjON]
us nous [noo]
  for us pour nous [poor noo]
USA les USA [œ-ess-a]
use utiliser [œteeleezay]
useful utile [œteel]

V

vacation les vacances **fpl**
valid (ticket etc) valable [val-abl]
value la valeur [valurr]
vanilla la vanille [vanee]
veal le veau [vo]
vegetables les légumes **mpl**
  [laygœm]
vegetarian le végétarien, la
  végétarienne [vayjaytaree-AN,
  -en]
very très [tray]
  I like it very much ça me plaît
  beaucoup [sa muh play bo-koo]
view la vue [vœ]
village le village [veelahj]
visit visiter [veezeetay]
vodka la vodka
voice la voix [vwa]

W

waist la taille [tī]
wait attendre [atONdr]
waiter le serveur [sairvurr], le

garçon [garsON]
  waiter! garçon!
waitress la serveuse [sairvurz]
  waitress! s'il vous plaît! [seel
  voo play]
wake-up call le réveil
  téléphonique [ray-vay
  taylayfoneek]
Wales le Pays de Galles [payee
  duh gal]
walk: is it a long walk? est-ce
  loin à pied? [es lwAN a p-yay]
wall le mur [mœr]
wallet le portefeuille [portfuh-ee]
want: I want a ... je veux
  un ... [juh vuh]
  I don't want any ... je ne
  veux pas de ... [juh nuh vuh pa
  duh]
  I don't want to non, je ne
  veux pas
  what do you want? que
  voulez-vous? [kuh voolay-voo]
warm chaud [sho]
wash laver [lavay]
  (oneself) se laver [suh]
washhand basin le lavabo
washing (clothes) la lessive
  [lesseev]
washing machine la machine
  à laver [lavay]
washing powder la lessive
  [lesseev]
wasp la guêpe [gep]
watch (wristwatch) la montre
  [mONtr]
water l'eau **f** [o]
way: it's this way c'est par ici
  [say par ee-see]

it's that way c'est par là
is it a long way to ...? est-ce que c'est loin d'ici à ...? [eskuh say lwAN dee-see]
no way! pas question! [pa kest-yON]

dialogue

could you tell me the way to ...? pouvez-vous m'indiquer le chemin pour aller à ...?
go straight on until you reach the traffic lights continuez tout droit jusqu'aux feux [kONteenꝏay too drwa jꝏsko fuh]
turn left tournez à gauche [toornay]
take the first on the right prenez la première à droite [pruhnay]

we nous [noo]
weather le temps [tON]
week la semaine [suhmen]
a week (from) today aujourd'hui en huit [ojoordwee ON weet]
weekend le week-end
weight le poids [pwa]
welcome: you're welcome (don't mention it) je vous en prie [juh voo zON pree]
well: she's not well elle ne se sent pas bien [el nuh suh sON pa b-yAN]
you speak English very well vous parlez très bien l'anglais
well done! bravo!
this one as well celui-là aussi [o-see]
well-done (meat) bien cuit [b-yAN kwee]
Welsh gallois [galwa]
west l'ouest **m** [west]
wet mouillé [mooyay]
what? quoi? [kwa]
what's that? qu'est-ce que c'est? [keskuh say]
wheel la roue [roo]
when? quand? [kON]
when's the train/ferry? à quelle heure part le train/ferry? [kel urr par]
where? où? [oo]
which: which bus? quel bus? [kel]
while: while I'm here pendant que je suis ici [pondON kuh]
whisky le whisky
white blanc, **f** blanche [blON, blONsh]
white wine le vin blanc [VAN blON]
who? qui? [kee]
whole: the whole week toute la semaine [toot]
whose: whose is this? à qui est ceci? [a kee ay suhsee]
why? pourquoi? [poorkwa]
why not? pourquoi pas? [pa]
wide large [larj]
wife la femme [fam]
wind le vent [vON]
window la fenêtre [fuhnetr]

in the window (of shop) en vitrine [ON veetreen]

wine le vin [VAN]

wine list la carte des vins [kart day VAN]

winter l'hiver **m** [eevair]

with avec [avek]

I'm staying with ... j'habite chez ... [jabeet shay]

without sans [SON]

woman la femme [fam]

wood (material) le bois [bwa]

wool la laine [len]

word le mot [mo]

work le travail [trav-I]

it's not working ça ne marche pas [sa nuh marsh pa]

worried inquiet, **f** inquiète [ANkee-ay, -et]

worse: it's worse c'est pire [say peer]

worst le pire [luh peer]

would: would you give this to ...? pourriez-vous donner ceci à ...? [pooree-ay-voo donay suhsee]

wrap: could you wrap it up? pourriez-vous me l'emballer? [pooree-ay-voo muh lONbalay]

wrist le poignet [pwAN-yay]

write écrire [aykreer]

could you write it down? pouvez-vous me l'écrire? [poovay-voo muh laykreer]

wrong: it's the wrong key ce n'est pas la bonne clef [suh nuh pa la bon klay]

there's something wrong with ... ... ne marche pas

Wi

bien [nuh marsh pa b-yAN]

what's wrong? qu'y a-t-il? [k-yateel]

Y

year l'année **f** [anay]

yellow jaune [jo-n]

yes oui [wee]

yesterday hier [yair]

the day before yesterday avant-hier [avONt-yair]

yet encore [ONkor]

you (polite or plural) vous [voo] (singular, familiar) tu [too]

this is for you c'est pour vous/toi [twa]

young jeune [jurn]

your votre, **pl** vos [votr, vo] (singular, familiar) ton, **f** ta, **pl** tes [tON, ta, tay]

yours le/la vôtre [luh/la vohtr], **pl** les vôtres (singular, familiar) le tien, **f** la tienne [t-yAN, t-yen], **pl** les tiens/tiennes

youth hostel l'auberge de jeunesse **f** [obairj duh jur-ness]

Z

zero zéro [zayro]

zip la fermeture éclair [fairmtOOr ayklair]

zoo le zoo [zo]

French → English

a: il/elle a he/she/it has

à [a] to; at; in; by

abonnements mpl [abonnuh-mON] season tickets

abord: d'abord [dabor] first

accès interdit no entry

accord: d'accord [dakor] OK

accueil m [akuh-ee] reception

acheter [ashtay] to buy

addition f [adeess-yON] bill

aérogare f [a-airogar] air terminal

aéroglisseur m [a-airogleessurr] hovercraft

affaires fpl [affair] business; things, belongings

agence de voyages f [ajONss duh vwyahj] travel agent's

ai: j'ai [jay] I have

aimer [aymay] to like; to love

Allemagne f [almañ] Germany

aller [alay] to go

aller-retour m [alay ruhtoor] return/round trip ticket

aller simple m [SANpl] single ticket, one-way ticket

allumez vos phares switch on your lights

amende f [amOnd] fine

ami m, amie f [amee] friend

amour m [amoor] love

an m [ON] year

anglais [ONglay] English

Angleterre f [ONgluhtair] England

année f [anay] year

anniversaire m [aneevairsair] anniversary; birthday

annuler [anœlay] to cancel

appareil m [aparay] device; camera

appeler [aplay] to call

apporter [aportay] to bring

apprendre [aprONdr] to learn

appuyer ici press here

après [apray] after

après-midi m afternoon

argent m [arjON] money; silver

arrêt m [aray] stop

arrêter [aretay] to stop; to arrest

arrière m [aree-air] back

arrivée(s) f(pl) [areevay] arrival(s)

arriver [areevay] to arrive; to happen

as: tu as [a] you have

ascenseur m [asONsurr] lift, elevator

assez (de) [assay] enough; quite

assiette f [ass-yet] plate

assurance f [assœrONss] insurance

attendre [atONdr] to wait

attention! [atONss-yON] look out!; caution!

au [o] to the; at the; in the; by the; with

auberge de jeunesse [jur-ness] youth hostel

aucun [okAN] none, not any

aujourd'hui [ojoordwee] today

aussi [o-see] also

 aussi grand que as big as

autre [ohtr] other

aux [o] to the; at the; in the; by the

avant before
avec [avek] with
avez: vous avez [voo zavay]
 you have
avion m [av-yON] plane
avocat m [avoka] lawyer
avoir [avwahr] to have
avons: nous avons [noo zavON]
 we have

bac m ferry
baignade interdite no
 swimming
bain m [bAN] bath
banlieue f [bON-l-yuh] suburbs
bateau m [bato] boat
beaucoup [bo-koo] a lot;
 much
beau, f belle [bo, bel]
 beautiful; fine
belge [belj] Belgian
Belgique f [beljeek] Belgium
besoin: j'ai besoin de ... [jay
 buhzwAN duh] I need ...
bien [b-yAN] well, fine
 bien du/de la/des many
 bien que [kuh] although
bientôt [b-yanto] soon
bienvenue! [b-yAN-vuhnoo]
 welcome!
billet m [bee-yay] ticket
billet de banque [bONk]
 banknote, bill
blanc, f blanche [blON, blONsh]
 white
bleu [bluh] blue
boire [bwahr] to drink
bon [bON] good
bon marché [bON marshay]

cheap
bouche f [boosh] mouth
boucherie f [booshree]
 butcher's
boulangerie f [boolONjree]
 baker's
bouteille f [bootay] bottle
bras m [bra] arm
brasserie f pub/bar/café
 serving food
brocante secondhand goods
brouillard m [broo-ee-yar] fog
brun [brAN] brown
brushing m blow-dry

ça [sa] it; that
 ça va? how's things?
 ça va it's OK, I'm OK;
 that's fine
cacher [kashay] to hide
cadeau m [kado] present
café m [kafay] (black) coffee;
 café, bar
caisse f [kess] till, cashier's
 desk, cash desk
camion m [kam-yON] lorry
camping m [kONpeeng]
 camping; campsite
car m coach, bus
carte f [kart] card; map; pass
carte orange [orONj] season
 ticket for transport in Paris
 and its suburbs
casser [kassay] to break
ce [suh] this; that; it
ceci [suhsee] this
cédez le passage give way,
 yield
cela [suhla] that

celle-ci [sel-see], celui-ci
[suhlwee-see] this one
centre-ville city centre
ces [say] these
c'est [say] it is; that's
  c'est ça that's it
c'était [saytay] it was
cette [set] this; that
chacun [shakAN] each one;
  everyone
chaise f [shez] chair
chambre f [shONbr] room
chambre à deux lits [duh lee]
  twin room
chantier m roadworks;
  building site
chariot obligatoire you must
  take a trolley
chaud [sho] warm, hot
chaussée déformée uneven
  road surface
chemin m [shuhmAN] path
chèque de voyage [duh vwyahj]
  traveller's cheque
cher [shair] expensive; dear
cheveux mpl [shuhvuh] hair
chez [shay] at; among
chien m [shee-AN] dog
chose f [shohz] thing
chute de pierres falling rocks
circuit touristique tourist
  route
circulation f [seerkOOlass-yON]
  traffic
clé f [klay] key
climatisation f [kleemateezass-
  yON] air-conditioning
coin m [kwAN] corner
col m collar; (mountain) pass

colis m [kolee] parcel, package
combien? [kONb-yAN] how
  many?; how much?
comme [kom] like; as; how
comment? [komON] how?;
  pardon?, sorry?
commissariat m [komeessaree-a]
  police station
communication internationale
  international call
complet full, no vacancies
composez le ... dial ...
compostez votre billet
  validate/punch your ticket
  in the machine
comprendre [kONprONdr] to
  understand; to include
comptant: payer comptant
  [kONtON] pay cash
conducteur m [kONdOOkturr]
  driver
confiserie f confectioner,
  sweet shop
connaître [konetr] to know
conserver au frais (et au sec)
  keep in a cool (dry) place
conservez votre titre de
  transport jusqu'à la sortie
  keep your ticket till you
  leave the station
consigne f [kONseeñ] left
  luggage
consommation au comptoir
  drink at the bar
consommation en salle drink
  in the lounge
consommer avant le ... best
  before ...
contenir: ne contient pas de ...

131

contains no ...
contre [kONtr] against
convoi exceptionnel long vehicle
cordonnier m cobbler
corps m [kor] body
correspondance f [koresspONdONss] connection
côté m [kotay] side
  à côté de next to
côte f [koht] coast; rib
côté non stabilisé soft verge
cou m [koo] neck
coup m [koo] blow, knock; stroke
coup de fil phonecall
couper [koopay] to cut
courrier m [kooree-ay] mail
cours du change m [koor dOO shONj] exchange rate
couteau m [kooto] knife
coûter [kootay] to cost
crayon m pencil
crêperie f [krepuhree] pancake restaurant
croire [krwahr] to believe
croisement m [krwazmON] junction, intersection
cuillère f [kwee-yair] spoon
cuir m [kweer] leather
cuisine f kitchen; cooking

dame f [dam] lady
dans [dON] in; into
date de naissance [nessONss] date of birth
date limite de vente sell-by date
de [duh] of; from

debout [duhboo] standing
décrire [daykreer] to describe
décrochez lift the receiver
défectueux [dayfektOO-uh] faulty
défendu [dayfONdOO] forbidden
défense de ... [dayfONss] ... forbidden, no ..., do not ...
défense d'entrer no entrance
défense de stationner no parking
dégustation f [daygOOstass-yON] wine tasting
dehors [duh-or] outside
déjà [dayja] already
déjeuner m [dayjuhnay] lunch; breakfast
demain [duhmAN] tomorrow
demander [duhmONday] to ask
démarrer [daymaray] to start
demi [duhmee] half
demi-heure f [-urr] half an hour
demi-pension f [-pONss-yON] half board, American plan
dent f [dON] tooth
dépenser [daypONsay] to spend
depuis [duhpwee] since
dérangement: en dérangement out of order
dernier [dairn-yay] last
derrière [dairyair] behind
des [day] of the; from the; some
descendre [duhsONdr] to go down; to get off
désinfectant m [dayzANfektON] disinfectant; antiseptic
dessous [duhsoo] underneath

dessus [duhsoo] above; on top

destinataire m/f addressee

devant [duhvON] in front (of)

devenir [duhvuhneer] to become

déviation f diversion

devoir to have to

Dieu m [d-yuh] God

dîner m [deenay] dinner

dire [deer] to say; to tell

direction f [deerex-yON] steering; direction

distributeur automatique de billets m ticket machine

doigt m [dwa] finger

dommage: c'est dommage [domahj] it's a pity

donc [dONk] then, therefore

donner [donay] to give

dormir [dormeer] to sleep

dos m [doh] back

douane f [dwan] Customs

doubler [dooblay] to overtake

douche f [doosh] shower

douleur f [doolurr] pain

doux, f douce [doo, dooss] soft; sweet

drap m [dra] sheet

droguerie f [drogree] drugstore, sells aspirins, toiletries, household goods etc

droit [drwa] straight

du [doo] of the; from the; some

dur [door] hard

durée de conservation ... keeps for ...

eau f [o] water

école f [aykol] school

écouter [aykootay] to listen (to)

église f [aygleez] church

elle [el] she; her; it

elles [el] they; them

emporter [ONportay] to take

empruntez le passage souterrain use the underpass

en [ON] in; to; by

encore [ONkor] again; still

encore une bière another beer

enfant m/f [ONfON] child

enfin [ONfAN] at last

enlever [ONluhvay] to take away; to remove

ennuyer [ON-nwee-yay] to bother; to bore

enregistrement des bagages m check-in

enseigner [ONsen-yay] to teach

ensemble [ONsONbl] together

ensuite [ONsweet] afterwards

entendre [ONtONdr] to hear

entre [ONtr] between; among

entrée f [ONtray] entrance, way in; entrée

entrer [ONtray] to go in; to come in; to enter

environ [ONveerON] about

envoyer [ONvwy-ay] to send

épicerie f [aypeesree] grocer's

épouse f [aypooz] wife

épouvantable [aypoovONtabl] terrible

es: tu es [ay] you are

escale f [eskal] stop-over

escalier m [eskal-yay] stairs

espérer [espayray] to hope

essence f [essONss] petrol, gas

est: il/elle est [ay] he/she/it is

est m east

est-ce que ...? [eskuh] to form questions

est-ce que vous pensez ...? do you think ...?

et [ay] and

étage m [aytahj] floor

état m [ayta] state

été m [aytay] summer

été been

éteignez vos phares switch off your lights

êtes: vous êtes [et] you are

étoile f [aytwal] star

étranger (**m**) [aytrONjay] foreigner; foreign

être [etr] to be

étroit [aytrwa] narrow; tight

étudiant m, étudiante f [aytœd-yON, -yONt] student

eux [uh] them

s'excuser [sexkœzay] to apologize

facile [fasseel] easy

facultatif optional; request

faire [fair] to do; to make

falaise f [falez] cliff

fatigué [fateegay] tired

faut: il faut que je/vous ... [eel fo kuh] I/you must ...

faux, f fausse [fo, fohss] wrong

femme f [fam] woman; wife

fenêtre f [fuhnetr] window

fermé [fairmay] closed

fermeture annuelle f annual holiday, annual closure

fermeture automatique des portes doors close automatically

fête f [fet] party; feast day

fête de village [veelajh] village fair

fête nationale 14 July (national holiday)

feu m [fuh] fire

feux de signalisation traffic lights

file f [feel] lane

fille f [fee] girl; daughter

fils m [feess] son

fin f [fAN] end

finir [feeneer] to finish

foire f [fwahr] fair

fois f [fwa] time

formidable [formeedabl] great

formulaire m [formœlair] form

fort [for] strong; loud; loudly

fou, f folle [foo, fol] mad

fourchette f [foorshet] fork

frais, f fraîche [fray, fresh] fresh

français [frONsay] French

Français m [frONsay] Frenchman

Française f [frONsez] French woman

frapper [frapay] to hit; to knock

frein moteur engage lower gear

frère m [frair] brother

froid [frwa] cold

fumer [fœmay] to smoke

fumeurs [fœmurr] smokers

134

garçon m [garson] boy; waiter
garder [garday] to keep
gare f [gar] train station
gare routière [root-yair] bus station
gas-oil m diesel
gauche f [gohsh] left
gênant [jenON] embarrassing
gendarmerie f police station
gens mpl [jON] people
gentil [jONtee] kind; nice
gérant m [jayrON] manager
gîte m rural holiday accommodation
glissant [gleessON] slippery
goût m [goo] taste
grand [grON] large; tall; great
grandes lignes main lines
grande surface f [sOOrfass] superstore
grand magasin m [magazAN] department store
gratuit [gratwee] free
gris [gree] grey
gros [gro] big; fat
grotte f [grot] cave
guerre f [gair] war
guichet m [geeshay] ticket office; box office; counter
guichet automatique cash dispenser

habiter [abeetay] to live
haut [o] high
 en haut upstairs
heure f [urr] hour; time
heures d'ouverture opening times
heureux [ur-ruh] happy

hexagone: l'hexagone m France (colloquial name)
hier [yair] yesterday
hiver m [eevair] winter
homme m [om] man
horodateur m parking meter, pay and display
hors service out of order
hôtel de ville [duh veel] town hall, city hall
huile f [weel] oil

ici [ee-see] here
il [eel] he; it
île f [eel] island
il n'y a pas ... [eel nya pa] there isn't ...; there aren't ...
ils [eel] they
il y a ... [eelya] there is ...; there are ...
 il y a trois jours three days ago
impasse cul-de-sac, dead end
imprimé printed matter
indicatif m [ANdeekateef] dialling code, area code
insérez votre carte insert your card
interdiction de ... [ANtairdeex-yON] no ...
interdit [ANtairdee] forbidden
introduire les pièces ici insert coins here
itinéraire bis alternative route
itinéraire conseillé recommended route
ivre [eevr] drunk

135

jamais [jamay] never; ever
jambe f [jONb] leg
jardin m [jardAN] garden
jaune [jo-n] yellow
je [juh] I
jeu m [juh] game
jeune [jurn] young
joli [jolee] pretty
jouer [joo-ay] to play
jour m [joor] day
jour férié [fayree-ay] public holiday
journal m [joornal] newspaper
journée f [joornay] day
journée continue open all day
jours ouvrables weekdays
jours pairs/impairs parking allowed only on even/odd days of the month
jusqu'à (ce que) [jœska(ss kuh)] until

kermesse f [kairmess] fair
klaxonner [klaxonay] to hoot

l' the; him; her; it
la the; her; it
là [la] there
laid [lay] ugly
laine f [len] wool
laisser [lessay] to let; to leave
langue f [lON-g] tongue; language
large [larj] wide
lave-auto m [lav-oto] car wash
laver [lavay] to wash
le [luh] the; him; it
lendemain m [lONduhmAN] the next day

lentement [lONtuhmON] slowly
les [lay] the; them
leur [lurr] their; (to) them
lever [luhvay] to lift, to raise
librairie f [leebrairee] bookshop, bookstore
libre [leebr] free, vacant
lieu m [l-yuh] place
lire [leer] to read
lit m [lee] bed
livraison f [leevrezzON] delivery
livre f [leevr] pound
livre m book
location f [lokass-yON] rental; theatre tickets
location de ... ... for hire
loi f [lwa] law
loin [lwAN] far away
longtemps [lONtON] a long time
lorsque [lorskuh] when
louer [loo-ay] to rent
lourd [loor] heavy; rich; muggy
lui [lwee] him; to him; to her
lumière f [lœm-yair] light

m' (to) me; myself
ma my
magasin m [magazAN] shop, store
main f [mAN] hand
maintenant [mANtnON] now
mais [may] but
maison f [mezzON] house
mal badly
malade [malad] ill
manger [mONjay] to eat
mari m [maree] husband

matin m [matAN] morning
mauvais [mo-vay] bad
me [muh] me; to me; myself
médecin m [maydsAN] doctor
meilleur [mayurr] better
  le meilleur the best
même [mem] even; same
mer f [mair] sea
merci [mairsee] thank you; no
  thank you
mère f [mair] mother
mes [may] my
messieurs [mess-yuh]
  gentlemen; men's room
mettre [metr] to put
Midi m South of France
midi m midday
mieux [m-yuh] better
  le mieux (the) best
milieu m [meel-yuh] middle
moi [mwa] me
mois m [mwa] month
moitié f [mwatee-ay] half
mon [mON] my
monde m [mONd] world
  tout le monde [too luh]
  everyone
monsieur m [muhss-yuh]
  gentleman, man
montagne f [mONtañ]
  mountain
monter [mONtay] to go up; to
  get in
mort [mor] dead
mot m [mo] word
mourir [mooreer] to die

nager [nahjay] to swim
navette f [navet] shuttle

service
neige f [nej] snow
ne pas ... do not ...
ne pas déranger do not
  disturb
ne ... que [kuh] only
nettoyer [net-wy-ay] to clean
neuf, f neuve [nuhf, nuhv] new
nez m [nay] nose
ni neither
noir [nwahr] black
nom m [nON] name
nom de famille [duh famee]
  surname, family name
non [nON] no; not
nord m [nor] north
nos [no] our
note f [not] bill; note
notre [notr] our
nous [noo] we; (to) us
nouveau, f nouvelle [noovo,
  -vel] new
nu [n∞] naked
nuit f [nwee] night
nul [n∞l] no; lousy
nulle part [n∞l par] nowhere
numéro m [n∞mayro] number
numérotez dial
numéro vert freephone

objets trouvés mpl [objay
  troovay] lost property office,
  lost and found
occasion: d'occasion [dokaz-
  yON] secondhand
œil m [uh-ee] eye
on [ON] one; someone; you;
  they; people; we
oncle m [ONkl] uncle

ont: ils/elles ont [ON] they have
or m gold
oreille f [oray] ear
ou [oo] or
où [oo] where
oublier [ooblee-ay] to forget
ouest m [west] west
oui [wee] yes
ouvert [oovair] open
ouvrir ici open here

papiers papers; litter
par by; through
parce que [parss-kuh] because
pardon [par-dON] excuse me, pardon me; thank you; sorry
parents mpl [parON] parents; relatives
parfait [parfay] perfect
parfois [parfwa] sometimes
parking courte durée short-term car park
parking longue durée long-term car park
parler [parlay] to speak
part f [par] piece; share
partir [parteer] to leave
partout [partoo] everywhere
pas [pa] not
pas de ... no ...
pas encore not yet
passage interdit no entry
passage piétons pedestrian crossing
passage protégé priority road
patientez SVP please wait

pauvre [pohvr] poor
payer [pay-ay] to pay
pays m [payee] country
péage m [payahj] toll
peau f [po] skin
pêche interdite no fishing
peinture fraîche wet paint
pellicule f film
pelouse f [puhlooz] lawn
pendant [pONdON] during
penser [pONsay] to think
pension f [pONS-yON] guesthouse
pension complète [kONplet] full board, European plan
père m [pair] father
périphérique m [payreefayreek] ring road
permis [pairmee] allowed
permis de conduire m [duh kONdweer] driving licence, driver's license
personne f [pairson] person
personne nobody
petit [puhtee] small
petit déjeuner m [dayjuhnay] breakfast
peu: peu de ... [puh] few ... un peu (de) a bit (of)
peut-être [puht-etr] maybe
pièce f [p-yess] coin; room; play
pièces de rechange [ruhshONj] spare parts
pied m [p-yay] foot
piétons passez en deux temps pedestrians cross in two stages
pile f [peel] battery; pile

pire [peer] worse
 le pire (the) worst
piscine f [peesseen] swimming pool
place f [plass] seat; square
place(s) assise(s) seat(s)
places debout standing passengers
places libres spaces free
plage f [plahj] beach
plan m [plON] map
plat m [pla] dish
plats à emporter take-away meals
plein [plAN] full
pluie f [plwee] rain
plupart: la plupart de [plʊpar duh] most of
plus [plʊ] more
 plus jamais never again
 plus de ... more; no more ...
 le plus [plʊss] (the) most
plutôt [plʊto] rather
pneu m [p-nuh] tyre
poids m [pwa] weight
poids lourds [pwa loor] heavy vehicles
poissonnerie f fishmonger
pont m [pON] bridge; deck
porte f [port] door; gate
poste f [posst] post office
pour [poor] for
pourquoi [poorkwa] why
pousser [poossay] to push
pouvoir [poovwahr] to be able to
préfecture f [prayfektʊr] regional administrative headquarters

premier [pruhm-yay] first
prendre [prONdr] to take; to catch
prénom m [praynON] Christian name, first name
près de [pray duh] near
préservatif m [prayzairvateef] condom
presque [presk] almost
pressing m dry-cleaner's
prêt [pray] ready
prière de ... please ...
prière de ne pas toucher please do not touch
printemps m [prANtON] spring
priorité à droite right of way for traffic coming from the right
privé [preevay] private
prix m [pree] price; fee; prize
prochain [proshAN] next
profond [profON] deep
PTT (Postes, Télégraphes, Téléphones) [pay-tay-tay] post office (with telephone)
puis [pwee] then
puisque [pweess-kuh] since

quand [kON] when
quart m [kar] quarter
quartier m [kart-yay] district
que [kuh] that; what; than; who(m); which
quel [kel] which
quelque chose [kelkuh shohz] something
quelque part [par] somewhere
quelque(s) [kelkuh] some

139

quelqu'un [kelkAN] somebody

qu'est-ce que ...? [keskuh] what ...?

qui [kee] who

quitter [kitay] to leave

quoi? [kwa] what?

ralentir [ralONteer] to slow down

rappel m reminder

rayon m [rayON] spoke; department

regarder [ruhgarday] to look (at); to watch

reine f [ren] queen

relais routier m [ruhlay root-yay] transport café (often good restaurant)

remonte-pente m [ruhmONt-pONt] ski lift; ski tow

renseignements information desk; directory enquiries

rentrer [rONtray] to return

repas m [ruhpa] meal

répondre [raypONdr] to answer

restoroute m roadside café

retard m [ruhtar] delay

retirez votre argent take your money

retour de suite back soon

retrait des bagages m [ruhtray day bagahj] baggage claim

revenir [ruhvuhneer] to come back

rez-de-chaussée m [rayd-shoh-say] ground floor, (US) first floor

rien [ree-AN] nothing
de rien you're welcome

rive f [reev] bank

riverains autorisés access only, residents only

RN (route nationale) f [air-en] national highway

roi m [rwa] king

roue f [roo] wheel

rouge [rooj] red

roulez au pas drive at walking pace

route f [root] road; route

route départementale secondary road

routier m [root-yay] lorry; lorry-driver; roadside café

Royaume-Uni m [rwy-ohm oonee] United Kingdom

rue f [roo] street

SA (société anonyme) [ess-ah] Ltd, Inc

sa his; her; its

salle à manger f [sal a mONjay] dining room

salle de bain [duh bAN] bathroom

salut! [saloo] hi!; cheerio!

sang m [sON] blood

sans [sON] without

sans plomb lead-free

santé! [sontay] cheers!; bless you!

sauf [sohf] except; safe

sauf riverains access only

savoir [savwahr] to know

se [suh] him; to him; himself; her; to her; herself; each other

sec, f sèche [sek, sesh] dry

séjour m [sayjoor] stay
selon [suhlON] according to
semaine f [suhmen] week
sens m [sONss] direction
serrez à droite keep to the right
ses [say] his; her; its
seul [surl] alone; single; only
seulement [surlmON] only
si if; so; yes
siège m [see-ej] seat
s'il vous plaît [seel voo play] please; excuse me
sœur f [surr] sister
soir m [swahr] evening
soirée f [swahray] evening; evening performance
soleil m [solay] sun
sommes: nous sommes [som] we are
son [sON] his; her; its
sont: ils/elles sont [sON] they are
sortie f [sortee] exit, way out
sortir [sorteer] to go out; to take out
sous [soo] under
sous-titres mpl [-teetr] subtitles
souvent [soovON] often
stationnement parking
stationner [stass-yonay] to park
sud m [sood] south
suis: je suis [swee] I am
Suisse f [sweess] Switzerland
suivre [sweevr] to follow
sur [soor] on
syndicat d'initiative m [sANdeeka deeneess-yateev] tourist information centre

t' (to) you; yourself
ta your
tabac-journaux m newsagent, tobacco store and news vendor (also sells stamps); newspaper kiosk
taille f [ti] size; waist
talon-minute heel bar
tant (de) [tON] so much; so many
tante f [tONt] aunt
tard [tar] late
te [tuh] (to) you; yourself
teinturerie f [tANtoor-uhree] dry cleaner's
télécartes en vente ici phonecards sold here
télécopie f fax
tellement [telmON] so
temps m [tON] time; weather
terminer [tairmeenay] to finish
tes [tay] your
tête f [tet] head
TGV (Train à grande vitesse) m [tay-jay-vay] high-speed train
timbre m [tANbr] stamp
tirer [teeray] to pull; to shoot
toi [twa] you
tomber [tONbay] to fall
ton [tON] your
tôt [toh] early
toujours [toojoor] always; still
tous [too] all; every
tout [too] everything; all; every
toutes directions all directions

traduction f [tradꝏx-yON] translation

travailler [travī-ay] to work

traversée f [travairsay] crossing

très [tray] very

triste [treest] sad

se tromper to be wrong

trop [tro] too; too much

trouver [troovay] to find

TTC (toutes taxes comprises) inclusive of tax

tu [tꝏ] you

tuer [tꝏ-ay] to kill

TVA (taxe sur la valeur ajoutée) f [tay-vay-ah] VAT

un, une [AN,ꝏn] a; one

usine f [ꝏzeen] factory

utiliser avant ... use before ...

valable jusqu'au ... valid until ...

valise f [valeez] suitcase

vélo m [vaylo] bike

vendre [vONdr] to sell

　à vendre for sale

venir [vuhneer] to come

vent m [vON] wind

vente f [vONt] sale; selling rate

ventre m [vONtr] stomach

verre m [vair] glass

vers towards; about

vert [vair] green

vêtements mpl [vetmON] clothes

veuillez ... [vuh-ee-yay] please ...

vide [veed] empty

vie f [vee] life

vieux, f vieille [v-yuh, v-yay] old

ville f [veel] town

vins et spiritueux wine merchant

virages sur ... km bends for ... km

vite [veet] quick; quickly

vitesse f speed; gear

vivre [veevr] to live

vœux: meilleurs vœux [may-yurr vuh] best wishes

voici [vwa-see] here is; here are; here you are

voilà [vwala] here is; here are; there you are

voir [vwahr] to see

voiture f [vwatꝏr] car; coach; carriage

vol m flight; theft

vos [vo] your

votre [votr] your

vous [voo] you; (to) you

vrai [vray] true; real

vraiment [vraymON] really

wagon-lit [-lee] sleeping car

y [ee] there; it

　y a-t-il ...? [yateel] is there ...?; are there ...?

yeux mpl [yuh] eyes

zone bleue f [zon bluh] restricted parking area

MENU READER

Food: Essential terms

bread le pain [pAN]
butter le beurre [burr]
cup la tasse [tass]
dessert le dessert [desair]
fish le poisson [pwassON]
fork la fourchette [foorshet]
glass: a glass of ... un verre de ...[AN vair duh]
knife le couteau [kooto]
main course le plat principal [pla prANseepal]
meat la viande [veeONd]
menu la carte [kart]
pepper le poivre [pwahvr]
plate l'assiette **f** [ass-yet]
salad la salade [sa-lad]

salt le sel
set menu le menu (à prix fixe) [muhnoo (a pree feex)]
soup le potage [potahj]
spoon la cuillère [kwee-yair]
starter l'entrée **f** [ONtray]
table la table [tahbl]

another ..., please encore un/une ..., s'il vous plaît [ONkor AN/OOn ... seel voo play]
excuse me! pardon [par-dON]
could I have the bill, please? l'addition, s'il vous plaît [seel voo play]

Food: Menu Reader

abricot [abreeko] apricot
agneau [an-yo] lamb
ail [i] garlic
ailloli [i-olee] garlic mayonnaise

amandes [amONd] almonds
ananas [anana] pineapple
anchois [ONshwa] anchovies
andouillette [ONdoo-yet] small, spicy tripe sausage

143

artichaut [artee-sho] artichoke
asperge(s) [aspairJ] asparagus
assiette anglaise [ass-yet ONglez] selection of cold meats
aubergine aubergine, eggplant
avocat [avoka] avocado
beignet [ben-yay] fritter, doughnut
betterave [betrahv] beetroot, (US) red beet
beurre [burr] butter
bifteck [beeftek] steak
bisque [beesk] shellfish soup
blanquette [blONket] stew
bœuf [burf] beef
boudin [boodAN] black pudding
bouillabaisse [booyabess] spicy fish soup
brioche [bree-osh] round bun
broche: à la broche [ala brosh] roasted on a spit
brochette [broshet] kebab
brugnon [broo-yON] nectarine
cabillaud [kabee-yo] cod
cacahuètes [kaka-wet] peanuts
cal(a)mar squid
canard [kanar] duck
caneton [kantON] duckling
câpres [kapr] capers
carrelet [karlay] plaice
carte [kart] menu
casse-croûte [kass-kroot] sandwich; snack
cassis [kasseess] blackcurrant
cassoulet [kassoolay] casserole with pork, sausages and beans
cerise [suhreez] cherry

champignons [shONpeen-yON] mushrooms
charcuterie [sharkOOtree] cold meats and pâtés
cheval [shuhval] horse
chèvre [shevr] goats' milk cheese
chevreuil [shevruh-ee] venison
chicorée [sheekoray] endive, chicory
chou [shoo] cabbage
choucroute [shookroot] sauerkraut
chou-fleur [shooflurr] cauliflower
choux de Bruxelles [shoo duh brOO-sel] Brussels sprouts
citron [seetrON] lemon
citron vert [vair] lime
civet [seevay] game stew
colin [kolAN] hake
cornichon [korneeshON] gherkin
confiture [kONfeetoor] jam
consommé [kONsommay] clear meat or chicken soup
coq au vin [kok o VAN] chicken in red wine
coques [kok] cockles
coquilles Saint-Jacques [kokee SAN Jak] scallops
côte/côtelette de porc [koht/kotlet duh por] pork chop
coulis [koolee] creamy sauce
coupe [koop] ice cream dessert
courgette courgette, zucchini
crème [krem] cream; creamy sauce or dessert
crème anglaise [ONglez] custard

144

crème Chantilly [shONtee-yee] whipped cream

crème de ... cream of ... soup

crème fouettée [foo-etay] whipped cream

crème pâtissière [pateessee-air] confectioner's custard

crêpe [krep] pancake

crêpes Suzette pancakes flambéd with orange sauce

cresson [kressON] cress

crevette grise [greez] shrimp

crevette rose [roz] prawn

croque-madame [krok ma-dam] toasted cheese sandwich with ham and eggs

croque-monsieur [krok muhss-yuh] toasted cheese sandwich with ham

croûte: en croûte [ON kroot] in pastry

cru [kroo] raw

crudités [kroodeetay] selection of salads or chopped raw vegetables

crustacés [kroostassay] shellfish

cuit cooked

cuisses de grenouille [kweess duh gruhnoo-yuh] frogs' legs

daube [dohb] casserole

dinde [dANd] turkey

écrevisse [aykruhveess] freshwater crayfish

endive [ONdeev] chicory, endive

entrecôte [ONtr-koht] rib steak

épinards [aypeenar] spinach

escargots [eskargo] snails

fait maison [fay mezzON] home-made

farci [farsee] stuffed

faux filet [fo feelay] fillet steak, sirloin steak

fenouil [fenoo-yuh] fennel

fines herbes [feen zairb] herbs

flan [flON] custard tart; crème caramel; egg custard

flétan [flaytON] halibut

foie [fwa] liver

four: au four [oh foor] baked

fraise [frez] strawberry

framboise [frONbwahz] raspberry

frit [free] deep-fried

frites [freet] chips, French fries

friture [freetoor] deep-fried small fish

fromage [fromahJ] cheese

fruits de mer [duh mair] seafood

fumé [foomay] smoked

galette [galet] round flat cake; buckwheat pancake

garni [garnee] with French fries or rice and/or vegetables

gaufre [gohfr] wafer; waffle

glace [glass] ice cream; ice

gras-double [gra-doobl] tripe

gratin: au gratin [o] baked in a milk, cream and cheese sauce

gratin dauphinois [gratAN dofeen-wa] potato gratin

grillade [gree-yad] grilled meat

groseille [grossay] currant; gooseberry

hachis [ashee] minced meat, ground beef

hareng [arON] herring

haricot de mouton [areeko duh mootON] mutton stew with beans

haricots [areeko] green beans; beans

haricots blancs [blON] haricot beans

haricots verts [vair] green beans

homard [omar] lobster

hors d'œuvres [or duhvr] starters, appetizers

huile [weel] oil

huître [weetr] oyster

îles flottantes [eel flotONt] poached whisked egg whites on top of custard

jambon [JONbON] ham

jardinière (de légumes) [Jardeen-yair (duh laygœm)] with mixed vegetables

laitue [lettœ] lettuce

langouste [lONgoost] crayfish

langoustine [lONgoosteen] scampi

lapin [lapAN] rabbit

lardons [lardON] cubes of bacon

légumes [laygœm] vegetables

lentilles [lONteel] lentils

lièvre [lee-evr] hare

limande [leemONd] dab; lemon sole

lotte [lot] burbot

loup [loo] bass

macédoine de légumes [massaydwan duh laygœm] chopped mixed vegetables

magret de canard [magray duh kanar] duck breast

maquereau [makro] mackerel

marrons [marrON] chestnuts

médaillon [maydî-ON] round piece of meat

merlan [mairlON] whiting

meunière [muhn-yair] dipped in flour and fried in butter

miel [mee-el] honey

millefeuille [meel-fuh-ee] custard slice

morue [morœ] cod

moules [mool] mussels

moules marinière [mareen-yair] mussels in white wine

moutarde [mootard] mustard

mouton [mootON] mutton

mûre [mœr] blackberry

myrtille [meertee] bilberry

nature [natœr] plain

navarin [navarAN] mutton stew with vegetables

noisette d'agneau [dan-yo] small, round lamb steak

noisettes [nwazet] hazelnuts

noix [nwa] walnuts

nouilles [noo-yuh] noodles

œuf [urf] egg

œuf à la coque [kok] (soft-)boiled egg

œuf dur [dœr] hard-boiled egg

œuf poché [poshay] poached egg

œufs à la neige [uh ala neJ] poached whisked egg whites on top of custard

œufs brouillés [broo-yay] scrambled eggs

œuf sur le plat [urf sœr luh pla] fried egg

oie [wa] goose

oignon [onyON] onion

pain [pAN] bread; loaf

pain complet [kONplay] wholemeal bread

pain de campagne [kONpañ] farmhouse loaf

palourdes [paloord] clams

pamplemousse [pONpl-mooss] grapefruit

pané [panay] breaded

parmentier [parmONtee-ay] with potatoes

pâte [paht] pastry; paste

pâtes [paht] pasta

pâtisserie [pateesree] cake, pastry

paupiettes de veau [pohp-yet duh vo] rolled-up stuffed slice of veal

pêche [pesh] peach

persil [pairsee] parsley

petit gâteau [puhtee] biscuit, cookie

petit pain [pAN] roll

petits pois [puhtee pwa] peas

piperade [peepayrad] scrambled eggs with peppers and tomatoes

piquant [peekON] hot, spicy

pissaladière [peessaladee-yair] Provençal dish similar to pizza

pistache [peestash] pistachio

plat du jour [pla dœ joor] dish of the day

poire [pwahr] pear

poireau [pwahro] leek

poire belle-Hélène [bel aylen] pear in chocolate sauce

pois chiches [pwa sheesh] chickpeas

poisson [pwassON] fish

poivre [pwahvr] pepper (seasoning)

poivron [pwahvrON] pepper (vegetable)

pomme [pom] apple

pomme de terre [duh tair] potato

pommes allumettes [pom alœmet] French fries

pommes dauphine [dofeen] potato fritters

pommes de terre à l'anglaise [pom duh tair a lONglez] boiled potatoes

pommes (de terre) en robe de chambre/des champs [ON rob duh shONbr/day shON] baked potatoes

pommes frites [freet] chips, French fries

pommes paille [pī] finely cut chips, French fries

porc [por] pork

potage [potahJ] soup

pot-au-feu [potofuh] beef and vegetable stew

potée [potay] vegetable and meat hotpot

poule au pot [pool o po] chicken and vegetable stew

poulet [poolay] chicken

praires [prair] small clams

prune [prœn] plum

pruneau [prOOno] prune
quenelle [kuhnel] dumpling
radis [radee] radish
ragoût [ragoo] stew
raie [ray] skate
raisin [rezzAN] grape(s)
râpé [rapay] grated
reine-claude [ren-klohd] greengage
religieuse [ruhleeJurz] iced cream puff
rillettes [ree-yet] potted meat
riz [ree] rice
rôti [rotee] roast, roast meat
rouget [roo-Jay] mullet
rouille [roo-yuh] spicy sauce to go with bouillabaisse
rumsteak steak
sablé [sablay] shortbread
saint-honoré [sANt-onoray] cake with cream and choux pastry decoration
salade composée [sa-lad kompozay] mixed salad
salade niçoise [neess-wahz] salad with olives, tomatoes, anchovies and hard-boiled eggs
salade verte [vairt] green salad
salé [salay] salted, salty; savoury
sauce blanche [blONsh] white sauce
saucisse [sosseess] sausage
saucisson [sosseessON] salami
saumon [somON] salmon
savarin [savarAN] ring-shaped rum baba
sel salt

service (non) compris service (not) included
sole bonne femme [bon fam] sole cooked in white wine and mushrooms
soupe au pistou [soop o peestoo] thick vegetable soup with basil
steak tartare raw minced beef with a raw egg
sucre [sOOkr] sugar
tartelette [tartuh-let] small tart/pie
tartine [tarteen] slice of bread
terrine [terreen] coarser type of pâté
thon [tON] tuna fish
tourte [toort] pie
tranche [trONsh] slice
truite au bleu [trweet o bluh] poached trout
veau [vo] veal
velouté [vuhlootay] creamy soup
viande [vee-ONd] meat
vinaigre [veenegr] vinegar
volaille [volī] poultry
yaourt [ya-oort] yogurt

Drink: Essential terms

beer la bière [bee-air]
bottle la bouteille [bootay]
brandy le cognac
coffee le café [kafay]
cup la tasse [tass]
  a cup of ... une tasse de ...
  [ꝏn ... duh]
fruit juice le jus de fruit [jꝏ
  duh frwee]
gin le gin [djeen]
  a gin and tonic un gin-tonic
glass le verre [vair]
  a glass of ... un verre de ...
  [ΛN ... duh]
milk le lait [lay]
mineral water l'eau minérale
  [o meenayral]
orange juice le jus d'orange
  [jꝏdorONj]

port le porto
red wine le vin rouge [VAN
  rooj]
rosé le rosé [rozzay]
soda (water) le soda
soft drink la boisson non-
  alcoolisée [bwassON nON-
  alkoleezay]
sugar le sucre [sꝏkr]
tea le thé [tay]
tonic (water) le schweppes®
vodka la vodka
water l'eau **f** [o]
whisky le whisky
white wine le vin blanc [VAN
  blON]
wine le vin [VAN]
wine list la carte des vins [kart
  day VAN]

Drink: Menu Reader

bière [bee-air] beer
bière (à la) pression [press-yON]
  draught beer
bière (blonde) lager
bière brune [brꝏn] bitter; dark
  beer
blanc [blON] white wine;
  white
boisson [bwassON] drink
café [kafay] espresso, very

strong black coffee
café au lait [o lay] white coffee
café crème [krem] white
  coffee
calvados apple brandy from
  Normandy
camomille [kamomee]
  camomile tea
champagne [shONpañ]
  champagne

149

chocolat chaud [shokola sho] hot chocolate

cidre [seedr] cider

citron pressé [seetrON pressay] fresh lemon juice

crème [krem] white coffee

crème de cassis [duh kasseess] blackcurrant liqueur

demi [duhmee] small draught beer; quarter of a litre of beer

diabolo menthe/fraise [d-yabolo mONt/frez] mint/strawberry cordial with lemonade

digestif [deejesteef] liqueur

eau [o] water

eau minérale gazeuse [gazurz] sparkling mineral water

frappé [frapay] well chilled, on ice

glaçon [glassON] ice cube

infusion [anfOOz-yON] herb tea

jus [jOO] juice

kir white wine with blackcurrant liqueur

lait [lay] milk

marc [mar] clear spirit distilled from grapes

menthe à l'eau [mONt a lo] mint cordial

millésime [meelay-zeem] vintage

mousseux [moossuh] sparkling

Noilly-Prat® [nwa-yee pra] an apéritif wine similar to Dry Martini

panaché [panashay] shandy

pastis [pasteess] aniseed-flavoured alcoholic drink

Pernod® [pairno] a brand of pastis

pétillant [paytee-ON] sparkling

porto port

pression [press-yON] draught beer, draught

Ricard® [reekar] a brand of pastis

rouge [rooj] red

sec [sek] dry; neat

sirop [seero] cordial

thé [tay] tea

thé au lait [o lay] tea with milk

thé nature [natOOr] tea without milk

tilleul [tee-yurl] lime-flower tea

vin [VAN] wine

vin blanc [blON] white wine

vin rouge [rooj] red wine

GERMAN

DICTIONARY PHRASEBOOK

Pronunciation

In this phrase book, the German has been written in a system of imitated pronunciation so that it can be read as though it were English. Bear in mind the notes on pronunciation given below:

ay	as in may
e	as in get
g	always hard as in goat
ī	as the 'i' sound in might
J	like the 's' sound in pleasure
KH	as in the Scottish way of saying loch
oo	as in book
oo	as in monsoon
∞	like the 'ew' in few but without any 'y' sound
ow	as in cow
uh	like the 'e' in butter
ur	as in fur but without any 'r' sound

The common German sound 'ei', as in Einstein, is written either with a 'y' or as 'ine'/'ite'/'ile' etc as in fine/kite/while.

Language Notes

There are three words for 'the' in German: **der**, **die**, **das** [dair, dee, dass] (masculine, feminine and neuter). The plural form is always **die** [dee].

The corresponding words for 'a' are **ein**, **eine**, **ein** [ine, **ine**-uh, ine]. Some examples:

der/ein Motor	**die/eine Reise**	**das/ein Mädchen**
the/an engine	the/a journey	the/a girl
die Motoren	**die Reisen**	**die Mädchen**
the engines	the journeys	the girls

German has a fairly complex system of cases, which means, amongst other things, that these words for 'the' and 'a' may often occur in a modified form. For example:

die Name des Hotels	**nach der Reise**
the name of the hotel	after the journey

    mit dem Mädchen
      with the girl

When an adjective is placed in front of a noun, it agrees with it:

eine lange Reise	**ein komisches Gesicht**
a long journey	a funny face

Here is a useful verb – 'to be':

ich bin [ish] I am	**wir sind** [veer zint] we are
du bist [doo] you are	**Sie sind** [zee zint] you are
(familiar form)	(plural or polite singular form)
er/sie/es ist [air/zee/ess]	**sie sind** [zee zint] they are
he/she/it is	

The familiar form **du** (which has a plural form **ihr seid** [eer zite]) is used to speak to people you are on friendly terms with.

Days

Monday Montag [**moh**ntahk]
Tuesday Dienstag [**dee**nstahk]
Wednesday Mittwoch [**mitt**voKH]
Thursday Donnerstag [**do**nnerstahk]
Friday Freitag [**fry**tahk]
Saturday Samstag [**za**mstahk]
Sunday Sonntag [**zo**nntahk]

Months

January Januar [**ya**nooar]
February Februar [**fay**brooar]
March März [mairts]
April April [a-**pril**l]
May Mai [my]
June Juni [**yoo**nee]
July Juli [**yoo**lee]
August August [owg**oo**st]
September September [**zep**tember]
October Oktober
November November
December Dezember [**dayts**ember]

Time

what time is it? wie spät ist es? [vee shpayt ist ess]
one o'clock ein Uhr [ine **oo**r]
two o'clock zwei Uhr [tsvy **oo**r]
it's one o'clock es ist ein Uhr [ess ist ine **oo**r]
it's two o'clock es ist zwei Uhr [ess ist tsvy **oo**r]
it's ten o'clock es ist zehn Uhr [ess ist tsayn **oo**r]
five past one fünf nach eins [f**oo**nf naKH ine-ss]
ten past two zehn nach zwei [tsayn nahKH tsvy]
quarter past one Viertel nach eins [**feer**tel nahKH ine-ss]
quarter past two Viertel nach zwei [**feer**tel naKH tsvy]
*half past ten halb elf [halp elf]
twenty to ten zwanzig vor zehn [tsv**a**ntsish for tsayn]
quarter to two Viertel vor zwei [**feer**tel for tsvy]
at half past four um halb fünf [oom halp f**oo**nf]
at eight o'clock um acht Uhr [oom aKHt **oo**r]
14.00 14 Uhr [**feer**tsayn **oo**r]
17.30 siebzehn Uhr dreißig [**zee**ptsayn **oo**r dr**y**ssish]
2 a.m. 2 Uhr morgens [tsvy **oo**r **mo**rgens]
2 p.m. 2 Uhr nachmittags [tsvy **oo**r n**ah**KHmittahks]
10 a.m. 10 Uhr vormittags [tsayn **oo**r f**o**rmittahks]

10 p.m. 10 Uhr abends [tsayn 00r **ah**bents]

noon Mittag [**mitt**ahk]

midnight Mitternacht [**mitt**ernaKHt]

an hour eine Stunde [**ine**-uh sht**oo**nd-uh]

a/one minute eine Minute [**ine**-uh min**00**t-uh]

two minutes zwei Minuten [tsvy min**00**ten]

a second eine Sekunde [**ine**-uh zek**oo**nd-uh]

a quarter of an hour eine Viertelstunde [**ine**-uh **feer**telshtoond-uh]

half an hour eine halbe Stunde [**ine**-uh halb-uh sht**oo**nd-uh]

three quarters of an hour eine Dreiviertelstunde [**ine**-uh **dry**feertel-shtoond-uh]

★ Note the difference here. German for 'half past ten/three/five' etc is, literally, 'half eleven/four/six' etc.

Numbers

0	null	[nooll]
1	eins	[ine-ss]
2	zwei	[tsvy]
3	drei	[dry]
4	vier	[feer]
5	fünf	[f00nf]
6	sechs	[zeks]
7	sieben	[**zee**ben]
8	acht	[aKHt]
9	neun	[noyn]
10	zehn	[tsayn]
11	elf	[elf]
12	zwölf	[tsvurlf]
13	dreizehn	[**dry**-tsayn]
14	vierzehn	[**veer**-tsayn]
15	fünfzehn	[**f00**nf-tsayn]
16	sechzehn	[**zesh**-tsayn]
17	siebzehn	[**zeep**-tsayn]
18	achtzehn	[**a**KH-tsayn]
19	neunzehn	[**noyn**-tsayn]
20	zwanzig	[**tsvan**tsish]
21	einundzwanzig	[**ine**-oont-tsvantsish]
22	zweiundzwanzig	[tsvy-oont-tsvantsish]
23	dreiundzwanzig	[**dry**-oont-tsvantsish]
30	dreißig	[**dry**ssish]
31	einunddreißig	[**ine**-oont-dryssish]
40	vierzig	[**feer**tsish]
50	fünfzig	[**f00**nftsish]
60	sechzig	[**zesh**tsish]
70	siebzig	[**zeep**tsish]
80	achtzig	[**a**KHtsish]
90	neunzig	[**noyn**tsish]
100	hundert	[**hoo**ndert]

110	hundertzehn	[hoondert-tsayn]
200	zweihundert	[tsvy-hoondert]
300	dreihundert	[dry-hoondert]
1,000	tausend [towzent]	
2,000	zweitausend	[tsvy-towzent]
10,000	zehntausend	[tsayn-towzent]
50,000	fünfzigtausend	[foonftsish-towzent]
100,000	hunderttausend	[hoondert-towzent]
1,000,000	eine Million	[ine-uh mill-yohn]

In German, thousands are written with a full-stop. A comma is used for decimals.

German	English
10.000	10,000
2,83	2.83

Ordinal numbers are formed by adding **-te** or **-ste** if the number ends in **-ig**. For example, **fünfte** [foonft-uh] (fifth), **zwanzigste** [tsvantsishst-uh] (twentieth).

1st	erste	[airst-uh]
2nd	zweite	[tsvite-uh]
3rd	dritte	[dritt-uh]
4th	vierte	[feert-uh]
5th	fünfte	[foonft-uh]
6th	sechste	[zekst-uh]
7th	siebte	[zeept-uh]
8th	achte	[aкнt-uh]
9th	neunte	[noynt-uh]
10th	zehnte	[tsaynt-uh]

English

→

German

A

a, an ein(e) [**ine**(-uh)]
about: about twenty etwa
zwanzig [**etvah**]
a film about Germany ein
Film über Deutschland
[**oober**]
above über [**oober**]
abroad im Ausland [**owss**lant]
to go abroad ins Ausland
gehen
accept akzeptieren
[aktsep**teer**en]
accident der Unfall [**oon**fal]
across: across the road über
die Straße [**oober**]
adapter der Adapter
address die Adresse [ad**ress**-
uh]
adult der Erwachsene
[air**vaks**en-uh]
advance: in advance im
voraus [**for**owss]
after nach [na**KH**]
afternoon der Nachmittag
[**na**KHmit-tahk]
aftersun cream die Après-
Lotion [ap**ray**-lohts-yohn]
afterwards danach [dan**a**KH]
again wieder [**vee**der]
against gegen [**gay**gen]
ago: a week ago vor einer
Woche [for **ine**-er]
AIDS Aids
air die Luft [**looft**]
by air mit dem Flugzeug
[fl**oo**ktsoyk]

airmail: by airmail per
Luftpost [pair l**oo**ftpost]
airport der Flughafen [fl**oo**k-
hahfen]
airport bus der Flughafenbus
[fl**oo**k-hafenbooss]
aisle seat der Sitz am Gang
alcohol der Alkohol
all alle [al-uh]
that's all, thanks das ist alles,
danke [al-ess]
allergic allergisch [all**air**gish]
all right okay
I'm all right ich bin okay
almost fast [fasst]
alone allein [al-**ine**]
already schon [shohn]
also auch [owKH]
altogether insgesamt
always immer
ambulance der
Krankenwagen [**kranken**-
vahgen]
America Amerika [a**maireeka**]
American der Amerikaner/
die Amerikanerin
(adj) amerikanisch
and und [oont]
angry wütend [v**oo**tent]
animal das Tier [teer]
annoying ärgerlich [**air**gerlish]
another ein anderer [ine
anderer]
another beer, please noch
ein Bier, bitte [noKH ine]
antiseptic das Antiseptikum
any: I don't have any ich habe
keine [ish h**ah**buh **kine**-uh]
apartment die Wohnung

[**voh**noong]
apartment block der
Wohnblock [**voh**nblock]
apple der **A**pfel
apricot die Aprikose [aprik**ohz**-uh]
arm der Arm
arrival die Ankunft [**a**nkoonft]
arrive **a**nkommen
art gallery die Kunstgalerie
[**koo**nstgal-leree]
as: as big as so groß wie [zoh
grohss vee]
ashtray der Aschenbecher
[**a**shen-besher]
ask fragen [**frah**gen]
I didn't ask for this das habe
ich nicht bestellt [dass h**a**hb-uh ish nisht besht**e**llt]
aspirin das
Kopfschmerzmittel [**ko**pf-shmairts-mittel]
at: at the hotel im Hotel
at the station am Bahnhof
at six o'clock um 6 Uhr
[oom]
at Günter's bei Günter [by]
Australia Australien
[owstr**ah**lee-en]
Australian (adj) australisch
[owstr**ah**lish]
Austria Österreich [**ur**ster-rysh]
Austrian der Österreicher
[**ur**ster-rysher]/die
Österreicherin
(adj) österreichisch [**ur**ster-rysh-ish]
automatic teller der
Geldautomat [g**e**lt-owtomaht]

autumn der Herbst [hairpst]
away: go away! gehen Sie
weg! [**gay**-en zee vek]
awful furchtbar [**foo**rsht-bar]

B

baby das Baby
back (of body) der Rücken
[**rœ**cken]
(back part) die Rückseite
[**rœ**ck-zite-uh]
at the back hinten
I'll be back soon ich bin bald
zurück [ish bin balt tsoor**œ**ck]
bad schlecht [shlesht]
badly schlecht [shlesht]
bag die Tasche [**ta**sh-uh]
(handbag) die Handtasche
[**ha**nt-tash-uh]
(plastic) die Tüte [t**œ**t-uh]
baggage das Gepäck [gep**e**ck]
baggage checkroom die
Gepäckaufbewahrung
[gep**e**ck-owfbevahroong]
bakery die Bäckerei [becker-**ī**]
balcony der Balkon [bal-k**oh**n]
ball (large) der Ball [bal]
(small: billiards etc) die Kugel
[k**oo**gel]
Baltic Sea die Ostsee [**o**st-zay]
banana die Banane [ban**ah**n-uh]
band (musical) die Band [bent]
bandage der Verband [fairb**a**nt]
bank (money) die Bank
bar die Bar
barber's der Frisör [friz**ur**]

basket der Korb [korp]
 (in shop) der Einkaufskorb
 [**ine**-kowfs-korp]
bath das Bad [baht]
bathroom das Bad
battery die Batterie [batter**ee**]
Bavaria Bayern [**by**-ern]
be sein [zine]
beach der Strand [shtrant]
beach umbrella der
 Sonnenschirm [**zo**nnen-
 sheerm]
beans die Bohnen
beautiful schön [shurn]
because weil [vile]
 because of ... wegen ...
 [**vay**gen]
bed das Bett
bed and breakfast
 Übernachtung mit
 Frühstück [œberna**к**Htoong mit
 frœshtœck]
bedroom das Schlafzimmer
 [shl**ah**f-tsimmer]
beef das Rindfleisch [rint-
 flysh]
beer das Bier [beer]
beer mug der Bierkrug
 [**beer**krook]
before vorher [**for**hair]
 before that davor [daf**or**]
 before me vor mir
begin: when does it begin?
 wann fängt es an? [van fengt
 ess an]
behind ... hinter ...
Belgian (adj) belgisch [**bel**gish]
Belgium Belgien [bel-gee-en]
below unten [**oo**nten]

below ... unter ... [**oo**nter]
belt der Gürtel [g**oo**rtel]
berth (on ship) die Kabine
 [kab**ee**n-uh]
beside: beside the ... neben
 dem/der ... [**nay**ben daym/dair]
best beste [**best**-uh]
better besser
between zwischen [tsv**i**shen]
beyond jenseits [**yayn**-zites]
bicycle das Fahrrad [**fahr**-raht]
big groß [grohss]
bikini der Bikini
bill die Rechnung [**resh**noong]
 (US: money) der Geldschein
 [**gelt**-shine]
 could I have the bill, please?
 kann ich bitte bezahlen?
 [kan ish b**itt**-uh bets**ah**len]
bird der Vogel [**foh**gel]
birthday der Geburtstag
 [geb**oo**rts-tahk]
 happy birthday! herzlichen
 Glückwunsch zum
 Geburtstag! [**hairts**-lishen
 gl**oo**ckvoonsh tsoom]
biscuit das Plätzchen [plets-
 shen]
bit: a little bit ein bißchen [ine
 biss-shen]
 a big bit ein großes Stück
 [gr**oh**ssess sht**oo**ck]
 a bit of ... ein Stück von ...
 a bit expensive etwas teuer
bite (by insect) der Stich [shtish]
black schwarz [shvarts]
blanket die Decke [**deck**-uh]
bless you! Gesundheit!
 [gez**oo**nt-hite]

blind blind [blint]
blinds die Jalousie [Jaloozee]
block of flats der Wohnblock [vohnblock]
blond blond [blont]
blood das Blut [bloot]
blouse die Bluse [blooz-uh]
blow-dry fönen [furnen]
blue blau [blow]
boat das Boot [boht]
  (for passengers) das Schiff [shiff]
body der Körper [kurper]
bone der Knochen [k-noKHen]
book das Buch [booKH]
  (verb) buchen [booKHen]
bookshop die Buchhandlung [booKH-hantloong]
boot (footwear) der Stiefel [shteefel]
border (of country) die Grenze [grents-uh]
borrow leihen [ly-en]
both beide [by-duh]
bottle die Flasche [flash-uh]
bottle-opener der Flaschen-öffner [flashen-urfner]
bottom (of person) der Hintern
  at the bottom of the hill am Fuß des Berges [fooss]
box die Schachtel [shaKHtel]
  (larger) der Karton
boy der Junge [yoong-uh]
boyfriend der Freund [froynt]
bra der BH [bay-hah]
bracelet das Armband [armbant]
brake die Bremse [bremz-uh]
brandy der Weinbrand [vine-brant]

bread das Brot [broht]
break brechen [breshen]
breakfast das Frühstück [frooshtcock]
breast die Brust [broost]
bridge (over river) die Brücke [brock-uh]
bring bringen
  I'll bring it back later ich bringe es später zurück [bring-uh ess shpayter tsooroock]
Britain Großbritannien [grohss-britannee-en]
British britisch [breetish]
brochure die Broschüre [broshoor-uh]
broken kaputt
brother der Bruder [brooder]
brown braun [brown]
brush (for hair, cleaning) die Bürste [boorst-uh]
building das Gebäude [geboyd-uh]
bulb (light bulb) die Birne [beern-uh]
bunk das Bett
burn die Verbrennung [fair-brennoong]
burst: a burst pipe ein geplatztes Rohr
bus der Bus [booss]
  what number bus is it to ...? welcher Bus fährt nach ...? [velsher booss fairt naKH]

dialogue

does this bus go to ...?
fährt dieser Bus nach ...?

[fairt]
no, you need a number ...
nein, Sie müssen mit der
... fahren
where does it leave from?
wo fährt er ab? [vo]

bus station der Busbahnhof
[**boo**ss-bahnhof]
bus stop die Bushaltestelle
[**boo**ss-halt-uh-shtell-uh]
busy (restaurant etc) voll [foll]
(telephone) besetzt [bez**e**tst]
but aber [**ah**ber]
butcher's der Metzger
[**m**etsger]
butter die Butter [**boo**tter]
button der Knopf [k-nopf]
buy kaufen [**kow**fen]
by: by bus/car mit dem
Bus/Auto [daym]
by the window am Fenster
by Thursday bis Donnerstag

C

cabbage der Kohl
cable car die Drahtseilbahn
[dr**ah**tzile-bahn]
café das Café [kaff**ay**]
cake der Kuchen [k**oo**KHen]
call rufen [r**oo**fen]
(phone) anrufen [**a**nr**oo**fen]
what's it called? wie heißt
das? [vee hyst dass]
he/she is called ... er/sie
heißt ...
camera die Kamera

camp zelten [ts**e**lten]
camping gas das Campinggas
[k**e**mping-gahss]
campsite der Campingplatz
[k**e**mpingplats]
can (tin) die Dose [d**oh**z-uh]
can: can you ...? kannst
du/können Sie ...?
[d**oo**/**kur**nen zee]
can I ...? kann ich ...?
I can't ... ich kann nicht...
[nisht]
Canada Kanada
Canadian (adj) kanadisch
[kan**ah**dish]
cancel (reservation) rückgängig
machen [r**oo**ck-gengish ma**kH**en]
candle die Kerze [**kai**rts-uh]
candy die Süßigkeiten
[z**oo**ssish-kyten]
can-opener der Dosenöffner
[**doh**zen-urfner]
car das Auto [**ow**to]
carafe die Karaffe [kar**aff**-uh]
card (birthday etc) die Karte
[**k**art-uh]
cardphone das Kartentelefon
car hire die Autovermietung
[**ow**to-fairmeetoong]
carnival der Karneval [k**arn**-
uh-val]
car park der Parkplatz
[**park**plats]
carpet der Teppich [**t**eppish]
carrot die Möhre [**mur**-uh]
carry tragen [**trah**gen]
cash das Bargeld [**bah**rgelt]
cash desk die Kasse [**kass**-uh]
cash dispenser der

Geldautomat [gelt-owtomaht]
castle das Schloß [shloss]
cat die Katze [kats-uh]
cathedral der Dom [dohm]
cave die Höhle [hurl-uh]
ceiling die Decke [deck-uh]
cellar (for wine) der Weinkeller [vine-keller]
centimetre der Zentimeter [tsentimayter]
centre das Zentrum [tsentroom]
certainly sicher [zisher]
chair der Stuhl [shtool]
chairlift der Sessellift [zessel-lift]
champagne der Champagner [shampan-yer]
change (noun: money) das Wechselgeld [veksel-gelt]
(verb: money) wechseln [wekseln]
to change a reservation umbuchen [oombookнen]

dialogue

do we have to change (trains/buses)? müssen wir umsteigen? [mʊssen veer oom-shtygen]
yes, change at Düsseldorf ja, Sie müssen in Düsseldorf umsteigen
no, it's direct nein, das ist eine Direktverbindung

cheap billig [billish]
check (verb) überprüfen [ʊber-prʊfen]
(US) der Scheck [sheck]
(in restaurant etc) die Rechnung [reshnoong]
check-in der Check-in
check in (at hotel) sich anmelden [zish]
cheers! (toast) Prost! [prohst]
cheese der Käse [kayz-uh]
chemist's die Apotheke [apotayk-uh]
cheque der Scheck [sheck]
cheque card die Scheckkarte [sheck-kart-uh]
chest (body) die Brust [broost]
chewing gum der Kaugummi [kow-goommee]
chicken (as food) das Hähnchen [haynshen]
child das Kind [kint]
chips die Pommes frites [pom frit]
(US) die Chips
chocolate die Schokolade [shokolahd-uh]
hot chocolate der Kakao [kakow]
Christmas Weihnachten [vynaкнten]
Christmas Eve der Heiligabend [hylish-ahbent]
merry Christmas! frohe Weihnachten [froh-uh]
church die Kirche [keersh-uh]
cider der Apfelwein [apfel-vine]
cigar die Zigarre [tsigarr-uh]
cigarette die Zigarette [tsigarett-uh]

cinema das Kino [**kee**no]
city die Stadt [**shtatt**]
city centre die Innenstadt [**innen**shtatt]
clean (adj) sauber [**zow**ber]
  can you clean this for me? können Sie dies für mich reinigen? [**kur**nen zee deess foor mish r**y**nigen]
clever klug [klook]
climbing das Bergsteigen [**ba**irk-shtygen]
clock die Uhr [00r]
close (verb) schließen [**shlee**ssen]
closed geschlossen [ge**shlo**ssen]
clothes die Kleider [kl**y**der]
cloudy wolkig [**vo**lkish]
coach (bus) der Bus [booss]
  (on train) der Wagen [**vah**gen]
coach trip die Busreise [**booss**-rize-uh]
coast die Küste [k**00**st-uh]
coat (long coat) der Mantel
  (jacket) die Jacke [**yack**-uh]
coathanger der Kleiderbügel [kl**y**derb00gel]
coffee der Kaffee [**kaffay**]
coin die Münze [m**00**nts-uh]
Coke® die Cola [**koh**la]
cold (adj) kalt
  I'm cold mir ist kalt [meer]
  I have a cold ich bin erkältet [ish bin air**kelt**et]
collar der Kragen [**krah**gen]
collect call das R–Gespräch [**air**-geshpraysh]
Cologne Köln [kurln]

colour die Farbe [**farb**-uh]
comb der Kamm
come kommen
come back zurückkommen [tsoor**00**ck-kommen]
come in hereinkommen [hair-**ine**-kommen]
comfortable (hotel etc) komfortabel [komfort**ah**bel]
complaint die Beschwerde [besh**vaird**-uh]
completely völlig [**fur**lish]
computer der Computer ['computer']
concert das Konzert [konts**air**t]
conditioner (for hair) der Festiger
condom das Kondom [kond**ohm**]
congratulations! herzlichen Glückwunsch! [**hairt**slishen gl**00**ckvoonsh]
connection (in travelling) die Verbindung [fair**bin**doong]
constipation die Verstopfung [fair-sht**op**foong]
consulate das Konsulat [konzool**aht**]
contact: where can I contact him? wo kann ich ihn erreichen? [vo – een air-r**y**shen]
contact lenses die Kontaktlinsen [kon**takt**-linzen]
cooker der Herd [hairt]
cookie das Plätzchen [**plets**-shen]
corkscrew der Korkenzieher [**korken**-tsee-er]
correct (right) richtig [**rish**tish]

165

cost kosten

cotton die Baumwolle [**bow**mvoll-uh]

cotton wool die Watte [**vat**-uh]

couchette der Liegewagen [**leeg**-uh-vahgen]

cough der Husten [**hoo**sten]

cough medicine das Hustenmittel [**hoo**sten-mittel]

could: could you ...? könnten Sie...? [**kurn**ten zee]

could I have ...? könnte ich ... haben? [**kurn**t-uh ish ... **hah**ben]

I couldn't ... (wasn't able to) ich konnte nicht... [ish **konn**t-uh nisht]

country das Land [lant]

couple (man and woman) das Paar [pahr]

a couple of ... ein paar... [ine pahr]

courier der Reiseleiter [**rize**-uh-lyter]

course (of meal) der Gang

of course natürlich [nat**oo**rlish]

crazy verrückt [fair-r**oo**ckt]

cream (on milk, in cake) die Sahne [**zahn**-uh]

(lotion) die Creme [kraym]

credit card die Kreditkarte [kred**eet**-kart-uh]

dialogue

can I pay by credit card? kann ich mit Kreditkarte bezahlen? [bets**ah**len]

which card do you want to use? mit welcher Karte möchten Sie bezahlen? [**vel**sher]

what's the number? was ist die Nummer? [**noo**mmer]

and the expiry date? und das Ablaufdatum? [**a**plowf-dahtoom]

crisps die Chips [chips]

crossroads die Kreuzung [**kroy**tsoong]

crowded (streets, bars) voll [foll]

cry weinen [**vy**nen]

cup die Tasse [**tass**-uh]

cupboard der Schrank [shrank]

curtains die Vorhänge [**for**heng-uh]

cushion das Kissen

Customs der Zoll [tsoll]

cyclist der Radfahrer [**raht**fahrer]/die Radfahrerin

Czech Republic die Tschechische Republik [**che**shish-uh rep00-b**leek**]

D

dad der Vater [**fah**ter]

damage beschädigen [besh**ay**digen]

damn! verdammt! [fair**dam**t]

damp feucht [foysht]

dance der Tanz [tants]

(verb) tanzen [**tant**sen]

dangerous gefährlich [gef**air**lish]

Danube die Donau [**doh**now]

dark dunkel [**doo**nkel]

date: what's the date today? der Wievielte ist heute? [dair vee**feelt**-uh ist h**oyt**-uh]

daughter die Tochter [**to**KHter]

day der Tag [tahk]

  the day after am Tag danach [dana**KH**]

  the day before am Tag zuvor [tsoo**for**]

dead tot [toht]

deaf taub [towp]

decaffeinated coffee koffeinfreier Kaffee [koffay-**een**-fry-er **kaffay**]

decide entscheiden [ent-**shy**den]

deckchair der Liegestuhl [**lee**g-uh-sht**oo**l]

deep tief [teef]

definitely bestimmt [be**shtimmt**]

delay die Verzögerung [fair-ts**urg**eroong]

delicious köstlich [**kurst**lish]

dentist der Zahnarzt [ts**ahn**-artst]

deodorant das Deodorant [De**o**dorant]

department store das Kaufhaus [**kowf**howss]

departure die Abreise [**ap**-rize-uh]

  (of plane) der Abflug [**ap**flook]

depend: it depends es kommt darauf an [ess kommt dar**owf**]

dessert der Nachtisch [**na**KHtish]

destination das Reiseziel [**rize**-uh-tseel]

develop entwickeln [ent**vick**eln]

dialling code die Vorwahl [**for**vahl]

diarrhoea der Durchfall [**doorsh**fal]

diesel der Diesel

difference der Unterschied [**oon**tersheet]

different verschieden [fair-**shee**den]

difficult schwer [shvair]

dining room das Speisezimmer [shp**ize**-uh-tsimmer]

dinner das Abendessen [**ah**bentessen]

direct (adj) direkt [dee**rekt**]

direction die Richtung [**rish**toong]

directory enquiries die Auskunft [**ows**skoonft]

dirty schmutzig [shm**oot**sish]

disco die Diskothek [diskot**ayk**]

disgusting widerlich [**veed**erlish]

district das Gebiet [geb**eet**]

divorced geschieden [ge**shee**den]

do tun [toon]

  what shall we do? was sollen wir tun? [vass **zol**len veer]

doctor der Arzt [artst]

dog der Hund [hoont]

don't! nicht!

door die Tür [toor]

double doppelt

double bed das Doppelbett
double room das Doppelzimmer [doppel-tsimmer]
down: down here hier unten [heer oonten]
downstairs unten [oonten]
dozen das Dutzend [dootsent]
draught beer das Faßbier [fassbeer]
dress das Kleid [klite]
drink (alcoholic) der Drink (non-alcoholic) das Getränk [getrenk]
(verb) trinken
what would you like to drink? was möchtest du/möchten Sie zu trinken? [murshtest doo/murshten zee]
drinking water das Trinkwasser [trinkvasser]
drive fahren
driver der Fahrer/die Fahrerin
driving licence der Führerschein [foorer-shine]
drug (medical) das Medikament
drugs (narcotics) die Drogen [drohgen]
drunk (adj) betrunken [betroonken]
dry (adj) trocken
dry-cleaner die chemische Reinigung [shaymish-uh rynigoong]
during während [vairent]
dustbin die Mülltonne [moolltonn-uh]

duvet das Federbett [fayderbet]

E

each (every) jeder [yayder]
ear das Ohr
early früh [froo]
earring der Ohrring
east der Osten
Easter Ostern [ohstern]
easy leicht [lysht]
eat essen
economy class die Touristenklasse [tooristen-klass-uh]
egg das Ei [i]
either: either ... or ... entweder... oder... [entvayder ... ohder]
either, I don't mind egal welcher [aygahl velsher]
elbow der Ellbogen
electric elektrisch [aylektrish]
electricity der Strom [shtrohm]
elevator der Aufzug [owf-tsook]
else: something else etwas anderes [etvass anderess]
somewhere else woanders [vo-anders]
embassy die Botschaft [bohtshafft]
emergency der Notfall [nohtfal]
empty leer [lair]
end das Ende [end-uh]
(verb) enden
at the end of the street am Ende der Straße

engaged (toilet, telephone) besetzt [bezetst]
(to be married) verlobt [fairlohpt]

England England [eng-lant]

English englisch [eng-lish]
I'm English ich bin Engländer/Engländerin [eng-lender]

enjoy: to enjoy oneself sich amüsieren [zish amoozeeren]

enormous enorm [aynorm]

enough genug [genook]
it's not big enough es ist nicht groß genug
that's enough das genügt [dass genookt]

entrance der Eingang [ine-gang]

envelope der Umschlag [oomshlahk]

equipment die Ausrüstung [owss- roostoong]

especially besonders [bezonders]

euro der Euro [oyro]

Eurocheque der Euroscheck [oyro-sheck]

Europe Europa [oyrohpa]

evening der Abend [ahbent]
this evening heute abend [hoyt-uh]

eventually schließlich [shleesslish]

ever jemals [yaymahls]

every jeder [yayder]

everyone jeder [yayder]

everything alles [al-ess]

everywhere überall [oober-al]

exactly! genau! [genow]

excellent ausgezeichnet [owss-getsyshnet]

except außer [owsser]

exchange rate der Wechselkurs [veckselkoorss]

exciting (day, holiday) aufregend [owf-raygent]
(film) spannend [shpannent]

excuse me (to get past) entschuldigen Sie! [ent-shooldigen zee]
(to get attention) Entschuldigung! [ent-shooldigoong]

exhibition die Ausstellung [owss-shtelloong]

exit der Ausgang [owssgang]

expensive teuer [toyer]

eye das Auge [owg-uh]

eyeglasses die Brille [brill-uh]

F

face das Gesicht [gezisht]

faint (verb) ohnmächtig werden [ohnmeshtish vairden]

fair (funfair) der Jahrmarkt [yahrmarkt]
(trade) die Messe [mess-uh]
(adj) fair

fairly ziemlich [tseemlish]

fall (verb) fallen [fal-en]
(US: autumn) der Herbst [hairpst]

family die Familie [fameelee-uh]

fantastic fantastisch

far weit [vite]

dialogue

is it far from here? ist es weit von hier? [fon heer]
no, not very far nein, nicht sehr weit [nisht zair]
it's about 10 kilometres es sind etwa zehn Kilometer [etvah]

farm der Bauernhof [bowernhohf]
fashionable modisch [mohdish]
fast schnell
fat (person) dick
father der Vater [fahter]
faucet der Wasserhahn [vasserhahn]
fault der Fehler [fayler]
sorry, it was my fault tut mir leid, es war mein Fehler [mine]
favourite Lieblings- [leeplings]
fax das Fax [faks]
feel fühlen [fœlen]
I feel unwell mir ist nicht gut [nisht goot]
felt-tip (pen) der Filzstift [filts-shtift]
ferry die Fähre [fair-uh]
fetch: I'll fetch him ich hole ihn [hohl-uh]
few: a few ein paar [ine pahr]
a few days ein paar Tage
fiancé der Verlobter [fairlohpter]
fiancée die Verlobte [fairlohpt-uh]

field das Feld [felt]
fight der Kampf
filling (in tooth) die Füllung [fœlloong]
film der Film
find finden
find out herausfinden [herowss-finden]
fine (weather) schön [shurn]
(punishment) die Geldstrafe [gelt-shtrahf-uh]
finger der Finger [fing-er]
finish beenden [buh-enden]
fire das Feuer [foy-er]
fire brigade die Feuerwehr [foy-er-vair]
first erster [airster]
at first zuerst [tsoo-airst]
first aid kit die Erste-Hilfe-Ausrüstung [airst-uh hilf-uh owssrœstoong]
first class erster Klasse [airster klass-uh]
first floor der erste Stock [airst-uh shtock]
(US) das Erdgeschoß [airt-geshoss]
first name der Vorname [fornahm-uh]
fish der Fisch [fish]
fit: it doesn't fit me es paßt mir nicht [ess passt meer nisht]
fix (arrange, sort out) regeln [raygeln]
fizzy sprudelnd [shproodelnt]
flat (apartment) die Wohnung [vohnoong]
(adj) flach [flaкн]
I've got a flat tyre ich habe

einen Platten [ish hahb-uh ine-en]

flavour der Geschmack [geshmack]

flight der Flug [flook]

flight number die Flugnummer [flook-noommer]

floor (of room) der Fußboden [foossbohden]

(storey) das Stockwerk [shtockvairk]

florist der Blumenhändler [bloomen-hentler]

flower die Blume [bloom-uh]

flu die Grippe [gripp-uh]

fluent: he speaks fluent German er spricht fließend Deutsch [air shprisht fleessent doytch]

fly (insect) die Fliege [fleeg-uh]

(verb) fliegen [fleegen]

food das Essen

foot der Fuß [fooss]

on foot zu Fuß [tsoo]

football der Fußball [foossbal]

for für [foor]

do you have something for ...? (headaches/diarrhoea etc) haben Sie etwas gegen ...? [hahben zee etvass gaygen]

foreign ausländisch [owsslendish]

foreigner der Ausländer [owsslender]/die Ausländerin

forest der Wald [vallt]

forget vergessen [fairgessen]

I forget, I've forgotten ich habe es vergessen [ish hahb-uh ess]

fork (for eating) die Gabel [gahbel]

fortnight zwei Wochen [tsvy voKHen]

forwarding address die Nachsendeadresse [naKHzend-uh-adress-uh]

fountain der Brunnen [broonnen]

foyer das Foyer [foy-yay]

France Frankreich [frank-rysh]

free frei [fry]

(no charge) kostenlos [kostenlohss], gratis [grahtiss]

freeway die Autobahn [owtobahn]

French französisch [frantsurzish]

French fries die Pommes frites [pom frit]

frequent häufig [hoyfish]

fresh frisch [frish]

fridge der Kühlschrank [koolshrank]

fried gebraten [gebrahten]

friend der Freund [froynt]/die Freundin [froyndin]

friendly freundlich [froyntlish]

from von [fon]

from Monday to Friday von Montag bis Freitag

from next Thursday ab nächsten Donnerstag

front die Vorderseite [forderzite-uh]

in front of the hotel vor dem Hotel [for]

at the front vorn [forn]

fruit das Obst [ohpst]

fruit juice der Fruchtsaft
[f[rooKHtzaft]
full voll [foll]
full board die Vollpension
[follpangz-yohn]
fun: it was fun es hat Spaß
gemacht [ess hat shpahss
gemaKHt]
funfair das Volksfest [follks-fest]
funicular railway die Seilbahn
[zile-bahn]
funny (strange) seltsam
[zeltzahm]
(amusing) komisch [kohmish]
further weiter [vyter]
future: in future in Zukunft
[tsOOkoonft]

G

game das Spiel [shpeel]
garage (for fuel) die Tankstelle
[tank-shtell-uh]
(for repairs) die Werkstatt
[vairkshtatt]
(for parking) die Garage
[garahj-uh]
garden der Garten
garlic der Knoblauch
[k-nohblowKH]
gas das Gas [gahss]
(US) das Benzin [bentseen]
gas station die Tankstelle
[tank-shtell-uh]
gate das Tor [tohr]
(at airport) der Flugsteig [flOOk-
shtike]
gay schwul [shvool]

gents (toilet) die
Herrentoilette [hairen-twalett-
uh]
German der/die Deutsche
[doytch-uh]
(adj, language) deutsch [doytch]
the Germans die Deutschen
[doytch]
Germany Deutschland
[doytch-lant]
get (obtain) bekommen
(fetch) holen [hohlen]
how do I get to ...? wie
komme ich nach...? [vee
komm-uh ish naKH]
get back (return)
zurückkommen [tsOOrück-
kommen
get off aussteigen [owss-
shtygen]
where do I get off? wo muß
ich aussteigen? [vo mooss ish]
get on (to train etc) einsteigen
[ine-shtygen]
get out (of car etc) aussteigen
[owss-shtygen]
get up (in the morning)
aufstehen [owf-shtay-en]
gift das Geschenk [geshenk]
gin der Gin
a gin and tonic einen Gin
Tonic [ine-en]
girl das Mädchen [maydshen]
girlfriend die Freundin
[froyndin]
give geben [gayben]
give back zurückgeben
[tsOOrück-gayben]
glad froh
glass das Glas [glahss]

a glass of wine ein Glas Wein

glasses die Brille [brill-uh]

gloves die Handschuhe [hant-shoo-uh]

go gehen [gay-en]
(by car, train etc) fahren

where are you going? wohin gehen/fahren Sie? [vohin]

where does this bus go? wohin fährt dieser Bus? [fairt]

let's go gehen wir

she's gone (left) sie ist gegangen

a hamburger to go ein Hamburger zum Mitnehmen [tsoom]

go away weggehen [vek-gay-en]

go away! gehen Sie weg! [zee]

go back (return) zurückgehen [tsoorock-gay-en]

go down (the stairs etc) hinuntergehen [hinoonter-gay-en]

go in hineingehen [hin-ine-gay-en]

go out (in the evening) ausgehen [owss-gay-en]

go through gehen durch [gay-en doorsh]

go up (the stairs etc) hinaufgehen [hinowf-gay-en]

God Gott

gold das Gold [gollt]

good gut [goot]

good! gut!

it's no good es hat keinen Zweck [ess hat kine-en tsveck]

goodbye auf Wiedersehen [owf-veederzayn]

good evening guten Abend [gooten ahbent]

good morning guten Morgen [gooten morgen]

good night gute Nacht [goot-uh nakht]

got: we've got to ... wir müssen ... [veer moossen]

I've got to ... ich muß ... [mooss]

have you got any ...? haben Sie ...? [hahben zee]

gradually allmählich [al-maylish]

gram(me) das Gramm

grapefruit die Grapefruit

grapes die Trauben [trowben]

grass das Gras [grahss]

grateful dankbar

great (excellent) großartig [grohss-artish]

green grün [groon]

grey grau [grow]

grilled gegrillt

grocer's der Lebensmittelhändler [laybensmittel-hentler]

ground: on the ground auf dem Boden [owf daym bohden]

ground floor das Erdgeschoß [airt-geshoss]

group die Gruppe [groop-uh]

guest der Gast

guesthouse die Pension [pangz-yohn]

guide (person) der Reiseleiter
[ry-zuh-lyter]
guidebook der Reiseführer
[ry-zuh-fOOrer]
guided tour die Rundfahrt
[roontfahrt]
(on foot) der Rundgang
[roontgang]

H

hair das Haar [hahr]
haircut der Haarschnitt
[hahrshnit]
hairdresser der Frisör [frizur]
hairdryer der Fön® [furn]
half halb [halp]
half an hour eine halbe
Stunde [ine-uh halb-uh shtoond-
uh]
half a litre ein halber Liter
half board die Halbpension
[halp-pangz-yohn]
half-bottle die halbe Flasche
[halb-uh flash-uh]
ham der Schinken [shinken]
hamburger der Hamburger
[hemburger]
hand die Hand [hant]
handbag die Handtasche
[hant-tash-uh]
hand luggage das
Handgepäck [hant-gepeck]
hangover der Kater [kahter]
happen geschehen [geshay-en]
what has happened? was ist
passiert? [passeert]
happy glücklich [glOOcklish]

harbour der Hafen [hahfen]
hard hart
(difficult) schwer [shvair]
hardly kaum [kowm]
hardly ever fast nie [fasst nee]
hardware shop die
Eisenwarenhandlung
[izenvahren-hantloong]
hat der Hut [hoot]
hate hassen
have haben [hahben]
can I have a ...? kann ich ein
... haben? [kan ish]
can we have some ...?
können wir etwas ... haben?
[kurnen veer etvass]
do you have ...? haben Sie...?
[zee]
do I have to ...? muß ich ...?
[mooss]
hayfever der Heuschnupfen
[hoy-shnoopfen]
he er [air]
head der Kopf
headache die
Kopfschmerzen [kopf-
shmairtsen]
headlights die Scheinwerfer
[shine-vairfer]
hear hören [hur-ren]
heat die Hitze [hits-uh]
heater (in room) der Ofen
[ohfen]
heating die Heizung
[hytsoong]
heavy schwer [shvair]
heel (of foot) die Ferse [fairz-uh]
(of shoe) der Absatz [apzats]
hello hallo

help die Hilfe [hilf-uh]
(verb) helfen
help! Hilfe!
can you help me? können
Sie mir helfen? [kurnen zee
meer]
her: I haven't seen her ich
habe sie nicht gesehen [zee]
give it to her geben Sie es ihr
[eer]
for her für sie
that's her das ist sie
that's her towel das ist ihr
Handtuch
herbal tea der Kräutertee
[kroyter-tay]
here hier [heer]
here is/are ... hier ist/sind ...
[zint]
here you are (offering) bitte
[bitt-uh]
hers: that's hers das gehört
ihr [dass gehurt eer]
hey! he! [hay]
hi! hallo
high hoch [hohкн]
highway die Autobahn
[owtobahn]
hill der Berg [bairk]
him: I haven't seen him ich
habe ihn nicht gesehen [een]
give it to him geben Sie es
ihm [eem]
for him für ihn
that's him das ist er [air]
hip die Hüfte [hooft-uh]
hire: for hire zu vermieten
[tsoo fairmeeten]
(verb) mieten [meeten]

his: it's his car es ist sein Auto
[zine]
that's his das ist seins [zine-ss]
hitch-hike trampen [trempen]
hole das Loch [loкн]
holiday der Urlaub [oorlowp]
on holiday im Urlaub
Holland Holland [hol-lant]
home das Zuhause [tsoohowz-
uh]
at home (in my house etc) zu
Hause
(in my country) bei uns [by
oonss]
we go home tomorrow wir
fahren morgen nach Hause
[veer fahren morgen naкн]
horrible schrecklich
horse das Pferd [pfairt]
hospital das Krankenhaus
[kranken-howss]
hot heiß [hice]
(spicy) scharf [sharf]
I'm hot mir ist heiß [meer]
hotel das Hotel
hour die Stunde [shtoond-uh]
house das Haus [howss]
house wine der Tafelwein
[tahfel-vine]
how wie [vee]
how many? wie viele? [feel-
uh]
how do you do? guten Tag!
[gooten tahk]

dialogues

how are you? wie geht es
dir/Ihnen? [gayt ess

deer/**ee**nen]
fine, thanks, and you?
danke, gut, und
dir/Ihnen? [dank-uh goot
oont]

how much is it? was kostet
das?
75 marks fünfundsiebzig
Mark
I'll take it ich nehme es
[ish **nay**m-uh ess]

Hungary Ungarn [**oo**ngarn]
hungry hungrig [**hoo**ngrish]
I'm hungry ich habe Hunger
[ish **hah**buh h**oo**ng-er]
hurry: I'm in a hurry ich habe
es eilig [ish **hah**b-uh ess **ī**lish]
hurt: it hurts es tut weh [toot
vay]
husband der Mann

I

I ich [ish]
ice das Eis [ice]
ice cream das Eis [ice]
ice lolly das Eis am Stiel [ice
am shteel]
idiot der Idiot [eedee-**oht**]
if wenn [ven]
ill krank
immediately sofort [zo**fort**]
important wichtig [**vi**shtish]
impossible unmöglich [**oo**n-
m**ur**glish]
in: it's in the centre es ist im

Zentrum
in my car in meinem Auto
in Munich in München
in May im Mai
in English auf Englisch [owf
eng-lish]
is he in? ist er da?
**include: does that include
meals?** ist das einschließlich
der Mahlzeiten? [**ine**-
shleeslish dair **mahl**-tsyten]
indigestion die
Magenverstimmung
[**mah**gen-fair-shtimmoong]
indoors drinnen
information die Information
[informats-y**ohn**]
injured verletzt [fair**letst**]
insect das Insekt [**in**zekt]
inside innen
inside the hotel im Hotel
instead of ... anstelle von ...
[an**shtell**-uh fon]
intelligent intelligent
[intelli**gent**]
interesting interessant
international international
[internats-yon**ahl**]
interpreter der Dolmetscher
[**dol**metcher]/die
Dolmetscherin
intersection die Kreuzung
[kr**oy**tsoong]
into in
I'm not into ... ich stehe nicht
auf ... [ish sht**ay**-uh nisht owf]
introduce vorstellen [**for**-
shtellen]
may I introduce ...? darf ich

Ihnen ... vorstellen? [ish **ee**nen]
invitation die Einladung [ine-lahdoong]
Ireland Irland [**ee**rlant]
Irish irisch [**ee**rish]
iron (for ironing) das Bügeleisen [b**oo**gel-īzen]
island die Insel [**in**zel]
it es [ess]
  it is ... es ist ...
  is it ...? ist es...?
  where is it? wo ist es? [vo]
  it was ... es war... [var]

J

jacket die Jacke [**ya**ckuh]
jam die Marmelade [marm-uh-**lah**d-uh]
jeans die Jeans
jellyfish die Qualle [k**va**ll-uh]
jewellery der Schmuck [sh**mooc**k]
job die Arbeit [**ar**bite]
joke der Witz [vits]
journey die Reise [**rize**-uh]
  have a good journey! gute Reise! [g**oo**t-uh]
juice der Saft [zaft]
jumper der Pullover [pooll**oh**ver]
just (only) nur [n**oo**r]
  just two nur zwei
  just for me nur für mich [f**oo**r mish]
  just here genau hier [gen**ow** heer]

K

keep behalten
  keep the change der Rest ist für Sie [dair rest ist f**oo**r zee]
key der Schlüssel [shl**oo**ssel]
kilo das Kilo
kilometre der Kilometer [keelo-m**ay**ter]
kind (generous) nett
kiss der Kuß [kooss]
kitchen die Küche [k**oo**sh-uh]
knee das Knie [k-nee]
knife das Messer
knock down (on road) anfahren
know (person, a place) kennen (something) wissen [**vi**ssen]
  I don't know ich weiß nicht [ish vice nisht]
  I didn't know that das wußte ich nicht [**voo**st-uh]

L

ladies' room die Damentoilette [dahmen-twalett-uh]
lady die Dame [dahm-uh]
lager das helle Bier [hell-uh beer]
lake der See [zay]
lamb das Lamm
lamp die Lampe [lamp-uh]
language die Sprache [shprahKH-uh]
large groß [grohss]
last letzter [letster]

177

last week letzte Woche [letst-uh voKH-uh]

last Friday letzten Freitag [letsten]

last night gestern abend [gestern ahbent]

late spät [shpayt]

later später [shpayter]

I'll come back later ich komme später wieder [ish komm-uh – veeder]

laugh lachen [laKHen]

launderette, laundromat der Waschsalon [vash-zallong]

laundry (clothes) die Wäsche [vesh-uh]

lawyer der Rechtsanwalt [reshts-anvallt]

leaflet der Prospekt

leak die undichte Stelle [oondisht-uh shtell-uh]

learn lernen [lairnen]

least: at least mindestens

leather das Leder [layder]

leave (something, someone) verlassen [fairlassen]

I am leaving tomorrow ich reise morgen ab [ish rize-uh morgen ap]

I left my coat in the bar ich habe meinen Mantel in der Bar gelassen [hahb-uh mine-en – gelassen]

when does the bus for Saarbrücken leave? wann fährt der Bus nach Saarbrücken? [vann fairt dair booss naKH]

left links

left luggage (office) die

Gepäckaufbewahrung [gepeck-owfbevahroong]

leg das Bein [bine]

lemon die Zitrone [tsitrohn-uh]

lemonade die Limonade [limonahd-uh]

lend leihen [ly-en]

less weniger [vayniger]

less expensive nicht so teuer [nisht zoh]

lesson die Stunde [shtoond-uh]

let (allow) lassen

let off: will you let me off at ...? können Sie mich in ... absetzen? [kurnen zee mish]

letter der Brief [breef]

letterbox der Briefkasten [breefkasten]

lettuce der Kopfsalat [kopfzalaht]

library die Bücherei [boosheri]

licence die Genehmigung [genaymigoong]

lift (in building) der Aufzug [owf-tsook]

could you give me a lift? könnten Sie mich mitnehmen? [kurnten zee mish mitnaymen]

light das Licht [lisht]

(not heavy) leicht [lysht]

do you have a light? (for cigarette) haben Sie Feuer? [hahben zee foyer]

light bulb die Glühbirne [gl>>beern-uh]

lighter (cigarette) das Feuerzeug [foyer-tsoyk]

like: I like it es gefällt mir [ess

gefelt meer]

I don't like it es gefällt mir nicht [nisht]

I'd like a beer ich möchte gern ein Bier [**mu**rsht-uh gairn]

would you like a drink? möchtest du/möchten Sie etwas trinken?

what's it like? wie ist es? [vee]

one like this so eins [zoh ine-ss]

line (on paper) die Linie [**lee**nee-uh]

(telephone) die Leitung [**ly**toong]

listen zuhören [ts**oo**-hur-ren]

litre der Liter

little klein [kline]

just a little, thanks danke, nur ein bißchen [**d**ank-uh n**oo**r ine biss-shen]

a little milk etwas Milch [**et**vass]

live (verb) leben [**lay**ben]

loaf das Brot [broht]

local örtlich [**urt**lish]

a local restaurant ein Restaurant am Ort

lock das Schloß [shloss]

(verb) abschließen [**ap**-shleessen]

lock out: I've locked myself out ich habe mich ausgesperrt [ish hahb-uh mish **ow**ss-geshpairt]

locker (for luggage etc) das Schließfach [shl**ee**ssfaкн]

long lang

a long time eine lange Zeit [ine-uh lang-uh tsite]

one day/two days longer ein Tag/zwei Tage länger [leng-er]

look: look out! passen Sie auf! [**p**assen zee owf]

can I have a look? kann ich mal sehen? [**zay**-en]

look after sich kümmern um [zish k**oo**mmern oom]

look at ansehen [**an**zay-en]

look for suchen [z**oo**кнen]

I'm looking for ... ich suche... [ish z**oo**кн-uh]

lorry der Lastwagen [**lasst**-vahgen]

lose verlieren [fairl**ee**ren]

I've lost my way ich habe mich verlaufen [ish hahb-uh mish fairl**ow**fen]

I've lost my handbag ich habe meine Handtasche verloren [fairl**oh**ren]

lost property (office) das Fundbüro [**foon**t-b**oo**r**oh**]

lot: a lot, lots viel [feel]

not a lot nicht sehr viel [nisht zair]

a lot of people viele Leute [**feel**-uh]

loud laut [lowt]

lounge (in house) das Wohnzimmer [**vohn**- tsimmer]

(in hotel) die Lounge

love die Liebe [**leeb**-uh]

(verb) lieben [**leeb**en]

lovely herrlich [**hair**lish]

low niedrig [**need**rish]

luck das Glück [glœck]
  good luck! viel Glück [feel]
luggage das Gepäck [gepeck]
lunch das Mittagessen
  [mittahkessen]

M

mad (insane) verrückt [fair-rœckt]
made: what is it made of?
  woraus ist es? [vohrowss]
  (food) was ist da drin? [vass]
magazine die Zeitschrift
  [tsite-shrift]
maid (in hotel) das
  Zimmermädchen [tsimmer-maydshen]
mail die Post
mailbox der Briefkasten
  [breefkasten]
main Haupt- [howpt]
main course das
  Hauptgericht [howpt-gerisht]
main road die Hauptstraße
  [howpt-shtrahss-uh]
make machen [maкнen]
make-up das Make-up
man der Mann
manager der Geschäftsführer
  [geshefts-fœrer]
  can I see the manager? kann
  ich den Geschäftsführer
  sprechen? [dayn – shpreshen]
many viele [feel-uh]
map (of city) der Stadtplan
  [shtat-plahn]
  (road map) die Straßenkarte

[shtrahssen-kart-uh]
  (geographical) die Landkarte
  [lantkart-uh]
market der Markt
marmalade die
  Orangenmarmelade [oronлen-marmelahd-uh]
married: I'm married ich bin
  verheiratet [ish bin fairhyrahtet]
match (football etc) das Spiel
  [shpeel]
matches die Streichhölzer
  [shtrysh-hurltser]
matter: it doesn't matter das
  macht nichts [maкнt nishts]
  what's the matter? was ist
  los? [vass ist lohss]
mattress die Matratze
  [matrats-uh]
may: may I see it? kann ich es
  sehen? [zay-en]
maybe vielleicht [feelysht]
mayonnaise die Mayonnaise
  [my-oh-nayz-uh]
me: that's for me das ist für
  mich [mish]
  me too ich auch [ish owкн]
meal die Mahlzeit
  [mahltsite]
mean (verb) bedeuten
  [bedoyten]
meat das Fleisch [flysh]
medicine die Medizin
  [meditseen]
medium (size) mittlerer
medium-dry (wine)
  halbtrocken [halp-trocken]
medium-rare (steak) medium
  [maydee-oom]

mend reparieren [repar**ee**ren]

mention: don't mention it gern geschehen [gairn gesh**ay**-en]

men's room die Herrentoilette [**hair**en-twalett-uh]

menu die Speisekarte [shp**ize**-uh-kart-uh]

message die Nachricht [**na**KHrisht]

metre der Meter [m**ay**ter]

midday der Mittag

middle: in the middle in der Mitte [dair mitt-uh]

midnight die Mitternacht [**mit**ter-naKHt]

milk die Milch [milsh]

mind: never mind macht nichts [maKHt nishts]

mine: it's mine es gehört mir [geh**ur**t meer]

mineral water das Mineralwasser [miner**ah**lvasser]

minute die Minute [min**oo**t-uh]

just a minute Moment mal [mohm**e**nt mahl]

mirror der Spiegel [shp**ee**gel]

Miss Frau [frow]

Miss! (waitress etc) Fräulein [**froy**line]

miss (bus, train) verpassen [fair**pa**ssen]

(regret absence of) vermissen [fair**mi**ssen]

missing: there's a suitcase missing ein Koffer fehlt [faylt]

mistake der Fehler [**fay**ler]

money das Geld [gelt]

month der Monat [**moh**naht]

moped das Moped [**moh**pet]

more mehr [mair]

can I have some more water, please? kann ich bitte noch etwas Wasser haben? [ish bitt-uh noKH **et**vass]

more expensive teurer [**toy**rer]

more than 50 über fünfzig [**oo**ber]

morning der Morgen

this morning heute morgen [**hoy**t-uh]

most: most of the time die meiste Zeit [dee myst-uh tsite]

mother die Mutter [**moo**tter]

motorbike das Motorrad [mot**oh**r-raht]

motorway die Autobahn [**ow**tobahn]

mountain der Berg [bairk]

mouse die Maus [mowss]

mouth der Mund [moont]

movie der Film

movie theater das Kino [**kee**no]

Mr Herr [hair]

Mrs Frau [frow]

Ms Frau [frow]

much viel [feel]

much better/worse viel besser/schlechter [**shle**shter]

not much nicht viel [nisht]

mum die Mutter [**moo**tter]

Munich München [**moo**nshen]

museum das Museum [moo**za**yoom]

Mu

mushrooms die Pilze [pilts-uh]
music die Musik [moozeek]
must: I must ich muß... [ish mooss]
mustard der Senf [zenf]
my mein [mine]; **f & pl** meine [mine-uh]
myself: I'll do it myself ich mache es selbst [ish maKH-uh ess zelpst]
by myself allein [alline]

N

nail (finger, metal) der Nagel [nahgel]
name der Name [nahmuh]
my name's John ich heiße John [ish hice-uh]
what's your name? wie heißen Sie? [vee hice-en zee]
napkin die Serviette [zairvee-ett-uh]
narrow eng
nasty (person) gemein [gemine] (weather, accident) furchtbar [foorshtbar]
national national [nats-yohnahl]
natural natürlich [natoorlish]
near nah
where is the nearest ...? wo ist der nächste ...? [vo ist dair naykst-uh]
nearly fast [fasst]
necessary notwendig [nohtvendish]
neck der Hals [halss]
necklace die Halskette [halskett-uh]

necktie die Krawatte [kravatt-uh]
need: I need ... ich brauche ... [ish browKH-uh]
needle die Nadel [nahdel]
neither ... nor ... weder ... noch ... [vayder ... noKH]
nephew der Neffe [neff-uh]
never nie [nee]
new neu [noy]
news (radio, TV etc) die Nachrichten [naKHrishten]
newsagent's der Zeitungshändler [tsytoongs-hentler]
newspaper die Zeitung [tsytoong]
New Year Neujahr [noy-yahr]
Happy New Year! frohes neues Jahr [froh-ess noyess yar]
New Year's Eve Silvester [zilvester]
New Zealand Neuseeland [noyzaylant]
next nächster [naykster]
next week nächste Woche
next to neben [nayben]
nice (food) gut [goot] (looks, view etc) hübsch [hoopsh] (person) nett
niece die Nichte [nisht-uh]
night die Nacht [naKHt]
no nein [nine]
I've no change ich habe kein Kleingeld [kine]
there's no ... left es ist kein ... übrig [oobrish]
nobody keiner [kine-er]

noisy: it's too noisy es ist zu laut [ts00 lowt]

non-alcoholic alkoholfrei [alkoho**ohl**fry]

none keiner [**kine**-er]

non-smoking compartment das Nichtraucherabteil [**ni**shtrowkHer-aptile]

no-one keiner [**kine**-er]

nor: nor do I ich auch nicht [owkH nisht]

normal normal [norm**ahl**]

north der Norden

northeast der Nordosten [nort-**o**sten]

North Sea die Nordsee [**no**rtzay]

northwest der Nordwesten [nortv**e**sten]

Northern Ireland Nordirland [nort-**ee**rlant]

nose die Nase [**nah**z-uh]

not nicht [nisht]

no, I'm not hungry nein, ich habe keinen Hunger [**kine**-en]

not that one nicht den [dayn]

note (banknote) der Geldschein [**ge**lt-shine]

nothing nichts [nishts]

nothing else sonst nichts [zonst]

now jetzt [yetst]

number die Nummer [**noo**mmer]

nuts die Nüsse [n**oo**ss-uh]

O

o'clock: it's nine o'clock es ist neun Uhr [00r]

odd (strange) merkwürdig [**ma**irk-v00rdish]

of von [fon]

the name of the hotel der Name des Hotels

off (lights) aus [owss]

it's just off Goethestraße es ist ganz in der Nähe der Goethestraße [gants in dair **na**y-uh]

often oft

how often are the buses? wie oft fahren die Busse? [vee]

oil das Öl [url]

ointment die Salbe [**za**lb-uh]

OK okay

are you OK? sind Sie okay?

that's OK thanks (it doesn't matter) danke, das ist in Ordnung

I'm OK (nothing for me) nein, danke [nine]

(I feel OK) mir geht's gut [meer gayts g00t]

old alt

olives die Oliven [ol**ee**ven]

omelette das Omelette [**om**lett]

on auf [owf]

on television im Fernsehen

I haven't got it on me ich habe es nicht bei mir [**hah**b-uh ess nisht by meer]

what's on tonight? was gibt es heute abend? [vass geept ess]

once (one time) einmal [**ine**-mahl]

at once (immediately) sofort [zo**fort**]

one ein(e) [**ine**(-uh)]

(as figure) eins [ine-ss]

the white one der weiße [dair]

one-way ticket die einfache Fahrkarte [**ine**-faкн-uh **fahr**-kartuh]

onion die Zwiebel [tsvee**bel**]

only nur [noor]

it's only 6 o'clock es ist erst sechs Uhr [airst]

open (adj) offen

(verb) öffnen [**urf**nen]

operator (telephone) die Vermittlung [fair**mitt**loong]

opposite: opposite my hotel gegenüber meinem Hotel

or oder [**oh**der]

orange (fruit) die Apfelsine [apfel**zeen**-uh], die Orange [oronJ-uh]

(colour) orange

orange juice der Orangensaft [oron**Jen**-zaft]

order: can we order now? können wir jetzt bestellen? [**kur**nen veer yetst beshtellen]

ordinary normal [nor**mahl**]

other andere [**ander**-uh]

the other one der andere

our unser [**oonz**er]; **f & pl** unsere [**oonz**er-uh]

ours unserer [**oonz**erer]

out: he's out (not at home) er ist nicht da [air ist nisht]

outdoors draußen [**drowss**en]

outside ... außerhalb ... [**owss**er-halp]

over: over here hier [heer]

over there dort drüben [dr**œ**ben]

over 500 über fünfhundert [**œ**ber]

overnight (travel) über Nacht [**œ**ber naкнt]

own: my own ... mein eigener ... [mine **ī**gener]

P

pack (verb) packen

a pack of ... eine Packung ... [**ine**-uh packoong]

package das Paket [pak**ayt**]

pain der Schmerz [shmairts]

I have a pain here ich habe hier Schmerzen [ish hahb-uh heer]

painful schmerzhaft [shm**airts**-haft]

painkillers das Schmerzmittel [shm**airts**-mittel]

pair: a pair of ... ein Paar ... [ine pahr]

panties das Höschen [**hurs**-shen]

pants (underwear: men's) die Unterhose [**oon**terhohz-uh]

(women's) das Höschen [**hurs**-shen]

(US) die Hose [**hoh**z-uh]

pantyhose die Strumpfhose [shtr**oo**mpf-hohz-uh]

paper das Papier [pap**eer**]
(newspaper) die Zeitung [ts**y**toong]

parcel das Paket [pak**ayt**]

pardon (me)? (didn't understand) wie bitte? [vee **bitt**-uh]

parents: my parents meine Eltern [**mine**-uh eltern]

park der Park
(verb) parken

parking lot der Parkplatz [**park**plats]

part der Teil [tile]

partner (boyfriend, girlfriend) der Partner/die Partnerin

party (group) die Gruppe [gr**oopp**-uh]
(celebration) die Fete [**fayt**-uh]

passport der Paß [pas]

past: just past the information office kurz hinter dem Auskunftsbüro [koorts]

pavement der Bürgersteig [b**oo**rgershtike]

pay zahlen [ts**ah**len]
can I pay, please? kann ich zahlen, bitte? [**bitt**-uh]

payphone der Münzfernsprecher [m**oo**nts-fairnshpresher]

peach der Pfirsich [**pfeer**zish]

peanuts die Erdnüsse [**airt**n**oo**ss-uh]

pear die Birne [**beern**-uh]

peas die Erbsen [**airp**sen]

pen der Stift [shtift]

pencil der Bleistift [**bly**-shtift]

people die Leute [**loyt**-uh]

pepper (spice) der Pfeffer
(vegetable) die Paprikaschote [**p**aprika-shoht-uh]

per: per night pro Nacht [nak**H**t]

per cent Prozent [prots**ent**]

perfume das Parfüm [parf**oo**m]

perhaps vielleicht [feel**ysht**]

person die Person [pairz**ohn**]

petrol das Benzin [bents**een**]

petrol station die Tankstelle [**t**ank-shtell-uh]

pharmacy die Apotheke [apot**ayk**-uh]

phone das Telefon [telef**ohn**]
(verb) anrufen [**an**-r**oo**fen]

phone book das Telefonbuch [telef**ohn**-b**oo**k**H**]

phonecard die Telefonkarte [-kartuh]

phone number die Telefonnummer [-n**oo**mmer]

photo das Foto

picture das Bild [bilt]

piece das Stück [sht**oo**ck]

pill die Pille [**pill**-uh]

pillow das Kopfkissen

pineapple die Ananas [**a**nanas]

pink rosa [**roh**za]

place der Platz [plats]
at your place (fam) bei dir [by deer]
(pol) bei Ihnen [**ee**nen]

plane das Flugzeug [fl**oo**ktsoyk]

plant die Pflanze [pflants-uh]

plaster (for cut) das Heftpflaster

185

plastic bag die Plastiktüte
[plastik-tοοt-uh]

plate der Teller

platform der Bahnsteig
[bahnshtike]

which platform is it, please?
welches Gleis, bitte? [velshess
glice bitt-uh]

play (verb) spielen [shpeelen]
(noun: in theatre) das Stück
[shtοοck]

pleasant angenehm [an-
genaym]

please bitte [bitt-uh]
yes please ja bitte [yah]

plenty: plenty of ... viel ...
[feel]

plug (electrical) der Stecker
[shtecker]
(in sink) der Stöpsel [shturpsel]

poisonous giftig [giftish]

Poland Polen

police die Polizei [politsr]

policeman der Polizist
[politsist]

police station die
Polizeiwache [politsī-vaκH-uh]

polite höflich [hurflish]

polluted verschmutzt
[fairshmοοtst]

pork das Schweinefleisch
[shvine-uh-flysh]

port (for boats) der Hafen
[hahfen]

possible möglich [murglish]
is it possible to ...? ist es
möglich, zu ...?
as ... as possible so ... wie
möglich [zo ... vee]

post (mail) die Post [posst]
(verb) absenden

postcard die Postkarte
[posstkart-uh]

post office die Post

poste restante postlagernd
[posst-lahgernt]

potato die Kartoffel

potato chips die Chips

potato salad der
Kartoffelsalat [kartoffel-zalaht]

pound (money, weight) das
Pfund [pfoont]

prefer: I prefer ... ich mag
lieber ... [ish mahk leeber]

pregnant schwanger [shvang-
er]

prescription (for chemist) das
Rezept [raytsept]

present (gift) das Geschenk
[geshenk]

pretty hübsch [hοοpsh]

price der Preis [price]

private privat [privaht]

probably wahrscheinlich
[vahrshine-lish]

problem das Problem
[problaym]
no problem! kein Problem
[kine]

pronounce: how is this
pronounced? wie spricht
man das aus? [vee shprisht man
dass owss]

public holiday der gesetzliche
Feiertag [gezetslish-uh fire-tahk]

pull ziehen [tsee-en]

purple violett [vee-oh-lett]

purse (for money) das

Portemonnaie [port-mon**ay**]
(US: handbag) die Handtasche
[h**a**nt-tash-uh]
push schieben [sh**ee**ben]
put tun [t**oo**n]
pyjamas der Schlafanzug
[shl**ah**f-ants**oo**k]

Q

quarter das Viertel [f**ee**rtel]
question die Frage [fr**ah**g-uh]
queue die Schlange [shl**a**ng-uh]
quick schnell [shnell]
quickly schnell [shnell]
quiet (place, hotel) ruhig [r**oo**ish]
quiet! Ruhe! [r**oo**-uh]
quite (fairly) ziemlich
[ts**ee**mlish]
(very) ganz [gants]
quite a lot eine ganze
Menge [**ine**-uh g**a**nts-uh m**e**ng-uh]

R

radiator (in room) der
Heizkörper [h**ite**s-kurper]
(of car) der Kühler [k**oo**ler]
radio das Radio [r**ah**dee-oh]
rail: by rail per Bahn
railway die Eisenbahn
[**ī**zenbahn]
rain der Regen [r**ay**gen]
it's raining es regnet [r**ay**gnet]
raincoat der Regenmantel

[r**ay**genmantel]
rape die Vergewaltigung
[fairgev**a**l-tigoong]
rare (steak) englisch [**e**ng-lish]
raspberry die Himbeere
[h**i**mbair-uh]
rather: I'd rather ... ich würde
lieber ... [ish v**oo**rd-uh l**ee**ber]
razor (electric) der
Rasierapparat [raz**ee**r-apparaht]
read lesen [l**ay**zen]
ready fertig [f**ai**rtish]
real echt [esht]
really wirklich [v**ee**rklish]
receipt die Quittung
[kv**i**ttoong]
recently kürzlich [k**oo**rtslish]
reception der Empfang
receptionist die
Empfangsperson [empf**a**ngs-pairzohn]
**recommend: could you
recommend ...?** könnten Sie
... empfehlen? [**kur**nten zee ...
empf**ay**len]
red rot [roht]
red wine der Rotwein
[r**o**htvine]
refund erstatten [air-sht**a**tten]
region das Gebiet [geb**ee**t]
registered: by registered mail
per Einschreiben [pair **ine**-shryben]
remember: I don't remember
ich kann mich nicht
erinnern [ish kan mish nisht air-**i**nnern]
rent die Miete [m**ee**t-uh]
(verb) mieten [m**ee**ten]

repair reparieren [repar**ee**ren]
repeat wiederholen [veeder**hoh**len]
reservation die Reservierung [rezairveer**oo**ng]
reserve reservieren [rezairveeren]

dialogue

can I reserve a table for tonight? kann ich für heute abend einen Tisch reservieren? [kan ish f**oo**r h**oy**t-uh **ah**bent **ine**-en tish]
yes madam, for how many people? ja, für wieviele Personen? [f**oo**r vee **veel**-uh pairz**oh**nen]
for two für zwei [tsvy]
and for what time? und für welche Zeit? [v**el**sh-uh tsite]
for eight o'clock für acht Uhr [**oo**r]
and could I have your name please? und kann ich bitte Ihren Namen haben? [**ee**ren n**ah**men]

restaurant das Restaurant [restor**ong**]
restaurant car der Speisewagen [shp**ize**-uh-vahgen]
rest room die Toilette [twal**ett**-uh]
return (ticket) die Rückfahr-karte [r**oo**ck-fahrkart-uh]

reverse charge call das R–Gespräch [**air**-geshpraysh]
rice der Reis [rice]
right (correct) richtig [**ri**shtish] (not left) rechts [reshts]
that's right das stimmt [shtimmt]
ring (on finger) der Ring
ring back zurückrufen [tsoor**oo**ck-r**oo**fen]
river der Fluß [flooss]
road die Straße [shtr**ah**ss-uh]
is this the road for ...? ist dies die Straße nach ...? [deess dee – nakH]
rob: I've been robbed ich bin bestohlen worden [ish bin besht**oh**len **vo**rden]
roll (bread) das Brötchen [br**ur**tchen]
roof das Dach [dakH]
room das Zimmer [ts**i**mmer]

dialogue

do you have any rooms? haben Sie Zimmer frei? [fry]
for how many people? für wie viele Personen? [f**oo**r vee **veel**-uh pairz**oh**nen]
for one/for two für eine Person/für zwei Personen
yes, we have rooms free ja, wir haben Zimmer frei
for how many nights will it be? für wie lange? [f**oo**r vee **lang**-uh]
just for one night nur für

eine Nacht **[ine**-uh na**KH**t]
how much is it? was kostet es?

**... with bathroom and ...
without bathroom** ... mit Bad und ... ohne Bad **[ohn**-uh baht]
can I see a room with bathroom? kann ich ein Zimmer mit Bad sehen? **[zay**-en]
ok, I'll take it gut, ich nehme es **[naym**-uh]

room service der Zimmerservice **[tsimmer**'service']
rosé (wine) der Roséwein **[rohzay**-vine]
round trip ticket die Rückfahrkarte **[rμck**-fahrkart-uh]
route die Strecke **[shtreck**-uh]
rubbish (waste) der Abfall **[ap**-fal]
(poor quality goods) der Mist
rucksack der Rucksack **[roockzack]**
rude unhöflich **[oon**-hurflish]
rum der Rum **[roomm]**
run (person) rennen, laufen **[lowfen]**

S

sad traurig **[trowrish]**
safe (not in danger) sicher **[zisher]**

(not dangerous) ungefährlich **[oon**-gefairlish]
salad der Salat **[zalaht]**
salad dressing die Salatsoße **[zalaht**-zohss-uh]
sale: for sale zu verkaufen **[tsoo fairkowfen]**
salt das Salz **[zalts]**
same: the same derselbe **[dairzelb**-uh]
the same again, please dasselbe nochmal, bitte **[noKHmahl** bitt-uh]
sand der Sand **[zant]**
sandals die Sandalen **[zandahlen]**
sandwich das belegte Brot **[belaykt**-uh broht]
sanitary napkin/towel die Damenbinde **[dahmenbind**-uh]
sauce die Soße **[zohss**-uh]
saucepan der Kochtopf **[koKHtopf]**
sausage die Wurst **[voorst]**
say: how do you say ... in German? was heißt ... auf Deutsch? **[vass hyst ... owf doytch]**
what did he say? was hat er gesagt? **[gezahkt]**
scarf (for neck) der Schal **[shahl]**
(for head) das Kopftuch **[kopftooKH]**
schedule (US) der Fahrplan **[fahrplahn]**
school die Schule **[shool**-uh]
scissors: a pair of scissors eine Schere **[shair**-uh]

Scotch tape® der Tesafilm® [tayzahfilm]

Scotland Schottland [shottlant]

Scottish schottisch [shottish]

sea das Meer [mair]
 by the sea am Meer

seafood die Meeresfrüchte [mairess-frOOsht-uh]

seasick: I feel seasick ich bin seekrank [ish bin zaykrank]

seat der Sitzplatz [zitsplats]
 is this anyone's seat? sitzt hier jemand? [zitst heer yaymant]

second (adj) zweiter [tsvyter]
 (of time) die Sekunde [zekoond-uh]

second class zweiter Klasse [tsvyter klass-uh]

see sehen [zay-en]
 can I see? kann ich mal sehen?
 have you seen ...? haben Sie ... gesehen? [hahben zee ... gezay-en]
 see you! bis später! [shpayter]
 I see (I understand) ich verstehe [fairstay-uh]

self-catering apartment die Ferienwohnung [fayree-en-vohnoong]

self-service die Selbstbedienung [zelpst-bedeenoong]

sell verkaufen [fairkowfen]

Sellotape® der Tesafilm® [tayzahfilm]

send senden [zenden]

separated: I'm separated ich

lebe getrennt [ish layb-uh]

separately (pay, travel) getrennt

serious ernst [airnst]

service station die Tankstelle (mit Werkstatt) [tankshtell-uh mit vairkshtatt]

serviette die Serviette [zairvee-ett-uh]

set menu die Tageskarte [tahgess-kart-uh]

several mehrere [mairer-uh]

sex der Sex

shade: in the shade im Schatten [shatten]

shampoo das Shampoo

share (room, table etc) sich teilen [zish tylen]

shaver der Rasierapparat [razeer-apparaht]

shaving foam die Rasierseife [razeer-zife-uh]

she sie [zee]

sheet (for bed) das Laken [lahken]

ship das Schiff [shiff]

shirt das Hemd [hemt]

shit! Scheiße! [shice-uh]

shoe der Schuh [shoo]

shoelaces die Schnürsenkel [shnOOr-zenkel]

shoe polish die Schuhcreme [shoo-kraym]

shoe repairer der Schuhmacher [shoo-maкher]

shop das Geschäft [gesheft]

short (time, journey) kurz [koorts]
 (person) klein [kline]

shorts die Shorts

should: what should I do? was
soll ich machen? [vass zoll ish
maкнen]
shoulder die Schulter
[shoolter]
show (in theatre) die
Vorstellung [for-shtelloong]
  could you show me?
  könnten Sie mir das zeigen?
  [kurnten zee meer dass tsygen]
shower (in bathroom) die
Dusche [doosh-uh]
shut (verb) schließen
[shleessen]
  when do you shut? wann
  machen Sie zu? [vann maкнen
  zee tsoo]
  they're shut sie sind
  geschlossen [geshlossen]
  shut up! halt den Mund!
  [dayn moont]
shutters (on window) die
Fensterläden [fenster-layden]
sick (ill) krank
side die Seite [zite-uh]
side salad die Salatbeilage
[zalaht-bylahg-uh]
sidewalk der Bürgersteig
[boorgershtike]
sight: the sights of ... die
Sehenswürdigkeiten von ...
[zay-ens-voordish-kyten fon]
silk die Seide [zyduh]
silly (person) albern [al-bairn]
  (thing to do etc) dumm [doomm]
silver das Silber [zilber]
since: since yesterday seit
gestern [zite]
sing singen [zingen]

single (not married)
unverheiratet [oon-fair-
hyrahtet]
  a single to ... eine einfache
  Fahrt nach ... [ine-uh ine-faкн-
  uh fahrt naкн]
single bed das Einzelbett [ine-
tsel-bett]
single room das
Einzelzimmer [ine-tsel-
tsimmer]
sister die Schwester [shvester]
sit: can I sit here? kann ich
mich hier hinsetzen? [ish
mish heer hinzetsen]
sit down sich hinsetzen [zish
hinzetsen]
size die Größe [grurss-uh]
skin die Haut [howt]
skirt der Rock
sky der Himmel
sleep schlafen [shlahfen]
sleeping bag der Schlafsack
[shlahfzack]
sleeping car der Schlafwagen
[shlahfvahgen]
slow langsam [langzahm]
  slow down! etwas langsamer
  bitte [etvass]
slowly langsam [langzahm]
small klein [kline]
smell: it smells es stinkt
[shtinkt]
smile (verb) lächeln [lesheln]
smoke der Rauch [rowкн]
  do you mind if I smoke?
  macht es Ihnen etwas aus,
  wenn ich rauche? [maкнt ess
  een-en etvass owss venn ish

rowKH-uh]

I don't smoke ich bin Nichtraucher [nishtrowKHer]

snow der Schnee [shnay]

it's snowing es schneit [shnite]

so: it's so good es ist so gut [zo gOOt]

not so fast nicht so schnell [nisht zo shnell]

so am I ich auch [ish owKH]

so do I ich auch

soap die Seife [zyfuh]

soap powder das Waschpulver [vashpoolver]

sober nüchtern [nOOshtern]

sock die Socke [zock-uh]

soda (water) das Sodawasser [zohda-vasser]

soft (material etc) weich [vysh]

soft drink das alkoholfreie Getränk [alkohohlfry-uh getrenk], der Soft drink

sole die Sohle [zohl-uh]

some: can I have some water/rolls? kann ich etwas Wasser/ein paar Brötchen haben? [etvass vasser/ine pahr brurt-shen hahben]

somebody jemand [yaymant]

something etwas [etvass]

sometimes manchmal [manshmahl]

somewhere irgendwo [eergentvo]

son der Sohn [zohn]

song das Lied [leet]

soon bald [balt]

sore: it's sore es tut weh [tOOt vay]

sorry: (I'm) sorry tut mir leid [tOOt meer lite]

sorry? (didn't understand) wie bitte? [vee bitt-uh]

sort: what sort of ...? welche Art von ...? [velsh-uh art fon]

soup die Suppe [zoop-uh]

south der Süden [zOOden]

South Africa Südafrika [zOOt-afrika]

southeast der Südosten [zOOt-osten]

southwest der Südwesten [zOOt-vesten]

souvenir das Souvenir

spa der Kurort [kOOr-ort]

speak: do you speak English? sprechen Sie Englisch? [shpreshen zee eng-lish]

I don't speak ... ich spreche kein ... [ish shpresh-uh kine]

spectacles die Brille [brill-uh]

spend ausgeben [owssgayben] (time) verbringen [fairbring-en]

spoon der Löffel [lurfel]

spring (season) der Frühling [frOOling]

square (in town) der Platz [plats]

stairs die Treppe [trepp-uh]

stamp die Briefmarke [breefmark-uh]

start der Anfang [anfang] (verb) anfangen

the car won't start das Auto springt nicht an [dass owto shpringt nisht an]

starter (food) die Vorspeise [for-shpize-uh]

station der Bahnhof [**bahn**hohf]

stay: where are you staying? wo wohnen Sie? [vo **voh**nen zee]

I'm staying at ... ich wohne in ... [ish **vohn**-uh]

I'd like to stay another two nights ich möchte gern noch zwei Nächte bleiben [**mursh**t-uh gairn noKH – **nesh**t-uh **bly**ben]

steak das Steak

steal stehlen [**shtay**len]

my bag has been stolen meine Tasche ist gestohlen worden [ge**shtoh**len **vor**den]

steep (hill) steil [shtile]

still: I'm still waiting ich warte immer noch [**var**t-uh – noKH]

stomach der Magen [**mah**gen]

stomach ache die Magenschmerzen [**mah**gen-**shmair**tsen]

stone (rock) der Stein [shtine]

stop anhalten

please, stop here (to taxi driver etc) bitte halten Sie hier [**bitt**-uh **hal**-ten zee heer]

storm der Sturm [shtoorm]

straight: it's straight ahead es ist geradeaus [gerahd-uh-**owss**]

strange (odd) seltsam [**zelt**zahm]

strawberry die Erdbeere [**airt**bair-uh]

street die Straße [**shtrah**ss-uh]

string die Schnur [shnoor]

strong (person, drink) stark [shtark]

(taste) kräftig [**kref**tish]

stuck: the key's stuck der Schlüssel steckt fest [shteckt]

student der Student [shtoo**dent**]/die Studentin

stupid dumm [doomm]

suburb die Vorstadt [**for**-shtatt]

subway (US) die U-Bahn [**oo**-bahn]

suddenly plötzlich [**plurts**lish]

sugar der Zucker [**tsoo**cker]

suit der Anzug [**ant**sook]

suitcase der Koffer

summer der Sommer [**zom**mer]

in the summer im Sommer

sun die Sonne [**zonn**-uh]

in the sun in der Sonne

sunblock die Sun-Block-Creme [-kraym]

sunburn der Sonnenbrand [**zonn**en-brant]

sunglasses die Sonnenbrille [**zonn**en-brill-uh]

sunstroke der Sonnenstich [**zonn**en-shtish]

suntanned braungebrannt [**brown**-gebrannt]

suntan oil das Sonnenöl [**zonn**en-url]

supermarket der Supermarkt [**zoo**permarkt]

supper das Abendessen [**ah**bent-essen]

supplement (extra charge) der Zuschlag [**tsoo**shlahk]

sure: are you sure? bist du/sind Sie sicher? [bist doo/zint zee **zi**sher]

sure! klar!
surname der Nachname
[naKHnahm-uh]
sweater der Pullover
[poolohver]
sweet (taste) süß [zooss]
(noun: dessert) der Nachtisch
[naKHtish]
sweets die Süßigkeiten
[zoossish-kyten]
swim schwimmen [shvimmen]
swimming costume der
Badeanzug [bahd-uh-antsook]
swimming pool das
Schwimmbad [shvimmbaht]
swimming trunks die
Badehose [bahd-uh-hohz-uh]
Swiss (adj) schweizerisch
[shvytserish]
switch der Schalter [shalter]
switch off ausschalten [owss-
shalten]
switch on einschalten [ine-
shalten]
Switzerland die Schweiz
[shvites]

T

table der Tisch [tish]
table wine der Tafelwein
[tahfelvine]
take bringen
(accept) nehmen [naymen]
fine, I'll take it gut, ich
nehme es [goot, ish naym-uh
ess]
a hamburger to take away

ein Hamburger zum
Mitnehmen [tsoom]
talk sprechen [shpreshen]
tall (person) groß [grohss]
(building) hoch [hohKH]
tampons die Tampons
tan die Bräune [broyn-uh]
tap der Wasserhahn
[vasserhahn]
taste der Geschmack
[geshmack]
taxi das Taxi

dialogue

to the airport/to Hotel ...
please zum
Flughafen/zum Hotel ...
bitte [tsoom]
how much will it be? was
kostet das?
thirty marks dreißig Mark
that's fine right here thanks
bis hierhin, danke [heer-
hin]

tea (drink) der Tee [tay]
teacher der Lehrer [lairer]/die
Lehrerin
telephone das Telefon
[telefohn]
television das Fernsehen
[fairn-zay-en]
tell: could you tell him ...?
können Sie ihm sagen ...?
[kurnen zee eem zahgen]
tennis das Tennis
terrible furchtbar [foorshtbar]
terrific sagenhaft [zahgenhaft]

than als [alss]
thanks, thank you danke [dank-uh]
thank you very much vielen Dank [feelen]
no thanks nein danke [nine]

dialogue

thanks danke
that's OK, don't mention it bitte [bitt-uh]

that: that man dieser Mann [deezer]
that woman diese Frau [deez-uh]
that one das da
that's nice das ist schön
is that ...? ist das ...?
the (singular) der/die/das [dair/dee/dass]
(plural) die [dee]
theatre das Theater [tayahter]
their ihr [eer]; f & pl ihre [eer-uh]
theirs ihrer [eer-er]
them sie [zee]
with them mit ihnen [een-en]
then (after that) dann
there da, dort
is/are there ...? gibt es ...? [geept]
there is/are ... es gibt ...
there you are (giving something) bitte [bitt-uh]
these diese [deez-uh]
they sie [zee]
thick dick

thief der Dieb [deep]
thin dünn [dʊn]
thing das Ding
my things meine Sachen [mine-uh zaкнen]
think denken
thirsty: I'm thirsty ich habe Durst [hahb-uh doorst]
this: this man dieser Mann [deezer]
this woman diese Frau [deez-uh]
this one dieser/diese/dieses [deezess]
is this ...? ist das ...?
those diese [deez-uh]
thread der Faden [fahden]
throat der Hals [halss]
through durch [doorsh]
thumb der Daumen [dowmen]
thunderstorm das Gewitter [gevitter]
ticket (train, bus, boat) die Fahrkarte [fahrkart-uh]
(plane) das Ticket
(theatre, cinema) die Eintrittskarte [ine-trittskart-uh]
(cloakroom) die Garderobenmarke [garderohben-mark-uh]

dialogue

a return ticket to Heidelberg eine Rückfahrkarte nach Heidelberg
coming back when? wann soll die Rückfahrt sein?

195

[r**oo**ck-fahrt]
today/next Tuesday
heute/nächsten Dienstag
**that will be two hundred
and ten marks** das macht
zweihundertzehn Mark

tie (necktie) die Krawatte
[krav**a**tt-uh]
tights die Strumpfhose
[shtr**oo**mpf-hohz-uh]
time die Zeit [ts**i**te]
what's the time? wie spät ist
es? [vee shp**a**yt ist ess]
next time nächstes Mal
[n**a**ykstess]
four times viermal [f**ee**rmahl]
timetable der Fahrplan
[f**a**hrplahn]
tin (can) die Dose [d**oh**z-uh]
tin opener der Dosenöffner
[d**oh**zen-urfner]
tip (to waiter etc) das Trinkgeld
[tr**i**nkgelt]
tired müde [m**oo**d-uh]
tissues die Papiertücher
[pap**ee**r-t**oo**sher]
to: to Freiburg/London nach
Fr**ei**burg/**E**ngland [nakH]
to the post office zum
P**o**stamt [ts**oo**m]
to the bank zur Bank [ts**oo**r]
toast (bread) der Toast
today heute [h**oy**t-uh]
toe der Zeh [tsay]
together zusammen
[ts**oo**z**a**mmen]
toilet die Toilette [twal**e**tt-uh]
toilet paper das

Toilettenpapier [twal**e**tten-
pap**ee**r]
tomato die Tomate [tom**aht**-
uh]
tomorrow morgen
tomorrow morning morgen
früh [fr**oo**]
the day after tomorrow
übermorgen [**oo**bermorgen]
tonic (water) das Tonic
tonight heute abend [h**oy**t-uh
ahbent]
too (excessively) zu [ts**oo**]
(also) auch [owkH]
too much zuviel [ts**oo**feel]
me too ich auch [ish]
tooth der Zahn [tsahn]
toothache die
Zahnschmerzen [ts**a**hn-
shmairtsen]
toothbrush die Zahnbürste
[ts**a**hn-b**oo**rst-uh]
toothpaste die Zahnpasta
[ts**a**hnpasta]
top: on top of ... oben auf...
[**oh**ben owf]
at the top oben
torch die Taschenlampe
[t**a**shenlamp-uh]
tour (journey) die Reise [r**ize**-
uh]
tourist der Tourist [t**oo**rist]/die
Touristin
tourist information office das
Fremdenverkehrsbüro
[fr**e**mden-fairkairs-b**oo**roh]
towards nach [nakH]
towel das Handtuch [h**a**nt-
t**oo**kH]

town die Stadt [shtatt]
  in town in der Stadt [dair]
town centre die Innenstadt
  [innen-shtatt]
toy das Spielzeug [shpeel-
  tsoyk]
track (US: at station) der
  Bahnsteig [bahnshtike]
traffic lights die Ampel
train der Zug [tsook]
  by train mit dem Zug
  [daym]
  is this the train for ...? fährt
  dieser Zug nach ...? [fairt
  deezer tsook nakh]
train station der Bahnhof
  [bahnhof]
tram die Straßenbahn
  [shtrahssen-bahn]
translate übersetzen [oober-
  zetsen]
trashcan die Mülltonne
  [moolltonn-uh]
travel reisen [ryzen]
travel agent's das Reisebüro
  [rize-uh-booro]
traveller's cheque der
  Reisescheck [rize-uh-sheck]
tree der Baum [bowm]
trip (excursion) der Ausflug
  [owssflook]
trousers die Hose [hohz-uh]
true wahr [vahr]
try versuchen [fairzookHen]
try on anprobieren [an-
  probeeren]
T-shirt das T-Shirt
tuna der Thunfisch
  [toonfish]

turn: turn left/right biegen Sie
  links/rechts ab [beegen zee
  links/reshts ap]
twice zweimal [tsvymahl]
twin room das
  Zweibettzimmer [tsvybett-
  tsimmer]
tyre der Reifen [ryfen]

U

umbrella der Schirm
  [sheerm]
uncle der Onkel
under unter [oonter]
underground (railway) die
  U-Bahn [oo-bahn]
underpants die Unterhose
  [oonter-hohz-uh]
understand: I understand ich
  verstehe [ish fairshtay-uh]
  I don't understand ich
  verstehe ich nicht [nisht]
university die Universität
  [oonivairzi-tayt]
unleaded petrol das bleifreie
  Benzin [bly-fry-uh bentseen]
until bis [biss]
up oben [ohben]
  up there da oben
upstairs oben [ohben]
urgent dringend [dring-ent]
us uns [oonss]
USA die USA [00-ess-ah]
use benutzen [benootsen]
useful nützlich [nootslish]

V

vacation der Urlaub [**oo**rlowp]
(from university) die
Semesterferien [zem**e**ster-
fairee-en]
value der Wert [vairt]
vanilla die Vanille [van**i**ll-uh]
veal das Kalbfleisch [kalp-flysh]
vegetables das Gemüse
[gem**oo**z-uh]
vegetarian der Vegetarier
[vegay**tah**ree-er]/die
Veget**a**rierin
very sehr [zair]
 I like it very much ich mag es
 sehr gern [gairn]
Vienna Wien [veen]
view der Blick
village das Dorf
visit besuchen [bez**oo**KHen]
vodka der Wodka [**vo**dka]
voice die Stimme [sht**i**mm-uh]

W

waist die Taille [tal-yuh]
wait warten [**va**rten]
waiter der Ober [**oh**ber]
 waiter! Herr Ober! [hair]
waitress die Kellnerin
 waitress! Fräulein!
 [**fro**yline]
wake-up call der Weckanruf
 [**ve**ck-anroof]
Wales Wales
walk: is it a long walk? geht

man lange dorthin? [gayt man
lang-uh]
wall die Wand [vant]
(external) die Mauer [**mo**wer]
wallet die Brieftasche
 [**bree**ftash-uh]
want: I want a ... ich möchte
 ein(e)... [ish m**u**rsht-uh **i**ne (-uh)]
 I don't want any ... ich
 möchte keinen ... [**ki**ne-en]
 I don't want to ich will nicht
 [nisht]
 what do you want? was
 wollen Sie? [vass **vo**llen zee]
warm warm [varm]
wash waschen [**va**shen]
 (oneself) sich waschen
 [zish]
washhand basin das
 Handwaschbecken [**ha**ntvash-
 becken]
washing (clothes) die Wäsche
 [**ve**sh-uh]
washing powder das
 Waschpulver [**va**shpoolver]
wasp die Wespe [**ve**sp-uh]
watch (wristwatch) die
 Armbanduhr [**a**rmbant-oor]
water das Wasser [**va**sser]
way: it's this way es ist hier
 entlang [heer]
 it's that way es ist dort
 entlang
 is it a long way to ...? ist es
 weit bis nach ...? [vite biss
 naKH]
 no way! auf keinen Fall! [owf
 kine-en fal]

dialogue

could you tell me the way to ...? können Sie mir sagen, wie ich nach ... komme? [**kur**nen zee meer **zah**gen vee ish naKH ... **komm**-uh]

go straight on until you reach the traffic lights fahren Sie geradeaus bis zur Ampel [ge**rah**d-uh-owss]

turn left biegen Sie links ab [**bee**gen]

take the first on the right nehmen Sie die erste Straße rechts [**nay**men zee dee **airst**-uh shtr**ah**ss-uh reshts]

we wir [veer]

weather das Wetter [**vetter**]

week die Woche [**voKH**-uh]

a week (from) today heute in einer Woche [**hoyt**-uh in **ine**-er]

weekend das Wochenende [**voKH**Hen-end-uh]

weight das Gewicht [ge**visht**]

welcome: you're welcome (don't mention it) keine Ursache [**kine**-uh **oor**zaKH-uh]

well: she's not well sie fühlt sich nicht wohl [zee f<s>oo</s>lt zish nisht vohl]

you speak English very well Sie sprechen sehr gut Englisch [shpr**esh**en zair g**oo**t **eng**-lish]

well done! gut gemacht! [ge**maKHt**]

this one as well diesen auch [**dee**zen owKH]

well-done (meat) gut durchgebraten [g**oo**t d**oor**sh-geb**rah**ten]

Welsh walisisch [val-**ee**zish]

west der Westen [**vesten**]

wet naß [nass]

what? was? [vass]

what's that? was ist das?

wheel das Rad [raht]

when? wann? [van]

when's the train/ferry? wann fährt der Zug/die Fähre? [van fairt dair ts**oo**k/dee **fair**-uh]

where? wo? [vo]

which: which bus? welcher Bus? [**velsher**]

while: while I'm here während ich hier bin [**vair**ent ish heer]

whisky der Whisky

white weiß [vice]

white wine der Weißwein [**vice**-vine]

who? wer? [vair]

whole: the whole week die ganze Woche [dee g**ants**-uh **voKH**-uh]

whose: whose is this? wem gehört das? [vaym ge**hurt**]

why? warum? [va**room**]

why not? warum nicht? [nisht]

wide breit [brite]

wife die Frau [**mine**-uh frow]

wind der Wind [vint]

window das Fenster

in the window (of shop) im Schaufenster [**show**-fenster]

wine der Wein [vine]

wine list die Weinkarte [**vine**-kart-uh]

winter der Winter [**vi**nter]

with mit

without ohne [**oh**n-uh]

woman die Frau [frow]

wood (material) das Holz [holts]

wool die Wolle [**voll**-uh]

word das Wort [vort]

work die Arbeit [**ar**bite]
  it's not working es funktioniert nicht [foonkts-yohn**eer**t nisht]

worry: I'm worried ich mache mir Sorgen [ish ma**KH**-uh meer **zor**gen]

worse schlimmer [**shli**mmer]

worst am schlimmsten [**shli**mmsten]

would: would you give this to ...? könnten Sie dies ... geben? [**kur**nten zee ess ine-**packen**]

wrap: could you wrap it up? können Sie es einpacken? [**kur**nen zee ess ine-**packen**]

wrist das Handgelenk [**hant**gelenk]

write schreiben [**shry**ben]
  could you write it down? könnten Sie es aufschreiben? [**kur**nten zee ess **owf**-shryben]

wrong: it's the wrong key es ist der falsche Schlüssel [dair **falsh**-uh]
  there's something wrong with ... mit ... stimmt etwas nicht [shtimmt **et**vass nisht]
  what's wrong? was ist los?

[vass ist lohss]

Y

year das Jahr [yahr]

yellow gelb [gelp]

yes ja [yah]

yesterday gestern
  the day before yesterday vorgestern [**for**gestern]

yet noch [noKH]

you (familiar: singular) du [doo]
  (plural) ihr [eer]
  (polite) Sie [zee]
  this is for you das ist für dich/euch [oych]/Sie

young jung [yoong]

your (familiar: singular) dein [dine]; f & pl deine [**dine**-uh]
  (plural) euer [**oy**er]; f & pl eure [**oyr**-uh]
  (polite) Ihr [eer]; f & pl Ihre [**eer**-uh]

yours (familiar: singular) deiner [**dine**-er]
  (plural) eurer [**oy**rer]
  (polite) Ihrer [**eer**er]

youth hostel die Jugendherberge [**yoo**gent-hairbairg-uh]

Z

zero null [nooll]

zip der Reißverschluß [**rice**-fairshlooss]

zoo der Zoo [tsoh]

German

→

English

ab [ap] from; off; down

Abend m [ahbent] evening

Abendessen n [ahbent-essen] dinner

aber [ahber] but

Abfahrt f [ap-fahrt] departure(s)

Abfall m [ap-fal] litter; garbage

Abfertigung f [ap-fairtigoong] check-in

Abflug m [ap-flook] departure(s)

Abstand m [ap-shtant] distance

Achtung! [aкнtoong] look out!; attention

alle [al-uh] all; everybody; finished

allein [aline] alone

alles [al-ess] everything

alles Gute [al-ess goot-uh] best wishes

als [alss] when; than; as

also [alzo] therefore

alt [alt] old

Alter n [alter] age

am at the; on (the)

Ampel f traffic lights

an at; to; on

andere [ander-uh] other(s)

Anfang m beginning

anhalten to stop

ankommen to arrive

Ankunft f [ankoonft] arrival(s)

Anlieger frei residents only

anrufen [anroofen] to phone

ans [anss] to the

Anschluß m [an-shlooss] connection

Anschrift f [an-shrift] address

anstatt [an-shtatt] instead of

Antwort f [antvort] answer

Anwohner frei residents only

Arbeit f [arbite] work; job

arm poor

Arzt m [artst] doctor

auch [owкн] too, also

auf [owf] on; to; in; open

Aufenthalt m [owf-ent-halt] stay

aufhören [owf-hur-ren] to stop

Aufzug m [owf-tsook] lift, elevator

Auge n [owg-uh] eye

aus [owss] from; off; out; out of; made of; finished

Ausfahrt f [owssfahrt] exit

Ausfahrt freihalten keep exit clear

Ausgang m [owssgang] exit, way out; gate; departure

ausgezeichnet [owss-getsyshnet] excellent

Auskunft f [owsskoonft] information

Ausland n [owsslant] overseas, abroad

außer [owsser] except

außer Betrieb out of order

Aussichtspunkt m [owss-zishts-poonkt] viewpoint

aussteigen [owss-shtygen] to get off

Ausstellung f [owss-shtelloong] exhibition

ausverkauft [owss-fairkowft] sold out

Ausweis m [owssvice] pass, identity card; identification

Autobahnkreuz motorway

junction

Autofahrer m [owtofahrer**]** car driver, motorist

Bäckerei f [becker-**ī]** baker's

Bad n [baht**]** bath; bathroom

Badezimmer n [bahd-uh-tsimmer**]** bathroom

Bahnhof m [bahn-hohf**]** station

Bahnsteig m [bahn-shtike**]** platform, (US) track

bald [balt**]** soon

bar cash

Bauernhof m [bowern-hohf**]** farm

Baumwolle f [bowmvoll-uh**]** cotton

Baustelle f building site; roadworks

Bayern [by-ern**]** Bavaria

bedeuten [bed**oy**ten**]** to mean

Bedienung f [bed**ee**noong**]** service (charge)

behalten [be**hal**ten**]** to keep

Behinderte m/f [be**hin**dert-uh**]** handicapped person

bei [by**]** by; at; next to; near

beide [bide-uh**]** both (of them)

beim at the

Bein n [bine**]** leg

bekommen to get

belegt [bel**aykt]** occupied, busy; no vacancies; full

Benzin n [bents**een]** petrol, gas(oline)

bequem [bek**vaym]** comfortable

bereit [ber**ite]** ready

Berg m [bairk**]** mountain

Bescheinigung f [beshy**nigoong]** certificate

beschweren: sich beschweren [zish beshv**airen]** to complain

besetzt [bez**etst]** busy; engaged, occupied

besonders [bez**onders]** especially

besser better

bestellen [besht**ellen]** to order

bestrafen [besht**rahfen]** to punish

besuchen [bez**ooкнen]** to visit

Betrag m [betr**ahk]** amount

Betreten auf eigene Gefahr enter at own risk, keep off/out

Betreten verboten keep out

Betrieb m [betr**eep]** company; operation; bustle

Bett n bed

Be- und Entladen erlaubt loading and off-loading permitted

bevor [bef**or]** before

bezahlen [bets**ahlen]** to pay

Bild n [bilt**]** picture

billig [billish**]** cheap

bin am

bis until; by

bißchen: ein bißchen [ine biss-shen**]** a little bit (of)

bist are

bitte [bittuh**]** please; you're welcome

bitte? pardon (me)?; can I help you?

bitte nicht ... please do not ...

blau [blow] blue
bleiben [blyben] to stay
bleifrei [blyfry] unleaded
Blick m [blick] look; view
Blut n [bloot] blood
Boden m [bohden] bottom; floor
Boot n [boht] boat
böse [burz-uh] angry
Botschaft f [bohtshaft] embassy
Brand m [brant] fire
Bräu n [broy] brew
braun [brown] brown
Brief m [breef] letter
Briefkasten m [breefkasten] letterbox, mailbox
Briefmarke f [breefmark-uh] stamp
Brücke f [brook-uh] bridge
Bruder m [brooder] brother
Buch n [bookH] book
Bücherei f [boosher-ī] library
Bühne f [boon-uh] stage
Bundeskanzler m [boondess-kantsler] chancellor
Burg f [boork] castle
Bürgersteig m [boorger-shtike] pavement, sidewalk

Chef m [shef] boss
chemische Reinigung f [shaymish-uh rynigoong] dry cleaner's

da there; as; since
Damen ladies' (room)
damit so that; with it
dankbar grateful
danke [dank-uh] thank you

dann then
darf am allowed to; is allowed to; may
das [dass] the; who; that; which
daß [dass] that
davon from there; of it; of them; from it; from them
dein [dine] your
denken to think
denn for, because; than
der [dair] the; who; that
deshalb [dess-halp] therefore
deutsch [doytch] German
Deutschland n [doytchlant] Germany
dich [dish] you
dick fat; thick
die [dee] the; who; that; which
dies [deess] this (one); that (one)
diese [deez-uh] this (one); that (one); these; those
dieser [deezer], **dieses** [deezess] this (one); that (one)
Ding n thing
dir [deer] (to) you
doch! [dokH] oh yes it is!; oh yes I am! etc
Dom m [dohm] cathedral
Dorf n village
dort there
dringend [dring-ent] urgent
drücken [drocken] to push
du [doo] you
dunkel [doonkel] dark
durch [doorsh] through; by; well-done

Durchgangsverkehr through traffic
durchgehend geöffnet open 24 hours
Dusche f [dOOsh-uh] shower

echt [esht] genuine
eigen [Igen] own
ein(e) [ine-(-uh)] a; one
Einbahnstraße f [ine-bahn-shtrahss-uh] one-way street
einfach [ine-faĸн] simple; single
Einfahrt f [ine-fahrt] way in
Eingang m [ine-gang] entrance, way in
einige [ine-ig-uh] a few; some
Einkaufszentrum n [ine-kowfss-tsentroom] shopping centre
Einladung f [ine-lahdoong] invitation
einmal [ine-mahl] once
eins [ine-ss] one
einsam [ine-zahm] lonely
einschl. (einschließlich) inclusive
Einschreiben n [ine-shryben] registered letter
einsteigen [ine-shtygen] to get in
Einstieg hinten enter at the rear
Eintritt frei admission free
einwerfen [ine-vairfen] to insert
Einzelzimmer n [ine-tsel-tsimmer] single room
Eisenbahn f [Izenbahn] railway
Eltern parents
Empfang m reception

endlich [entlish] at last; finally
Endstation f [ent-shtats-yohn] terminus
entfernt [entfairnt] away; distant
Entfernung f [entfairnoong] distance
enthält ... contains ...
Entschuldigung [entshooldigoong] sorry; excuse me
entweder ... oder ... [entvayder ohder] either ... or ...
Entwerter m [entvairter] ticket-stamping machine
er [air] he
Erdgeschoß n [airt-geshoss] ground floor, (US) first floor
Erfrischung f [airfrishoong] refreshment
erlauben [airlowben] to allow
Ersatzteile npl [airzatz-tile-uh] spare parts
erst [airst] only just; only
erste(r,s) [airst-uh, -er, -es] first
es [ess] it
essen to eat
Etage f [aytahj-uh] floor, storey
etwa [etvah] about; perhaps
etwas [etvass] something; some; somewhat
euch [oysh] you
euer [oyer] your

Fabrik f [fabreek] factory
Fahrausweis m [fahr-owssvice] ticket
Fähre f [fair-uh] ferry
fahren to drive; to go

Fahrer m driver
Fahrgäste passengers
Fahrkarte f [**fahr**kart-uh] ticket
Fahrplan m [-rplahn] timetable, (US) schedule
Fahrrad n [-raht] bicycle
Fahrschein m [-shine] ticket
Fahrstuhl m [-shtool] lift, elevator
Fahrt f journey
Fahrzeug n [-tsoyk] vehicle
Fall m [fal] fall; case
falls [falss] if
falsch [falsh] wrong; false
Farbe f [**farb**-uh] colour; paint
fast [fasst] almost, nearly
Feierabend m [**fy**-erahbent] closing time; time to stop
Feiertag m [**fy**-ertahk] public holiday
Fenster n window
Ferien fpl [**fai**ree-en] holidays, vacation
Fernsehen n [**fai**rnzay-en] television
Fernsprecher m telephone
fertig [**fair**tish] ready; finished
Feuer n [**foy**er] fire
Flasche f [**flash**-uh] bottle
fliegen [**flee**gen] to fly
Flug m [flook] flight
Flughafen m [-hahfen] airport
Flugsteig m [-shtike] gate
Flugzeug n [-tsoyk] (aero)plane
folgen [**fol**-gen] to follow
Frage f [**frah**g-uh] question
fragen [**frah**gen] to ask
Frankreich n [**frank**-rysh] France

Frau f [frow] woman; wife; Mrs; Ms
Fräulein n [**froy**line] Miss
frei [fry] free, vacant
Freibad n [**fry**baht] outdoor swimming pool
fremd [fremt] strange; foreign
Fremdenzimmer npl [fremden-tsimmer] room(s) to let/rent
Freund m [froynt] friend; boyfriend
Freundin f [froyndin] friend; girlfriend
freut mich! [froyt mish] pleased to meet you!
frisch gestrichen wet paint
früh [froo] early
Frühling m [**froo**ling] spring
Frühstück n [**froo**shtook] breakfast
Führer m [**foo**rer] guide; guidebook
Führerschein m [**foo**rer-shine] driving licence
Fundbüro n [**foont**-booro] lost property office
für [foor] for
Fuß m [fooss] foot
Fußgänger m [**foo**ss-geng-er] pedestrian

Gabel f [**gah**bel] fork; hook
ganz [gants] whole; quite; very
Gasthaus n [**gast**-howss] inn
Gaststätte f [**gast**-shtett-uh] restaurant; pub; inn
Gebäude n [geb**oy**d-uh] building

207

geben [**gay**ben] to give
Gebrauch m [gebr**ow**KH] use; custom
gebraucht [gebr**ow**KHt] second-hand
Gebühren fpl [geb**oo**ren] charges
Geburtsort m [geb**oo**rts-ort] place of birth
Geburtstag m [geb**oo**rts-tahk] birthday
Gefahr f [gef**ah**r] danger
gefährlich [gef**air**lish] dangerous
gegen [**gay**gen] against
gegenüber [gaygen-**oo**ber] opposite
gehen [**gay**-en] to go; to walk **geht das?** is that OK?
gelb [gelp] yellow
Geld n [gelt] money
Geldstrafe f [**gel**tshtrahf-uh] fine
genau [gen**ow**] exact; exactly
geöffnet von ... bis ... open from ... to ...
Gepäck n [gep**eck**] baggage
gerade [ger**ah**d-uh] just; straight
geradeaus [gerahd-uh-**ow**ss] straight on
Gericht n [ger**i**sht] court; dish
gern(e) [**gair**n(uh)] gladly
Geschäft n [gesh**e**ft] shop; business
Geschäftsführer m [gesh**e**fts-f**oo**rer] manager
geschlossen von ... bis ... closed from ... to ...
Geschwindigkeit f [geshvindish-kite] speed

Geschwindigkeits-beschränkung f [geshvindish-kites-beshr**e**nkoong] speed limit
Gesellschaft f [gez**e**llshafft] society; company
Gesetz n [gez**e**ts] law
Gesicht n [gez**i**sht] face
gesperrt closed; no entry
gestern [**ge**stern] yesterday
gibt [geept] **es gibt ...** there is/are ...
glauben [**glow**ben] to believe
gleich [glysh] equal; same; in a moment
Gleis n [glice] platform, (US) track
GmbH [gay-em-bay-h**ah**] Ltd, Inc
Grenze f [**grents**-uh] border
groß [grohss] big; tall
Größe f [gr**ur**ss-uh] size
grün [gr**oo**n] green
grüß Gott [gr**oo**ss] hello (South German)
gültig [**goo**ltish] valid
günstig [**goo**nstish] favourable; convenient; inexpensive
gut [g**oo**t] good; well

Haar n [hahr] hair
habe have
haben [**hah**ben] to have
halb [halp] half
Hälfte f [**hel**ft-uh] half
Hals n [halss] neck
Haltbar bis ... best before ...
Haltestelle f [**hal**lt-uh-shtell-uh] stop
Halteverbot no stopping; no

waiting

hält nicht in ... does not stop in ...

häßlich [hesslish] ugly

hast have

hat has

Hauptbahnhof m [howpt-bahnhohf] central station

Hauptstraße f [howpt-shtrahss-uh] main road; high street

Haus n [howss] house

Haut f [howt] skin

Hbf (Hauptbahnhof) central station

heiß [hice] hot

heißen f [hyssen] to be called

Heizung f [hytsoong] heating

helfen to help

Herbst m [hairpst] autumn, (US) fall

hergestellt in ... made in ...

Herr m [hair] Mr; gentleman

Herren gents, men's room

Herz n [hairts] heart

heute [hoyt-uh] today

hier [heer] here

hinten at the back

hinter behind

hoch [hohkH] high

höflich [hurflish] polite

holen [hohlen] to fetch, to get

Holz n [holts] wood

hören [hur-ren] to hear

hübsch [hoopsh] pretty

Hügel m [hoogel] hill

Hund m [hoont] dog

ich [ish] I; me

ihm [eem] him; to him

ihn [een] him

Ihnen [eenen] you; to you

ihnen them; to them

Ihr [eer] your

ihr you; her; to her; their

im in (the)

immer always

Inhalt contents

Inlandsflüge domestic flights

ins into the; to the

Insel f [inzel] island

irgendwo [eergent-vo] somewhere

ist is

ja [yah] yes

Jahr n [yahr] year

je [yay] ever

jede [yayd-uh] each; every

jeder [yayder] everyone; each

jemand [yaymant] somebody

jetzt [yetst] now

Jugendherberge f [yoogent-hairbairg-uh] youth hostel

jung [yoong] young

Junge m [yoong-uh] boy

kalt cold

Kasse f [kass-uh] cashdesk; box office

kaufen [kowfen] to buy

Kaufhaus n [kowfhowss] department store

kaum [kowm] hardly

kein(e) ... [kine(-uh)] no ...; not ...

kein Zugang no entry

Kellner m waiter

Kellnerin f waitress

kennen to know

Ki

Kind n [kint] child
Kino n [keeno] cinema, movie theater
Kirche f [keersh-uh] church
klar clear; OK, sure
Kleider [klyder] clothes
klein [kline] small
klug [klook] clever
Kneipe f [k-nipe-uh] pub
Koffer m bag; suitcase
komisch [kohmish] funny
kommen to come
Konditorei f [kondeetor-ī] cake shop
können [kurnen] to be able to; can
Kopf m head
Körper m [kurper] body
köstlich [kurstlish] delicious
krank ill, sick
Krankenhaus n [kranken-howss] hospital
Kreis m [krice] circle
Krieg m [kreek] war
kriegen [kreegen] to get
Küche f [koosh-uh] cooking, cuisine; kitchen
Kundenparkplatz customer car park/parking lot
Kunst f [koonst] art
Kurs m [koorss] rate; exchange rate; course

Laden m [lahden] shop
Landkarte f [lantkart-uh] map
Landschaft f [lantshafft] countryside; landscape
lang long
langsam [langzahm] slow; slowly
lassen to let; to leave
Lastwagen m [lasst-vahgen] lorry, truck
laufen [lowfen] to run
laut [lowt] loud; noisy
Lawinengefahr danger of avalanches
leben to live
Lebensgefahr f [laybens-gefahr] danger
Lebensmittelhandlung f [laybensmittel-hantloong] grocer's
leer [lair] empty
legen [laygen] to put
Lehrer m [lairer] teacher
leicht [lysht] easy; light
leider [lyder] unfortunately
lernen [lairnen] to learn
letzter [letster] last
Leute pl [loyt-uh] people
Licht n [lisht] light
lieben [leeben] to love
lieber [leeber] rather
Lied n [leet] song
links left
Löffel m [lurfel] spoon
Luft f [looft] air

machen [makhen] to make; to do
mach's gut [goot] take care
Mädchen n [mayt-shen] girl
Mahlzeit f [mahl-tsite] meal
Mal n [mahl] time
man one; you
manchmal [manshmahl] sometimes

Mann m man; husband
Mauer f [mower] wall
Meer n [mair] sea
mehr [mair] more
Mehrwertsteuer f [mairvairt-shtoyer] value-added tax
mein [mine] my
meiste: das meiste (von) [myst-uh (fon)] most (of)
Menge f [meng-uh] crowd
Mensch m [mensh] person
Messe f [mess-uh] (trade) fair
Messegelände n [messuh-gelenduh] fair (site)
Messer n knife
Metzger m [metsger] butcher's
mich [mish] me
Miete f [meet-uh] rent
mieten [meeten] to rent
mir [meer] me; to me
mit with
mitnehmen [mit-naymen] to take; to give a lift to
zum Mitnehmen to take away, (US) to go
Mittag m [mittahk] midday
Mittagessen n [mittahk-essen] lunch
Mitte f [mitt-uh] middle
Möbel pl [murbel] furniture
möglich [murklish] possible
Monat m [mohnaht] month
morgen tomorrow
Morgen m [morgen] morning
müde [mood-uh] tired
Münzen fpl [moontsen] coins
Mutter f [mootter] mother
MWSt VAT

nach [naKH] after; to
nachdem [naKHdaym] after
Nachmittag m [naKHmittahk] afternoon
Nachname m [naKHnahm-uh] surname
Nachrichten fpl [naKHrishten] news
nächste [naykst-uh] next; nearest
Nacht f [naKHt] night
Nähe: in der Nähe [in dair nay-uh] near here
Nahverkehrszug m [nah-fairkairs-tsook] local train
Nase f [nahz-uh] nose
naß [nass] wet
natürlich [natoorlish] natural; of course
neben [nayben] next to
nehmen [naymen] to take
nein [nine] no
nett nice
neu [noy] new
nicht [nisht] not
nicht berühren do not touch
Nichtraucher non-smokers
nichts [nishts] nothing
nie [nee] never
niemals [neemalss] never
niemand [neemant] nobody
nirgends [neergents] nowhere
noch [noKH] still; even; more
noch ein(e) ... [ine(-uh)] another ...
noch nicht [nisht] not yet
nochmal [noKHmahl] again
Norden m north
Notarzt m [noht-artst]

emergency doctor
Notausgang m [**noh**t-owssgang]
emergency exit
Notfall m [**noh**tfal] emergency
nötig [**nur**tish] necessary
nun [n00n] now
nur [n00r] only; just

ob [op] whether; if
oben [**oh**ben] top; at the top;
upstairs
oder [**oh**der] or
offen open
öffentlich [**urf**entlish] public
öffnen [**urf**nen] to open
oft often
ohne [**oh**n-uh] without
Ohr n [ohr] ear
Ort m town; place
Osten m east
Österreich n [**ur**ster-rysh]
Austria

paar: ein paar ... a few ...
Panne f [**pann**-uh] breakdown
Parkdauer parking allowed
for ...
Parken verboten no parking
Parkplatz m [**park**plats] car
park, parking lot
Pkw m [pay-kah-**vay**] private
car
Platz m [plats] seat; square;
place; space
plötzlich [**plurt**slish] sudden(ly)
Polizeiwache f [polits-ī-vaкн-uh]
police station
Porto n postage
postlagernd poste restante,

(US) general delivery
Postwertzeichen n(pl) postage
stamp(s)
Präservativ n [prezairvate**ef**]
condom
preisgünstig [**price**-g00nstish]
cheap; inexpensive
pro: pro Woche per week
prost! [prohst] cheers!
prüfen [pr00fen] to check

Quittung f [kvittoong] receipt

Rabatt m reduction, discount
Rad n [raht] wheel
Radfahren n [**raht**-fahren]
cycling
Rathaus n [**raht**-howss] town
hall
rauchen [**row**кнen] to smoke
Rauchen verboten no
smoking
Raucherabteil n [**row**кнer-apt**ile**]
smoking compartment
Rechnung f [**resh**noong] bill,
(US) check
rechts [reshts] right
Rechtsanwalt m [**reshts**-anvalt]
lawyer
rechts fahren keep to the
right
Reformkost f health food
Regen m [**ray**gen] rain
Regierung f [reg**ee**roong]
government
reich [rysh] rich
reine Schurwolle pure wool
Reise f [**rize**-uh] journey
Reisebedarf m [**rize**-uh-bedarf]

travel requisites

Reisebüro n [rize-uh-bꝏro] travel agency

Reiseführer m [rize-uh-fꝏrer] guide; guidebook

Reisescheck m [rize-uh-sheck] travellers' cheque

richtig [rishtish] right; correct

Richtung f [rishtoong] direction

rot [roht] red

Rücken m [rꝏcken] back

Rückfahrkarte f [rꝏckfahrkart-uh] return/round trip ticket

rufen [rꝏfen] to call; to shout

Ruhetag closed all day

ruhig [rꝏo-ish] quiet

Rundfahrt f [rꝏontfahrt] guided tour

Sache f [zaкн-uh] thing; matter; affair

Sackgasse f [zack-gass-uh] cul-de-sac, dead end

sagen [zahgen] to say

sauber [zowber] clean

S-Bahn f [ess-bahn] local railway

schade: das ist schade [shahd-uh] it's a pity

Schiff n [shiff] ship; boat

Schlafwagen m [shlahfvahgen] sleeping car

Schlafzimmer n [shlahf-tsimmer] bedroom

schlagen [shlahgen] to hit

schlecht [shlesht] bad; badly; unwell

schließen [shleessen] to close

Schließfächer luggage lockers

Schloß n [shloss] castle; lock

Schlüssel m [shlꝏssel] key; spanner, wrench

schmecken [shmecken] to taste; to taste good

Schmerz m [shmairts] pain

schmutzig [shmꝏtsish] dirty

Schnee m [shnay] snow

Schneiderei f [shnyder-I] tailor's

schnell [shnell] fast

Schnellimbiß m [shnell-imbiss] snackbar

schön [shurn] beautiful; nice

schon [shohn] already

schreiben [shryben] to write

Schule f [shool-uh] school

schwach [shvaкн] weak

schwarz [shvartz] black

Schweiz f [shvites] Switzerland

schwer [shvair] heavy; difficult

Schwester f [shvester] sister

schwierig [shveerish] difficult

See m [zay] lake

See f sea

sehen [zay-en] to see

sehr [zair] very

Seide f [zide-uh] silk

sein [zine] to be; his; its

seit [zite] since

Seite f [zite-uh] side; page

selbe [zelb-uh] same

selbst [zelpst] even

Selbstbedienung f [zelpst-bedeenoong] self-service

seltsam [zeltzahm] strange

setzen [zetsen] to put

sicher [zisher] sure; safe

sie [zee] she; her; they; them

Sie you

sind [zint] are
sofort [zofort] immediately
Sohn m [zohn] son
Sommer m [zommer] summer
Sommerschlußverkauf
summer sale
Sonderangebot n [zonder-angeboht] special offer
sondern [zondern] but
Sonne f [zonn-uh] sun
sonst [zonst] otherwise
Spaß m [shpahss] fun; joke
spät [shpayt] late
Speisewagen m [shpize-uh-vahgen] restaurant car
Speisezimmer n [shpize-uh-tsimmer] dining room
Spiel n [shpeel] game; match
spielen [shpeelen] to play
Sprache f [shprahKH-uh]
language
sprechen [shpreshen] to speak;
to talk
Staatsangehörigkeit f [shtahts-an-gehur-rish-kite] nationality
Stadt f [shtatt] town; city
Stadtmitte f [shtatt-mitt-uh] city
centre
Station f [shtats-yohn]
(hospital) ward; stop
stehen [shtay-en] to stand
Steinschlag falling rocks
Stelle f [shtell-uh] place
sterben [shtairben] to die
Stockwerk n [shtockvairk] floor,
storey
stören [shtur-ren] to disturb
Strafe f [shtrahf-uh] penalty;
punishment

Strand m [shtrant] beach
Straße f [shtrahss-uh] street;
road
Straßenbahn f [shtrahssenbahn]
tram
strengstens untersagt strictly
prohibited
Stück n [shtock] piece; play
Stuhl m [shtool] chair
Stunde f [shtoond-uh] hour;
lesson
Süden m [zooden] south
süß [zooss] sweet

Tag m [tahk] day
täglich [tayklish] daily
Tal n [tahl] valley
Tankstelle f [tankshtell-uh]
petrol/gas station
Tante f [tant-uh] aunt
Teil m [tile] part
teuer [toyer] expensive
tief [teef] deep; low
Tiefgeschoß basement
Tisch m [tish] table
Tochter f [toKHter] daughter
Tod m [toht] death
Tor n goal; gate
tot [toht] dead
tragen [trahgen] to carry
traurig [trowrish] sad
trocken dry
tschüs [chooss] cheerio
tun [toon] to do; to put
Tür f [toor] door

über [oober] over; above
überall [oober-al] everywhere
überholen [ooberhohlen] to

overtake

Übernachtung f
[ɷbernaкнtoong] night

übersetzen [ɷberzetsen] to
translate

Ufer n [**oo**fer] shore

Uhr f [**oo**r] clock; o'clock

um [**oo**m] around; at
  um zu in order to

und [**oo**nt] and

Unfall m [**oo**nfal] accident

ungefähr [**oo**n-gefair]
  approximately

unmöglich [**oo**n-m**u**rklish]
  impossible

uns [**oo**nss] us

unser [**oo**nzer] our

unten [**oo**nten] down; at the
  bottom; downstairs

unter [**oo**nter] under;
  underneath; among

Unterkunft f [**oo**nterkoonft]
  accommodation

untersagt prohibited

Unterschrift f [**oo**ntershrift]
  signature

Urlaub m [**oo**rlowp] holiday,
  vacation

usw. (und so weiter) etc

Vater m [**fah**ter] father

verantwortlich [fair-**a**ntvortlish]
  responsible

Verbindung f [fairb**i**ndoong]
  connection

verboten [fairb**oh**ten]
  forbidden, prohibited

vergessen [fairg**e**ssen] to
  forget

verkaufen [fairk**ow**fen] to sell

Verkehr m [fairk**ai**r] traffic

verlangen [fairl**a**ngen] to ask
  for

verlassen [fairl**a**ssen] to leave

verrückt [fair-r**oo**ckt] mad

Versicherung f [fairz**i**sheroong]
  insurance

verspätet [fairshp**ay**tet] late,
  delayed

Verspätung f [fairshp**ay**toong]
  delay

verstehen [fairsht**ay**-en] to
  understand

viel [feel] much, a lot (of)

viele [feel-uh] many

vielleicht [feel**y**sht] maybe

voll [fol] full; crowded

Vollpension f [fol-pangz-yohn]
  full board, (US) American
  plan

von [fon] of; by; from

vor [for] before; in front of
  vor ... Tagen ... days ago

voraus: im voraus [v**o**rowss] in
  advance

vorbei [forb**y**] over
  vorbei an ... past ...

Vorfahrt f [f**o**rfahrt] right of
  way

Vorfahrt beachten give way,
  yield

vorher [forhair] before

vorn [forn] at the front

Vorname m [f**o**rnahm-uh] first
  name

Vorsicht f [f**o**rzisht] caution

Vorsicht Stufe! mind the step!

Vorwahl f [f**o**rvahl] dialling

code, area code

Wagen m [**vah**gen] car; coach; carriage
wahr [vahr] true
während [**vai**rent] during; while
Wald m [valt] forest
wann [van] when
warum? [var**oom**] why?
was? [vass] what?
Wäsche f [**vesh**-uh] washing
Wasser n [**va**sser] water
Wechselkurs m [**vek**sel-koors] exchange rate
wechseln [**vek**seln] to change
Wechselstube f [**vek**sel-shtoob-uh] bureau de change
weder ... noch [**vay**der – noKH] neither ... nor ...
Weg m [vayk] path
wegen [**vay**gen] because of
weich [vysh] soft
Weihnachten n [**vy**naKHten] Christmas
weil [vile] because
weiß [vice] white; knows
weit [vite] far; wide
weiter [**vy**ter] further
welche? [**velsh**-uh] which?
Welt f [velt] world
wenig [**vay**nish] little; few
weniger [**vay**niger] less
wenn [venn] if
wer? [vair] who?
Werktag m [**vairk**tahk] weekday
Westen m [**ve**sten] west
wichtig [**vish**tish] important
wider [**vee**der] against
wie [vee] how; like

wieder [**vee**der] again
wieviel? [vee**feel**] how much?
willkommen! welcome!
wir [veer] we
wirklich [**veer**klish] really
wissen [**vi**ssen] to know
wo? [vo] where?
Woche f [**vo**KH-uh] week
woher? [vo-**hair**] where from?
wohin? [vo-**hin**] where to?
wohnen [**voh**nen] to live
Wohnung f [**voh**noong] flat, apartment
Wolle f [**vol**l-uh] wool
wollen [**vol**len] to want
Wort n [vort] word

Zahl f [tsahl] number
zahlen [**tsah**len] to pay
Zahlung f [**tsah**loong] payment
Zahn m [tsahn] tooth
Zahnarzt m [**tsahn**-artst] dentist
Zeit f [tsite] time
Zeitung f [**tsy**toong] newspaper
ziehen [**tsee**-en] to pull
ziemlich [**tseem**lish] rather
Zimmer n [**tsim**mer] room
Zimmernachweis m [-na**KH**vice] accommodation service
Zoll m [tsol] Customs
zu [tsoo] to; too; shut
Zug m [tsook] train
zum [tsoom], [tsoor] to the
zurück [tsoo**rück**] back
zusammen [tsoo**tsam**men] together
Zuschlag m [**tsoo**shlahk] supplement
zwischen [**tsvi**shen] between

MENU READER

Food: Essential terms

bread das Brot [broht]
butter die Butter [**boo**ter]
cup die Tasse [**ta**ss-uh]
dessert der Nachtisch
  [na**KH**tish]
fish der Fisch [fish]
fork die Gabel [**gah**bel]
glass: a glass of ... ein Glas ...
  [ine glahss]
knife das Messer
main course das
  Hauptgericht [**how**pt-gerisht]
meat das Fleisch [flysh]
menu die Speisekarte [shpize-
  uh-kart-uh]
pepper der Pfeffer
plate der Teller

salad der Salat [zal**aht**]
salt das Salz [zalts]
set menu die Tageskarte
  [**tah**gess-kart-uh]
soup die Suppe [**zoo**p-uh]
spoon der Löffel [**lur**fel]
starter die Vorspeise [for-
  shpize-uh]
table der Tisch [tish]

another ..., please noch ein
  ..., bitte [no**KH** ine bitt-uh]
excuse me! Entschuldigung!
  [ent-sh**oo**ldigoong]
could I have the bill, please?
  kann ich bitte bezahlen?
  [kan ish bitt-uh betsahlen]

Food: Menu Reader

Ananas [**a**nanass] pineapple
Apfelkuchen [-ko**OKH**en] apple
  pie
Apfelmus [-m**OO**ss] apple
  purée

Apfelsinen [apfelz**ee**nen]
  oranges
Aprikosen [aprik**oh**zen]
  apricots
Arme Ritter [**arm**-uh] bread

217

soaked in milk and egg then fried

Auflauf [owf-lowf] (baked) pudding or omelette

Aufschnitt [owf-shnitt] sliced cold meats, cold cuts

Austern [owstern] oysters

Baiser [bezzay] meringue

Bauernauflauf [bowern-owflowf] bacon and potato omelette

Bauernfrühstück [-frŒshtŒk] bacon and potato omelette

Beilagen [bylahgen] side dishes; side salads, vegetables

belegtes Brot [belayktess broht] sandwich

Bierschinken [beer-shinken] ham sausage

Birnen [beernen] pears

Blumenkohl [bloomenkohl] cauliflower

blutig [blootish] rare

Blutwurst [bloot-voorst] black pudding, blood sausage

Bockwurst large frankfurter

Bohnen beans

Bouletten meat balls

Braten [brahten] roast meat

Brathähnchen [braht-haynshen] roast chicken

Bratheringe [-hairing-uh] (pickled) fried herrings (served cold)

Bratkartoffeln fried potatoes

Bratwurst [-voorst] grilled pork sausage

Brombeeren [brombairen] blackberries

Brot [broht] bread

Brötchen [brurtshen] roll

Buttercremetorte [bootterkraym-tort-uh] cream cake

Champignons [shampinyongs] mushrooms

Currywurst [-voorst] curried pork sausage

deutsches Beefsteak [doytshess] mince patty

durchgebraten [doorsh-gebrahten] well-done

Ei [ī] egg

eingelegt [ine-gelaykt] pickled

Eintopf [ine-topf] stew

Eis [ice] ice; ice cream

Eisbein [-bine] knuckles of pork

Eissplittertorte [-shplitter-tort-uh] ice chip cake

Entenbraten [entenbrahten] roast duck

Erbsen [airpsen] peas

Erdäpfel [airt-epfel] potatoes

Erdbeeren [airtbairen] strawberries

Essig vinegar

Fasan [fazahn] pheasant

Fleisch [flysh] meat

Fleischkäse [-kayz-uh] meat loaf

Forelle [forell-uh] trout

Forelle Müllerin (Art) [mŒllerin] trout coated with breadcrumbs and served with butter and lemon

Frikadelle [frickadell-uh] rissole

Gänsebraten [genz-uh-brahten] roast goose

Gebäck [gebeck] pastries, cakes

gebacken fried

gebraten [gebrahten] roast

gedämpft [gedempft] steamed

Geflügel [geflﬂgel] poultry

gehackt minced; chopped

Gehacktes minced meat, ground beef

gekochtes Ei [i] boiled egg

Gemüse [gemﬂz-uh] vegetable(s)

gepökelt [gepurkelt] salted, pickled

geräuchert [geroyshert] smoked

geschmort [geshmohrt] braised, stewed

Geschnetzeltes strips of meat in thick sauce

Gewürze [gevﬂrts-uh] spices

Goldbarsch [goltbarsh] type of perch

Götterspeise [gurttershpize-uh] jelly

grüne Nudeln [grﬂn-uh noodeln] green pasta

Grünkohl (curly) kale

Gurkensalat [-zalaht] cucumber salad

Hackfleisch [-flysh] minced meat, ground meat

Hähnchen [haynshen] chicken

Hammelfleisch [-flysh] mutton

Handkäse [hant-kayz-uh] very strong-smelling cheese

Hasenbraten [hahzenbrahten] roast hare

Hasenpfeffer jugged hare

Hauptgerichte main dishes

Hausfrauenart [howssfrowenart] home-made style

hausgemacht [howss-gemaKHt] homemade

Hecht [hesht] pike

Heidelbeeren [hydelbairen] bilberries

Heilbutt [hile-boott] halibut

Heringstopf pickled herrings

Himbeeren [himbairen] raspberries

Himmel und Erde [oont aird-uh] potato and apple purée with liver sausage

Hirschbraten [heershbrahten] roast venison

Hoppelpoppel bacon and potato omelette

Huhn [hoon] chicken

Hühnerbrühe [hﬂner-broo-uh] chicken broth

Hummer [hoommer] lobster

Imbiß [imbiss] snack

Jägerschnitzel [yaygershnitsel] pork with mushrooms

Kabeljau [kahbelyow] cod

Kalbfleisch [kalpflysh] veal

Kalbshaxe leg of veal

Kalbsschnitzel [-shnitsel] veal cutlet

kalte Speisen cold dishes

Kaninchen [kaneenshen] rabbit

Karbonade [karbonahd-uh] carbonade, beef and onion stew cooked in beer

Karfiol [karf-yohl] cauliflower

Karpfen carp

Kartoffel potato

Kartoffelpuffer [-pooffer] potato fritters

Kartoffelsalat [-zalaht] potato salad

Käse [kayz-uh] cheese

Käsekuchen [-kooкнen] cheesecake

Käseplatte [-plat-uh] selection of cheeses, cheeseboard

Kasseler Rippenspeer [rippen-shpair] salted ribs of pork

Keule [koyl-uh] leg, haunch

Kinderteller children's portion

Klöße [klurss-uh] dumplings

Knackwurst [-voorst] frankfurter

Knoblauch [k-nohb-lowкн] garlic

Knödel [k-nurdel] dumplings

Kohl cabbage

Kohl und Pinkel cabbage, potatoes, sausage and smoked meat

Königinpastete [kurnigin-pastayt-uh] chicken vol-au-vent

Kopfsalat [kopfzalaht] lettuce

Krabben shrimps, prawns

Kraftbrühe [kraftbroo-uh] beef consommé, beef tea

Kräuter [kroyter] herbs

Krautsalat [krowtzalaht] coleslaw

Kuchen [kooкнen] cake; pie

Labskaus [lapskowss] meat, fish and potato stew

Lachs [lacks] salmon

Lachsforelle [-forell-uh] sea trout

Lammrücken [-rooken] saddle of lamb

Languste [langoost-uh] crayfish

Leber [layber] liver

Leberkäse [-kayz-uh] baked pork and beef loaf

Leberwurst [-voorst] liver sausage

Leipziger Allerlei [lipe-tsiger al-er-ly] mixed vegetables

Linsensuppe [-zoop-uh] lentil soup

Mandeln almonds

Matjesfilet [matyess-fillay] fillet of herring

Medaillons [maydah-yongs] small fillets

Meeresfrüchte [-froosht-uh] seafood

Meerrettich [mair-rettish] horseradish

Milchreis [-rice] rice pudding

Möhren [mur-ren] carrots

Mus [mooss] purée

Nachspeisen [naкн-shpyzen] desserts

Nachtisch [naкнtish] dessert

nicht gar underdone

Nudeln [noodeln] pasta

Nudelsuppe [-zoop-uh] noodle soup

Nüsse [nooss-uh] nuts

Obst [ohpst] fruit

Ochsenschwanzsuppe [oksen-shvants-zoop-uh] oxtail soup

paniert [paneert] with breadcrumbs

Paprikaschote [-shoht-uh] pepper

Paradeiser [paradyzer] tomatoes

Pellkartoffeln potatoes boiled in their jackets

Petersilie [payterzeel-yuh] parsley

Pfannkuchen [-kooKHen] pancake

Pfirsiche [pfeerzish-uh] peaches

Pflaumen [pflowmen] plums

Pilze [pilts-uh] mushrooms

Plätzchen [plets-shen] biscuit

Preßkopf [presskopf] brawn

Putenschenkel [pootenshenkel] turkey leg

Radieschen [radeess-shen] radishes

Rahm (sour) cream

Räucheraal [roysher-ahl] smoked eel

Rehbraten [ray-brahten] roast venison

Reibekuchen [ribe-uh-kooKHen] potato waffles

Reis [rice] rice

Rhabarber [rabarber] rhubarb

Rinderbraten [rinder-brahten] pot roast

Rinderfilet [-fillay] fillet steak

Rinderrouladen [-roolahden] stuffed beef rolls

Rindfleisch [rintflysh] beef

Rippchen [ripshen] spareribs

Risi-Pisi [reezee-peezee] rice and peas

roh raw

Rostbraten [-brahten] roast

Röstkartoffeln [rurst-] fried potatoes

rote Bete [roht-uh bayt-uh] beetroot, red beet

rote Grütze [roht-uh groots-uh] red fruit jelly

Rotkohl [roht-] red cabbage

Roulade [roolahd-uh] beef olive

Rühreier [roor-ī-er] scrambled eggs

Russische Eier [roossish-uh ī-er] egg mayonnaise

Sachertorte [zaKHertort-uh] rich chocolate cake

Sahne [zahn-uh] cream

Salat [zalaht] salad; lettuce

Salz [zalts] salt

Salzburger Nockerln [zaltsboorger] sweet soufflés

Salzkartoffeln boiled potatoes

Sauerkraut [zowerkrowt] white cabbage, finely chopped and pickled

Schaschlik [shashlik] (shish-) kebab

Schellfisch haddock

Schinken [shinken] ham

Schlagsahne [-zahn-uh] whipped cream

Schmorbraten [shmohrbrahten] pot roast

Schnecken [shnecken] snails

Schnittlauch [shnitt-lowKH] chives

Schnitzel [shnitsel] cutlet

Scholle [sholl-uh] plaice

Schwarzwälder Kirschtorte [shvartsvelder keershtort-uh] Black Forest cherry gateau

Schweinebraten [-brahten] roast pork

Schweinefilet [-fill**ay**] fillet of pork

Schweinefleisch [-flysh] pork

Schweinshaxe [shv**ine**-ss-hacks-uh] knuckle of pork

Seelachs [**zay**lacks] pollack

Senf [zenf] mustard

Soße [**zoh**ss-uh] sauce; gravy

Spargel [shp**a**rgel] asparagus

Spätzle [shp**e**ts-luh] home-made noodles

Speckkartoffeln [shp**eck**-] potatoes with bacon

Spiegeleier [shp**ee**gel-ī-er] fried eggs

Spießbraten [shp**ee**ss-brahten] joint roasted on a spit

Spinat [shpin**aht**] spinach

Stachelbeeren [shta**ka**ĸel-bairen] gooseberries

Steinbutt [sht**ine**-boott] turbot

Stollen [sht**o**llen] type of fruit loaf

Strammer Max [shtr**a**mmer] ham and fried egg on bread

Sülze [z**ʊ**lts-uh] brawn

Suppe [z**oo**p-uh] soup

Süßigkeiten [z**oo**ssish-kyten] sweets

Tageskarte [-kart-uh] menu of the day; set menu

Teigmantel [t**ike**-mantel] pastry covering

Teigwaren [-vahren] pasta

Thunfisch [t**oo**nfish] tuna

Törtchen [t**ur**tshen] tart(s)

Truthahn [tr**oo**t-] turkey

Vorspeisen [f**o**rshpyzen] hors d'oeuvres, starters

Weißkohl white cabbage

Wiener Schnitzel [v**ee**ner shn**i**tsel] veal in breadcrumbs

Wild [vilt] game

Wildbret [-brayt] venison

Wildschweinsteak [v**i**ltshvine-] wild boar steak

Windbeutel [v**i**ntboytel] cream puff

Wurst [voorst] sausage

Würstchen [v**ʊ**rstshen] frankfurter(s)

Wurstplatte [v**oo**rst-plat-uh] selection of sausages

Ziegenkäse [ts**ee**gen-kayz-uh] goat's cheese

Zigeunerschnitzel [tsig**oy**ner-shnitsel] veal or pork with peppers and relishes

Zitrone [tsitr**oh**n-uh] lemon

Zucker [ts**oo**cker] sugar

Zuckererbsen [-airpsen] mange-tout peas

Zwiebel [tsv**ee**bel] onion

Zwiebeltorte [-tort-uh] onion tart

Drink: Essential terms

beer das Bier
bottle die Flasche [**fla**sh-uh]
brandy der Weinbrand [**vine**-brant]
coffee der Kaffee [**ka**ffay]
cup: a cup of ... eine Tasse ... [**ine**-uh **ta**ss-uh]
fruit juice der Fruchtsaft [**froo**KHtzaft]
gin der Gin
  a gin and tonic einen Gin Tonic [**ine**-en]
glass: a glass of ... ein Glas ... [ine **glah**ss]
milk die Milch [**mil**sh]
mineral water das Mineralwasser [miner**ahl**vasser]
orange juice der Orangensaft [o**ron**Jen-zaft]
red wine der Rotwein [**roht**vine]

rosé der Roséwein [rohz**ay**-vine]
soda (water) das Sodawasser [**zoh**da-vasser]
soft drink das alkoholfreie Getränk [alko**hohl**fry-uh get**renk**], der Soft drink
sugar der Zucker [ts**oo**cker]
tea der Tee [tay]
tonic (water) das Tonic
vodka der Wodka [**vo**dka]
water das Wasser [**va**sser]
whisky der Whisky
white wine der Weißwein [**vice**-vine]
wine der Wein [vine]
wine list die Weinkarte [**vine**-kart-uh]

another ..., please noch ein ..., bitte [noKH ine ... **bit**t-uh]

Drink: Menu Reader

Alt(bier) [**alt**(beer)] light brown beer, not sweet
Apfelschorle [**a**pfel-shorl-uh] sparkling apple juice
Apfelwein [-vine] cider
Auslese [**ow**sslayz-uh] wine selected from ripest grapes in top wine category

Berliner Weiße [bairl**ee**ener **vice**-uh] fizzy beer
Bockbier [**bo**ckbeer] strong beer
Bowle [**bo**hl-uh] punch
Doppelkorn grain schnapps
Eierlikör [**ier**-likur] advocaat
Eiswein [**ice**-vine] wine made from grapes picked after frost

Erdbeermilch [**ai**rtbair-milsh] strawberry milk shake

Federweißer [**fay**der-vysser] new wine

Gespritzter [geshpr**i**tster] wine and soda, spritzer

Glühwein [gl**oo**-vine] mulled wine

Hefeweizen [**hay**f-uh-vytsen] fizzy beer made with yeast and wheat

Helles [**h**elless] lager

Kabinett light, usually dry, wine in top wine category

Kaffee [kaff**ay**] coffee

Kännchen (Kaffee) [**k**ennshen (kaff**ay**)] pot (of coffee)

koffeinfrei [koffay-**een**-fry] decaffeinated

Korn type of schnapps

Kräutertee [kr**oy**ter-tay] herbal tea

Limo [**lee**mo] lemonade

Malzbier [**ma**ltsbeer] sweet stout

Milchmixgetränk [milshmix-getrenk] milkshake

Most [mosst] fruit wine

Nektar fruit squash

Obstler [**oh**pstler] fruit schnapps

offener Wein [vine] wine by the glass

Pikkolo quarter bottle of Champagne

Radler(maß) [**ra**htler-mahss] shandy

Rotwein [**roh**tvine] red wine

Saft [zaft] juice

Schokomilch [sh**o**ko-milsh] chocolate milk shake

schwarzer Tee [shv**a**rtser tay] tea

Sekt [zekt] sparkling wine, champagne

Spezi [shp**ay**tsee] cola and lemonade

Steinhäger® [sht**ine**-hayger] type of schnapps

Sturm [shtoorm] new wine

Tafelwasser [**ta**hfel-vasser] still mineral water

Tee [tay] tea

vom Faß [fom fass] draught

Weinbrand [**vine**-brant] brandy

Weißbier [**vice**beer] fizzy, light-coloured beer made with wheat

Weizenbier [**vy**ts-tenbeer] wheat beer

GREEK

DICTIONARY PHRASEBOOK

Pronunciation

Greek words have been transliterated into a romanized form (see The Greek Alphabet page 268) so that they can be read as though they were English bearing, in mind the notes on pronunciation given below:

a   as in c**a**t

e   as in g**e**t

eh   represents e at end of a word; should always be pronounced as in g**e**t

g   a throaty version of the g in **g**ap

i   as in sk**i**

kh   like the ch in the Scottish way of saying lo**ch**

o   as in h**o**t

th   as in **th**en

TH   as in **th**eme

Letters given in bold type indicate the part of the word to be stressed. When two vowels (such as 'ea') are next to each other in the pronunciation, both should be pronounced, as for example in the word: amfiTH**e**atro (amphitheatre).

Language Notes

There are three words for 'the' in Greek: **o, i, to**. The plural forms are **i, i, ta**. These forms correspond to masculine, feminine and neuter genders. Some examples:

o pateras	**i mitera**	**to moro**
the father	the mother	the baby
i paterathes	**i miteres**	**ta mora**
the fathers	the mothers	the babies

The corresponding words for 'a' are **enas, mia, ena**. Some examples:

enas anthras	**mia yineka**	**ena pethi**
a man	a woman	a child

Greek has a fairly complex system of cases, which means, amongst other things, that these words for 'the' and 'a' may often occur in a modified form. For example:

o skilos too yitona	**stin paralia**
the neighbour's dog	to the beach

The Greek words for 'I', 'you', 'he' etc are usually omitted as subjects unless special emphasis is required. For example:

efiyeh khTHes	**afti efiyeh khTHes**
he/she left yesterday	she left yesterday (but he stayed behind)
tin itha	**ego tin itha**
I saw her	I saw her (although nobody else seems to have)

Here is a useful verb – 'to be':

imeh I am	**imasteh** we are
iseh you are (familiar form)	**isasteh/isteh** you are (plural or polite singular form)
ineh he/she/it is	**ineh** they are

The familiar form is used to speak to people you are on friendly terms with.

Days

Monday i Theftera
Tuesday i Triti
Wednesday i Tetarti
Thursday i Pempti
Friday i Paraskevi
Saturday to Savato
Sunday i Kiriaki

Months

January o I-anooarios
February o Fevrooarios
March o Martios
April o Aprilios
May o Ma-ios
June o I-oonios
July o I-oolios
August o Avgoostos
September o Septemvrios
October o Oktovrios
November o No-emvrios
December o Thekemvrios

Time

what time is it? τί ώρα είναι;
ti ora ineh?
one o'clock μία η ώρα mia i
ora
two o'clock δύο η ώρα thio i
ora
...e o'clock είναι μία η
...neh mia i ora

it's two o'clock είναι δύο η
ώρα ineh thio i ora
it's ten o'clock είναι δέκα η
ώρα ineh theka i ora
five past one μία και πέντε
mia keh pendeh
ten past two δύο και δέκα
thio keh theka
quarter past one μία και
τέταρτο mia keh tetarto
quarter past two δύο και
τέταρτο thio keh tetarto
twenty past ten δέκα και
είκοσι theka keh ikosi
half past ten δέκα και μισή
theka keh misi
twenty to ten δέκα παρά
είκοσι theka para ikosi
quarter to two δύο παρά
τέταρτο thio para tetarto
at half past four στις
τέσσερις και μισή stis
teseris keh misi
at eight o'clock στις οκτώ stis
okto
14.00 δεκατέσσερις theka-
teseris
17.30 δεκαεφτά και τριάντα
theka-efta keh trianda
2 a.m. δύο η ώρα το βράδυ
thio i ora to vrathi
2 p.m. δύο η ώρα το
μεσημέρι thio i ora to
mesimeri
6 a.m. έξι η ώρα το πρωί exi

i ora to pro-i
6 p.m. έξι η ώρα το απάγευμα exi i ora to apoyevma
noon το μεσημέρι to mesimeri
midnight τα μεσάνυχτα ta mesanikhta

an hour η ώρα i ora
a minute το λεπτά to lepto
one minute ένα λεπτά ena lepto
two minutes δύο λεπτά thio lepta
a second το δευτεράλεπτο to thefterolepto
a quarter of an hour ένα τέταρτο ena tetarto
half an hour μισή ώρα misi ora
three quarters of an hour τρία τέταρτα της ώρας tria tetarta tis oras

Numbers

0	μηδέν	mithen
1	ένα	ena
2	δύο	thio
3	τρία	tria
4	τέσσερα	tesera
5	πέντε	pendeh
6	έξι	exi
7	επτά	epta
8	οχτώ	okhto
9	εννιά	enia
10	δέκα	theka
11	έντεκα	endeka
12	δώδεκα	thotheka
13	δεκατρία	theka-tria
14	δεκατέσσερα	theka-tesera
15	δεκαπέντε	theka-pendeh
16	δεκαέξι	theka-exi
17	δεκαεπτά	theka-epta
18	δεκαοχτώ	theka-okhto
19	δεκαεννιά	theka-enia
20	είκοσι	ikosi
21	εικοσιένα	ikosi-ena
22	εικοσιδύο	ikosi-thio
30	τριάντα	trianda
31	τριανταένα	trianda-ena
40	σαράντα	saranda
50	πενήντα	peninda
60	εξήντα	exinda
70	εβδομήντα	evthominda

80	ογδάντα ogthonda
90	ενενήντα eneninda
100	εκατό ekato
110	εκατά δέκα ekato theka
200	διακάσια thiakosia
300	τριακάσια triakosia
1,000	χίλια khilia
2,000	δύο χιλιάδες thio khiliathes
5,000	πέντε χιλιάδες pendeh khiliathes
10,000	δέκα χιλιάδες theka khiliathes
20,000	είκοσι χιλιάδες ikosi khiliathes
50,000	πενήντα χιλιάδες peninda khiliathes
100,000	εκατά χιλιάδες ekato khiliathes
1,000,000	ένα εκατομμύριο ena ekatomirio

Ordinals

1st	πρώτος protos
2nd	δεύτερος thefteros
3rd	τρίτος tritos
4th	τέταρτος tetartos
5th	πέμπτος pemptos
6th	έκτος ektos
7th	έβδομος evthomos
8th	άγδοος ogtho-os
9th	ένατος enatos
10th	δέκατος thekatos

English

→

Greek

a, an enas, mia, ena
about: about 20 peripoo ikosi
a film about Greece ena ergo
ya tin Elatha
above pano apo
abroad sto exoteriko
accept thekhomeh
accident to thistikhima
across: across the road
apenandi sto thromo
adapter to polaplo
(for voltage change) i briza taf
address i thi-efTHinsi
adult (man/woman) o enilikos/i
eniliki
advance: in advance
prokatavolika
after meta
afternoon apo-yevma
aftersun cream to galaktoma
ya ton ilio
afterwards meta
again xana
against enandion
ago: a week ago prin apo mia
evthomatha
AIDS to AIDS
air o a-eras
by air a-eroporikos
air-conditioning o
klimatismos
airmail: by airmail a-
eroporikos
airport to a-erothromio
airport bus to leoforio a-
erothromi-oo

Albania i Alvania
Albanian (adj) Alvanikos
alcohol to alko-ol
all ola
that's all, thanks afta ineh
ola, efkharisto
allergic to ... aleryikos meh ...
all right entaxi
I'm all right imeh entaxi
are you all right? (fam) iseh
entaxi?
(pol) esis entaxi?
almost skhethon
alone monos
alphabet to alfavito
see page 268
already ithi
also episis
always panda
ambulance to asTHenoforo
America i Ameriki
American (adj) Amerikanikos
Ancient Greece i arkhea
Elatha
Ancient Greek ta arkhea
Elinika
and keh
angry THimomenos
animal to zo-o
annoying enokhlitikos
another alos, ali, alo
another beer, please ali mia
bira, parakalo
antiseptic to andisiptiko
any: I don't have any then
ekho kaTHoloo
apartment to thiamerisma
apple to milo
apricot to verikoko

archaeology i arkheoloyia
arm to kheri
arrival i afixi
arrive ftano
art gallery i pinakoTHiki
as: as big as ... megalo san ...
ashtray to tasaki
ask roto
  I didn't ask for this then zitisa afto
aspirin i aspirini
at: at the hotel sto xenothokhio
  at the station sto staTHmo
  at six o'clock stis exi i ora
  at Yanni's stoo Yanni
Athens i ATHina
aunt i THia
Australia i Afstralia
Australian (adj) Afstralezikos
autumn to fTHinoporo
away: go away! fiyeh
awful apesios

B
—

baby to moro
back (of body) i plati
  (back part) piso
  at the back sto piso meros
  I'll be back soon THa yiriso sindoma
bad kakos
badly askhima
bag i tsanda
baggage i aposkeves
baggage checkroom o khoros filaxis aposkevon

bakery o foornaris
balcony to balkoni
ball (large) i bala
  (small) to balaki
banana i banana
band (musical) to singrotima
bandage o epithesmos
Bandaid® to lefkoplast
bank i trapeza
bar to bar
barber's to koorio
basket to kalaTHi
bath to banio
bathroom to lootro, to banio
battery i bataria
be imeh
beach i paralia
beach umbrella i ombrela
beans ta fasolia
  green beans ta fasolakia
beautiful oreos
because epithi
  because of ... exetias ...
bed to krevati
  I'm going to bed now pao ya ipno tora
bed and breakfast thomatio meh pro-ino
bedroom to ipnothomatio
beef to moskhari
beer i bira
before prin
begin arkhizo
  when does it begin? poteh arkhizi?
behind piso
below apo kato
belt i zoni
berth (on ship) i klini

beside the ... thipla sto ...
best aristos
better kaliteros
  better than ... kaliteros
  apo ...
between metaxi
beyond pera apo
bicycle to pothilato
big megalos
bikini to bikini
bill o logariasmos
  (US) to khartonomisma
  could I have the bill, please?
  boro na ekho ton
  logariasmo, parakalo?
bin o skoopithotenekes
bird to pooli
birthday ta yeneTHlia
  happy birthday! khronia
  pola!
biscuit to biskoto
bit: a little bit ligo
  a big bit ena megalo komati
  a bit of ... ligo apo ...
  a bit expensive ligo akrivo,
  akrivootsiko
bite (by insect) to tsibima
black mavros
blanket i kooverta
blind tiflos
blinds ta pantzooria
block of flats i polikatikia
blond xanTHos
blood to ema
blouse i blooza
blow-dry to khtenisma
blue bleh
  blue eyes galana matia
boat (small) to ka-iki

(for passengers) to plio
body to soma
bone to kokalo
book to vivlio
  (verb) klino
bookshop, book store to
  vivliopolio
boot (footwear) i bota
border (of country) ta sinora
borrow thanizomeh
both keh i thio
bottle to bookali
bottle-opener to anikhtiri
bottom (of person) o kolos
  at the bottom of the hill sto
  vaTHos too lofoo
  at the bottom of the road sto
  telos too thromoo
box to kooti
boy to agori
boyfriend o filos
bra to sooti-en
bracelet to vrakhioli
brake to freno
  (verb) frenaro
brandy to koniak
bread to psomi
break spao
breakfast to pro-ino
breast to stiTHos
bridge (over river) i yefira
bring ferno
  I'll bring it back later THa to
  fero piso argotera
Britain i Vretania
British Vretanikos
brochure to prospektoos
broken spasmenos
  it's broken ineh spasmeno

brother o athelfos
brown kafeh
  brown hair kastana malia
  brown eyes kastana matia
brush i voortsa
building to ktirio
bulb (light bulb) i lamba
Bulgaria i Voolgaria
Bulgarian (adj) Voolgarikos
bumper o profilaktiras
bunk i kooketa
burn to kapsimo
burst: a burst pipe mia
  spasmeni solina
bus to leoforio

dialogue

does this bus go to ...?
piyeni afto to leoforio
sto ...?
no, you need a number ...
okhi, prepi na pareteh to
leoforio ariTHmos ...

bus station to praktorio
  leoforion
bus stop i stasi leoforioo
busy (restaurant etc)
  polisikhnastos
but ala
butcher's o khasapis
butter to vootiro
button to koobi
buy agorazo
by: by bus/car meh to
  leoforio/aftokinito
  by the window thipla sto
  paraTHiro

by Thursday prin apo tin
  Pempti

C

cabbage to lakhano
cabin (on ship) i kabina
café i kafeteria, to kafenio
cake to cake
call fonazo
  (to phone) tilefono
  what's it called? pos to
  leneh?
  he/she is called ... ton/tin
  leneh ...
camera i fotografiki mikhani
camp (verb) kataskinono
camping gas to igra-erio
campsite to kambing
can to kooti, i konserva
can: can you ...? boriteh
  na ...?
  can I have ...? boro na
  ekho ...?
  I can't ... then boro ...
Canada o Kanathas
Canadian Kanathezikos
cancel akirono
candies i karameles
candle to keri
can-opener to anikhtiri
car to aftokinito
carafe i karafa
card (birthday etc) i karta
cardphone i tilekarta
car hire enikiasis aftokiniton
car park to parking
carpet to khali

(fitted) i mok**e**ta
carrot to kar**o**to
carry metaf**e**ro
cash ta metrit**a**
cash desk to tam**io**
cash dispenser i mikhan**i** ya
   metrit**a**
cat i g**a**ta
cathedral o kaTHethrik**o**s
   na**o**s
cave i sp**i**lia
ceiling to tav**a**ni
cellar (for wine) to kel**a**ri
centimetre **e**na ekatost**o**
centre to k**e**ndro
certainly s**i**goora
chair i kar**e**kla
champagne i samp**a**nia
change (money) ta r**e**sta
   (verb: money, trains) al**a**zo

dialogue

> **do we have to change**
> **(trains)?** pr**e**pi na
> alaxoomeh tr**e**no?
> **yes, change at Corinth/no,**
> **it's a direct train** neh,
> al**a**xteh stin
> KorinTHo/**o**khi, pi**e**ni
> katefTH**i**an

cheap ftin**o**s
check (verb) epaliTH**e**vo
   (US: cheque) i epitay**i**
   (US: bill) o logariasm**o**s
checkbook to karn**e**h
   epitag**o**n
check-in to check-in

cheers! (toast) stin iy**a** sas!
cheese to tir**i**
chemist's to farmak**io**
cheque i epitay**i**
cheque card i k**a**rta epitag**o**n
chest to st**i**THos
chewing gum i ts**i**khla
chicken to kot**o**poolo
chickenpox i anemovloy**i**a
child to peth**i**
chips i tiganit**e**s pat**a**tes
   (US) ta tsips
chocolate i sokol**a**ta
   a hot chocolate i zest**i**
   sokol**a**ta
Christmas ta khrist**oo**yena
   Christmas Eve i paramon**i**
   ton khristooy**e**non
   merry Christmas! kal**a**
   khrist**oo**yena!
church i eklis**i**a
cicada o tz**i**tzikas
cider cider
cigar to p**oo**ro
cigarette to tsig**a**ro
cinema o kinimatograf**o**s, to
   s**i**nema
city i p**o**li
city centre to k**e**ndro tis p**o**lis
clean (adj) kaTHar**o**s
   can you clean these for me?
   moo plen**e**teh aft**a**?
clever **e**xipnos
clock to rol**o**-i
close (verb) kl**i**no
closed klist**o**s
clothes ta r**oo**kha
clothes peg to mandal**a**ki
cloudy sinefiasm**e**nos

Co

coach (bus) to poolman
(on train) to vagoni
coach station o staTHmos
iperastikon leoforion
coach trip to taxithi meh
poolman
coast i akti
coat (long coat) to palto
(jacket) to sakaki
coathanger i kremastra
code (for phoning) o kothikos
coffee o kafes
coin to kerma
Coke® i koka-kola
cold krios
I'm cold kriono
I have a cold imeh
kriomenos
collar o yakas
collect call tilefono collect
colour to khroma
comb i khtena
come erkhomeh
come back epistrefo
come in beno mesa
comfortable (chair)
anapaftikos
(clothes) anetos
(room, hotel) volikos
complaint to parapono
completely telios
computer o ipolo-yistis
concert i sinavlia
conditioner (for hair) to
kondisioner
condom to profilaktiko
congratulations!
sinkharitiria!
connection (travel) i sinthesi

constipation i thiskiliotis
consulate to proxenio
contact erkhomeh seh epafi
contact lenses i faki epafis
cooker i koozina
cookie to biskoto
Corfu i Kerkira
corkscrew to anikhtiri
correct (right) sostos
cost (verb) stikhizo
cotton vamvaki
cotton wool vamvaki
couchette i kooketa
cough o vikhas
cough medicine to farmako
ya ton vikha
could: could you ...? boriteh
na ...?
could I have ...? boro na
ekho ...?
I couldn't ... (wasn't able to)
then boresa na ...
country (nation) i khora
(countryside) i exokhi
couple (man and woman) to
zevgari
a couple of ... thio apo ...
courier o/i sinothos
course (main course etc) to
piato
of course veveh-a
cousin (male/female) o
xathelfos/
i xathelfi
crazy trelos
cream (on milk, in cake) i
krema
(lotion) i krema thermatos
credit card i pistotiki karta

dialogue

> can I pay by credit card?
> boro na pliroso meh
> pistotiki karta?
> which card do you want to
> use? ti karta THeleteh na
> khrisimopi-iseteh?
> yes, sir entaxi, kiri-eh
> what's the number? ti
> ariTHmo ekhi?
> and the expiry date? keh
> poteh ineh i imerominia
> lixeos?

Crete i Kriti
crisps ta tsips
crossroads to stavrothromi
crowded yematos kosmo
cry (weep) kleo
cup to flidzani
cupboard to doolapi
curtains i koortines
cushion to maxilaraki
Customs to Telonio
cut to kopsimo
 (verb) kovo
 I've cut myself kopika
cutlery ta makheropiroona
cycling i pothilasia
cyclist o/i pothilatis
Cyprus i Kipros

D

dad o babas
damage katastrefo
damn! na pari i oryi!

damp (adj) igros
dance o khoros
 (verb) khorevo
dangerous epikinthinos
dark (colour) skotinos
 (hair) mavros
date: what's the date today?
 poso ekhi o minas simera?
daughter i kori
day i mera
 the day after tin epomeni
 mera
 the day before tin pro-
 igoomeni mera
dead peTHamenos, nekros
deaf koofos
decaffeinated coffee o kafes
 khoris kafe-ini
decide apofasizo
deckchair i poliTHrona, i sez
 long
deep vaTHis
definitely oposthipoteh
delay i kaTHisterisi
delicatessen ta delicatessen
delicious nostimotatos
demotic i dimotiki
dentist o/i othondiatros
deodorant to aposmitiko
department store to megalo
 katastima
departure i anakhorisi
depend: it depends exartateh
dessert to glikisma
destination o pro-orismos
develop anaptiso
 (a film) emfanizo
dialling code o kothikos
 ariTHmos

diarrhoea i thiaria
diesel i dizel
difference i thiafora
different thiaforetikos
difficult thiskolos
dining room i trapezaria
dinner to thipno
direct (adj) kat-efTHian
direction i katefTHinsi
directory enquiries i plirofori-
es
dirty vromikos
disco i diskotek
disgusting a-ithiastikos
district i sinikia
divorced: I'm divorced
(man/woman)
khorismenos/khorismeni
do kano
  what shall we do? ti THa
  kanoomeh?
doctor o/i yatros
dog o skilos
donkey o ga-itharos
don't! mi!
door i porta
double thiplo
double bed to thiplo krevati
double room to thiplo
  thomatio
down kato
  down here etho kato
downstairs kato
dozen mia doozina
draught beer varelisia bira
dress to forema
drink to poto
  (verb) pino
  what would you like to drink?

ti THa THelateh na pi-iteh?
drinking water to posimo
nero
drive othiga-o
driver o/i othigos
driving licence i athia
othiyiseos
drug to farmako
  drugs (narcotics) ta narkotika
drunk (adj) meTHismenos
dry (adj) stegnos
  (wine) xiros
dry-cleaner to stegno-
kaTHaristirio
during kata ti thiarkia
dustbin o skoopithodenekes
duvet to paploma

E

each kaTHeh
ear to afti
early noris
earrings ta skoolarikia
east i anatoli
Easter to Paskha
Easter Sunday i Kiriaki too
Paskha
easy efkolos
eat tro-o
economy class tooristiki
THesi
egg to avgo
either: either ... or ... i ... i ...
elbow o angonas
electric ilektrikos
electricity to ilektriko revma
elevator to asanser

else: something else kati alo
  somewhere else kapoo aloo
embassy i presvia
emergency i ektakti anangi
empty (adj) athios
end to telos
  (verb) teliono
  at the end of the street sto
  telos too thromoo
  when does it end? poteh
  telioni?
engaged (toilet, telephone)
  katilimenos
  (to be married: man/woman)
  aravoniasmenos/aravoniasm
  eni
England i Anglia
English ta Anglika
enjoy: to enjoy oneself
  thiaskethazo
enormous terastios
enough arketa
  it's not big enough then ineh
  arketa megalo
  that's enough ftani, arki
entrance i isothos
envelope o fakelos
equipment o exoplismos
especially ithika
euro to evro
Eurocheque to Eurocheque
Europe i Evropi
evening to vrathi
  this evening simera to
  vrathi
eventually telika
ever poteh
every kaTHeh
everyone oli

everything kaTHeh ti
everywhere pandoo
exactly! akrivos!
excellent exokhos
  excellent! exokha!
except ektos
exchange rate sinalagmatiki
  isotimia
exciting sinarpastikos
excuse me (to get past)
  signomi
  (to get attention) parakalo
exhibition i ekTHesi
exit i exothos
expensive akrivos
eye to mati
eyeglasses ta yialia

F

face to prosopo
faint (verb) lipoTHimao
fair (funfair) to paniyiri
  (trade) i ekTHesi
  (adj) thikeos
fairly arketa
fall (US) to fThinoporo
fall (verb) pefto
family i iko-yenia
fantastic fandastikos
far makria

dialogue

  is it far from here? ineh
  makria apo etho?
  no, not very far okhi, okhi
  keh poli makria

it's about 20 kilometres
ineh peripoo ikosi
khiliometra

farm to agroktima
fashionable tis mothas
fast grigoros
fat (person) pakhis
father o pateras
faucet i vrisi
fault to elatoma
  sorry, it was my fault
  signomi, itan sfalma moo
favourite agapimenos
fax to fax
feel esTHanomeh
  I feel unwell then
  esTHanomeh kala
felt-tip pen o markathoros
ferry to feri bot
fetch pa-o na fero
  I'll fetch him THa pa-o na
  ton fero
few: a few liyi, liyes, liga
  a few days liyes meres
fiancé o aravoniastikos
fiancée i aravoniastikia
field to khorafi
fight o agonas
figs ta sika
filling (in tooth) to sfra-yisma
film to film
find vrisko
find out anakalipto
fine (weather) oreos
  (punishment) to prostimo
finger to thakhtilo
finish teliono
fire i pirkaya

fire brigade i pirosvestiki
  ipiresia
first protos
  at first stin arkhi
first aid kit to kooti proton
  vo-iTHi-on
first class (travel etc) proti
  THesi
first floor to proto patoma
  (US) to iso-yio
first name to onoma
fish to psari
fisherman o psaras
fit: it doesn't fit me then moo
  khora-i
fix ftiakhno
  (arrange) kanonizo
fizzy meh anTHrakiko
flat (apartment) to thiamerisma
  (adj) epipethos
  I've got a flat tyre me epiaseh
  lastikho
flavour i gefsi
flight i ptisi
flight number ariTHmos ptisis
floor (of room) to patoma
  (of building) o orofos
  on the floor sto patoma
florist o anTHopolis
flower to looloothi
flu i gripi
fluent: he speaks fluent Greek
  mila-i aptesta elinika
fly i miga
  (verb) peto
food to fa-yito
foot to pothi
  on foot meh ta pothia
football (game) to pothosfero

(ball) i bala
for ya
  **do you have something
  for ...?** (headache/diarrhoea etc)
  ekheteh kati ya ...?
foreign xenos
foreigner (man/woman) o
  xenos/i xeni
forest to thasos
forget xekhno
  I forget xekhno
  I've forgotten xekhasa
fork (for eating) to pirooni
fortnight to theka-
  penTHimero
forwarding address i thi-
  efTHinsi apostolis
fountain i piyi
foyer to foyer
free elefTHeros
  (no charge) thorean
freeway i eTHniki othos
French (adj) galikos
  (language) ta galika
French fries i tiganites patates
frequent sikhnos
fresh (weather, breeze) throseros
  (fruit etc) freskos
fridge to psiyio
fried tiganismenos
friend (male/female) o filos/i fili
friendly filikos
from apo
  from Monday to Friday apo
  theftera os Paraskevi
  from next Thursday apo tin
  ali Pempti
front: in front of the hotel
  mbrosta apo to

xenothokhio
  at the front sto mbrostino
  meros
fruit ta froota
fruit juice o khimos frooton
full yematos
full board fool pansion
fun: it was fun kala itan
funeral i kithia
funny (strange) paraxenos
  (amusing) astios
further parapera
future: in future sto melon

G

game (cards etc) to pekhnithi
  (match) o agonas
garage (for fuel) to
  venzinathiko
  (for repairs) to sineryio
  (for parking) to garaz
garden o kipos
garlic to skortho
gas to gazi
  (US) i venzini
gas station to venzinathiko
gate i avloporta
  (at airport) i exothos
gay (adj) omofilofilos
gents (toilet) i too-aleta ton
  anthron
Germany i Yermania
get (fetch) perno
  how do I get to ...? pos boro
  na pao sto ...?
get back (return) epistrefo
get off kateveno

where do I get off? poo THa katevo?

get on (to train etc) aneveno

get out (of car etc) vyeno

get up (in the morning) sikonomeh

gift to thoro

gin to tzin

a gin and tonic ena tzin meh tonik

girl to koritsi

girlfriend i filenatha

give thino

give back epistrefo, thino piso

glad efkharistimenos

glass (material) to yali

(tumbler, wine glass) to potiri

a glass of wine ena potiri krasi

glasses ta yalia

go pao

where are you going? poo pateh?

where does this bus go? poo pa-i afto to leoforio?

let's go! pameh

she's gone (left) efiyeh

hamburger to go khamboorger ya to spiti

go away fevgo

go away! fiyeh!

go back (return) epistrefo

go down (the stairs etc) kateveno

go in beno

go out (in the evening) v-yeno

go through thiaskhizo, pao thia mesoo

go up (the stairs etc) aneveno

God o THeos

gold o khrisos

good kalos

good! kala!

it's no good (product etc) afto then ineh kalo

(not worth trying) then ofeli

goodbye ya khara, adio

good evening kalispera

good morning kalimera

good night kalinikhta

got: we've got to ... prepi na ...

I've got to ... prepi na ...

have you got any ...? ekheteh kaTHoloo ...?

gradually siga-siga

gram(me) ena gramario

grapefruit to grapefruit

grapes ta stafilia

grass to khortari

grateful evgnomon

great (excellent) poli kalo

Greece i Elatha

Greek (adj) Elinikos

(language) ta Elinika

(man) o Elinas

(woman) i Elinitha

the Greeks i Elines

Greek coffee Elinikos kafes

Greek-Cypriot (adj) Elinokiprios

Greek Orthodox Elinikos OrTHothoxos

green prasinos

greengrocer's o manavis

grey grizos

grilled psitos sti skhara

grocer's to bakaliko
ground: on the ground sto
 ethafos
ground floor to iso-yio
group to groop
guest (man/woman) o
 filoxenoomenos/i
 filoxenoomeni
guesthouse i pansion
guide o/i xenagos
guidebook o tooristikos
 othigos
guided tour i xenayisi

H

hair ta malia
haircut (man's) to koorema
 (woman's) to kopsimo
hairdresser's to komotirio
 (men's) to koorio
hairdryer to pistolaki
half misos
 half an hour misi ora
 half a litre miso litro
half board demi-pansion
half-bottle miso bookali
half price misotimis
ham to zambon
hamburger to khamboorger
hand to kheri
handbag i tsanda
hand luggage to sakvooa-yaz
hangover o ponokefalos
happen simveni
 what has happened? ti
 sinevi?
happy eftikhismenos

harbour to limani
hard skliros
 (difficult) thiskolos
hardly meta vias
 hardly ever s-khethon poteh
hardware shop ta ithi
 kingalerias
hat to kapelo
hate miso
have ekho
 can I have a ...? boro na
 ekho ena ...?
 do you have ...? ekheteh ...?
 do I have to ...? prepi na ...?
hayfever aler-yia sti yiri
he aftos
head to kefali
headache o ponokefalos
headlights i provolis
hear akoo-o
heat i zesti
heater i THermansi
 (radiator) to kalorifer
heating i THermansi
heavy varis
heel (of foot) i fterna
 (of shoe) to takooni
hello ya sas
 (familiar) ya soo
 (on phone) embros
help i vo-iTHia
 (verb) vo-iTHo
help! vo-iTHia!
 can you help me? boriteh na
 meh vo-iTHiseteh?
her: I haven't seen her then
 tin ekho thi
 to her saftin
 for her yaftin

that's her afti ineh
that's her towel afti ineh i
   petseta tis
herbal tea tsa-i too voonoo
here etho
   here is/are ... na ...
   here you are (offering) oristeh
hers thiko tis
hey! eh!
hi! ya soo
high psilos
highway i eTHniki othos
hill o lofos
him: I haven't seen him then
   ton ekho thi
   to him safton
   for him yafton
   that's him aftos ineh
hip o gofos
hire niki-azo
   for hire eniki-azonteh
his: it's his car ineh to
   aftokinito too
   that's his ineh thiko too
hitch-hike kano otostop
holiday i thiakopes
   on holiday seh thiakopes
home to spiti
   at home (in my house etc) sto
   spiti
   (in my country) stin patritha
   moo
   we go home tomorrow
   piyeno stin patritha moo
   avrio
horrible friktos
horse to alogo
hospital to nosokomio
hot zestos

(spicy) kafteros, kaftos
   I'm hot zestenomeh
hotel to xenothokhio
hour i ora
house to spiti
house wine to krasi too
   magazioo
how pos
   how many? posi?
   how do you do? khero poli

dialogue

> how are you? pos iseh?
> fine, thanks, and you? poli
> kala, efkharisto; ki esi?
>
> how much is it? poso kani
> afto?
> 5000 drachmas pendeh
> khiliathes thrakhmes
> I'll take it THa to paro

hungry pinasmenos
hurry: I'm in a hurry viazomeh
hurt: it hurts pona-i
husband o sizigos

I

I ego
ice o pagos
   with ice meh pago
ice cream to pagoto
iced coffee to frapeh
ice lolly to pagoto xilaki
idiot o vlakas
if an

ill arostos
immediately amesos
important spootheos
impossible athinaton
in: it's in the centre ineh sto kendro
in my car mesa sto aftokinito moo
in Athens stin ATHina
in May sto Ma-io
in English sta Anglika
is he in? ineh eki?
in five minutes seh pendeh lepta
include: does that include meals? afto perilamvani keh fayito?
indigestion i thispepsia
indoors mesa
information i plirofori-es
injured travmatismenos
insect to endomo
inside mesa
  inside the hotel mesa sto xenothokhio
instead andi
  instead of ... sti THesi too ...
intelligent exipnos
interesting enthiaferon
international thi-ethnis
interpreter o/i thi-ermineas
intersection to stavrothromi
into mesa
  I'm not into ... then moo aresi ...
introduce sistino
  may I introduce ...? boro na sas sistiso ton ...?
invitation i prosklisi

Ionian Sea to I-onio pelagos
Ireland i Irlanthia
Irish Irlanthos
iron (for ironing) to ilektriko sithero
island to nisi
it afto
  it is ... ineh ...
  is it ...? ineh ...?
  where is it? poo ineh?
  it was ... itan ...

J

jacket to sakaki
jam i marmelatha
jeans ta tzins
jellyfish i tsookhtra
jewellery ta kosmimata
job i thoolia
joke to astio
journey to taxithi
  have a good journey! kalo taxithi!
juice o khimos
jumper to poolover
just (only) monon
  just two mono thio
  just for me mono ya mena
  just here akrivos etho

K

keep krato
  keep the change krata ta resta
key to klithi

kilo ena kilo
kilometre ena khiliometro
kind (generous) evyenikos
kiss to fili
(verb) filao
kitchen i koozina
knee to gonato
knife to makheri
knock down khtipo
know (somebody) gnorizo
(something, a place) xero
I don't know then xero
I didn't know that then to
ixera

L

ladies' room i too-aleta ton
yinekon
lady i kiria
lager i bira
lake i limni
lamb (meat) to arni
lamp i lamba
language i glosa
large megalos
last telefteos
last week i perasmeni
evthomatha
last Friday tin perasmeni
Paraskevi
last night kh-THes vrathi
late arga
later argotera
I'll come back later THa
yiriso argotera
laugh yelo
launderette, laundromat to

plindirio rookhon
laundry (clothes) i boogatha
lawyer o/i thikigoros
leaflet to thiafimistiko
leak i thiaro-i
learn maTHeno
least: at least toolakhiston
leather to therma
leave (bag etc) afino
(go away) fevgo
(forget) xekhnao
I am leaving tomorrow fevgo
avrio
may I leave this here? boro
nafiso afto etho?
I left my coat in the bar afisa
tin tsanda moo sto bar
left aristera
left luggage (office) o khoros
filaxis aposkevon
leg to pothi
lemon to lemoni
lemonade i lemonatha
lend thanizo
less ligotero
less expensive ligotero
akrivo
lesson to maTHima
let (allow) epitrepo
let off: will you let me off at ...?
THa meh katevaseteh
sto ...?
letter to grama
letterbox to gramatokivotio
lettuce to marooli
library i vivlioTHiki
licence i athi-a
lift (in building) to asanser
could you give me a lift?

boriteh na meh pateh?
light to fos
(not heavy) elafros
do you have a light? (for cigarette) ekhis fotia?
light bulb i lamba
lighter (cigarette) o anaptiras
like moo aresi
I like it moo aresi afto
I don't like it then moo aresi afto
I'd like a beer THa iTHela mia bira
would you like a drink? THa iTHeles ena poto?
what's it like? meh ti miazi?
I want one like this THelo ena san ki afto
line (on paper) i grami
(phone) i tilefoniki grami
lips ta khilia
listen akoo-o
litre ena litro
little mikros
just a little, thanks ligo mono, efkharisto
a little milk ligo gala
live zo
loaf i fradzola
local dopios
a local wine ena dopio krasi?
lock i klitharia
(verb) klithono
lock out: I've locked myself out klithoTHika apexo
locker (for luggage etc) i THiritha

London to LonTHino
long makris
how long does it take? posi ora kani?
a long time poli ora
one day/two days longer mia mera/thio meres parapano
look: look out! prosexe!
can I have a look? boro na tho?
look after prosekho, frondizo
look at kitazo
look for psakhno
I'm looking for ... psakhno ya ...
look forward to perimeno meh khara
lorry to fortigo
lose khano
I've lost my way ekho khaTHi
I've lost my bag ekhasa tin tsanda moo
lost property (office) to grafio apolesTHendon
lot: a lot, lots pola
not a lot okhi pola
a lot of people poli anTHropi
loud thinatos
lounge to saloni
love i agapi
(verb) agapo
lovely oreos
low khamilos
luck i tikhi
good luck! kali tikhi!
luggage i aposkeves

lunch to yevma

M

Macedonia i Makethonia
mad (insane) trelos
magazine to periothiko
maid (in hotel) i servitora
mail ta gramata, to
takhithromio
(verb) takhithromo
mailbox to gramatokivotio
main kirios
main course to kirio piato
Mainland Greece i Ipirotiki
Elatha
main road (in town) o
kendrikos thromos
(in country) o aftokinito-
thromos
make (verb) kano
make-up to make-up
man o andras
manager o thi-efTHindis, o
manager
can I see the manager? boro
na tho ton thi-efTHindi?
many pola
map o khartis
market i agora
marmalade i marmelatha
married: I'm married (said by a
man/woman) imeh
pandremenos/pandremeni
mascara i maskara
match (football etc) to mats, o
agonas
matches ta spirta

matter: it doesn't matter then
pirazi
what's the matter? ti
simveni?
mattress to stroma
may: may I see it? boro na to
tho?
maybe isos
mayonnaise i ma-yoneza
me emena
that's for me afto ineh ya
mena
me too ki ego episis
meal to fa-yito
mean: what does it mean? ti
simeni?
meat to kreas
medicine to farmako
medium (adj: size) metrios
medium-dry imixiro krasi
medium-rare misopsimeno
mend thiorTHono
men's room i too-aleta ton
anthron
mention: don't mention it
parakalo
menu to menoo
message to minima
metre to metro
midday to mesimeri
middle: in the middle sti mesi
midnight ta mesanikhta
milk to gala
mind: never mind then pirazi
mine: it's mine ineh thiko
moo
mineral water to
emfialomeno nero
minute to lepto

just a minute ena lepto

mirror o kaTHreftis

Miss thespinis

miss khano

missing lipi

there's a suitcase missing lipi
mia valitsa

mistake to laTHos

Modern Greek ta Nea Elinika

monastery to monastiri

money ta lefta

month o minas

moped to mikhanaki

more perisoteros

can I have some more water,
please? akomi ligo nero,
parakalo

more expensive pio akrivo

more than 50 perisotero apo
peninda

morning to pro-i

this morning simera to pro-i

most: most of the time
siniTHos

mother i mitera

motorbike i motosikleta

motorway i eTHniki othos

mountain to voono

mouse to pondiki

mouth to stoma

movie to film

movie theater o kinimato-
grafos, to sinema

Mr kiri-eh

Mrs kiria

Ms thespinis

much poli

much better/much worse
poli kalitera/poli khirotera

much hotter poli pio zesta

not much okhi poli

mum i mama

museum to moosio

mushrooms ta manitaria

music i moosiki

must: I must ... prepi na ...

mustard i moostartha

my o/i/to ... moo

myself: I'll do it myself THa to
kano o ithios

by myself apo monos moo

N

nail (finger) to nikhi

name to onoma

my name's John meh leneh
John

what's your name? pos seh
leneh?

napkin i petseta

narrow (street) stenos

nasty (person) apesios

(weather, accident) askhimos

national eTHnikos

natural fisikos

near konda

where is the nearest ...? poo
ineh to plisi-estero ...?

nearly skhethon

necessary aparetitos,
anangeos

neck o lemos

necklace to koli-e

necktie i gravata

need: I need ...
khriazomeh ...

needle i velona
neither: neither ... nor ... ooteh ... ooteh ...
nephew o anipsios
never poteh
new neos, kenooryos
news (radio, TV etc) ta nea
newsagent's to praktorio efimerithon
newspaper i efimeritha
New Year to neo etos
  Happy New Year! eftikhismenos o kenooryos khronos!
New Year's Eve i protokhronia
New Zealand i Nea Zilanthia
next epomenos
  next week tin ali evthomatha
  next to thipla apo
nice (food) nostimos
  (looks, view etc) oreos
  (person) kalos
niece i anipsia
night i nikhta
no okhi

  I've no change then ekho psila
  there's no ... left then emineh kaTHoloo ...
nobody kanenas
noisy: it's too noisy ekhi poli fasaria
non-alcoholic khoris alko-ol
none kanis
nonsmoking compartment o khoros ya mi kapnizondes
no-one kanenas

nor: nor do I ooteh kego
normal fisiolo-yikos
north o voras
northeast o vorio-anatolikos
northwest o vorio-thitikos
Northern Ireland i Vorios Irlanthia
nose i miti
not then
  no, I'm not hungry okhi, then pina-o
  not that one okhi afto
note (banknote) to khartonomisma
nothing tipoteh
  nothing else tipoteh alo
now tora
number o ariTHmos
nuts to karithi

O

o'clock i ora
odd (strange) paraxenos
of too
off (lights) klisto
  it's just off Omonia Square ligo pio eki apo tin Omonia
often sikhna
  how often are the buses? kaTHeh poteh ekhi leoforia?
oil (for car) ta lathia
  (for salad) to lathi
ointment i alifi
OK entaxi
  are you OK? iseh kala?

that's OK thanks (it doesn't matter) ineh entaxi, efkharisto

I'm OK (nothing for me) tipoteh ya mena

(I feel OK) imeh mia khara

old (person) yeros

(thing) palios

olive oil to eleolatho

olives i eli-es

omelette i omeleta

on pano

(lights) anikhto

on television stin tileorasi

I haven't got it on me then to ekho mazi moo

what's on tonight? ti pezi simera?

once (one time) mia fora

at once (immediately) amesos

one enas, mia, ena

the white one to aspro

one-way ticket ena aplo

onion to kremithi

only mono

it's only 6 o'clock ineh mono exi i ora

open (adj) aniktos

(verb) anigo

operator (telephone: man/woman) o tilefonitis/i tilefonitria

opposite: opposite my hotel apenandi apo to xenothokhio moo

or i

orange (fruit) to portokali

(colour) portokali

orange juice i portokalatha

order: can we order now?

boroomeh na paragiloomeh tora?

ordinary kanonikos

other alos, ali, alo

the other one to alo

our o/i/to ... mas

ours thikos mas

out: he's out then ineh etho

outdoors exo

outside ... exo ...

over: over here etho

over there eki, eki pera

over 500 pano apo pendakosia

overnight (travel) oloniktio

own: my own ... thiko moo ...

P

pack (verb) ftiakhno tis valitses

a pack of ... ena paketo ...

package (parcel) to paketo

pain o ponos

I have a pain here esTHanomeh ena pono etho

painful othiniros

painkillers to pafsipono

pair: a pair of ... ena zevgari ...

panties to slip, i kilotes

pants (underwear: men's) to sovrako

(women's) to slip, i kilotes

(US: trousers) to pandaloni

pantyhose to kalson

paper to kharti

(newspaper) i efimeriTHa

parcel to thema
pardon (me)? (didn't understand/hear) pardon!, signomi?
parents: my parents i gonis moo
park to parko
(verb) parkaro
parking lot to parking
part to meros
partner (boyfriend) o filos (girlfriend) i fili
party (group) i omatha (celebration) to parti
passport to thiavatirio
past: just past the information office amesos meta to grafio pliroforion
pavement to pezothromio
pay plirono
can I pay, please? boro na pliroso, parakalo?
pay phone to tilefono meh kermata
peach to rothakino
peanuts fistikia arapika
pear to akhlathi
peas ta bizelia
pen to stilo
pencil to molivi
people i anTHropi
pepper (spice) to piperi (vegetable) i piperia
per: per night tin vrathia
per cent tis ekato
perfume to aroma
perhaps isos
person to atomo
petrol i venzini

petrol station to venzinathiko
pharmacy to farmakio
phone to tilefono
(verb) perno tilefono, tilefono
phone book o tilefonikos katalogos
phonecard i tilekarta
phone number o ariTHmos tilefonoo
photo i fotografia
picture i ikona
piece to komati
pill to khapi
pillow to maxilari
pineapple o ananas
pink roz
place to meros
at your place (fam) esi soo (pol) sti THesi sas
plane to a-eroplano
plant to fito
plasters to lefkoplast
plastic bag i plastiki sakoola
plate to piato
plate-smashing spasimo pi-aton
platform i platforma
which platform is for Patras, please? pia platforma ya tin Patra, parakalo?
play (in theatre) to THeatriko ergo
(verb) pezo
pleasant efkharistos
please parakalo
yes please neh, parakalo
plenty: plenty of ... poli/ pola ...

plug (electrical) i briza
  (in sink) i tapa
poisonous thilitiriothis
police i astinomia
policeman o astifilakas
police station to astinomiko
  tmima
polite evgenikos
polluted molismenos
pool (for swimming) i pisina
pork to khirino
port (for boats) to limani
possible thinatos
  is it possible to ...? ineh
  thinaton na ...?
  as ... as possible oso to
  thinaton ...
post (mail) ta gramata
  (verb) takhithromo
postcard i kartpostal
postcode o takhithromikos
  kothikos
post office to takhithromio
poste restante post restand
potato i patata
potato chips ta tsips
pottery ta keramika
pound (money) i lira
  (weight) i libra
prefer: I prefer ... protimo ...
pregnant engios
prescription (for chemist) i
  sindayi
present (gift) to thoro
pretty (beautiful) omorfos,
  oreos
  (quite) arketa
price i timi
private ithiotikos

probably piTHanon
problem to provlima
  no problem! kanena
  provlima!
pronounce: how is this
  pronounced? pos to proferis
  afto?
public holiday i thimosia arya
pull travao
purple mov
purse (for money) to portofoli
  (US: handbag) i tsanda
push sprokhno
put vazo
pyjamas i pitzames

Q

quarter to tetarto
question i erotisi
queue i oora
quick grigora
quickly grigora
quiet (place, hotel) isikhos
  quiet! siopi!
quite (fairly) arketa
  (very) telios
  quite a lot arketa

R

radiator (in room) to kalorifer
  (of car) to psiyio aftokinitoo
radio to rathiofono
rail: by rail sithirothromikos
railway o sithirothromos
rain i vrokhi

it's raining vrekhi
rape o viasmos
rare (steak) okhi poli
  psimeno
raspberry to vatomooro
rather: I'd rather ... THa
  protimoosa na ...
razor (dry) to xirafaki
  (electric) i xiristiki mikhani
read thiavazo
ready etimos
real pragmatikos
really pragmatika
  (very) poli
receipt i apothixi
recently prosfata
reception (in hotel) i resepsion
  (for guests) i thexiosi
receptionist i/o resepsionist
recommend: could you
  recommend ...? boriteh na
  moo sististeh ...?
red kokinos
red wine to kokino krasi
refund i epistrofi
  khrimaton
region i periokhi
registered: by registered mail
  sistimeno
remember: I don't remember
  then THimameh
rent (for apartment etc) to
  enikio
  (verb) niki-azo
repair i episkevi
repeat epanalamvano
reservation (train, bus) to
  klisimo THesis
reserve krato

dialogue

can I reserve a table for
tonight? boro na kliso ena
trapezi ya apopseh?
yes madam, for how many
people? malista, kiria
moo; ya posa atoma?
for two ya thio
and for what time? keh ya
ti ora?
for eight o'clock ya tis
okhto
and could I have your
name please? to onoma
sas, parakalo?

restaurant to estiatorio
rest room i too-aleta
return: a return to ... ena
  isitirio met epistrofis ya
  to ...
reverse charge call to
  tilefonima kolekt
Rhodes i Rothos
rice to rizi
right (correct) sostos
  (not left) thexia
  that's right sosta
ring (on finger) to thaktilithi
ring back THa seh paro piso
river to potami
road (country) o thromos
  (in town) i othos
  is this the road for ...? ineh
  aftos o thromos ya ...?
rob: I've been robbed meh
  listepsan
roll (bread) to psomaki

roof i orofi, i steyi
 (flat) i taratsa
room to thomatio
 (space) to meros

dialogue

> do you have any rooms?
> ekheteh kaTHoloo
> thomatia?
> for how many people? ya
> posa atoma?
> for one/for two ya ena/ya
> thio
> yes, we have some
> vacancies neh,
> ekhoomeh elefTHera
> thomatia
> for how many nights will it
> be? ya posa vrathia to
> THeleteh?
> just for one night mono ya
> ena vrathi
> how much is it? poso
> kani?
> ... drachmas with
> bathroom and ... drachmas
> without bathroom ...
> thrakhmes meh mbanio
> keh ... thrakhmes khoris
> mbanio
> can I see a room with
> bathroom? boro na tho
> ena thomatio meh
> mbanio?
> OK, I'll take it entaxi, THa
> to paro

room service to servis

thomatioo
rosé (wine) to rozeh
round trip ticket ena isitirio
 met epistrofis
route i poria
rubbish (waste) ta skoopithia
 (poor quality goods) kaki piotita
rucksack to sakithio
rude a-yenis
rum to roomi
run (person) trekho

S

sad lipimenos
safe (not in danger) asfalis
 (not dangerous) akinthinos,
 avlavis
salad i salata
salad dressing to lathoxitho
sale: for sale politeh
Salonika i THesaloniki
salt to alati
same: the same o ithios
 the same again, please to
 ithio xana, parakalo
sand i amos
sandals ta santhalia
sandwich to sandwich
sanitary napkins i servi-etes
sauce i saltsa
saucepan i katsarola
sausage to lookaniko
say: how do you say ... in
 Greek? pos to leneh ... sta
 Elinika?
 what did he say? ti ipeh?
scarf (for neck) to kaskol

(for head) to mandili
schedule (US) to programa
school to skholio
scissors: a pair of scissors to psalithi
Scotch tape® to sellotape®
Scotland i Skotia
Scottish Skotsezikos
sea i THalasa
 by the sea konda sti THalasa
seafood ta THalasina
seasick: I feel seasick esthanomeh naftia
seat i THesi
 is this anyone's seat? ineh kanenos afti i THesi?
second (of time) to theftero-lepto
 (adj) thefteros
second class (travel) thefteri THesi
see vlepo, kitazo
 can I see? boro na tho?
 have you seen ...? ekhis thi ...?
 see you! ta xanalemeh!
 I see (I understand) katalava
self-catering apartment to anexartito thiamerisma
self-service self-servis
sell poolo
Sellotape® to sellotape®
send stelno
separated: I'm separated imeh khorismenos/khorismeni
separately (pay, travel) xekhorista
serious sovaros

service station to venzinathiko
serviette i petseta
set menu to tabl-dot
several arketi
sex to sex
shade: in the shade sti skia
shampoo to samboo-an
share (verb: room, table etc) mirazomeh
shaver i xiristiki mikhani
shaving foam o afros xirismatos
she afti
sheet (for bed) to sendoni
shellfish ta ostraka
ship to plio
shirt to pookamiso
shit! skata!
shoe to papootsi
shoelaces ta korthonia papootsion
shoe polish to verniki papootsion
shoe repairer o tsangaris
shop to magazi
short (person) kondos
 (time) ligos
 (journey) sindomos
shorts to sorts
should: what should I do? ti prepi na kano?
shoulder o omos
show (in theatre) to ergo
 could you show me? boriteh na moo thixeteh?
shower (in bathroom) to doos
 (rain) i bora
shut (verb) klino

when do you shut? poteh
klineteh?
they're shut ineh klista
shut up! skaseh!
shutter (on window) to exofilo
sick (ill) arostos
side i plevra
side salad i salata ya
garnitoora
sidewalk to pezothromio
sight: the sights of ... ta
axioTHeata too ...
silk to metaxi
silly ano-itos
silver to asimi
since: since yesterday apo
kh-THes
sing tragootho
single monos
  a single to ... ena aplo ya ...
  I'm single imeh
  elefTHeros/elefTHeri
single bed to mono krevati
single room to mono
  thomatio
sister i athelfi
sit: can I sit here? boro na
kaTHiso etho?
sit down kaTHomeh
site to axioTHeato
  (archaeological) arkheoloyikos
  khoros
size to meh-yeTHos
skin to therma
skirt i foosta
sky o ooranos
sleep (verb) kimameh
sleeping bag to sleeping bag
sleeping car i klinamaxa

slow argos
  slow down! pio arga
slowly siga-siga
small mikros
smell: it smells (smells bad)
  vroma-i
smile (verb) khamo-yelo
smoke o kapnos
  do you mind if I smoke? sas
  pirazi an kapniso?
  I don't smoke then kapnizo
snake to fithi
snow to khioni
so: it's so good ineh poli
  kalo
  not so fast okhi toso grigora
  so am I keh ego to ithio
  so do I keh ego epsis
soap to sapooni
soap powder to
  aporipandiko
sober xemeTHistos
socks i kaltses
soda (water) i sotha
soft (material etc) apalos
soft drink to anapsiktiko
sole i sola
some: can I have some
  water/rolls? moo thineteh
  ligo nero?/liga psomakia?
somebody kapios
something kati
sometimes merikes fores
somewhere kapoo
son o yos
song to tragoothi
soon sindoma
sore: it's sore ineh
  ereTHismeno

sorry: (I'm) sorry signomi
  sorry? (didn't understand/hear)
  pardon?, signomi?
sort: what sort of ...? ti
  ithos ...?
soup i soopa
south notos
  south of noti-a
  to the south noti-a
South Africa i Noti-os Afriki
South African (adj) Notio-
  afrikanos
southeast notio-anatolikos
southwest notio-thitikos
souvenir to enTHimio
Spain i Ispania
speak: do you speak English?
  milateh Anglika?
  I don't speak ... then milo ...
spectacles ta yali-a
spend xothevo
spoon to kootali
spring (season) i anixi
square (in town) i platia
stairs ta skalopatia, i skales
stamp to gramatosimo
start i arkhi, to xekinima
  (verb) arkhizo
  the car won't start to
  aftokinito then xekina
starter (food) to proto piato
starving: I'm starving
  peTHeno tis pinas
station o staTHmos
stay: where are you staying?
  poo meneteh?
  I'm staying at ... meno sto ...
  I'd like to stay another two
  nights THa iTHela na mino

ales thio nikhtes
steak i brizola
steal klevo
  my bag has been stolen
  klepsaneh tin tsanda moo
steep (hill) apotomos
still: I'm still waiting akoma
  perimeno
stomach to stomakhi
stomach ache o ponos sto
  stomakhi
stone (rock) i petra
stop stamatao
  please, stop here (to taxi driver
  etc) parakalo, stamatisteh
  etho
storm i THi-ela
straight: it's straight ahead
  ineh olo efTHia
strange (odd) paraxenos
strawberry i fraoola
street o thromos
string o spangos
strong thinatos
stuck frakarismenos
student i fititis, i fititria
stupid vlakas
suburb ta pro-astia
subway (US) o ipo-yios
suddenly xafnika
sugar i zakhari
suit (man's) to koostoomi
  (woman's) to ta-yer
suitcase i valitsa
summer to kalokeri
  in the summer to kalokeri
sun o ilios
  in the sun ston ilio
sunblock (cream) to andiliako

sunburn to kapsimo apo ton ilio
sunglasses ta yalia ilioo
sunstroke i ili-asi
suntanned iliokamenos
suntan oil to lathi mavrismatos
supermarket to supermarket
supper to thipno
supplement (extra charge) epipleon, to prosTHeto
sure: are you sure? iseh sigooros?
 sure! veveos!
surname to epiTHeto
sweater to poolover
sweet (taste) glikos
 (dessert) to gliko
sweets i karameles
swim kolimbao
 I'm going for a swim pao ya kolibi
swimming costume to ma-yo
swimming pool i pisina
swimming trunks to ma-yo
switch o thiakoptis
switch off (TV, lights) klino
switch on (TV, lights) anigo

T

table to trapezi
table wine to epitrapezio krasi
take perno
 (accept) thekhomeh
 fine, I'll take it entaxi THa to paro

hamburger to take away khamboorger ya to spiti
talk (verb) milo
tall psilos
tampons ta tabon
tan to mavrisma
tap i vrisi
taste i yefsi
taxi to taxi

dialogue

to the airport/to the Hilton Hotel please sto a-erothromio/sto xenothokhio Khilton, parakalo
how much will it be? poso THa stikhisi?
1,500 drachmas khili-es pendakosi-es thrakmes
that's fine, right here, thanks entaxi, etho pera ineh, efkharisto

tea to tsa-i
teacher (man/woman) o thaskalos/i thaskala
telephone to tilefono
television i tileorasi
tell: could you tell him ...? boriteh na too piteh ...?
temple (church) o na-os
tennis to tennis
terrible foveros
terrific exeretikos
than apo
thanks, thank you efkharisto
 thank you very much

efkharisto para poli
no thanks okhi efkharisto

dialogue

thanks efkharisto
that's OK, don't mention it
parakalo, then kani
tipoteh

that ekinos, ekini, ekino
 that one ekino
 that's nice ti orea!
 is that ...? afto ineh ...?
the o, i, to; (pl) i, i, ta
theatre to THeatro
their o/i/to ... toos
theirs thiki toos
them toos, tis, ta
 for them ya ekinoos
 who? – them pi-i? – afti
then (after that) katopin
there eki
 is there ...? iparkhi ...?
 there is ... iparkhi ...
 are there ...? iparkhoon ...?
 there are ... iparkhoon ...
 there you are (giving something)
 oristeh
these afti, aftes, afta
 can I have these? boro na
 ekho afta?
Thessaly i THesalia
they afti, aftes, afta
thick pakhis
thief (man/woman) o kleftis/i
 kleftra
thin leptos
 (person) athinatos

thing to pragma
 my things ta pragmata moo
think skeptomeh
 (believe) nomizo
 I'll think about it THa to
 skepto
thirsty: I'm thirsty thipso
this aftos, afti, afto
 this one afto etho
 is this ...? ineh ...?
those ekini, ekines, ekina
 which ones? – those pi-a? –
 afta
Thrace i THraki
thread i klosti
throat o lemos
through thiamesoo
thumb o andikhiras
thunderstorm i kateyitha, i
 THi-ela
ticket to isitirio

dialogue

a return to Athens ena
isitirio epistrofis ya tin
ATHina
coming back when? poteh
ineh i epistrofi?
today/next Tuesday
simera/tin epomeni Triti
that will be 2,000
drachmas please thio
khiliathes thrakhmes,
parakalo

tie (necktie) i gravata
tights to kalson
time o khronos

(occasion) i fora
what's the time? ti ora ineh?
next time tin epomeni fora
four times teseris fores
timetable to programa
tin (can) i konserva
tin-opener to anikhtiri
tip (to waiter etc) to filothorima
tired koorasmenos
tissues ta khartomandila
to: to Salonika/London ya tin
THesaloniki/to Lonthino
to Greece/England ya tin
Elatha/Anglia
to the post office sto
takhithromio
toast (bread) to tost
today simera
toe to thakhtilo too pothioo
together mazi
toilet i too-aleta
toilet paper kharti iyias
tomato i domata
tomorrow avrio
tomorrow morning avrio to
pro-i
the day after tomorrow
methavrio
tonic (water) to tonik
tonight apopseh
too (excessively) poli
(also) episis
too much para poli
me too kego episis
tooth to thondi
toothache o ponothondos
toothbrush i othondovoortsa
toothpaste i othondokrema
top: on top of ... pano apo ...

at the top stin korifi
torch o fakos
tour i peri-iyisis, i xenayisi
tourist (man/woman) o
tooristas/i tooristria
tourist information office
Grafio Pliroforion E-OT
towards pros
towel i petseta
town i poli
in town stin poli
town centre to kendro tis
polis
toy to pekh-nithi
track (US: at station) i
platforma
traffic lights ta fanaria tis
trokheas
train to treno
by train meh treno
is this the train for ...? afto
ineh to treno ya ...?
train station o sithiro-
thromikos staTHmos
translate metafrazo
trashcan o
skoopithodenekes
travel taxithevo
travel agent's to taxithiotiko
grafio
traveller's cheque i
taxithiotiki epitayi
tree to thendro
trip (excursion) to taxithi
trousers to pandaloni
true aliTHinos
try prospaTHo, thokimazo
try on provaro
T-shirt to bloozaki

tuna o tonos
turn: turn left/right stripseh aristera/thexia
twice thio fores
twin room to thomatio meh thio krevatia
tyre to lastikho

U

umbrella i ombrela
uncle o THios
under apo kato
 (less than) ligotero apo
underground (railway) o ipo-yios
underpants to sovrako, to slip
understand: I understand katalaveno
 I don't understand then katalaveno
university to panepistimio
unleaded petrol i amolivthi venzini
until mekhri
up pano
 (upwards) pros ta pano
 up there eki pano
upstairs pano
urgent epigon
us mas
 for us ya mas
USA i IPA
use khrisimopi-o
useful khrisimos

V

vacation i thiakopes
valid (ticket etc) engiros
value i axia
vanilla i vanilia
veal to moskhari
vegetables ta lakhanika
vegetarian o/i khortofagos
very poli
 I like it very much moo aresi para poli
view i THea
village to khorio
visit episkeptomeh
vodka i votka
voice i foni

W

waist i mesi
wait perimeno
waiter o servitoros
 waiter! garson!
waitress i garsona, i servitora
 waitress! sas parakalo!
wake-up call tilefonima ya xipnima
Wales i Oo-alia
walk: is it a long walk? ineh poli perpatima?
wall o tikhos
wallet to portofoli
want: I want a ... THelo ena ...
 I don't want any ... then THelo ...

I don't want to then THelo
what do you want? ti THelis?
warm zestos
wash pleno
  (oneself) plenomeh
washhand basin o niptiras
washing (clothes) i boogatha
washing machine to
  plindirio
washing powder i skoni
  plindirioo, to
  aporipandiko
wasp i sfinga
watch (wristwatch) to rolo-i
water to nero
way: it's this way apo etho
  ineh
  it's that way apo eki ineh
  is it a long way to ...? ineh
  makri-a ya to ...?
  no way! apokli-eteh!

dialogue

could you tell me the way
to? boriteh na moo
thixeteh to thromo ya ...?
go straight on until you
reach the traffic lights
piyeneteh olo isia mekhri
na ftaseteh sta fanaria
turn left stripsteh aristera
take the first on the right
parteh ton proto thromo
sta thexia

we emis
weather o keros
week i evthomatha

a week (from) today seh mia
evthomatha apo simera
weekend to Savatokiriako
weight to varos
welcome: you're welcome
(don't mention it) parakalo
well: she's not well ekini then
ineh kala
you speak English very well
milateh poli kala Anglika
well done! bravo
this one as well ki afto episis
well-done (meat)
kalopsimenos
Welsh Oo-alos
west thitikos
wet vregmenos
what? ti?
  what's that? ti ineh ekino?
wheel i rotha
when? poteh?
  when's the train/ferry?
  poteh fevyi to treno/to
  karavi?
where? poo?
which: which bus? pio
leoforio?
while: while I'm here oso imeh
etho
whisky to whisky
white aspros
white wine to aspro krasi
who? pios?
whole: the whole week oli tin
evthomatha
whose: whose is this? pianoo
ineh afto?
why? yati?
  why not? yati okhi?

wide platis
wife: my wife i sizigos moo
wind o anemos
window to paraTHiro
 in the window (of shop) sti
 vitrina
wine to krasi
wine list o katalogos ton
 krasion
winter o khimonas
with meh
without khoris
woman i yineka
wood (material) to xilo
wool to mali
word i lexi
work i thoolia
 it's not working then
 thoolevi
worry: I'm worried
 stenokhori-emeh
worry beads to kombolo-i
worse: it's worse ineh
 khirotera
worst o khiroteros
would: would you give this
 to ...? boriteh na thoseteh
 afto ston ...?
wrap: could you wrap it up?
 boriteh na to tilixeteh?
wrist o karpos
write grafo
 could you write it down?
 boriteh na moo to
 grapseteh?
wrong: it's the wrong key afto
 ineh laTHos klithi
 there's something wrong
 with ... iparkhi kapio laTHos

meh ...
what's wrong? ti simveni?

Y

year o khronos
yellow kitrinos
yes neh
yesterday kh-THes
 the day before yesterday
 prokh-THes
yet akomi
you (fam) esi
 (pl or polite) esis
 this is for you afto ineh ya sas
young neos
your (fam) o/i/to ... soo
 (pl or polite) o/i/to ... sas
 your camera i fotografiki
 mikhani soo/sas
yours (fam) thiko soo
 (pl or polite) thiko sas
youth hostel o xenonas neon

Z

zero mithen
zip to fermoo-ar
zoo o zo-oloyikos kipos

Greek

→

English

The Greek Alphabet

A, α	**alfa**	a as in c**a**t
B, β	**vita**	v as in **v**et
Γ, γ	**Gama**	y as in **y**es, except before consonants and a, o or long i, when it's a throaty version of the g in **g**ap
Δ, δ	**thelta**	th as in **th**en
E, ε	**epsilon**	e as in g**e**t
Z, ζ	**zita**	z
H, η	**ita**	i as in sk**i**
Θ, θ	**THita**	as the th in **th**eme (represented by TH)
I, ι	**yota**	i as in b**i**t
K, κ	**kapa**	k
Λ, λ	**lamtha**	l
M, μ	**mi**	m
N, ν	**ni**	n
Ξ, ξ	**ksi**	x
O, o	**omikron**	o as in h**o**t
Π, π	**pi**	p
P, ρ	**ro**	r
Σ, σ, ς*	**siGma**	s
T, τ	**taf**	t
Y, υ	**ipsilon**	long i, indistinguishable from **i**ta
Φ, φ	**fi**	f
X, χ	**khi**	h as in **h**at or harsh ch in the Scottish pronunciation of lo**ch** (represented by kh)
Ψ, ψ	**psi**	ps as in li**ps**
Ω, ω	**omeGa**	o as in h**o**t, indistinguishable from **o**mikron

* this letter is used only at the end of a word in lower case αγαπώ [agapo] to love

ΑΓΓΛΙΑ Αγγλία (η) [Anglia (i)] England

ΑΓΓΛΙΚΟΣ Αγγλικός [Anglikos] English

ΑΓΟΡΑ αγορά (η) [agora (i)] market

αγοράζω [agorazo] to buy

αγόρι (το) [agori (to)] boy

άδεια οδηγήσεως (η) [athia othiyiseos (i)] driving licence

άδειος [athios] empty, vacant

αδελφή (η) [athelfi (i)] sister

αδελφός (ο) [athelfos (o)] brother

ΑΕΡΟΔΡΟΜΙΟ αεροδρόμιο (το) [aerothromio (to)] airport

αεροπλάνο (το) [aeroplano (to)] plane

αεροπορική εταιρεία (η) [aeroporiki eteria (i)] airline

ΑΘΗΝΑ Αθήνα (η) [ATHina (i)] Athens

ΑΙΓΑΙΟ Αιγαίο (το) [E-yeo (to)] Aegean

αίμα (το) [ema (to)] blood

ΑΚΑΤΑΛΛΗΛΟ ακατάλληλο adults only

ακολουθώ [akolooTHo] to follow

ακόμα, ακόμη [akoma, akomi] still, yet; even; also

ακούω [akoo-o] to hear; to listen

ακριβός [akrivos] expensive

ΑΚΤΗ ακτή (η) [akti (i)] beach; coast; shore

ακυρώνω [akirono] to cancel

αλλά [alla] but

αλλάζω [allazo] to change

άλλος [alos] other; else

άλλος ένας [alos enas] another

αλλού [aloo] elsewhere

ΑΜΑΞΟΣΤΟΙΧΙΑ αμαξοστοιχία (η) [amaxostikhia (i)] train

ΑΜΕΡΙΚΗ Αμερική (η) [Ameriki (i)] America

αμέσως [amesos] immediately

αν [an] if

αναγκαίος [anangeos] necessary

ανάμεσα [anamesa] among; between

ανατολή (η) [anatoli (i)] east; dawn

ΑΝΑΧΩΡΕΙ ΚΑΘΗΜΕΡΙΝΑ ΓΙΑ ... αναχωρεί καθημερινά γιά ... departs daily to ...

ΑΝΑΧΩΡΗΣΗ αναχώρηση (η) [anakhorisi (i)] departure

άνδρας (ο) [anthras (o)] man

ΑΝΔΡΙΚΑ ανδρικά (τα) [anthrika (ta)] menswear

ΑΝΔΡΙΚΑΙ ΚΟΜΜΩΣΕΙΣ ανδρικαί κομμώσεις [anthrikeh komosis] men's hairdresser

ΑΝΔΡΩΝ ανδρών gents, men's room

ΑΝΕΛΚΥΣΤΗΡΑΣ ανελκυστήρας (ο) [anelkistiras (o)] lift, elevator

ΑΝΘΟΠΩΛΕΙΟ ανθοπωλείο (το) [anTHopolio (to)] florist's

άνθρωποι (οι) [anTHropi (i)] people

αν και [an keh] although

ανοίγω [anigo] to open; to switch on

ΑΝΟΙΚΤΑ ανοικτά [anikta]

open
ΑΝΤΑΛΛΑΚΤΙΚΑ
ανταλλακτικά (τα) spare parts
αντί [adi] instead of
ΑΝΩ άνω [ano] up
ΑΠΑΓΟΡΕΥΕΤΑΙ
απαγορεύεται it is prohibited
ΑΠΑΓΟΡΕΥΕΤΑΙ Η ΕΙΣΟΔΟΣ
απαγορεύεται η είσοδος no
entry, no admission
ΑΠΑΓΟΡΕΥΕΤΑΙ Η ΣΤΑΣΗ
απαγορεύεται η στάση no
waiting, no stopping
ΑΠΑΓΟΡΕΥΕΤΑΙ ΤΟ
ΚΑΠΝΙΣΜΑ απαγορεύεται
το κάπνισμα no smoking
απαγορευμένος [apagorevmenos]
forbidden
απάντηση (η) [apadisi (i)]
answer
από [apo] from; since; than
από κάτω [apo kato] under
από πάνω [apo pano] over
απόγευμα (το) [apoyevma (to)]
afternoon
ΑΠΟΣΚΕΥΕΣ αποσκευές (οι)
[aposkeves (i)] baggage
απόψε [apopseh] tonight
ΑΠΩΛΕΣΘΕΝΤΑ
ΑΝΤΙΚΕΙΜΕΝΑ
απωλεσθέντα αντικείμενα
[apolesTHeda adikimena] lost
property, lost and found
αργά [arga] late; slowly
αργίες (οι) [aryies (i)] public
holidays
αργός [argos] slow
αργότερα [argotera] later
ΑΡΙΘΜΟΣ αριθμός (ο)

[ariTHmos (o)] number
αριστερά [aristera] left
αρκετά [arketa] enough; quite
αρκετοί [arketi] several
ΑΡΤΟΠΟΙΕΙΟ αρτοποιείο (το)
[artopi-io (to)] bakery
αρχαίος [arkheos] ancient
αρχή (η) [arkhi (i)] beginning
αρχίζω [arkhizo] to begin
ΑΣΑΝΣΕΡ ασανσέρ (το)
[asanser (to)] lift, elevator
ΑΣΗΜΕΝΙΟΣ ασημένιος
[asimenios] silver
άσπρος [aspros] white
αστείος [astios] funny,
amusing
αστέρι (το) [asteri (to)] star
ΑΣΤΥΝΟΜΙΑ αστυνομία (η)
[astinomia (i)] police
ΑΣΦΑΛΕΙΑ ασφάλεια (η)
[asfalia (i)] fuse; insurance
άσχημα [askhima] badly
άσχημος [askhimos] ugly
άτομο (το) [atomo (to)] person
αύριο [avrio] tomorrow
αυτά, αυτές [afta, aftes] these;
they; them
αυτή [afti] she; this (one)
αυτί (το) [afti (to)] ear
αυτό [afto] it; this
αυτοί [afti] these; they
ΑΥΤΟΚΙΝΗΤΟ αυτοκίνητο
(το) [aftokinito (to)] car
αυτό που [afto poo] what
αυτός [aftos] he; this (one)
αυτούς [aftoos] them
ΑΦΕΤΗΡΙΑ αφετηρία (η)
[afetiria (i)] terminus
αφήνω [afino] to leave

ΑΦΙΞΗ άφιξη (η) **[afixi (i)]** arrival

βαλίτσα (η) **[valitsa (i)]** bag, suitcase

ΒΑΜΒΑΚΕΡΟ βαμβακερό (το) **[vamvakero (to)]** cotton

ΒΑΡΚΑ βάρκα (η) **[varka (i)]** small boat; dinghy

ΒΑΡΟΣ βάρος (το) **[varos (to)]** weight

βαρύς **[varis]** heavy; rich (food)

βγάζω φωτογραφία **[vgazo fotografia]** to photograph

ΒΓΑΛΤΕ ΤΗΝ ΚΑΡΤΑ βγάλτε την κάρτα remove your card

ΒΕΝΖΙΝΗ βενζίνη (η) **[venzini (i)]** petrol, gas(oline)

βιβλίο (το) **[vivlio (to)]** book

ΒΙΒΛΙΟΠΩΛΕΙΟ βιβλιοπωλείο (το) **[vivliopolio (to)]** bookshop, bookstore

βλέπω **[vlepo]** to see

βοήθεια (η) **[voithia (i)]** help

βουνό (το) **[voono (to)]** mountain

βουτάω **[vootao]** to dive

βράδυ (το) **[vrathi (to)]** evening

ΒΡΕΤΑΝΝΙΑ Βρεταννία (η) **[vretania (i)]** Britain

βρίσκω **[vrisko]** to find

βροχή (η) **[vrokhi (i)]** rain

γειά σου! **[yia soo!]** hello!; bless you!; cheers!

γεμάτος **[yematos]** full

γενέθλια (τα) **[yenethlia (ta)]** birthday

γέρος **[yeros]** old

ΓΕΥΜΑ γεύμα (το) **[yevma (to)]** meal

για **[ya]** for

γιατί; **[yati?]** why?

ΓΙΑ ΤΟ ΣΠΙΤΙ για το σπίτι **[ya to spiti]** to take away, to go

ΓΙΑΤΡΟΣ γιατρός (ο/η) **[yatros (o/i)]** doctor

γιός (ο) **[yos (o)]** son

ΓΚΑΡΑΖ γκαράζ (το) **[garaz (to)]** garage

γλυκός **[glikos]** sweet

γλώσσα (η) **[glosa (i)]** language; tongue

γνωρίζω **[gnorizo]** to know

γονείς (οι) **[gonis (i)]** parents

γράμμα (το) **[grama (to)]** letter

ΓΡΑΜΜΑΤΟΚΙΒΩΤΙΟ γραμματοκιβώτιο (το) **[gramatokivotio (to)]** letterbox, mailbox

γραμματόσημο (το) **[gramatosimo (to)]** stamp

ΓΡΑΦΕΙΟ ΤΑΞΙΔΙΩΝ γραφείο ταξιδίων **[grafio taxithion]** travel agency

γράφω **[grafo]** to write

γρήγορα **[grigora]** quick; quickly

γυναίκα (η) **[yineka (i)]** woman; wife

ΓΥΝΑΙΚΕΙΑ γυναικεία (τα) **[yinekia (ta)]** ladies' wear

ΓΥΝΑΙΚΩΝ γυναικών ladies' (room)

δάσκαλος (ο) **[thaskalos (o)]**

A
B
Γ
Δ
E
Z
H
Θ
I
K
Λ
M
N
Ξ
O
Π
P
Σ
T
Y
Φ
X
Ψ
Ω

instructor; teacher
δε [theh] not
ΔΕΙΠΝΟ δείπνο (το) [thipno (to)] evening meal
δέμα (το) [thema (to)] parcel
δεν [then] not
ΔΕΝ ΛΕΙΤΟΥΡΓΕΙ δεν λειτουργεί [then litooryi] out of order
δεξιός [thexios] right
ΔΕΡΜΑ δέρμα (το) [therma (to)] skin; leather
ΔΕΣΠΟΙΝΙΔΑ δεσποινίδα (η) [thespinitha (i)] young woman; Miss; Ms
ΔΕΣΠΟΙΝΙΣ δεσποινίς [thespinis] Miss; Ms
δέχομαι [thekhomeh] to accept; to receive
ΔΗΜΑΡΧΕΙΟ δημαρχείο (το) [thimarkhio (to)] town hall
διαβάζω [thiavazo] to read
ΔΙΑΒΑΤΗΡΙΟ διαβατήριο (το) [thiavatirio (to)] passport
ΔΙΑΔΡΟΜΗ ΜΕΤ' ΕΠΙΣΤΡΟΦΗΣ διαδρομή μετ' επιστροφής (η) [thiathromi met' epistrofis (i)] return/round trip fare
ΔΙΑΜΕΡΙΣΜΑ διαμέρισμα (το) [thiamerisma (to)] apartment, flat
διά μέσου [thia mesoo] through
διαμονή (η) [thiamoni (i)] accommodation; stay
ΔΙΑΝΥΚΤΕΡΕΥΟΝ διανυκτερεύον open all night
διαφορετικός [thiaforetikos] different

διαχειριστής (ο) [thiakhiristis (o)] manager
διδάσκω [thithasko] to teach
ΔΙΕΥΘΥΝΣΗ διεύθυνση (η) [thiefrHinsi (i)] address
δικός μας [thikos mas] ours
δικός μου [thikos moo] mine
δικός σας, δικά σου [thikos sas, thikos soo] yours
δικός της [thikos tis] hers
δικός του [thikos too] his, its
δικός τους [thikos toos] theirs
δικηγόρος (ο/η) [thikigoros (o/i)] lawyer
δίνω [thino] to give
διπλό [thiplo] double
δόντι (το) [thodi (to)] tooth
δουλειά (η) [thoolia (i)] job; work
δουλεύω [thoolevo] to work
ΔΡΟΜΟΛΟΓΙΑ δρομολόγια (τα) [thromoloyia (ta)] timetable, (US) schedule
δρόμος (ο) [thromos (o)] road; street
δροσερός [throseros] cool
δυνατός [thinatos] loud; possible; strong
ΔΩΜΑΤΙΟ δωμάτιο (το) [thomatio (to)] room

εβδομάδα (η) [evthomatha (i)] week
έγγραφο (το) [engrafo (to)] document
εγώ [ego] I
εδώ [etho] here
ΕΘΝΙΚΗ ΟΔΟΣ εθνική οδός (η) [eTHniki othos (i)]

motorway, highway

ΕΘΝΙΚΟΤΗΤΑ εθνικότητα (η)
[eΤΗnik**o**tita (i)] nationality

είμαι [**i**meh] I am

είμαστε [**i**masteh] we are

είναι [**i**neh] he/she/it is; they
are

είστε [**i**steh] you are

είσαι [**i**seh] you are

ΕΙΣΙΤΗΡΙΟ εισιτήριο (το)
[isi**ti**rio (to)] ticket

ΕΙΣΙΤΗΡΙΟ ΜΕ ΕΠΙΣΤΡΟΦΗ
εισιτήριο με επιστροφή [isi**ti**rio
meh epist**ro**fi] return/round
trip ticket

ΕΙΣΟΔΟΣ είσοδος (η) [**i**sothos
(i)] entrance, way in

ΕΙΣΟΔΟΣ ΕΛΕΥΘΕΡΑ
είσοδος ελευθέρα admission
free

ΕΚΔΟΣΗ ΕΙΣΙΤΗΡΙΩΝ
έκδοση εισιτηρίων [**e**kthosi
isi**ti**rion] ticket office

εκεί [e**ki**] there, over there

εκείνοι [e**ki**ni] those

εκείνος [e**ki**nos] that

εκτός [ek**tos**] except

ΕΛΕΥΘΕΡΑ ΕΙΣΟΔΟΣ
ελευθέρα είσοδος [elef**ΤΗ**era
isothos] admission free

ΕΛΕΥΘΕΡΟΝ ελεύθερον
[elef**ΤΗ**eron] free; for hire

ΕΛΛΑΔΑ Ελλάδα (η) [E**la**tha
(i)] Greece

ΕΛΛΗΝΙΚΑ Ελληνικά (τα)
[E**li**nika (ta)] Greek (language)

ΕΛΛΗΝΙΚΟ ΠΡΟΙΟΝ
Ελληνικό προιόν produce of
Greece

ΕΛ.ΤΑ. Greek Post Office

εμάς [e**mas**] us

εμείς [e**mis**] we

εμένα [e**mena**] me

εμπρός [e**bros**] come in; hello
(on phone)

ένα(ν) [**e**na(n)] a; one

εναντίον [e**na**dion] against

ένας [**e**nas] a; one

ΕΝΗΛΙΚΟΣ ενήλικος (ο)
[e**ni**likos (o)] adult

ΕΝΟΙΚΙΑΖΟΝΤΑΙ
ενοικιάζονται [eni**ki**azodeh] for
hire, to rent

**ΕΝΟΙΚΙΑΖΟΝΤΑΙ
ΑΥΤΟΚΙΝΗΤΑ**
ενοικιάζονται αυτοκίνητα car
rental

ΕΝΟΙΚΙΑΖΟΝΤΑΙ ΔΩΜΑΤΙΑ
ενοικιάζονται δωμάτια rooms
to let

ενοίκιο (το) [e**ni**kio (to)] rent

εντάξει [e**ntaxi**] that's all right;
OK

ΕΞΟΔΟΣ έξοδος (η) [**e**xothos
(i)] exit; gate; door

ΕΞΟΔΟΣ ΚΙΝΔΥΝΟΥ έξοδος
κινδύνου emergency exit

ΕΞΠΡΕΣ εξπρές [ex**pres**]
special delivery; express

εξωτερικός [exoteri**kos**]
external

στο εξωτερικό [sto exoteri**ko**]
abroad

επείγον [e**pigon**] urgent

επειδή [epi**thi**] because

ΕΠΙΘΕΤΟ επίθετο (το)
[e**pi**ΤΗeto (to)] surname

επικίνδυνος [epi**ki**nthinos]

dangerous

έπιπλα (τα) **[epipla (ta)]**
furniture

επίσης **[episis]** too, also

επισκευή (η) **[episkevi (i)]** repair

ΕΠΙΣΤΟΛΕΣ επιστολές letters

ΕΠΙΤΑΓΗ επιταγή (η) **[epitayi (i)]** cheque, (US) check

επιτρέπεται **[epitrepeteh]** it is permitted

επόμενος (ο) **[epomenos (o)]** next

ΕΡΓΑ ΕΠΙ ΤΗΣ ΟΔΟΥ ΣΕ ΜΗΚΟΣ...ΧΙΛ. έργα επί της οδού σε μήκος...χιλ. roadworks for ... kms

εργάζομαι **[ergazomeh]** to work

έρχομαι **[erkhomeh]** to come

εσάς, εσείς, εσένα **[esas, esis, esena]** you

ΕΣΤΙΑΤΟΡΙΟ εστιατόριο (το) **[estiatorio (to)]** restaurant

εσύ **[esi]** you

ΕΤΟΙΜΑ ΓΥΝΑΙΚΕΙΑ έτοιμα γυναικεία ladies' clothing

έτοιμος **[etimos]** ready

έτσι **[etsi]** so; like this

ευγενικός **[evyenikos]** kind; polite

εύκολος **[efkolos]** easy

ευχαριστώ **[efkharisto]** thank you

έχει **[ekhi]** he/she/it has

έχεις **[ekhis]** you have

έχετε **[ekheteh]** you have

έχουμε **[ekhoomeh]** we have

έχουν **[ekhoon]** they have

έχω **[ekho]** I have

ΖΑΧΑΡΟΠΛΑΣΤΕΙΟ
ζαχαροπλαστείο (το) **[zakharoplastio (to)]** cake shop or café selling cakes and soft drinks

ζέστη (η) **[zesti (i)]** heat

ζεστός **[zestos]** hot; warm

ζω **[zo]** to live

η **[i]** the

ή **[i]** or

ήδη **[ithi]** already

ήλιος (ο) **[ilios (o)]** sun

ημέρα (η) **[imera (i)]** day

ΗΜΕΡΟΜΗΝΙΑ ΛΗΞΗΣ
ημερομηνία λήξης best before

ΗΜΙΔΙΑΤΡΟΦΗ ημιδιατροφή (η) **[imithiatrofi (i)]** half board, American plan

Η.Π.Α. (οι) **[I.P.A. (i)]** USA

θάλασσα (η) **[THalasa (i)]** sea

ΘΑΛΑΣΣΙΟ ΣΚΙ θαλάσσιο σκι (το) **[THalasio ski (to)]** waterskiing

θάνατος (ο) **[THanatos (o)]** death

θεά (η) **[THea (i)]** goddess

θέα (η) **[THea (i)]** view

θεία (η) **[THia (i)]** aunt

θείος (ο) **[THios (o)]** uncle

θέλω **[THelo]** to want

θεός (ο) **[THeos (o)]** God

θέση (η) **[THesi (i)]** seat

θυμάμαι **[THimameh]** to remember

ιδιοκτήτης (ο) **[ithioktitis (o)]** owner

ΙΔΙΟΚΤΗΤΟ ΠΑΡΚΙΝΓΚ
ιδιόκτητο πάρκινγκ private parking

ίδιος [ithios] same

ΙΔΙΩΤΙΚΟΣ ιδιωτικός [ithiotikos] private

ίσια [isia] straight

ΙΣΟΓΕΙΟ ισόγειο (το) [isoyio (to)] ground floor, (US) first floor

ιστιοπλο≍κό σκάφος (το) [istioplo-iko skafos (to)] sailing boat

ίσως [isos] maybe, perhaps

Κ. κ. Mr

ΚΑ. κα. Mrs

ΚΑΘΑΡΙΣΤΗΡΙΟ
καθαριστήριο (το) [kaTHaristirio (to)] laundry and dry cleaner's

καθαρός [kaTHaros] clean (adj)

κάθε [kaTHeh] every

καθεμία, καθένα, καθένας [kaTHemia, kaTHena, kaTHenas] each

κάθε τι [kaTHeh ti] everything

καθηγητής (ο) [kaTHiyitis (o)] teacher; professor

καθόλου [kaTHoloo] not at all; none; any

ΚΑΘΥΣΤΕΡΗΣΗ
καθυστέρηση (η) [kaTHisterisi (i)] delay

και [keh] and

και οι δύο [k i thio] both of them

καιρός (ο) [keros (o)] weather

κακός [kakos] bad

καλά [kala] well; good

ΚΑΛΟΚΑΙΡΙ καλοκαίρι (το) [kalokeri (to)] summer

καλός [kalos] good; kind

καλύτερος (ο) [kaliteros (o)] better; the best

καλώς ήλθατε! [kalos ilTHateh!] welcome!

καμμία [kamia] no-one

καμμιά φορά [kamia fora] sometimes

κανένα [kanena] nothing

κανένας [kanenas] nobody

κάνω [kano] to do; to make

ΚΑΠΝΙΖΟΝΤΕΣ καπνίζοντες [kapnizodes] smoking

κάποιος [kapios] somebody

κάπου [kapoo] somewhere

καρδιά (η) [karthia (i)] heart

καρέκλα (η) [karekla (i)] chair

κατά [kata] against; about

καταδύσεις (οι) [katathisis (i)] skin-diving

καταλαβαίνω [katalaveno] to understand

κατάλογος (ο) [katalogos (o)] list; menu

ΚΑΤΑΝΑΛΩΣΗ ΠΡΙΝ ...
κατανάλωση πριν ... use by ...

κατά τη διάρκεια [kata ti thiarkia] while; during

κατεβαίνω [kateveno] to get off; to go down

κατειλημμένος [katilimenos] engaged, occupied

κατευθείαν [katefrhian] direct

κάτι [kati] something

ΚΑΤΩ κάτω [kato] down; downstairs

κάτω από [kato apo] under
καυτός [kaftos] hot (to taste)
καφέ [kafe] brown
ΚΑΦΕΚΟΠΤΕΙΟ καφεκοπτείο
  (το) [kafekoptio (to)] coffee
  shop
ΚΑΦΕΝΕΙΟ καφενείο (το)
  [kafenio (to)] coffee house,
  where Greek coffee is
  served with traditional
  sweets
ΚΑΦΕΤΕΡΙΑ καφετέρια (η)
  [kafeteria (i)] café, coffee shop
ΚΕΝΤΡΟ κέντρο (το) [kedro
  (to)] centre
ΚΕΡΚΥΡΑ Κέρκυρα (η)
  [Kerkira (i)] Corfu
ΚΕΣ. κες. Mrs
κεφάλι (το) [kefali (to)] head
ΚΙΛΟ κιλό (το) [kilo (to)] kilo
ΚΙΝΗΜΑΤΟΓΡΑΦΟΣ
  κινηματογράφος (ο)
  [kinimatografos (o)] cinema,
  movie theater
κίτρινος [kitrinos] yellow
κλειδί (το) [klithi (to)] key;
  spanner, wrench
κλείνω [klino] to close; to
  switch off
ΚΛΕΙΣΤΟΣ κλειστός [klistos]
  closed; off
ΚΛΙΜΑΤΙΖΟΜΕΝΟΣ
  κλιματιζόμενος
  [klimatizomenos] air-
  conditioned
κόκκινος [kokinos] red
ΚΟΛΥΜΒΗΤΗΡΙΟ
  κολυμβητήριο (το) [kolimvitirio
  (to)] swimming pool

κολύμπι (το) [kolibi (to)]
  swimming
κολυμπώ [kolibo] to swim
κομμάτι (το) [komati (to)] piece
ΚΟΜΜΩΤΗΡΙΟ κομμωτήριο
  (το) [komotirio (to)] hairdresser's
κοντά [koda] near, close by
κόρη (η) [kori (i)] daughter
κορίτσι (το) [koritsi (to)] girl
κόσμος (ο) [kosmos (o)] world;
  people, crowd
κόστος (το) [kostos (to)] cost
ΚΟΥΖΙΝΑ κουζίνα (η) [koozina
  (i)] cooker; kitchen
κουρασμένος [koorasmenos]
  tired
ΚΟΥΡΕΙΟ κουρείο (το) [koorio
  (to)] barber's shop
κουτάλι (το) [kootali (to)] spoon
κρατάω [kratao] to hold; to
  keep
κράτηση θέσης (η) [kratisi thesis
  (i)] reservation
κρεβάτι (το) [krevati (to)] bed
ΚΡΕΟΠΩΛΕΙΟ κρεοπωλείο
  (το) [kreopolio (to)] butcher's
κρίμα: είναι κρίμα [ineh krima]
  it's a pity
κρύο (το) [krio (to)] cold
κρύος [krios] cold (adj)
Κ.Τ.Ε.Λ. long-distance bus
  station
κυκλοφορία (η) [kikloforia (i)]
  traffic
ΚΥΠΡΟΣ Κύπρος (η) [Kipros
  (i)] Cyprus
κυρία (η) [kiria (i)] lady;
  madam; Mrs
κύριε [kiri-eh] sir

κύριος (ο) [**kirios** (o)] gentleman

κυττάζω [**kitazo**] to look

ΚΩΔΙΚΟΣ κωδικός (ο) [**kothikos** (o)] code

ΛΑΔΙ λάδι (το) [**lathi (to)**] oil

λάθος (το) [**laTHos (to)**] mistake

λάθος [**laTHos**] wrong

λαιμός (ο) [**lemos (o)**] neck; throat

λάστιχο (το) [**lastikho (to)**] rubber; tyre

λείπω [**lipo**] to be missing; to be out; to be away

λέξη (η) [**lexi (i)**] word

ΛΕΦΤΑ λεφτά (τα) [**lefta (ta)**] money

λέω [**leo**] to say

ΛΕΩΦΟΡΕΙΟ λεωφορείο (το) [**leoforio (to)**] bus

λίγα [**liga**] a few

λίγο [**ligo**] a little bit

λίγος [**ligos**] little; short

ΛΙΜΑΝΙ λιμάνι (το) [**limani (to)**] harbour

λίμνη (η) [**limni (i)**] lake

ΛΙΡΑ ΑΓΓΛΙΑΣ λίρα Αγγλίας (η) [**lira Anglias (i)**] pound sterling

ΛΙΤΡΟ λίτρο (το) [**litro (to)**] litre

ΛΟΓΑΡΙΑΣΜΟΣ λογαριασμός (ο) [**logariasmos (o)**] bill, (US) check

ΛΟΝΔΙΝΟ Λονδίνο (το) [**Lonthino (to)**] London

ΛΟΥΤΡΟ λουτρό (το) [**lootro (to)**] bathroom

μαγαζί (το) [**magazi (to)**] shop

μαζί [**mazi**] together

μακριά [**makria**] far

μακρύς [**makris**] long

ΜΑΛΛΙ μαλλί (το) [**mali (to)**] wool

μαλλιά (τα) [**malia (ta)**] hair

ΜΑΝΑΒΗΣ μανάβης (ο) [**manavis (o)**] greengrocer's

ΜΑΡΙΝΑ μαρίνα (η) [**marina (i)**] marina

μας [**mas**] us; our

μάτι (το) [**mati (to)**] eye; ring (on cooker)

μαύρος [**mavros**] black

μαχαίρι (το) [**makheri (to)**] knife

με [**meh**] with; by; me

μεγάλος [**megalos**] big

μεθαύριο [**meTHavrio**] the day after tomorrow

μεθυσμένος [**meTHismenos**] drunk

μένω [**meno**] to live; to stay

μέρα (η) [**mera (i)**] day

μερικά, μερικές, μερικοί [**merika, merikes, meriki**] some

μέρος (το) [**meros (to)**] part; place; WC

μέσα [**mesa**] in; inside

μεσημέρι (το) [**mesimeri (to)**] midday

Μεσόγειος (η) [**Mesoyios (i)**] Mediterranean

μετά [**meta**] after; afterwards

ΜΕΤΑΞΙ μετάξι (το) [**metaxi (to)**] silk

μεταξύ [**metaxi**] between

μεταφράζω [**metafrazo**] to translate

ΜΕΤΡΗΤΑ μετρητά [metrita] cash

μέχρι [mekhri] until

ΜΗ μη do not

ΜΗ ΚΑΠΝΙΖΟΝΤΕΣ μη καπνίζοντες [mi kapnizontes] non-smoking

μήνας (ο) [minas (o)] month

μητέρα (η) [mitera (i)] mother

μία [mia] a; one

ΜΙΚΡΟ ΟΝΟΜΑ μικρό όνομα (το) [mikro onoma (to)] Christian name

ΜΙΚΡΟΣ μικρός [mikros] little

μιλάω [milao] to speak

μισός [misos] half

μόνο [mono] only

ΜΟΝΟΔΡΟΜΟΣ μονόδρομος one-way street

ΜΟΝΟ ΔΩΜΑΤΙΟ μονό δωμάτιο (το) [mono thomatio (to)] single room

μόνος [monos] alone

μου [moo] my

ΜΟΥΣΕΙΟ μουσείο (το) [moosio (to)] museum

μουσική (η) [moosiki (i)] music

μπαίνω [beno] to go in, to enter

ΜΠΑΚΑΛΙΚΟ μπακάλικο (το) [bakaliko (to)] grocer's

ΜΠΑΝΙΟ μπάνιο (το) [banio (to)] bath

ΜΠΑΡ μπαρ (το) [bar (to)] bar

μπλε [bleh] blue

μπρος [bros] forwards; in front of

μπουκάλι (το) [bookali (to)] bottle

μύτη (η) [miti (i)] nose

μωρό (το) [moro (to)] baby

να [na] here is/are

ναι [neh] yes

νέα (τα) [nea (ta)] news

νέος [neos] new; young

ΝΕΡΟ νερό (το) [nero (to)] water

νησί (το) [nisi (to)] island

νοικιάζω [nikiazo] to rent

νομίζω [nomizo] to think

νόμος (ο) [nomos (o)] law

νύχτα (η) [nikhta (i)] night

νωρίς [noris] early

ξανά [xana] again

ΞΕΝΟΔΟΧΕΙΟ ξενοδοχείο (το) [xenothokhio (to)] hotel

ξένος [xenos] foreign

ΞΕΝΩΝΑΣ ξενώνας (ο) [xenonas (o)] guesthouse

ΞΕΝΩΝΑΣ ΝΕΟΤΗΤΑΣ ξενώνας νεότητας [xenonas neotitas] youth hostel

ξέρω [xero] to know

ξεχνώ [xekhno] to leave; to forget

ξηρός [xiros] dry

ξύλο (το) [xilo (to)] wood

ο [o] the

Ο/Γ ferry

οδηγός (ο/η) [othigos (o/i)] driver

ΟΔΙΚΑ ΕΡΓΑ οδικά έργα roadworks

ΟΔΟΣ οδός (η) [othos (i)] road; street

οι [i] the
όλα [ola] all
όλα πληρωμένα [ola pliromena]
  all inclusive
όλες, όλη [oles, oli] all
όμορφος [omorfos] fine,
  beautiful
ONOMA όνομα (το) [onoma
  (to)] name; first name
όπως [opos] like; as
όρεξη (η) [orexi (i)] appetite
  καλή όρεξη! [kali orexi!] enjoy
  your meal!
όροφος (ο) [orofos (o)] floor,
  storey
όταν [otan] when
ότι [oti] that
οτιδήποτε [otithipoteh] anything
OYZEΡI ουζερί [oozeri] bar
  serving ouzo and beer with
  snacks or full meals
OYPA ουρά (η) [oora (i)]
  queue; tail; queue here
ούτε ... ούτε ... [oote ... oote ...]
  neither ... nor ...
OXI όχι [okhi] no; not
  όχι άλλο [okhi allo] no more

ΠΑΓΟΣ πάγος (ο) [pagos (o)]
  ice
ΠΑΙΔΙ παιδί (το) [pethi (to)]
  child
παίζω [pezo] to play
παίρνω [perno] to get; to take
παλαιός [paleos] old, ancient
ΠΑΝΕΠΙΣΤΗΜΙΟ
  πανεπιστήμιο (το) [panepistimio
  (to)] university
ΠΑΝΣΙΟΝ πανσιόν (η)

[pansion (i)] guesthouse
πάντα [pada] always; still
ΠΑΝΤΟΠΩΛΕΙΟ
  παντοπωλείο (το) [padopolio
  (to)] grocery store
πάντοτε [padoteh] always
παντού [padoo] everywhere
πάνω [pano] on; up; upstairs
πάνω από [pano apo] above
παραγγελία (η) [parangelia (i)]
  message
παραδοσιακός [parathosiakos]
  traditional
παράθυρο (το) [paraThiro (to)]
  window
παρακαλώ [parakalo] please;
  excuse me; don't mention
  it; can I help you?
ΠΑΡΑΚΑΜΠΤΗΡΙΟΣ
  παρακαμπτήριος (η) diversion
ΠΑΡΑΛΙΑ παραλία (η) [paralia
  (i)] beach
παραμένω [parameno] to stay
παραπονούμαι [paraponoomeh]
  to complain
ΠΑΡΚΙΝΓΚ πάρκινγκ (το)
  [parking (to)] car park, parking
  lot
πάρκο (το) [parko (to)] park
πατέρας (ο) [pateras (o)] father
πάτωμα (το) [patoma (to)] floor
παχύς [pakhis] fat; thick
πάω [pao] to go
πεζοδρόμιο (το) [pezothromio
  (to)] pavement, sidewalk
πεθαίνω [peTHeno] to die
πεθαμένος [peTHamenos] dead
περιμένω [perimeno] to wait
  (for); to expect

περιοχή (η) [periokhi (i)] area
περίπου [peripoo] about,
approximately
ΠΕΡΙΠΤΕΡΟ περίπτερο
[periptero] newspaper kiosk
περισσότερος [perisoteros]
more, most (of)
πηρούνι (το) [pirooni (to)] fork
πιάνω [piano] to catch
ΠΙΝΑΚΟΘΗΚΗ πινακοθήκη
(η) [pinakoTHiki (i)] art gallery
πίνω [pino] to drink
ΠΙΣΙΝΑ πισίνα (η) [pisina (i)]
swimming pool
ΠΙΣΤΩΤΙΚΗ ΚΑΡΤΑ
πιστωτική κάρτα (η) [pistotiki
karta (i)] credit card
πίσω [piso] back; behind
ΠΛΑΤΕΙΑ πλατεία (η) [platia
(i)] square; stalls
πλατύς [platis] wide
ΠΛΑΤΦΟΡΜΑ πλατφόρμα (η)
[platforma (i)] platform, (US)
track
ΠΛΗΡΕΣ πλήρες no
vacancies, full
ΠΛΗΡΟΦΟΡΙΕΣ πληροφορίες
(οι) [plirofories (i)]
information; directory
enquiries
πλοίο (το) [plio (to)] boat, ship
πόδι (το) [pothi (to)] foot; leg
ποδόσφαιρο (το) [pothosfero (to)]
football
ποιό; [pio?] which?
ποιός; [pios?] who?
πόλη (η) [poli (i)] city; town
πολλά, πολλές, πολλή, πολλοί
[pola, poles, poli, poli] many, a

lot (of)
πάρα πολύ [para poli] too
much; very much
πόνος (ο) [ponos (o)] ache; pain
πορεία (η) [poria (i)] route
πόρτα (η) [porta (i)] door
ΠΟΣΙΜΟ ΝΕΡΟ πόσιμο νερό
(το) [posimo nero (to)] drinking
water
πόσο; [poso?] how much?
πόσοι; [posi?] how many?
ΠΟΣΤ ΡΕΣΤΑΝΤ ποστ
ρεστάντ [post restant] poste
restante, (US) general
delivery
ποτάμι (το) [potami (to)] river
ποτέ [poteh] never
πότε; [poteh?] when?
ποτήρι (το) [potiri (to)] glass
που [poo] who, which, that
πού; [poo?] where?
πουλώ [poolo] to sell
πούρο (το) [pooro (to)] cigar
πράγμα (το) [pragma (to)] thing
πρακτορείο (το) [praktorio (to)]
agency
πράσινος [prasinos] green
ΠΡΑΤΗΡΙΟ ΒΕΝΖΙΝΗΣ
πρατήριο βενζίνης (το) [pratirio
venzinis (to)] petrol station, gas
station
πρέπει να ... [prepi na ...]
I must ...
ΠΡΕΣΒΕΙΑ πρεσβεία (η)
[presvia (i)] embassy
πριν [prin] before; ago
ΠΡΟΒΛΗΤΑ προβλήτα (η)
[provlita (i)] quay
ΠΡΟΓΕΥΜΑ πρόγευμα (το)

[proyevma (to)] breakfast
ΠΡΟΓΡΑΜΜΑ πρόγραμμα (το) [programa (to)] timetable, (US) schedule; programme
προκαταβολικά [prokatavolika] in advance
ΠΡΟΞΕΝΕΙΟ προξενείο (το) [proxenio (to)] consulate
ΠΡΟΣΕΧΕ! πρόσεχε! [prosekheh!] look out!
ΠΡΟΣΟΧΗ ΑΡΓΑ προσοχή αργά caution: slow
ΠΡΟΣΟΧΗ ΚΙΝΔΥΝΟΣ προσοχή κίνδυνος caution: danger
προσπερνώ [prosperno] to overtake
ΠΡΟΣΤΙΜΟ πρόστιμο (το) [prostimo (to)] fine
προσφέρω [prosfero] to offer; to give
προς [pros] towards
ΠΡΟΦΥΛΑΚΤΙΚΟ προφυλακτικό (το) [profilaktiko (to)] condom
προχτές [prokhtes] the day before yesterday
πρωί (το) [proi (to)] morning
ΠΡΩΙΝΟ πρωινό (το) [pro-ino (to)] breakfast
πρώτα [prota] first, firstly
ΠΡΩΤΕΣ ΒΟΗΘΕΙΕΣ πρώτες βοήθειες (οι) [protes voiTHi-es (i)] first aid
πρώτο! [proto!] great!
πρώτος [protos] first
ΠΤΗΣΗ πτήση (η) [ptisi (i)] flight
πυρκαγιά (η) [pirkaya (i)] fire

ΠΩΛΕΙΤΑΙ πωλείται for sale
πώς; [pos?] how?; what?

ΡΑΦΕΙΟ ραφείο (το) [rafio (to)] tailor's
ΡΕΣΕΨΙΟΝ ρεσεψιόν (η) [resepsion (i)] reception
ρόδα (η) [rotha (i)] wheel
ρούχα (τα) [rookha (ta)] clothes
ρωτώ [roto] to ask

σαββατοκύριακο (το) [savatokiriako (to)] weekend
σακάκι (το) [sakaki (to)] jacket
σακβουαγιάζ (το) [sakvooayaz (to)] hand baggage
σάκος (ο) [sakos (o)] backpack
ΣΑΛΟΝΙ σαλόνι (το) [saloni (to)] lounge
σαν [san] like, as
σας [sas] you; your
σε [seh] you; to; at; in
ΣΗΚΩΣΤΕ ΤΟ ΑΚΟΥΣΤΙΚΟ σηκώστε το ακουστικό lift receiver
ΣΗΜΕΡΑ σήμερα [simera] today
σιγά-σιγά [siga-siga] slowly; slow down
ΣΙΔΗΡΟΔΡΟΜΙΚΟΣ ΣΤΑΘΜΟΣ σιδηροδρομικός σταθμός (ο) [sithrothromikos staTHmos (o)] railway station
ΣΙΔΗΡΟΥΡΓΕΙΟ σιδηρουργείο (το) [sithiirooryio (to)] hardware store
ΣΙΝΕΜΑ σινεμά (το) [sinema (to)] cinema, movie theater
σκέπτομαι [skeptomeh] to think

σκληρός [sklirós] hard
σκοτεινός [skotinós] dark
σκουπίδια (τα) [skoopíthia (ta)] rubbish, garbage
σκύλος (ο) [skílos (o)] dog
σοβαρός [sovarós] serious
σου [soo] you; your
ΣΟΥΠΕΡΜΑΡΚΕΤ σούπερμάρκετ (το) [soopermárket (to)] supermarket
σπασμένος [spasménos] broken
σπάω [spao] to break
σπηλιά (το) [spiliá (to)] cave
σπίτι (το) [spíti (to)] house
σπουδαίος [spootheos] important
σπρώχνω [sprokhno] to push
ΣΤΑΘΜΟΣ σταθμός (ο) [staTHmos (o)] station
ΣΤΑΘΜΟΣ ΛΕΩΦΟΡΕΙΩΝ σταθμός λεωφορείων [staTHmos leoforion] bus station
ΣΤΑΘΜΟΣ ΤΑΞΙ σταθμός ταξί [staTHmos taxi] taxi stand
ΣΤΑΘΜΟΣ ΧΩΡΟΦΥΛΑΚΗΣ σταθμός χωροφυλακής [staTHmos khorofilakis] police station
σταματάω [stamatao] to stop
ΣΤΑΣΗ στάση (η) [stasi (i)] stop (for bus, train)
ΣΤΕΓΝΟΚΑΘΑΡΙΣΤΗΡΙΟ στεγνοκαθαριστήριο (το) [stegnokaTHaristirio (to)] dry cleaner's
στεγνός [stegnos] dry
στέλνω [stelno] to send
στην [stin] at; in; to; on

στο [sto] at; in; to; on
στόμα (το) [stoma (to)] mouth
στον [ston] at; in; to; on
ΣΤΟΠ! στοπ! stop!
συγγνώμη [signomi] sorry; excuse me
σύζυγος (ο) [sizigos (o)] husband
ΣΥΝΑΛΛΑΓΜΑ συνάλλαγμα (το) [sinalagma (to)] foreign exchange
ΣΥΝΑΛΛΑΓΜΑΤΙΚΗ ΙΣΟΤΙΜΙΑ συναλλαγματική ισοτιμία (η) [sinalagmatiki isotimia (i)] exchange rate
σύνορα (τα) [sinora (ta)] border
σύντομα [sidoma] soon
ΣΥΡΑΤΕ σύρατε pull
συχνά [sikhna] often
σχεδόν [skhethon] almost
ΣΧΟΛΕΙΟ σχολείο (το) [skholio (to)] school
σώμα (το) [soma (to)] body
σωστός [sostos] correct

τα [ta] the; them
ΤΑΒΕΡΝΑ ταβέρνα (η) [taverna (i)] restaurant
ΤΑΜΕΙΟ ταμείο (το) [tamio (to)] box office; cash desk
τάξη (η) [taxi (i)] class
ΤΑΞΙ ταξί (το) [taxi (to)] taxi
ταξίδι (το) [taxithi (to)] journey, trip
ΤΑΧΥΔΡΟΜΕΙΟ ταχυδρομείο (το) [takhithromio (to)] post office
τέλειος [telios] perfect
τελευταίος [telefteos] last

ΤΕΛΟΣ τέλος (το) [telos (to)] end

ΤΕΛΩΝΕΙΟ Τελωνείο (το) [Telonio (to)] Customs

τέχνη (η) [tekhni (i)] art

τη [ti] the

ΤΗΛΕΚΑΡΤΑ τηλεκάρτα (η) [tilekarta (i)] phonecard

ΤΗΛΕΟΡΑΣΗ τηλεόραση (η) [tileorasi (i)] television

ΤΗΛΕΦΩΝΗΜΑ τηλεφώνημα [tilefonima] call

ΤΗΛΕΦΩΝΟ τηλέφωνο (το) [tilefono (to)] phone

την [tin] her; on; per; the

της [tis] her; to her; of her

τι; [ti?] what?

ΤΙΜΗ τιμή (η) [timi (i)] price

τίποτε [tipoteh] nothing

τις [tis] them

το [to] in; it; the; per

τον [ton] him; the

τόσο [toso] so (much)

τότε [toteh] then

του [too] his; its; to him

ΤΟΥΑΛΕΤΑ τουαλέτα (η) [tooaleta (i)] toilet, rest room

ΤΟΥΡΙΣΤΙΚΗ ΑΣΤΥΝΟΜΙΑ Τουριστική Αστυνομία (η) [Tooristiki Astinomia (i)] Tourist Police

ΤΟΥΡΚΙΑ Τουρκία (η) [Toorkia (i)] Turkey

τους [toos] them; to them

τραβάω [travao] to pull

ΤΡΑΠΕΖΑΡΙΑ τραπεζαρία (η) [trapezaria (i)] dining room

ΤΡΑΠΕΖΑ τράπεζα (η) [trapeza (i)] bank

τραπέζι (το) [trapezi (to)] table

τρελλός [trelos] mad

ΤΡΕΝΟ τρένο (το) [treno (to)] train

τρώω [troo] to eat

τσάντα (η) [tsada (i)] bag; handbag, (US) purse

ΤΣΙΓΑΡΟ τσιγάρο (το) [tsigaro (to)] cigarette

των [ton] of them

τώρα [tora] now

υπάρχει [iparkhi] there is

υπάρχουν [iparkhoon] there are

υπερβολικά [ipervolika] too

υπνοδωμάτιο (το) [ipnothomatio (to)] bedroom

ύπνος (ο) [ipnos (o)] sleep

ΥΠΟΓΕΙΟ υπόγειο (το) [ipoyio (to)] basement

ΥΠΟΓΕΙΟΣ υπόγειος (ο) [ipoyios (o)] underground, (US) subway

υπογράφω [ipografo] to sign

υπολογιστής (ο) [ipoloyistis (o)] computer

ΦΑΓΗΤΟ φαγητό (το) [fayito (to)] food; meal; lunch

ΦΑΡΜΑΚΕΙΟ φαρμακείο (το) [farmakio (to)] pharmacy

φάρμακο (το) [farmako (to)] medicine

φέρνω [ferno] to bring

ΦΕΡΡΥ ΜΠΩΤ φέρρυ μπωτ (το) [feri bot (to)] ferry

φεύγω [fevgo] to go away

φθινόπωρο (το) [fтhinoporo (to)] autumn, (US) fall

φιλενάδα (η) [filenatha (i)] girlfriend; friend

ΦΙΛΜ φιλμ (το) [film (to)] film, movie

ΦΙΛΟΔΩΡΗΜΑ φιλοδώρημα (το) [filothorima (to)] service charge; tip

φίλος (ο) [filos (o)] boyfriend; friend

φοβερός [foveros] terrible

φοιτητής (ο) [fititis (o)], φοιτήτρια (η) [fititria (i)] student

φορά (η) [fora (i)] time, occasion

ΦΟΥΛ ΠΑΝΣΙΟΝ φουλ πανσιόν (η) [fool pansion (i)] full board, European plan

ΦΟΥΡΝΟΣ φούρνος (ο) [foornos (o)] baker's; oven

ΦΡΕΣΚΟΣ φρέσκος [freskos] fresh

φτάνω [ftano] to arrive

ΦΤΗΝΟΣ φτηνός [ftinos] cheap

φτωχός [ftokhos] poor

ΦΥΛΑΞΗ ΑΠΟΣΚΕΥΩΝ φύλαξη αποσκευών [filaxi aposkevon] left luggage, baggage check

φώτα (τα) [fota (ta)] lights

ΦΩΤΙΑ φωτιά (η) [fotia (i)] fire

φωτογραφία (η) [fotografia (i)] photograph

φωτογραφική μηχανή (η) [fotografiki mikhani (i)] camera

χαμηλός [khamilos] low

ΧΑΡΤΗΣ χάρτης (ο) [khartis (o)] map

ΧΑΡΤΙ χαρτί (το) [kharti (to)] paper

χαρτονόμισμα [khartonomisma] banknote, (US) bill

ΧΑΣΑΠΗΣ χασάπης (ο) [khasapis (o)] butcher's

ΧΕΙΜΕΡΙΝΟΣ χειμερινός [khimerinos] (winter) cinema/movie theater

χειμώνας (ο) [khimonas (o)] winter

χειρότερος [khiroteros] worse

χέρι (το) [kheri (to)] arm; hand

χθες [khTHes] yesterday

χιλιόμετρο (το) [khiliometro (to)] kilometre

Χριστούγεννα (τα) [KHristooyena (ta)] Christmas

χρονιά (η) [khronia (i)] year

χρόνος (ο) [khronos (o)] time; year

ΧΡΥΣΟΣ χρυσός (ο) [khrisos (o)] gold

χρώμα (το) [khroma (to)] colour

χωριό (το) [khorio (to)] village

ΧΩΡΙΣ χωρίς [khoris] without

ψεύτικος [pseftikos] false

ΨΩΜΑΔΙΚΟ ψωμάδικο [psomathiko] baker's

ψηλός [psilos] high; tall

ΩΘΗΣΑΤΕ ωθήσατε push

ώρα (η) [ora (i)] hour

ωραίος [oreos] beautiful; handsome; lovely

ως [os] as, since

MENU READER

Food: Essential terms

bread to psomi
butter to vootiro
cup to flidzani
dessert to glikisma
fish to psari
fork to pirooni
glass to potiri
knife to makheri
main course to kirio piato
meat to kreas
menu to menoo
pepper to piperi
plate to piato
salad i salata

salt to alati
set menu to tabl-dot
soup i soopa
spoon to kootali
starter to proto piato
table to trapezi

another ..., please ali mia ...,
 parakalo
excuse me! parakalo
could I have the bill, please?
 boro na ekho ton
 logariasmo, parakalo?

Food: Menu Reader

ΑΓΓΙΝΑΡΕΣ ΑΥΓΟΛΕΜΟΝΟ
 αγγινάρες αυγολέμονο
 [aginares avgolemono]
 artichokes in egg and lemon
 sauce
ΑΓΓΟΥΡΙ αγγούρι [agoori]
 cucumber
ΑΚΤΙΝΙΔΙΟ ακτινίδιο
 [aktinithio] kiwi fruit

ΑΛΑΤΙ αλάτι [alati] salt
ΑΛΛΑΝΤΙΚΑ αλλαντικά
 [aladika] sausages, salami,
 ham etc
ΑΜΥΓΔΑΛΑ αμύγδαλα
 [amigthala] almonds
ΑΝΑΝΑΣ ανανάς [ananas]
 pineapple
ΑΡΑΚΑΣ αρακάς [arakas] peas

285

ΑΡΝΑΚΙ αρνάκι [**arn**aki] lamb

ΑΡΝΙ αρνί [**arni**] mutton, lamb

ΑΣΤΑΚΟΣ αστακός [ast**ak**os] lob er

ΑΤΖΕΜ ΠΙΛΑΦΙ ατζέμ πιλάφι [at**zem** pil**afi**] rice pilaf

ΑΥΓΑ ΜΕ ΜΑΝΙΤΑΡΙΑ αυγά με μανιτάρια [av**ga** meh manit**aria**] mushroom omelette

ΑΥΓΟ αυγό [av**go**] egg

ΑΥΓΟΛΕΜΟΝΟ ΣΟΥΠΑ αυγολέμονο σούπα [avgo**lemono soopa**] chicken broth with egg and lemon

ΑΧΛΑΔΙ αχλάδι [akhl**athi**] pear

ΒΑΤΟΜΟΥΡΟ βατόμουρο [vat**o**mooro] blackberry

ΒΕΡΙΚΟΚΟ βερίκοκο [ver**ikoko**] apricot

ΒΟΔΙΝΟ βοδινό [voth**in**o] beef

ΒΟΥΤΥΡΟ βούτυρο [v**oo**tiro] butter

ΒΡΑΣΤΟ βραστό [vrast**o**] boiled

ΒΥΣΣΙΝΟ βύσσινο [v**is**ino] sour cherries

ΓΑΛΟΠΟΥΛΑ γαλοπούλα [galop**oo**la] turkey

ΓΑΡΙΔΕΣ γαρίδες [gar**ithes**] prawns

ΓΑΡΙΔΕΣ ΚΟΚΤΑΙΗΛ γαρίδες κοκταίηλ [gar**ithes** cocktail] shrimp cocktail

ΓΑΡΝΙΤΟΥΡΑ γαρνιτούρα [garnit**oora**] vegetables

ΓΕΜΙΣΤΑ γεμιστά [yemist**a**]

stuffed, usually with rice and/or minced meat

ΓΙΑΟΥΡΤΙ γιαούρτι [ya-**oorti**] yoghurt

ΓΙΓΑΝΤΕΣ γίγαντες [**yi**gandes] white haricot beans; butter beans

ΓΙΟΥΒΑΡΛΑΚΙΑ γιουβαρλάκια [yoovarl**akia**] meatballs, rice and seasoning in a sauce

ΓΙΟΥΒΕΤΣΙ γιουβέτσι [yoo**vetsi**] oven-roasted lamb with pasta

ΓΚΡΕΙΠΦΡΟΥΤ γκρέιπφρουτ [grapefruit] grapefruit

ΓΛΥΚΑ γλυκά [**glika**] cakes, desserts

ΓΛΩΣΣΑ γλώσσα [**glosa**] sole; tongue

ΓΡΑΝΙΤΑ γρανίτα [gran**ita**] sorbet

ΔΑΜΑΣΚΗΝΟ δαμάσκηνο [thamaskino] plum; prune

ΔΙΠΛΕΣ δίπλες [**thiples**] pancakes

ΕΛΑΙΟΛΑΔΟ ελαιόλαδο [ele**olatho**] olive oil

ΕΛΙΕΣ ελιές [eli-**es**] olives

ΖΑΜΠΟΝ ζαμπόν [zab**on**] ham

ΖΑΧΑΡΗ ζάχαρη [**zakhari**] sugar

ΖΕΛΕ ζελέ [zel**eh**] jelly

ΖΥΜΑΡΙΚΑ ζυμαρικά [zimar**ika**] pasta and rice

ΘΑΛΑΣΣΙΝΑ θαλασσινά [THalas**ina**] seafood

ΚΑΒΟΥΡΙΑ καβούρια

[kavooria] crab

ΚΑΚΑΒΙΑ κακαβιά [kakavia] mixed fish soup

ΚΑΛΑΜΑΡΙΑ καλαμάρια [kalamaria] squid

ΚΑΝΕΛΛΟΝΙΑ ΓΕΜΙΣΤΑ κανελλόνια γεμιστά [kanelonia yemista] stuffed canelloni

ΚΑΠΑΜΑΣ ΑΡΝΙ καπαμάς αρνί [kapamas arni] lamb cooked in spices and tomato sauce

ΚΑΠΝΙΣΤΟ καπνιστό [kapnisto] smoked

ΚΑΠΠΑΡΗ κάππαρη [kapari] caper

ΚΑΡΑΒΙΔΕΣ καραβίδες [karavithes] king prawns; crayfish

ΚΑΡΟΤΑ καρότα [karota] carrots

ΚΑΡΠΟΥΖΙ καρπούζι [karpoozi] watermelon

ΚΑΡΥΔΙ καρύδι [karithi] nut

ΚΑΡΥΔΟΠΙΤΤΑ καρυδόπιττα [karithopita] walnut cake; cake with nuts and syrup

ΚΑΡΧΑΡΙΑΣ καρχαρίας [karkharias] shark

ΚΑΤΑΪΦΙ καταΐφι [kata-ifi] shredded filo pastry with honey and nuts

ΚΕΙΚ κέικ [cake] cake

ΚΕΡΑΣΙΑ κεράσια [kerasia] cherries

ΚΕΦΤΕΔΕΣ κεφτέδες [keftethes] meatballs

ΚΙΜΑΣ κιμάς [kimas] minced meat

ΚΛΕΦΤΙΚΟ κλέφτικο [kleftiko] meat, potatoes and vegetables cooked together in a pot or foil

ΚΟΚΚΙΝΙΣΤΟ κοκκινιστό [kokinisto] in tomato sauce

ΚΟΛΙΟΙ κολιοί [koli-i] mackerel

ΚΟΛΟΚΥΘΑΚΙΑ κολοκυθάκια [kolokiThakia] courgettes, zucchini

ΚΟΜΠΟΣΤΑ κομπόστα [kobosta] fruit compote

ΚΟΤΑ κότα [kota] chicken

ΚΟΤΟΠΟΥΛΟ κοτόπουλο [kotopoolo] chicken

ΚΟΥΚΙΑ ΛΑΔΕΡΑ κουκιά λαδερά [kookia lathera] broad beans in tomato sauce

ΚΟΥΝΕΛΙ κουνέλι [kooneli] rabbit

ΚΟΥΝΟΥΠΙΔΙ κουνουπίδι [koonoopithi] cauliflower

ΚΡΑΣΑΤΟ κρασάτο [krasato] cooked in wine sauce

ΚΡΕΑΣ κρέας [kreas] meat, usually beef

ΚΡΕΑΤΙΚΑ κρεατικά [kreh-atika] meat dishes

ΚΡΕΜΑ κρέμα [krema] cream

ΚΡΕΜΜΥΔΙΑ κρεμμύδια [kremithia] onions

ΚΡΕΜΜΥΔΟΣΟΥΠΑ κρεμμυδόσουπα [kremithosoopa] onion soup

ΚΡΕΠΑ κρέπα [krepa] pancake

ΚΥΔΩΝΙΑ κυδώνια [kithonia] quinces

ΚΥΝΗΓΙ κυνήγι [kiniyi] game

ΚΥΡΙΟ ΠΙΑΤΟ κύριο πιάτο [kirio piato] main course

ΛΑΓΟΣ λαγός [lagos] hare

ΛΑΔΕΡΑ λαδερά [lathera] in olive oil and tomato sauce

ΛΑΔΟΛΕΜΟΝΟ λαδολέμονο [latholemono] olive oil and lemon dressing

ΛΑΔΟΞΥΔΟ λαδόξυδο [lathoxitho] oil and vinegar salad dressing

ΛΑΖΑΝΙΑ λαζάνια [lazania] lasagne

ΛΑΧΑΝΙΚΑ λαχανικά [lakhanika] vegetables

ΛΑΧΑΝΟ λάχανο [lakhano] cabbage

ΛΑΧΑΝΟ ΝΤΟΛΜΑΔΕΣ λάχανο ντολμάδες [lakhano dolmathes] cabbage leaves stuffed with minced meat and rice

ΛΕΜΟΝΙ λεμόνι [lemoni] lemon

ΛΙΘΡΙΝΙ λιθρίνι [liTHrini] red snapper

ΛΟΥΚΑΝΙΚΑ λουκάνικα [lookanika] sausages

ΛΟΥΚΟΥΜΑΔΕΣ λουκουμάδες [lookoomathes] doughnuts

ΛΟΥΚΟΥΜΙΑ λουκούμια [lookoomia] Turkish delight

ΜΑΚΑΡΟΝΑΚΙ ΚΟΦΤΟ μακαρονάκι κοφτό [makaronaki kofto] macaroni

ΜΑΚΑΡΟΝΙΑ μακαρόνια [makaronia] pasta

ΜΑΝΙΤΑΡΙΑ μανιτάρια [manitaria] mushrooms

ΜΑΡΙΔΕΣ ΤΗΓΑΝΗΤΕΣ μαρίδες τηγανητές [marithes tiganites] small fried fish

ΜΑΡΜΕΛΑΔΑ μαρμελάδα [marmelatha] jam, marmalade

ΜΑΡΟΥΛΙ μαρούλι [marooli] lettuce

ΜΑΡΟΥΛΙΑ ΣΑΛΑΤΑ μαρούλια σαλάτα [maroolia salata] green salad

ΜΕ ΛΑΔΟΛΕΜΟΝΟ με λαδολέμονο [meh latholemono] with olive oil and lemon dressing

ΜΕΛΙ μέλι [meli] honey

ΜΕΛΙΤΖΑΝΕΣ μελιτζάνες [melidzanes] aubergines, eggplants

ΜΕ ΣΑΛΤΣΑ με σάλτσα [meh saltsa] with sauce, usually tomato sauce

ΜΗΛΟ μήλο [milo] apple μισοψημένο [misopsimeno] medium (steak)

ΜΟΣΧΑΡΙ μοσχάρι [moskhari] veal; tender beef

ΜΟΣΧΑΡΙ ΣΝΙΤΖΕΛ ΜΕ ΠΑΤΑΤΕΣ ΤΗΓΑΝΗΤΕΣ μοσχάρι σνίτζελ με πατάτες τηγανητές [moskhari schnitzel meh patates tiganites] steak and chips/fries

ΜΟΥΣΑΚΑΣ μουσακάς [moosakas] moussaka – layers of vegetables and minced meat topped with béchamel sauce

ΜΠΑΚΑΛΙΑΡΟΣ μπακαλιάρος [bakaliaros] cod; salt cod; haddock

ΜΠΑΚΛΑΒΑΔΕΣ μπακλαβάδες [baklavathes] baklava – layers of thin pastry with nuts and syrup

ΜΠΑΜΙΕΣ μπάμιες [bami-es] okra

ΜΠΑΡΜΠΟΥΝΙΑ μπαρμπούνια [barboonia] red mullet

ΜΠΕΙΚΟΝ μπέικον [bacon] bacon

ΜΠΙΖΕΛΙΑ μπιζέλια [bizelia] peas

ΜΠΙΦΤΕΚΙ μπιφτέκι [bifteki] hamburger; grilled meatballs

ΜΠΟΝ ΦΙΛΕ μπον φιλέ [bon fileh] fillet steak

ΜΠΟΥΓΑΤΣΑ μπουγάτσα [boogatsa] puff pastry with various fillings

ΜΠΡΙΑΜΙ μπριάμι [briami] ratatouille

ΜΠΡΙΖΟΛΑ μπριζόλα [brizola] chop; steak

ΜΠΡΟΚΟΛΟ μπρόκολο [brokolo] broccoli

ΜΥΑΛΑ μυαλά [miala] brains

ΜΥΔΙΑ μύδια [mithia] mussels

ΝΕΦΡΑ νεφρά [nefra] kidneys

ΝΤΟΛΜΑΔΕΣ ντολμάδες [dolmathes] vine or cabbage leaves stuffed with minced meat and/or rice

ΝΤΟΜΑΤΕΣ ντομάτες [domates] tomatoes

ΞΙΦΙΑΣ ξιφίας [xifias] swordfish

ΟΜΕΛΕΤΑ ομελέτα [omeleta] omelette

ΟΡΕΚΤΙΚΑ ορεκτικά [orektika] hors d'oeuvres, starters

ΟΣΤΡΑΚΟΕΙΔΗ οστρακοειδή [ostrako-ithi] shellfish

ΠΑΓΩΤΟ παγωτό [pagoto] ice cream

ΠΑΠΙΑ πάπια [papia] duck

ΠΑΣΤΑ πάστα [pasta] cake

ΠΑΣΤΙΤΣΙΟ παστίτσιο [pastitsio] macaroni cheese or lasagne-type dish, with minced meat and white sauce

ΠΑΤΑΤΕΣ πατάτες [patates] potatoes

ΠΑΤΑΤΕΣ ΤΗΓΑΝΙΤΕΣ πατάτες τηγανιτές [patates tiganites] chips, French fries

ΠΑΤΣΑΣ πατσάς [patsas] tripe; soup made from lambs' intestines

ΠΕΠΟΝΙ πεπόνι [peponi] melon

ΠΕΣΤΡΟΦΑ πέστροφα [pestrofa] trout

ΠΙΛΑΦΙ πιλάφι [pilafi] rice

ΠΙΠΕΡΙ πιπέρι [piperi] pepper (spice)

ΠΙΠΕΡΙΕΣ πιπεριές [piperi-es] peppers

ΠΙΡΟΣΚΙ πιροσκί [piroski] minced meat or sausage rolls

ΠΙΤΣΑ πίτσα [pizza] pizza

ΠΙΤΤΑ πίττα [pita] pie

ΠΛΑΚΙ πλακί [plaki] baked in the oven in a tomato sauce

πολύ ψημένο [poli psimeno] overdone

ΠΟΡΤΟΚΑΛΙ πορτοκάλι [portokali] orange

ΠΟΥΛΕΡΙΚΑ πουλερικά [poulerika] poultry

ΠΟΥΤΙΓΚΑ πουτίγκα [pootiga] pudding

ΠΡΑΣΑ πράσα [prasa] leeks

ΠΡΩΤΟ ΠΙΑΤΟ πρώτο πιάτο [proto piato] starter

ΡΑΒΙΟΛΙΑ ραβιόλια [raviolia] ravioli

ΡΟΔΑΚΙΝΟ ροδάκινο [rothakino] peaches

ΡΟΣΜΠΙΦ ΑΡΝΙ ΜΟΣΧΑΡΙ ροσμπίφ αρνί μοσχάρι [rozbif arni moskhari] roast beef, veal or lamb

ΡΥΖΙ ρύζι [rizi] rice

ΡΥΖΟΓΑΛΟ ρυζόγαλο [rizogalo] rice pudding

ΣΑΛΑΜΙ σαλάμι [salami] salami

ΣΑΛΑΤΑ σαλάτα [salata] salad

ΣΑΛΙΓΚΑΡΙΑ σαλιγκάρια [saligaria] snails

ΣΑΛΤΣΑ σάλτσα [saltsa] sauce

ΣΑΜΑΛΙ σάμαλι [samali] semolina cake with honey

ΣΑΝΤΙΓΥ σαντιγύ [sadiyi] whipped cream

ΣΑΝΤΟΥΙΤΣ σάντουιτς [sandwich] sandwich

ΣΑΡΔΕΛΛΕΣ σαρδέλλες [sartheles] sardines

ΣΕΛΙΝΟ σέλινο [selino] celery

ΣΙΡΟΠΙ σιρόπι [siropi] syrup

ΣΚΟΡΔΑΛΙΑ σκορδαλιά [skorthalia] thick garlic sauce

ΣΟΛΟΜΟΣ σολομός [solomos] salmon

ΣΟΥΒΛΑΚΙΑ σουβλάκια [soovlakia] meat grilled on a skewer, served in pitta bread

ΣΟΥΠΑ σούπα [soopa] soup

ΣΟΥΠΙΕΣ σουπιές [soopi-es] cuttlefish

ΣΟΥΤΖΟΥΚΑΚΙΑ σουτζουκάκια [sootzookakia] spicy meatballs in red sauce

ΣΟΥΦΛΕ σουφλέ [soofleh] soufflé

ΣΠΑΝΑΚΙ σπανάκι [spanaki] spinach

ΣΠΑΝΑΚΟΠΙΤΤΑ σπανακόπιττα [spanakopita] spinach (and sometimes feta) in filo pastry

σπάνιος [spanios] rare (steak)

ΣΠΑΡΑΓΓΙΑ ΣΑΛΑΤΑ σπαράγγια σαλάτα [sparagia salata] asparagus salad

ΣΠΕΣΙΑΛΙΤΕ σπεσιαλιτέ [spesialiteh] speciality

ΣΤΑΦΙΔΕΣ σταφίδες [stafithes] dried fruit

ΣΤΑΦΥΛΙΑ σταφύλια [stafilia] grapes

ΣΤΙΦΑΔΟ στιφάδο [stifatho] chopped meat with onions; hare or rabbit stew with onions

ΣΤΟ ΦΟΥΡΝΟ στο φούρνο

[sto **foo**rno] baked in the oven

ΣΤΡΕΙΔΙΑ στρείδια [**stri**thia] oysters

ΣΥΚΑ σύκα [**si**ka] figs

ΣΥΚΩΤΑΚΙΑ συκωτάκια [si**ko**takia] liver

ΣΥΝΑΓΡΙΔΑ ΨΗΤΗ συναγρίδα ψητή [sina**gri**tha psi**ti**] grilled sea bream

ΣΩΤΕ σωτέ [so**teh**] lightly fried, sautéed

ΤΑΡΑΜΑΣ ταραμάς [tara**mas**] cod roe

ΤΑΡΑΜΟΣΑΛΑΤΑ ταραμοσαλάτα [taramosa**la**ta] cod roe dip

ΤΑΡΤΑ τάρτα [**tar**ta] tart

ΤΖΑΤΖΙΚΙ τζατζίκι [**dza**dziki] yoghurt, cucumber and garlic dip

ΤΗΓΑΝΗΤΟΣ τηγανητός [tiga**ni**tos] fried

ΤΗΣ ΚΑΤΣΑΡΟΛΑΣ της κατσαρόλας [tis katsa**ro**las] casseroled

ΤΗΣ ΣΟΥΒΛΑΣ της σούβλας [tis **soo**vlas] roast on a spit

ΤΗΣ ΣΧΑΡΑΣ της σχάρας [tis **skha**ras] grilled over charcoal

ΤΟΝΝΟΣ τόννος [**to**nos] tuna

ΤΟΣΤ τοστ [**tost**] toasted sandwich

ΤΟΥ ΑΤΜΟΥ του ατμού [too at**moo**] steamed

ΤΟΥΡΣΙ τουρσί [**toor**si] pickled

ΤΟΥΡΤΑ τούρτα [**toor**ta] gâteau

ΤΣΙΠΟΥΡΕΣ τσιπούρες

[tsi**poo**res] sea bream

ΤΣΙΠΣ τσιπς [**tsips**] crisps, (US) potato chips

ΦΑΒΑ φάβα [**fa**va] chick pea soup

ΦΑΚΕΣ φακές [**fa**kes] lentil soup

ΦΑΣΟΛΑΚΙΑ φασολάκια [faso**la**kia] green beans

ΦΑΣΟΛΙΑ φασόλια [fa**so**lia] beans

ΦΕΤΑ φέτα [**fe**ta] feta cheese

ΦΙΛΕΤΟ φιλέτο [fi**le**to] fillet steak

ΦΟΥΝΤΟΥΚΙΑ φουντούκια [food**oo**kia] hazelnuts

ΦΡΑΟΥΛΕΣ φράουλες [fra-**oo**les] strawberries

ΦΡΙΚΑΣΕ ΑΡΝΙ φρικασέ αρνί [frika**seh** ar**ni**] lamb cooked in lettuce with cream sauce

ΦΡΟΥΤΑ φρούτα [**froo**ta] fruit

ΦΡΥΓΑΝΙΑ φρυγανιά [friga**nia**] toast

ΦΡΥΓΑΝΙΕΣ φρυγανιές [friga**ni-es**] French toast

ΦΥΛΛΟ ΠΙΤΤΑΣ φύλλο πίττας [**fi**lo **pi**tas] filo pastry

ΦΥΣΤΙΚΙΑ ΑΙΓΙΝΗΣ φυστίκια Αιγίνης [fi**sti**kia **Ey**inis] pistachios

ΧΑΒΙΑΡΙ χαβιάρι [kha**via**ri] caviar

ΧΑΛΒΑΣ χαλβάς [khal**vas**] halva, sweet made from semolina, sesame seeds, nuts and honey

ΧΑΜΠΟΥΡΓΚΕΡ χάμπουργκερ [**kham**burger]

hamburger

ΧΗΝΑ χήνα [khina] goose

ΧΟΙΡΙΝΟ χοιρινό [khirino] pork

ΧΟΡΤΑΡΙΚΑ χορταρικά [khortarika] vegetables

ΧΤΑΠΟΔΙ χταπόδι [khtapothi] octopus

ΧΥΛΟΠΙΤΕΣ χυλοπίτες [khilopites] tagliatelle

ΧΩΡΙΑΤΙΚΗ ΣΑΛΑΤΑ χωριάτικη σαλάτα [khoriatiki salata] Greek salad – tomatoes, cucumber, peppers, feta, olives and boiled eggs with olive oil and vinegar dressing

ΨΑΡΙ ψάρι [psari] fish

ΨΑΡΟΣΟΥΠΑ ψαρόσουπα [psarosoopa] fish soup

ΨΗΤΟ ψητό [psito] grilled over charcoal; oven-roasted

ΨΗΤΟ ΣΤΗ ΣΧΑΡΑ ψητό στη σχάρα [psito sti skhara] grilled

ΨΩΜΙ ψωμί [psomi] bread

ΩΜΟΣ ωμός [omos] raw

MENU READER

Drink: Essential terms

beer i bira
bottle to bookali
brandy to koniak
coffee o kafes
cup: a cup of ... ena flidzani ...
fruit juice o khimos frooton
gin to tzin
 a gin and tonic ena tzin meh
 tonik
glass: a glass of ... ena
 potiri ...
milk to gala
mineral water to
 emfialomeno nero
orange juice i portokalatha
red wine to kokino krasi

rosé to rozeh
soda (water) i sotha
soft drink to anapsiktiko
sugar i zakhari
tea to tsa-i
tonic (water) to tonik
vodka i votka
water to nero
whisky to whisky
white wine to aspro krasi
wine to kras
wine list o katalogos ton
 krasion

another ..., please ali mia ...,
 parakalo

Drink: Menu Reader

ΑΝΑΝΑΣ ΧΥΜΟΣ ανανάς
 χυμός [ananas khimos]
 pineapple juice
ΑΝΑΨΥΚΤΙΚΟ αναψυκτικό
 [anapsiktiko] soft drink
ΑΣΠΡΟ ΚΡΑΣΙ άσπρο κρασί

[aspro krasi] white wine
ΒΟΤΚΑ βότκα [votka] vodka
ΒΥΣΣΙΝΑΔΑ βυσσινάδα
 [visinatha] black cherry juice
ΓΑΛΑ γάλα [gala] milk
ΓΑΛΛΙΚΟΣ ΚΑΦΕΣ γαλλικός

καφές [galikos kafes] filter
coffee; French coffee

ΓΛΥΚΟ ΚΡΑΣΙ γλυκό κρασί
[gliko krasi] sweet wine

ΕΛΛΗΝΙΚΟΣ ΚΑΦΕΣ
ελληνικός καφές [elinikos
kafes] Greek coffee

ΖΕΣΤΗ ΣΟΚΟΛΑΤΑ ζεστή
σοκολάτα [zesti sokolata] hot
chocolate

ΚΑΦΕΣ ΜΕΤΡΙΟΣ καφές
μέτριος [kafes metrios]
medium-sweet Greek
coffee

ΚΑΦΕΣ ΒΑΡΥΣ ΓΛΥΚΟΣ
καφές βαρύς γλυκός [kafes varis
glikos] sweet Greek coffee

ΚΑΦΕΣ ΜΕ ΓΑΛΑ καφές με
γάλα [kafes meh gala] coffee
with milk

ΚΟΚΚΙΝΟ ΚΡΑΣΙ κόκκινο
κρασί [kokino krasi] red wine

ΚΟΝΙΑΚ κονιάκ [koniak]
brandy

ΚΡΑΣΙ κρασί [krasi] wine

ΚΡΑΣΙ ΜΑΥΡΟΔΑΦΝΗ
κρασί μαυροδάφνη [krasi
mavrothafni] sweet red wine

ΚΡΑΣΙ ΤΟΥ ΜΑΓΑΖΙΟΥ
κρασί του μαγαζιού [krasi too
magazi-oo] house wine

ΛΕΜΟΝΑΔΑ λεμονάδα
[lemonatha] lemonade

ΛΙΚΕΡ λικέρ [liker] liqueur

ΜΕΤΑΛΛΙΚΟ ΝΕΡΟ
μεταλλικό νερό [metaliko nero]
mineral water

ΜΗΛΟΧΥΜΟΣ μηλοχυμός
[milokhimos] apple juice

ΜΠΥΡΑ μπύρα [bira] beer

ΝΕΣΚΑΦΕ νέσκαφέ [neskafeh]
Nescafé®, instant coffee

ΝΕΡΟ νερό [nero] water

ΝΤΟΜΑΤΑ ΧΥΜΟΣ ντομάτα
χυμός [domata khimos] tomato
juice

ΟΥΖΟ ούζο [oozo] ouzo

ΟΥΙΣΚΥ ουίσκυ whisky

ΠΑΓΟΣ πάγος [pagos] ice

ΠΟΡΤΟΚΑΛΑΔΑ
πορτοκαλάδα [portokalatha]
orange juice

ΠΟΡΤΟΚΑΛΙ ΧΥΜΟΣ
πορτοκάλι χυμός [portokali
khimos] orange juice

ΡΑΚΗ ρακή [raki] strong
spirit, eau-de-vie

ΡΕΤΣΙΝΑ ρετσίνα [retsina]
retsina

ΡΟΖΕ ΚΡΑΣΙ ροζέ κρασί
[rozeh krasi] rosé wine

ΡΟΥΜΙ ρούμι [roomi] rum

ΣΤΑΦΥΛΙ ΧΥΜΟΣ σταφύλι
χυμός [stafili khimos] grape
juice

ΤΖΙΝ ΜΕ ΤΟΝΙΚ τζιν με
τόνικ [tzin meh tonik] gin and
tonic

ΤΣΑΙ ΜΕ ΛΕΜΟΝΙ τσάι με
λεμόνι [tsa-i meh lemoni]
lemon tea

ΤΣΙΠΟΥΡΟ τσίπουρο [tsipooro]
type of ouzo

ΦΡΑΠΕ φραπέ [frapeh] iced
coffee

ΧΥΜΟΣ χυμός [khimos] juice

ITALIAN

DICTIONARY PHRASEBOOK

Pronunciation

In this phrase book, the Italian has been written in a system of imitated pronunciation so that it can be read as though it were English, bearing in mind the notes on pronunciation given below:

ay	as in may	ow	as in now
e	as in get	y	as in yes
g	always hard as in goat		

Letters given in bold type indicate the part of the word to be stressed.

When double consonants are given in the pronunciation such as j-j, t-t and so on, both consonants should be pronounced, for example **formaggio** [formaj-jo], **biglietto** [beel-yet-to].

Language Notes

Italian nouns have one of two genders – masculine or feminine. Words for 'the' are **il** (m) and **la** (f):

il letto	**la casa**
the bed	the house

Il changes to **lo** in front of a noun starting with **s**+consonant, **gn**, **pn**, **ps** or **z**:

lo scontrino	**lo zaino**
the receipt	the backpack

Both **il** and **la** change to **l'** in front of a vowel:

l'albergo	**l'autostrada**
the hotel	the motorway

The corresponding words for 'a' are **un** (m) and **una** (f). **Lo** becomes **uno**:

un treno	**uno specchio**	**una stanza**
a train	a mirror	a room

In the plural **il** becomes **i**; **lo** and **l'** (m) become **gli**; **la** and **l'** (f) become **le**.

The Italian words for 'I', 'you', 'he' etc are usually omitted as subjects unless special emphasis is required. For example:

è partito	**lui è partito**
he has left	he left (but not the others)

Here is a useful verb – 'to be':

sono I am	**siamo** [s-yamo] we are
sei [say] you are (familiar form)	**siete** [s-yaytay] you are (plural polite or familiar form)
è [ay] he/she/it is; you are (polite singular form)	**sono** they are

The familiar form is used to people you are on friendly terms with. When speaking to one person, and using the polite form, the verb takes the same form as for 'he/she/it':

(lei) è molto gentile
you are very kind

297

Days

Monday lunedì [loonedee]
Tuesday martedì [martedee]
Wednesday mercoledì [mairkoledee]
Thursday giovedì [jovedee]
Friday venerdì [venairdee]
Saturday sabato
Sunday domenica [domayneeka]

Months

January gennaio [jen-na-yo]
February febbraio [feb-bra-yo]
March marzo [martzo]
April aprile [apreelay]
May maggio [maj-jo]
June giugno [joon-yo]
July luglio [lool-yo]
August agosto
September settembre [set-tembray]
October ottobre [ot-tobray]
November novembray
December dicembre [deechembray]

Time

what time is it? che ore sono? [kay oray sono]
one o'clock l'una [loona]
two o'clock le due [lay doo-ay]
it's one o'clock è l'una [ay loona]
it's two o'clock sono le due [sono lay doo-ay]
it's ten o'clock sono le dieci [sono lay dee-echee]
five past one l'una e cinque [loona ay cheenkway]
ten past two le due e dieci [lay doo-ay ay dee-echee]
quarter past one l'una e un quarto [loona ay oon kwarto]
quarter past two le due e un quarto [lay doo-ay]
half past ten le dieci e mezza [lay dee-echee ay medza]
twenty to ten le dieci meno venti [lay dee-echee mayno ventee]
quarter to two le due meno un quarto [lay doo-ay mayno oon kwarto]
at eight o'clock alle otto
at half past four alle quattro e mezza [al-lay kwat-tro ay medza]
14.00 le quattordici [lay kwat-

tordeechee]

17.30 le diciassette e trenta [lay deechas-**set**-tay ay **tren**ta]

2 a.m. le due di notte [lay **doo**-ay dee **not**-tay]

2 p.m. le due del pomeriggio [pomer**eej**-jo]

6 a.m. le sei del mattino [lay **say**]

6 p.m. le sei di sera [dee **sai**ra]

noon mezzogiorno [medzo-**jor**no]

midnight mezzanotte [medzan**ot**-tay]

an hour un'ora [**o**ra]

a minute un minuto [meen**oo**to]

a second un secondo [sek**on**do]

a quarter of an hour un quarto d'ora [**kwar**to **do**ra]

half an hour mezz'ora [med**zo**ra]

three quarters of an hour tre quarti d'ora [tray **kwar**tee **do**ra]

Numbers

0	zero [**tz**airo]
1	uno [**oo**no]
2	due [**doo**-ay]
3	tre [tray]
4	quattro [**kwat**-tro]
5	cinque [**cheenk**way]
6	sei [say]
7	sette [**set**-tay]
8	otto [**ot**-to]
9	nove [**no**-vay]
10	dieci [dee-**ay**chee]
11	undici [**oon**-deechee]
12	dodici [**doh**-deechee]
13	tredici [**tray**-deechee]
14	quattordici [kwat-**tor**-deechee]
15	quindici [**kween**-deechee]
16	sedici [**say**-deechee]
17	diciassette [deechas-**set**-tay]
18	diciotto [deech**ot**-to]
19	diciannove [deechan-**no**-vay]
20	venti [**ven**tee]
21	ventuno [vent-**oo**no]
22	ventidue [ventee-**doo**-ay]
23	ventitré [ventee-**tray**]
30	trenta [**tren**ta]
31	trentuno [trent**oo**no]
40	quaranta [kwar**an**ta]
50	cinquanta [cheenk**wan**ta]
60	sessanta [ses-**san**ta]

70	settanta [set-**tan**ta]
80	ottanta [ot-**tan**ta]
90	novanta [no**van**ta]
100	cento [**chen**to]
110	centodieci [chento-dee-**ay**chee]
200	duecento [doo-ay-**chen**to]
300	trecento [tray-**chen**to]
1,000	mille [**mee**lay]
2,000	duemila [doo-ay-**mee**la]
5,000	cinquemila [cheenkway-**mee**la]
5,720	cinquemilasette-centoventi [cheenkway-**mee**la-set-tay-**chen**to-**ven**tee]
10,000	diecimila [dee-echee**mee**la]
10,550	diecimilacinque-centocinquanta [dee-echee**mee**la-cheenkway-**chen**to-cheenk**wan**ta]
20,000	ventimila [ventee**mee**la]
50,000	cinquantamila [cheenkwanta**mee**la]
100,000	centomila [chento**mee**la]
1,000,000	un milione [oon meel-**yo**nay]

In Italian, thousands are written with a full stop instead of a comma, e.g. 1.000, 10.000. Decimals are written with a comma, e.g. 3.5 would be 3,5 in Italian.

Ordinals

1st	primo [**pree**mo]
2nd	secondo [se**kon**do]
3rd	terzo [**tairt**zo]
4th	quarto [**kwar**to]
5th	quinto [**kween**to]
6th	sesto
7th	settimo [**set**-teemo]
8th	ottavo [ot-**tav**o]
9th	nono
10th	decimo [**day**cheemo]

English

→

Italian

A

a, an uno/una [**oo**no/**oo**na]
about circa [**cheer**ka]
  a film about Italy un film
  sull'Italia
above ... sopra a ...
abroad all'estero [al-**le**stairo]
accept accettare [achet-**ta**ray]
accident l'incidente m
  [eencheed**ay**ntay]
across: across the road
  dall'altra parte della strada
  [**par**tay]
adapter il riduttore [reedoot-
  toray]
address l'indirizzo m
  [eendeer**eet**zo]
Adriatic il mare Adriatico
  [**ma**ray]
adult l'adulto m [ad**oo**lto]
advance: in advance in
  anticipo [een ant**ee**cheepo]
after dopo
afternoon il pomeriggio
  [pomair**eej**-jo]
aftersun cream la crema
  doposole [dopos**o**lay]
afterwards dopo
again di nuovo [dee nw**o**vo]
against contro
ago: a week ago una
  settimana fa
AIDS l'aids m [a-eeds]
air l'aria f
  by air per via aerea [pair **vee**-a
  a-**ai**ray-a]
air-conditioning l'aria

condizionata [kondeetz-yon**a**ta]
airmail: by airmail per via
  aerea [a-**ai**ray-a]
airport l'aeroporto m
  [a-airop**or**to]
airport bus l'autobus
  dell'aeroporto m [**low**toboos]
alcohol l'alcool m [**al**kol]
all tutti [**toot**-tee]
  that's all, thanks è tutto,
  grazie [ay – gr**at**zee-ay]
allergic allergico [al-**lair**jeeko]
all right (I agree) va bene,
  d'accordo [**be**nay]
  I'm all right sto bene
  are you all right? (fam) stai
  bene? [sty]
  (pol) sta bene?
almost quasi [kw**a**zee]
alone solo
already già [ja]
also anche [**an**kay]
altogether in tutto [een t**oot**-to]
always sempre [**sem**pray]
ambulance l'ambulanza f
  [amboo**lan**tza]
America l'America f
  [am**ai**reeka]
American americano
  [amair**ee**kano]
ancient antico
and e [ay]
angry arrabbiato [ar-rab-y**a**to]
animal l'animale m [aneem**a**lay]
annoying seccante [sek-**kan**tay]
another un altro, un'altra
  [oon]
  another beer, please ancora
  una birra, per favore

antiseptic l'antisettico m
any: I don't have any non ne
ho [non nay o]
apartment l'appartamento m
apple la mela [mayla]
apricot l'albicocca f [albeekok-
ka]
arm il braccio [bracho]
arrival l'arrivo m [ar-reevo]
arrive arrivare [ar-reevaray]
art gallery la galleria d'arte
[gal-lairee-a]
as: as big as (così) grande
come [kozee granday komay]
ashtray il portacenere
[portachenairay]
ask chiedere [k-yaydairay]
I didn't ask for this non ho
chiesto questo [non o k-yesto
kwesto]
aspirin l'aspirina f
at: at the hotel in albergo
at the station alla stazione
at six o'clock alle sei
[al-lay]
at Giovanni's da Giovanni
aunt la zia [tzee-a]
Australia l'Australia f [owstral-
ya]
Australian australiano [owstral-
yano]
autumn l'autunno m [owtoon-
no]
away: go away! vattene! [vat-
tenay]
awful terribile [tair-reebeelay]

B

baby (male/female) il bambino,
la bambina
back (of body) la schiena [sk-
yayna]
(back part) la parte posteriore
[partay postair-yoray]
at the back dietro [d-yetro]
I'll be back soon torno fra
poco
bad cattivo [kat-teevo]
badly male [malay]
bag la borsa
(handbag) la borsetta
baggage i bagagli [bagal-yee]
baggage checkroom il
deposito bagagli
bakery la panetteria [panet-
tairee-a]
balcony il balcone [balkonay]
ball (large) la palla
(small) la pallina
banana la banana
band (musical) il gruppo
[groop-po]
bandage la fasciatura
[fashatoora]
Bandaids® i cerotti [chairot-
tee]
bank (money) la banca
bar il bar
barber's il barbiere [barb-
yairay]
basket il cestino [chesteeno]
(in shop) il cestello [chestel-lo]
bath il bagno [ban-yo]
bathroom il bagno

bathtub la vasca da bagno
battery la batteria [bat-tairee-a]
be essere [es-sairay]
beach la spiaggia [spee-aj-ja]
beach umbrella l'ombrellone
  m [ombrel-lonay]
beans i fagioli [fajolee]
beautiful bello
because perché [pairkay]
  because of ... a causa di...
  [kowza]
bed il letto
  I'm going to bed vado a letto
bed and breakfast camera
  con prima colazione [preema
  – kolatz-yonay]
bedroom la camera da letto
beef il manzo [mantzo]
beer la birra [beer-ra]
before prima di [preema]
begin cominciare
  [komeencharay]
  when does it begin? quando
  comincia? [kwando komeencha]
behind dietro (a) [d-yetro]
bell (church) la campana
  (doorbell) il campanello
below sotto (a)
belt la cintura [cheentoora]
berth la cuccetta [koochet-ta]
beside accanto a [ak-kanto]
best il migliore [meel-yoray]
better meglio [mayl-yo]
between tra, fra
beyond oltre [oltray]
bicycle la bicicletta
  [beecheeklet-ta]
big grande [granday]
bikini il bikini

bill il conto
  could I have the bill, please?
  il conto, per favore
bin la pattumiera [pat-toom-
  yaira]
bird l'uccello **m** [oochel-lo]
birthday il compleanno
  [komplay-an-no]
  happy birthday! buon
  compleanno! [bwon]
biscuit il biscotto
bit: a little bit un po'
  a big bit un grosso pezzo
  [petzo]
  a bit of ... un pezzetto di...
  [petzet-to dee]
  a bit expensive un po' caro
bite (by insect) la puntura
  [poontoora]
black nero [nairo]
blanket la coperta [kopairta]
blind cieco [chee-ayko]
blinds gli avvolgibili [av-
  voljeebeelay]
block of flats il caseggiato
  [kasej-jato]
blond biondo [b-yondo]
blood il sangue [sangway]
blouse la camicetta
  [kameechet-ta]
blow-dry l'asciugatura col fon
  f [ashoogatoora]
blue blu [bloo]
  blue eyes gli occhi azzurri
  [ok-kee adzoor-ree]
boat la barca
  (for passengers) il battello
body il corpo
boiler lo scaldabagno

[skaldaban-yo]
bone l'**o**sso m
book il l**i**bro
 (verb) prenotare [prenotaray]
bookshop, bookstore la
 libreria [leebrairee-a]
boot (footwear) lo stivale
 [steevalay]
border (of country) il confine
 [konf**ee**nay]
borrow prendere a prestito
 [prendairay]
both tutti e due [**too**t-tee ay
 d**oo**-ay]
bottle la bottiglia [bot-t**ee**l-ya]
bottle-opener il cavatappi
bottom (of person) il sedere
 [sed**ai**ray]
 at the bottom of ... (hill etc) ai
 piedi di... [a-ee p-y**ay**dee]
 (street, sea etc) in fondo a...
box la scatola
 (wooden) la cassetta
boy il ragazzo [rag**a**tzo]
boyfriend il ragazzo
bra il reggiseno [rej-jees**ay**no]
bracelet il braccialetto
 [brachal**e**t-to]
brake il freno [fr**ay**no]
brandy il brandy
bread il pane [p**a**nay]
break rompere [r**o**mpairay]
breakfast la (prima)
 colazione [kolatz-y**o**nay]
breast il seno [s**ay**no]
bridge (over river) il ponte
 [p**o**ntay]
bring portare [port**a**ray]
 I'll bring it back later lo

riporterò più tardi
 [reeportair**o**]
Britain la Gran Bretagna
 [bretan-ya]
British britannico
brochure l'opuscolo m
 [op**oo**skolo]
broken rotto [r**o**t-to]
brother il fratello
brown marrone [mar-r**o**nay]
 (hair, eyes) castano
brush (for hair) la spazzola
 [sp**a**tzola]
building l'edificio m
 [edeef**ee**cho]
bulb (light bulb) la lampadina
bunk la cuccetta [kooch**e**t-ta]
burn la bruciatura
 [broochat**oo**ra]
burst: a burst pipe una
 tubatura scoppiata [toobat**oo**ra
 skop-y**a**ta]
bus l'**a**utobus m [**ow**toboos]
 what number bus is it to ...?
 che numero va a...? [kay
 n**oo**mairo]

dialogue

 does this bus go to ...?
 questo autobus va a...?
 [kw**e**sto]
 no, you need a number ...
 no, deve prendere il...
 [d**ay**vay prend**ai**ray]

bus station la stazione degli
 autobus [statz-y**o**nay d**ay**l-yee
 owtoboos]

bus stop la fermata dell'autobus [fairmata]

busy (restaurant etc) animato

but ma

butcher's il macellaio [machella-yo]

butter il burro [boor-ro]

button il bottone [bot-tonay]

buy comprare [kompra-ray]

by: by bus/car in autobus/macchina [een]

by the window vicino al finestrino [veecheeno]

by Thursday per giovedì [pair]

C

cabbage il cavolo

cabin (on ship) la cabina

cable car la funivia [fooneevee-a]

café il caffè [kaf-fay]

cake la torta

call chiamare [k-yamaray] (phone) telefonare [telefonaray]

what's it called? come si chiama? [komay see k-yama]

he/she/it is called ... si chiama...

camera la macchina fotografica [mak-keena]

camp campeggiare [kampej-jaray]

camping gas il gas liquido [leekweedo]

campsite il campeggio [kampej-jo]

can la lattina

can: can you ...? puoi/può...? [pwoy/pwo]

can I ...? posso ...?

I can't ... on posso...

Canada il Canada

Canadian canadese [kanadayzay]

cancel annullare [an-nool-laray]

candies le caramelle [karamel-lay]

candle la candela [kandayla]

can opener l'apriscatole m [apreeskatolay]

car la macchina [mak-keena], l'auto(mobile) f [owtomobeelay]

carafe la caraffa

card (birthday etc) il biglietto [beel-yet-to]

cardphone il telefono a scheda [telayfono a skayda]

car hire l'autonoleggio m [owtonolej-jo]

carnival il carnevale [karnevalay]

car park il parcheggio [parkej-jo]

carpet il tappeto [tap-payto] (wall to wall) la moquette [moket]

carrot la carota

carry portare [portaray]

cash il contante [kontantay]

cash desk la cassa

cash dispenser il bancomat®

castle il castello

cat il gatto

cathedral la cattedrale [kattedralay], il duomo [dwomo]

cave la grotta

ceiling il soffitto

cellar (for wine) la cantina

centimetre il centimetro
[chenteemetro]

centre il centro [chentro]

certainly certamente
[chairtamentay]

chair la sedia [sayd-ya]

chair lift la seggiovia [sej-jovee-a]

change (money) gli spiccioli
[speecholee]
(verb: money, trains) cambiare
[kamb-yaray]

dialogue

do we have to change
(trains)? dobbiamo
cambiare? [dob-yamo]
yes, change at Rome/no
it's a direct train sì,
cambiate a Roma/no, è
diretto [kamb-yatay – ay]

cheap a buon mercato [bwon
mairkato]

check (verb) controllare
[kontrol-laray]
(US: noun) l'assegno m [as-sen-yo]
(US: bill) il conto

checkbook il libretto degli
assegni [dayl-yee as-sen-yee]

check-in il check-in

cheers! (toast) alla salute!
[salootay]

cheese il formaggio [formaj-jo]

chemist's la farmacia
[farmachee-a]

cheque l'assegno m [as-sen-yo]

cheque card la carta assegni

chest il petto

chewing gum il chewing gum

chicken il pollo

child (male/female) il bambino,
la bambina

chips le patatine fritte
[patateenay freet-tay]
(US) le patatine

chocolate il cioccolato [chok-kolato]

a hot chocolate una
cioccolata calda

Christmas il Natale [natalay]
Christmas Eve la vigilia di
Natale [veejeel-ya]
merry Christmas! Buon
Natale! [bwon]

church la chiesa [k-yayza]

cider il sidro

cigar il sigaro

cigarette la sigaretta

cinema il cinema [cheenema]

city la città [cheet-ta]

city centre il centro [chentro]

clean (adj) pulito [pooleeto]
can you clean these for me?
me li/le può pulire? [may
lee/lay pwo pooleeray]

clever intelligente [eentel-leejentay]

climbing l'alpinismo m

clock l'orologio m [orolojo]

close (verb) chiudere

[k-yoodairay]
closed chiuso [k-yoozo]
clothes gli abiti
clothes peg la molletta da
 bucato
cloudy nuvoloso [noovolozo]
coach (bus) il pullman
 (on train) la carrozza [kar-rotza]
coach station la stazione dei
 pullman [statz-yonay day]
coach trip la gita in pullman
 [jeeta]
coast la costa
coat (long coat) il cappotto
 (jacket) la giacca [jak-ka]
coathanger la gruccia
 [groocha]
code (for telephoning) il prefisso
 [prayfees-so]
coffee il caffè [kaf-fay]
coin la moneta [monayta]
Coke® la Coca-Cola
cold (adj) freddo
 I'm cold ho freddo [o]
 I have a cold ho il
 raffreddore [raf-fred-doray]
collar il colletto
collect call la telefonata a
 carico del destinatario
colour il colore [koloray]
comb il pettine [pet-teenay]
come venire [veneeray]
come back ritornare
 [reetornaray]
come in entrare [entraray]
comfortable comodo
complaint il reclamo [reklamo]
completely completamente
 [kompleta-mentay]

computer il computer
concert il concerto
 [konchairto]
conditioner (for hair) il balsamo
condom il preservativo
 [prezairvateevo]
congratulations!
 congratulazioni!
 [kongratoolatz-yonee]
connection la coincidenza
constipation la stitichezza
 [steeteeketza]
consulate il consolato
contact mettersi in contatto
 con
contact lenses le lenti a
 contatto
cooker la cucina [koocheena]
cookie il biscotto
corkscrew il cavatappi
correct (right) esatto
cost costare [kostaray]
cotton il cotone [kotonay]
cotton wool l'ovatta f
couchette la cuccetta [koochet-
 ta]
cough la tosse [tos-say]
cough medicine lo sciroppo
 per la tosse [sheerop-po pair]
could: could you ...?
 potresti/potrebbe...? [potrayb-
 bay]
 could I have ...? vorrei... [vor-
 ray]
 I couldn't ... (wasn't able to)
 non ho potuto... [o potooto]
country il paese [pa-ayzay]
 (countryside) la campagna
couple (two people) la coppia

[kop-ya]
a couple of ... un paio di...
[pa-yo dee]
courier la guida turistica
[gweeda]
course (main course etc) la
portata
of course naturalmente
[natooralmentay]
cousin (male/female) il cugino
[koojeeno], la cugina
crazy pazzo [patzo]
cream (on milk, in cake) la panna
(lotion) la crema [krayma]
credit card la carta di credito
[kraydeeto]

dialogue

> can I pay by credit card?
> posso pagare con una
> carta di credito? [pagaray]
> which card do you want to
> use? con quale carta
> vuole pagare? [kwalay –
> vwolay]
> yes, sir sì, signore [seen-
> yoray]
> what's the number? qual è
> il numero? [kwal ay eel
> noomairo]
> and the expiry date? e la
> data di scadenza? [ay –
> skadentza]

crisps le patatine [patateenay]
crossroads l'incrocio m
[eenkrocho]
crowded affollato

cry piangere [p-yanjairay]
cup la tazza [tatza]
cupboard l'armadio m [armad-
yo]
(in kitchen) la credenza
[kredentza]
curtains le tende [tenday]
cushion il cuscino [koosheeno]
Customs la dogana
cut il taglio [tal-yo]
cyclist il ciclista [cheekleesta]

D

dad il papà
damage danneggiare [dan-nej-
jaray]
damn! accidenti! [acheedentee]
damp umido [oomeedo]
dance il ballo
(verb) ballare [bal-laray]
dangerous pericoloso
[paireekolozo]
dark (colour) scuro [skooro]
(hair) bruno [broono]
date: what's the date today?
che giorno è oggi? [kay jorno
ay oj-jee]
daughter la figlia [feel-ya]
day il giorno [jorno]
the day after il giorno dopo
the day before il giorno
prima
dead morto
deaf sordo
decaffeinated coffee il caffè
decaffeinato [kaf-fay dekaf-fee-
aynato]

decide decidere [decheedairay]

deckchair la sedia a sdraio [sayd-ya a zdra-yo]

deep profondo

definitely certamente [chairtamentay]

delay il ritardo

delicatessen la gastronomia

delicious delizioso [deleetz-yozo]

dentist il dentista **m/f**

deodorant il deodorante [day-odorantay]

department store il grande magazzino [granday magatzeeno]

departure la partenza [partentza]

depend: it depends dipende [deependay]

dessert il dessert [des-sair]

destination la destinazione [desteenatz-yonay]

develop sviluppare [zveeloop-paray]

dialling code il prefisso telefonico [prefees-so]

diarrhoea la diarrea [dee-aray-a]

diesel il gasolio [gaz-ol-yo]

difference la differenza [deef-fairentza]

different diverso [deevairso]

difficult difficile [deef-feecheelay]

dining room la sala da pranzo [prantzo]

dinner la cena [chayna]

direct (adj) diretto [deeret-to]

direction la direzione [deeretz-yonay]

directory enquiries informazioni elenco abbonati [eenformatz-yonee]

dirty sporco

disco la discoteca

disgusting disgustoso [deesgoostozo]

district la zona

divorced divorziato [deevortz-yato]

do fare [faray]
  what shall we do? che facciamo? [kay fachamo]

doctor il medico [maydeeko]

dog il cane [kanay]

donkey l'asino **m**

don't!: don't do that! non farlo!

door (of room) la porta (of train, car) lo sportello

double doppio [dop-yo]

double bed il letto a due piazze [doo-ay p-yatzay]

double room la camera doppia [dop-ya]

down giù [joo]
  down here quaggiù [kwaj-joo]

downstairs di sotto

dozen la dozzina [dotzeena]

draught beer la birra alla spina [beer-ra]

dress il vestito

drink bere [bairay]
  something to drink qualcosa da bere [kwalkoza]
  what would you like to drink? cosa vuoi bere? [koza vwoy]

drinking water l'acqua
potabile [akwa potabeelay]
drive guidare [gweedaray]
can you drive? sa guidare?
driver (of car) l'autista m/f
[owteesta]
(of bus) il/la conducente
[kondoochentay]
driving licence la patente
[patentay]
drug la medicina
[medeecheena]
drugs (narcotics) la droga
drunk (adj) ubriaco [oobree-
ako]
dry asciutto [ashoot-to]
(wine) secco
dry-cleaner il lavasecco
during durante [doorantay]
dustbin la pattumiera [pat-
toom-yaira]
duvet il piumone [p-yoo-
monay]

E

each (every) ciascuno
[chaskoono]
ear l'orecchio m [orek-yo]
early presto
earrings gli orecchini [orek-
keenee]
east l'est m
Easter la Pasqua [paskwa]
easy facile [facheelay]
eat mangiare [manjaray]
economy class la classe
turistica [klas-say]

egg l'uovo m [wovo]
either: either ... or ... o... o...
elbow il gomito
electric elettrico
electricity l'elettricità f [elet-
treecheeta]
elevator l'ascensore m
[ashensoray]
else: something else
qualcos'altro [kwalkoz]
somewhere else da qualche
altra parte [kwalkay – partay]
embassy l'ambasciata f
[ambashata]
emergency l'emergenza f
[emairjentza]
empty vuoto [vwoto]
end la fine [feenay]
(verb) finire [feeneeray]
at the end of the street in
fondo alla strada
engaged (toilet, telephone)
occupato [ok-koopato]
(to be married) fidanzato
[feedantzato]
England l'Inghilterra f
[eengheeltair-ra]
English inglese [eenglayzay]
enjoy: to enjoy oneself
divertirsi
enormous enorme [enormay]
enough abbastanza [ab-
bastantza]
it's not big enough non è
grande abbastanza [ay]
that's enough basta
entrance l'entrata f
envelope la busta [boosta]
equipment l'attrezzatura f [at-

tretzat**oora**]
especially specialmente
[spech**al**mentay]
euro l'euro m [ay-**oo**ro]
Eurocheque l'eurocheque m
[ay-**oo**rochek]
Europe l'Europa f [ay-oor**o**pa]
evening la sera [**sai**ra]
 this evening questa sera
 [**kwe**sta]
eventually alla fine [**fee**nay]
ever mai [my]
every ogni [**on**-yee]
everyone ognuno [on-y**oo**no]
everything tutto [**toot**-to]
everywhere dappertutto [dap-
pair**toot**-to]
exactly! esattamente! [esat-
tamentay]
excellent eccellente
[eche**len**tay]
excellent! ottimo!
except eccetto [e**chet**-to]
exchange rate il tasso di
cambio [**kamb**-yo]
exciting emozionante [emotz-
yo**nan**tay]
excuse me (to get past)
permesso [pair**mes**-so]
 (to get attention) mi scusi [mee
sk**oo**zee]
exhibition la mostra
exit l'uscita f [oosh**ee**ta]
expensive caro
eye l'occhio m [**ok**-yo]
eyeglasses gli occhiali [**ok**-
y**a**lee]

face la faccia [**fa**cha]
faint (verb) svenire [sven**ee**ray]
fair (funfair) il luna park [**loo**na]
 (trade) la fiera [f-**yai**ra]
 (adj) giusto [**joo**sto]
fairly abbastanza [ab-bas**tan**tza]
fall (verb) cadere [ka**dai**ray]
 (US) l'autunno m [owt**oon**-no]
family la famiglia [fam**eel**-ya]
fantastic fantastico
far lontano

dialogue

is it far from here? è
lontano da qui? [ay – kwee]
no, not very far no, non è
molto lontano
it's about 20 kilometres
circa venti chilometri
[**cheer**ka]

farm la fattoria [fat-tor**ee**-a]
fashionable di moda
fast veloce [vel**o**chay]
fat (person) grasso
father il padre [**pa**dray]
father-in-law il suocero
 [sw**o**chairo]
faucet il rubinetto
fault il difetto
 sorry, it was my fault mi
 dispiace, è stata colpa mia
 [mee deesp-**ya**chay ay – **mee**-a]
favourite preferito [prefair**ee**to]
fax il fax

feel sentire [senteeray]
 I feel unwell non mi sento bene [baynay]
felt-tip (pen) il pennarello
ferry il traghetto [traget-to]
fetch (andare a) prendere [prendairay]
 I'll fetch him vado a prenderlo [prendairlo]
few: a few alcuni/alcune [alkoonee/alkoonay]
 a few days alcuni giorni
fiancé il fidanzato [feedantzato]
fiancée la fidanzata
field il campo
fight la lite [leetay]
filling (in tooth) l'otturazione f [ot-tooratz-yonay]
film (movie) il film [feelm]
 (for camera) la pellicola
find trovare [trovaray]
find out scoprire [skopreeray]
fine (weather) bello
 (punishment) la multa
finger il dito
finish finire [feeneeray]
fire il fuoco [fwoko]
fire brigade i vigili del fuoco [veejeelee del fwoko]
first primo [preemo]
 at first all'inizio [eeneetz-yo]
first aid kit la cassetta del pronto soccorso
first class (travel etc) in prima classe [klassay]
first floor (UK) il primo piano
 (US) il piano terra [tair-ra]
first name il nome di battesimo [nomay dee bat-

tayseemo]
fish il pesce [peshay]
fit: it doesn't fit me non mi sta
fix (repair) riparare [reepararay]
 (arrange) fissare [fees-saray]
fizzy frizzante [freetzantay]
flat (noun: apartment) l'appartamento m
 (adj) piatto [p-yat-to]
 I've got a flat tyre ho una gomma a terra [o – tair-ra]
flavour il sapore [saporay]
flight il volo
flight number il numero del volo [noomairo]
floor (of room) il pavimento
 (of building) il piano
florist il fioraio [f-yora-yo]
flower il fiore [f-yoray]
flu l'influenza f
fluent: he speaks fluent Italian parla l'italiano correntemente [eetal-yano kor-rentementay]
fly la mosca
 (verb) volare [volaray]
food il cibo [cheebo]
foot il piede [p-yayday]
 on foot a piedi
football il calcio [kalcho]
 (ball) il pallone [pal-lonay]
for per [pair], da
 do you have something for ...? (headache/diarrhoea etc) avete qualcosa contro...? [avaytay kwalkoza]
foreign straniero [stran-yairo]
foreigner (man/woman) lo straniero [stran-yairo], la

straniera
forest la foresta
forget dimenticare
[deementeekaray]
I forget non ricordo
I've forgotten ho
dimenticato
fork la forchetta [forket-ta]
fortnight quindici giorni
[kweendeechee jornee]
forwarding address il nuovo
recapito [nwovo]
fountain la fontana
foyer (of hotel) l'atrio m
(theatre) il foyer
France la Francia [francha]
free libero [leebairo]
(no charge) gratuito [gratoo-
eeto]
freeway l'autostrada f
[owtostrada]
French francese [franchayzay]
French fries le patatine fritte
[patatee-nay freet-tay]
frequent frequente [frekwentay]
fresh fresco
fridge il frigo
fried fritto
friend (male/female) l'amico m,
l'amica f
friendly cordiale [kord-yalay]
from da
from Monday to Friday dal
lunedì al venerdì
from next Thursday da
giovedì prossimo
front il davanti
in front of the hotel davanti
all'albergo

at the front sul davanti [sool]
fruit la frutta [froot-ta]
fruit juice il succo di frutta
[sook-ko dee froot-ta]
full pieno [p-yayno]
full board la pensione
completa [pens-yonay
komplayta]
fun: it was fun è stato
divertente [deevairtentay]
funny (strange) strano
(amusing) buffo [boof-fo]
further più avanti [p-yoo]
future il futuro [footooro]

G

game (cards etc) il gioco [jo-ko]
(match) la partita
garage (for fuel) il distributore
di benzina [deestreebootoray
dee bentzeena]
(for repairs) l'autofficina f
[owtof-feecheena]
(for parking) l'autorimessa f
[owtoreemes-sa]
garden il giardino [jardeeno]
garlic l'aglio m [al-yo]
gas il gas
(US) la benzina [bentzeena]
gas station la stazione di
servizio [statz-yonay dee
sairveetz-yo]
gate il cancello [kanchel-lo]
(at airport) l'uscita f [oosheeta]
gay gay
gents (toilet) la toilette (degli
uomini) [twalet dayl-yee wo-

meenee]

German tedesco

Germany la Germania

get (fetch) prendere [prendairay]
 how do I get to ...? come si arriva a...? [komay]

get back (return) tornare [tornaray]

get in (arrive) arrivare [arreevaray]

get off scendere [shendairay]
 where do I get off? dove devo scendere? [dovay dayvo]

get on (to train etc) salire [saleeray]

get out (of car etc) scendere [shendairay]

get up (in the morning) alzarsi [altzarsee]

gift il regalo

gin il gin
 a gin and tonic un gin tonic

girl la ragazza [ragatza]

girlfriend la ragazza

give dare [daray]

dialogue

how much do you want for this? quanto vuole per questo? [kwanto vwolay pair kwesto]
100,000 lire 100.000 (centomila) lire [leeray]
I'll give you 80,000 lire gliene do ottantamila [l-yee-aynee]

give back restituire

[resteetweeray]

glad contento

glass (material) il vetro
 (tumbler) il bicchiere [beek-yairay]
 a glass of wine un bicchiere di vino

glasses (spectacles) gli occhiali [ok-yalee]

gloves i guanti [gwantee]

go andare [andaray]
 where are you going? dove stai andando? [dovay sty]
 where does this bus go? dove va questo autobus? [dovay va kwesto]
 let's go! andiamo! [and-yamo]
 she's gone (left) se n'è andata [say nay]
 pizza to go una pizza da portare via [portaray vee-a]

go away andare via [andaray]
 go away! vattene! [vat-tenay]

go back (return) tornare [tornaray]

go down (the stairs etc) scendere [shendairay]

go in entrare [entraray]

go out (in the evening) uscire [oosheeray]

go through attraversare [attravairsaray]

go up (stairs) salire [saleeray]

God Dio [dee-o]

gold l'oro m

gondola la gondola

gondolier il gondoliere [gondol-yairay]

good buono [bwono]

good! bene! [**bay**nay]
  it's no good non va bene
goodbye arrivederci [arreeved**air**chee]
good evening buonasera [bwonas**ai**ra]
good morning buongiorno [bwonj**or**no]
good night buonanotte [bwonan**ot**-tay]
got: we've got to leave dobbiamo partire [dob-y**a**mo part**ee**ray]
I've got to ... devo... [**day**vo]
have you got any ...? avete...? [av**ay**tay]
gradually gradualmente [gradoo-alm**en**tay]
gram(me) il grammo
grapefruit il pompelmo
grapes l'uva **f** [**oo**va]
grass l'erba **f** [**air**ba]
grateful grato
great (excellent) fantastico
green verde [**vair**day]
greengrocer's il fruttivendolo [froot-teev**en**dolo]
grey grigio [**gree**jo]
grilled alla griglia
grocer's il negozio di alimentari [neg**ot**z-yo]
ground la terra [**tair**-ra]
  on the ground per terra [pair]
ground floor il piano terra [**tair**-ra]
group il gruppo [**groo**p-po]
guest l'ospite **m/f** [**os**peetay]
guesthouse la pensione [pens-y**o**nay]

guide la guida [**gwee**da]
guidebook la guida
guided tour la visita guidata [**vee**zeeta gwee**da**ta]

H

hair i capelli
haircut il taglio di capelli [**tal**-yo]
hairdresser (men's) il barbiere [barb-y**ai**ray]
  (women's: man/woman) il parrucchiere [par-rook-y**ai**ray], la parrucchiera
hairdryer il fon
half la metà
  half an hour mezz'ora [metz**o**ra]
  half a litre mezzo litro [**metz**o]
half board la mezza pensione [**metz**a pens-y**o**nay]
half bottle mezza bottiglia [bot-**teel**-ya]
half price metà prezzo [**pretz**o]
ham il prosciutto [prosh**oot**-to]
hamburger l'hamburger **m** [am**boor**gair]
hand la mano
handbag la borsetta
hand luggage il bagaglio a mano [bag**al**-yo]
hangover i postumi della sbornia [**zborn**-ya]
happen succedere [sooch**ay**dairay]
  what has happened? che è successo? [ay sooch**ays**-so]

Ha

317

happy felice [feleechay]
harbour il porto
hard duro [dooro]
(difficult) difficile [deef-feecheelay]
hardly a mala pena
hardly ever quasi mai [kwazee my]
hardware shop il negozio di ferramenta [negotz-yo dee fair-ramenta]
hat il cappello
hate detestare [detestaray]
have avere [avairay]
can I have ...? vorrei... [vorray]
do you have ...? ha...? [a]
do I have to ...? devo...?
hayfever la febbre da fieno [feb-bray da f-yayno]
he lui [loo-ee]
head la testa
headache il mal di testa
headlights i fari
hear sentire [senteeray]
heat il caldo
heater (in room) il radiatore [rad-yatoray]
heating il riscaldamento
heavy pesante [pezantay]
heel (of foot) il tallone [tal-lonay]
(of shoe) il tacco
hello (in the daytime) buongiorno [bwonjorno]
(late afternoon, in the evening) buonasera [bwonasaira]
(on the phone) pronto
help l'aiuto m [a-yooto]

(verb) aiutare [a-yootaray]
help! aiuto!
can you help me? mi può aiutare? [pwo]
her: I haven't seen her non l'ho vista [lo]
to her a lei [lay], le [lay]
for her per lei
that's her è lei
that's her towel è il suo asciugamano [ay eel soo-o]
herbal tea la tisana [teezana]
here qui [kwee]
here is/are ... ecco...
here you are ecco a te/lei [tay/lay]
hers: that's hers quello è suo [kwel-lo ay soo-o]
hey! ehi! [ay-ee]
hi! ciao! [chow]
high alto
highway l'autostrada f [owtostrada]
hill la collina
him: I haven't seen him non l'ho visto [lo]
to him a lui [loo-ee], gli [l-yee]
for him per lui [pair]
that's him è lui [ay]
hip il fianco [f-yanko]
hire noleggiare [nolej-jaray]
for hire a nolo
his: it's his car è la sua macchina [ay la soo-a]
that's his quello è suo [kwel-lo ay soo-o]
hitch-hike fare l'autostop [faray lowtostop]
hole il buco [booko]

holiday la vacanza [vakantza]
 on holiday in vacanza
home la casa [kaza]
 at home (in my house etc) a casa
 (in my country) in patria
 we go home tomorrow
 torniamo in patria domani
 [torn-yamo]
horrible orribile [or-reebeelay]
horse il cavallo
hospital l'ospedale m
 [ospedalay]
hot caldo
 (spicy) piccante [peek-kantay]
 I'm hot ho caldo [o]
hotel l'albergo m [albairgo]
hour l'ora f
house la casa [kaza]
house wine il vino della casa
how come [komay]
 how many? quanti? [kwantee]
 how much? quanto?
 how do you do? piacere
 [p-yachairay]

dialogues

 how are you? come
 stai/sta? [komay sty]
 fine, thanks, and you?
 bene, grazie, e lei? [baynay
 – ay lay]

 how much is it? quanto
 costa? [kwanto]
 ... lire ... lire [leeray]
 I'll take it lo/la prendo

hungry: I'm hungry ho fame [o

famay]
hurry: I'm in a hurry ho fretta
 [o]
hurt: it hurts mi fa male
 [malay]
husband il marito [mareeto]

I

I io [ee-o]
ice il ghiaccio [g-yacho]
ice cream il gelato [jelato]
ice lolly il ghiacciolo
 [g-yacholo]
idiot l'idiota m/f [eed-yota]
if se [say]
ill malato
immediately immediatamente
 [eem-med-yatamentay]
important importante
 [eemportantay]
impossible impossibile
 [eempos-seebeelay]
in: it's in the centre è in
 centro [chentro]
 in my car con la mia
 macchina
 in Florence a Firenze
 in five minutes tra cinque
 minuti
 in May a maggio
 in English in inglese [een]
 is he in? c'è? [chay]
include: does that include
 meals? sono compresi i
 pasti? [komprayzee]
indigestion l'indigestione f
 [eendeejest-yonay]

indoors all'interno [eentairno]
information l'informazione f
[eenformatz-yonay]
injured ferito [faireeto]
insect l'insetto m
inside dentro
  inside the hotel nell'albergo
instead invece [eenvaychay]
  instead of ... invece di...
intelligent intelligente [eentel-leejentay]
interesting interessante
[eentaires-santay]
international internazionale
[eentairnatz-yonalay]
interpreter l'interprete m/f
[eentairpretay]
intersection l'incrocio m
[eenkrocho]
into in
  I'm not into ... non
  m'interesso di...
introduce presentare
[presentaray]
  may I introduce ...? posso
  presentarle...? [presentarlay]
invitation l'invito m
Ireland l'Irlanda f [eerlanda]
Irish irlandese [eerlandayzay]
iron (for ironing) il ferro da stiro
[fair-ro]
island l'isola f [eezola]
it esso
  it is ... è... [ay]
  is it ...? è...?
  where is it? dov'è? [dovay]
  it was ... era... [aira]
Italian (adj) italiano [eetal-yano]
  (language, man) l'italiano m

  (woman) l'italiana f
  the Italians gli Italiani
Italy l'Italia f [eetal-ya]

J

jacket la giacca [jak-ka]
jam la marmellata
jeans i jeans
jellyfish la medusa [medooza]
jewellery i gioielli [joy-el-lee]
job l'impiego m [eemp-yaygo]
joke lo scherzo [skairtzo]
  (story) la barzelletta [bartzel-letta]
journey il viaggio [vee-aj-jo]
  have a good journey! buon
  viaggio! [bwon]
juice il succo [sook-ko]
jumper il maglione [mal-yonay]
just (only) solo
  just two soltanto due
  just for me solo per me [pair may]
  just here proprio qui [kwee]

K

keep tenere [tenairay]
  keep the change tenga il
  resto
key la chiave [k-yavay]
kilo il chilo [keelo]
kilometre il chilometro
[keelometro]
kind (generous) gentile
[jenteelay]

kiss il bacio [**ba**cho]
(verb) baciare [**ba**charay]
kitchen la cucina [koo**chee**na]
knee il ginocchio [jeen**ok**-yo]
knife il coltello
knock down: he's been knocked down è stato investito [ay]
know (somebody, a place) conoscere [ko**no**-shairay]
(something) sapere [sa**pa**iray]
I don't know non lo so
I didn't know that non lo sapevo [sa**pay**vo]

L

ladies' room la toilette delle donne [tw**al**et **del**-lay **don**-nay]
lady la signora [seen-**yo**ra]
lager la birra chiara [**bee**r-ra k-**ya**ra]
lake il lago
lamb l'agnello **m** [an-**yel**-lo]
lamp la lampada
language la lingua [**leen**gwa]
large grande [**gran**day]
last ultimo [**ool**teemo]
last week la settimana scorsa
last Friday venerdì scorso
last night la notte scorsa
late tardi
later più tardi [p-yoo]
I'll come back later torno più tardi
laugh ridere [**ree**dairay]
launderette, laundromat la lavanderia automatica
[lavandair**ee**-a owto-ma**tee**ka]
laundry (clothes) il bucato
lawyer l'avvocato **m**
laxative il lassativo
leaflet il dépliant [dayplee-**an**]
leak la perdita [**pair**deeta]
learn imparare [eempa**ra**ray]
least: at least come minimo
[**ko**may]
leather il cuoio [**kwo**-yo], la pelle [**pel**-lay]
leave (depart) partire [par**tee**ray]
(leave behind) lasciare [la**sha**ray]
I am leaving tomorrow parto domani
may I leave this here? posso lasciarlo qui? [la**shar**lo kwee]
I left my coat in the bar ho lasciato il cappotto al bar [o]
leek il porro
left la sinistra [seen**ees**tra]
left luggage (office) il deposito bagagli [ba**gal**-yee]
leg la gamba
lemon il limone [lee**mo**nay]
lemonade la gassosa [gas-**so**za]
lend prestare [pres**ta**ray]
less meno [**may**no]
less expensive più a buon mercato [p-yoo]
lesson la lezione [letz-**yo**nay]
let (allow) permettere [pairmet-**tai**ray]
let off: will you let me off at ...? può farmi scendere a...? [pwo]
letter la lettera [**let**-taira]
letterbox la buca delle lettere [**boo**ka **del**-lay]

lettuce la lattuga [lat-**too**ga]

library la biblioteca [beeblee-o**tay**ka]

licence il permesso [pairmes-so]

lift (in building) l'ascensore m [ashen**sor**ay]

could you give me a lift? mi puoi/può dare un passaggio? [mee pwoy/pwo **da**ray oon pas-**saj**-jo]

light la luce [**loo**chay]

(not heavy) leggero [lej-**jai**ro]

do you have a light? (for cigarette) può farmi accendere? [pwo **far**mee a**chen**dairay]

light bulb la lampadina

lighter (cigarette) l'accendino m [achen-**dee**no]

like piacere [p-ya**chai**ray]

I like it mi piace [mee pee-**a**chay]

I don't like it non mi piace

I'd like a beer vorrei una birra

would you like a drink? vuoi/vuole qualcosa da bere? [vwoy/**vwo**lay kwal**ko**za da **bai**ray]

what's it like? com'è? [ko**may**]

like this così [ko**zee**]

one like this uno come questo

line la linea [**leen**-ay-a]

lips le labbra

listen ascoltare [askol**ta**ray]

litre il litro

little piccolo

just a little, thanks solo un po', grazie

a little milk un po' di latte

live (verb) vivere [**vee**vairay]

loaf la pagnotta [pan-**yot**-ta]

local locale [lo**ka**lay]

a local wine/restaurant un vino/un ristorante del posto

lock la serratura [sair-ra**too**ra]

(verb) chiudere a chiave [k-**yoo**dairay a k-**ya**vay]

lock out: I've locked myself out mi sono chiuso/chiusa fuori [k-**yoo**zo]

locker (for luggage etc) l'armadietto m [armad-**yet**-to]

London Londra

long lungo [**loon**go]

how long does it take? quanto tempo ci vuole? [chee **vwo**lay]

a long time tanto tempo

one day/two days longer ancora un giorno/due giorni

look: **look out!** attenzione! [at-tentz-**yo**nay]

can I have a look? posso dare un'occhiata? [**da**ray]

look after badare a [ba**da**ray]

look at guardare [gwar**da**ray]

look for cercare [chair**ka**ray]

I'm looking for ... sto cercando... [chair**kan**do]

lorry il camion [**kam**-yon]

lose perdere [**pair**dairay]

I've lost my bag ho perso la borsa [o]

lost property (office) l'ufficio oggetti smarriti m [oof-**fee**cho

oj-**jet**-tee zmar-**ree**tee]
lot: a lot, lots molto
  not a lot non molto
  a lot of people molta gente
  [**jen**tay]
loud forte [**for**tay]
lounge (in house, hotel) il salone
  [sal**on**ay]
love l'amore **m** [am**or**ay]
  (verb) amare [am**a**ray]
lovely bello
  (meal) delizioso [deleetz-**yoz**o]
low basso
luck la fortuna [fort**oo**na]
  good luck! buona fortuna!
  [**bwo**na]
luggage i bagagli [bag**a**l-yee]
lunch il pranzo [**pran**tzo]

M

mad (insane) pazzo [**pa**tzo]
magazine la rivista
maid (in hotel) la cameriera
  [kamair-**ya**ira]
mail la posta
  (verb) impostare [eempost**a**ray]
mailbox la buca delle lettere
  [**boo**ka del-lay **let**-tairay]
main principale
  [preencheep**a**lay]
main course la portata
  principale
main road (in town) la strada
  principale [preencheep**a**lay]
  (in country) la strada maestra
  [m**y**stra]
make fare [**fa**ray]

make-up il trucco [**troo**k-ko]
man l'uomo **m** [**wo**mo]
manager il direttore [deerett-
  toray]
  can I see the manager? posso
  parlare con il direttore?
  [parl**a**ray]
many molti/molte [**mol**tay]
map (city plan) la pianta
  [p-**yan**ta]
  (road map, geographical) la
  cartina
market il mercato [mair**ka**to]
marmalade la marmellata
  d'arance [dar**an**chay]
married: I'm married (said by a
  man/woman) sono
  sposato/sposata
mascara il mascara
match (football etc) la partita
matches i fiammiferi [f-yam-
  meefairee]
matter: it doesn't matter non
  importa
  what's the matter? che c'è?
  [kay chay]
mattress il materasso
may: may I see it? posso
  vederlo/vederla?
  [ved**air**lo/ved**air**la]
maybe forse [**for**say]
mayonnaise la maionese [ma-
  yon**ay**zay]
me: that's for me è per me [ay
  pair may]
  me too anch'io [ank**ee**-o]
meal il pasto
mean (verb) significare [seen-
  yeefeek**a**ray]

meat la carne [**ka**rnay]

medicine la medicina [medee**chee**na]

medium (adj: size) medio [**mayd**-yo]

medium-dry semisecco

medium-rare non troppo cotto

mend riparare [reepa**raray**]

men's room la toilette (degli uomini) [twa**let dayl**-yee **wo**-meenee]

mention: don't mention it prego [**pray**go]

menu il menù [men**oo**]

message il messaggio [mes-**saj**-jo]

metre il metro

midday mezzogiorno [met-**zo**jorno]

middle: in the middle nel mezzo [**met**zo]

midnight mezzanotte [metza**not**-tay]

milk il latte [**lat**-tay]

mind: never mind non fa niente [n-**yen**tay]

mine: it's mine è mio/mia [ay]

mineral water l'acqua minerale f [**akwa** meen-ai**ra**lay]

minute il minuto [meen**oo**to]

just a minute un attimo

mirror lo specchio [**spek**-yo]

Miss (la) signorina [seen-yo**ree**na]

missing smarrito

there's a suitcase missing manca una valigia

mistake lo sbaglio [**zbal**-yo]

money i soldi

month il mese [**may**zay]

moped il motorino

more più [p-yoo]

can I have some more water, please? vorrei ancora acqua, per favore [vor-**ray**]

more expensive più caro [p-yoo]

more than 50 più di cinquanta

morning la mattina

this morning questa mattina [**kwes**ta]

most: most of the time la maggior parte del tempo [**maj**-jor **par**tay]

mother la madre [**mad**ray]

motorbike la motocicletta [moto-cheek**let**-ta]

motorway l'autostrada f [owto**stra**da]

mountain la montagna [mon**tan**-ya]

mouse il topo

mouth la bocca

movie il film [feelm]

movie theater il cinema [**chee**nema]

Mr (il) signor [seen-**yor**]

Mrs (la) signora [seen-**yo**ra]

Ms (la) signora

much molto

much better/much worse molto meglio/peggio [**mayl**-yo/**pej**-jo]

much hotter molto più caldo [p-yoo]

not much non molto

mum la mamma

museum il museo [moozay-o]

mushrooms i funghi [foongee]

music la musica [moozeeka]

must: I must devo [dayvo]

mustard la senape [saynapay]

my il mio, la mia; pl i miei [mee-yay], le mie [lay mee-ay]

myself: I'll do it myself lo farò da me [may]

by myself da solo

N

nail (finger) l'unghia f [oong-ya]

name il nome [nomay]

my name's John mi chiamo John [k-yamo]

what's your name? come si chiama? [komay see k-yama]

napkin il tovagliolo [toval-yolo]

narrow (street) stretto

nasty (person) antipatico (weather, accident) brutto [broot-to]

national nazionale [natz-yonalay]

natural naturale [natooralay]

near vicino a [veecheeno]

where is the nearest ...? dov'è il... più vicino? [dovay eel ... p-yoo]

nearly quasi [kwazee]

necessary necessario [neches-sar-yo]

neck il collo

necklace la collana

necktie la cravatta

need: I need ... ho bisogno di... [o beezon-yo dee]

needle l'ago m

neither: neither ... nor ... né... né... [nay]

nephew il nipote [neepotay]

never mai [ma-ee]

new nuovo [nwovo]

news (radio, TV etc) le notizie [noteetzee-ay]

newsagent's il giornalaio [jornala-yo]

newspaper il giornale [jornalay]

New Year l'anno nuovo m [nwovo]

Happy New Year! felice anno nuovo! [felee-chay]

New Year's Eve la notte di Capodanno [not-tay dee]

New Zealand la Nuova Zelanda [nwova tzaylanda]

next prossimo

next week la settimana prossima

next to vicino a [veecheeno]

nice (food) buono [bwono] (looks, view etc) bello (person) simpatico

niece la nipote [neepotay]

night la notte [not-tay]

no no

I've no change non ho spiccioli [o speech-yolee]

there's no ... left non c'è più... [cheh p-yoo]

nobody nessuno [nes-soono]

noisy: it's too noisy c'è troppo

rumore
non-alcoholic analcolico
none nessuno [nes-soono]
nonsmoking compartment la carrozza per non fumatori [kar-rotza pair non foomatoree]
no-one nessuno [nes-soono]
nor: nor do I nemmeno io [nem-mayno ee-o]
normal normale [normalay]
north il nord
Northern Ireland l'Irlanda del Nord **f** [eerlanda]
nose il naso
not non
  no, I'm not hungry no, non ho fame [o famay]
  not that one non quello [kwel-lo]
note (banknote) la banconota
nothing niente [n-yentay]
  nothing else nient'altro
now adesso
number il numero [noomairo]
nuts le noci [nochee]

O

o'clock: at 7 o'clock alle sette [al-lay]
odd (strange) strano
of di [dee]
off (lights) spento
  it's just off the via ... è una traversa di via ... [ay – travairsa]
often spesso
  how often are the buses?

ogni quanto passano gli autobus? [on-yee kwanto]
oil l'olio **m** [ol-yo]
ointment l'unguento **m** [oongwento]
OK d'accordo
  are you OK? tutto bene? [toot-to baynay]
  that's OK thanks va bene così grazie [kozee]
  I'm OK (nothing for me) io sono a posto [ee-o]
  (I feel OK) sto bene
old vecchio [vek-yo]
olive oil l'olio di oliva **m** [ol-yo]
olives le olive [oleevay]
omelette la frittata
on su [soo]
  on television alla televisione
  I haven't got it on me non ce l'ho con me [non chay lo kon may]
  what's on tonight? cosa c'è da vedere stasera? [koza chay da vedairay stasaira]
once (one time) una volta
  at once (immediately) immediatamente [eem-med-yatamentay]
one uno [oono], una [oona]
  the white one quello bianco [kwel-lo]
one-way ticket il biglietto di sola andata [beel-yet-to]
onions le cipolle [cheepol-lay]
only solo
open (adj) aperto [apairto]
  (verb) aprire [apreeray]

operator (telephone) il/la
  centralinista [chentraleen**ee**sta]
opposite: opposite my hotel
  di fronte al mio albergo
  or o
orange (fruit) l'arancia **f**
  [ar**a**ncha]
  (colour) arancione [aranch**o**nay]
orange juice il succo
  d'arancia [s**oo**k-ko]
  (freshly squeezed) la spremuta
  d'arancia [sprem**oo**ta]
  (fizzy) l'aranciata **f** [aranch**a**ta]
order: can we order now?
  possiamo ordinare ora? [pos-
  y**a**mo ordeen**a**ray]
ordinary ordinario
other altro
  the other one l'altro, l'altra
our/ours il nostro, la nostra; **pl**
  i nostri, le nostre
out: he's out è fuori [ay fw**o**ree]
outdoors all'aperto [ap**a**irto]
outside fuori (di) [fw**o**ree dee]
over: over here qui [kwee]
  over there lì
  over 500 più di cinquecento
  [p-yoo]
overnight (travel) di notte [dee
  n**o**t-tay]
own: my own ... il mio...

P

pack (verb) fare le valigie
  [f**a**ray lay val**ee**jay]
  a pack of ... un pacco di...
package (small parcel) il pacco

pain il dolore [dol**o**ray]
  I have a pain here mi fa male
  qui [mee fa m**a**lay kwee]
painful doloroso
painkillers gli analgesici
  [analj**ay**zeechee]
pair: a pair of ... un paio di...
  [p**a**-yo]
panties le mutande
  [moot**a**nday]
pants (underwear) le mutande
  (US) i pantaloni
pantyhose il collant [kol-l**a**n]
paper la carta
  (newspaper) il giornale
  [jorn**a**lay]
parcel il pacco
pardon (me)? prego? [pr**ay**go]
parents i genitori [jeneet**o**ree]
park il parco
  (verb) parcheggiare [parkej-
  j**a**ray]
parking lot il parcheggio
  [parkej-jo]
part la parte [p**a**rtay]
partner (boyfriend, girlfriend etc)
  il/la partner
party (group) il gruppo [gr**oo**p-
  po]
  (celebration) la festa
passport il passaporto
**past: just past the information
  office** appena dopo l'ufficio
  informazioni [ap-p**ay**na]
pavement il marciapiede
  [marchap-y**ay**day]
pay pagare [pag**a**ray]
  can I pay, please? il conto,
  per favore

pay phone il telefono pubblico

peach la pesca

peanuts le arachidi [arakeedee]

pear la pera [pairla]

peas i piselli

pen la penna

pencil la matita

people la gente [jentay]

pepper (spice) il pepe [paypay]
(vegetable) il peperone [peperonay]

per: per night a notte [not-tay]
per cent per cento [pair chento]

perfume il profumo [profoomo]

perhaps forse [forsay]

person la persona [pairsona]

petrol la benzina [bentzeena]

petrol station la stazione di servizio [statz-yonay dee sairveetz-yo]

pharmacy la farmacia [farmachee-a]

phone il telefono [telayfono]
(verb) telefonare [telefonaray]

phone book l'elenco telefonico **m**

phone box la cabina telefonica

phonecard la scheda telefonica [skayda]

phone number il numero di telefono [noomairo dee telayfono]

photo la fotografia [fotografee-a]

picture (painting) il quadro [kwadro]

(photo) la fotografia [fotografee-a]

piece il pezzo [petzo]

pill la pillola

pillow il cuscino [koosheeno]

pineapple l'ananas **m**

pink rosa

place il posto
at your place (fam) a casa tua [too-a]
(pol) a casa sua [soo-a]

plane l'aereo **m** [a-airay-o]

plant la pianta [p-yanta]

plasters i cerotti [chairot-tee]

plastic bag il sacchetto di plastica [sak-ket-to]

plate il piatto [p-yat-to]

platform il marciapiede [marchapyayday]
which platform is it for Milan, please? su quale binario parte il treno per Milano, per favore? [soo kwalay beenar-yo partay eel trayno pair]

play (verb: game, sport) giocare [jokaray]
(instrument) suonare [swonaray]
(noun: in theatre) la commedia [kom-mayd-ya]

pleasant piacevole [p-yachayvolay]

please per favore [pair favoray]
yes please sì, grazie [see gratzee-ay]

plenty: plenty of ... molto...

plug (electrical) la spina
(in sink) il tappo

poisonous velenoso [velenozo]

police la polizia [poleetzee-a]

policeman il poliziotto [poleetz-yot-to]

police station il commissariato

polite educato [edookato]

polluted inquinato [eenkweenato]

pool (for swimming) la piscina [peesheena]

pork il maiale [ma-yalay]

port il porto

possible possibile [pos-seebeelay]

is it possible to ...? è possibile...? [ay]

as soon as possible al più presto possibile [p-yoo]

post (mail) la posta

(verb) impostare [eempostaray]

postcard la cartolina

postcode il codice postale [kodeechay postalay]

post office l'ufficio postale **m** [oof-feecho postalay]

poste restante il fermo posta [fairmo]

potato la patata

potato chips le patatine [patateenay]

pound (money) la sterlina [stairleena]

(weight) la libbra

prefer: I prefer ... preferisco... [prefaireesko]

pregnant incinta [eencheenta]

prescription la ricetta [reechetta]

present il regalo

pretty grazioso [gratz-yozo]

price il prezzo [pretzo]

private privato

probably probabilmente [probabeelmentay]

problem il problema [problayma]

no problem! nessun problema

pronounce: how is this pronounced? come si pronuncia? [komay see pronooncha]

public holiday la festa nazionale [natzyonalay]

pull tirare [teeraray]

purple viola [v-yola]

purse (for money) il portamonete [portamonaytay] (US) la borsetta

push spingere [speenjairay]

put mettere [met-tairay]

pyjamas il pigiama [peejama]

Q

quarter il quarto [kwarto]

question la domanda

queue la fila

quick veloce [velochay]

quickly velocemente [velochementay]

quiet (place, hotel) tranquillo [trankweel-lo]

quiet! silenzio! [seelentz-yo]

quite (fairly) abbastanza [ab-bastantza]

(very) molto

quite a lot moltissimo

329

R

radiator il radiatore [rad-yatoray]
radio la radio
rail: by rail in treno [trayno]
railway la ferrovia [fair-rovee-a]
rain la pioggia [p-yoj-ja]
  it's raining piove [p-yovay]
rape lo stupro [stoopro]
rare (steak) al sangue [sangway]
raspberry il lampone [lamponay]
rather: I'd rather ...
  preferirei... [prefaireeray]
razor il rasoio [raso-yo]
read leggere [lej-jairay]
ready pronto
real reale [ray-alay]
really veramente [vairamentay]
receipt la ricevuta [reechevoota]
recently recentemente [rechentementay]
reception (in hotel) la reception (for guests) il ricevimento [reecheveemento]
receptionist il/la receptionist
recommend: could you recommend ...? mi potrebbe consigliare...? [mee potreb-bay konseel-yaray]
red rosso
red wine il vino rosso
refund il rimborso
region la regione [rejonay]
registered: by registered mail (per) raccomandata

remember: I don't remember non ricordo
rent (for apartment etc) l'affitto m (verb) noleggiare [nolej-jaray]
repair riparare [reepararay]
repeat ripetere [repetairay]
reservation la prenotazione [prenotatz-yonay]
reserve prenotare [prenotaray]

dialogue

can I reserve a table for tonight? vorrei prenotare un tavolo per stasera [vor-ray – pair stasaira]
yes madam, for how many people? sì, signora, per quante persone? [seen-yora, pair kwantay pairsonay]
for two per due
and for what time? per che ora? [pair kay]
for eight o'clock per le otto [lay]
and could I have your name please? il suo nome, per favore? [soo-o nomay]

restaurant il ristorante [reestorantay]
restaurant car il vagone ristorante [vagonay reestorantay]
rest room la toilette [twalet]
return (ticket) il biglietto di andata e ritorno [beel-yet-to]
reverse charge call la telefonata a carico del

destinatario
rice il riso [**ree**zo]
right (correct) giusto [**joo**sto]
(not left) destro
that's right è giusto [ay]
ring (on finger) l'anello **m**
ring back ritelefonare
[reetelefon**a**ray]
river il fiume [f-**yoo**may]
road la strada
is this the road for ...? è
questa la strada per...? [ay
k**we**sta – pair]
rob: I've been robbed sono
stato derubato/derubata!
[dairoo**ba**to]
roll (bread) il panino
Roman (adj) romano
Rome Roma
roof il tetto
room la camera, la stanza
[**stan**tza]

dialogue

do you have any rooms?
ha una camera? [a]
for how many people? per
quante persone? [pair
k**wan**tay pairs**o**nay]
for one/for two per
una/due
yes, we have rooms free sì,
abbiamo una camera
libera [ab-**ya**mo]
for how many nights will it
be? per quante notti la
vuole? [k**wan**tay – v**wo**lay]
just for one night solo per

una notte [**not**-tay]
how much is it? quanto
costa? [k**wan**to]
... with bathroom and ...
without bathroom ... con
bagno e... senza bagno
[**ban**-yo – **sen**tza]
can I see a room with
bathroom? posso vedere
una camera con bagno?
[ved**ai**ray]
OK, I'll take it va bene, la
prendo [**bay**nay]

room service il servizio in
camera [sairv**ee**tz-yo een]
rosé il rosé
round trip ticket il biglietto di
andata e ritorno [beel-**yet**-to]
route il tragitto [traj**ee**t-to]
rubbish (waste) i rifiuti [reef-
yootee]
(poor quality goods) la porcheria
[porkair**ee**-a]
rucksack lo zaino [**tza**-eeno]
rude sgarbato [zgar**ba**to]
rum il rum [room]
run (person) correre [**kor**-rairay]

S

sad triste [**tree**stay]
safe (not in danger) sicuro
[seek**oo**ro]
(not dangerous) non pericoloso
[paireekol**o**zo]
salad l'insalata **f**
salad dressing il condimento

per l'insalata [pair]

sale: for sale vendesi [vendesee]

salt il sale [salay]

same: the same lo stesso

the same again, please un altro/un'altra, per favore

sand la sabbia

sandals i sandali

sandwich il panino imbottito

sanitary napkins/towels gli assorbenti igienici [assorbentee eejayneechee]

sauce la salsa

saucepan la pentola

sausage la salsiccia [salseecha]

say: how do you say ... in Italian? come si dice... in italiano? [komay see deechay ... een eetal-yano]

what did he/she say? cos'ha detto? [koz a]

scarf (for neck) la sciarpa [sharpa]

(for head) il foulard [foolar]

schedule (US) l'orario m

school la scuola [skwola]

scissors: a pair of scissors un paio di forbici [pa-yo dee forbeechee]

scooter lo scooter

Scotch tape® lo scotch

Scotland la Scozia [skotz-ya]

Scottish scozzese [skotzayzay]

sea il mare [maray]

by the sea sul mare [sool]

seafood i frutti di mare [froottee dee]

seasick: I feel seasick ho mal di mare [o – maray]

seat il posto

is this anyone's seat? è libero questo posto? [ay leebairo kwesto]

second (adj) secondo

(of time) il secondo

second class (travel) in seconda classe [klassay]

see vedere [vedairay]

can I see? posso vedere?

have you seen ...? hai/ha visto...? [a-ee/a]

see you! ci vediamo! [chee ved-yamo]

I see (I understand) capisco

self-catering apartment l'appartamento (per le vacanze) m [pair lay vakantzay]

self-service il self-service

sell vendere [vendairay]

Sellotape® lo scotch

send mandare [mandaray]

separated: I'm separated sono separato/separata

separately (pay) a parte [partay]

(travel) separatamente [separatamentay]

serious serio [sair-yo]

service station la stazione di servizio [statz-yonay dee sairveetz-yo]

serviette il tovagliolo [tovalyolo]

set menu il menù fisso [menoo]

several diversi [deevairsee]

sex il sesso

(sexual intercourse) il rapporto sessuale [ses-swalay]

shade: in the shade all'ombra

shampoo lo shampoo

share (room, table etc) dividere [deeveedairay]

shaver il rasoio [razo-yo]

shaving foam la schiuma da barba [sk-yooma]

she lei [lay]

sheet (for bed) il lenzuolo [lentz-wolo]

shellfish i frutti di mare [froot-tee dee maray]

ship la nave [navay]

shirt la camicia [kameecha]

shit! merda! [mairda]

shoe la scarpa

shoelaces i lacci

shoe polish il lucido per le scarpe [loocheedo pair lay skarpay]

shoe repairer il calzolaio [kalzola-yo]

shop il negozio [negotz-yo]

short (person) basso
(time) poco
(journey) corto

shorts i calzoncini [kaltzoncheenee]

should: what should I do? cosa dovrei fare? [koza dovray faray]

shoulder la spalla

show (in theatre) lo spettacolo
could you show me? mi può far vedere? [mee pwo far vedairay]

shower (in bathroom) la doccia

[docha]

shut (verb) chiudere [k-yoodairay]
when do you shut? quando chiudete? [kwando k-yoodaytay]
they're shut sono chiusi [k-yoosee]
shut up! stai zitto! [sty tzeet-to]

shutter (on window) l'imposta f

sick malato

side il lato

side salad l'insalata f

sidewalk il marciapiede [marchap-yayday]

sight: the sights of ... le attrazioni turistiche di... [at-tratz-yonee tooreesteekay]

silk la seta [sayta]

silly sciocco [shok-ko]

silver l'argento m [arjento]

since: since yesterday da ieri [yairee]

sing cantare [kantaray]

single: a single to ... un biglietto di sola andata per... [beel-yet-to – pair]
I'm single (man/woman) sono celibe/nubile [chaylee-bay/noobeelay]

single bed il letto a una piazza [p-yatza]

single room la camera singola

sister la sorella

sit: can I sit here? posso sedere qui? [sedairay kwee]

size la taglia [tal-ya]

skin la pelle [pel-lay]

skirt la gonna

sky il cielo [**chay**lo]
sleep dormire [dor**mee**ray]
sleeping bag il sacco a pelo [**pay**lo]
sleeping car il vagone letto [va**go**nay]
slow lento
slow down! (driving) rallenta! (speaking) parla/parli più lentamente! [p-yoo lenta**men**tay]
slowly lentamente
small piccolo
smell: it smells (smells bad) puzza [**poot**za]
smile sorridere [sor-**ree**dairay]
smoke il fumo [**foo**mo]
do you mind if I smoke? le/ti dispiace se fumo? [lay/tee deespeea**chay** say]
I don't smoke non fumo
snow la neve [**nay**vay]
it's snowing nevica [**nay**veeka]
so: it's so expensive è così caro [ay]
it's so good è proprio buono [**bwo**no]
not so fast più piano [p-yoo]
so am I anch'io [an**kee**-o]
so do I anch'io
soap il sapone [sap**o**nay]
soap powder il detersivo (in polvere) [detair**see**vo een **pol**vairay]
sober sobrio
sock il calzino [kal**tzee**no]
soda (water) il seltz
soft (material etc) morbido
soft drink la bibita (analcolica)

sole la suola [**swo**la]
some: can I have some water/rolls? potrei avere dell'acqua/dei panini? [**pot**ray a**vai**ray – day]
somebody qualcuno [kwal-**koo**no]
something qualcosa [kwal**ko**za]
sometimes qualche volta [**kwal**kay]
somewhere da qualche parte [**par**tay]
son il figlio [**feel**-yo]
song la canzone [kan**tzo**nay]
soon presto
sore: it's sore mi fa male [**ma**lay]
sorry: (I'm) sorry scusa/mi scusi [**skoo**za/mee **skoo**zee]
sorry? (didn't understand) prego? [**pray**go]
sort: what sort of ...? che tipo di...? [kay]
soup la minestra, la zuppa [**tzoo**p-pa]
south il sud [sood]
South Africa il Sudafrica [sooda**free**ka]
South African sudafricano [soodafree-**ka**no]
southeast il sud-est [sood**est**]
southwest il sud-ovest [sood**o**vest]
souvenir il souvenir
speak: do you speak English? parla inglese? [eeng**lay**zay]
I don't speak ... non parlo...
spectacles gli occhiali [ok-**ya**lee]

spend spendere [spendairay]

spoon il cucchiaio [kook-ya-yo]

spring (season) la primavera [preema-vaira]

square (in town) la piazza [p-yatza]

stairs le scale [skalay]

stamp il francobollo

start l'inizio **m** [eeneetz-yo] (verb) cominciare [komeencharay]

the car won't start la macchina non parte [mak-keena]

starter (food) l'antipasto **m**

station la stazione [statz-yonay]

stay: where are you staying? dove'è alloggiato/ alloggiata? [dovay ay al-loj-jato] **I'm staying at ...** sono (alloggiato/alloggiata) a...

I'd like to stay another two nights vorrei fermarmi ancora due notti [vor-ray fair-marmee]

steak la bistecca

steal rubare [roobaray]

my bag has been stolen mi hanno rubato la borsa [mee an-no roobato]

steep (hill) ripido

still ancora

I'm still waiting sto ancora aspettando

stomach lo stomaco

stomach ache il mal di stomaco

stone (rock) la pietra [p-yetra]

stop fermare [fairmaray]

please, stop here (to taxi driver etc) fermi qui, per favore [fairmee kwee]

storm la tempesta

straight: straight ahead avanti diritto

strange (odd) strano

strawberry la fragola

street la strada

string lo spago

strong forte [fortay]

stuck bloccato

student (man/woman) lo studente/la studentessa [stoodentay/stoodentes-sa]

stupid stupido [stoopeedo]

suburb la periferia

subway (US) la metropolitana

suddenly improvvisamente [eemprov-veezamentay]

sugar lo zucchero [tzook-kairo]

suit il completo [komplayto]

suitcase la valigia [valeeja]

summer l'estate **f** [estatay]

in the summer d'estate

sun il sole [solay]

in the sun al sole

sunblock (cream) la crema a protezione totale [krayma a protetz-yonay totalay]

sunburn la scottatura [skot-tatoora]

sunglasses gli occhiali da sole [ok-yalee da solay]

sunstroke il colpo di sole

suntanned abbronzato [ab-brontzato]

suntan oil l'olio solare **m** [ol-yo

solaray]

supermarket il supermercato [soopair-mairkato]

supper la cena [chayna]

supplement (extra charge) il supplemento [soop-plemento]

sure sicuro [seekooro]
sure! certo! [chairto]

surname il cognome [konyomay]

sweater il maglione [malyonay]

sweet (taste) dolce [dolchay]
(noun: dessert) il dolce

sweets le caramelle [karamellay]

swim nuotare [nwotaray]
I'm going for a swim vado a fare una nuotata [faray oona nwotata]

swimming costume il costume da bagno [kostoomay da ban-yo]

swimming pool la piscina [peesheena]

swimming trunks il costume da bagno [kostoomay da ban-yo]

Swiss svizzero [zveetzairo]

switch l'interruttore m [eentair-root-toray]

switch off spegnere [spenyairay]

switch on accendere [achendairay]

Switzerland la Svizzera [sveetzaira]

T

table il tavolo
table wine il vino da tavola
take prendere [prendairay]
(accept) accettare [achetaray]
fine, I'll take it va bene, lo/la prendo [baynay]
pizza to take away una pizza da portare via [portaray vee-a]
talk parlare [parlaray]
tall alto
tampons i tamponi
tan l'abbronzatura f [abbrontzatoora]
tap il rubinetto [roobeenet-to]
taste il gusto [goosto]
taxi il taxi

dialogue

to the airport/to Hotel Centrale please
all'aeroporto/all'albergo Centrale, per favore
how much will it be?
quanto verrà a costare? [kwanto – kostaray]
50,000 cinquantamila lire
that's fine, right here, thanks va bene qui, grazie [baynay kwee]

tea (drink) il tè [tay]
teacher l'insegnante m/f [eensen-yantay]
telephone il telefono

[tel**ay**fono]

television la televisione
[televeez-y**o**nay]

tell: could you tell him ...?
potr**e**sti/potr**e**bbe dirgli...?
[potr**eb**-bay d**ee**rl-yee]

temple (building) il t**e**mpio

tennis il tennis

terrible terribile [tair-r**ee**beelay]

terrific fant**a**stico

than di [dee]

thanks, thank you grazie
[gr**a**tzee-ay]

thank you very much grazie
mille [m**ee**l-lay]

no thanks no grazie

dialogue

thanks grazie [gr**a**tzee-ay]
that's OK, don't mention it
prego [pr**ay**go]

that: that man quell'uomo
[kwel w**o**mo]

that woman quella donna
[kwel-la]

that one quello/quella lì
[kwel-lo]

that's nice (food) è
bu**o**no/bu**o**na [bw**o**no]

is that ...? (quello/quella)
è...?

the il, lo, la [eel]; **pl** i, gli, le
[l-yee, lay]

theatre il teatro [tay-**a**tro]

their/theirs il loro, la loro;
pl i loro, le loro

them: for them per loro

who? – them chi? – loro
[kee]

then (after that) poi [poy]

there là

is there ...? c'è...? [chay]

there is ... c'è...

are there ...? ci sono...?

there is ... ci sono...

there you are (giving something)
ecco qua [kwa]

these questi [kw**e**stee], queste
[kw**e**stay]

they loro

thick spesso

thief il ladro

thin sottile [sot-t**ee**lay]
(person) magro

thing la cosa [k**o**za]

my things le mie cose [lay
m**ee**-ay k**o**zay]

think pensare [pens**a**ray]

I'll think about it ci penserò
[chee pensair**o**]

thirsty: I'm thirsty ho sete [o
s**ay**tay]

this questo [kw**e**sto], questa

this man quest'uomo

this woman questa donna

this one questo/questa (qui)
[kwee]

is this ...? (questo/questa)
è...?

those quelli... [kwel-lee]

thread il filo

throat la gola

through attraverso [at-trav**a**irso]

thumb il pollice [p**o**l-leechay]

thunderstorm il temporale
[temporal-ay]

ticket il biglietto [beel-yet-to]

dialogue

a return to Rome un biglietto di andata e ritorno per Roma [pair]
coming back when? il ritorno per quando? [kwando]
today/next Tuesday oggi/martedì prossimo [oj-jee]
that will be 48,000 quarantottomila lire

tie (necktie) la cravatta
tights il collant [kol-lan]
time il tempo
what's the time? che ore sono? [kay oray]
next time la prossima volta
four times quattro volte [kwat-tro voltay]
timetable l'orario m
tin (can) il barattolo
tin opener l'apriscatole m [apree-skatolay]
tip (to waiter etc) la mancia [mancha]
tired stanco
tissues i fazzolettini di carta [fatzolet-teenee]
to: to Naples/London a Napoli/Londra
to Italy/England in Italia/Inghilterra [een]
to the post office all'ufficio postale

toast (bread) il pane tostato [panay]
today oggi [oj-jee]
toe il dito del piede [p-yayday]
together insieme [eens-yaymay]
toilet la toilette [twalet]
toilet paper la carta igienica [eejayneeka]
tomato il pomodoro
tomorrow domani
tomorrow morning domani mattina
the day after tomorrow dopodomani
tonic (water) l'acqua tonica f [akwa]
tonight (before 10 p.m.) stasera (after 10 p.m.) stanotte [stanot-tay]
too (excessively) troppo (also) anche [ankay]
too much troppo
me too anch'io [ankee-o]
tooth il dente [dentay]
toothache il mal di denti
toothbrush lo spazzolino da denti [spatzoleeno]
toothpaste il dentifricio [denteefreecho]
top: on top of ... su... [soo]
at the top in cima [cheema]
torch la torcia elettrica [torcha]
tour il giro [jeero]
tourist il/la turista [tooreesta]
tourist information office l'ufficio informazioni m [oof-feecho eenformatz-yonay]

towards verso [**vair**so]

towel l'asciugamano **m** [ashooga**ma**no]

tower la torre [**tor**-ray]

town la città [**cheet**ta]
  in town in città

town centre il centro (della città) [**chen**tro **del**-la **cheet**a]

toy il giocattolo [jokat-**to**lo]

track (US: at station) il marciapiede [marchapy**ay**day]

traffic lights il semaforo

train il treno [**tray**no]
  by train in treno
  is this the train for ...? questo treno va a...? [**kwes**to]

train station la stazione ferroviaria [statz-y**o**nay fair-rov-**yar**-ya]

tram il tram

translate tradurre [trad**oor**-ray]

trashcan la pattumiera [pat-toom-**yai**ra]

travel viaggiare [v-yaj-**ja**ray]

travel agent's l'agenzia di viaggi **f** [a**jentz**-ya dee vee-**aj**-jee]

traveller's cheque il travellers' cheque

tree l'albero **m** [**al**bairo]

trip (excursion) la gita [**jee**ta]

trousers i pantaloni

true vero [**vai**ro]

try provare [pro**va**ray]

try on provare

T-shirt la maglietta [mal-y**et**-ta]

tuna il tonno

turn: turn left/right giri a sinistra/destra [**jee**ree]

twice due volte [**doo**-ay **vol**tay]

twin room la camera a due letti [**doo**-ay]

tyre lo pneumatico [p-nay-oo**ma**teeko]

U

umbrella l'ombrello **m**

uncle lo zio [**tzee**-o]

under (in position) sotto
  (less than) meno di [**may**no]

underground (railway) la metropolitana

underpants le mutande [moo**tan**day]

understand capire [kap**ee**ray]
  I understand capisco
  I don't understand non capisco

university l'università **f** [ooneevair**see**ta]

unleaded petrol la benzina senza piombo [bentz**ee**na **sen**za p-y**om**bo]

until finché [feen**kay**]

up: up there lassù [las-s**oo**]

upstairs di sopra

urgent urgente [oor**jen**tay]

us noi [noy], ci [chee]
  for us per noi [pair]

USA gli USA [**oo**-sa]

use usare [oo**za**ray]

useful utile [**oo**teelay]

V

vacation la vacanza [vak**a**ntza]
(from university) le vacanze
[vak**a**ntzay]
valid (ticket etc) valido
value il valore [val**o**ray]
vanilla la vaniglia [van**ee**l-ya]
veal il vitello
vegetables la verdura
[vaird**oo**ra]
vegetarian (man/woman) il
vegetariano [vejetar-y**a**no], la
vegetaria**n**a
very molto
I like it very much mi piace
moltissimo [mee pee-a**chay**]
view la vista
village il paese [pa-**ay**zay]
visit visitare [veezeet**a**ray]
vodka la vodka
voice la voce [v**o**chay]
volcano il vulcano

W

waist la vita
wait aspettare [aspet-t**a**ray]
waiter il cameriere [kamair-
y**a**iray]
waiter! cameriere!
waitress la cameriera [kamair-
y**a**ira]
waitress! cameriera!
wake-up call la sveglia
Wales il Galles [g**a**l-les]
walk: is it a long walk? ci si

mette molto a piedi? [chee
see met-tay – p-y**ay**day]
wall il muro [m**oo**ro]
wallet il portafoglio [porta-f**o**l-
yo]
want: I want a ... voglio un...
[v**o**l-yo]
I don't want to non voglio
what do you want? cosa
vuole? [vw**o**lay]
warm caldo
wash lavare [lav**a**ray]
(oneself) lavarsi
washhand basin il lavabo
washing (clothes) il bucato
washing machine la lavatrice
[lavatr**ee**chay]
washing powder il detersivo
per bucato [detairs**ee**vo pair]
wasp la vespa
watch (wristwatch) l'orologio m
[orol**o**jo]
water l'acqua f [**a**kwa]
way: it's this way da questa
parte [kw**e**sta p**a**rtay]
it's that way da quella parte
[kw**e**l-la]
is it a long way to ...? ... è
molto lontano? [ay]
no way! assolutamente no!
[as-solootam**e**ntay]

dialogue

**could you tell me the way
to ...?** come si fa per
andare a...? [k**o**may – pair
and**a**ray]
go straight on until you

reach the traffic lights
vada dritto fino al
semaforo
turn left giri a sinistra
[**jee**ree]
take the first on the right
prenda la prima a destra

we noi [noy]
  we are ... siamo ... [s-yamo]
weather il tempo
week la settimana
  a week (from) today oggi a
otto [**oj**-jee]
weekend il fine settimana
[**fee**nay]
weight il peso [**pay**zo]
welcome: you're welcome
  (don't mention it) prego [**pray**go]
well: she's not well non sta
bene [**bay**nay]
  you speak English very well
parla inglese molto bene
[eenglay-zay]
  well done! bravo!
  this one as well anche
questo [**ankay kwesto**]
well-done (meat) ben cotto
Welsh gallese [gal-la**yzay**]
west l'ovest **m**
wet umido [**oo**meedo],
bagnato [ban-**yato**]
what? cosa?
  what's that? cos'è? [ko**zay**]
wheel la ruota [**rwota**]
when? quando? [**kwando**]
  when's the train/ferry? a che
ora parte il treno/il
traghetto? [kay – par**tay**]

where? dove? [**do**vay]
which: which bus? quale
autobus? [kwalay **owt**oboos]
while: while I'm here mentre
sono qui [mentray – kwee]
whisky il whisky
white bianco [b-yanko]
white wine il vino bianco
who? chi? [kee]
whole: the whole week tutta la
settimana [**toot**-ta]
whose: whose is this? di chi è
questo? [dee kee ay kw**esto**]
why? perché? [pair**kay**]
  why not? perché no?
wide largo
wife la moglie [mol-yay]
wind il vento
window (of house) la finestra
(of shop) la vetrina
  in the window (of shop) in
vetrina
wine il vino
wine list la lista dei vini [day]
winter l'inverno **m** [eenvairno]
with con
  I'm staying with ... sono
ospite di... [**o**speetay]
without senza [**sentza**]
woman la donna
wood (material) il legno [len-yo]
wool la lana
word la parola
work il lavoro
  it's not working non
funziona [foontz-**yona**]
worry: I'm worried sono
preoccupato [pray-ok-koo**pato**]
worse: it's worse è peggio [ay

pej-jo]
worst il peggio [pej-jo]
would: would you give this
to ...? può dare questo a...?
[pwo daray kwesto]
wrap: could you wrap it up?
può incartarlo? [pwo]
wrist il polso
write scrivere [skreevairay]
could you write it down? può
scrivermelo? [pwo
skreevairmelo]
wrong: it's the wrong key è la
chiave sbagliata [ay la k-yavay
zbal-yata]
there's something wrong
with ... c'è qualcosa che non
va nel... [chay kwalkoza kay]
what's wrong? cosa c'è che
non va? [koza]

Y

year l'anno m
yellow giallo [jal-lo]
yes sì
yesterday ieri [yairee]
the day before yesterday
l'altro ieri
yet ancora
you (singular, polite) lei [lay]
(singular, familiar) tu
(plural) voi [voy]
this is for you questo è per
te/lei [kwesto ay pair tay/lay]
young giovane [jovanay]
your/yours (singular, polite) (il)
suo [soo-o], (la) sua; pl (i) suoi

[swoy], (le) sue [soo-ay]
(singular, familiar) (il) tuo [too-
o], (la) tua; pl (i) tuoi [twoy], le
tue [too-ay]
(plural) (il) vostro, (la) vostra;
pl (i) vostri, (le) vostre
[vostray]
youth hostel l'ostello della
gioventù m [joventoo]

Z

zero lo zero [tzairo]
zip la cerniera lampo [chairn-
yaira]
zoo lo zoo [tzo-o]

Italian

→

English

a at; in; to; per

abbastanza [ab-bast**a**ntza] enough; quite

abbiamo we have

abbigliamento clothing

abbonamento m [ab-bonam**e**nto] season ticket

abitare [abeet**a**ray] to live

abiti mpl [ab**e**etee] clothes

accendere [achend**a**iray] to switch on; to light

accesso riservato ai viaggiatori muniti di biglietto access only for passengers in possession of tickets

accettazione f [achet-tatz-y**o**nay] check-in

accomodi: si accomodi [ak-k**o**modee] come in; take a seat

accordo: d'accordo all right, OK

acqua f [**a**kwa] water

adesso now

affari mpl business

affittare [af-feet-t**a**ray] to rent

affittasi to let, to rent

affrancatura per l'estero postage abroad

agenzia di viaggio [ajentz**e**e-a dee vee-aj-jee] travel agency

agitare prima dell'uso shake before use

agli [al-yee], **ai** [a-ee] at the; to the; for the; with

aiutare [a-yoot**a**ray] to help

al at the; to the

albergo m hotel

alla, alle [al-lay], **allo** at the; to the

alloggio m [al-l**o**j-jo] accommodation

allora then

alt stop, halt

alto high, tall

altra, altri, altre [**a**ltray] other

altro other

amare [am**a**ray] to love

ambasciata f [ambash**a**ta] embassy

ambulatorio m [amboolat**o**r-yo] out-patients' department; surgery

amico m, **amica** f friend

amore m [am**o**ray] love

anche [**a**nkay] also; even

ancora [ank**o**ra] still

　ancora un/uno/una... another ...

　non ancora not yet

andare [and**a**ray] to go

andarsene [and**a**rsenay] to go away

anno m year

annullare [an-nool-l**a**ray] to cancel

anticipo: in anticipo [ant**e**echeepo] in advance; early

aperto open

appena [ap-p**a**yna] just; hardly

aprire [apr**e**eray] to open

argento m [arj**e**nto] silver

arrivare [ar-reev**a**ray] to arrive

arrivederci [ar-reeved**ai**rchee] goodbye

ascensore f [ashens**o**ray] lift, elevator

asciutto [ash**oo**t-to] dry

ascoltare [askolt**a**ray] to listen

aspettare [aspet-t**a**ray] to wait (for)

assegno m [as-s**e**n-yo] cheque, (US) check

assicurazione f [as-seekooratz-y**o**nay] insurance

attenti al cane beware of the dog

attenzione f [at-tentz-y**o**nay] care, attention

attimo: un attimo just a minute

attraente [at-tra-**e**ntay] attractive

auguri: tanti auguri [tant**ee** owg**oo**ree] best wishes

autista m/f [owt**ee**sta] driver

autolavaggio m [owtolav**aj**-jo] car wash

autonoleggio m car rental

avanti come in; cross now

  avanti diritto straight ahead

  più avanti further on

avere to have

avete [av**ay**tay] you have

avvocato m lawyer

bagagli mpl [bag**a**l-yee] baggage

bagno m [b**a**n-yo] bath; bathroom

  fare il bagno to have a bath; to have a swim

ballare [bal-l**a**ray] to dance

bambino m, **bambina f** child

banchina f [bank**ee**na] platform, (US) track; quayside

banchina non transitabile soft verge

banco informazioni [eenformatz-y**o**nee] information desk

bancomat® m cash dispenser, automatic teller

barca f boat

basso low

basta (così)! [koz**ee**] that's enough!

bastare [bast**a**ray] to be enough

battello m passenger ferry; steamer

bello beautiful

bene [b**ay**nay] good; fine; well

benissimo! excellent!

benvenuto! [benv**ay**nooto] welcome!

benzina f [bendz**ee**na] petrol, (US) gas

benzina senza piombo [s**e**ntza p-y**o**mbo] unleaded petrol/gas

benzina verde [v**air**day] unleaded petrol/gas

bere [b**ai**ray] to drink

bianco [b-y**a**nko] white

bibita f [b**ee**beeta] soft drink

bicchiere m [beek-y**ai**ray] glass

bicicletta f [beecheekl**e**t-ta] bicycle

biglietteria f [beel-yet-tair-**ee**-a] ticket office; box-office

biglietteria automatica [owtom**a**teeka] ticket vending machine

biglietto m [beel-y**e**t-to] ticket; banknote, (US) bill

biglietto di andata e ritorno [reet**o**rno] return (ticket),

round trip ticket
biglietto di sola andata single (ticket), one-way ticket
binario m [beenar-yo] platform, (US) track
bisogno: ho bisogno di [o beezon-yo] I need
borgo medioevale m [med-yo-ayvalay] medieval village
bosco m wood, forest
braccio m [bracho] arm
breve [brayvay] short
brutto [broot-to] ugly
buca delle lettere f [del-lay let-tairay] letter box, mailbox
bucato f laundry
buffo [boof-fo] funny
buio (m) [boo-yo] dark
buono [bwono] good

C (caldo) hot
cadere [kadairay] to fall
caduta massi falling rocks
caffetteria f [kaf-fet-tairee-a] coffee bar, coffee house
calcio m [kalcho] football; kick
caldo (m) heat; warm; hot
calzature fpl [kaltzatooray] footwear
calzolaio m [kaltzola-yo] shoe repairer's
cambiare [kamb-yaray] to change
cambiavalute m [kamb-yavalootay] bureau de change
cambio m [kamb-yo] change; bureau de change; gears
camera f [kamaira] room
camera da letto bedroom

camera doppia [dop-ya] double room
cameriera f [kamair-yaira] maid; waitress
cameriere m [kamair-yairay] waiter
camion m [kam-yon] truck
campagna f [kampan-ya] countryside; campaign
campeggio m [kampej-jo] camping; campsite
campo m course; court; field
cane m [kanay] dog
cantare [kantaray] to sing
capelli mpl hair
capire [kapeeray] to understand
non capisco [kapeesko] I don't understand
capo m boss
capolinea m [kapoleenay-a] terminus
carabinieri mpl [karabeen-yairee] police
carino nice, pleasant
caro dear; expensive
carrozza f [kar-rotza] carriage, car
carta geografica [jay-ografeeka] map
cartina f map
cartolina f postcard
casa f [kaza] house
cassa f [kas-sa] cashdesk
cassetta delle lettere [del-lay let-tairay] postbox, mailbox
cattivo [kat-teevo] bad
cavallo m horse
c'è [chay] there is

non c'è he/she/it is not here

cena f [chayna] dinner; supper

centralino m [chentraleeno] local exchange, operator

centro città [cheet-ta] city centre

centro storico old town

cestino m [chesteeno] basket; wastepaper basket

che [kay] that, which; than

che? what?

chi? [kee] who?

chiamare [k-yamaray] to call

chiamata f [k-yamata] call

chiaro [k-yaro] clear; light

chiave f [k-yavay] key; wrench

chiedere [k-yaydairay] to ask

chiesa f [k-yayza] church

chilo m [keelo] kilo

chilometro m [keelometro] kilometre

chiudere [k-yoodairay] to close

ci [chee] here; there; us; each other; to us; ourselves

ci sono there are

ciao! [chow] hello!; cheerio!

ciascuno [chaskoono] each

cibo m [cheebo] food

ciò [cho] this; that

circa [cheerka] about

città f [cheet-ta] town(s); city, cities

code traffic queues ahead

cognome m [kon-yomay] surname

coi [koy], **col** with the

colle m [kol-lay] hill

collo m neck

colpa: è colpa mia it's my fault

colpire [kolpeeray] to hit; to knock

come [komay] like; as

come? how?; what?; pardon me?

come va? how are things?

commissariato (di polizia) m [kom-mees-sar-yato dee poleetzee-a] police station

comodo comfortable

compleanno m [komplay-an-no] birthday

comprare [kompraray] to buy

compreso [komprayzo] included

comunicazione f [komooneekatz-yonay] phone call

comunque [komoonkway] however

con with

conducente m/f [kondoochentay] driver

conoscere [konoshairay] to know

contanti mpl cash

conto m bill, (US) check; account

contro against

coperto m cover charge

al coperto indoors

corpo m body

corriera f [kor-yaira] long-distance bus

corsia di emergenza f [emairjentza] emergency lane

corso m course; main street

cosa f [koza] thing

cosa? what?

così [ko**zee**] like this; so
costare [ko**sta**ray] to cost
credere [kray**dair**ay] to believe
cuoio m [**kwo**-yo] leather
cuore m [**kwo**ray] heart
curva pericolosa dangerous bend

da from; by; at; to
dagli [**dal**-yee] from the; by the
dai [**da**-ee] from the; by the; you give
dallo, dal, dalla, dalle [**dal**-lay] from the; by the
dare [**da**ray] to give
data di nascita [na**shee**ta] date of birth
davanti m [da**van**tee] front
davanti a in front of
da vendersi entro... sell by ...
davvero [dav-**vai**ro] really?
del, dei [day], **degli** [**dayl**-yee], **dello, della, delle** [**del**-lay] some; of the
denaro m money
dente m [**den**tay] tooth
dentro inside
deposito bagagli [ba**gal**-yee] left luggage, baggage checkroom
destra f right
di of; than
dica? yes?
dietro m [d-**yay**tro] back, rear
dietro (a) behind
difettoso [deefet-**to**zo] faulty
dimenticare [deementee**ka**ray] to forget

Dio m [**dee**-o] God
dire [**dee**ray] to say; to tell
dispiacere: mi dispiace (tanto)! [deesp-**ya**chay] I'm (so) sorry!
disporsi su due file get into two lanes
distributore (automatico) di biglietti [owtoma**tee**ko dee beel-**yet**-tee] ticket machine
dito m finger
ditta f [**deet**-ta] firm, company
divieto di accesso no entry
divieto di balneazione no bathing
divieto di fermata no stopping
divieto di sosta no parking
doccia f [**do**cha] shower
Dogana f Customs
dolci mpl [**dol**chee] confectionery; cakes
dolore m [do**lo**ray] pain
domanda f question
domani [do**ma**nee] tomorrow
donna f woman
donne ladies (rest room)
dopo after; afterwards
doppio [**dop**-yo] double
dormire [dor**mee**ray] to sleep
dove? [**do**vay] where?
dovere (m) [do**vai**ray] to have to, must; to owe; duty
dritto straight on
drogheria f [droga**ir**ee-a] grocer's
dunque [**doon**kway] therefore, so; well (then)
duomo m [**dwo**mo] cathedral
durante [doo**ran**tay] during
duro [**doo**ro] hard

E

e [ay] and

è [ay] he/she/it is; you are

ecco [ek-ko] here is/are; here you are; that's it

elenco telefonico m [telayfoneeko] telephone directory

enoteca f [enotayka] wine-tasting shop

entrare [entraray] to come/go in

entrata f entrance

esatto [esat-to] correct

esaurito sold out

escluso frontisti residents only

essere [es-sairay] to be

esso [es-so] it

est m east

estate f [estatay] summer

estero: all'estero [al-lestairo] abroad

età f [ayta] age

etto(grammo) m hundred grams

F (freddo) cold

fa he/she/it does; you do; ago

fabbrica f factory

faccia f [facha] face

facile [facheelay] easy

famiglia f [fameel-ya] family

fa' pure! [pooray] please, do!

fare [faray] to make; to do

favore m [favoray] favour

per favore please

felice [feleechay] happy

feriali mpl working days

fermare [fairmaray] to stop

fermata f [fairmata] (bus) stop

fermata facoltativa [fakoltateeva] request stop

fermo posta m poste restante, (US) general delivery

ferrovia f [fair-rovee-a] railway

festa f party; holiday, vacation

festivi mpl public holidays

figlia f [feel-ya] daughter

figlio m son

finché [feenkay] until

fine (f) [feenay] end; thin; fine

fine settimana [set-teemana] weekend

finestra f window

finire [feeneeray] to finish

fino thin; fine; even

fino a until

firma f signature

firmare [feermaray] to sign

fiume m [f-yoomay] river

fondo m bottom

forno m oven

forse [forsay] maybe

forte [fortay] strong; loud

fra between; in; through

francobollo m [frankobol-lo] stamp

fratello m brother

freddo (m) cold

freno m [frayno] brake

fumare [foomaray] to smoke

fumatori smokers

fuori [fworee] outside

fuori servizio out of order

gabinetto m [gabeenet-to] toilet, rest room

gamba f leg
gara f sporting event; race; competition
gelato m [jelato] ice cream
genitori mpl [jeneetoree] parents
gente f [jentay] people
gentile [jenteelay] kind
ghiaccio m [g-yacho] ice
già [ja] already
giallo [jal-lo] yellow
giardino m [jardeeno] garden
giocare [jokaray] to play
gioco m [joko] game
gioielli mpl [jo-yel-lee] jewellery
giornale m [jornalay] newspaper
giornata f [jornata] day
giorno m [jorno] day
giro m [jeero] turn; walk; tour
gita f [jeeta] excursion; hike
giù [joo] down
gli [l-yee] the; to him; to them
gola f throat
gomma f rubber; tyre
grande [granday] big
grasso fat
gratis free
gratuito [gratoo-eeto] free
grazie [gratzee-ay] thank you
grazioso [gratz-yozo] pretty
grosso big; thick
grotta f cave
guardare [gwardaray] to look (at)
guasto (m) [gwasto] breakdown; broken, out of order; rotten

guerra f [gwair-ra] war
guidare [gweedaray] to lead; to drive

ha [a] he/she it has; you have
hai [a-ee] you have
hanno [an-no] they have
ho [o] I have

i [ee] the
ieri [yairee] yesterday
il [eel] the
imbucare [eembookaray] to post, to mail
imposta f tax
in in; into; to; by
incidente m [eencheedentay] accident
incrocio pericoloso dangerous junction
indietro [eend-yaytro] behind; back
indirizzo m [eendeereetzo] address
Inghilterra f [eengheeltair-ra] England
inglese (m/f) [eenglayzay] English; Englishman; Englishwoman
ingorgo m traffic jam
ingresso gratuito/libero admission free
insieme [eens-yaymay] together
intero whole
inverno m winter
investire [eenvesteeray] to invest; to knock over
inviare [eenv-yaray] to send; to post, to mail

io [**ee**-o] I
isola f [**ee**zola] island
I.V.A. (Imposta sul Valore Aggiunto) f [**eeva**] VAT

la the; her; it; you
là there
 di là [dee] over there; that way; from there
laggiù [laj-**joo**] over there
lago m lake
lana f wool
largo wide
lasciare [lash**a**ray] to leave; to let; to allow
lavare [lav**a**ray] to wash
lavasecco m dry-cleaner's
lavorare [lavor**a**ray] to work
lavori stradali roadworks
lavoro m work
le [lay] the; to her; to you
legge f [**lej**-jay] law
leggere [**lej**-jairay] to read
legno m [**len**-yo] wood
lei [lay] she; her; you
lentamente [lentament**ay**] slowly
lento slow
letto m bed
li [lee] them
lì there
libbra f pound
libero vacant, free
libreria f [leebrair**ee**-a] bookshop, bookstore; bookcase
libro m book
lingua f [**lee**ngwa] tongue; language

lista f list; menu
lo the; him; it
locanda f guesthouse, hotel
lontano far away
loro they; them; you
 il/la loro their(s); your(s)
luce f [**loo**chay] light
lui [**loo**-ee] he; him
lungo long; along
luogo di nascita m [l**wo**go dee n**a**sheeta] place of birth

ma but
macchina f [mak-**kee**na] car; machine
macelleria f [machel-lair**ee**-a] butcher's
madre f [**ma**dray] mother
maggior: la maggior parte (di) [maj-**jor** p**a**rtay] most (of)
maggiore [maj-**jo**ray] bigger
mai [ma-**ee**] never
malato ill
male badly
mandare [mand**a**ray] to send
mangiare [manj**a**ray] to eat
mano f hand
marcia a senso unico alternato temporary one-way system in operation
marcia normale normal speed lane
marciapiede m [marchap-**yay**day] pavement, sidewalk; platform, (US) track
mare m [**ma**ray] sea
marito m husband
mattina f, mattino m morning
me [may] me

medusa f [med**oo**za] jellyfish
meglio [may**l**-yo] better
meno (di) [**may**no dee] less (than)
mentre [**men**tray] while
mercato m [mair**ka**to] market
 a buon mercato [bwon] cheap, inexpensive
mese m [**may**zay] month
metà f half
mettere [met-**tai**ray] to put
mezzanotte f [medza**not**-tay] midnight
mezza pensione f [**med**za pens-**yo**nay] half board, (US) European plan
mezzo (m) [**med**zo] half; middle
mezzogiorno m [medzo**jor**no] midday
mezz'ora f [med**zo**ra] half an hour
mi [mee] me; myself; to me
migliore [meel-**yo**ray] best; better
mio [**mee**-o] my; mine
mobili mpl [**mo**beelee] furniture
modulo m form
moglie f [**mol**-yay] wife
molto a lot; much; very
mondo m world
moneta f [mon**ay**ta] coin; small change
morbido soft
morire [mor**ee**ray] to die
morte f [**mor**-tay] death
morto dead
mostra f exhibition; show
multa f fine

muro m wall

naso m [**na**zo] nose
nastro m tape; ribbon
Natale m [na**ta**lay] Christmas
nato born
nave f [**na**vay] ship
ne [nay] of him/her/them/it; about him/her/them/it
 non ne ho [o] I don't have any
né... né... [nay] neither ... nor ...
neanche [nay-**an**kay] not even
negli [**nay**l-yee] in the
negozio m [ne**got**z-yo] shop
nello, nel, nella, nei [nay], **nelle** [**nel**-lay] in the
nero (m) [**nai**ro] black; dark
nessun no; not any
nessuno no; none; nobody; not any
netto clean
nevicata f snowfall
niente [n-**yen**tay] nothing
 di niente don't mention it
 niente pesce oggi no fish today
no no; not
noi [noy] we; us
noleggiare [nolej-**ja**ray] to rent
noleggio sci [shee] ski hire
nolo: a nolo for hire, to rent
nome m [**no**may] name
nome di battesimo [bat-**tay**zeemo] Christian name
non not
non ferma a... does not stop at ...

non toccare do not touch
nord m north
nostro our(s)
notte f [not-tay] night
novello new
nulla nothing; anything
numero di volo flight number
nuotare [nwotaray] to swim
nuovo new

o or
occasione f [ok-kas-yonay] chance; bargain
 d'occasione secondhand; bargain (price)
occhio m [ok-yo] eye
oggetti smarriti lost property, lost and found
oggi [oj-jee] today
ogni [on-yee] each, every; all
ogni abuso sarà punito penalty for misuse
ognuno [on-yoono] everyone
olio m [ol-yo] oil
oltre [oltray] beyond
ora (f) hour; now; in a moment
orario m [orar-yo] timetable, (US) schedule
orario di apertura opening hours
oriente m [or-yentay] east
ormai [orma-ee] by now
oro m gold
ospedale m [ospaydalay] hospital
ospite m/f [ospeetay] guest; host
osteria f [ostairee-a] inn

ottimo excellent
ovest m west

pacchetto m [pak-ket-to] package; packet
padre m [padray] father
paese m [pa-ayzay] country; town; village
pagamento m payment
pagare [pagaray] to pay
panetteria f [panet-tairee-ya] baker's
paninoteca f [paneenotayka] bar selling sandwiches
parcheggiare [parkej-jaray] to park
parcheggio m [parkej-jo] car park, parking lot
parecchi [parek-kee] several
parlare [parlaray] to talk; to speak
parola f word
parrucchiere m [par-rook-yairay], parrucchiera f hairdresser
parte f [partay] part
 da qualche parte somewhere
partenza f [partentza] departure
partire [parteeray] to leave
partita f match (sport)
patente f [patentay] driving licence
pazzo [patzo] mad
pedaggio m toll
pedoni mpl pedestrians
peggio [pej-jo] worse
pensare [pensaray] to think
pensione f [pens-yonay] guesthouse

pensione completa [kompl**ay**ta] full board

per [pair] for; by; through; in order to

perché [pair**kay**] because
  perché? why?

perfino even

pericolo di valanghe [val**ang**ay] danger of avalanches

pericoloso: è pericoloso sporgersi it is dangerous to lean out of the window

però [pair**o**] but

peso m [**pay**zo] weight

piacere di conoscerla [p-yach**ai**ray dee konosh**ai**rla] pleased to meet you
  per piacere please

piano (m) floor, storey; quietly; slowly

pianta f plant; map

pianterreno m [p-yantair-r**ay**no] ground floor, (US) first floor

piatto (m) plate; dish; flat (adj)

piccolo small

piede m [p-y**ay**day] foot

pieno [p-y**ay**no] full

pinacoteca f gallery

pioggia f [p-y**o**j-ja] rain

piscina f [pee**shee**na] swimming pool

più [p-yoo] more

po': un po' (di) a little bit (of)

poca few

pochi [p**o**kee] few

pochino: un pochino [pok**ee**no] a little bit

poco few
  fra poco in a little while

poi [poy] then

pomeriggio m [pomair**eej**-jo] afternoon

ponte m [p**on**tay] bridge; deck

porta f door

portare [port**a**ray] to carry; to take; to bring

pranzo m [pr**an**dzo] lunch

prefisso m dialling code, area code

pregare [preg**a**ray] to request
  si prega di (non)... please do (not) ...

prego [pr**ay**go] please; pardon; you're welcome; after you

prendere [pr**en**dairay] to take; to catch

prenotare [prenot**a**ray] to book, to reserve

prenotazione f [prenotatz-y**o**nay] reservation, booking

presto soon; early

prezzo m [pr**et**zo] price

prima colazione f [kolatz-y**o**nay] breakfast

primavera f spring

primo m first

pronto ready; hello (on phone)

proprio exactly; just; really; own

prossimo next

pulire [pool**ee**ray] to clean

pulito clean

pulitura f dry-cleaner's

pullman m coach, long-distance bus

qua [kwa] here

qualche [kw**al**kay] some, a few

qualcosa [kwalkoza]
something; anything
qualcuno [kwalkoono]
somebody
quale [kwalay] which
quando [kwando] when
quanti? [kwantee], quante?
[kwantay] how many?
quanto? [kwanto] how much?
quasi [kwazee] almost, nearly
quello [kwel-lo] that (one)
questo [kwesto] this (one)
qui [kwee] here
quindi [kweendee] therefore

raccordo autostradale m [owto-
stradalay] motorway junction,
highway intersection
ragazza f [ragatza] girl;
girlfriend
ragazzo m [ragatzo] boy;
boyfriend
rallentare [ral-lentaray] reduce
speed, slow down
re m [ray] king
reclamo m complaint
regalo m present
regina f [rejeena] queen
ricco [reek-ko] rich
ricevuta f [reechevoota] receipt
ridotto reduced
rifiuti mpl [reef-yootee] rubbish
riservato viacard for magnetic
toll card holders only
ritardo m delay
ritirata f toilet, rest room (on
train)
rosso red
rotto broken

roulotte f [roolot] caravan, (US)
trailer
R.U. (Regno Unito) m UK
ruota f [rwota] wheel

sala da pranzo [prandzo]
dining room
sala d'aspetto waiting room
salire [saleeray] to go up; to
get on/in
salumeria f [saloomairee-a]
delicatessen
salute f [salootay] health
sapere [sapairay] to know
sbagliato [zbal-yato] wrong
scale fpl [skalay] stairs
scheda f [skayda] card
sciare [shee-aray] to ski
scomodo uncomfortable
scontrino m receipt
scorso: l'anno scorso last year
scrivere [skreevairay] to write
scuola f [skwola] school
scuro dark
scusa f [skooza] apology;
excuse
scusa! sorry!
scusi! [skoozee] sorry!
se [say] if
sé [say] himself; herself; itself;
oneself; themselves
sebbene [seb-baynay] although
secco dry
secolo m [saykolo] century
sedia f [sayd-ya] chair
seguire [segweeray] to follow
sei [say] you are; six
semaforo m traffic lights
sempre [sempray] always

sempre d(i)ritto straight on

senso unico one way

sentiero m [sent-yairo] path

senza [sentza] without

sera f [saira] evening

sesso m sex

seta f [sayta] silk

settimana f week

si [see] himself; herself; itself; themselves

sì [see] yes

siamo we are

siccome [seek-komay] as

siete [s-yaytay] you are

signore fpl ladies' (room)

signori mpl gents, men's room

simpatico nice

sinistra f [seeneestra] left

so: non (lo) so I don't know

soccorso m help

soccorso stradale [stradalay] breakdown service

soldi mpl [soldee] money

sole m [solay] sun

solito [soleeto] usual

solo alone; only

soltanto only

sono I am; they are

sopra on; above

di sopra upstairs

sorella f sister

sorpassare [sorpas-saray] to overtake

sosta vietata no parking

sotto under; below

di sotto downstairs

spedire [spedeeray] to send; to post, to mail

spegnere [spen-yairay] to

switch off

sperare [speraray] to hope

spesso often

spiace: mi spiace [spee-achay] I'm sorry

spiaggia f [sp-yaj-ja] beach

spiccioli mpl [speecholee] (small) change

sporco dirty

sposato married

spuntino m snack

stanco tired

stanotte [stanot-tay] tonight

stanza f [stantza] room

stare [staray] to be; to stand; to stay; to suit

stesso same

strada f road

straniero m [stran-yairo], straniera f foreigner

strano strange

su [soo] on; up

subito [soobeeto] immediately

sud m south

sul [sool], sulla, sullo, sui [soo-ee], sugli [sool-yee], sulle [sool-lay] on the

suo [soo-o] his; her(s); its; your(s)

superstrada f motorway/ highway without toll

Svizzera f [zveetzaira] Switzerland

taglia f [tal-ya] size

tagliare [tal-yaray] to cut

tanti, tante [tantee, tantay] many, lots of

tanto a lot; so much

tardi late
tassa f tax
tassista m/f taxi driver
tavola f [tavola] table
tavola calda snack bar
te [tay] you
tè m [tay] tea
tedesco (m/f) [tedesko] German
tempo m time; weather
tenere [tenayray] to hold; to keep
testa f head
ti [tee] you; yourself; to you
tifoso m, **tifosa** f fan
tintoria f [teentoree-a] drycleaner's
tirare [teeraray] to pull
togliere [tol-yairay] to take away; to remove
tra among; between
tradurre [tradoor-ray] to translate
treno m [trayno] train
triste [treestay] sad
troppo too; too much
trovare [trovaray] to find
trucco m make-up
tu [too] you
tuo [too-o] your(s)
tuttavia however
tutti all; every; everybody
  tutti e due [ay doo-ay] both
tutto all; everything

ubriaco drunk
uccidere [oocheedairay] to kill
ultimo [oolteemo] last
un, una, uno a; one

uomini mpl [womeenee] men; gents, mens' room
uomo m [womo] man
uscire [oosheeray] to go out
uscita f [oosheeta] exit; gate
uscita di sicurezza emergency exit

vecchio (m) old; old man
vedere [vedairay] to see
vendere [vendairay] to sell
vendesi for sale
venire [veneeray] to come
verde [vairday] green
vernice fresca wet paint
vero [vairo] true; real
vetro m glass
vi [vee] you; yourselves; to you; each other
via (f) [vee-a] road, street; way; away
viaggiare [v-yaj-jaray] to travel
viaggio m [v-yaj-jo] journey; tour
viale m [vee-alay] avenue
vicino (a) near; nearby
vietato [v-yaytato] forbidden
vietato l'ingresso no entry
vigili urbani mpl traffic police
vivere [veevairay] to live
voi [voy] you
volo m flight
volta f time
vostro your(s)

zia f [tzee-a] aunt
zio m uncle
zitto [tzeet-to] quiet; silent

MENU READER

Food: Essential terms

bread il pane [**pa**nay]
butter il burro [**boo**r-ro]
cup la tazza [**ta**tza]
dessert il dessert [des-**sair**]
fish il pesce [**pe**shay]
fork la forchetta [for**ket**-ta]
glass il bicchiere [beek-**ya**iray]
knife il coltello
main course la portata
  principale [preencheepalay]
meat la carne [**ka**rnay]
menu il menù [me**noo**]
pepper il pepe [**pay**pay]
plate il piatto [p-**yat**-to]
salad l'insalata

salt il sale [**sa**lay]
set menu il menù fisso
  [me**noo**]
soup la minestra, la zuppa
  [tz**oo**p-pa]
spoon il cucchiaio [kook-ya-yo]
starter l'antipasto m
table il tavolo

another ..., please ancora
  un/una ..., per favore
excuse me! mi scusi [mee
  sk**oo**zee]
could I have the bill, please? il
  conto, per favore

Food: Menu Reader

acciughe [ach**oo**gay] anchovies
aceto [a**che**to] vinegar
affumicato smoked
aglio [**al**-yo] garlic
agnello [an-**yel**-lo] lamb
albicocca apricot
ananas pineapple
anatra duck

anguria water melon
antipasti starters
aragosta spiny lobster
arancia [a**ran**cha] orange
aringa herring
arrosto roast
asparagi [aspara**jee**] asparagus
astice [**a**steechay] lobster

359

baccalà dried cod
basilico [bazeeleeko] basil
bignè [been-yay] cream puff
biscotto biscuit
bistecca steak
bollito boiled
bombolone [bombolonay] doughnut
bra full-fat white cheese
braciola di maiale [brachola dee my-alay] pork chop
branzino al forno [brantzeeno] baked sea bass
brasato [brazato] braised; braised beef with herbs
bresaola [breza-ola] dried, salted beef sliced thinly and eaten cold
brodetto fish casserole
brodo clear broth
budino pudding
burro butter
calamari fritti fried squid
calzone [kaltzonay] folded pizza with tomato and mozzarella or ricotta and ham, or other fillings inside
cannella cinnamon
caponata di melanzane [melandzanay] fried aubergines or eggplants and celery with tomato, capers and olives
capperi capers
capretto al forno roast kid
caramella sweet
carciofi [karchofee] artichokes
carne [karnay] meat
carote [karotay] carrots
carpaccio [karpacho] finely

sliced raw beef fillets with oil, lemon and grated Parmesan
cassata siciliana [seecheel-yana] Sicilian ice-cream cake
castagne [kastan-yay] chestnuts
cavoletti di Bruxelles [brooksel] Brussels sprouts
cavolfiore [kavolf-yoray] cauliflower
cavolo cabbage
ceci [chaychee] chickpeas
cervella al burro [chairvel-la] brains cooked in butter
cetriolo [chetree-olo] cucumber
chiacchiere [k-yak-yairay] sweet pastries fried in lard and sprinkled with fine sugar
chiodi di garofano [k-yodee] cloves
cicoria [cheekoree-a] chicory
ciliege [cheel-yay-jay] cherries
cioccolata [chok-kolata] chocolate
cipolle [cheepol-lay] onions
coniglio [koneel-yo] rabbit
contorni vegetable side dishes
cornetto croissant
cosciotto di agnello al forno [koshot-to dee an-yel-lo] baked leg of lamb
costoletta chop
cotoletta veal cutlet
cotto cooked
cozze [kotzay] mussels
crema [krayma] custard
crema di ... cream of ... soup
crostata di frutta fruit tart
crostini ai funghi [a-ee foongee]

croutons with mushrooms in oil with garlic and parsley

crudo raw

datteri dates

erbe aromatiche [**air**bay aro**ma**teekay] herbs

fagiano [fa**ja**no] pheasant

fagioli [fa**jo**lee] beans

fagiolini [fajol**ee**nee] green beans

faraona [fara-**o**na] guinea fowl

fegatini di pollo chicken livers

fegato [**fay**gato] liver

ferri: ai ferri [**a**-ee] grilled

fettuccine [fet-too**chee**nay] ribbon-shaped pasta

fichi [**fee**kee] figs

filetto fillet

finocchio [fee**no**k-yo] fennel

focaccia [fo**ka**cha] flat bread sprinkled with olive oil and baked or grilled

fonduta fondue made with cheese, milk and eggs

formaggio [for**maj**-jo] cheese

forno: al forno roast

fragole [**fra**golay] strawberries

frittata type of omelette

fritto fried

fritto misto mixed seafood in batter

frutta fruit

frutti di mare [**ma**ray] seafood

funghi [**foon**gee] mushrooms

gallina chicken

gamberetti shrimps

gamberi crayfish; prawns

gamberoni king prawns

gelato [je**la**to] ice cream

gnocchi [n-**yo**k-kee] small flour and potato dumplings

grancevola [gran**chay**vola] spiny spider crab

granchio [**grank**-yo] crab

gratin di patate [gra**teen** dee pa**ta**tay] potatoes with grated cheese

griglia: alla griglia [al-la **greel**-ya] grilled

grigliata di pesce [greel-**ya**ta di **pe**shay] grilled fish

grissini breadsticks

gruviera [groov-**yai**ra] Gruyère cheese

impanato breaded, in breadcrumbs

indivia [een**deev**-ya] endive

insalata salad

insalata caprese [ka**pray**zay] sliced tomatoes, mozzarella and oregano

krapfen doughnut

lamponi raspberries

lattuga lettuce

legumi pulses

lenticchie [len**teek**-yay] lentils

lepre [**le**pray] hare

lesso boiled

limone [lee**mo**nay] lemon

lingua [**lee**ngwa] tongue

macedonia di frutta [mached**on**-ya] fruit salad

maggiorana [maj-jo**ra**na] marjoram

maiale [my-**a**lay] pork

maionese [my-on**ay**zay] mayonnaise

mandorle [**man**dorlay] almonds

manzo [**ma**ndzo] beef
marroni chestnuts
mela [**may**la] apple
melanzane [melandz**a**nay]
aubergines, eggplants
melone [mel**o**nay] melon
menta mint
merluzzo [mairl**oo**tzo] cod
miele [m-**yay**lay] honey
minestra di verdure [vaird**oo**ray]
vegetable soup
Montebianco [monteb-**ya**nko]
puréed chestnut and
whipped cream pudding
more [**mo**ray] mulberries,
blackberries
mostarda di Cremona preserve
of candied fruit in grape
must or sugar with mustard
nasello [naz**e**l-lo] hake
nocciole [noch**o**lay] hazelnuts
noce moscata [**no**chay]
nutmeg
noci [**no**chee] walnuts
nodino veal chop
oca goose
olio [**o**l-yo] oil
oliva olive
orzo [**o**rdzo] barley
ossobuco stewed shin of veal
ostriche [**o**streekay] oysters
paglia e fieno [**pa**l-ya ay f-**yay**no]
mixture of ordinary and
green tagliatelle
pancetta [panch**e**t-ta] bacon
pancotto stale bread cooked
with tomatoes etc
pan di Spagna [**spa**n-ya]
sponge cake

pane [**pa**nay] bread
pane nero [**na**iro] wholemeal
bread
panettone [panet-**to**nay] cake
with sultanas and candied
fruit eaten at Christmas
panforte [panf**o**rtay] nougat-
type spiced delicacy
panini sandwiches; filled rolls
panna cream
panna cotta kind of pudding
typical of Tuscany
panzanella [pantzan**e**l-la] Tuscan
dish of bread with fresh
tomatoes, onions basil and
olive oil
pappa col pomodoro tomato
soup with toasted home-
made bread
parmigiano reggiano
[parmeej**a**no rej-**ja**no] Parmesan
cheese
passato di patate [pat**a**tay]
cream of potato soup
pasta pasta; cake; pastry
pasta e fagioli [ay faj**o**lee] very
thick soup with blended
borlotti beans and small pasta
patate [pat**a**tay] potatoes
patatine [patat**ee**nay] crisps, (US)
potato chips
patatine fritte [**free**t-tay] chips,
French fries
pecorino strong, hard ewes
milk cheese
penne [**pe**n-nay] pasta quills
pepe [**pay**pay] pepper (spice)
peperonata peppers cooked
in olive oil with onion,

tomato and garlic

peperoncino [pepaironch**ee**no] chilli pepper

peperone [pepair**o**nay] pepper (vegetable)

pera [p**ai**ra] pear

pernice [pairn**ee**chay] partridge

pesca [p**e**ska] peach

pesce [p**e**shay] fish

pesce spada swordfish

piccata di vitello al limone [leem**o**nay] veal in sour lemon sauce

piccione [peech**o**nay] pigeon

piedini di maiale [p-yayd**ee**nee dee my-**a**lay] pigs' trotters

pinoli pine nuts

piselli peas

pistacchi [peest**a**k-kee] pistachios

pizzaiola [peetza-ee-**o**la] slices of cooked beef in tomato sauce, oregano and anchovies

polenta yellow cornmeal porridge, left to set and cut in slices

pollame [pol-l**a**may] poultry

pollo chicken

polpette [polp**et**-tay] meatballs

polpettone [polpet-t**o**nay] meat-loaf

polpo octopus

pomodori tomatoes

pompelmo grapefruit

porchetta [pork**et**-ta] roast sucking pig

porro leek

portata course (of meal)

prezzemolo [pretz**ay**molo] parsley

prosciutto [prosh**oo**t-to] ham

provolone [provol**o**nay] oval-shaped cheese, with a slight smoked and spicy flavour

prugne [pr**oo**n-yay] plums

purè di patate [poor**ay** dee pat**a**tay] creamed potatoes

quaglie [kw**a**l-yay] quails

radicchio [rad**ee**k-yo] chicory

ragù sauce made with minced beef and tomatoes

rapa type of white turnip with flavour similar to radish

ravanelli radishes

razza [r**a**tza] skate

ribollita vegetable soup with toasted home-made bread

ripieno [reep-y**ay**no] stuffed

riso rice

risi e bisi risotto with peas and small pieces of ham

rombo turbot

rosmarino rosemary

rucola rocket

sale [s**a**lay] salt

salmone [salm**o**nay] salmon

salsa sauce

salsiccia [sals**ee**cha] sausage

saltimbocca alla romana slices of veal rolled up with ham and sage and fried

salvia [s**a**lv-ya] sage

sangue: al sangue [s**a**ngway] rare

sarde ai ferri [s**a**rday a-ee] grilled sardines

scaloppine [skalop-p**ee**nay] veal escalopes

scarola type of endive

sedano [**say**dano] celery

selvaggina [selvaj-**jee**na] game

semifreddo ice cream and sponge dessert

senape [**se**napay] mustard

seppie in umido [**sep**-yay] stewed cuttlefish

sogliola [**sol**-yola] sole

sorbetto sorbet; soft ice cream

sottaceti [sot-tach**ay**tee] pickles

speck type of dry-cured, smoked ham

spezie [sp**ay**tz-yay] spices

spiedini [sp-yayd**ee**nee] small pieces of a variety of meat or fish roasted on a spit

spiedo: allo spiedo [sp-y**ay**do] on a spit

spigola sea bass

spinaci [speen**a**chee] spinach

spuntino snack

stoccafisso dried cod

stufato stewed

sugo al tonno tomato sauce with garlic, tuna and parsley

svizzera [zv**ee**tzaira] hamburger

tacchino [tak-**kee**no] turkey

tagliatelle [tal-yat**el**-lay] thin, flat strips of egg pasta

timo thyme

tiramisù coffee-soaked sponge, eggs, Marsala, mascarpone cheese and cocoa powder

toast [tost] toasted sandwich

tonno tuna fish

torrone [tor-r**o**nay] nougat

torta cake; tart; flan

torta lorenese [loren**ay**zay] quiche lorraine

tortelli ravioli filled with ricotta and spinach

tortellini small pasta filled with pork loin, ham, Parmesan and nutmeg

tournedos [toorn**ay**do] round, thick slice of beef fillet

tramezzino [tramedz**ee**no] sandwich

triglia [**treel**-ya] mullet

trippa tripe

trota trout

umido stewed

uova [**wo**va] eggs

uva grapes

vaniglia [van**eel**-ya] vanilla

verdura [vaird**oo**ra] vegetables

vitello veal

vitello tonnato sliced veal in blended tuna, anchovy, oil and lemon sauce

vongole [**von**golay] clams

würstel [**voor**stel] frankfurter

zabaglione/zabaione [tzabal-**yo**nay] beaten eggs, sugar and Marsala

zafferano [tzaf-fair**a**no] saffron

zucca [tz**oo**k-ka] pumpkin

zucchero [tz**oo**k-kairo] sugar

zucchine [tzook-**kee**nay] courgettes

zuccotto [tzook-**kot**-to] ice-cream cake with sponge, fresh cream and chocolate

zuppa [tz**oo**p-pa] soup

zuppa inglese [eenglay**zay**] trifle

Drink: Essential terms

beer la birra [**beer**-ra]
bottle la bottiglia [bot-**teel**-ya]
brandy il brandy
coffee il caffè [kaf-**fay**]
cup: a cup of una tazza di [**tatza**]
fruit juice il succo di frutta [**soo**k-ko dee fr**oo**t-ta]
gin il gin
a gin and tonic un gin tonic
glass: a glass of ... un bicchiere di ... [beek-**yai**ray]
milk il latte [**lat**-tay]
mineral water l'acqua minerale **f** [**akwa** meen-air**alay**]
orange juice il succo d'arancia [**soo**k-ko daran**cha**]]

red wine il vino rosso
rosé il rosé [ro**zay**]
soda (water) il seltz
soft drink la bibita (analcolica)
sugar lo zucchero [tz**oo**k-kairo]
tea il tè [**tay**]
tonic (water) l'acqua tonica **f** [**akwa**]
vodka la vodka
water l'acqua **f** [**akwa**]
whisky il whisky
white wine il vino bianco
wine il vino
wine list la lista dei vini [**day**]

another ..., please ancora un/una ..., per fav**o**re

Drink: Menu Reader

acqua minerale gassata [**akwa** meenair**alay**] sparkling mineral water
acqua naturale [natoor**alay**] still mineral water
Amaretto liqueur made from apricot kernels, giving it a strong almond-type flavour
amaro dark, bitter, herbal digestive liqueur
analcolici [analk**o**leechee] non-alcoholic drinks
aranciata [aran**cha**ta]

orangeade
Bardolino dry red wine from area around Verona
bianco [b-**yanko**] white
bibita analcolica soft drink
birra alla spina [**beer**-ra] draught beer
birra chiara [k-**yara**] amber-coloured light beer, lager
birra grande [**granday**] large beer (40 cl, approx. 1 pint)
birra rossa darker, maltier beer

365

birra scura [skoora] beer similar to bitter, darker than birra rossa

bitter bitter-tasting, red or orange alcoholic aperitif

caffè corretto [kaf-fay] espresso with a dash of liqueur or spirit

caffellatte [kaf-fel-lat-tay] half espresso, half milk

caffè lungo weak black coffee

caffè macchiato [mak-yato] espresso coffee with a dash of milk

caffè ristretto extra-strong espresso coffee

china [keena] liqueur made from chinchona bark

Cirò [cheero] slightly sweet, red, rosé or white wine

digestivo [deejesteevo] digestive liqueur

D.O.C. (Denominazione di Origine Controllata) certifies the origin of a wine

frappé [frap-pay] whisked milkshake or fruit drink with crushed ice

frizzante [freedzantay] fizzy

frullato di frutta milkshake with fruit and crushed ice

gazzosa [gatz-zoza] clear lemonade

ghiaccio [g-yacho] ice

granita drink with crushed ice

grappa very strong, clear spirit distilled from grape husks

latte macchiato con cioccolato [lat-tay mak-yato kon chok-kolato] foaming milk with a sprinkling of cocoa or chocolate powder

liquore [leekworay] liqueur

Marsala thick, very sweet wine similar to sherry

Moscato sweet, sparkling fruity wine

Nebbiolo [neb-yolo] dry red wine from Piedmont region

Orvieto [orvee-ayto] crisp white wine, usually dry

Pinot grigio [greejo] dry white wine from the north

Prosecco sparkling or still white wine from Veneto, can be either sweet or dry

rosatello [rozatel-lo] dry rosé wine

rosso red

Sambuca (con la mosca) aniseed liqueur (served with a coffee bean in the glass)

sidro cider

spremuta d'arancia [darancha] freshly squeezed orange juice

spumante [spoomantay] sparkling wine, like champagne

Strega® [strayga] sweet liqueur made from a secret recipe

succo [sook-ko] juice

vino da pasto table wine

Vin Santo type of dessert wine from Tuscany

PORTUGUESE

DICTIONARY PHRASEBOOK

Pronunciation

In this phrasebook, the Portuguese has been written in a system of imitated pronunciation so that it can be read as though it were English, bearing in mind the notes on pronunciation given below:

a	as in hat
ay	as in may
eh	as in get
g	as in goat
i	as in it
ī	as the 'i' sound in might
J	as the 's' sound in pleasure
o	as in not
oh	like the exclamation oh
oo	as in boot
ow	as in now

In words such as **não** [nowng] and **bem** [bayng], the final 'g' in the pronunciation signifies a nasal sound and should barely be sounded.

Letters given in bold type indicate the part of the word to be stressed.

Language Notes

Portuguese nouns have one of two genders - masculine or feminine. Words for 'the' are **o** [oo] **(m)** and **a** [uh] **(f)**:

o dinheiro	**the money**
a cama	the bed

The corresponding words for 'a' are **um** [oong] **(m)** and **uma (f)**:

um selo	**uma mulher**
a stamp	a woman

In the plural **o** becomes **os** [oosh] and **a** becomes **as** [ash]:

os condutores
the drivers

as mulheres
the women

The Portuguese words for 'I', 'you', 'he' etc are usually omitted as subjects unless special emphasis is required. For example:

está cansado
he is tired

ele não está cansado
he isn't tired (although the others all are)

Here is a useful verb – 'to be'. Portuguese has two verbs for this. One is **ser**:

sou [soh] I am
és [ehsh] you are
(familiar form)
é [eh] he/she/it is; you are
(polite singular form)

somos [sohmoosh] we are
são [sowng] you are (plural polite
or familiar form)
são [sowng] they are

And the other **estar**:

estou [stoh] I am
estás [shtash] you are
(familiar form) .
está [shta] he/she/it is;
you are (polite singular form)

estamos [shtamoosh] we are
estão [shtowng] you are
(plural polite or familiar form)
estão [shtowng] they are

Ser is used for permanent conditions and **estar** for conditions which can change. For example:

somos escoceses
we're Scottish

estamos cansados
we're tired

The familiar forms are used to speak to people you are on friendly terms with. When using the polite form, the verb takes the same form as for 'he/she/it' or, if plural, as for 'they'.

Days

Monday segunda-feira [sigoonda **fay**ra]
Tuesday terça-feira [**tay**rsa **fay**ra]
Wednesday quarta-feira [**kwar**ta **fay**ra]
Thursday quinta-feira [**keen**ta **fay**ra]
Friday sexta-feira [**says**hta **fay**ra]
Saturday sábado [**sa**badoo]
Sunday domingo [doo**meen**goo]

Months

January Janeiro [Jan**ay**roo]
February Fevereiro [fivr**ay**roo]
March Março [**mar**soo]
April Abril [ab**reel**]
May Maio [**mī**-oo]
June Junho [**Joon**-yoo]
July Julho [**Jool**-yoo]
August Agosto [ag**oh**shtoo]
September Setembro [sit**ay**mbroo]
October Outubro [oht**oo**broo]
November Novembro [noov**ay**mbroo]
December Dezembro [diz**ay**mbroo]

Time

what time is it? que horas são? [k-yo**rash** sowng]
one o'clock uma hora [**oo**ma **o**ra]
two o'clock duas horas [d**oo**-az **o**rash]
it's one o'clock é uma hora [eh **oo**ma **o**ra]
it's two o'clock são duas horas [sowng doo-az**o**rash]
it's three o'clock são três horas [trayz**o**rash]
five past one uma e cinco [**oo**mi s**een**koo]
ten past two duas e dez [d**oo**-azi dehsh]
quarter past one uma e um quarto [**oo**mi-oong kw**ar**too]
quarter past two duas e um quarto [d**oo**-azi-oong]
half past ten dez e meia [dehz ee **may**-a]
twenty to ten dez menos vinte [dehJ **may**nooJ veent]
quarter to ten dez menos um quarto [dehJ **may**nooz oong kw**ar**too]
at eight o'clock às oito horas [az**oh**-itoo **o**rash]
at half past four às quatro e meia [ash kw**a**troo ee **may**-a]
2 a.m. duas da manhã [d**oo**-aJ da man-y**ang**]
2 p.m. duas da tarde [tard]
6 a.m. seis da manhã [saysh da man-y**ang**]
6 p.m. seis da tarde [tard]

noon meio-dia [**may**-oo **dee**-a]
midnight meia-noite [m**ay**-a n**oh**-it]
an hour uma hora [**oo**ma **o**ra]
a minute um minuto [oong min**oo**too]
two minutes dois minutos [**doh**-ij min**oo**toosh]
a second um segundo [oong sig**oo**ndoo]
a quarter of an hour um quarto de hora [kw**a**rtoo d**o**ra]
half an hour meia hora [m**ay**-a **o**ra]
three quarters of an hour três quartos de hora [traysh kw**a**rtoosh d**o**ra]

Numbers

0 zero [**zeh**roo]
1 um [oong]
2 dois [**doh**-ish]
3 três [traysh]
4 quatro [kw**a**troo]
5 cinco [**see**nkoo]
6 seis [saysh]
7 sete [seht]
8 oito [**oh**-itoo]
9 nove [nov]
10 dez [dehsh]
11 onze [ohnz]
12 doze [dohz]
13 treze [trayz]
14 catorze [kat**oh**rz]
15 quinze [keenz]
16 dezasseis [diza**saysh**]
17 dezassete [diza**seht**]
18 dezoito [diz**oh**-itoo]
19 dezanove [diz**anov**]
20 vinte [veent]
21 vinte e um [**veen**ti-oong]
22 vinte e dois [**veen**ti d**oh**-ish]
23 vinte e três [**veen**ti traysh]
30 trinta [**treen**ta]
31 trinta e um [**treen**ti-oong]
32 trinta e dois [**treen**tid**oh**-ish]
40 quarenta [kwar**ayn**ta]
50 cinquenta [sink**wayn**ta]
60 sessenta [ses**ayn**ta]
70 setenta [set**ayn**ta]
80 oitenta [oh-it**ayn**ta]
90 noventa [noov**ayn**ta]
100 cem [sayng]
101 cento e um [**sayn**twee oong]
120 cento e vinte [veent]
200 duzentos [dooz**ayn**toosh], duzentas [dooz**ayn**tash]
300 trezentos [triz**ayn**toosh], trezentas [triz**ayn**tash]
400 quatrocentos [kwatros**ayn**toosh], quatrocentas [kwatros**ayn**tash]
500 quinhentos [keen-y**ayn**toosh], quinhentas [keen-y**ayn**tash]
600 seiscentos [sayshs**ayn**toosh], seiscentas [sayshs**ayn**tash]
700 setecentos [setes**ayn**toosh], setecentas [setes**ayn**tash]

800	oitocentos [oh-itoos**ay**ntoosh], oitocentas [oh-itoos**ay**ntash]
900	novecentos [noves**ay**ntoosh], novecentas [noves**ay**ntash]
1,000	mil [meel]
2,000	dois mil [**doh**-ish]
5,000	cinco mil [**seen**koo]
10,000	dez mil [dehsh]
1,000,000	um milhão [mil-**yow**ng]

With multiples of a hundred, the **-as** ending is used with feminine nouns:

trezentos homens
triz**ay**ntooz **oh**mayngsh
300 men

quinhentas mulheres
keen-y**ay**ntaɹ mool-y**eh**rish
500 women

Ordinals

1st	primeiro [prim**ay**roo]
2nd	segundo [sig**oo**ndoo]
3rd	terceiro [tirs**ay**roo]
4th	quarto [**kwar**too]
5th	quinto [**keen**too]
6th	sexto [**say**shtoo]
7th	sétimo [**seh**timoo]
8th	oitavo [oh-it**a**voo]
9th	nono [**noh**noo]
10th	décimo [**deh**simoo]

English

→

Portuguese

a, an um, uma [oong, **oo**ma]
about: about 20 mais ou
menos vinte [mīz oh m**ay**noosh
veent]
  a film about Portugal um
filme sobre Portugal [oong
feelm sohbr poortoog**al**]
above acima [as**ee**ma]
abroad no estrangeiro [noo
shtranJ**ay**roo]
accelerator o acelerador
[asilirad**ohr**]
accept aceitar [asay**tar**]
accident o acidente
[aseed**aynt**]
across: across the road do
outro lado da rua [doo **oh**troo
l**a**doo da r**oo**-a]
adapter o adaptador
[adaptad**ohr**]
address a morada [moor**a**da]
adult o adulto [ad**oo**ltoo], a
adulta
advance: in advance
adiantado [ad-yant**a**doo]
after depois [dip**oh**-ish]
afternoon a tarde [tard]
aftersun cream a loção para
depois do sol [loos**ow**ng –
dip**oh**-ish doo]
afterwards depois [dip**oh**-ish
again outra vez [**oh**tra vaysh]
against contra
ago: a week ago há uma
semana [a **oo**ma simana]
AIDS a SIDA [**see**da]

air o ar
  by air de avião [dav-y**ow**ng]
air-conditioning o ar
condicionado [kondis-
yoon**a**doo]
airmail: by airmail por via
aérea [poor v**ee**-a-**eh**r-ya]
airport o aeroporto
[a-ayroop**oh**rtoo]
airport bus o autocarro do
aeroporto [owtook**a**rroo doo]
alcohol o álcool [**a**lko-ol]
all todos [**toh**dooz]
  that's all é tudo [eh **too**doo]
allergic alérgico [al**ehr**Jikoo]
all right está bem [shta bayng]
  I'm all right estou bem [shtoh]
  are you all right? (fam) estás
bem? [shtash]
  (pol) está bem? [shta]
almost quase [kwaz]
alone só [saw]
already já [Ja]
also também [tamb**ayng**]
altogether totalmente
[tootalm**aynt**]
always sempre [**say**mpr]
ambulance a ambulância
[ambool**a**ns-ya]
America a América
American americano
[amirik**a**noo]
and e [ee]
angry zangado
animal o animal
annoying aborrecido
[aboorris**ee**doo]
another outro [**oh**troo]
  another beer, please outra

cerveja, por favor [sirvayja poor favohr]

antiseptic o anti-séptico

any: I don't have any não tenho [nowng tayn-yoo]

apartment o apartamento [apartamayntoo]

apartment block o bloco de apartamentos [blokoo dapartamayntoosh]

apple a maçã [masang]

apricot o damasco [damashkoo]

Arab (adj) árabe [arabi]

arm o braço [brasoo]

arrival a chegada [shigada]

arrive chegar

art gallery a galeria de arte [galiree-a dart]

as: as big as tão grande quanto [towng grand kwantoo]

ashtray o cinzeiro [sinzayroo]

ask perguntar [pirgoontar], pedir [pideer]

I didn't ask for this não pedi isto [nowng pidee eeshtoo]

aspirin a aspirina [ashpireena]

at: at the hotel no hotel [noo]

at the station na estação [nashtasowng]

at six o'clock às seis horas [ash sayz orash]

at Américo's na casa do Américo [dwamehrikoo]

aunt a tia [tee-a]

Australia a Austrália [owshtral-ya]

Australian (adj) australiano [owshtral-yanoo]

automatic teller o caixa automático [kīsha owtoomatikoo]

autumn o Outono [ohtohnoo]

away: go away! vá-se embora! [vasi aymbora]

awful horrível [ohrreevil]

B

baby o bebé [bebeh]

back (of body) as costas [koshtash]

(back part) a parte posterior [part pooshteriohr]

at the back atrás [atrash]

I'll be back soon estarei de volta em breve [shtaray di vohltayng]

bad mau [mow], f má

badly mal

bag o saco [sakoo]

(handbag) a mala de mão [di mowng]

baggage a bagagem [bagajayng]

baggage checkroom o depósito de bagagem [dipozitoo di baga-jayng]

bakery a padaria [padaree-a]

balcony a varanda

ball a bola

(small) a bolinha [boleen-ya]

banana a banana

band (musical) a banda

bandage a ligadura [ligadoora]

Bandaid® o adesivo [adezeevoo]

bank (money) o banco [bankoo]

bar o bar

barber's o barbeiro [barbayroo]

basket o cesto [sayshtoo]
 (in shop) o cesto de compras
 [di kohmprash]

bath o banho [ban-yoo]

bathroom a casa de banho
 [kaza di]

bathtub a banheira [ban-yayra]

battery a pilha [peel-ya]
 (for car) a bateria [batiree-a]

be ser [sayr]; estar [shtar]

beach a praia [prī-a]
 on the beach na praia

beach umbrella o chapéu de
 sol [shapeh-oo]

beans os feijões [faiJoyngsh]

beautiful bonito [booneetoo]

because porque [poorkay]
 because of ... por causa
 do ... [poor kowza doo]

bed a cama

 I'm going to bed now vou
 para a cama agora [voh]

bed and breakfast cama e
 pequeno almoço [ee pikaynoo
 almohsoo]

bedroom o quarto [kwartoo]

beef a carne de vaca [karn di]

beer a cerveja [sirvayJa]

before antes [antsh]

begin começar [koomesar]
 when does it begin? quando
 é que começa? [kwandoo eh ki
 koomehsa]

behind atrás [atrash]

below abaixo [abīshoo]

belt o cinto [seentoo]

berth (on ship) o beliche
 [bileesh]

beside the ... junto da ...
 [Joontoo]

best o melhor [mil-yor]

better melhor

between entre [ayntr]

beyond para além de
 [paralayng di]

bicycle a bicicleta [bisiklehta]

big grande [grand]

bikini o bikini

bill a conta
 (US) a nota

 could I have the bill, please?
 pode-me dar a conta, por
 favor? [pod-mi – poor favohr]

bin o caixote de lixo [kīshot di
 leeshoo]

bird o pássaro [pasaroo]

birthday o dia de anos [dee-a
 danoosh]

 happy birthday! feliz
 aniversário! [fileez anivirsar-yoo]

biscuit a bolacha [boolasha]

bit: a little bit um pouco [oong
 pohkoo]

 a big bit um pedaço grande
 [pidasoo grand]

 a bit of ... um pedaço de ...

 a bit expensive um pouco
 caro [pohkoo karoo]

bite (by insect) a picada [pikada]

black preto [praytoo]

blanket o cobertor [koobirtohr]

blind cego [sehgoo]

blinds as persianas [pirs-yanash]

blond louro [lohroo]

blood o sangue [sang]

blouse a blusa [blooza]

blow-dry secar com secador [kong sikadohr]
blue azul [azool]
boat o barco [barkoo]
  (for passengers) o ferry-boat
body o corpo [kohrpoo]
bone o osso [ohsoo]
  (in fish) a espinha [shpeen-ya]
book o livro [leevroo]
  (verb) reservar [rizirvar]
bookshop, bookstore a livraria [livraree-a]
boot (footwear) a bota
border (of country) a fronteira [frontayra]
borrow pedir emprestado [pideer aymprishtadoo]
both ambos [amboosh]
bottle a garrafa
bottle-opener o abre-garrafas [abrigarrafash]
bottom (of person) o traseiro [trazayroo]
  at the bottom of ... (hill) no sopé do ... [noo soopeh doo]
box a caixa [kīsha]
boy o rapaz [rapash]
boyfriend o namorado [namooradoo]
bra o soutien [soot-yang]
bracelet a pulseira [poolsayra]
brake o travão [travowng]
brandy o brandy
Brazil Brasil [brazeel]
Brazilian brasileiro [brazilayroo]
bread o pão [powng]
break partir
breakfast o pequeno almoço [pikaynoo almohsoo]
breast o peito [paytoo]
bridge (over river) a ponte [pohnt]
bring trazer [trazayr]
  I'll bring it back later trago isto de volta mais tarde [tragoo eeshtoo di – mīsh tard]
Britain a Grã-Bretanha [grang britan-ya]
British britânico [britanikoo]
brochure o folheto [fool-yaytoo]
broken partido [parteedoo]
brother o irmão [eermowng]
brown castanho [kashtan-yoo]
brush (for hair, cleaning) a escova [shkova]
building o edifício [idifees-yoo]
bulb (light bulb) a lâmpada
bullfight a tourada [tohrada]
bullfighter o toureiro [tohrayroo]
bullring a praça de touros [prasa di tohroosh]
bull-running as garraiadas [garrī-adash]
bunk o beliche [bileesh]
burn a queimadura [kaymadoora]
burst: a burst pipe um cano rebentado [oong kanoo ribayntadoo]
bus o autocarro [owtookarroo]
  what number bus is it to ...? qual é o número do autocarro para ...? [kwal-eh oo noomiroo doo]

dialogue

does this bus go to ...?
este autocarro vai para ...?
[aysht – vī]
no, you need a number ...
não, tem que apanhar o
número ... [nowng tayng
k-yapang-yar oo noomiroo]

bus station a estação dos
autocarros [shtasowng dooz
owtookarroosh]
bus stop a paragem do
autocarro [parajayng doo
owtookarroo]
busy (restaurant etc)
frequentado [frikwayntadoo]
but mas [mash]
butcher's o talho [tal-yoo]
butter a manteiga [mantayga]
button o botão [bootowng]
buy comprar
by: by bus de autocarro
[dowtookarroo]
by car de carro [di karroo]
by the window à janela
by Thursday na quinta-feira

C

cabbage a couve [kohv]
cabin (on ship) o camarote
[kamarot]
cable car o teleférico
[telefehrikoo]
café o café [kafeh]
cake o bolo [bohloo]

call chamar [shamar]
(to phone) telefonar [telefoonar]
what's it called? como se
chama isto? [kohmoo si shama
eeshtoo]
he/she is called ... ele/ela
chama-se ... [ayl/ehla shamasi]
camera a máquina
fotográfica [makina
footoografika]
camp acampar
camping gas o gás para
campismo [gash par
kampeejmoo]
campsite o parque de
campismo [park di
kampeejmoo]
can a lata
can: can you ...? você
pode ...? [vosay pod]
can I ...? posso ...? [posoo]
I can't ... não posso ...
[nowng]
Canada o Canadá
Canadian canadiano [kanad-
yanoo]
cancel cancelar [kansilar]
candle a vela
candies os rebuçados
[riboosadoosh]
can-opener o abre-latas
[abrilatash]
car o carro [karroo]
card (birthday etc) o cartão
[kartowng]
cardphone o telefone de
cartão [telefohn di kartowng]
car hire o aluguer de
automóveis [aloogehr

dowtoom**o**vaysh]
carnival o carnaval
car park o parque de
   estacionamento [park di shtas-
   yonam**ay**ntoo]
carpet a carpete [karp**eh**t]
carrot a cenoura [sin**oh**ra]
carry levar [liv**ar**]
cash o dinheiro [deen-**yay**roo]
cash desk a caixa [k**ī**sha]
cash dispenser o caixa
   automático [owtoom**a**tikoo]
castle o castelo [kasht**eh**loo]
cat o gato [g**a**too]
cathedral a catedral [katidr**al**]
cave a caverna
ceiling o tecto [t**eh**too]
cellar (for wine) a cave [k**a**v]
centimetre o centímetro
   [sent**ee**mitroo]
central central [sen-tr**al**]
central heating o
   aquecimento central
   [akesim**ay**ntoo]
centre o centro [s**ay**ntroo]
certainly certamente
   [sirtam**ay**nt]
chair a cadeira [kad**ay**ra]
champagne o champanhe
   [shampan-y**i**]
change (money) o troco
   [tr**oh**koo]
   (verb: money) trocar [trook**ar**]

dialogue

**do we have to change
(trains)?** temos de mudar?
[t**ay**moosh di mood**ar**]

yes, change at
Coimbra/no, it's a direct
train sim, troque em
Coimbra/não, é um
comboio directo [seeng
tro-k**ee**ng kw**ee**mbra/nowng eh
oong komb**oh**-yo dir**eh**too]

cheap barato [bar**a**too]
check (US) o cheque [shehk]
   (US: bill) a conta [k**o**nta]
check verificar
checkbook o livro de
   cheques [**lee**vroo di shehksh]
check card o cartão de
   garantia [kart**ow**ng di garant**ee**-a]
check-in o check-in
cheers! (toast) saúde! [sa-**oo**d]
cheese o queijo [k**ay**Joo]
chemist's a farmácia [farmas-
   ya]
cheque o cheque [shehk]
cheque card o cartão de
   garantia [kart**ow**ng di
   garant**ee**-a]
chest o peito [p**ay**too]
chewing gum a pastilha
   elástica [pasht**ee**l-ya ila**sh**tika]
chicken o frango [fr**a**ngoo]
child a criança [kry-**a**nsa]
chips as batatas fritas [bat**a**tash
   fr**ee**tash]
chocolate o chocolate
   [shook**oo**lat]
   a hot chocolate um
   chocolate quente [oong –
   kaynt]
Christmas o Natal
   Christmas Eve a Véspera de

Natal [**veh**shpira di]

merry Christmas! feliz Natal! [fil**eeJ**]

church a igreja [ig**ray**Ja]

cider a cidra [**seed**ra]

cigar o charuto [sha**root**oo]

cigarette o cigarro [sig**arr**oo]

cinema o cinema [sin**ay**ma]

city a cidade [sid**ad**]

city centre o centro da cidade [**sayn**troo]

clean (adj) limpo [**leemp**oo]

can you clean this for me? pode limpar isto para mim? [pod leempar **ee**shtoo – meeng]

clever inteligente [intiliJ**aynt**]

climb escalar [shk**alar**]

clock o relógio [riloJ-yoo]

close (verb) fechar [fi**shar**]

closed fechado [fi**shad**oo]

clothes a roupa [**rohp**a]

clothes peg a mola de roupa [di **rohp**a]

cloudy enevoado [iniv**wad**oo]

coach (bus) o autocarro [owtook**arr**oo]
(on train) a carruagem [karrwa-**Jayng**]

coach station a estação dos autocarros [shtas**own**g dooz owtook**arr**oosh]

coach trip a excursão [shkoors**own**g]

coast a costa [**kosht**a]

coat (long coat) o sobretudo [soobrit**ood**oo]
(jacket) o casaco [ka**zak**oo]

coathanger a cruzeta [krooz**ayt**a]

code (for phoning) o indicativo [indikat**eev**oo]

coffee o café [kaf**eh**]

coin a moeda [m**weh**da]

Coke® a coca-cola

cold frio [**free**-oo]

I'm cold tenho frio [**tayn**-yoo]

I have a cold estou constipado [shtoh konshtip**ad**oo]

collar o colarinho [koolar**een**-yoo]

collect call a chamada paga no destinatário [sham**ad**a **pag**a noo dishtinat**ar**-yoo]

colour a cor [kohr]

comb o pente [**paynt**]

come vir [veer]

come back voltar

come in entrar [ayn**trar**]

comfortable confortável [konfoort**av**il]

complaint a reclamação [riklamas**own**g]

completely completamente [komplitam**aynt**]

computer o computador [kompootad**ohr**]

concert o concerto [kons**ayrt**oo]

conditioner (for hair) o creme amaciador [kraym amas-yad**ohr**]

condom o preservativo [prizirvat**eev**oo]

congratulations! parabéns! [parab**ayng**sh]

connection a ligação

constipation a prisão de ventre [priz**own**g di **vayn**tr]

consulate o consulado [konsool**ad**oo]

contact contactar
contact lenses as lentes de contacto [layntsh di kontatoo]
cooker o fogão [foogowng]
cookie a bolacha [boolasha]
corkscrew o saca-rolhas [saka-rohl-yash]
correct (right) certo [sehrtoo]
cost custar [kooshtar]
cotton a algodão [algoodowng]
cotton wool o algodão em rama [ayng]
couchette o beliche [bileesh]
cough a tosse [tos]
cough medicine o xarope [sharop]
could: could you ...? podia ...? [poodee-a]
could I have ...? queria ...? [kiree-a]
I couldn't ... (wasn't able to) não pude ... [nowng pood]
country o país [pa-eesh] (countryside) o campo [kampoo]
couple (people) o casal [kazal]
a couple of ... um par de ... [oong par di]
courier o/a guia [gee-a]
course (main course etc) o prato [pratoo]
of course é claro [eh klaroo]
cousin (male/female) o primo [preemoo], a prima
crazy doido [doh-idoo]
cream as natas [natash] (lotion) o creme [kraym]
credit card o cartão de crédito [kartowng di krehdeetoo]

dialogue

can I pay by credit card? posso pagar com cartão de crédito? [posoo – kong]
which card do you want to use? que cartão deseja utilizar? [ki kartowng disayja ootilizar]
yes, sir sim, senhor [seeng sin-yor]
what's the number? qual é o número? [kwaleh oo noomiroo]
and the expiry date? e a data de validade? [ya data de validad]

crisps as batatas fritas [batatash freetash]
crossroads o cruzamento [kroozamayntoo]
crowded apinhado [apeen-yadoo]
cry chorar [shoorar]
cup a chávena [shavena]
cupboard o armário [armar-yoo]
curtains a cortinas [koorteenash]
cushion a almofada [almoofada]
customs a alfândega [alfandiga]
cyclist o/a ciclista [sikleeshta]

D

dad o papá
damage avariar [avari-ar]
damn! raios me partam! [ra-

yoosh mi **part**owng]

damp húmido [**oo**meedoo]

dance a dança [**dan**sa]

(verb) dançar

dangerous perigoso

[pirig**oh**zoo]

dark (adj) escuro [shk**oo**roo]

date: what's the date today?

qual é a data hoje? [kwal eh –

ohJ]

daughter a filha [**feel**-ya]

day o dia [**dee**-a]

the day after o dia seguinte

[sig**eent**]

the day before o dia anterior

[antir-y**ohr**]

dead morto [**mohr**too]

deaf surdo [**soor**doo]

decaffeinated coffee o café

descafeinado [kaf**eh** dishkafay-

ee**na**doo]

decide decidir [disid**eer**]

deckchair a cadeira de lona

[kad**ayr**a di **loh**na]

deep fundo [**foon**doo]

definitely de certeza [di

sirt**ayz**a]

delay o atraso [atr**az**oo]

delicatessen a charcutaria

[sharkootar**ee**-a]

delicious delicioso [dilis-y**oh**zo]

dentist o/a dentista

[dent**eesh**ta]

deodorant o desodorizante

[dizoodoori**zant**]

department store os grandes

armazéns [grandz armaza**yngsh**]

departure a saída [sa-**ee**da]

depend: it depends depende

[dip**aynd**]

dessert a sobremesa

[sobrim**ayz**a]

destination o destino

[disht**ee**noo]

develop desenvolver

[disaynvolv**ayr**]

dialling code o indicativo

[indikat**ee**voo]

diarrhoea a diarreia [dy-

array-a]

diesel o gasóleo [gaz**ol**-yoo]

difference a diferença

[difir**ayn**sa]

different diferente [difir**aynt**]

difficult difícil [dif**eesil**]

dining room a sala de jantar

[di J**antar**]

dinner o jantar

direct (adj) directo [dir**eh**too]

direction a direcção

[direhs**owng**]

directory enquiries as

informações [infoormas**oy**ngsh]

dirty sujo [**soo**Joo]

disco o disco [**dee**shkoo]

disgusting nojento

[nooJ**ayn**too]

district o bairro [**bir**roo]

divorced divorciado [divoors-

yadoo]

do fazer [faz**ayr**]

what shall we do? que

vamos fazer? [ki-va**moosh**]

doctor o médico [**meh**dikoo], a

médica

dog o cão [kowng]

donkey o burro [**boor**roo]

don't! não! [nowng]

door a porta
double duplo [dooploo]
double bed a cama de casal [di kazal]
double room o quarto de casal [kwartoo]
down embaixo [aymbishoo]
down here aqui embaixo [akee]
downstairs embaixo
dozen a dúzia [dooz-ya]
draught beer imperial [eempir-yal]
dress o vestido [vishteedoo]
drink a bebida [bibeeda] (verb) beber [bibayr]
what would you like to drink? o que gostaria de beber? [gooshtaree-ya di]
drinking water a água potável [agwa pootavil]
drive conduzir [kondoozeer]
driver (of car) o condutor [kondootohr], a condutora (of bus) o/a motorista [mootooreeshta]
driving licence a carta de condução [di kondoosowng]
drug o medicamento [medikamayntoo]
drugs (narcotics) a droga
drunk bêbado [baybadoo]
dry seco [saykoo]
dry-cleaner a tinturaria [teentooraree-a]
during durante [doorant]
dustbin o caixote de lixo [kishot di leeshoo]
duvet o edredão [idridowng]

E

each (every) cada
ear a orelha [orayl-ya]
early cedo [saydoo]
earrings os brincos [breenkoosh]
east o leste [lehsht]
Easter Semana Santa [simana], Páscoa [pashkwa]
easy fácil [fasil]
eat comer [koomayr]
economy class classe económica [klas-ekoonohmika]
egg o ovo [ohvoo]
either: either ... or ... ou ... ou ... [oh]
elbow o cotovelo [kootoovayloo]
electric eléctrico [elehtrikoo]
electricity a electricidade [eletrisidad]
elevator o elevador [elevadohr]
else: something else outra coisa [ohtra koh-iza]
somewhere else noutro sítio [nohtroo seet-yoo]
embassy a embaixada [aymbishada]
emergency a emergência [emirjayns-ya]
empty vazio [vazee-oo]
end o fim [feeng] (verb) acabar
at the end of the street no fim da rua [noo feeng da roo-a]
engaged (toilet, telephone) ocupado [okoopadoo]

(to be married) noivo [**noh**-ivoo]

England a Inglaterra [inglate**hr**ra]

English (adj, language) inglês [ingl**ay**sh]

enjoy: to enjoy oneself divertir-se [divirt**eer**si]

enormous enorme [en**or**m]

enough suficiente [soofis-y**aynt**]

it's not big enough não é suficientemente grande [eh soofis-yayntim**ay**nt]

that's enough, thanks está bem, obrigado/obrigada [shta bayng obrig**a**doo]

entrance a entrada [ayntr**a**da]

envelope o envelope [aynvil**op**]

equipment o equipamento [ekipam**ay**ntoo]

especially especialmente [shpis-yalm**ay**nt]

euro o euro [**ay**-ooroo]

Eurocheque o Eurocheque [ay-oroosh**ehk**]

Europe a Europa [ay-oor**o**pa]

evening a noite [**noh**-it]

this evening esta noite [**ehsh**ta]

eventually no fim [noo feeng]

ever já [Ja]

every cada

everyone toda a gente [**toh**da a Jaynt]

everything tudo [**too**doo]

everywhere em toda a parte [ayng **toh**da part]

exactly! exactamente! [ezatam**ay**nt]

excellent excelente [ish-sil**ay**nt]

except excepto [ish-**seh**too]

exchange rate a cotação cambial [kootas**ow**ng kamby**al**]

exciting emocionante [emoos-yoon**ant**]

excuse me (to get past) com licença [kong lis**ay**nsa]

(to get attention) se faz favor [si fash fav**ohr**]

exhibition a exposição [shpoozis**ow**ng]

exit a saída [sa-**ee**da]

expensive caro [**ka**roo]

eye o olho [**oh**l-yoo]

eyeglasses os óculos [**o**kooloosh]

F

face a cara

faint (verb) desmaiar [diJmī-**ar**]

fair (funfair, tradefair) a feira [**fay**ra]

(adj) justo [**Joo**shtoo]

fairly bastante [bash**tant**]

fall cair [ka-**eer**]

fall (US) o Outono [oht**oh**noo]

in the fall no Outono [noo]

family a família [fam**eel**-ya]

fantastic fantástico [fant**ash**tikoo]

far longe [lohnJ]

dialogue

is it far from here? é longe daqui? [eh – dak**ee**]

no, not very far não, não é

muito longe [nowng –
mweeingtoo]
it's about 20 kilometres são
mais ou menos vinte
quilómetros [sowng mīz oh
maynoosh veengt kilomitroosh]

farm a quinta [keenta]
fashionable na moda
fast rápido [rapidoo]
fat (person) gordo [gohrdoo]
father o pai [pī]
faucet a torneira [toornayra]
fault o defeito [difaytoo]
sorry, it was my fault
desculpe, foi culpa minha
[foh-i koolpa meen-ya]
favourite favorito [favooreetoo]
fax o fax
feel sentir [saynteer]
I feel unwell não me sinto
bem [nowng mi seentoo bayng]
felt-tip (pen) a caneta de feltro
[kanayta di fayltroo]
ferry o ferry-boat
fetch buscar [booshkar]
I'll fetch him vou buscá-lo
[voh booshka-loo]
few: a few alguns [algoonsh]
a few days poucos dias
[pohkoosh dee-ash]
fiancé o noivo [noh-ivoo]
fiancée o noiva
field o campo [kampoo]
fight a briga [breega]
filling (in tooth) o chumbo
[shoomboo]
film o filme [feelm]
find encontrar [aynkontrar]

find out descobrir
[dishkoobreer]
fine (weather) bom [bong]
(punishment) a multa [moolta]
finger o dedo [daydoo]
finish terminar
fire o fogo [fohgoo]
fire brigade os bombeiros
[bombayroosh]
first primeiro [primayroo]
at first ao princípio [ow
prinseep-yoo]
first aid kit a caixa de
primeiros socorros [kīsha di
first class (travel etc) primeira
classe [klas]
first floor o primeiro andar
(US) o rés de chão [rehj doo]
first name o nome próprio
[nohm propr-yoo]
fish o peixe [paysh]
fit: it doesn't fit me não me
serve [nowng mi sehrv]
fix (repair) reparar
fizzy gasoso [gazohzoo]
flat (apartment) o apartamento
[apartamayntoo]
(adj) plano [planoo]
I've got a flat tyre tenho um
pneu furado [tayn-yoo oong
pnay-oo fooradoo]
flavour o sabor [sabohr]
flight o voo [voh-oo]
flight number o número de
voo [noomiroo di]
floor (of room) o chão [showng]
(storey) o andar
on the floor no chão
florist a florista [flooreeshta]

flower a flor [flohr]
flu a gripe [greep]
fluent: he speaks fluent
  Portuguese ele fala
  português fluentemente [el –
  poortoogaysh flwentimaynt]
fly a mosca [mohshka]
  (verb: person) ir de avião [eer
  dav-yowng]
food a comida [koomeeda]
foot o pé [peh]
  on foot a pé
football (game) o futebol
  [footbol]
  (ball) a bola de futebol
for: do you have something
  for ...? (headache/diarrhoea etc)
  tem alguma coisa para ...?
  [tayng algooma koh-iza]
foreign estrangeiro
  [shtranJayroo]
foreigner o estrangeiro
  [shtranJayroo], a estrangeira
forest a floresta [floorehshta]
forget esquecer [shkisayr]
  I forget, I've forgotten
  esqueci-me [shkiseemi]
fork o garfo [garfoo]
fortnight a quinzena
  [keenzayna]
forwarding address a nova
  morada [moorada]
fountain a fonte [fohnt]
foyer o foyer [fwi-ay]
France a França [fransa]
free livre [leevr]
  (no charge) gratuito [gratoo-
  eetoo]
freeway a autoestrada

[owtooshtrada]
French (adj, language) francês
  [fransaysh]
French fries as batatas fritas
  [batatash freetash]
frequent frequente [frikwaynt]
fresh fresco [frayshkoo]
fridge o frigorífico [frigoo-
  reefikoo]
fried frito [freetoo]
friend (male/female) o amigo
  [ameegoo], a amiga
friendly simpático [simpatikoo]
from de [di]
  from Monday to Friday de
  segunda a sexta-feira [di
  sigoonda-a sayshta fayra]
  from next Thursday a partir
  da próxima quinta-feira [a
  parteer da prosima keenta fayra]
front a frente [fraynt]
  in front of the hotel em frente
  ao hotel [ow]
  at the front na frente [na]
fruit a fruta [froota]
fruit juice o sumo de fruta
  [soomoo di froota]
full cheio [shay-oo]
full board a pensão completa
  [paynsowng komplehta]
fun: it was fun foi divertido
  [foh-i divirteedoo]
funny (strange) estranho
  [shtran-yoo]
  (amusing) engraçado
  [ayngrasadoo]
further mais longe [mīj lohnJ]
future: in future no futuro
  [footooroo]

G

game (cards, match etc) o jogo [**Joh**goo]

garage (for fuel) a bomba de gasolina [di gazoo**lee**na]
(for repairs, parking) a garagem [gara**J**ayng]

garden o jardim [**J**ard**ee**ng]

garlic o alho [**al**-yoo]

gas o gás [gash]
(US) a gasolina [gazoo**lee**na]

gas station a bomba de gasolina [**boh**mba di gazoo**lee**na]

gate o portão [poort**ow**ng]
(at airport) o portão de embarque [daym**bark**]

gay o homossexual [ohmoosekswal]

gents (toilet) a casa de banho dos homens [**kaza** di **ban**-yoo dooz **oh**mayngsh]

Germany a Alemanha [aliman-ya]

get (fetch) ir buscar [eer]
how do I get to ...? como vou para ...? [**koh**moo voh]

get back (return) voltar

get off sair [sa-**eer**]
where do I get off? onde é que saio? [ohnd**eh** ki s**ī**-yoo]

get on (to train etc) apanhar [apan-**yar**]

get out (of car etc) sair [sa-**eer**]

get up (in the morning) levantar-se [livant**ar**si]

gift a lembrança [laymbr**a**nsa]

gin o gin [Jeeng]

a gin and tonic um gin-tónico [oong Jeeng **t**onikoo]

girl a rapariga [rapar**ee**ga]

girlfriend a namorada

give dar

give back devolver [divolv**ayr**]

glad contente [kont**a**ynt]

glass (material) o vidro [**vee**droo]
(for drinking) o copo [**ko**poo]
a glass of wine um copo de vinho [oong – di **vee**n-yoo]

glasses os óculos [**o**kooloosh]

gloves as luvas [**loo**vash]

go ir [eer]
where are you going? onde vai? [ohnd v**ī**]
where does this bus go? para onde vai este autocarro? [aysht owtook**a**rroo]
let's go! vamos! [**vam**oosh]
she's gone (left) ele foi-se embora [ayl f**oh**-isaymbora]
hamburger to go o hamburger para levar

go away ir embora [eer aymbora]
go away! vá-se embora! [**vas**-aymbora]

go back (return) voltar

go down (the stairs etc) descer [dish**sayr**]

go in entrar [ayntrar]

go out (in the evening) sair [sa-**eer**]

go through atravessar

go up (the stairs etc) subir [soob**eer**]

God Deus [**day**-oosh]

gold o ouro [**oh**roo]
good bom [bong]
  good! bem! [**bay**ng]
  it's no good não presta [nowng pr**eh**shta]
goodbye adeus [ad**ay**-oosh]
good evening boa noite [b**oh**-a n**oh**-it]
good morning bom dia [bong d**ee**-a]
good night boa noite [b**oh**-a n**oh**-it]
got: we've got to leave temos que ir [**tay**moosh ki-**eer**]
  I've got to ... tenho di ... [**tayn**-joo di]
  have you got any ...? tem ...? [**tayng**]
gradually gradualmente [gradwalm**ay**nt]
gram(me) o grama
grapefruit a toranja [toor**an**Ja]
grapes as uvas [**oo**vash]
grass a relva [**reh**lva]
grateful agradecido [agradis**ee**doo]
great (excellent) óptimo [**oti**moo]
green verde [vayrd]
greengrocer's o lugar [l**oo**gar]
grey cinzento [sinz**ay**ntoo]
grilled grelhado [gril-**ya**doo]
grocer's o merceeiro [mirs-**yay**roo]
ground: on the ground no chão [noo sh**ow**ng]
ground floor o rés de chão [rehJ doo]
group o grupo [gr**oo**poo]

guest o convidado [konvid**a**doo], a convidada
guesthouse a pensão [payns**ow**ng]
guide (person) a guia [**gee**-a]
guidebook o livro–guia [**lee**vroo–]
guided tour a excursão com guia [shkoors**ow**ng kong]

H

hair o cabelo [kab**ay**loo]
haircut o corte de cabelo [kort]
hairdresser's (unisex, women's) o cabeleireiro [kabilayr**ay**roo] (men's) o barbeiro [barb**ay**roo]
hairdryer o secador de cabelo [sikad**ohr** di kab**ay**loo]
half a metade [mit**ad**]
  half an hour meia hora [m**ay**-a **o**ra]
  half a litre meio litro [m**ay**-oo l**ee**troo]
half board a meia pensão [m**ay**-a payns**ow**ng]
half-bottle a meia garrafa
half price metade do preço [mit**ad** doo pr**ay**soo]
ham o fiambre [f-y**a**mbr]
hamburger o hamburger [amb**oo**rger]
hand a mão [m**ow**ng]
handbag a mala de mão [di]
hand luggage a bagagem de mão [baga**J**ayng]
hangover a ressaca [ris**a**ka]

happen acontecer [akontis**ayr**]
  what has happened? o que
    aconteceu? [oo ki-akoontis**ay**-
    oo]
happy contente [kont**aynt**]
harbour o porto [**poh**rtoo]
hard duro [**doo**roo]
  (difficult) difícil [dif**ee**sil]
hardly mal
  hardly ever quase nunca
    [kwaz n**oo**nka]
hardware shop a loja de
  ferragens [**lo**Ja di firra**J**ayngsh]
hat o chapéu [shap**eh**-oo]
hate detestar [ditisht**ar**]
have ter [tayr]
  can I have a ...? pode dar-
    me ...? [pod d**ar**mi]
  do you have ...? tem ...?
    [tayng]
  do I have to ...? tenho de ...?
    [di]
hayfever a febre dos fenos
  [**fehb**r doosh **fay**noosh]
he ele [el]
head a cabeça [kab**ay**sa]
headache a dor de cabeça
  [di]
headlights o farol
hear ouvir [ohv**eer**]
heat o calor [kal**ohr**]
heater o aquecedor [akesid**ohr**]
heating o aquecimento
  [akesim**ayn**too]
heavy pesado [piz**a**doo]
heel (of foot) o calcanhar
  [kalkan-**yar**]
  (of shoe) o salto
hello olá

(on phone) está [shta]
help a ajuda [a**J**oo**da**]
  (verb) ajud**ar**
  help! socorro! [sook**oh**rroo]
  can you help me? pode
    ajudar-me? [pod – mi]
her: I haven't seen her não a
  vi [nowng a vee]
  to her para ela [**eh**la]
  for her para ela
  that's her é ela [eh]
  that's her towel esta é a
    toalha dela [**eh**shta-**eh** – **deh**la]
herbal tea o chá de ervas [sha
  dehrvash]
here aqui [ak**ee**]
  here is/are ... aqui
    está/estão ... [shta/shtowng]
  here you are aqui tem [tayng]
hers dela [**deh**la]
  that's hers isso é dela [**ee**soo]
hey! eh!
hi! olá! [o**ola**]
high alto [**al**too]
highway a autoestrada
  [owt**oosh**trada]
hill o monte [mohnt]
him: I haven't seen him não o
  vi [nowng oo vee]
  to him para ele [ayl]
  for him para ele
  that's him é ele [eh]
hip a anca
hire alugar [aloog**ar**]
  for hire para alugar
his: it's his car é o carro dele
  [**eh**-oo k**a**rroo dayl]
  that's his isto é dele
    [eeshtw**eh**]

hitch-hike andar à boleia
 [boolay-a]
hole o buraco [boorakoo]
holiday as férias [fehr-yash]
 on holiday de férias [shtoh di]
home a casa [kaza]
 at home (in my house etc) em
 casa [ayng]
 (in my country) no meu país
 [noo may-oo pa-eesh]
 we go home tomorrow
 vamos embora amanhã
 [vamoosh aymbora aman-yang]
horrible horrível [ohrreevil]
horse o cavalo [kavaloo]
hospital o hospital [oshpital]
hot quente [kaynt]
 (spicy) picante [pikant]
 I'm hot tenho calor [tayn-yoo
 kalohr]
hotel o hotel [ohtehl]
hour a hora [ora]
house a casa [kaza]
house wine o vinho da casa
 [veen-yoo]
how como [kohmoo]
 how many? quantos?
 [kwantoosh]
 how do you do? muito
 prazer [mweengtoo prazair]

dialogues

how are you? como está?
 [shta]
fine, thanks, and you? bem,
 obrigado/obrigada, e
 você? [bayng obrigadoo – ee
 vosay]

how much is it? quanto é?
 [kwantweh]
it's 500 escudos são
 quinhentos escudos
 [sowng kin-yayntooz-
 shkoodoosh]
I'll take it vou levar [voh]

hunger a fome [fohm]
hungry: I'm hungry tenho
 fome [tayn-joo]
hurry: I'm in a hurry estou
 com pressa [shtoh kong prehsa]
hurt: it hurts dói-me [doymi]
husband o marido [mareedoo]

I

I eu [ay-oo]
ice gelo [Jayloo]
ice cream o gelado [Jiladoo]
ice lolly o gelado [Jiladoo]
idiot o idiota [id-yota]
if se [si]
ill doente [dwaynt]
immediately imediatamente
 [imed-yatamaynt]
important importante
 [importnt]
impossible impossível
 [impooseevil]
in: it's in the centre fica no
 centro [feeka noo sayntroo]
in my car no meu carro [noo
 may-oo karroo]
in Beja em Beja [ayng behJa]
in five minutes em cinco
 minutos [minootoosh]

in May em Maio [mī-oo]
in English em inglês [inglaysh]
is he in? ele está? [el shta]
include: does that include
meals? isso inclui as
refeições? [eesoo inkloo-i
refaysoyngsh]
indigestion a indigestão
[indiJishtowng]
indoors dentro de casa
[dayntroo di kaza]
information a informação
[infoormasowng]
injured ferido [fireedoo]
insect o insecto [insehtoo]
inside dentro [dayntroo]
  inside the hotel dentro do
  hotel [dwohtehl]
instead em vez [ayng vaysh]
  instead of ... em vez de ... [di]
intelligent inteligente
[intiliJaynt]
interesting interessante
[intrisant]
international internacional
[intayrnas-yoonal]
interpreter o/a intérprete
[intehrprit]
intersection o cruzamento
[kroozamayntoo]
into para
  I'm not into ... não me
  interesso por ... [nowng
  mintrehsoo poor]
introduce apresentar
[aprizentar]
  may I introduce ...? posso
  apresentar ... [posoo]
invitation o convite [konveet]

Ireland a Irlanda [eerlanda]
Irish irlandês [eerlandaysh]
iron (for ironing) o ferro de
engomar [fehrroo dayngoomar]
island a ilha [eel-ya]
it ele [ayl], ela [ehla]
  it is ... é ... [eh]; está ... [shta]
  is it ...? é ...?; está ...?
  it was ... era ... [ehra];
  estava ... [shtava]

J

jacket o casaco [kazakoo]
jam a compota
jeans os jeans
jellyfish a alforreca [alfoorrehka]
jewellery a joalharia [Jwal-
yaree-a]
job o emprego [aympraygoo]
joke a piada [p-yada]
journey a viagem [v-yaJayng]
  have a good journey! boa
  viagem! [boh-a]
juice o sumo [soomoo]
jumper a camisola [kamizola]
just (only) só [saw]
  just two só dois/duas
  just for me só para mim
  just here aqui mesmo [akee
  mayJmoo]

K

keep guardar [gwardar]
  keep the change guarde o
  troco [gward oo trohkoo]

key a chave [shav]
kilo o quilo [keeloo]
kilometre o quilómetro
  [kilomitroo]
kind (generous) amável
kiss o beijo [bayJoo]
  (verb) beijar [bayJar]
kitchen a cozinha [koozeen-ya]
knee o joelho [Jwayl-yoo]
knife a faca [faka]
knock down atropelar
  [atropilar]
know (somebody, a place)
  conhecer [koon-yisair]
  (something) saber
  I don't know não sei [nowng
  say]
  I didn't know that não sabia
  isso [nowng sabee-a eesoo]

L

ladies' room o quarto do
  banho das senhoras [kwartoo
  di ban-yoo dash sin-yorash]
lady a senhora [sin-yora]
lager a cerveja [sirvay-Ja]
lake o lago [lagoo]
lamb (meat) o borrego
  [boorraygoo]
lamp o candeiro [kand-yayroo]
language a língua [leengwa]
large grande [grand]
last o último [ooltimoo]
  last week semana passada
  [simana]
  last Friday sexta-feira
  passada [sayshta-fayra]

last night ontem à noite
  [ohntayng a noh-it]
late tarde [tard]
later, later on mais tarde [mīsh]
  I'll come back later volto
  mais tarde [voltoo]
laugh rir [reer]
launderette, laundromat a
  lavandaria automática
  [lavandaree-a owtoomatika]
laundry (clothes) a roupa para
  lavar [rohpa]
lawyer o advogado
  [advoogadoo], a advogada
leaflet o panfleto [panflaytoo]
leak a fuga [fooga]
learn aprender [aprayndayr]
least: at least pelo menos
  [piloo maynoosh]
leather o cabedal [kabidal]
leave (depart) partir [parteer]
  (behind) deixar [dayshar]
  I am leaving tomorrow parto
  amanhã [partoo aman-yang]
  may I leave this here? posso
  deixar isto aqui? [posoo –
  eeshtwakee]
  I left my coat in the bar
  deixei meu casaco no bar
  [dayshay may-oo kazakoo noo]
left esquerdo [shkayrdoo]
left luggage (office) o
  depósito de bagagem
  [dipozitoo di bagaJayng]
leg a perna [pehrna]
lemon o limão [limowng]
lemonade a limonada
  [limoonada]
lend emprestar [aymprishtar]

less menos [**may**nosh]
less expensive mais barato
[mīⱼ bara**too**]
lesson a lição [lis**ow**ng]
let (allow) deixar [day**shar**]
let off: will you let me off at ...?
é capaz de parar em ...? [eh
ka**pa**ⱼ di – ayng]
letter a carta
letterbox o marco de correio
[**mar**koo di koo**ray**-oo]
lettuce a alface [al**fas**]
library a biblioteca [bibl-
yoo**teh**ka]
licence a licença [li**sayn**sa]
lift (in building) o elevador
[eleva**dohr**]
could you give me a lift?
pode dar-me uma boleia?
[pod dar**moo**ma boo**lay**-a]
light a luz [loosh]
(not heavy) leve [lehv]
do you have a light? (for
cigarette) tem lume? [tayng
loom]
light bulb a lâmpada
lighter (cigarette) o isqueiro
[shk**ay**roo]
like gostar [goosh**tar**]
I like it gosto [**go**shtoo]
I don't like it não gosto
[nowng]
I'd like a beer queria uma
cerveja [kir**ee**-a **oo**ma sirvay**ⱼa**]
would you like a drink?
gostaria duma bebida?
[gooshtar**ee**-a **doo**ma bi**bee**da]
what's it like? como é?
[**koh**moo eh]

one like this um como este
[oong koh**mway**sht]
line a linha [**leen**-ya]
lips os lábios [**lab**-yoosh]
Lisbon Lisboa [liⱼb**oh**-a]
listen escutar [shk**oo**tar]
litre o litro [**lee**troo]
little pequeno [pi**kay**noo]
just a little, thanks só um
pouco, por favor [saw oong
pohkoo poor fa**vohr**]
a little milk pouco leite [layt]
live (verb) viver [vi**vayr**]
loaf o pão [powng]
local local [**loo**kal]
a local wine? um vinho da
região? [oong **veen**-yoo da riⱼ-
yowng]
lock a fechadura [fisha**doo**ra]
(verb) fechar à chave [fi**shar** a
shav]
lock out: I've locked myself
out (of room) fechei o quarto
com a chave lá dentro [fis**hay**
oo **kwar**too kong – **day**ntroo]
locker (for luggage etc) o cacifo
[ka**see**foo]
London Londres [**lohn**drish]
long comprido [kompr**ee**doo]
how long does it take?
quanto tempo demora?
[di**mo**ra]
a long time muito tempo
[m**ween**gtoo]
one day/two days longer
mais um dia/dois dias [mīz
oong **dee**-a/**do**-iⱼ **dee**-ash]
look: look out! cuidado!
[kwi**da**doo]

can I have a look? posso ver?
[posoo vayr]
look after tomar conta de
[toomar kohnta]
look at olhar para [ol-yar]
look for procurar [prookoorar]
I'm looking for ... procuro ...
[prookooroo]
lorry o camião [kam-yowng]
lose perder [pirdayr]
I've lost my way perdi-me
[pirdeem]
I've lost my bag perdi o
meu saco [pirdee oo may-oo
sakoo]
lost property (office) a secção
de perdidos e achados
[sehksowng di pirdeedooz ee-
ashadoosh]
lot: a lot, lots muito
[mweengtoo]
not a lot não muito [nowng]
a lot of people muita gente
[mweengta Jayngt]
loud alto [altoo]
lounge a sala
love o amor [amohr]
(verb) amar
lovely (meal, food) delicioso
[dilis-yohzoo]
(view) encantador
[aynkantadohr]
(weather) excelente [ish-silaynt]
(present) adorável
low baixo [bīshoo]
luck a sorte [sort]
good luck! boa sorte! [boh-a]
luggage a bagagem [bagaJayng]
lunch o almoço [almohsoo]

M

mad (insane) doido [doh-idoo]
Madeira a Madeira [madayra]
(wine) o (vinho da) Madeira
[veen-yoo]
magazine a revista [riveeshta]
maid (in hotel) a criada [kr-yada]
mail o correio [koorray-oo]
(verb) pôr no correio [pohr
noo]
mailbox o marco de correio
[markoo di kooray-oo]
main principal [prinsipal]
main course o prato principal
[pratoo prinsipal]
main road (in town) a rua
principal [roo-a prinsipal]
(in country) a estrada principal
[shtrada]
make (verb) fazer [fazayr]
make-up a maquilhagem
[makil-yaJayng]
man o homem [ohmayng]
manager o gerente [Jeraynt]
can I see the manager? pode
chamar o gerente? [pod
shamar]
many muitos [mweengtoosh]
map o mapa
market o mercado [mirkadoo]
marmalade a compota de
laranja [di laranJa]
married: I'm married sou
casado/casada [soh kazadoo]
mascara o rímel [reemil]
match (football etc) o jogo
[Johgoo]

matches os fósforos [**fosh**fooroosh]

matter: it doesn't matter não faz mal [**now**ng faJ mal]

what's the matter? o que se passa? [oo ki si]

mattress o colchão [koolsh**ow**ng]

may: may I see it? posso vê-lo/vê-la? [**po**soo **vay**loo/**vay**la]

maybe talvez [tal**vay**sh]

mayonnaise a maionese [mī-on**ehz**]

me mim [meeng]

that's for me isto é para mim [**ee**shtweh para meeng]

me too eu também [**ay**-oo tamb**ayng**]

meal a refeição [rifays**ow**ng]

mean (verb) significar

meat a carne [karn]

medicine o remédio [rim**ehd**-yoo]

medium médio [**mehd**-yoo]

medium-dry meio seco [**may**-oo s**ay**koo]

medium-rare médio [**mehd**-yoo]

mend consertar [konsir**tar**]

men's room a casa de banho dos homens [**ka**za di b**an**-yoo dooz **oh**mayngsh]

mention: don't mention it não tem de quê [nowng tayng di kay]

menu a ementa [ema**ynta**]

message o recado [rik**a**doo]

metre o metro [**meh**troo]

midday o meio-dia [**may**-oo dee-a]

middle: in the middle no meio [noo m**ay**-oo]

midnight a meia-noite [**may**-a n**oh**-it]

milk o leite [layt]

mind: never mind não faz mal [nowng faJ mal]

mine: it's mine é meu [eh m**ay**-oo]

mineral water a água mineral [**a**gwa]

minute o minuto [min**oo**too]

just a minute um momento [oong]

mirror o espelho [shp**ayl**-yoo]

Miss a Senhora [sin-y**o**ra]

Miss! se faz favor! [si fash fav**ohr**]

missing falta

there's a suitcase missing falta uma mala [**oo**ma]

mistake o erro [**ayr**roo]

money o dinheiro [deen-y**ay**roo]

month o mês [maysh]

Moor o mouro [m**oh**-ooroo]

Moorish mourisco [mor**eesh**koo]

moped a motorizada [mootooriz**a**da]

more mais [mīsh]

can I have some more water, please? mais água, por favor [mīz **a**gwa por fav**ohr**]

more expensive mais caro [mīsh k**a**roo]

more than 50 mais de cinquenta [mīz di sinkw**ay**nta]

morning a manhã [man-**yang**]
 this morning esta manhã
 [**eh**shta]
most: most of the time a
 maior parte do tempo [a mi-
 or part doo **tay**mpoo]
mother a mãe [mayng]
motorbike a motocicleta
 [mootoosikl**eh**ta]
motorway a autoestrada
 [owtooshtr**a**da]
mountain a montanha
 [mont**an**-ya]
mouse o rato [**ra**too]
mouth a boca [**boh**ka]
movie o filme [feelm]
movie theater o cinema
 [s**in**ayma]
Mr o Senhor [sin-y**ohr**]
Mrs a Senhora [sin-y**o**ra]
much muito [m**wee**ngtoo]
 much better/worse muito
 melhor/pior [mil-y**or**/pi-**or**]
 much hotter muito mais
 quente [m**ish** kaynt]
 not much não muito [nowng]
mum a mamã [mam**ang**]
museum o museu [mooz**ay**-oo]
mushrooms os cogumelos
 [kogoom**eh**loosh]
music a música [**moo**zika]
must: I must ... tenho de ...
 [**tayn**-yoo di]
mustard a mostarda
 [moosht**a**rda]
my o meu [**may**-oo], a minha
 [**meen**-ya]; **pl** os meus [**may**-
 oosh], as minhas [**meen**-yash]
myself: I'll do it myself eu

mesmo/mesma faço isso
 [**ay**-oo m**ay**Jmoo – fasoo **ee**soo]
 by myself sozinho [soz**een**-
 yoo]/sozinha

N

nail (finger) a unha [**oo**n-ya]
name o nome [nohm]
 my name's John o meu
 nome é John [oo m**ay**-oo nohm
 eh]
 what's your name? como se
 chama? [**koh**moo si **sha**ma]
napkin o guardanapo
 [gwardan**a**poo]
narrow (street) estreito
 [shtr**ay**too]
nasty (person) mau [mow], **f** má
 (weather, accident) grave [grav]
national nacional [nas-yoon**a**l]
natural natural [natoor**a**l]
near perto [**pehr**too]
 where is the nearest ...? onde
 fica o/a ... mais
 próximo/próxima ...? [ohnd
 f**ee**ka oo/a ... m**ish** pr**o**simoo]
nearly quase [kwaz]
necessary necessário [nisis**a**r-
 yoo]
neck o pescoço [pishk**oh**soo]
necklace o colar [kool**a**r]
necktie a gravata
need: I need ... preciso de ...
 [pris**ee**zoo di]
needle a agulha [ag**oo**l-ya]
neither: neither ... nor ...
 nem ... nem ... [nayng]

nephew o sobrinho [soobreen-yoo]

never nunca [noonka]

new novo [nohvoo]

news (radio, TV etc) as notícias [nootees-yash]

newsagent's a tabacaria [tabakaree-a]

newspaper o jornal [Joornal]

New Year Ano Novo [anoo nohvoo]

Happy New Year! Feliz Ano Novo! [fileez anoo nohvoo]

New Year's Eve a véspera do dia de Ano Novo [vehshpira doo dee-a danoo]

New Zealand Nova Zelândia [nova ziland-ya]

next próximo [prosimoo]

next week na próxima semana [simana]

next to próximo de [di]

nice (food, person) agradável (looks, view etc) bonito [booneetoo]

niece a sobrinha [soobreen-ya]

night a noite [noh-it]

no não [nowng]

I've no change não tenho troco [tayn-yoo trohkoo]

there's no ... left não há mais ... [a mīsh]

nobody ninguém [ningayng]

noisy: it's too noisy é barulhento demais [eh barool-yayntoo dimīsh]

non-alcoholic não alcoólico [nowng alkwolikoo]

none nenhum [nin-yoong]

non-smoking carriage a carruagem para não fumadores [karrwaJayng – nowng foomadohrish]

no-one ninguém [ningayng]

nor: nor do I nem eu [nayng ay-oo]

normal normal

north o norte [nort]

northeast o nordeste [noordehsht]

Northern Ireland a Irlanda do Norte [eerlanda doo nort]

northwest o noroeste [norwehsht]

nose o nariz [nareesh]

not não [nowng]

no, I'm not hungry não, não tenho fome [tayn-yoo fohm]

not that one esse não [ays]

note (banknote) a nota

nothing nada

nothing else mais nada [mīJ]

now agora

number o número [noomiroo]

nuts a noz [nosh]

O

o'clock horas [orash]

odd (strange) estranho [shtran-yoo]

of de [di]

off (lights) desligado [diJligadoo]

it's just off Praça do Comércio mesmo ao lado da Praça do Comércio [meJmoo ow ladoo da prasa doo koom**ehrs**-yoo]

often muitas vezes [m**wee**ngta**ɹ**
vay**zish**]

  how often are the buses?
com que frequência há
autocarros? [kong ki frikw**ay**nsya
a owtoo**ka**rroosh]

oil o óleo [**ol**-yoo]

ointment a pomada [poom**a**da]

OK está bem [shta bayng]

  are you OK? você está bem?
[vos**ay** shta bayng]

  that's OK thanks está bem
obrigado/obrigada
[obrig**a**doo]

  I'm OK, thanks (nothing for me)
não quero, obrigado/
obrigada [nowng k**eh**ro]

  (I feel OK) sinto-me bem
[**seen**toom]

old velho [**vehl**-yoo]

olive oil o azeite [a**zayt**]

olives a azeitona [azayt**oh**na]

omelette a omeleta [omil**ay**ta]

on sobre [**sohbr**]

  on television na televisão

  I haven't got it on me não o
tenho comigo [nowng oo t**ay**n-
yoo koom**ee**goo]

  what's on tonight? qual é o
programa para esta noite?
[kwal**eh** oo pro**o**grama par**ehsh**ta
n**oh**-it]

  once (one time) uma vez [**oo**ma
vaysh]

  at once (immediately)
imediatamente [imid-
yatam**aynt**]

one um [oong], uma [**oo**ma]

  the white one o/a
branco/branca [oo/a br**an**koo]

one-way ticket o bilhete
simples [bil-**yayt** s**ee**mplish]

onion a cebola [sib**oh**la]

only só [saw], somente
[som**aynt**]

  it's only 6 o'clock ainda são
só seis horas [a-**een**da sowng
saw sayz **o**rash]

open (adj) aberto [ab**eh**rtoo]
(verb) abrir [ab**reer**]

operator o/a telefonista
[telefoon**ee**shta]

opposite: opposite my hotel
em frente ao meu hotel
[ayng fraynt ow]

or ou [oh]

orange (fruit) a laranja [lar**an**Ja]
(colour) cor de laranja [kohr di]

orange juice (fresh) o sumo de
laranja [**soo**moo]
(fizzy) a laranjada com gás
[laranJada kong**ash**]
(diluted) o refresco de laranja
[rifr**ay**shkoo di]

order: can we order now?
podemos pedir agora?
[pood**ay**moosh pid**eer**]

ordinary vulgar [vool**gar**]

other outro [**oh**troo]

  the other one o outro [oo]

our/ours nosso [**no**soo], nossa
[**no**sa]; **pl** nossos [**no**soosh],
nossas [**no**sash]

out: he's out saiu [sa-**ee**-oo]

outdoors fora de casa [di k**a**za]

outside do lado de fora [doo
l**a**doo di]

over: over here aqui [akee]
over there ali [alee]
over five hundred mais de quinhentos/quinhentas [mish di]
overnight (travel) de noite [di noh-it]
own: my own ... o meu próprio ... [oo may-oo propr-yoo]

P

pack fazer as malas [fazayr aJ malash]
a pack of ... um pacote de ... [oong pakot di]
package (parcel) a encomenda [aynkoomaynda]
pain a dor [dohr]
I have a pain here tenho uma dor aqui [tayn-yoo ooma dohr akee]
painful doloroso [dooloorohzoo]
painkillers os analgésicos [analJehzikoosh]
pair: a pair of ... um par de ... [oong di]
panties as cuecas [kwehkash]
pants (underwear) as cuecas [kwehkash]
(US) as calças [kalsash]
pantyhose os collants [koolansh]
paper o papel [papehl]
(newspaper) o jornal [Joornal]
paragliding o parapentismo [parapaynteeJmoo]

parcel a encomenda [aynkoomaynda]
pardon (me)? (didn't understand/hear) desculpe? [dishkoolp], como? [kohmoo]
parents os pais [pish]
park o jardim público [Jardeeng pooblikoo]
(verb) estacionar [shtas-yoonar]
parking lot o parque de estacionamento [park di shtas-yoonamayntoo]
part a parte [part]
partner (boyfriend) o companheiro [kompan-yayroo]
(girlfriend) a companheira [kompan-yayra]
party (group) o grupo [groopoo]
(celebration) a festa [fehshta]
passport o passaporte [pasaport]
past: just past the information office logo a seguir ao escritório de informações [logoo a sigeer owshkritor-yoo dinformasoyngsh]
pavement o passeio [pasay-oo]
pay pagar
can I pay, please? por favor, queria pagar [poor favohr kiree-a]
pay phone o telefone público [telefohn pooblikoo]
peach o pêssego [paysigoo]
peanuts os amendoins [amayndweensh]
pear a pêra [payra]
peas as ervilhas [irveel-yash]
pen a caneta [kanayta]
pencil o lápis [lapsh]

people a gente [Jaynt]
 too many people gente
 demais [dimīsh]
pepper (spice) a pimenta
 [pim**ay**nta]
 (vegetable) o pimento
 [pimayntoo]
per: per night por noite [poor
 n**oh**-it]
 per cent por cento [**say**ntoo]
perfume o perfume [pirf**oo**m]
perhaps talvez [talv**ay**sh]
person a pessoa [pis**oh**-a]
petrol a gasolina [gazool**ee**na]
petrol station a bomba de
 gasolina [**boh**mba di]
pharmacy a farmácia [farmas-
 ya]
phone o telefone [telef**oh**n]
 (verb) telefonar [telef**oo**nar]
phone book a lista telefónica
 [**lee**shta telef**oh**nika]
phone box a cabina telefónica
 [kab**ee**na]
phonecard o cartão de
 telefone [kart**ow**ng di telef**oh**n]
phone number o número de
 telefone [**noo**miroo]
photo a fotografia
 [footoograf**ee**-a]
picture (drawing, painting) a
 pintura [peent**oo**ra]
 (photograph) a fotografia
 [footoograf**ee**-a]
piece o pedaço [pid**a**soo]
pilchards as sardinhas
 [sard**een**-yash]
pill a pílula [**pee**loola]
pillow a almofada [alm**oo**fada]

pineapple o ananás [anan**ash**]
pink cor de rosa [kohr di r**oza**]
place o lugar [loog**ar**]
 at your place (fam) na tua
 casa [**too**-a k**aza**]
 (pol) na sua casa [**soo**-a]
plane o avião [av-y**ow**ng]
plant a planta
plasters o adesivo [adiz**ee**voo]
plastic bag o saco de plástico
 [**sako** di]
plate o prato [pr**a**too]
platform o cais [kīsh]
 **which platform is it for
 Fátima?** qual é o cais para
 Fátima? [kwal**eh** oo]
play (verb) jogar [Joog**ar**]
 (in theatre) a peça de teatro
 [**peh**sa di t-y**a**troo]
pleasant agradável
please se faz favor [si fash
 fav**ohr**], por favor [poor]
 yes please sim, por favor
 [seeng]
plenty: plenty of ... muito ...
 [mw**ee**ngtoo]
plug (electrical) a tomada
 [too**ma**da]
 (in sink) a tampa do ralo [doo
 r**a**loo]
poisonous venenoso
 [vinin**oh**zoo]
police a polícia [pool**ees**-ya]
policeman o polícia [oo
 pool**ees**-ya]
police station o Posto da
 Polícia [**poh**shtoo]
polite bem-educado [bayng
 idook**a**doo]

polluted contaminado
[kontaminadoo]

pool (for swimming) a piscina
[pish-seena]

pork a carne de porco [karn di pohrkoo]

port (for boats) o porto
[pohrtoo]

Portugal Portugal [poortoogal]

Portuguese (adj) português
[poortoogaysh]
(language) português
(man) o português
(woman) a portuguesa
the Portuguese os
portugueses [poortoogayzish]

possible possível [pooseevil]
is it possible to ...? é
possível ...? [eh]
as ... as possible tão ...
quanto possível [towng ...
kwantoo]

post (mail) o correio [koorray-oo]
(verb) pôr no correio [pohr noo]

postcard o postal [pooshtal]

postcode o código postal
[kodigoo pooshtal]

poste restante a posta-
restante [poshta rishtant]

post office os correios
[koorray-oosh]

potato a batata

potato chips as batatas fritas
[batatash freetash]

pound (money, weight) a libra
[leebra]

prefer: I prefer ... prefiro ...
[prifeeroo]

pregnant grávida

prescription (for medicine) a
receita [risayta]

present (gift) o presente
[prizaynt]

pretty bonito [booneetoo]

price o preço [praysoo]

private privado [privadoo]

probably provavelmente
[proovavilmaynt]

problem o problema
[prooblayma]
no problem! tudo bem!
[toodoo bayng]

public holiday o feriado [fir-yadoo]

pull puxar [pooshar]

purple roxo [rohshoo]

purse (for money) a carteira
[kartayra]
(US) a mala de mão [di]

push empurrar [aympoorrar]

put pôr [pohr]

pyjamas o pijama [piJama]

Q

quarter a quarta parte [kwarta part]

question a pergunta [pirgoonta]

queue a bicha [beesha]

quick rápido [rapidoo]

quickly depressa [diprehsa]

quiet (place, hotel) silencioso
[silayns-yohzoo]
quiet! cale-se! [kalsi]

quite (fairly) bastante [bashtant]

R

radiator o radiador [rad-yad**oh**r]
radio o rádio [**rad**-yoo]
rail: by rail por caminho de ferro [poor kam**een**-yoo di **feh**rroo]
railway o caminho de ferro
rain a chuva [sh**oo**va]
it's raining está a chover [sh**ta**-a shoov**ay**r]
rape a violação [v-yoolas**ow**ng]
rare (uncommon) raro [**raroo**]
(steak) mal passado [pas**ad**oo]
raspberry a framboesa [frambw**ay**za]
rather: I'd rather ... prefiro ... [prif**ee**roo]
razor (electric) a máquina de barbear [**makina di barb-yar**]
read ler [layr]
ready pronto [pr**oh**ntoo]
real verdadeiro [virdad**ay**roo]
really realmente [r-yalm**ay**nt]
reasonable (prices etc) razoável [razw**a**vil]
receipt o recibo [ris**ee**boo]
recently há pouco [a p**oh**koo]
reception a recepção [risehs**ow**ng]
receptionist o/a recepcionista [risehs-yoon**ee**shta]
recommend: could you recommend ...? podia

recomendar ...? [poodee-a rikoomaynd**ar**]
red vermelho [virm**ayl**-yoo]
red wine o vinho tinto [**veen**-yoo **tee**ntoo]
refund o reembolso [ri-aymb**oh**lsoo]
region a região [riJ-y**ow**ng]
registered: by registered mail por correio registado [poor koorr**ay**-oo riJisht**ad**oo]
remember: I remember lembro-me [**laym**broomi]
rent (noun: for apartment etc) o aluguer [aloog**eh**r]
(verb: car etc) alugar
repair reparar
repeat repetir [ripit**eer**]
reservation a reserva [riz**eh**rva]
reserve reservar [rizirv**ar**]

dialogue

can I reserve a table for tonight? posso reservar uma mesa para esta noite? [p**os**oo – **oo**ma m**ay**za para **eh**shta n**oh**-it]
yes madam, for how many people? sim senhora, para quantas pessoas? [seeng sin-y**o**ra para kwantash pis**oh**-ash]
for two para duas [d**oo**-ash]
and for what time? e para que hora? [i – ki-**o**ra]
for eight o'clock para as oito horas [az**oh**-itorash]
and could I have your name, please? pode

dizer-me o seu nome, por favor? [pod diz**ay**rmoo **say**-oo nohm poor fav**oh**r]

restaurant o restaurante [rishtowr**ant**]
restaurant car a carruagem restaurante [karrwa**J**ayng rishtowr**ant**]
rest room a casa de banho [k**a**za di b**a**n-yoo]
return: a return to ... um bilhete de ida e volta a ... [oong bil-**yay**t d**ee**da ee]
return ticket o bilhete de ida e volta
reverse charge call a chamada paga no destinátario [sham**a**da – noo dishtinat**a**r-yoo]
rice o arroz [arr**oh**sh]
right (correct) certo [**seh**rtoo] (not left) direito [dir**ay**too] **that's right** está certo [shta]
ring (on finger) o anel [an**eh**l]
ring back voltar a telefonar [telefoon**a**r]
river o rio [r**ee**-oo]
road (in town) a rua [r**oo**-a] (in country) a estrada [sht**ra**da] **is this the road for ...?** é esta a estrada para ...? [**eh**shta]
rob: I've been robbed fui roubado/roubada [fwee rohb**a**doo]
roll (bread) o paposseco [papoos**ay**koo]
roof o telhado [til-y**a**doo] (of car) o tejadilho [ti**J**ad**eel**-yoo]

room o quarto [kw**a**rtoo]

dialogue

do you have any rooms?
tem quartos vagos? [tayng kw**a**rtoosh v**a**goosh]
for how many people?
para quantas pessoas? [kw**a**ntash pis**oh**-ash]
for one/for two para uma/para duas [**oo**ma/ – d**oo**-ash]
yes, we have rooms free
sim, temos quartos vagos [seeng t**ay**moosh]
for how many nights will it be? para quantas noites? [n**oh**-itsh]
just for one night só para uma noite [saw – n**oh**-it]
how much is it? quanto é o quarto? [kw**a**ntweh]
... with bathroom and ... without bathroom ... com casa de banho e ... sem casa banho [kong k**a**za di ban-yoo ee ... sayng]
can I see a room with bathroom? posso ver um quarto com casa de banho? [p**o**soo vayr oong]
OK, I'll take it está bem, fico com ele [shta bayng f**ee**koo kong ayl]

room service o serviço de quartos [sirv**ee**soo di kw**a**rtoosh]
rosé (wine) rosé [rooz**ay**]

round trip ticket o bilhete de
ida e volta [bil-**yay**t **dee**da ee]
route o trajecto [traj**eh**too]
rubbish (waste) o lixo [**lee**shoo]
(poor quality goods) o refugo
[rif**oo**goo]
rucksack a mochila
[moo**shee**la]
rude grosseiro [groos**ay**roo]
rum o rum [roong]
run (person) correr [koorr**ayr**]

S

sad triste [treesht]
safe (adj) seguro [sig**oo**roo]
salad a salada
salad dressing o tempero da
salada [taymp**ay**roo]
sale: for sale à venda [**vay**nda]
salt o sal
same: the same o mesmo
[**may**ʃmoo]
the same again, please o
mesmo, por favor [poor
fav**ohr**]
sand a areia [a**ray**-a]
sandals as sandálias [sandal-
yash]
sandwich a sandes [sandsh]
sanitary napkins/towels os
pensos higiénicos [**pay**nsooz
ij-y**eh**nikoosh]
sauce o molho [**mohl**-yoo]
saucepan a panela [pan**eh**la]
sausage a salsicha [sals**ee**sha]
say dizer [diz**ayr**]
how do you say ... in

Portuguese? como se diz ...
em português? [**koh**moo si
deez ... ayng poortoog**ay**sh]
what did he say? o que é
que ele disse? [oo k-yeh kayl
dees]
scarf (for neck) o lenço de
pescoço [**lay**nsoo di pishk**oh**soo]
(for head) o lenço de cabeça
[kab**ay**sa]
schedule (US) o horário [oo
orar-yoo]
school a escola [shk**o**la]
scissors: a pair of scissors a
tesoura [tiz**oh**ra]
scooter a motoreta
[mootoor**ay**ta]
Scotch tape® a fita gomada
[**fee**ta goomada]
Scotland a Escócia [shk**o**s-ya]
Scottish escocês [shkoos**ay**sh]
sea o mar
by the sea à beira-mar
[**bay**ra]
seafood os mariscos
[mar**ee**shkoosh]
seasick: I feel seasick estou
enjoado/enjoada [shtoh
aynʃw**a**doo]
seat o assento [as**ay**ntoo]
is this seat taken? este lugar
está ocupado? [aysht loogar
shta okoopadoo]
second (adj) segundo
[sig**oo**ndoo]
(of time) o segundo
second class (travel) segunda
classe [sig**oo**nda klas]
see ver [vayr]

can I see? posso ver? [**po**soo]

have you seen the ...? viu o/a ...? [**vee**-oo]

see you! até logo! [a**teh lo**goo]

I see (I understand) percebo [pir**say**boo]

self-catering apartment o aparthotel [apartoh**tehl**]

self-service o self-service

sell vender [vayn**dayr**]

Sellotape® a fita gomada [**fee**ta goo**ma**da]

send mandar

separated: I'm separated estou separado/separada [**shtoh**]

separately (pay, travel) separadamente [siparada**maynt**]

serious sério [**sehr**-yoo]

service station a estação de serviço [shtasa**owng**]

serviette o guardanapo [gwardana**poo**]

set menu a ementa fixa [e**mayn**ta **feek**sa]

several vários [**var**-yoosh]

sex o sexo [**sehx**oo]

shade: in the shade à sombra [**sohm**bra]

shampoo o champô [sham**poh**]

share (room, table etc) partilhar [partil-**yar**]

shaver a máquina de barbear [**ma**kina di barb-**yar**]

shaving foam a espuma de barbear [shp**oo**ma]

she ela [**ehl**a]

sheet (for bed) o lençol [layn**sol**]

shellfish os mariscos [ma**ree**shkoosh]

ship o navio [na**vee**-o]

shirt a camisa [ka**mee**za]

shit! merda! [**mehr**da]

shoe os sapatos [sa**pa**toosh]

shoelaces os atacadores [ataka**doh**rish]

shoe polish a graxa para sapatos [**gra**sha para sa**pa**toosh]

shoe repairer o sapateiro [sapa**tay**roo]

shop a loja [**lo**ʒa]

short (person) baixo [**bī**shoo] (time, journey) curto [**koor**too]

shorts os calções [kal**soy**ngsh]

should: what should I do? que devo fazer? [ki **day**voo fa**zayr**]

shoulder o ombro [**ohm**broo]

show (in theatre) o espetáculo [shpita**koo**loo]

could you show me? podia mostrar-me? [poo**dee**-a mooshtrarmi]

shower (in bathroom) o duche [**doosh**]

shrimp a gamba

shut (verb) fechar [fi**shar**]

when do you shut? a que horas fecha? [k-**yo**rash **feh**sha]

it's shut está fechado/fechada [shta fisha**doo**]

shut up! cale-se! [**ka**lisi]

shutter (on window) os postigos [poosh**tee**goosh]

sick (unwell) doente [**dwaynt**]

side o lado [**la**doo]
side salad a salada a
  acompanhar [akompan-**yar**]
sidewalk o passeio [pas**ay**-oo]
sight: the sights of ... os
  centros de interesse de ...
  [oosh **sayn**troosh dintr**ays** di]
silk a seda [**say**da]
silly tolo [**toh**loo]
silver a prata
since: since last week desde a
  semana passada [**day**Jda
  sim**an**a]
sing cantar
single: a single to ... uma
  bilhete simples para ... [**oo**ng
  bil-**yayt** se**emplish**]
I'm single sou
  solteiro/solteira [soh
  soolt**ay**roo]
single bed a cama individual
  [individwal]
single room o quarto
  individual [**kwar**too]
single ticket o bilhete simples
  [bil-**yayt** se**emplish**]
sister a irmã [eer**mang**]
sit: can I sit here? posso
  sentar-me aqui? [**pos**oo
  sayn**tar**mi ak**ee**]
size o tamanho [tam**an**-yoo]
skin a pele [pehl]
skirt a saia [**sī**-ya]
sky o céu [**seh**-oo]
sleep dormir [door**meer**]
sleeping bag o saco de
  dormir [**sak**oo di door**meer**]
sleeping car a carruagem–
  cama [karrwa**Jayng kam**a]

slow lento [**layn**too]
  slow down! (driving) mais
  devagar! [mīJ diva**gar**]
slowly devagar
small pequeno [pik**ay**noo]
smell: it smells (smells bad)
  cheira mal [**shay**ra]
smile sorrir [soor**reer**]
smoke o fumo [**foo**moo]
  do you mind if I smoke?
  importa-se que fume?
  [im**por**tasi ki **foo**mi]
  I don't smoke não fumo
  [nowng]
snow a neve [nehv]
so: it's so good! é tão bom!
  [eh towng bong]
  it's so expensive! é tão caro!
  [**kar**oo]
  it's not so bad não é tão
  mau/má [eh towng mow]
  so am I, so do I eu também
  [**ay**-oo tamb**ayng**]
soap o sabonete [saboon**ayt**]
soap powder o detergente
  [deter**Jaynt**]
sober sóbrio [**sobr**-yoo]
sock a peúga [p-**yoo**ga]
soda (water) a soda
soft (material etc) mole [mol]
soft drink a bebida não
  alcoólica [bib**ee**da nowng alko-
  olika]
sole a sola
some: can I have some water?
  pode trazer-me água?
  [traz**ayrm**]
somebody alguém [alg**ayng**]
something alguma coisa

[algooma koh-iza]

sometimes às vezes [ash vayzish]

somewhere nalguma parte [nalgooma part]

son o filho [feel-yoo]

song a canção [kansowng]

soon em breve [ayng brev]

sore: it's sore dói-me [doymi]

sorry: (I'm) sorry tenho muita pena [tayn-yoo mweengta payna]
sorry? (didn't understand) como? [kohmoo]

sort: what sort of ...? que tipo de ...? [ki teepoo di]

soup a sopa [sohpa]

south o sul [sool]

South Africa a África do Sul [doo]

South African sul-africano [soolafrikanoo]

southeast o sudeste [soodehsht]

southwest o sudoeste [soodwehsht]

souvenir a lembrança [laymbransa]

Spain a Espanha [shpan-ya]

sparkling wine o vinho espumante [veen-yooshpoomant]

speak: do you speak English? fala inglês? [inglaysh]
I don't speak ... não falo ... [nowng faloo]

spectacles os óculos [okooloosh]

spend gastar [gashtar]

spoon a colher [kool-yehr]

spring (season) a Primavera [primavehra]

square (in town) a praça [prasa]

stairs a escada [shkada]

stamp o selo [sayloo]

start o começo [koomaysoo] (verb) começar [koomisar]
the car won't start o carro não pega [oo karroo nowng pehga]

starter (food) a entrada [ayntrada]

starving: I'm starving estou morto/morta de fome [shtoh mohrtoo – di fohm]

station a estação [shtasowng]

stay: where are you staying? onde está hospedado/hospedada? [ohndshta oshpidadoo]
I'm staying at ... estou hospedado/hospedada em ... [shtoh – ayng]
I'd like to stay another two nights gostaria de ficar mais duas noites [gooshtaree-a di fikar mish doo-aJ noh-itsh]

steak o bife [beef]

steal roubar [rohbar]
my bag has been stolen roubaram-me a mala [rohbarowng m-ya mala]

steep (hill) íngreme [eengrim]

still: I'm still here ainda estou aqui [a-eenda shtoh akee]

stomach o estômago [shtohmagoo]

stomach ache a dor de estômago [dohr dishtohmagoo]

stone (rock) a pedra [**peh**dra]

stop par**ar**

please, stop here (to taxi driver etc) pare aqui, por favor [par ak**ee** poor fav**ohr**]

storm a tempestade [taympisht**ad**]

straight: it's straight ahead sempre em frente [**say**mprayng fraynt]

strange (odd) esquisito [shkiz**ee**too]

strawberry o morango [moor**ang**oo]

street a rua [**roo**-a]

string o cordel [koord**ehl**]

strong forte [fort]

stuck emperrado [aympirr**ad**oo]

student (male/female) o/a estudante [shtood**ant**]

stupid estúpido [sht**oo**pidoo]

suburb os arredores [arred**or**ish]

subway (US) o metro [**meh**troo]

suddenly subitamente [soobitam**aynt**]

sugar o açúcar [as**oo**kar]

suit o fato [f**at**oo]

suitcase a mala [m**al**a]

summer o Verão [vir**ow**ng]

in the summer no Verão [noo]

sun o sol

in the sun ao sol [ow]

sunblock o creme écran total [kraym ekrang toot**al**]

sunburn a queimadura de sol [kaymad**oo**ra di]

sunglasses os óculos de sol [**ok**ooloosh di]

sunstroke a insolação [insoolas**ow**ng]

suntanned bronzeado [bronz** yad**oo]

suntan oil o óleo de bronzear [**ol**-yoo di]

supermarket o supermercado [soopermerk**ad**oo]

supper o jantar [**J**antar]

supplement (extra charge) o suplemento [sooplim**aynt**oo]

sure: are you sure? tem a certeza? [tayng a sirt**ay**za]

sure! claro! [kl**ar**oo]

surname o apelido [apil**ee**doo]

sweater a camisola [kamiz**ol**a]

sweet (taste) doce [dohs]

(dessert) a sobremesa [sobrim**ay**za]

sweets os rebuçados [riboos**ad**oosh]

swim nad**ar**

I'm going for a swim vou nadar [voh]

swimming costume o fato de banho [**f**atoo di b**an**-yoo]

swimming pool a piscina [pish**seena**]

swimming trunks os calções de banho [kals**oy**ngsh di b**an**-yoo]

switch o interruptor [intiroopt**ohr**]

switch off (engine, TV) desligar [diJlig**ar**]

(lights) apag**ar**

switch on (engine, TV) lig**ar**

(lights) acender [asaynd**ayr**]

Switzerland a Suíça [sw**ee**sa]

T

table a mesa [**may**za]
table wine o vinho de mesa
[**veen**-yoo]
take levar
(accept) aceitar [asay**tar**]
fine, I'll take it está bem, fico
com ele [shta bayng **fee**koo kong
ayl]
hamburger to take away o
hamburger para levar
talk falar
tall alto [**al**too]
tampons o tampão [tamp**owng**]
tan o bronzeado [bronz-**ya**doo]
tap a torneira [toor**nay**ra]
taste o sabor [sa**bohr**]
taxi o táxi

dialogue

to the airport/Borges
Hotel, please para o
aeroporto/Hotel Borges,
se faz favor [paroo-
ayroop**oh**rtoo/oh**tehl** bor**j**ish si
fash fav**ohr**]
how much will it be?
quanto vai custar?
[**kwan**too vī koosh**tar**]
two thousand escudos
dois contos [**doh**-ish
kohntoosh]
that's fine right here,
thanks aqui está bem,
obrigado/obrigada [a**kee**
shta bayng obri**ga**doo]

tea (drink) o chá [sha]
teacher o professor
[proofes**ohr**], a profess**o**ra
telephone o telefone [telef**ohn**]
television a televisão
[televiz**owng**]
tell: could you tell him ...?
pode dizer-lhe ...? [pod
di**zayr**l-yi]
tennis o ténis [**teh**nish]
terrible terrível [tir**ree**vil]
terrific (weather) esplêndido
[shpl**ayn**didoo]
(food, teacher) excelente [ish-
sel**ayn**t]
than do que [doo ki]
thanks, thank you (said by man)
obrigado [obri**ga**doo]
(said by woman) obrigada
thank you very much muito
obrigado/obrigada
[m**wee**ngtoo]
no thanks não
obrigado/obrigada [nowng]

dialogue

thanks obrigado/
obrigada
that's OK, don't mention it
está bem, não se
preocupe com isso [shta
bayng nowng si pri-ook**oop** kong
eesoo]

that: that ... esse/essa ...
[ays/**eh**sa]
(further away) aquele/aquela ...
[a**kayl**/a**keh**la]

that one esse/essa/isso [**ee**soo]
(further away)
aquele/aquela/aquilo
[a**kee**loo]
that's nice! que bom! [bong]
is that ...? isso é ...? [eh]
the o [oo], a
(pl) os [oosh], as [ash]
theatre o teatro [t-y**a**troo]
their/theirs deles [**day**lish],
delas [**deh**lash]
them os [oosh]
(feminine) as [ash]
for them para eles/elas
[aylsh/**eh**lash]
to them para eles/elas
who? – them quem? –
eles/elas [kayng]
then (after that) depois [dip**oh**-
ish]
there ali [a**lee**], lá
is/are there ...? há ...? [a]
there is/are ... há ...
there you are (giving something)
tome lá [tohm]
these estes [**ay**shtish], estas
[**eh**shtash]
they eles [**ay**lish], f elas [**eh**lash]
thick espesso [shp**ay**soo]
thief o ladrão [ladr**ow**ng], a
ladra
thin fino [**fee**noo]
(person) magro [**ma**groo]
thing a coisa [**koh**-iza]
my things as minhas coisas
[aJ m**ee**n-yash k**oh**-izash]
think pensar [payn**sar**]
I'll think about it vou pensar
[voh]

thirsty: I'm thirsty tenho sede
[**tay**n-yoo sayd]
this: this boy este menino
[aysht min**ee**noo]
this girl esta menina [**eh**shta
min**ee**na]
this one este [**ay**sht]/esta
[**eh**shta]/isto [**ee**shtoo]
is this ...? isto é ...?
[**ee**eeshtweh]
those esses/essas [**ay**sish,
ehsash]
(further away) aqueles/aquelas
... [ak**ay**lish/ak**eh**lash]
thread o fio [**fee**-oo]
throat a garganta
through por, através de
[atrav**eh**J di]
thumb o pôlegar [poo**ligar**]
thunderstorm a trovoada
[troov**wa**da]
ticket o bilhete [bil-**yayt**]

dialogue

a return to Setúbal um
bilhete de ida e volta para
Setúbal [oong – **dee**dī –
sit**oo**bal]
coming back when?
quando volta? [kw**a**ndoo]
today/next Tuesday
hoje/na próxima terça-
feira [ohJ/na pr**o**sima t**ay**rsa
f**ay**ra]
that will be 500 escudos
são quinhentos escudos
[sowng keen-**yayn**tooz-
shk**oo**doosh]

tie (necktie) a gravata

tights os collants [koolansh]

time o tempo [taympoo]

what's the time? que horas são? [k-yorash sowng]

next time a próxima vez [prosima]

three times três vezes [traysh vayzish]

timetable o horário [oo orar-yoo]

tin (can) a lata

tin-opener o abre-latas [abrilatash]

tip (to waiter etc) a gorgeta [goorJayta]

tired cansado [kansadoo]

tissues os lenços de papel [laynsoosh di papehl]

to: to Lisbon/England para Lisboa/Inglaterra

to the museum/to the post office ao museo/aos correios [ow moosay-oo/owsh koorray-oosh]

toast (bread) a torrada [toorrada]

today hoje [ohJ]

toe o dedo do pé [daydoo doo peh]

together juntos [Joontoosh]

toilet a casa de banho [kaza di ban-yoo]

toilet paper o papel higiénico [papehl iJ-yehnikoo]

tomato o tomate [toomat]

tomorrow amanhã [aman-yang]

tomorrow morning amanhã de manhã [aman-yang di man-

yang]

the day after tomorrow depois de amanhã [dipoh-ish daman-yang]

tonic (water) a água tónica [agwa]

tonight esta noite [ehshta noh-it]

too (excessively) demasiado [dimaz-yadoo]

(also) também [tambayng]

too much demais [dimīsh]

me too eu também [ay-oo tambayng]

tooth o dente [daynt]

toothache a dor de dentes [dohr di dayntsh]

toothbrush a escova de dentes [shkohva]

toothpaste a pasta de dentes [pashta]

top: on top of ... em cima de ... [ayng seema di]

at the top no alto [noo altoo]

torch a lanterna [lantehrna]

tour a excursão [shkoorsowng]

tourist o/a turista [tooreeshta]

tourist information office o turismo [tooreeJmoo]

towards para

towel a toalha [twal-ya]

town a cidade [sidad]

in town na cidade

town centre o centro da cidade [sayntroo]

toy o brinquedo [breenkaydoo]

track (US: at station) o cais [kīsh]

traffic lights os semáforos [simafooroosh]

train o comboio [komb**oy**-oo]
 by train de comboio [di]
 is this the train for ...? é este
 o comboio para ...? [eh
 ayshtoo]
train station a estação de
 comboios [shtas**ow**ng di
 komb**oy**-oosh]
tram o eléctrico [el**eh**trikoo]
translate traduzir [tradooz**eer**]
trash (waste) o lixo [l**ee**shoo]
trashcan o caixote de lixo
 [kish**ot** di l**ee**shoo]
travel viajar [v-ya**Jar**]
travel agent's a agência de
 viagens [aJ**aynsy**a di v-
 ya**Jaynsh**]
traveller's cheque o cheque
 de viagem [shehk di
 v-ya**Jayng**]
tree a árvore [**ar**voori]
trip (excursion) a excursão
 [shkoors**owng**]
trousers as calças [k**al**sash]
true verdadeiro [virdad**ay**roo]
try tentar
try on experimentar
T-shirt a T-shirt
tuna o atum [at**oong**]
turn: turn left/right vire à
 esquerda/direita [**vee**ra
 shk**ay**rda/dir**ay**ta]
twice duas vezes [d**oo**-aJ
 v**ay**zish]
twin room o quarto com duas
 camas [kw**ar**too kong d**oo**-ash]
tyre o pneu [p-n**ay**-oo]

U

umbrella o guarda-chuva
 [gwarda sh**oo**va]
uncle o tio [t**ee**-oo]
under debaixo de [dib**ee**shoo di]
 (less) menos de [**may**noosh]
underground (railway) o metro
 [m**eh**troo]
underpants as cuecas
 [kw**eh**kash]
understand: I understand já
 percebi [Ja pirsib**ee**]
 I don't understand não
 percebo [nowng pirs**ay**boo]
university a universidade
 [oonivirsid**ad**]
unleaded sem chumbo [sayng
 sh**oom**boo]
until até a [at**eh**]
up acima [as**ee**ma]
 up there lá em cima [ayng
 s**ee**ma]
upstairs lá em cima
urgent urgente [oor**Jaynt**]
us nos [noosh]
 for us para nós [nosh]
USA os Estados Unidos
 [shtadooz oon**ee**doosh]
use usar [ooz**ar**]
useful útil [**oo**til]

V

vacation as férias [**fehr**-yash]
 on vacation de férias [shtoh
 di]

valid (ticket etc) válido [**valid**oo]
value o valor
vanilla a baunilha [bown**eel**-ya]
veal a vitela [vit**eh**la]
vegetables os legumes
  [lig**oo**mish]
vegetarian o vegetariano
  [viJitar-**yan**oo], a vegetariana
very muito [**mwee**ngtoo]
  I like it very much gosto
  muito disso [**g**oshtoo – **dee**soo]
view a vista [**vee**shta]
village a aldeia [ald**ay**-a]
visit visitar [vizi**tar**]
vodka o vodka
voice a voz [vosh]

W

waist a cintura [sint**oo**ra]
wait esperar [shpi**rar**]
waiter o empregado de mesa
  [aympreg**a**doo di **may**za]
  waiter! se faz favor! [si fash
  fav**ohr**]
waitress a empregada de
  mesa [aympreg**a**da di **may**za]
  waitress! se faz favor!
wake-up call a chamada para
  despertar [sham**a**da para
  dishpir**tar**]
Wales o País de Gales [pa-**ee**J
  di **g**alish]
walk: is it a long walk? é
  muito longe a pé? [eh
  m**wee**ngtoo lohnJ a peh]
wall (outside) o muro [**moo**roo]
  (inside) a parede [par**ay**d]

wallet a carteira [kart**ay**ra]
want: I want a ... queria
  um ... [kir**ee**-a oong]
  I don't want any ... não
  quero ... [nowng k**eh**roo]
  I don't want to não quero
  what do you want? o que
  deseja? [oo ki dis**ay**Ja]
warm quente [kaynt]
wash lavar
  (oneself) lavar-se [–si]
washhand basin o lavatório
  [lavat**or**-yoo]
washing (clothes) a roupa para
  lavar [**roh**pa]
washing machine a máquina
  de lavar [**mak**ina di]
washing powder o detergente
  [deterJ**aynt**]
wasp a vespa [**vay**shpa]
watch (wristwatch) o relógio
  (de pulso) [ril**o**J-yoo (di p**oo**lsoo)]
water a água [**ag**wa]
way: it's this way é por aqui
  [eh por ak**ee**]
  it's that way é por ali [al**ee**]
  is it a long way to ...? é
  muito longe até ...?
  [m**wee**ngtoo lohnJ at**eh**]
  no way! de maneira
  nenhuma! [di man**ay**ra nin-
  yooma]

dialogue

could you tell me the way
to ...? pode indicar-me o
caminho para ...?
[podindik**ar**moo kam**een**-yoo]

go straight on until you reach the traffic lights siga em frente até chegar ao semáforo [**see**gayng fr**ay**nt at**eh** shigar ow sem**a**fooroo]
turn left vire à esquerda [**vee**ra shk**ay**rda]
take the first on the right vire na primeira à direita [veer na prim**ay**ra dir**ay**ta]

we nós [nosh]
weather o tempo [**tay**mpoo]
week a semana [si**ma**na]
 a week (from) today de hoje a uma semana [dohJ a **oo**ma]
weekend o fim de semana [feeng di]
weight o peso [**pay**zoo]
welcome: welcome to ... bem vindo a ... [bayng v**ee**ndwa]
 you're welcome (don't mention it) não tem de quê [nowng tayng di kay]
well: she's not well ela não está bem [**eh**la nowng shta bayng]
 you speak English very well fala inglês muito bem [ingl**ay**sh]
 well done! muito bem!
 this one as well este também [aysht tamb**ay**ng]
well-done (meat) bem passado [bayng pas**a**doo]
Welsh galês [gal**ay**sh]
west o oeste [wesht]
wet molhado [mool-y**a**doo]
what? o quê? [oo kay]

what's that? o que é isso? [oo k-yeh **ee**soo]
wheel a roda
when? quando? [kw**a**ndoo]
 when's the train/ferry? quando é o comboio/ferry? [kw**a**ndweh o komb**oy**-oo]
where? onde? [ohnd]
which: which bus? qual autocarro? [kwal owto**o**karroo]
while: while I'm here enquanto estou aqui [aynkw**a**ntoo shtoh ak**ee**]
whisky o whisky [**wee**shkee]
white branco [**bra**nkoo]
white wine o vinho branco [veen-yoo]
who? quem? [kayng]
whole: the whole week toda a semana [**toh**da si**ma**na]
whose: whose is this? de quem é isto? [di kayng eh **ee**shtoo]
why? porquê? [poork**ay**]
 why not? porque não? [nowng]
wide largo [**lar**goo]
wife a mulher [mool-y**eh**r]
wind o vento [**vay**ntoo]
window a janela [Jan**eh**la]
 (of shop) a montra [**moh**ntra]
 in the window (of shop) na montra
wine o vinho [veen-yoo]
wine list a lista dos vinhos [**lee**shta dooJ veen-y**oo**sh]
winter o Inverno [inv**eh**rnoo]
with com [kong]
 I'm staying with ... estou na

casa do/da ... [shtoh na kaza doo]

without sem [sayng]
woman a mulher [mool-yehr]
wood (material) a madeira [madayra]
wool a lã [lang]
word a palavra
work o trabalho [trabal-yoo]
  it's not working não funciona [nowng foons-yohna]
worry: I'm worried estou preocupado/preocupada [shtoh pri-okoopadoo]
worse: it's worse está pior [shta p-yor]
worst o pior [oo]
would: would you give this to ...? pode dar isto a ...? [pod dar eeshtwa]
wrap: could you wrap it up? pode embrulhá-lo? [aymbrool-yaloo]
wrist o pulso [poolsoo]
write escrever [shkrivayr]
  could you write it down? pode escrever isso? [pod – eesoo]
wrong: it's the wrong key não é esta a chave [nowng eh ehshta shav]
  there's something wrong with ... passa-se qualquer coisa com ... [pasasi kwalkehr koh-iza kong]
  what's wrong? o que se passa? [oo ki si]

Y

year o ano [anoo]
yellow amarelo [amarehloo]
yes sim [seeng]
yesterday ontem [ohntayng]
  the day before yesterday anteontem [antiohntayng]
yet ainda [a-eenda], já [Ja]
you (pol) você [vosay]
  (more formal: to man/woman) o senhor [oo sin-yohr], a senhora
  (fam) tu [too]
  this is for you isto é para si [eeshtweh para see]
  (fam) isto é para ti
young jovem [Jovayng]
your/yours (pol) seu [say-oo], sua [soo-a]; pl seus [say-oosh], suas [soo-ash]
  (fam) teu [tay-oo], tua [too-a]; pl teu [tay-oosh], tua [too-ash]
youth hostel o albergue da juventude [albehrg da Joovayntood]

Z

zero zero [zehroo]
zip o fecho éclair [fayshwayklehr]
zoo o jardim zoológico [Jardeeng zwoloJikoo]

Portuguese

→

English

a the; to; her; it; to it; you
à to the
abaixo [abīshoo] below; down
aberto das ... às ... horas
open from ... to ... o'clock
acabar to finish
acampar to camp
aceitar [asaytar] to accept; to
take
acenda os médios switch on
dipped headlights
acima [aseema] up; above
adega f cellar; old-style bar
adeus [aday-oosh] goodbye,
bye
adiantado [ad-yantadoo] in
advance
advogada f [advoogada],
advogado m [advoogadoo]
lawyer
agência de viagens [di v-ya-
Jayngsh] travel agency
agora [agora] now
agradável [agradavil] nice
agradecer [agradisayr] to
thank
água f [agwa] water
água potável [pootavil]
drinking water
aguardar [agwardar] to wait
for
aí [a-ee] there
ainda [a-eenda] yet, still
ajudar [aJoodar] to help
albergaria f [albirgaree-a]
luxury hotel
albergue da juventude m
[albehrg da Joovayntood] youth
hostel

aldeia f [alday-a] village
alfaiate m [alfi-at] tailor
alfândega f [alfandiga]
Customs
algodão m [algoodowng]
cotton
alguém [algayng] anybody;
somebody
algum [algoong], **alguma**
[algooma] some
alguma coisa [koh-iza]
something
ali [alee] (over) there
alimento m [alimayntoo] food
almoço m [almohsoo] lunch
alojamento m [alooJamayntoo]
accommodation
alto [altoo] high; tall; loud
alugam-se quartos rooms for
rent
aluga-se [alooga-si] to rent
aluguer de automóveis
[dowtoomovaysh] car rental
amanhã [aman-yang]
tomorrow
amar to love
amarelo [amarehloo] yellow
ambos [amboosh] both
amiga f [ameega] friend
amigo m [ameegoo] friend
amor m [amohr] love
andar (m) floor, storey; to
walk
aniversário natalício [natalees-
yoo] birthday
ano m [anoo] year
anteontem [anti-ohntayng] the
day before yesterday
antes [antsh] before

antigo [anteegoo] ancient, old

ao [ow] to the; at the

ao pé de [ow peh di] near

aos [owsh] to the; at the

apagar to switch off

aparthotel m [apartohtehl] self-catering apartment

apelido m [apileedoo] surname; family name

aprender [aprayndayr] to learn

aquecimento m [akesimayntoo] heating

aquela [akehla], **aquele** [akayl] that (one)

aqui [akee] (over) here

aquilo [akeeloo] that (one)

areia f [aray-a] sand

artigos em pele [pehl] leather goods

árvore f [arvoori] tree

as [ash] the; them; you

às to the; at the

ascensor m [ashsaynsohr] lift, elevator

a senhora [sin-yora] you

assim [aseeng] this way

  assim está bem? is that OK?

assinar to sign

assinatura f [asinatoora] signature

às vezes [aJ vayzish] sometimes

até [ateh] until

atenção please note; caution; warning

atrás [atrash] behind

atrasado [atrazadoo] late, delayed

atraso m [atrazoo] delay

através de [atravehJ di] through

autocarro m [owtookarroo] coach, bus

autoestrada f [owtooshtrada] motorway, highway

avaria f [avaree-a] breakdown

avariado [avari-adoo] damaged; faulty; out of order

avião m [av-yowng] plane

azul [azool] blue

bagagem f [bagaJayng] baggage

bairro m [bīrroo] district

baixo [bīshoo] low; short

balcão de informações [dinfoormasoyngsh] information desk

banheiros [ban-yayroosh] toilets

banho m [ban-yoo] bath

barato [baratoo] cheap

barco m [barkoo] boat

bebida f [bibeeda] drink

beco sem saída cul-de-sac, dead end

beira: à beira do mar [bayra doo] at the seaside

belo [behloo] beautiful

bem [bayng] fine; well; OK; properly

bem-vindo [veendoo] welcome

bengaleiro m [bengalayroo] cloakroom, checkroom

bicicleta f [bisiklehta] bicycle

bilhete m [bil-yayt] fare; ticket

bilhete de ida [deeda] single

ticket, one-way ticket

bilhete de ida e volta [**deed**ī] return ticket, round trip ticket

bilheteira f [bil-yi**tay**ra] ticket office

boa [**boh**-a] good

boate f [bwat] nightclub; disco

boca f [**boh**ka] mouth

bocadinho m [bookadeen-yoo] little bit

bocado m [booka**doo**] piece

bom [bong] good; fine

bonito [boo**nee**too] beautiful; nice; pretty

bosque m [boshk] woods, forest

braço m [bra**soo**] arm

branco [**bran**koo] white

breve: em breve [ayng brev] soon

buscar [boosh**kar**] to collect; to fetch

cá here

cabeça f [ka**bay**sa] head

cabedais mpl [kabi**dī**sh] leather goods

cabedal m [kabi**dal**] leather

cabeleireiro m [kabilay**ray**roo] hairdresser's

cabelo m [ka**bay**loo] hair

cada each, every

cais m [kīsh] quay; platform, (US) track

caixa f [**kī**sha] box; cash desk; cashpoint, ATM; savings bank

caixa do correio [doo koor**ray**-oo] postbox; mailbox

calçado m [kal**sa**doo] footwear

calor m [ka**lohr**] heat

cama f bed

cama de casal [di ka**zal**] double bed

cama de solteiro [sool**tay**roo] single bed

câmbio m [**kamb**-yoo] bureau de change; exchange rate

camião m [kam-**yowng**] truck

caminho m [ka**meen**-yoo] path

caminho de ferro railway

campo m [**kam**poo] field; countryside

cansado [kan**sa**doo] tired

cão m [kowng] dog

cara f face

caro [**ka**roo] expensive

carro m [**kar**roo] car

carruagem-cama f [karrwa**Jayng**] sleeping car

carta f letter

carta de condução [di kondoo**sowng**] driver's licence

cartão m [kar**towng**] card; identity card; cardboard

carteirista m/f [kartay**reesh**ta] pickpocket

casa f [**ka**za] home; house

casa de banho [di ban-yoo] bathroom; toilet, rest room

casado [ka**za**doo] married

castanho [kash**tan**-yoo] brown

cavalo m [ka**va**loo] horse

caverna f [ka**veh**rna] cave

cedo [**say**doo] early

certidão f [sirti**downg**]

certificate
certo [**seh**rtoo] correct, right; sure
cervejaria f [sirvayJa**ree**-a] beer cellar/tavern serving food
chamada f [sha**ma**da] call
chamar [sha**ma**r] to call
chão m [**show**ng] ground; floor
charuto m [sha**roo**too] cigar
chave f [**sha**v] key
chávena f [**sha**vena] cup
chega [**shay**ga] that's enough
chegada f [shi**ga**da] arrival
chegar [shi**ga**r] to arrive; to reach
cheio [**shay**-oo] full
cheque de viagem m [shehk di v-ya**Jay**ng] travellers' cheque
chuva f [**shoo**va] rain
cidade f [si**da**d] town; city
cigarro m [si**ga**rroo] cigarette
claro [**kla**roo] pale; light; clear; of course
coisa f [**koh**-iza] thing
com [kong] with
comboio m [kom**boy**-oo] train
começar [koome**sa**r] to begin
começo m [koo**may**soo] start
comer [koo**may**r] to eat
comida f [koo**mee**da] food; meal
como [**koh**moo] how; like; since, as
como? pardon (me)?, sorry?
comprar [kom**pra**r] to buy
compreender [kompr-yaynd**ay**r] to understand
comprido [kom**pree**doo] long

condutor m [kondoo**toh**r] driver
conduzir [kondoo**zee**r] to lead; to drive
confecções de homem [**doh**mayng] menswear
conhecer [kon-yi**say**r] to know
consigo [kon**see**goo] with you
constipação f [konshtipas**ow**ng] cold
conta f [**koh**nta] bill; account
contigo [kon**tee**goo] with you
conto m [**koh**ntoo] tale; a thousand escudos
contra against
cor f [**koh**r] colour
coração m [koora**sow**ng] heart
corpo m [**koh**rpoo] body
correio m [koorr**ay**-oo] post, mail; post office
correio azul express mail
correr [koorr**ay**r] to run
corte m [kort] cut
costa f [**koh**shta] coast
couro m [**koh**roo] leather
cozinha f [koo**zeen**-ya] kitchen
crer [krayr] to believe
criada f [kr-**ya**da] maid
criança f [kr-**yan**sa] child
cuidado m [**kwida**doo] care
cumprimento: com os melhores cumprimentos with best wishes

da of the; from the
damas f [**da**mash] ladies' (room)
daqui [da**kee**] from now on
dar to give
das [dash] of the; from the

da senhora [sin-yora] your(s)
de [di] from; of; by; in
debaixo de ... [dibīshoo di] under ...
dedo m [daydoo] finger
defeito m [difaytoo] fault, defect
deixar [dayshar] to leave (behind), to let
dela [dehla] her; hers
dele [dayl] his
deles [daylish] their(s)
demais [dimīsh] too much
demasiado [dimaz-yadoo] too much
demora f delay
dente m [daynt] tooth
dentro de ... [dayntroo] inside ...
de onde? [dohnd] where from?
depois [dipoh-ish] then; after
descer [dishsayr] to go down; to get off
desculpas fpl [diskoolpash] apologies
desde [dayづdi] since; from
desgarradas fpl [diづgarradash] improvised popular songs
desligar [diづligar] to turn off
desocupar antes das ... vacate before ...
desporto m [dishpohrtoo] sport
desvio m [diづvee-oo] detour, diversion
Deus [day-oosh] God
devagar [divagar] slow; slowly
dever (m) [divayr] duty; to owe; to have to
de vocês [di vosaysh] your(s)

dia m [dee-a] day
dia de anos m [dee-a danoosh] birthday
diariamente [d-yar-yamaynt] daily
dias de semana weekdays
dinheiro m [deen-yayroo] money
direito [diraytoo] straight; right
divisas fpl foreign currency
dizer [dizayr] to say; to tell
do of the; from the
dobro [dohbroo] twice as much
doença f [dwaynsa] disease
doer [dwayr] to hurt
doido [doh-idoo] crazy
Dona Mrs
donde [dohnd] where from
dono m [dohnoo] owner
do que [doo ki] than
dor f [dohr] pain
dormidas rooms to let
dos of the; from the
do senhor [doo sin-yohr] your(s)
dto. right
duche m [doosh] shower
durante [doorant] during

e [ee] and
e. left
é [eh] he/she/it is; you are
ela [ehla] she; her; it
elas [ehlash] they; them
ele [ayl] he; him; it
eles [aylish] they; them
em [ayng] in; at; on
embaixada f [aymbīshada]

embassy

embaixo [aymbīshoo] down, downstairs; underneath

embora [aymbora] although

ementa f [emaynta] menu

empregada f [aympregada] waitress

empregada de quarto [kwartoo] chambermaid

empregado (de mesa) m [aympregadoo (di mayza)] waiter

emprego m [aympraygoo] job

empresa f [aymprayza] company, firm

empurrar [aympoorrar] to push

encomendas fpl parcels

encontrar [aynkontrar] to find; to meet

endereço m [ayndiraysoo] address

enganado [aynganadoo] wrong

ensinar [aynsinar] to teach

então [ayntowng] then, at that time

entrada f [ayntrada] entrance; starter

entre [ayntr] among; between

entregar [ayntrigar] to deliver

enviar [aynv-yar] to send

equipa f [ekeepa] team

és [ehsh] you are

escola f [shkola] school

escrever [shkrivayr] to write

escritório m [shkritor-yoo] office

escuro [shkooroo] dark

esperar [shpirar] to expect; to hope; to wait

esposa f [shpohza] wife

esq. left

esquadra da polícia f [shkwarda da poolees-ya] police station

esquecer [shkisayr] to forget

esquerdo [shkayrdoo] left

essa [ehsa] that; that one

essas [ehsash] those

esse [ays] that

esses [aysish] those

esta [ehshta] this; this one

está [shta] hello (on the phone); he/she/it is; you are

estação f [shtasowng] station; season

estacionamento m [shtasyoonamayntoo] car park, parking lot

estacionamento proibido no parking

estacionar [shtas-yoonar] to park

estadia f [shtadee-a] stay

estalagem f [shtalaJayng] luxury hotel

estamos [shtamoosh] we are

esta noite [ehshta noh-it] tonight

estão [shtowng] they are; you are

estar [shtar] to be

estas [ehshtash] these

estás [shtash] you are

este [aysht] this; this one

este m [ehsht] east

estes [ayshtish] these

estou [shtoh] I am

estrada f [shtrada] road

estragado [shtragadoo] out of order

estrangeiro (m) [shtranJ**ay**roo] foreign; foreigner

estudante m/f [shtoo**dant**] student

eu [**ay**-oo] I

E.U.A. USA

exposição f [shpoozis**ow**ng] exhibition

F cold

fábrica f [**fa**brika] factory

fácil [**fa**sil] easy

fado m [**fa**doo] traditional Portuguese song, usually sad and romantic

faixa f [**fi**sha] lane

falar to speak; to talk

faróis máximos mpl [far**oy**J **ma**simoosh] headlights

favor: por favor [fav**ohr**] please

fazer [fa**zayr**] to do; to make

fechado [fish**a**doo] closed; overcast

feio [**fay**-oo] ugly

feliz [fil**ee**sh] happy

feriado m [fir-**ya**doo] public holiday

ficar [fi**kar**] to remain

onde fica ...? [**fee**ka] where is ...?

ficar com [kong] to keep

filha f [**feel**-ya] daughter

filho m [**feel**-yoo] son

fim m [**feeng**] end

fim de semana [di si**ma**na] weekend

fita f [**fee**ta] tape, cassette

floresta f [floor**eh**shta] forest

fogo m [**foh**goo] fire

fora: lá fora outside

forte [fort] strong; rich

frente f [**fraynt**] front

frio [**free**-oo] cold

fumadores smokers

funcionar [foons-yo**nar**] to work

fundo (m) [**foon**doo] deep; bottom

garrafa f [ga**rra**fa] bottle

gasóleo m [gaz**ol**-yoo] diesel

gastar [gash**tar**] to spend

gelataria f [Jilata**ree**-a] ice-cream parlour

gelo [**Jay**loo] ice

gente f [**Jaynt**] people

geral [Je**ral**] general

gerente m/f [Je**raynt**] manager; manageress

guerra f [**geh**rra] war

H gents, men's room

há ... [a] there is ...; there are ...

há uma semana a week ago

hoje [ohJ] today

homem m [**oh**mayng] man

homens mpl [**oh**mayngsh] men; gents', men's room

hora f [**o**ra] hour; time

horário m [o**rar**-yoo] timetable, (US) schedule

hospedaria f [oshpida**ree**-a] guesthouse

hóspede m/f [**o**shpidi] guest

idade f [ee**dad**] age

igreja f [ig**ray**Ja] church

igual [**igwal**] same
ilha f [**eel**-ya] island
impresso m [impr**ehs**oo] form,
  document
incêndio m [ins**aynd**-yoo] fire
indicativo m [indikat**eev**oo]
  dialling code, area code
Inglaterra f [inglat**ehr**ra]
  England
introduza a moeda na ranhura
  insert coin in slot
Inverno m [inv**ehr**noo] winter
ir [eer] to go
irmã f [eerm**ang**] sister
irmão m [eerm**owng**] brother
isso [**ees**oo] that (one)
isto [**eesh**too] this (one)

já [Ja] ever; already
janela f [Jan**ehl**a] window
jardim público [**poob**likoo] park
jogo m [**Johg**oo] game, match
jornal m [Jo**ornal**] newspaper
jovem [**Jov**ayng] young
jovens mpl [**Jov**ayngsh] young
  people
junto: junto da ... [**Joo**ntoo da]
  beside the ...
juntos [**Joo**ntoosh] together

lá over there, there
lã f [lang] wool
lado m [**lad**oo] side
ladrão m [ladr**owng**] thief
lá fora outside
lago m [**lag**oo] lake; pond
largo (m) [**larg**oo] wide;
  square
lavabos mpl [lava**boosh**] toilets,

rest room
lavagem a seco f [lavaJayng a
  saykoo] dry-cleaning
lavagem automática
  [owtoom**atik**a] carwash
lavar to wash
lei f [lay] law
lento [**layn**too] slow
ler [layr] to read
leste m [**lehsht**] east
levar to take; to carry
leve [lehv] light (not heavy)
lhe [l-yi] (to) him; (to) her;
  (to) you
lhes [l-yaysh] (to) them; (to)
  you
libra f [**leebr**a] pound
lição f [lis**owng**] lesson
licença f [lis**aynsa**] licence;
  permit
com licença [kong] excuse
  me
ligação f [ligas**owng**]
  connection
ligação com ... connects
  with ...
ligar to turn on
limpar [leemp**ar**] to clean
limpeza a seco f [leemp**ayz**a a
  saykoo] dry-cleaning
limpo [**leemp**oo] clean
língua f [**leeng**wa] language;
  tongue
liquidação sale
livraria f [livrar**ee**-a] bookshop,
  bookstore
livre [leevr] free, vacant
livro m [**leevr**oo] book
lixo m [**leesh**oo] rubbish; litter

logo [**lo**goo] immediately
loja f [**lo**Ja] shop
longe [lohnJ] far
lugar m [**loo**gar] greengrocer's; seat; place
lume m [loom] light; fire
luz f [loosh] light
Lx Lisbon

má bad
madeira f [mad**ay**ra] wood
mãe f [mayng] mother
maior [mī-**or**] greater; bigger
mais [mīsh] more
mais nada no more; nothing else
mal hardly; badly
mala f [bag; suitcase; handbag
mandar to send
manhã f [man-**yang**] morning
mão f [mowng] hand
mar m sea
marcar to dial
marco de correio m [**ma**rkoo di koor**ay**-oo] letterbox, mailbox
marido m [mar**ee**doo] husband
marisqueira f [marishk**ay**ra] seafood restaurant
mas [mash] but
mau [mow] bad
medida f [mid**ee**da] size
meia hora f [**o**ra] half an hour
meia pensão f [payns**ow**ng] half board, American plan
meio m [**may**-oo] middle; half
meio-dia m [**may**-oo d**ee**-a] midday
melhor [mil-**yor**] best; better
menina f [min**ee**na] girl; young

lady
menino m boy
menor [min**or**] smaller
menos [**may**noosh] less
mercado m [mirk**a**doo] market
mercearia f [mirs-yar**ee**-a] grocery store
mês m [maysh] month
mesa f [**may**za] table
mesmo [**may**Jmoo] same; myself
metade f [mit**a**d] half
meu [**may**-oo] my; mine
mim [meeng] me
minha [**meen**-ya] my; mine
mobília f [moob**eel**-ya] furniture
moeda f [mw**eh**da] coin
molhado [mool-y**a**doo] wet
monte m [mohnt] hill
morada f [moor**a**da] address
morar [moor**ar**] to live
morrer [moorr**ayr**] to die
morte f [mort] death
morto [**moh**rtoo] dead
mostrar [moosht**rar**] to show
mudar [mood**ar**] to move
mudar em ... change at ...
muito [m**wee**ngtoo] a lot (of); very
muito bem [bayng] very well
mulher f [mool-y**ehr**] woman; wife
multa f [m**oo**lta] fine
mundo m [m**oo**ndoo] world

na in the; at the; on the
nada nothing
nadar to swim

não [nowng] no; not
não contém ... does not
  contain ...
não fumar no smoking
não funciona out of order
não mexer do not touch
nariz m [nareesh] nose
nas [nash] in the; at the; on
  the
natação f [natasowng]
  swimming
Natal m Christmas
navio m [navee-o] ship
negócio m [nigos-yoo] deal;
  business
nem ... nem ... [nayng] neither
  ... nor ...
nenhum [nin-yoong], nenhuma
  [nin-yooma] none; no ...
neve f [nehv] snow
ninguém [ningayng] nobody
no [noo] in; in the; at the; on
  the
noite f [noh-it] evening; night
nome m [nohm] name
nome próprio [propr-yoo] first
  name
norte m [nort] north
nos [noosh] in the; at the; on
  the; (to) us; ourselves
nós [nosh] we; us
nosso [nosoo] our(s)
noutro [nohtroo] in/on
  another
novidades fpl [noovidadsh]
  news
novo [nohvoo] new
num [noong], numa [nooma]
  in a

nunca [noonka] never

o [oo] the; him; it; to it; you
objectos perdidos lost
  property, lost and found
obliterador m [obli.tiradohr]
  ticket-stamping machine
obras (na estrada) roadworks
oeste m [wesht] west
óleo m [ol-yoo] oil
olho m [ohl-yoo] eye
onde? [ohnd] where?
ontem [ohntayng] yesterday
o que [oo kay] what?
orelha f [orayl-ya] ear
os [oosh] the; them; you
o senhor [oo sin-yohr], os
  senhores [oosh sin-yohrish]
  you
ou [oh] or
ouro m [ohroo] gold
Outono [ohtohnoo] autumn,
  (US) fall
outra coisa [ohtra koh-iza]
  something else
outra vez [ohtra vaysh] again
outro [ohtroo] different,
  another; other
ouvir [ohveer] to hear

padaria f [padaree-a] bakery
pagar to pay
pai m [pī] father
país m [pa-eesh] country
pais mpl [pīsh] parents
palavra f word
papéis waste paper
papel m [papehl] paper
par m pair

428

para into; for; to; towards
paragem f [para**Jay**ng] stop
para levar to take away, (US) to go
parar to stop
parentes mpl [par**ay**ntsh] relatives
partida f [part**ee**da] departure
partir [part**ee**r] to break; to leave
passado (**m**) [pas**a**doo] past; last
passageiro m [pasaJ**ay**roo] passenger
passeio m [pas**ay**-oo] pavement, sidewalk; walk
patrão m [pat**row**ng] boss
pé m [peh] foot
pedaço m [pid**a**soo] piece
pedir [pid**ee**r] to ask; to order
pela [**pi**la], **pelo** [**pi**loo] through the; by the; about the
pensão f [payns**ow**ng] guesthouse
pensão completa [kompl**eh**ta] full board, European plan
pensar [payns**ar**] to think
peões mpl [p-y**oy**ngsh] pedestrians
pequeno [pik**ay**noo] little
pequeno almoço m [alm**oh**soo] breakfast
perceber [pirsib**ay**r] to understand
perder [pird**ay**r] to lose; to miss
perdidos e achados lost property, lost and found

pergunta f [pirg**oo**nta] question
perguntar [pirgoont**ar**] to ask
perigo m [pir**ee**goo] danger
perigoso [pirig**oh**zoo] dangerous
perna f [**peh**rna] leg
perto [**peh**rtoo] near
pesado [piz**a**doo] heavy
pescoço m [pishk**oh**soo] neck
peso m [**pay**zoo] weight
pessoa f [pis**oh**-a] person
pessoal m [pisoo-**al**] staff
pintado de fresco wet paint
pior [p-yor] worse; worst
piscina f [pish-**see**na] swimming pool
piso m [**pee**zoo] floor, storey
piso escorregadio slippery road surface
pneu m [p**nay**-oo] tyre
poder [pood**ay**r] to be able to
por [poor] through; by
pôr [pohr] to put
porque [poork**ay**] because; why
porta de embarque f [daymb**ar**k] gate
portagem f [pohrt**a**jayng] toll
possível [poos**ee**vil] possible
pouco [**poh**koo] a little
pouquinho: um pouquinho [oong pohk**een**-yoo] a little bit
pousada f [pohs**a**da] state-owned hotel, often a historic building
praça f [pr**a**sa] square; market
praça de táxis [di t**a**xish] taxi rank
praça de touros [t**oh**roosh]

bullring
praia f [prī-a] seafront; beach
prata f [prata] silver
prato m [pratoo] course, dish; plate
precisar [prisizar] to need
preço m [praysoo] price
prendas fpl [prayndash] gifts
pré-pagamento choose your food, drink etc then pay at the cash desk before being served
preservativo m [prizirvateevoo] condom
preto [praytoo] black
Primavera f [primavehra] spring
primeiro [primayroo] first
professor m [proofesohr], **professora** f [proofesohra] teacher
proibida a paragem no stopping
proibido [proo-ibeedoo] forbidden
proibido ultrapassar no overtaking
pronto [prohntoo] ready
próximo [prosimoo] near; next
puxar [pooshar] to pull

qual? [kwal] which?
qualquer [kwalkehr] any
qualquer coisa [koh-iza] anything
quando? [kwandoo] when?
quanto? [kwantoo] how much?
quantos? [kwantoosh] how

many?
quarto (m) [kwartoo] bedroom; room; quarter
quase [kwaz] almost
que that; than
quê? [kay] what?
quebrar [kibrar] to break
queimadura f [kaymadoora] burn
queixas complaints
quem? [kayng] who?
quente [kaynt] warm; hot
querer [kirayr] to want
quilo m [keeloo] kilo
quinta f [keenta] farm
quinzena f [keenzayna] fortnight

rainha f [ra-een-ya] queen
rapaz m [rapash] boy
recado m [rikadoo] message
receber [risibayr] to receive
recepção f [risehsowng] reception
recibo m [riseeboo] receipt
reclamação f [riklamasowng] complaint
reclamação de bagagens [di bagaJayngsh] baggage claim
refeição f [rifaysowng] meal
refugo m [rifoogoo] rubbish
rei m [ray] king
Reino Unido m United Kingdom
rés de chão m [rehJ doo showng] ground floor, (US) first floor
residencial m [rizidayns-yal] bed and breakfast hotel
retretes fpl [ritrehtsh] toilets,

rest rooms
rico [**ree**koo] rich
rio m [**ree**-oo] river
roda f [**ro**da] wheel
roupa f [**roh**pa] clothes
rua f [**roo**-a] road; street

S ladies' (room)
saber [sa**bayr**] to know; to be able to
saída f [sa-**ee**da] departure; exit
sala f lounge
saldos mpl [**sal**doosh] sale
sangue m [sang] blood
são [sowng] healthy; they are; you are
sapateiro m [sapa**tay**roo] shoe repairer's
saúde [sa-**oo**d] health
se [si] if; yourself; himself; herself; themselves; yourselves
secar [si**kar**] to dry
secção f [sehk**sowng**] department
seco [**say**koo] dry
seda f [**say**da] silk
seguinte [si**gee**ngt] following
seguir [si**geer**] to follow
seguro de viagem [di v-ya**Jayng**] travel insurance
selo m [**say**loo] stamp
sem [sayng] without
semana f [si**ma**na] week
sempre [**say**mpr] always
senha f [**sayn**-ya] ticket; receipt
senhor (m) sir; gentleman;

you
senhora madam; lady; you
senhoras ladies' (room)
sentido proibido no entry
sentido único one way
ser [sayr] to be
serviço m [sir**vee**soo] service
seu [**say**-oo] his; her(s); its; your(s); their(s)
si [see] you
sim [seeng] yes
só [saw] alone; just; only
sobre [**sohbr**] about; on
sol m sun
somente [so**may**nt] only; just
somos [**soh**moosh] we are
sono m [**soh**noo] sleep
sopé: no sopé do ... [noo soo**peh** doo] at the bottom of ...
sou [soh] I am
sozinho [so**zeen**-yoo] by myself
sua [**soo**-a] his; her(s); its; your(s); their(s)
sujo [**soo**Joo] dirty
sul m [sool] south

talho m [**tal**-yoo] butcher's
talvez [tal**vaysh**] maybe
tamanho m [ta**man**-yoo] size
também [tam**bayng**] also
tanto [**tan**too] so much
tão [towng] so
tarde f [tard] afternoon; late
te [ti] you; to you; yourself
teleférico m [tele**feh**rikoo] cable car
tem [tayng] he/she/it has; you have

têm [**tay**-ayng] they have; you have

temos [**tay**moosh] we have

tempo m [**tay**mpoo] time; weather

tenho [**tayn**-yoo] I have; I am

não tenho [nowng] I don't have any

tenho de/que ... [di/ki] I must ...

ter [tayr] to have; to hold; to be; to contain; to have to

teu [**tay**-oo] your(s)

ti you

tia f [**tee**-a] aunt

tio m [**tee**-oo] uncle

tipo m [**tee**poo] sort

todo [**toh**doo] all

toda a gente [**toh**da a Jaynt] everyone

tomar [**too**mar] to take

tourada f [**toh**rada] bullfight

trabalhar [trabal-**yar**] to work

trabalho m [trabal-yoo] work

tradução f [tradoos**ow**ng] translation

trânsito m [**tran**zitoo] traffic

traseiro (m) [tra**zay**roo] bottom (of person); back

trazer [tra**zayr**] to bring

trespassa-se premises for sale

trocar [troo**kar**] to change

tu [too] you

tua [**too**-a] your(s)

tudo [**too**doo] everything

turismo m [too**ree**Jmoo] tourist information office

um [oong], uma [**oo**ma] a; one

umas [**oo**mash], uns [oonsh] some

validação de bilhetes punch your ticket here

vedado ao trânsito no thoroughfare

velho [**veh**l-yoo] old

venda f [**vayn**da] sale

vendem-se [**vayn**daynsi] for sale

vender [vayn**dayr**] to sell

vende-se [**vayn**di-si] for sale

ver [vayr] to look; to see

Verão m [vi**row**ng] summer

verde [vayrd] green

vermelho [vir**mayl**-yoo] red

vestir [vish**teer**] to dress

vez f [vaysh] time

em vez [ayng] instead

viagem f [v-ya**Jay**ng] journey

vida f [**vee**da] life

viola f [v-**yo**la] Portuguese guitar

vir [veer] to come

viver [vi**vayr**] to live

você [vo**say**], vocês [vo**saysh**] you

voo m [**voh**-oo] flight

zona azul f [zohna**zool**] parking permit zone

MENU READER

Food: Essential terms

bread o pão [**pow**ng]
butter a manteiga [mant**ay**ga]
cup a chávena [**sha**vena]
dessert a sobremesa
  [sobri**may**za]
fish o peixe [**pay**-ish]
fork o garfo [**gar**foo]
glass o copo [**ko**poo]
knife a faca
main course o prato principal
  [**pra**too prinsi**pal**]
meat a carne [karn]
menu a ementa [e**mayn**ta]
pepper a pimenta [pi**mayn**ta]
plate o prato [**pra**too]
salad a salada

salt o sal
set menu a ementa fixa
  [e**mayn**ta **feek**sa]
soup a sopa [**soh**pa]
spoon a colher [kool-**yehr**]
starter a entrada [ayn**tra**da]
table a mesa [**may**za]

another ..., please outro/
  outra ..., por favor [**oh**troo –
  poor fa**vohr**]
excuse me! se faz favor! [si
  fash]
could I have the bill, please?
  pode-me dar a conta, por
  favor? [**pod**-mi – poor fa**vohr**]

Food: Menu Reader

abóbora [a**bo**boora] pumpkin
acepipes [asi**pee**pish] hors
  d'oeuvres
açorda de alho [a**sohr**da dal-yoo]
  thick soup of bread and

garlic
açúcar [a**soo**kar] sugar
agriões [agr-**yoyng**sh]
  watercress
aipo [**ī**poo] celery

433

alcachofra [alkashohfra] artichoke

alface [alfas] lettuce

alheira [al-yayra] garlic sausage

alho [al-yoo] garlic

alho francês [fransaysh] leek

almóndegas [almohndigash] meatballs

alperces [alpehrsish] apricots

amêijoas [amayJwash] clams

ameixa [amaysha] plum

ameixas secas [saykas] prunes

amêndoas [amayndwash] almonds

amoras [amorash] blackberries

ananás [ananash] pineapple

anchovas [anshohvash] anchovies

anho à moda do Minho [an-yoo a moda doo meen-yoo] roast lamb served with rice

aniz [aneesh] aniseed

ao natural [ow natooral] plain

arroz [arrohsh] rice

ao ponto [pohntoo] medium-rare

assado [asadoo] roasted

atum [atoong] tuna

avelãs [avilangsh] hazelnuts

aves [avish] poultry

azeite [azayt] olive oil

azeitonas [azaytohnash] olives

bacalhau [bakal-yow] dried salted cod

batata assada [batatasada] baked potato

batatas [batatash] potatoes

batatas fritas [freetash] chips,

bem passado [bayng pasadoo] well-done

berbigão [birbeegowng] shellfish similar to mussels

berinjela [bireenJehla] aubergine, eggplant

besugos [bizoogoosh] sea bream

beterraba [biterraba] beetroot

bife [beef] steak

bolacha [boolasha] biscuit, cookie

bola de carne [di karn] meatball

bolo [bohloo] cake

bolos e bolachas [bohlooz ee boolashash] cakes and biscuits/cookies

borrego [boorraygoo] lamb

broa [broh-a] maize/corn bread or rye bread

cabreiro [kabrayroo] goat's cheese

cabrito [kabreetoo] kid

caça [kasa] game

cachorro [kashohrroo] hot dog

caldeirada [kaldayrada] fish stew

caldo [kaldoo] broth

caldo verde [vayrd] cabbage soup

camarões [kamaroyngsh] prawns

canela [kanehla] cinammon

caracóis [karakoysh] snails

caranguejo [karangayJoo] crab

carapau [karapow] mackerel

caril [kareel] curry

carne [karn] meat

carne de cabrito [di kabr**ee**too] kid

carne de porco [di p**oh**rkoo] pork

carne de vaca [**vaka**] beef

carneiro [karn**ay**roo] mutton

carnes frias [**karn**ish fr**ee**-ash] selection of cold meats

caseiro [kaz**ay**roo] home-made

castanhas [kashtan-yash] chestnuts

cebola [sib**oh**la] onion

cenoura [sin**oh**ra] carrot

cerejas [sir**ay**jash] cherries

cherne [shehrn] sea bream

chocos [sh**oh**koosh] cuttlefish

chouriço [shoor**ee**soo] spiced sausage

churros [sh**oo**rrosh] long thin fritters

codorniz [koodoorn**ee**sh] quail

coelho [kw**ay**l-yoo] rabbit

coêntros [kw**ay**ntroosh] coriander

cogumelos [kogoom**eh**loosh] mushrooms

compota stewed fruit

compota de laranja [di laranJa] marmalade

conquilhas [konk**ee**l-yash] baby clams

consomme [konsoom**ay**] consommé, clear meat soup

coração [koorasowng] heart

costeleta [kooshtil**ay**ta] chop

couve [kohv] cabbage

couve-flor [kohv flohr] cauliflower

couves de bruxelas [kohvsh di br**oo**sh**ehl**ash] Brussels sprouts

cozido [kooz**ee**doo] boiled; stewed; poached; cooked (either in a sauce or with olive oil); stew

creme de mariscos [mar**ee**shkoosh] cream of shellfish soup

cru/crua [kroo/kr**oo**-a] raw

damasco [dam**ash**koo] apricot

dobrada [doobr**ada**] tripe with chickpeas

doce [dohs] jam; any sweet dish or dessert

dourada [dohr**ada**] dory (saltwater fish); browned, golden brown

eirozes [ayr**o**zish] eels

empada pie

enguias [ayng**ee**-ash] eels

ensopado de ... [aynsoop**ado** di] ... stew

entradas [ayntr**ada**sh] starters, appetizers

ervas [**ehr**vash] herbs

ervilhas [irv**ee**l-yash] peas

espaguete à bolonhesa [shpag**eh**t a booloon-y**ay**za] spaghetti bolognese

espargos [shp**argoo**sh] asparagus

esparregado [shparrig**ado**o] stew made from chopped green vegetables

especiaria [shpis-yar**ee**-a] spice

espetada mista [m**ee**shta] mixed kebab

espinafre [shpin**afr**] spinach

estragão [shtragowng] tarragon
estufado [shtoofadoo] stewed
faisão [fizowng] pheasant
farturas [fartoorash] long thin fritters
favas [favash] broad beans
feijão [fayJowng] beans
feijoada [fayJwada] bean and meat stew
feijões verdes [vayrdish] French beans
fiambre [f-yambr] ham
fígado [feegadoo] liver
figos [feegoosh] figs
framboesa [frambwayza] raspberry
frango [frangoo] chicken
frito [freetoo] fried
fruta [froota] fruit
fumado [foomadoo] smoked
funcho [foonshoo] fennel
galinha [galeen-ya] chicken
galinha de África [dafreeka] guinea fowl
gambas [gambash] prawns
ganso [gansoo] goose
garoupa [garohpa] fish similar to bream
gaspacho [gaspashoo] chilled vegetable soup
gelado [Jiladoo] ice cream
geleia [Jilay-a] preserve
gengibre [JaynJeebr] ginger
grão [growng] chickpeas
grelhado [gril-yadoo] grilled
guisado [geezadoo] stewed
hortaliças [ortaleesash] green vegetables
hortelã [ortilang] mint

jantar [Jantar] evening meal, dinner; supper
jardineira [Jardinayra] mixed vegetables
lagosta [lagohshta] lobster
lampreia [lampray-a] lamprey
laranja [laranJa] orange
lasanha [lasan-ya] lasagne
legumes [ligoomish] vegetables
leitão assado [laytowng asadoo] roast sucking pig
leite [layt] milk
limão [limowng] lemon
língua [leengwa] tongue
linguado [lingwadoo] sole
lombo [lohmboo] loin
louro [lohroo] bay leaf
lulas [loolash] squid
maçã [masang] apple
maionese [mī-oonehz] mayonnaise
mal passado [pasadoo] rare
manjericão [manJirikowng] basil
manteiga [mantayga] butter
mariscos [mareeshkoosh] shellfish
marmelada [marmilada] quince jam
marmelos [marmehloosh] quinces
massa pasta
mel [mehl] honey
melancia [milansee-a] watermelon
melão [milowng] melon
melocotão [milookootowng] peach
mexilhões [mishil-yoyngsh] mussels

migas à Alentejana [**mee**gaz a alaynti**J**ana] thick bread soup

miolos [m-y**o**loosh] brains

míscaros [**mee**shkaroosh] mushrooms

moleja [moolay**J**a] soup made from pig's blood

molho [**moh**l-yoo] sauce

morangos [moor**a**ngoosh] strawberries

morcela [moors**eh**la] black pudding, blood sausage

mostarda [moosht**a**rda] mustard

na brasa [br**a**za] charcoal-grilled

natas [**na**tash] cream

nêsperas [**nay**shpirash] loquats (yellow fruit similar to a plum)

no churrasco [noo shoorr**a**shkoo] barbecued

no espeto [noosh**pay**too] spit-roasted

no forno [**foh**rno] baked

nozes [**no**zish] walnuts

óleo [**ol**-yoo] oil

ostras [**oh**shtrash] oysters

ovo [**oh**voo] egg

pão [powng] bread

pargo [**pa**rgoo] sea bream

parrilhada [pareel-y**a**da] grilled fish

passas [**pa**sash] raisins

pastéis [pasht**eh**-ish] pastries

pastel [pasht**eh**l] cake; pie

pataniscas [patan**ee**shkash] dried cod fritters

pato [**pa**too] duck

peixe [paysh] fish

peixe espada [sh**pa**da] swordfish

pepino [pip**ee**noo] cucumber

pequeno almoço [pik**ay**noo alm**oh**soo] breakfast

pêra [**pay**ra] pear

pêra abacate [abak**a**t] avocado

percebes [pirs**eh**bish] shellfish similar to barnacles

perdiz [pird**ee**sh] partridge

perna [**peh**rna] leg

peru [pir**oo**] turkey

pescada [pishk**a**da] hake

pêssego [**pay**sigoo] peach

pêssego careca [kar**eh**ka] nectarine

petiscos [pit**ee**shkoosh] savouries

picante [pik**a**nt] hot, spicy

pimenta [pim**ay**nta] pepper

pimentos [pim**ay**nt**oo**sh] peppers, capsicums

piperate [peepir**a**t] pepper stew

piri-piri [**pee**ree-**pee**ree] seasoning made from chillies and olive oil

polvo [**poh**lvoo] octopus

porco [**poh**rkoo] pork

prato [**pra**too] dish; course

presunto [priz**oo**ntoo] ham

puré de batata [poor**ay** di] mashed potatoes

p.v. (preço variado) [**pray**soo var-y**a**doo] price varies

queijo [**kay**Joo] cheese

raia [**rī**-a] skate

requeijão [rikay**Jo**wng] curd cheese

rins [reensh] kidneys

robalo [roob**a**loo] rock bass

rolo de carne [**roh**loo di karn]
meat loaf

sal salt

salada salad

salgado [salg**a**doo] savoury,
salty

salmão [salm**ow**ng] salmon

salmonete [salmoon**ayt**] red
mullet

salsa parsley

salsicha [sals**ee**sha] sausage

salteado [salt-y**a**doo] sautéed

sandes [**san**dish] sandwich

santola spider crab

sapateira [sapat**ay**ra] spider
crab

sarda mackerel

sardinha [sard**een**-ya] sardine

sobremesas [sobrim**ay**zash]
desserts

solha [**sohl**-ya] flounder

sopa [**sohp**a] soup

taxa de serviço [**ta**sha di
sirv**ee**soo] service charge

tempero da salada [taymp**ay**roo
da sal**a**da] salad dressing

tomar [too**mar**] fresh soft goat's
cheese

tomate [too**mat**] tomato

tomilho [too**mee**l-yoo] thyme

toranja [toor**an**Ja] grapefruit

torrada [toor**ra**da] toast

torta tart

tortilha [toort**eel**-ya] Spanish–
style omelette with potato

tosta [**tosh**ta] toasted sandwich

tripas [**tree**pash] tripe

truta [**troo**ta] trout

uvas [**oo**vash] grapes

veado assado [v-y**a**doo as**a**doo]
roast venison

vieiras recheadas [v-y**ay**rash
rish-y**a**dash] scallops filled
with seafood

vitela [vit**eh**la] veal

Drink: Essential terms

beer a cerveja [sirvayJa]
bottle a garrafa
brandy o brandy
coffee o café [kafeh]
cup: a cup of ... uma chávena di ...[ooma shavena di]
gin o gin [Jeeng]
 a gin and tonic um gin-tónico [oong Jeeng tonikoo]
glass: a glass of ... um copo de ... [oong kopoo di]
milk o leite [layt]
mineral water a água mineral [agwa]
orange juice o sumo de laranja [soomoo di laranJa]
port o vinho do Porto [veen-yoo doo pohrtoo]
red wine o vinho tinto [teentoo]

rosé rosé [roozay]
soda (water) a soda
soft drink a bebida não alcoólica [bibeeda nowng alko-oleeka]
sugar o açúcar [asookar]
tea o chá [sha]
tonic (water) a água tónica
vodka o vodka
water a água [agwa]
whisky o whisky [weeshkee]
white wine o vinho branco [veen-yoo brankoo]
wine o vinho [veen-yoo]
wine list a lista dos vinhos [leeshta dooJ veen-yoosh]

another ..., please outro/outra ..., por favor [ohtroo – poor favohr]

Drink: Menu Reader

aguardente [agwardaynt] clear spirit/brandy
aguardente de figo [feegoo] fig brandy
aguardentes bagaceiras [agwardayntish bagasayrash] clear spirit/brandy distilled from grape skins
amêndoa amarga [amayndwa amarga] bitter almond liqueur

bagaço [bagasoo] clear spirit/brandy
batido de leite [bateedoo di layt] milkshake
bica [beeka] small black espresso–type coffee
café com pingo [kafeh kong peengoo] espresso with brandy
café duplo [dooploo] two

439

espressos in the same cup

capilé [kapileh] drink made from water, sugar and syrup

carapinhada de café [karapeen-yada di kafeh] coffee drink with crushed ice

carioca [kar-yoka] small weak black coffee

cerveja [sirvayJa] beer

cerveja branca [branka] lager

cerveja de pressão [di prisowng] draught beer

cerveja preta [prayta] bitter, dark beer

chá de limão [sha di limowng] infusion of hot water with a lemon rind

chá de lucialima [loos-yaleema] herb tea

cimbalino small espresso

doce [dohs] sweet (usually very sweet)

figo [feegoo] fig brandy

galão [galowng] large weak milky coffee in a tall glass

garoto [garohtoo] small coffee with milk

garrafeira [garrafayra] high-quality red wine

gelo [Jayloo] ice

ginja [JeenJa], **ginjinha** [JeenJeen-ya] brandy with sugar and cherries added

italiana [ital-yana] half a very strong espresso

leite [layt] milk

licor de medronho [di midrohn-yoo] berry liqueur

licor de whisky [weeshkee]

whisky liqueur

limonada [limoonada] fresh lemon juice with water and sugar

Malvasia [malvasee-a] Malmsey wine, a sweet heavy Madeira wine

Madeira [madayra] sweet and dry fortified wine

mazagrin [mazagrang] iced coffee with lemon

meia de leite [may-a di layt] large white coffee

meio seco [may-oo saykoo] medium-dry (usually fairly sweet)

morena [moorayna] mixture of lager and bitter

pingo [peengoo] small coffee with milk

seco [saykoo] dry

sumo de lima lime juice

sumo de limão [limowng] lemon juice

vinho branco [veen-yoo brankoo] white wine

vinho da casa [kaza] house wine

vinho de Xerêz [shiraysh] sherry

vinho espumante [shpoomant] sparkling wine

vinho tinto [teentoo] red wine

vinho verde [vayrd] young, slightly sparkling white, red, or rosé wine

xarope de morango [moorangoo] strawberry cordial

SPANISH

DICTIONARY PHRASEBOOK

Pronunciation

In this phrasebook, the Spanish has been written in a system of imitated pronunciation so that it can be read as though it were English, bearing in mind the notes on pronunciation given below:

- air   as in h**air**
- ay   as in m**ay**
- e   as in g**e**t
- g   always hard as in **g**oat
- H   a harsh 'ch' as in the Scottish way of pronouncing lo**ch**
- ī   as the 'i' sound in m**i**ght
- ow   as in n**ow**
- y   as in **y**es

Letters given in bold type indicate the part of the word to be stressed.

As **i** and **u** are always pronounced 'ee' and 'oo' in Spanish, pronunciation has not been given for all words containing these letters unless they present other problems for the learner. Thus **María** is pronounced 'mar**ee**-a' and **fútbol** is 'f**oo**tbol'.

Language Notes

Spanish nouns have one of two genders – masculine or feminine. Words for 'the' are **el (m)** and **la (f)**:

el piso	**la cama**
the apartment	the bed

The corresponding words for 'a' are **un (m)** and **una (f)**:

un sello	**una chica**
a stamp	a girl

In the plural **el** becomes **los** and **la** becomes **las**.

When **el** is used together with **a** (to, at) or **de** (of, from) it changes:

vamos al museo
let's go to the museum

el precio del coche
the price of the car

The Spanish words for 'I', 'you', 'he' etc are usually omitted as subjects unless special emphasis is required. For example:

está cansada
she is tired

ella non está cansada
she isn't tired (although the others all are)

Here is a useful verb - 'to be'. Spanish has two verbs for this. One is **ser**:

soy I am

eres [airess] you are
(familiar form)

es [ess]he/she/it is; you are
(polite singular form)

somos we are

sois [soyss] you are
(plural familiar form)

son they are; you are
(plural polite form)

And the other **estar**:

estoy [est**oy]** I am

estás [est**ass]** you are
(familiar form)

está [est**a]** he/she/it is;
you are (polite singular form)

estamos [estamoss] we are

estaís [esta-eesss] you are
(plural familiar form)

están [estan] they are;
you are (plural polite form)

Ser is used for permanent conditions and **estar** for conditions which can change. For example:

somos escoceses
we're Scottish

estamos cansados
we're tired

The familiar forms are used to speak to people you are on friendly terms with. When using the polite form, the verb takes the same form as for 'he/she/it' or, if plural, as for 'they'.

Days

Monday lunes [**loo**ness]
Tuesday martes [**mar**tess]
Wednesday miércoles [m-**yair**koless]
Thursday jueves [Hway**bess]
Friday viernes [b-**yair**ness]
Saturday sábado
Sunday domingo

Months

January enero [e**nair**o]
February febrero [fe**brair**o]
March marzo [**mar**tho]
April abril [a**bril**]
May maio [**ma**-yo]
June junio [**H**oon-yo]
July julio [**H**ool-yo]
August agosto
September septiembre [sept-**yem**bray]
October octubre [ok**too**bray]
November noviembre [nob-**yem**bray]
December diciembre [deeth-**yem**bray]

Time

what time is it? ¿qué hora es? [kay **o**ra ess]
one o'clock la una [la **oo**na]
two o'clock las dos [lass doss]
it's one o'clock es la una [ess la **oo**na]

it's two o'clock son las dos [son lass doss]
it's ten o'clock son las diez [son lass d-yeth]
five past one la una y cinco [la **oo**na ee **th**eenko]
ten past two las dos y diez [lass doss ee d-yeth]
quarter past one la una y cuarto [la **oo**na ee **kwar**to]
quarter past two las dos y cuarto [lass doss ee **kwar**to]
half past ten las diez y media [lass d-yeth ee **mayd**-ya]
twenty to ten las diez menos veinte [lass d-yeth **may**noss **bay**-eentay]
quarter to ten las diez menos cuarto [lass d-yeth **may**noss **kwar**to]
at eight o'clock a las ocho [a lass **o**cho]
at half past four a las cuatro y media [a lass **kwat**ro ee **mayd**-ya]
2 a.m. las dos de la mañana [lass doss day la man-**ya**na]
2 p.m. las dos de la tarde [lass doss day la **tar**day]
6 a.m. las seis de la mañana [lass say-eess day la man-**ya**na]
6 p.m. las seis de la tarde [lass say-eess day la **tar**day]
noon mediodía [**mayd**-yo **dee**-a]
midnight medianoche [**mayd**-ya **no**chay]
an hour una hora [**oo**na **o**ra]
a minute un minuto [oon

meen**oo**to]

two minutes dos minutos
[doss meen**oo**toss]

a second un segundo [oon
seg**oo**ndo]

a quarter of an hour un
cuarto de hora [kw**a**rto day
ora]

half an hour media hora
[**may**d-ya **o**ra]

three quarters of an hour
tres cuartos de hora [tress
kw**a**rtoss day **o**ra]

Numbers

0   cero [th**ai**ro]
1   uno, una [**oo**no, **oo**na]
2   dos [doss]
3   tres [tress]
4   cuatro [kw**a**tro]
5   cinco [**theen**ko]
6   seis [say-eess]
7   siete [s-y**ay**tay]
8   ocho [**o**cho]
9   nueve [nw**ay**bay]
10 diez [d-yeth]
11 once [**on**thay]
12 doce [**do**thay]
13 trece [**tray**thay]
14 catorce [kat**or**thay]
15 quince [**keen**thay]
16 dieciséis [d-yethees**ay**-eess]
17 diecisiete [d-yethees-y**ay**tay]
18 dieciocho [d-yethee-**o**cho]
19 diecinueve
    [d-yetheen**way**bay]
20 veinte [b**ay-ee**ntay]

21 veintiuno [bay-eentee-
    oono]
22 veintidós [bay-eented**oss**]
23 veintitrés [bay-eentee**tress**]
30 treinta [**tray-ee**nta]
31 treinta y uno [**tray-ee**ntĭ
    oono]
40 cuarenta [kw**a**renta]
50 cincuenta [theenkw**e**nta]
60 sesenta [ses**e**nta]
70 setenta [set**e**nta]
80 ochenta [och**e**nta]
90 noventa [nob**e**nta]
100 cien [th-yen]
120 ciento veinte [th-y**e**nto
    bay-**ee**ntay]
200 doscientos, doscientas
    [dosth-y**e**ntoss, dosth-
    y**e**ntass]
300 trescientos, trescientas
    [tresth-y**e**ntoss, tresth-
    y**e**ntass]
400 cuatrocientos, cuatro-
    cientas [kwatroth-y**e**ntoss,
    kwatroth-y**e**ntass]
500 quinientos, quinientas
    [keen-y**e**ntoss, keen-y**e**ntass]
600 seiscientos, seiscientas
    [say-eesth-y**e**ntoss, say-eesth-
    y**e**ntass]
700 setecientos, setecientas
    [seteth-y**e**ntoss, seteth-yen-
    tass]
800 ochocientos, ochocien-
    tas [ochoth-y**e**ntoss, ochoth-
    y**e**ntass]
900 novecientos, novecien-
    tas [nobeth-y**e**ntoss, nobeth-
    y**e**ntass]

1,000	mil [meel]
2,000	dos mil [doss meel]
5,000	cinco mil [theenko meel]
10,000	diez mil [d-yeth meel]
1,000,000	un millón [meel-yon]

With multiples of a hundred, the **-as** ending is used with feminine nouns:

trescientos hombres
tresth-yentoss ombress
300 men

quinientas mujeres
keen-yentass mooHairess
500 women

Ordinals

1st	primero [preemairo]
2nd	segundo [segoondo]
3rd	tercero [tairthairo]
4th	cuarto [kwarto]
5th	quinto [keento]
6th	sexto [sesto]
7th	séptimo [septeemo]
8th	octavo [oktabo]
9th	noveno [nobayno]
10th	décimo [detheemo]

English

→

Spanish

a, an un, una [oon, **oo**na]
about aproximadamente
[aproxima**da**mentay]
  about 20 unos veinte
  a film about Spain una
  película sobre España
  [**so**bray]
above ... encima de ...
[en**thee**ma day]
abroad en el extranjero
[estran**H**airo]
accept aceptar [athep**tar**]
accident el accidente
[akthee**den**tay]
across: across the road al
  otro lado de la calle [**ka**-yay]
adapter el adaptador
address la dirección
[**D**eerekth-**yon**]
adult el adulto
advance: in advance por
  adelantado
after después (de) [des**pwess**
  day]
afternoon la tarde [**tar**day]
aftersun cream la crema para
  después del sol [**kray**ma **pa**ra
  des**pwess**]
afterwards después [des**pwess**]
again otra vez [beth]
against contra
ago: a week ago hace una
  semana [**a**thay]
AIDS el SIDA [**see**da]
air el aire [a-**ee**ray]
  by air en avión [ab-**yon**]

air-conditioning el aire
  acondicionado [a-eeray
  akondeeth-**yo**nado]
airmail: by airmail por avión
  [ab-**yon**]
airport el aeropuerto
  [a-airop**wair**to]
airport bus el autobús del
  aeropuerto [owto**booss**]
alcohol el alcohol [**al**kol]
all todos
  that's all, thanks eso es todo,
  gracias [**ay**so]
allergic alérgico/alérgica
  [a**lair**Heeko]
all right ¡bien! [b-yen]
  I'm all right estoy bien
  are you all right? (fam) ¿estás
  bien?
  (pol) ¿se encuentra bien?
  [say enk**way**ntra]
almost casi
alone solo
already ya
also también [tamb-**yen**]
altogether del todo
always siempre [s-**yem**pray]
ambulance la ambulancia
  [amboo**lanth**-ya]
America América
American (adj) americano
and y [ee]
angry enfadado
animal el animal
annoying molesto
another otro
  another beer, please otra
  cerveza, por favor
antiseptic el antiséptico

any: I don't have any no tengo

apartment el apartamento, el piso

apple la manzana [man**tha**na]

apricot el albaricoque [albari**ko**kay]

arm el brazo [**bra**tho]

arrival la llegada [ye**ga**da]

arrive llegar [ye**gar**]

art gallery el museo de bellas artes [moos**ay**-o day **bay**-yass **art**ess]

(smaller) la galería de arte [galai**ree**-a]

as: as big as tan grande como [**gran**day]

ashtray el cenicero [thaynee**thai**ro]

ask preguntar [pregoon**tar**]

I didn't ask for this no había pedido eso [ab**ee**-a – **ay**so]

aspirin la aspirina

at: at the hotel en el hotel

at the station en la estación

at six o'clock a las seis

at Pedro's en la casa de Pedro

aunt la tía [**tee**-a]

Australia Australia [**owstral**-ya]

Australian (adj) australiano

automatic teller el cajero automático [ka**Hai**ro]

autumn el otoño [o**ton**-yo]

away: go away! ¡lárguese! [**largay**say]

awful terrible [te**rree**blay]

B

baby el bebé [bay**bay**]

back (of body) la espalda

(back part) la parte de atrás [**partay** day]

at the back en la parte de atrás

I'll be back soon volveré pronto [bolbair**ay** ayng brev]

bad malo

badly mal

(injured) gravemente [grabem**ay**ntay]

bag la bolsa

(handbag) el bolso

baggage el equipaje [ekeepa**Hay**]

baggage checkroom la consigna [kon**see**gna]

bakery la panadería [panadai**ree**-a]

balcony el balcón

Balearic Islands las Baleares [balay-**ar**ess]

ball (large) la pelota

(small) la bola

banana el plátano

band (musical) el grupo

bandage la venda [**ben**da]

Bandaid® la tirita

bank (money) el banco

bar el bar

barber's el barbero [bar**bai**ro]

basket el cesto [**thes**to]

(in shop) la cesta

bath el baño [**ban**-yo]

bathroom el cuarto de baño

[kwarto]
battery la pila
(car) la batería [batairee-a]
Bay of Biscay el Golfo de
Vizcaya [day beethkaya]
be ser [sair]; estar [aystar]
beach la playa [pla-ya]
beach umbrella la sombrilla
[sombree-ya]
beans las judías [Hoodee-ass]
beautiful bonito
because porque [porkay]
because of ... debido a ...
[debeedo]
bed la cama
I'm going to bed now me
voy a acostar ya [may boy]
bed and breakfast habitación
y desayuno [abeetath-yon ee
desa-yoono]
bedroom el dormitorio
[dormeetor-yo]
beef la carne de vaca [karnay
day baka]
beer la cerveza [thairbaytha]
before antes [antess]
begin empezar [empethar]
when does it begin? ¿cuándo
empieza? [kwando emp-yetha]
behind detrás
below abajo [abaHo]
belt el cinturón [theentooron]
berth (on ship) el camarote
[kamarotay]
beside ... al lado de ...
best el mejor [meHor]
better mejor
between entre [entray]
beyond más allá [a-ya]

bicycle la bicicleta
[beetheeklayta]
big grande [granday]
bikini el bikini [beekeenee]
bill la cuenta [kwenta]
(US: banknote) el billete [bee-
yaytay]
could I have the bill, please?
la cuenta, por favor
bin el cubo de la basura
[koobo day]
bird el pájaro [paHaro]
birthday el cumpleaños
[koomplayan-yoss]
happy birthday! ¡feliz
cumpleaños! [feleeth]
biscuit la galleta [ga-yeta]
bit: a little bit un poquito
[pokeeto]
a big bit un pedazo grande
[pedatho granday]
a bit of ... un pedazo de ...
a bit expensive un poco caro
bite (by insect) la picadura
black negro [naygro]
blanket la manta
blind ciego [th-yaygo]
blinds las persianas [pers-
yanass]
block of flats el bloque de
apartamentos [blokay day]
blond rubio [roob-yo]
blood la sangre [sangray]
blouse la blusa [bloosa]
blow-dry secar a mano
blue azul [athool]
boat el barco
body el cuerpo [kwairpo]
boiler la caldera [kaldaira]

bone el hueso [**way**so]
book el libro [**lee**bro]
(verb) reservar [resair**bar**]
bookshop, bookstore la
librería [leebrair**ee**-a]
boot (footwear) la bota
border (of country) la frontera
[fron**tair**a]
borrow pedir prestado
both los dos
bottle la botella [bo**tay**-ya]
bottle-opener el abrebotellas
[abraybo**tay**-yass]
bottom (of person) el trasero
[tra**ssair**o]
at the bottom of the ...
(hill/road) al pie del/de la ...
[p-**yay** del/day]
box la caja [**ka**Ha]
boy el chico
boyfriend el amigo
bra el sujetador [sooHeta**dor**]
bracelet la pulsera [pool**sair**a]
brake el freno [**frayn**o]
brandy el coñac [kon-**yak**]
bread el pan
break romper [rom**pair**]
breakfast el desayuno [desa-**yoon**o]
breast el pecho [**paych**o]
bridge (over river) el puente
[**pwent**ay]
bring traer [tra-**air**]
I'll bring it back later lo
devolveré después [lo
daybolbair**ay** despw**ess**]
Britain Gran Bretaña [bretan-ya]
British británico

brochure el folleto [fo-**yet**o]
broken roto
brother el hermano [air**man**o]
brown marrón
(hair, eyes) castaño [cas**tan**-yo]
brush (for hair, cleaning) el
cepillo [the**pee**-yo]
building el edificio [edeefe**eeth**-yo]
bulb (light bulb) la bombilla
[bom**bee**-ya]
bull el toro
bullfight la corrida de toros
[day]
bullfighter el torero [to**rair**o]
bullring la plaza de toros
[**plath**a day]
bunk la litera [lee**tair**a]
burn la quemadura
[kema**door**a]
burst: a burst pipe una
cañería rota [kan-yair**ee**-a]
bus el autobús [owto**booss**]
what number bus is it to ...?
¿qué número es para ...?
[kay **noo**mairo]

dialogue

does this bus go to ...?
¿este autobús va a ...?
[**estay** owto**booss** ba]
no, you need a number ...
no, tiene que coger el ...
[t-**yay**nay kay ko**Hair**]

bus station la estación de
autobuses [estath-**yon** day
owto**boo**sess]

bus stop la parada de autobús
busy (restaurant etc) concurrido
but pero [pairo]
butcher's la carnicería [karneethairee-a]
butter la mantequilla [mantekee-ya]
button el botón
buy comprar
by: by bus/car en autobús/coche
by the window junto a la ventana [Hoonto]
by Thursday para el jueves

C

cabbage el repollo [repo-yo]
cabin (on ship) el camarote [kamarotay]
cable car el teleférico [telefaireeko]
café la cafetería [kafetairee-a]
cake el pastel [pastayl]
call (verb) llamar [yamar]
(to phone) llamar (por teléfono)
what's it called? cómo se llama esto? [say yama]
he/she is called ... se llama ...
camera la máquina de fotos [makeena]
camp acampar
camping gas el butano [bootano]

campsite el camping
can la lata
can: can you ...? ¿puede ...? [pwayday]
can I have ...? ¿me da ...? [may]
I can't ... no puedo ...
Canada el Canadá
Canadian canadiense [kanad-yensay]
Canaries las Islas Canarias [eeslass kanar-yass]
cancel anular [anoolar]
candies los caramelos [karamayloss]
candle la vela [bayla]
can-opener el abrelatas
car el coche [kochay]
carafe la garrafa
card (birthday etc) la tarjeta [tarHayta]
cardphone el teléfono de tarjeta [telayfono day tarHeta]
car hire el alquiler de coches [alkeelair day]
car park el aparcamiento [aparkam-yento]
carpet la moqueta [mokayta]
carrot la zanahoria [thana-or-ya]
carry llevar [yebar]
cash el dinero [deenairo]
cash desk la caja [kaHa]
cash dispenser el cajero automático [kaHairo owtomateeko]
castanets las castañuelas [kastan-ywaylass]
Castilian castellano [kastay-

yano]

castle el castillo [kastee-yo]

cat el gato

cathedral la catedral

cave la cueva [kwayba]

ceiling el techo [taycho]

cellar (for wine) la bodega [bodayga]

centimetre el centímetro [thenteemetro]

centre el centro [thentro]

certainly desde luego [desday lwaygo]

chair la silla [see-ya]

champagne el champán

change (money) el cambio [kamb-yo]
(verb) cambiar [kamb-yar]

dialogue

do we have to change (trains)? ¿tenemos que cambiar de tren?
[tenaymoss kay kamb-yar]
yes, change at Córdoba/no it's a direct train sí, cambie en Córdoba/no, es un tren directo [kamb-yay]

cheap barato

check (US) el cheque [chaykay]
(US: bill) la cuenta [kwaynta]
(verb) revisar [rebeesar]

check book el talonario de cheques [chaykess]

check-in la facturación [faktoorath-yon]

cheers! (toast) ¡salud! [saloo]

cheese el queso [kayso]

chemist's la farmacia [farmath-ya]

cheque el cheque [chaykay]

cheque card la tarjeta de banco [tarHayta]

chest el pecho [paycho]

chewing gum el chicle [cheeklay]

chicken el pollo [po-yo]

child el niño [neen-yo]/la niña

chips las patatas fritas

chocolate el chocolate [chokolatay]
a hot chocolate la taza de chocolate [tatha]

Christmas Navidad [nabeeda]
Christmas Eve Nochebuena [nochay-bwayna]
merry Christmas! ¡Feliz Navidad! [feleeth]

church la iglesia [eeglays-ya]

cider la sidra [seedra]

cigar el puro [pooro]

cigarette el cigarro [theegarro], el cigarrillo [theegarree-yo]

cinema el cine [theenay]

city la ciudad [thee-oo-da]

city centre el centro de la ciudad [thentro day]

clean (adj) limpio [leemp-yo]
can you clean these for me? ¿puede limpiarme estos?
[pwayday leemp-yarmay]

clever listo

climbing el alpinismo

clock el reloj [reloH]

close (verb) cerrar [therrar]
closed cerrado [thairrado]
clothes la ropa
clothes peg la pinza de la
  ropa [peentha day]
cloudy nublado
coach (bus) el autocar
  [owtokar]
  (on train) el vagón [bagon]
coach station la estación de
  autobuses [estath-yon day
  owtoboosess]
coach trip la excursión (en
  autobús) [eskoorss-yon]
coast la costa
coat (long coat) el abrigo
  (jacket) la chaqueta [chakayta]
coathanger la percha [paircha]
code (for phoning) el prefijo
  [prefeeHo]
coffee el café [kafay]
coin la moneda [monayda]
Coke® la Coca-Cola
cold frío [free-o]
  I'm cold tengo frío
  I have a cold tengo catarro
collar el cuello [kway-yo]
collect call la llamada a cobro
  revertido [yamada –
  rebairteedo]
colour el color
comb el peine [pay-eenay]
come venir [bayneer]
come back volver [bolbair]
come in entrar
comfortable cómodo
complaint la queja [kayHa]
completely completamente
  [komplaytamentay]

computer el ordenador
concert el concierto [konth-
  yairto]
conditioner (for hair) el
  acondicionador de pelo
  [akondeeth-yonador day paylo]
condom el condón
congratulations!
  ¡enhorabuena! [enorabwayna]
connection el enlace [enlathay]
constipation el estreñimiento
  [estren-yeem-yento]
consulate el consulado
  [konsoolado]
contact ponerse en contacto
  con [ponairsay]
contact lenses las lentes de
  contacto, las lentillas [lentess
  – lentee-yass]
cooker la cocina [kotheena]
cookie la galleta [ga-yayta]
corkscrew el sacacorchos
correct (right) correcto
cost costar
cotton el algodón
cotton wool el algodón
couchette la litera [leetaira]
cough la tos
cough medicine la medicina
  para la tos [medeetheena]
could: could you ...?
  ¿podría ...?
  could I have ...? quisiera ...
  [kees-yaira...]
  I couldn't ... (wasn't able to) no
  podía ...
country (nation) el país [pa-
  eess]
  (countryside) el campo

couple (two people) la pareja [parayHa]

a couple of ... un par de ... [day]

courier el/la guía turístico [gee-a]

course (main course etc) el plato

of course por supuesto [soopwesto]

cousin el primo [preemo]/la prima

crazy loco

cream (on milk, in cake) la nata (lotion) la crema [krayma]

credit card la tarjeta de crédito [tarHayta day]

dialogue

can I pay by credit card? ¿puedo pagar con tarjeta? [pwaydo]
which card do you want to use? ¿qué tarjeta quiere usar? [kay – k-yairay oosar]
yes, sir sí, señor [sen-yor]
what's the number? ¿qué número es? [noomairo]
and the expiry date? ¿y la fecha de caducidad? [fecha day kadootheeda]

crisps las patatas fritas (de bolsa)

crossroads el cruce [kroothay]

crowded lleno [yayno]

cry llorar [yorar]

cup la taza [tatha]

cupboard el armario [armar-yo]

curtains las cortinas

cushion el cojín [koHeen]

Customs la aduana [adwana]

cyclist el/la ciclista [theekleesta]

D

dad el papá

damn! ¡maldita sea! [say-a]

damp húmedo [oomaydo]

dance el baile [ba-eelay]
(verb) bailar [ba-eelar]

dangerous peligroso

dark (adj: colour) oscuro [oskooro]
(hair) moreno [morayno]

date: what's the date today? ¿qué día es hoy? [kay – oy]

dates (fruit) los dátiles [dateeless]

daughter la hija [eeHa]

day el día

the day after el día siguiente [seeg-yentay]

the day before el día anterior [antair-yor]

dead muerto [mwairto]

deaf sordo

decaffeinated coffee el café descafeinado [kafay deskafay-eenado]

decide decidir [detheedeer]

deckchair la tumbona

deep profundo

definitely claramente, ¡desde

luego! [klaramentay desday lwaygo]

delay el retraso

delicatessen la charcutería [charkootairee-a]

delicious delicioso [deleeth-yoso]

dentist el/la dentista

deodorant el desodorante [desodorantay]

department store los grandes almacenes [grandess almathayness]

departure la salida

depend: it depends depende [dependay]

dessert el postre [postray]

destination el destino

develop (photos) revelar [rebelar]

diarrhoea la diarrea [d-yarray-a]

dialling code el prefijo [prefeeHo]

diesel el gasoil

difference la diferencia [deefairenth-ya]

different diferente [deefairentay]

difficult difícil [deefeetheel]

dining room el comedor [komaydor]

dinner la cena [thayna]

direct (adj) directo

direction la dirección [deerekth-yon]

directory enquiries información [eenformath-yon]

dirty sucio [sooth-yo]

disco la discoteca

disgusting repugnante [repoognantay]

district el distrito

divorced divorciado [deeborth-yado]

do hacer [athair]

what shall we do? ¿qué hacemos? [kay athaymoss]

doctor el/la médico

dog el perro [pairro]

donkey el burro [boorro]

don't! ¡no lo haga! [aga]

door la puerta [pwairta]

double doble [doblay]

double bed la cama de matrimonio [matreemon-yo]

double room la habitación doble [abeetath-yon doblay]

down: down here aquí abajo [akee abaHo]

downstairs abajo [abaHo]

dozen la docena [dothayna]

draught beer la cerveza de grifo [thairbaytha day]

dress el vestido [besteedo]

drink (alcoholic) la copa (non-alcoholic) la bebida (verb) beber [bebair]

what would you like to drink? ¿qué le apetece beber? [kay lay apetaythay]

drinking water agua potable [agwa potablay]

drive conducir [kondootheer]

driver el conductor [kondooktor]/la conductora

driving licence el permiso de conducir [pairmeeso day

kondootheer]

drug la medicina
[maydeetheena]
 drugs (narcotics) la droga
drunk (adj) borracho
dry (adj) seco [sayko]
 (sherry) fino
dry-cleaner la tintorería
[teentorairee-a]
during durante [doorantay]
dustbin el cubo de la basura
[koobo day]
duvet el edredón

E

each cada
ear la oreja [orayHa]
early temprano
earring el pendiente [pend-
yentay]
east este [estay]
Easter la Semana Santa
easy fácil [fatheel]
eat comer [komair]
economy class la clase turista
[klassay]
egg el huevo [waybo]
either: either ... or ... o ... o ...
elbow el codo
electric eléctrico
electricity la electricidad
[elektreetheeda]
elevator el ascensor [asthensor]
else: something else algo más
 somewhere else en otra
parte [partay]
embassy la embajada

[embaHada]
emergency la emergencia
[emairHenth-ya]
empty vacío [bathee-o]
end el final [feenal]
 (verb) terminar [tairmeenar]
 at the end of the street al
final de la calle [day la ka-yay]
engaged (toilet) ocupado
 (telephone) comunicando
 (to be married) prometido
England Inglaterra
[eenglatairra]
English inglés [eenglayss]
enjoy: to enjoy oneself
divertirse [deebairteersay]
enormous enorme [enormay]
enough suficiente [soofeeth-
yentay]
 it's not big enough no es
suficientemente grande
[soofeeth-yentementay]
 that's enough es suficiente
entrance la entrada
envelope el sobre [sobray]
equipment el equipo [ekeepo]
especially especialmente
[espeth-yalmentay]
euro el euro [ay-ooro]
Eurocheque el eurocheque
[ay-oorochekay]
Europe Europa [ay-ooropa]
evening (early evening) la tarde
[tarday]
 (after nightfall) la noche
[nochay]
 this evening esta
tarde/noche
eventually finalmente

[feenalmentay]
ever alguna vez [beth]
every cada
everyone todos
everything todo
everywhere en todas partes
[partess]
exactly! ¡exactamente!
[exactamentay]
excellent excelente
[esthelentay]
excellent! ¡estupendo!
except excepto [esthepto]
exchange rate el cambio
[kamb-yo]
exciting emocionante [emoth-yonantay]
excuse me (to get past) con permiso
(to get attention) ¡por favor!
[fabor]
exhibition la exposición
[exposeeth-yon]
exit la salida
expensive caro
eye el ojo [oHo]
eyeglasses las gafas

F

face la cara
faint (verb) desmayarse [desma-yarsay]
fair la feria [fair-ya]
(adj) justo [Hoosto]
fairly bastante [bastantay]
fall (US) el otoño [oton-yo]
fall caerse [ka-airsay]

family la familia [fameel-ya]
fantastic fantástico
far lejos [layHoss]

dialogue

is it far from here? ¿está lejos de aquí? [day akee]
no, not very far no, no muy lejos [mwee]
it's about 20 kilometres unos veinte kilómetros

farm la granja [granHa]
fashionable de moda
fast rápido
fat (person) gordo
father el padre [padray]
faucet el grifo [greefo]
fault el defecto
sorry, it was my fault lo siento, fue culpa mía [s-yento fway koolpa mee-a]
favourite favorito [faboreeto]
fax el fax
feel sentir
I feel unwell no me siento bien [may s-yento b-yen]
felt-tip (pen) el rotulador
ferry el ferry
fetch: I'll fetch him yo iré a recogerle [eeray a raykoHairlay]
few: a few unos pocos
a few days unos pocos días
fiancé el novio [nob-yo]
fiancée la novia
field el campo
fight la pelea [pelay-a]
figs los higos [eegoss]

filling (in tooth) el empaste
[empastay]
film la película
find encontrar
find out enterarse [enterarsay]
fine (weather) bueno [bwayno]
(noun) la multa [moolta]
finger el dedo [daydo]
finish terminar [tairmeenar],
acabar
fire el fuego [fwaygo]
fire brigade los bomberos
[bombaiross]
first primero [preemairo]
at first al principio
[preentheep-yo]
first aid kit el botiquín
[boteekeen]
first class (travel etc) de
primera (clase) [preemaira
klasay]
first floor la primera planta
(US) la planta baja [baHa]
first name el nombre de pila
[nombray day]
fish el pez [peth]
(food) el pescado
fit: it doesn't fit me no me
viene bien [b-yaynay b-yen]
fix (mend) arreglar
(arrange) fijar [feeHar]
fizzy con gas
flat (apartment) el piso
(adj) llano [yano]
I've got a flat tyre tengo un
pinchazo [peenchatho]
flavour el sabor
flight el vuelo [bwaylo]
flight number el número de

vuelo [noomairo day]
floor (of room) el suelo [swaylo]
(of building) el piso
on the floor en el suelo
florist la floristería
[floreestairee-a]
flower la flor
flu la gripe [greepay]
fluent: he speaks fluent
Spanish domina el
castellano [kastay-yano]
fly la mosca
(verb) volar [bolar]
can we fly there? ¿podemos
ir en avión allí? [podaymoss
eer en ab-yon a-yee]
food la comida
foot el pie [p-yay]
on foot a pie
football (game) el fútbol
(ball) el balón
for para, por
do you have something
for ...? (headache/diarrhoea etc)
¿tiene algo para ...?
[t-yaynay]
foreign extranjero [estranHairo]
foreigner el extranjero/la
extranjera
forest el bosque [boskay]
forget olvidar [olbeedar]
I forget no me acuerdo [no
may akwairdo]
I've forgotten me he
olvidado [ay olbeedado]
fork el tenedor
fortnight quince días
[keenthay]
forwarding address la nueva

dirección [nwayba deerekth-yon]
fountain la fuente [fwentay]
foyer el hall [Hol]
France Francia [franth-ya]
free libre [leebray]
  (no charge) gratuito [gratweeto]
freeway la autopista [owtopeesta]
French francés [franthess]
French fries las patatas fritas
frequent frecuente [frekwentay]
fresh fresco
fridge el frigorífico
fried frito
friend el amigo/la amiga
friendly simpático
from de, desde [day, desday]
  from Monday to Friday de
  lunes a viernes [day]
  from next Thursday desde el
  próximo jueves
front la parte delantera [partay
  delantaira]
  in front of the hotel delante
  del hotel
  at the front delante
fruit la fruta
fruit juice el zumo de frutas
  [thoomo]
full lleno [yayno]
full board pensión completa
  [pens-yon komplayta]
fun: it was fun fue muy
  divertido [fway mwee
  deebairteedo]
funny (strange) raro
  (amusing) gracioso [grath-yoso]
further más allá [a-ya]

future el futuro [footooro]
  in the future en lo sucesivo
  [sootheseebo]

G

game (cards etc) el juego
  [Hwaygo]
  (match) el partido
garage (for fuel) la gasolinera
  [gasoleenaira]
  (for repairs) el taller (de
  reparaciones) [ta-yair day
  reparath-yoness]
  (for parking) el garaje [garaHay]
garden el jardín [Hardeen]
garlic el ajo [aHo]
gas el gas
  (US) la gasolina
gas station la gasolinera
  [gasoleenaira]
gate la puerta [pwairta]
  (at airport) la puerta de
  embarque [embarkay]
gay el gay
gents (toilet) el aseo de
  caballeros [asay-o day kaba-
  yaiross]
Germany Alemania [aleman-
  ya]
get (fetch) traer [tra-air]
  how do I get to ...? ¿cómo se
  va a ...? [say ba]
get back (return) volver
  [bolbair]
get off bajarse [baHarsay]
  where do I get off? ¿dónde
  tengo que bajarme? [donday

– kay baHarmay]
get on (to train etc) subirse [soobeersay]
get out (of car etc) bajarse [baHarsay]
get up (in the morning) levantarse [lebantarsay]
gift el regalo
gin la ginebra [Heenaybra]
  a gin and tonic un gintónic [Heentoneek]
girl la chica [cheeka]
girlfriend la novia [nob-ya]
give dar
give back devolver [debolbair]
glass (material) el cristal [kreestal]
  (tumbler) el vaso [baso]
  (wine glass) la copa
glasses las gafas
gloves los guantes [gwantess]
go ir [eer]
  where are you going? ¿adónde va? [adonday ba]
  where does this bus go? ¿adónde va este autobús? [estay]
  let's go! ¡vamos! [bamoss]
  she's gone (left) se ha marchado [say a]
  a hamburger to go una hamburguesa para llevar [yebar]
go away irse [eersay]
  go away! ¡váyase! [bayasay]
go back (return) volver [bolbair]
go down (the stairs etc) bajar

[baHar]
go in entrar
go out salir
go through pasar por
go up (the stairs etc) subir
God Dios [d-yoss]
gold el oro
good bueno [bwayno]
  good! ¡muy bien! [mwee b-yen]
  it's no good es inútil [eenooteel]
goodbye adiós [ad-yoss]
good evening buenas tardes [bwenass tardess]
good morning buenos días [bwaynoss]
good night buenas noches [nochess]
got: we've got to ... tenemos que ... [taynaymoss kay]
  I've got to ... tengo que ...
  have you got any apples? ¿tiene manzanas? [t-yaynay]
gradually gradualmente [gradwalmentay]
gram(me) el gramo
grapefruit el pomelo [pomaylo]
grapes las uvas [oobass]
grass la hierba [yairba]
grateful agradecido [agradetheedo]
great (excellent) muy bueno [mwee bwayno]
green verde [bairday]
greengrocer's la frutería [frootairee-a]
grey gris

grilled a la parrilla

grocer's (la tienda de) comestibles [t-yenda day komesteebless]

ground: on the ground en el suelo [swaylo]

ground floor la planta baja [baHa]

group el grupo

guest el invitado [eembeetado]/la invitada

guesthouse la casa de huéspedes [day wespedess]

guide el/la guía [gee-a]

guidebook la guía

guided tour la visita con guía [beeseeta]

H

hair el pelo [paylo]

haircut el corte de pelo [kortay]

hairdresser's (men's) la barbería
(women's) la peluquería [pelookairee-a]

hairdryer el secador de pelo [day paylo]

half la mitad [la meeta]

half an hour media hora [mayd-ya ora]

half a litre medio litro

half board la media pensión [pens-yon]

half-bottle la botella pequeña [botay-ya pekayn-ya]

half price la mitad del precio [meeta del preth-yo]

ham el jamón [Hamon]

hamburger la hamburguesa [amboorgaysa]

hand la mano

handbag el bolso

hand luggage el equipaje de mano [ekeepaHay]

hangover la resaca

happen suceder [soothedair]
what has happened? ¿qué ha pasado? [a]

happy contento

harbour el puerto [pwairto]

hard duro [dooro]
(difficult) difícil [deefeetheel]

hardly apenas [apaynass]
hardly ever casi nunca

hardware shop la ferretería [fairretairee-a]

hat el sombrero

hate odiar

have tener [tenair]
can I have a ...? ¿me da ...? [may]
do you have ...? ¿tiene ...? [t-yaynay]
do I have to ...? ¿tengo que ...?

hayfever la alergia al polen [alairHee-a al polayn]

he él

head la cabeza [kabaytha]

headache el dolor de cabeza

headlights el faro

hear oír [o-eer]

heat el calor

heater el calefactor

heating la calefacción

heavy pesado
heel (of foot) el talón
  (of shoe) el tacón
hello ¡hola! [ola]
  (on phone) ¡dígame!
  [deegamay]
help la ayuda [a-yooda]
  (verb) ayudar [a-yoodar]
  help! ¡socorro!
  can you help me? ¿puede
  ayudarme? [pwayday a-
  yoodarmay]
her: I haven't seen her no la
  he visto [ay]
  to her a ella [ay-ya]
  for her para ella
  that's her ésa es (ella) [aysa]
  that's her towel ésa es su
  toalla
herbal tea el té de hierbas
  [tay day yairbass]
here aquí [akee]
  here is/are ... aquí
  está/están ...
  here you are (offering) tenga
hers (el) suyo [soo-yo], (la)
  suya
  that's hers es de ella [day ay-
  ya], es suyo/suya
hey! ¡oiga!
hi! ¡hola! [ola]
high alto
highway la autopista
  [owtopeesta]
hill la colina
him: I haven't seen him no le
  he visto [lay ay]
  to him a él
  for him para él

that's him ése es (él) [aysay]
hip la cadera [kadaira]
hire alquilar [alkeelar]
  for hire de alquiler
  [alkeelair]
his: it's his car es su coche
  that's his eso de él [ayso day],
  eso es suyo [soo-yo]
hitchhike hacer autostop
  [athair owtostop]
hole el agujero [agooHairo]
holiday las vacaciones [bakath-
  yoness]
  on holiday de vacaciones
home la casa
  at home (in my house) en
  casa
  (in my country) en mi país [pa-
  eess]
  we go home tomorrow
  volvemos a casa mañana
  [bolbaymoss]
horrible horrible [orreeblay]
horse el caballo [kaba-yo]
hospital el hospital
  [ospeetal]
hot caliente [kal-yentay]
  (spicy) picante [peekantay]
  I'm hot tengo calor
hotel el hotel [otel]
hour la hora [ora]
house la casa
house wine el vino de la casa
  [beeno day]
how como
  how many? ¿cuántos?
  [kwantoss]
  how do you do? ¡mucho
  gusto! [moocho]

dialogues

how are you? ¿cómo está?
fine, thanks, and you?
bien gracias, y usted
[b-yen – ee oostay]

how much is it? ¿cuánto
es? [kwanto]
1,000 pesetas mil pesetas
[pesaytass]
I'll take it me lo quedo
[may lo kaydo]

hungry hambriento [ambr-
yento]
I'm hungry tengo hambre
[ambray]
hurry: I'm in a hurry tengo
prisa
hurt: it hurts me duele [may
dwaylay]
husband el marido

I
■

I yo
ice el hielo [yaylo]
ice cream el helado [elado]
ice lolly el polo
idiot el/la idiota [eed-yota]
if si
ill enfermo [enfairmo]
immediately ahora mismo
[a-ora meesmo]
important importante
[eemportantay]
impossible imposible

[eemposeeblay]
in: it's in the centre está en el
centro
in my car en mi coche
in Córdoba en Córdoba
in five minutes dentro de
cinco minutos
in May en mayo
in English en inglés
is he in? ¿está?
include: does that include
meals? ¿eso incluye las
comidas? [ayso eenkloo-yay]
indigestion la indigestión
[eendeeHest-yon]
indoors dentro
information la información
[eenformath-yon]
injured herido [ereedo]
insect el insecto
inside dentro de [day]
inside the hotel dentro del
hotel
instead: instead of ... en lugar
de ... [day]
intelligent inteligente
[eenteleeHentay]
interesting interesante
[eenteresantay]
international internacional
[internath-yonal]
interpreter el/la intérprete
intersection el cruce
[krroothay]
into en
I'm not into ... no me
gusta ... [may goosta]
introduce presentar
may I introduce ...? le

presento a ...
invitation la invitación
[eembeetath-yon]
Ireland Irlanda [eerlanda]
Irish irlandés [eerlandayss]
iron (for ironing) la plancha
island la isla [eessla]
it ello, lo [ay-yo]
  it is ... es ...; está ...
  is it ...? ¿es ...?; ¿está ... ?
  where is it? ¿dónde está?
  [donday]
  it was ... era ...; estaba ...
  [aira]

J

jacket la chaqueta [chakayta]
jam la mermelada
  [mairmaylada]
jeans los vaqueros [bakaiross]
jellyfish la medusa [medoosa]
jewellery las joyas [Hoyass]
job el trabajo [trabaHo]
joke el chiste [cheestay]
journey el viaje [b-yaHay]
  have a good journey! ¡buen
  viaje! [bwen b-yaHay]
juice el zumo [thoomo]
jumper el jersey [Hairsay]
just (only) solamente
  [solamentay]
  just two sólo dos
  just for me sólo para mí
  just here aquí mismo [akee
  meesmo]

K

keep quedarse [kedarsay]
  keep the change quédese
  con el cambio [kay-daysay –
  kamb-yo]
key la llave [yabay]
kilo el kilo
kilometre el kilómetro
kind (nice) amable [amablay]
kiss el beso [bayso]
  (verb) besarse [baysarsay]
kitchen la cocina [kotheena]
knee la rodilla [rodee-ya]
knife el cuchillo [koochee-yo]
knock down atropellar
  [atropay-yar]
know (somebody, a place)
  conocer [konothair]
  (something) saber [sabair]
  I don't know no sé [say]
  I didn't know that no lo sabía

L

ladies' room el aseo de
  señoras [asay-o day sen-yorass]
lady la señora [sen-yora]
lager la cerveza [thairbaytha]
lake el lago
lamb (meat) el cordero
  [kordairo]
lamp la lámpara
language el idioma [eed-yoma]
large grande [granday]
last último [oolteemo]
  last week la semana pasada

last Friday el viernes pasado
last night anoche [anochay]
late tarde [tarday]
later más tarde
 I'll come back later volveré
 más tarde [bolbairay]
laugh reirse [ray-eersay]
launderette/laundromat la
 lavandería [labandairee-a]
laundry (clothes) la ropa sucia
 [sooth-ya]
lawyer el abogado/la
 abogada
leaflet el folleto [fo-yayto]
leak (in roof) la gotera [gotaira]
 (gas, water) el escape [eskapay]
learn aprender [aprendair]
least: at least por lo menos
 [maynoss]
leather (fine) la piel [p-yel]
 (heavy) el cuero [kwairo]
leave (go away) irse [eersay]
 I am leaving tomorrow me
 marcho mañana [may]
 may I leave this here?
 ¿puedo dejar esto aquí?
 [pwaydo dayHar – akee]
 I left my coat in the bar me
 he dejado el abrigo en el
 bar [ay dayHado]

dialogue

 when does the bus for
 Montoro leave? ¿cuándo
 sale el autobús para
 Montoro? [kwando salay]
 it leaves at 9 o'clock sale a
 las nueve

left izquierda [eethk-yairda]
left luggage (office) la
 consigna [konseegna]
leg la pierna [p-yairna]
lemon el limón [leemon]
lemonade la limonada
lend prestar
less menos [maynoss]
 less expensive menos caro
lesson la lección [lekth-yon]
let (allow) dejar [dayHar]
 let off: will you let me off at ...?
 ¿me para en ...? [may]
letter la carta
letterbox el buzón [boothon]
lettuce la lechuga [lechooga]
library la biblioteca [beebl-
 yotayka]
licence el permiso
lift (in building) el ascensor
 [asthensor]
 could you give me a lift?
 ¿podría llevarme en su
 coche? [yebarmay – kochay]
light la luz [looth]
 (not heavy) ligero [leeHairo]
 do you have a light? (for
 cigarette) ¿tiene fuego?
 [t-yaynay fwaygo]
light bulb la bombilla
 [bombee-ya]
lighter (cigarette) el
 encendedor [enthendedor]
like gustar [goostar]
 I like it me gusta [may]
 I don't like it no me gusta
 I'd like a beer quisiera una
 cerveza [kees-yaira oona
 thairbaytha]

would you like a drink? ¿le
apetece beber algo?
[apaytaythay bebair]
what's it like? ¿cómo es?
one like this uno como éste
[estay]
line la línea [leenay-a]
lips el labio [lab-yo]
listen escuchar [eskoochar]
litre el litro
little pequeño [paykayn-yo]
just a little, thanks sólo un
poco, gracias
a little milk un poco de
leche [lechay]
live (verb) vivir [beebeer]
loaf el pan
local local
a local wine un vino local
lock la cerradura
[thairradoora]
(verb) cerrar [thairrar]
**lock out: I've locked myself
out** he cerrado la puerta
con las llaves dentro [ay – la
pwairta – yabayss]
locker (for luggage etc) la
consigna automática
[konseegna owtomateeka]
London Londres [londress]
long largo
how long does it take?
¿cuánto tiempo se tarda?
[say]
a long time mucho tiempo
[moocho]
one day/two days longer un
día/dos días más
look: look out! ¡cuidado!

[kweedado]
can I have a look? ¿puedo
mirar? [pwaydo]
look after cuidar [kweedar]
look at mirar
look for buscar
I'm looking for ... estoy
buscando ...
lorry el camión [kam-yon]
lose perder [pairdair]
I've lost my way me he
perdido [may ay pairdeedo]
I've lost my bag he perdido
el bolso [ay]
lost property (office) (la
oficina de) objetos perdidos
[ofeetheena day obHaytoss
pairdeedoss]
lot: a lot, lots mucho, muchos
[moocho]
not a lot no mucho
a lot of people mucha gente
[Hentay]
loud fuerte [fwairtay]
lounge el salón
love el amor
(verb) querer [kairair]
lovely encantador
low bajo [baHo]
luck la suerte [swairtay]
good luck! ¡buena suerte!
[bwayna]
luggage el equipaje
[ekeepaHay]
lunch el almuerzo
[almwairtho]

Li

M

mad (insane) loco

magazine la revista [rebeesta]

maid (in hotel) la camarera [kamaraira]

mail el correo [korray-o]

mailbox el buzón [boothon]

main principal [preentheepal]

main course el plato principal

main road (in town) la calle principal [ka-yay preentheepal]
(in country) la carretera principal [karretaira]

make hacer [athair]

make-up el maquillaje [makee-yaHay]

man el hombre [ombray]

manager el gerente [Hairentay]
can I see the manager? ¿puedo ver al gerente? [pwaydo bair]

many muchos [moochoss]
not many no muchos

map el mapa
(of city plan) el plano

market el mercado [mairkado]

marmalade la mermelada de naranja [mairmelada day naranHa]

married: **I'm married** estoy casado/casada

mascara el rímel

match (football etc) el partido

matches las cerillas [thairee-yass]

matter: **it doesn't matter** no importa
what's the matter? ¿qué pasa? [kay]

mattress el colchón

may: **may I see it?** ¿puedo verlo? [pwaydo bairlo]

maybe tal vez [beth]

mayonnaise la mayonesa [ma-yonaysa]

me: **that's for me** eso es para mí [ayso]
me too yo también [tamb-yen]

meal la comida

mean (verb) querer decir [kairair detheer]

meat la carne [karnay]

medicine la medicina [medeetheena]

medium (adj: size) medio [mayd-yo]

medium-dry semi-seco [sayko]
(sherry) amontillado [amontee-yado]

medium-rare poco hecho [aycho]

mend arreglar

men's room el servicio de caballeros [sairbeeth-yo day kaba-yaiross]

mention: **don't mention it** de nada [day]

menu el menú [menoo]

message un recado

metre el metro

midday el mediodía [mayd-yodee-a]

middle: **in the middle** en el

469

medio [**may**d-yo]
midnight la medianoche
[**may**d-ya-**no**chay]
milk la leche [**le**chay]
mind: never mind ¡qué más
da! [kay]
mine: it's mine es mío
mineral water el agua mineral
[**a**gwa meen**ai**ral]
minute el minuto [meen**oo**to]
just a minute un momento
mirror el espejo [esp**ay**HO]
Miss Señorita [sen-yor**ee**ta]
miss: there's a suitcase
missing falta una maleta
mistake el error
monastery el monasterio
[monast**air**-yo]
money el dinero [deen**ai**ro]
month el mes
moped el ciclomotor
[theeklomot**or**]
more más
can I have some more water,
please? más agua, por favor
more expensive más caro
more than 50 más de
cincuenta
morning la mañana [man-**ya**na]
this morning esta mañana
most: most of the time la
mayor parte del tiempo
[ma-**yor partay del t-yempo**]
mother la madre [**ma**dray]
motorbike la moto
motorway la autopista
[owtop**ee**sta]
mountain la montaña [montan-
ya]

mouse el ratón
mouth la boca
movie la película [pel**ee**koola]
movie theater el cine [the**e**nay]
Mr Señor [sen-**yor**]
Mrs Señora [sen-**yo**ra]
Ms Señorita [sen-yor**ee**ta]
much mucho [**moo**cho]
much better/worse mucho
mejor/peor [ma-**yor**/pay-**or**]
much hotter mucho más
caliente [kal-**yen**tay]
not much no mucho
mum la mamá
museum el museo [moos**ay**-o]
mushrooms los champiñones
[champeen-**yo**ness]
music la música [**moo**seeka]
must: I must tengo que [kay]
mustard la mostaza [most**a**tha]
my mi; pl mis
myself: I'll do it myself lo haré
yo mismo [ar**ay** yo m**ee**smo]
by myself yo solo

N

nail (finger) la uña [**oo**n-ya]
name el nombre [**no**mbray]
my name's John me llamo
John [may **ya**mo]
what's your name? ¿cómo se
llama usted? [say – oost**ay**]
napkin la servilleta [sairbee-
yayta]
narrow (street) estrecho
[estr**ay**cho]
nasty (person) desagradable

[desagradablay]
(weather, accident) malo
national nacional [nath-yonal]
natural natural [natooral]
near cerca [thairka]
 where is the nearest ...?
 ¿dónde está el ... más
 cercano? [donday – thairkano]
nearly casi
necessary necesario [nethesar-yo]
neck el cuello [kway-yo]
necklace el collar [ko-yar]
necktie la corbata
need: I need ... necesito
 un ... [netheseeto]
needle la aguja [agooHa]
neither ... nor ... ni ... ni ...
nephew el sobrino
never nunca [noonka]
new nuevo [nwaybo]
news (radio, TV etc) las noticias
 [noteeth-yass]
newsagent's el kiosko de
 prensa [day]
newspaper el periódico [pair-yodeeko]
New Year el Año Nuevo [an-yo nwaybo]
 Happy New Year! ¡Feliz Año
 Nuevo [feleeth]
New Year's Eve Nochevieja
 [nochay-b-yayHa]
New Zealand Nueva Zelanda
 [nwayba thelanda]
next próximo
 next week la próxima
 semana
 next to al lado de [day]

nice (food) bueno [bwayno]
 (looks, view etc) bonito
 (person) simpático
niece la sobrina
night la noche [nochay]
no no
 I've no change no tengo
 cambio [kamb-yo]
 there's no ... left no queda ...
 [kayda]
nobody nadie [nad-yay]
noisy: it's too noisy hay
 demasiado ruido [i daymas-yado]
non-alcoholic sin alcohol
 [alko-ol]
none ninguno
non-smoking compartment
 no fumadores [foomadoress]
no-one nadie [nad-yay]
nor: nor do I yo tampoco
normal normal
north norte [nortay]
northeast nordeste [nordestay]
northwest noroeste [noro-estay]
Northern Ireland Irlanda del
 Norte [eerlanda del nortay]
nose la nariz [nareeth]
not no
 no, I'm not hungry no, no
 tengo hambre [ambray]
 not that one ése no [aysay]
note (banknote) el billete [bee-yaytay]
nothing nada
 nothing else nada más
now ahora [a-ora]
number el número [noomairo]

nuts los frutos secos

O

o'clock en punto [**poo**nto]
odd (strange) raro
of de [day]
off (lights) apagado
  it's just off calle Corredera
  está cerca de calle
  Corredera [tha**ir**ka day ka-yay]
often a menudo
  how often are the buses?
  ¿cada cuánto son los
  autobuses? [kwanto]
oil el aceite [athay-**ee**tay]
ointment la pomada
OK vale [**ba**lay]
  are you OK? ¿está bien?
  [b-yen]
  that's OK thanks está bien,
  gracias
  I'm OK (nothing for me) yo no
  quiero [k-y**air**o]
  (I feel OK) me siento bien
  [may s-**yen**to]
old viejo [b-**yay**Ho]
olive la aceituna [athay-
  eet**oo**na], la oliva
olive oil el aceite de oliva
  [athay-**ee**tay day ol**ee**ba]
omelette la tortilla [tort**ee**-ya]
on en
  on television en la tele
  [**tay**lay]
  I haven't got it on me no lo
  llevo encima [**yay**bo enth**ee**ma]
  what's on tonight? ¿qué

ponen esta noche? [kay]
once (one time) una vez [**oo**na
  beth]
  at once (immediately) en
  seguida [seg**ee**da]
one uno [**oo**no], una
  the white one el blanco, la
  blanca
one-way ticket el billete de
  ida [bee-**yay**tay day **ee**da]
onion la cebolla [theb**o**-ya]
only sólo
  it's only 6 o'clock son sólo
  las seis
open (adjective) abierto [ab-
  yairto]
  (verb) abrir [ab**reer**]
operator el operador/la
  operadora
opposite: opposite my hotel
  enfrente de mi hotel
or o
orange (fruit) la naranja
  [naran**Ha**]
  (colour) (color) naranja
orange juice (fresh) el zumo
  de naranja [th**oo**mo day]
  (fizzy, diluted) la naranjada
  [naran**Ha**da]
order: can we order now?
  ¿podemos pedir ya?
  [pod**ay**moss]
ordinary corriente [korr-**yen**tay]
other otro
  the other one el otro
our/ours nuestro [**nwe**stro],
  nuestra; (pl) nuestros, nuestras
out: he's out no está
outdoors fuera de casa [f**wai**ra

Nu

day]

outside ... fuera de ...

over: over here por aquí [akee]

over there por allí [a-yee]

over 500 más de quinientos

overnight (travel) de noche [day nochay]

own: my own ... mi propio ... [prop-yo]

P

pack: a pack of ... un paquete de ... [pakaytay day]
(verb) hacer las maletas [malaytass]

package el paquete [pakaytay]

pain el dolor

I have a pain here me duele aquí [may dwaylay akee]

painful doloroso

painkillers los analgésicos [analHayseekoss]

pair: a pair of ... un par de ... [day]

panties las bragas

pants (underwear: men's) los calzoncillos [kalthonthee-yoss]
(women's) las bragas
(US: trousers) los pantalones [pantaloness]

pantyhose los panties

paper el papel
(newspaper) el periódico [pair-yodeeko]

parcel el paquete [pakaytay]

pardon (me)? (didn't understand/hear) ¿cómo?

parents: my parents mis padres [padress]

park el parque [parkay]
(verb) aparcar

parking lot el aparcamiento [aparcam-yento]

part la parte [partay]

partner (boyfriend, girlfriend etc) el compañero [kompan-yairo]

party (group) el grupo
(celebration) la fiesta

passport el pasaporte [pasaportay]

past: just past the information office justo después de la oficina de información [Hoosto despwayss day]

pavement la acera [athaira]

pay pagar
can I pay, please? la cuenta, por favor [kwenta]

pay phone el teléfono público [telayfono poobleeko]

peach el melocotón

peanuts los cacahuetes [kakawaytess]

pear la pera [paira]

peas los guisantes [geesantess]

pen la pluma [plooma]

pencil el lápiz [lapeeth]

people la gente [Hentay]
too many people demasiada gente [daymas-yada]

pepper (spice) la pimienta [peem-yenta]
(vegetable) el pimiento

per: per night por noche [nochay]

per cent por ciento [th-yento]

perfume el perfume [pairfoomay]

perhaps quizás [keethass]

person la persona [pairsona]

petrol la gasolina

petrol station la gasolinera [gasoleenaira]

pharmacy la farmacia [far-math-ya]

phone el teléfono [telayfono]
(verb) llamar por teléfono [yamar]

phone book la guía telefónica [gee-a]

phone box la cabina telefónica [kabeena]

phonecard la tarjeta de teléfono [tarHayta day taylayfono]

phone number el número de teléfono [noomairo]

photo la foto

picture el cuadro [kwadro]

piece el pedazo [pedatho]

pill la píldora

pillow la almohada [almo-ada]

pineapple la piña [peen-ya]

pink rosa

place el sitio [seet-yo]
at your place (fam) en tu casa
(pol) en su casa

plane el avión [ab-yon]

plant la planta

plasters las tiritas

plastic bag la bolsa de plástico

plate el plato

platform el andén

which platform is it for Saragossa, please? ¿qué andén para Zaragoza, por favor? [kay]

play (in theatre) la obra
(verb) jugar [Hoogar]

pleasant agradable [agradablay]

please por favor [fabor]
yes please sí, por favor

plenty: plenty of ... mucho ... [moocho]

plug (electrical) el enchufe [enchoofay]
(in sink) el tapón

poisonous venenoso [benenoso]

police la policía [poleethee-a]

policeman el (agente de) policía [aHentay day]

police station la comisaría de policía

polite educado [edookado]

polluted contaminado

pool (for swimming) la piscina [peestheena]

pork la carne de cerdo [karnay day thairdo]

port (for boats) el puerto [pwairto]

possible posible [poseeblay]
is it possible to ...? ¿es posible ...?
as ... as possible tan ... como sea posible [say-a]

post (mail) el correo [korray-o]
(verb) echar al correo

postcard la postal

post office Correos [korray-oss]

poste restante la lista de Correos [leesta]

potato la patata

potato chips las patatas fritas (de bolsa)

pound (money, weight) la libra

prefer: I prefer ... prefiero ... [pref-yairo]

pregnant embarazada [embarathada]

prescription (for chemist) la receta [rethayta]

present (gift) el regalo

pretty mono

price el precio [preth-yo]

private privado [preebado]

probably probablemente [probablementay]

problem el problema [problayma]

no problem! ¡con mucho gusto! [moocho goosto]

pronounce: how is this pronounced? ¿cómo se pronuncia esto? [say pronoonth-ya]

public holiday el día de fiesta [day]

pull tirar

purple morado

purse (for money) el monedero [monedairo]

(US: handbag) el bolso

push empujar [empooHar]

put poner [ponair]

pyjamas el pijama [peeHama]

quarter la cuarta parte [kwarta partay]

question la pregunta [pregoonta]

queue la cola

quick rápido

quickly rápidamente [rapeedamentay]

quiet (place, hotel) tranquilo [trankeelo]

quiet! ¡cállese! [ka-yaysay]

quite (fairly) bastante [bastantay]

(very) muy [mwee]

quite a lot bastante

radiator el radiador [rad-yador]

radio la radio [rad-yo]

rail: by rail en tren

railway el ferrocarril

rain la lluvia [yoob-ya]

it's raining está lloviendo [yob-yendo]

rape la violación [b-yolath-yon]

rare (steak) (muy) poco hecho [mwee – aycho]

raspberry la frambuesa [frambwaysa]

rather: I'd rather ... prefiero ... [pref-yairo]

razor la maquinilla de afeitar [makeenee-ya day afay-eetar]

(electric) la máquina de

afeitar eléctrica [makeena]
read leer [lay-**air**]
ready preparado
real verdadero [bairdad**air**o]
really realmente [ray-
almentay]
receipt el recibo [reth**ee**bo]
recently recientemente [reth-
yentem**en**tay]
reception la recepción
[rethepth-y**on**]
receptionist el/la
recepcionista [rethepth-
yon**ee**sta]
**recommend: could you
recommend ...?** ¿puede
usted recomendar ...?
[pw**ay**day oost**ay**]
red rojo [ro**H**o]
red wine el vino tinto [b**ee**no
t**ee**nto]
refund el reembolso [ray-
emb**o**lso]
region la zona [th**o**na], la
región [re**H**-yon]
registered: by registered mail
por correo certificado
[k**o**rray-o thairteefeek**a**do]
remember: I don't remember
no recuerdo [rekw**ai**rdo]
rent (for apartment etc) el
alquiler [alkeel**air**]
(verb) alquilar
repair reparar
repeat repetir
reservation la reserva
[res**ai**rba]
reserve reservar [res**air**bar]

dialogue

**can I reserve a table for
tonight?** ¿puedo reservar
una mesa para esta
noche? [pw**ay**do – m**ay**sa –
n**o**chay]
**yes madam, for how many
people?** sí, señora, ¿para
cuántos? [sen-**yo**ra –
kw**a**ntoss]
for two para dos
and for what time? ¿y para
qué hora? [kay **o**ra]
for eight o'clock para las
ocho
**and could I have your
name please?** ¿me dice su
nombre, por favor? [may
d**ee**thay soo n**o**mbray]

restaurant el restaurante
[restowr**a**ntay]
restaurant car el vagón-
cafetería [bagon kafetair**ee**-a]
rest room los servicios
[sairb**ee**th-yoss]
return (ticket) el billete de ida
y vuelta [bee-y**ay**tay day **ee**da ee
bw**e**lta]
reverse charge call la llamada
a cobro revertido [yam**a**da –
rebert**ee**do]
rice arroz [arr**o**th]
right (correct) correcto
(not left) derecho
that's right eso es [**ay**so]
ring (on finger) la sortija
[sort**ee**Ha]

ring back volver a llamar [bolbair a yamar]
river el río
road la carretera [karretaira]
  is this the road for ...? ¿es ésta la carretera que va a ...? [kay ba]
rob: I've been robbed ¡me han robado! [may an]
roll (bread) el bollo [bo-yo]
roof el tejado [teHado]
room la habitación [abeetath-yon]

dialogue

do you have any rooms? ¿tiene habitaciones? [t-yaynay abeetath-yoness]
for how many people? ¿para cuántos? [kwantoss]
for one/two para uno/dos
yes, we have rooms free sí, tenemos habitaciones libres [tenaymoss – leebress]
for how many nights will it be? ¿para cuántas noches? [kwantass nochess]
just for one night sólo para una noche [oona]
how much is it? ¿cuánto es? [kwanto]
... with bathroom and ... without bathroom ... con baño y ... sin baño [ban-yo – ee seen]
can I see a room with bathroom? ¿me enseña una habitación con

baño? [may ensen-ya]
OK, I'll take it vale, me la quedo [balay may la kaydo]

room service el servicio de habitaciones [sairbeeth-yo day]
rosé (wine) vino rosado [beeno]
round trip ticket el billete de ida y vuelta [bee-yaytay day eeda ee bwelta]
route la ruta [roota]
rubbish (waste) la basura (poor quality goods) las porquerías [porkairee-ass]
rucksack la mochila
rude grosero [grosairo]
rum el ron
run (person) correr [korrair]

S

sad triste [treestay]
safe seguro [segooro]
salad la ensalada
salad dressing el aliño para la ensalada [aleen-yo]
sale: for sale en venta [em baynta]
salt la sal
same: the same mismo [meesmo]
  the same again, please lo mismo otra vez, por favor [beth]
sand la arena [arayna]
sandals las sandalias [sandal-

477

yass]

sandwich el sandwich

sanitary napkin/towel la compresa [komp**ray**sa]

sauce la salsa

saucepan el cazo [**ka**tho]

sausage la salchicha

say: how do you say ... in Spanish? ¿cómo se dice ... en español? [say **dee**thay en espan-y**ol**]

what did he say? ¿que ha dicho? [kay a]

scarf (for neck) la bufanda (for head) el pañuelo [pan-y**way**lo]

schedule (US) el horario [or**ar**-yo]

school la escuela [esk**way**la]

scissors: a pair of scissors las tijeras [tee**Hai**rass]

Scotch tape® la cinta adhesiva [**thee**nta ades**ee**ba]

Scotland Escocia [esk**oth**-ya]

Scottish escocés [eskoth**ayss**]

sea el mar

by the sea junto al mar [**Hoo**nto]

seafood los mariscos

seasick: I feel seasick estoy mareado [maray-**a**do]

seat el asiento [as-y**en**to]

is this anyone's seat? ¿es de alguien este asiento? [day **a**lg-yen es**tay**]

second (adjective) segundo [seg**oo**ndo]

(of time) el segundo

second class (travel) en

segunda clase [kl**a**ssay]

see ver [bair]

can I see? ¿puedo ver? [pw**ay**do]

have you seen ...? ¿ha visto ...? [a **bee**sto]

see you! ¡hasta luego! [**a**sta lw**ay**go]

I see (I understand) ya comprendo

self-catering apartment el apartamento

self-service autoservicio [owtosairb**eeth**-yo]

sell vender [bend**air**]

Sellotape® la cinta adhesiva [**thee**nta ades**ee**ba]

send enviar [emb-y**ar**]

separated: I'm separated estoy separado/separada

separately (pay, travel) por separado

serious serio [**sair**-yo]

service station la estacion de servicio [estath-y**on** day]

serviette la servilleta [sairbee-y**ay**ta]

set menu el menu del día [men**oo**]

several varios [**bar**-yoss]

sex el sexo

shade: in the shade a la sombra

shallow (water) poco profundo [prof**oo**ndo]

shame: what a shame! ¡que lástima! [kay]

shampoo el champú

share (room, table etc)

compartir

shaver la máquina de afeitar [makeena day afay-eetar]

shaving foam la espuma de afeitar

she ella [**ay**-ya]

sheet (for bed) la sábana

shellfish los mariscos

sherry el jerez [Hereth]

ship el barco

shirt el camisa

shit! ¡mierda! [m-y**ai**rda]

shoes los zapatos [thap**a**toss]

shoelaces los cordones para zapatos [kord**o**ness]

shoe polish la crema para los zapatos [kr**ay**ma]

shoe repairer's la zapatería [thapatair**ee**-a]

shop la tienda [t-y**e**nda]

short (time, journey) corto (person) bajo [b**a**Ho]

shorts los pantalones cortos [pantal**o**ness]

should: what should I do? ¿que hago? [kay **a**go]

shoulder el hombro [**o**mbro]

shout gritar

show (in theatre) el espectáculo [espekt**a**koolo]

could you show me? ¿me lo enseña? [may lo ensen-ya]

shower (in bathroom) la ducha [d**oo**cha]

shut (verb) cerrar [th**ai**rrar]

when do you shut? ¿a qué hora cierran? [a kay **o**ra th-y**ai**rran]

they're shut está cerrado [thair**ra**do]

shut up! ¡cállese! [ka-yesay]

shutter (on window) la contraventana [kontrabent**a**na]

sick (ill) enfermo [enf**ai**rmo]

side el lado

side salad la ensalada aparte [ap**a**rtay]

sidewalk la acera [ath**ai**ra]

sight: the sights of ... los lugares de interés de ... [loog**a**ress day eentair**e**ss]

silk la seda [s**ay**da]

silly tonto

silver la plata

since: since yesterday desde ayer [**d**esday a-y**ai**r]

sing cantar

single: a single to ... un billete para ... [bee-y**ay**tay]

I'm single soy soltero [solt**ai**ro]

single bed la cama individual [eendeebeed**wa**l]

single room la habitación individual [abeetath-y**o**n]

sister la hermana [air**ma**na]

sit: can I sit here? ¿puedo sentarme aquí? [pw**ay**do sent**a**rmay ak**ee**]

sit down sentarse [sent**a**rsay]

size el tamaño [tam**a**n-yo] (of clothes) la talla [t**a**-ya]

skin la piel [p-yel]

skirt la falda

sky el cielo [th-y**ay**lo]

sleep dormir

sleeping bag el saco de dormir [day]

sleeping car el coche-cama [kochay-kama]

slow lento

slow down! ¡más despacio! [despath-yo]

slowly despacio

small pequeño [peken-yo]

smell: it smells! (smells bad) ¡apesta!

smile sonreír [sonray-eer]

smoke el humo [oomo]

do you mind if I smoke? ¿le importa si fumo? [lay – foomo]

I don't smoke no fumo

snow la nieve [n-yaybay]

it's snowing está nevando

so: it's so good es tan bueno [bwayno]

not so fast no tan de prisa [preesa]

so am I yo también [tamb-yen]

so do I yo también

soap el jabón [Habon]

soap powder el jabón en polvo [em polbo]

sober sobrio [sobr-yo]

sock el calcetín [kaltheteen]

soda (water) la soda

soft (material etc) suave [swabay]

soft drink el refresco

sole la suela [swayla]

some: can I have some water? ¿me da un poco de agua? [may – day]

can I have some rolls? ¿me da unos bollos? [bo-yoss]

somebody alguien [alg-yen]

something algo

sometimes a veces [baythess]

somewhere en alguna parte [partay]

son el hijo [eeHo]

song la canción [kanth-yon]

soon pronto

sore: it's sore me duele [may dwaylay]

sorry: (I'm) sorry perdone [pairdonay]

sorry? (didn't understand) ¿cómo?

sort: what sort of ...? ¿qué clase de ...? [kay klassay day]

soup la sopa

south el sur [soor]

South Africa Sudáfrica

South African (adj) sudafricano

southeast el sudeste [sood-estay]

southwest el sudoeste [soodo-estay]

souvenir el recuerdo [rekwairdo]

Spain España [espan-ya]

Spaniard el español [espan-yol]/la española

Spanish español

the Spanish los españoles [espan-yoless]

speak: do you speak English? ¿habla inglés? [abla]

I don't speak ... no hablo ... [ablo]

spectacles las gafas

spend gastar

spoon la cuchara
spring (season) la primavera
[preemabaira]
square (in town) la plaza
[platha]
stairs las escaleras [eskalairass]
stamp el sello [say-yo]
start el principio [preentheep-yo]
(verb) comenzar [komenthar]
the car won't start el coche
no arranca [kochay]
starter (food) la entrada
starving: I'm starving me
muero de hambre [may
mwairo day ambray]
station la estación del
ferrocarril [estath-yon]
stay: where are you staying?
¿dónde se hospedan?
[donday say ospaydan]
I'm staying at ... me hospedo
en ... [may ospaydo]
I'd like to stay another two
nights me gustaría
quedarme otras dos noches
[may – kedarmay – nochess]
steak el filete [feelaytay]
steal robar
my bag has been stolen me
han robado el bolso [may an]
steep (hill) empinado
still: I'm still waiting todavía
estoy esperando [todabee-a]
stomach el estómago
stomach ache el dolor de
estómago [day]
stone (rock) la piedra [p-yedra]
stop parar

please, stop here (to taxi driver
etc) pare aquí, por favor
[paray akee]
storm la tormenta
straight: straight ahead todo
derecho [dairecho]
strange (odd) extraño [estran-yo]
strawberry la fresa [fraysa]
street la calle [ka-yay]
string la cuerda [kwairda]
strong fuerte [fwairtay]
stuck atascado
student el/la estudiante
[estood-yantay]
stupid estúpido [estoopeedo]
suburb el suburbio [sooboorb-yo]
subway (US) el metro
suddenly de repente
[repentay]
sugar el azúcar [athookar]
suit el traje [traHay]
suitcase la maleta [malayta]
summer el verano [bairano]
in the summer en el verano
sun el sol
in the sun en el sol
sunblock la crema protectora
[krayma]
sunburn la quemadura de sol
[kemadoora]
sunglasses las gafas de sol
sunstroke la insolación
[eensolath-yon]
suntanned bronceado
suntan oil el aceite
bronceador [athay-eetay]
supermarket el

supermercado
[soopairmairkado]
supper la cena [thayna]
supplement (extra charge) el
suplemento
sure: are you sure? ¿está
seguro?
sure! ¡por supuesto¡
[soopwesto]
surname el apellido [apay-
yeedo]
sweater el suéter [swetair]
sweet (dessert) el postre
[postray]
(adj: taste) dulce [doolthay]
(sherry) oloroso
sweets los caramelos
[karamayloss]
swim nadar
I'm going for a swim voy a
nadar [boy]
swimming costume el
bañador [ban-yador]
swimming pool la piscina
[peestheena]
swimming trunks el traje de
baño [traHay day banyo]
switch el interruptor
[eentairrooptor]
switch off apagar
switch on encender
[enthendair]

T

table la mesa [maysa]
table wine el vino de mesa
[beeno day maysa]

take coger [koHair]
(accept) aceptar [atheptar]
fine, I'll take it está bien, lo
compro [b-yen]
a hamburger to take away
una hamburguesa para llevar
[yebar]
talk hablar [ablar]
tall alto
tampons los tampones
[tamponess]
tan el bronceado [bronthay-
ado]
tap el grifo
taste el sabor
taxi el taxi

dialogue

to the airport/to Hotel Sol
please al aeropuerto/al
hotel Sol, por favor
[a-airopwairto/otel]
how much will it be?
¿cuánto costará? [kwanto]
1,000 pesetas mil pesetas
[pesaytass]
that's fine, right here,
thanks está bien, aquí
mismo, gracias [b-yen akee
meesmo]

tea (drink) el té [tay]
teacher (primary) el maestro
[ma-estro]/la maestra
(secondary) el profesor/la
profesora
telephone el teléfono
[telayfono]

television la televisión [telebees-yon]
tell: could you tell him ...? ¿podría decirle ...? [detheerlay]
tennis el tenis
terrible terrible [terreeblay]
terrific fabuloso [fabooloso]
than que [kay]
thanks, thank you gracias [grath-yass]
thank you very much muchas gracias [moochass]
no thanks no gracias

dialogue

thanks gracias
that's OK, don't mention it no hay de qué [ī day kay]

that: that man ese hombre [aysay ombray]
that woman esa mujer [mooHair]
that one ése
that's nice (clothes, souvenir etc) es bonito
is that ...? ¿es ése ...? [aysay]
the el, la; (pl) los, las
theatre el teatro [tay-atro]
their su; (pl) sus [sooss]
theirs su, sus; (pl) suyos [soo-yoss], suyas; de ellos [day ay-yoss], de ellas
them (things) los, las (people) les
for them para ellos [ay-yoss]/ellas

who? – them ¿quién? – ellos/ellas [k-yen]
then entonces [entonthess]
there allí [a-yee]
is/are there ...? ¿hay ...? [ī]
there is/are ... hay ...
there you are (giving something) aquí tiene [akee t-yaynay]
these estos/estas
which ones? – these ¿cuáles? – éstos/éstas
they ellos [ay-yoss], f ellas [ay-yass]
thick grueso [grwayso]
thief el ladrón/la ladrona
thin delgado
thing la cosa
my things mis cosas [meess]
think pensar
I'll think about it lo pensaré [pensaray]
thirsty: I'm thirsty tengo sed [seth]
this: this man este hombre [estay]
this woman esta mujer
this one éste/ésta
is this ...? ¿es éste/ésta ...?
those aquellos/aquellas [akay-yoss]
which ones? – those ¿cuáles? – aquéllos/aquéllas [kwaless]
thread el hilo [eelo]
throat la garganta
through a través de [day]
thumb el dedo pulgar [daydo]
thunderstorm la tormenta
ticket el billete [bee-yaytay]

483

dialogue

a return to Salamanca un billete de ida y vuelta a Salamanca [day **ee**da ee b**wel**ta]
coming back when? ¿cuándo piensa volver? [kwando p-yensa bolb**air**]
today/next Tuesday hoy/el martes que viene [oy/el martess kay b-ya**ynay**]
that will be 2,000 pesetas son dos mil pesetas [pes**ay**tass]

tie (necktie) la corbata
tights los panties
time el tiempo [t-y**em**po]
  what's the time? ¿qué hora es? [kay **o**ra]
  next time la próxima vez
  four times cuatro veces [b**eth**ess]
timetable el horario [or**ar**-yo]
tin (can) la lata
tin opener el abrelatas
tip (to waiter etc) la propina
tired cansado
tissues los Kleenex®
to: to Barcelona/England a Barcelona/Inglaterra
  to the post office a la oficina de Correos
toast (bread) la tostada
today hoy [oy]
toe el dedo del pie [**day**do del p-yay]
together junto [H**oon**to]

toilet los servicios [sairb**eeth**-yoss]
toilet paper el papel higiénico [eeH-**yay**neeko]
tomato el tomate [tom**a**tay]
tomorrow mañana [man-**ya**na]
  tomorrow morning mañana por la mañana
  the day after tomorrow pasado mañana
tonic (water) la tónica
tonight esta noche [**no**chay]
too (excessively) demasiado [demass-**ya**do]
  (also) también [tamb-**yen**]
  too much demasiado
  me too yo también
tooth el diente [d-y**en**tay]
toothache el dolor de muelas [day mw**ay**lass]
toothbrush el cepillo de dientes [theep**ee**-yo day d-y**en**tess]
toothpaste la pasta de dientes
top: on top of ... encima de ... [enth**ee**ma day]
  at the top en lo alto
torch la linterna [leent**air**na]
tour el viaje [b-ya**Hay**]
tourist el/la turista
tourist information office la oficina de información turística [ofeeth**ee**na day eenformath-y**on**]
towards hacia [**ath**-ya]
towel la toalla [to-**a**-ya]
town la ciudad [th-y**oo**da]
  in town en el centro [th**en**tro]

town centre el centro de la ciudad
toy el juguete [Hoog**ay**tay]
track (US: at station) el andén
traffic lights los semáforos
train el tren
  by train en tren
  is this the train for ...? ¿es éste el tren para ...? [**e**stay]
train station la estación de trenes [estath-y**o**n day tr**ay**ness]
translate traducir [trad**ootheer**]
trashcan el cubo de la basura [k**oo**bo day la bas**oo**ra]
travel viajar [b-ya**H**ar]
travel agent's la agencia de viajes [a**H**enth-ya day b-ya**H**ess]
traveller's cheque el cheque de viaje [ch**ay**kay day b-ya**H**ay]
tree el árbol
trip (excursion) la excursión [eskoors-y**o**n]
trousers los pantalones [pantal**o**ness]
true verdadero [bairdad**ai**ro]
try intentar
try on probar
T-shirt la camiseta [kamees**ay**ta]
tuna el atún [at**oo**n]
tunnel el túnel [**too**nel]
turn: turn left/right gire a la izquierda/derecha [**H**ee**r**ay]
twice dos veces [b**ay**thess]
twin room la habitación doble [abeetath-y**o**n d**o**blay]
tyre la rueda [rw**ay**da]

U

umbrella el paraguas [para**g**wass]
uncle el tío
under (in position) debajo de [deba**H**o day]
  (less than) menos de [**may**noss]
underground (railway) el metro
underpants los calzoncillos [kalthonth**ee**-yoss]
understand: I understand lo entiendo [ent-y**e**ndo]
  I don't understand no entiendo
university la universidad [ooneebairs**ee**da]
unleaded petrol la gasolina sin plomo [gasol**ee**na seen]
until hasta que [**a**sta kay]
up arriba
  up there allí arriba [a-y**ee**]
upstairs arriba
urgent urgente [oor**H**entay]
us: for us para nosotros
USA EE.UU., Estados Unidos [oon**ee**doss]
use usar [**oo**sar]
useful útil [**oo**teel]

V

vacation las vacaciones [bakath-y**o**ness]
valid (ticket etc) válido [b**a**leedo]
value el valor

485

vanilla vainilla [ba-eenee-ya]

veal la ternera [tairnaira]

vegetables las verduras [bairdoorass]

vegetarian el vegetariano [beHetar-yano]/la vegetariana

very muy [mwee]

I like it very much me gusta mucho [may goosta moocho]

view la vista [beesta]

village el pueblo [pwayblo]

visit visitar [beeseetar]

vodka el vodka [bodka]

voice la voz [both]

W

waist la cintura [theentoora]

wait esperar [espairar]

waiter el camarero [kamarairo]

waiter! ¡camarero!

waitress la camarera [kamaraira]

waitress! ¡señorita! [sen-yoreeta]

wake-up call la llamada para despertar [yamada]

Wales Gales [galess]

walk: is it a long walk? ¿se tarda mucho en llegar andando? [say – moocho en yegar]

wall (inside) la pared [paray] (outside) la tapia

wallet la billetera [bee-yetaira]

want: I want a ... quiero un/una ... [k-yairo]

I don't want any ... no quiero

ninguno/ninguna ...

I don't want ... no quiero ...

what do you want? ¿qué quiere? [kay]

warm caliente [kal-yentay]

wash lavar [labar] (oneself) lavarse [-say]

washhand basin el lavabo [lababo]

washing (clothes) la ropa sucia [sooth-ya]

washing machine la lavadora [labadora]

washing powder el detergente [detairHentay]

wasp la avispa [abeespa]

watch (wristwatch) el reloj [rayloH]

water el agua [agwa]

way: it's this way es por aquí [akee]

it's that way es por allí [a-yee]

is it a long way to ...? ¿queda lejos...? [kayda layHoss]

no way! ¡de ninguna manera! [day – manaira]

dialogue

could you tell me the way to ...? podría indicarme el camino a ...? [eendeekarmay]
go straight on until you reach the traffic lights siga recto hasta llegar al semáforo [asta yegar]
turn left gire a la

izquierda [**H**eeray]
take the first on the right
tome la primera a la
derecha [**to**may]

we nosotros, nosotras
weather el tiempo [t-y**e**mpo]
week la semana
 a week (from) today dentro
 de una semana [**d**ay]
weekend el fin de semana
 [feen]
weight el peso [**pay**so]
welcome: you're welcome
 (don't mention it) de nada [**d**ay]
well: she's not well no se
 siente bien [say s-y**e**ntay b-y**e**n]
 you speak English very well
 habla inglés muy bien [**a**bla
 – mwee]
 well done! ¡bravo! [**br**abo]
 this one as well éste también
 [**e**stay tamb-y**e**n]
well-done (meat) muy hecho
 [mwee **ay**cho]
Welsh galés [gal**ay**ss]
west el oeste [o-**e**stay]
wet mojado [mo**H**ado]
what? ¿qué? [kay]
 what's that? ¿qué es eso?
 [**ay**so]
wheel la rueda [rw**ay**da]
when? ¿cuándo? [kw**a**ndo]
 when's the train/ferry?
 ¿cuándo es el tren/ferry?
where? ¿dónde? [**d**onday]
which: which bus? ¿qué
 autobús? [kay]
while: while I'm here mientras

esté aquí [m-y**e**ntrass est**ay**
 ak**ee**]
whisky el whisky
white blanco
white wine el vino blanco
 [**bee**no]
who? ¿quién? [k-y**e**n]
whole: the whole week toda la
 semana
whose: whose is this? ¿de
 quién es esto? [day k-y**e**n]
why? ¿por qué? [kay]
 why not? ¿por qué no?
wide ancho
wife la mujer [moo**H**air]
wind el viento [b-y**e**nto]
window la ventana [bent**a**na]
 (of ticket office, vehicle) la
 ventanilla [bentan**ee**-ya]
 in the window (of shop) en el
 escaparate [escapar**a**tay]
wine el vino [**bee**no]
wine list la lista de vinos
 [**lee**sta day bee**no**ss]
winter el invierno [eemb-
 y**air**no]
with con
without sin [seen]
woman la mujer [moo**H**air]
wood (material) la madera
 [mad**air**a]
wool la lana
word la palabra
work el trabajo [trab**a**Ho]
 it's not working no funciona
 [foonth-y**o**na]
worry: I'm worried estoy
 preocupado/preocupada
 [pray-okoop**a**do]

worse: it's worse es peor [pay-or]

worst el peor

would: would you give this to ...? ¿le puede dar esto a ...? [lay pwayday]

wrap: could you wrap it up? ¿me lo envuelve? [may lo embwelbay]

wrist la muñeca [moon-yayka]

write escribir [eskreebeer]
could you write it down? ¿puede escribírmelo? [pwayday]

wrong: it's the wrong key no es ésa la llave [aysa la yabay]
there's something wrong with ... le pasa algo a ... [lay]
what's wrong? ¿qué pasa? [kay]

Y

year el año [an-yo]
yellow amarillo [amaree-yo]
yes sí
yesterday ayer [a-yair]
the day before yesterday anteayer [antay-ayair]
yet
you (fam, sing) tú [too]
(pol, sing) usted [oostay]
(fam, pl) vosotros [bosotross]
(pol, pl) ustedes [oostaydess]
this is for you esto es para tí/usted
young joven [Hoben]
your (fam, sing) tu; (pl) tus

[tooss]
(fam, pl) vuestro [bwestro], vuestra; (pl) vuestros, vuestras
(polite, sing) su; (pl) sus [sooss]

yours (fam, sing) tuyo [too-yo], tuya
(fam pl) vuestro [bwestro], vuestra
(polite, sing) suyo [soo-yo], suya; de usted [day oostay]

youth hostel el albergue juvenil [albairgay Hoobayneel]

Z

zero cero [thairo]
zip la cremallera [krema-yaira]
zoo el zoo(lógico) [tho(loHeeko)]

Spanish → English

a to; at; per; from
abajo [aba**H**o] downstairs
abierto [ab-y**ai**rto] open
abogado m/f lawyer
abonos mpl season tickets
ábrase aquí open here
abrir to open
acabar to finish
 acabo de ... I have just ...
acceso prohibido no
 admittance
acerca de [ath**ai**rka day] about,
 concerning
adelantar to overtake
adentro inside
adiós [ad-y**o**ss] goodbye
aduana f [ad-w**a**na] customs
agencia de viajes [a-**H**enth-ya
 day b-ya**H**ess] travel agency
agua f [**a**gwa] water
ahora [a-**o**ra] now
albergue m [alb**ai**rgay] country
 hotel; hostel
albergue juvenil [Hooben**ee**l]
 youth hostel
Alemania f [aleman-ya]
 Germany
alfombra f rug; carpet
algo something
algodón m cotton; cotton
 wool, absorbent cotton
alguien [**a**lg-yen] somebody;
 anybody
algún, alguno some; any
allá: más allá [a-y**a**] further
allí [a-y**ee**] there
almacén m [alma**th**en]
 department store;
 warehouse

almuerzo m [alm**wai**rtho] lunch
alojamiento m [aloHam-y**e**nto]
 accommodation
alquilar [alkeel**a**r] to rent; to
 hire
alquiler de coches [k**o**chess]
 car rental
alrededor (de) [alray-day-d**o**r]
 around
alto high; tall
¡alto! stop!
amarillo [amar**ee**-yo] yellow
ambos both
amiga f friend
amigo m friend
amor m love
ancho wide
andar to walk
andén m platform, (US) track
anoche last night
anteayer [antay-a-y**ai**r] the day
 before yesterday
antes de before
anulado cancelled
año m [**a**n-yo] year
apague el motor switch off
 your engine
aparcamiento privado private
 parking
aparecer [aparet**hai**r] to appear
apellido m [apay-y**ee**do]
 surname
aquel [ak**e**l] that
aquél that (one)
aquí [ak**ee**] here
árbol m tree
arena f [ar**ay**na] sand
arriba up; upstairs; on top
ascensor m [asthens**o**r] lift,

elevator

aseos mpl [asay-oss] toilets, rest room

así like this; like that

atención [atenth-yon] please note; caution

atrás at the back; behind

aun even

aún [a-oon] still; yet

aunque [a-oonkay] although

avería f [abairee-a] breakdown

averiado out of order

avión m [ab-yon] aeroplane

ayer [a-yair] yesterday

ayuda f [a-yooda] help

ayuntamiento m [ayoontam-yento] town hall

azul [athool] blue

bajo [baHo] low; short; under(neath)

bañarse [ban-yarsay] to go swimming; to have a bath

baño m [ban-yo] bathroom; bath

barato cheap, inexpensive

barco m boat

barrio m [barr-yo] district, area

bastante [bastantay] enough

bastante más quite a lot more

basura f litter

beber [bebair] to drink

bello [bay-yo] beautiful

bien [b-yen] well

  ¡**bien!** good!

  bien ... bien either ... or ...

¡**bienvenido!** welcome!

billete m [bee-yaytay] ticket

billete de ida single ticket, one-way ticket

billete de ida y vuelta [bwelta] return ticket, round trip ticket

blanco white

boca f mouth

bodega f [bodayga] wine cellar; wine bar

bolsa f bag; stock exchange

bomberos mpl [bombaiross] fire brigade

botella f [botay-ya] bottle

buceo m [boothay-o] skin-diving

¡**buenas!** [bwaynass] hello!

bueno [bwayno] good; good-natured

buscar to look for

buzón [boothon] letter box, mail box

c/ (calle) street

caballeros mpl [kaba-yaiross] gents, men's rest room

caballo m [kaba-yo] horse

cabello m [kabay-yo] hair

cabeza f [kabetha] head

cada every

caduca ... expires ...

cafetería f cafe

caja f [kaHa] cash desk

caja de ahorros [a-orross] savings bank

cajero automático [owtomateeko] cash dispenser, ATM

calle f [ka-yay] street

calle de dirección única

[deerekth-yon] one-way street
calor m heat
cama f bed
cama de matrimonio double bed
cama individual single bed
camarero m waiter
cambiar [kamb-yar] to change
cambio m change; exchange; exchange rate
camino m path
camión m lorry, truck
cansado tired
caña f [kan-ya] small glass of beer
cara f face
caro expensive
carretera f [karretaira] road
carterista m pickpocket
casa f house
casa de huéspedes [wespedess] boarding house
casado married
casi almost
cena f [thayna] dinner
cerca de [thairka] near
cerrado [thairrado] closed
CH (casa de huespedes) f [wespedess] boarding house, low-price hostel
cheque de viaje m [chaykay day b-yaHay] travellers' cheque
chica f girl
chico m boy
cinturón de seguridad m seat belt
circulación f [theerkoolath-yon] traffic; circulation
ciudad f [thee-oo-da] town,
city
climatizado [-thado] air-conditioned
coche m [kochay] car
coche-cama m sleeper, sleeping car
coche comedor dining car
coche de línea [leenay-a] long-distance bus
cocina f [kotheena] kitchen; cooker
coger [koHair] to catch; to take
comedor m dining room
comer [komair] to eat
comida f lunch; food; meal
comisaría f police station
como as; like
¿cómo? pardon?; how?
completo full, no vacancies
comprar to buy
comprender [komprendair] to understand
con with
conducir [kondootheer] to drive
conductor m, **conductora** f driver
conmigo with me
conocer [konothair] to know
consigna f [konseeg-na] left luggage, baggage check
consigo with himself; with herself; with yourself; with themselves; with yourselves
consúmase antes de ... best before ...
contado: pagar al contado to pay cash
contenido m contents

contestar to reply, to answer
contigo with you
contra against
copa f glass
corazón m [korathon] heart
correo m [korray-o] mail
correos m post office
correr [korrair] to run
corrida de toros f bullfight
corto short
cosa f thing
costar to cost
creer [kray-air] to believe
cruce m [kroothay] junction,
  intersection; crossing;
  crossroads
cuadro m [kwadro] painting
cual [kwal] which; who
¿cuándo? [kwando] when?
¿cuánto? [kwanto] how
  much?
  en cuanto... as soon as...
¿cuántos? how many?
cuarto (m) [kwarto] quarter;
  fourth; room
cubierto (m) covered;
  overcast; meal
cuchara f spoon
cuchillo m [koochee-yo] knife
cuello m [kway-yo] neck;
  collar
cuero m [kwairo] leather
cuerpo m [kwairpo] body
cuidado (m) [kweedado] take
  care; look out; care
cumpleaños m [koomplay-an-
  yoss] birthday
cura m priest

damas fpl ladies' toilet,
  ladies' restroom
daños mpl [dan-yoss] damage
dar to give
dcha. (derecha) right
de of; from
debajo de [debaHo] under
decir [detheer] to say; to tell
dedo m [daydo] finger
dejar [dayHar] to leave; to let
delante de [delantay] in front
  of
demás: los demás the others
demasiado [demass-yado] too
demasiados too many
demora f delay
dentro (de) inside
derecha f right
derecho: todo derecho
  straight ahead
desayuno m [desa-yoono]
  breakfast
descuelgue el auricular lift
  the receiver
desde (que) [desday] since
desde luego [lwaygo] of
  course
desear [desay-ar] to want; to
  wish
despachador automático m
  ticket machine
despacho de billetes m [bee-
  yaytess] ticket office
despacio [despath-yo] slowly
después [despwess] afterwards
desviación f [desb-yath-yon]
  diversion
desvío m [desbee-o] detour,
  diversion

detrás (de) behind
día m [dee-a] day
día festivo public holiday
días azules [athooless] cheap travel days
días laborables weekdays
diente m [d-yentay] tooth
difícil [deefeetheel] difficult
dígame [deegamay] hello, yes
Dios m [dee-oss] God
dirección f [deerekth-yon] direction; address; steering; management
dirección única one-way traffic
dirección prohibida no entry
divisas fpl foreign currency
doble [doblay] double
doler [dolair] to hurt
dolor m pain
don Mr
donde [donday] where
doña [don-ya] Miss; Mrs
dormir to sleep
ducha f shower
durante [doorantay] during

e and
edad f age
educado polite
EE.UU. (Estados Unidos) USA
efectivo: en efectivo in cash
el the
él he; him
ella [ay-ya] she; her
ellas they; them
ellos they; them
embajada f [embaHada] embassy

en in; at; on; by
encima [entheema] above
enfadado angry
enfermedad f [enfairmeda] disease
enfermo [enfairmo] ill
enfrente de [enfrentay] opposite
enseñar [ensen-yar] to teach
entender [entendair] to understand
entero [entairo] whole
entonces [entonthess] then; therefore
entrada f entrance, way in; ticket
entre [entray] among; between
enviar [emb-yar] to send
equipaje m [ekeepaHay] luggage, baggage
equipajes mpl left-luggage office, (US) baggage check
equipo m [ekeepo] team
equivocado [ekeebokado] wrong
eres you are
es he is; you are
ésa [aysa] that one
esa that
ésas those ones
esas those
escribir to write
ése [aysay] that one
ese that
eso [ayso] that
  eso es that's it, that's right
ésos those ones
esos those

español (m) [espan-yol] Spanish; Spaniard

esperar [espairar] to wait; to hope

esposa f wife

esposo m husband

esquí m [eskee] ski; skiing

esta this

ésta this one

estacionamiento limitado restricted parking

estar to be

estas these

éstas these ones

este m [estay] east

este this

éste this one

esto this

estos these

éstos these ones

estoy I am

estropear [estropay-ar] to damage

exprés m slow night train stopping at all stations

extranjero (m) [estranHairo] foreign; abroad; overseas; foreigner

fábrica f factory

fácil [fatheel] easy

facturación f [faktoorath-yon] check-in

falta f lack; mistake; defect; fault

favor [fabor]: por favor please

fecha f date

fecha de caducidad [kadootheeda] expiry date

fecha de nacimiento [natheem-yento] date of birth

fecha límite de venta sell-by date

feliz [feleeth] happy

feo [fay-o] ugly

ferretería f [fairraytairee-a] hardware store

festivos bank holidays, public holidays

fiesta f public holiday; party

fiesta nacional [nath-yonal] bullfighting

fin m [feen] end; purpose

fin de semana weekend

final de autopista end of motorway/highway

firma f signature; company

firmar to sign

firme deslizante slippery surface

fondo m bottom; background

frío [free-o] cold

frontera f [frontaira] border

frutería f fruit shop/store; greengrocer

fuego m [fwaygo] fire

fuera de servicio out of order

fuerte [fwairtay] strong; loud

fumadores smoking

gasóleo m [gasolay-o] diesel

gasolinera f [gasoleenaira] petrol/gas station, filling station

gente f [Hentay] people

gerente m [Hairentay] manager

gobierno m [gob-yairno]

government
gracias [grath-yass] thank you
gracioso [grath-yoso] funny
grande [granday] big, large
grandes almacenes mpl
  [almathayness] large
  department store
guapo [gwapo] handsome
guardarropa m [gwardarropa]
  cloakroom, checkroom
guardia civil m/f [gward-ya
  theebeel] police;
  policeman/policewoman
guerra f [gairra] war
guía m/f [gee-a] guide

ha he/she/it has; you have
habéis [abay-eess] you have
habitación f [abeetath-yon]
  room
habitar to live
hablar to speak
hace [athay]: **hace ... días** ...
  days ago
hacer [athair] to make; to do
hacerse [athairsay] to become
hacia [ath-ya] towards
han [an] they have; you have
has [ass] you have
hasta [asta] even; until
hay [ī] there is; there are
he [ay] I have
heladería f [eladairee-a] ice-
  cream parlour
helado f [elado] ice-cream
hemos we have
hermana f [airmano] sister
hermano m brother
hermoso [airmoso] beautiful

hielo m [yaylo] ice
hierba f [yairba] grass
hija f [eeHa] daughter
hijo m son
hombre m [ombray] man
hora f [ora] hour
horario de autobuses
  [owtoboosess] bus
  timetable/schedule
hostal m [ostal] restaurant
  specializing in regional
  dishes; boarding house
hostal-residencia m
  [reseedenth-ya] long-stay
  boarding house
hostería f [ostairee-a]
  restaurant specializing in
  regional dishes
hoy [oy] today
huésped m/f [wesped] guest
huevo m [waybo] egg

idioma m [eed-yoma] language
iglesia f [eeglays-ya] church
igual [eegwal] equal; like
importe m [eemportay] amount
incendio m [eenthend-yo] fire
Inglaterra f [eenglatairra]
  England
inglés (m) [een-glayss] English;
  Englishman
insolación f [eensolath-yon]
  sunstroke
intentar to try
invierno m [eemb-yairno]
  winter
ir to go
**IVA (impuesto sobre el valor
  añadido)** [eeba] VAT

lv

497

izq. (izquierda) left
izquierda f [eethk-yairda] left

jardines públicos [Hardeeness] park, public gardens
jefe m [Hayfay] boss
joven (m/f) [Hoben] young; young man; young woman
joyería f [Hoyairee-a] jewellery; jeweller's
juego (m) [Hwaygo] game; I play
junto (a) [Hoonto] next (to)
juntos together

la the; her; it
laborables [laborabless] weekdays, working days
lado m side
ladrón m thief
lago m lake
lana f wool
largo (m) length; long
las the; them; you
lástima: es una lástima it's a pity
lata f can; nuisance
lavabos toilets, rest room
lavar en seco dry clean
le [lay] him; her; you
leer [lay-air] to read
lejos [layHoss] far away
lento slow
les them; you
ley f [lay-ee] law
libra f pound
libre [leebray] free; vacant
librería f [leebrairee-a] bookshop, bookstore

libro m book
líder m [leedair] leader
limpieza en seco dry-cleaning
limpio [leemp-yo] clean
liquidación f [leekeedath-yon] sale
lista de correos [korray-oss] poste restante, (US) general delivery
llamada f [yamada] call
llave f [yabay] key; wrench
llegada f [yaygada] arrival
llegar [yegar] to arrive; to get to
lleno [yayno] full
llevar [yebar] to carry; to take; to bring; to give a lift to
lluvia f [yoob-ya] rain
lo it; the
loco (m) mad; madman
los the
luego [lwaygo] then
lugar m place
luz f [looth] light

madera f [madaira] wood
madre f [madray] mother
mal (m) badly; unwell, ill, sick; evil
mandar to send; to order
mano f hand
manténgase alejado de los niños keep out of the reach of children
mañana (f) [man-yana] morning; tomorrow
mañana por la mañana

tomorrow morning
marcharse [marcharsay] to go
away
marido m husband
marque ... dial ...
marrón brown
marroquinería f [marrokeen-
airee-a] fancy leather goods
más more
mayor [mayor] adult; bigger;
older; biggest; oldest
media pensión f [pens-yon]
half board, European plan
mejor [mayHor] best; better
menor [menor] smaller;
younger; smallest; youngest
menos [maynoss] less; fewest;
least
a menos que unless
menudo tiny, minute
a menudo often
mercado m market
mes m month
mesa f table
meta [mayta] goal
mí me
mi my
mía [mee-a] mine
mientras [m-yentrass] while
mío [mee-o] mine
mis my
mismo same
mitad f half
modo de empleo instructions
for use
molestar to disturb; to
bother
montaña f [montan-ya]
mountain

moreno [morayno] dark-haired
morir to die
mostrar to show
mozo m [motho] porter
muchacha f girl
muchacho m boy
mucho much; a lot; a lot of
muebles mpl [mwaybless]
furniture
muerte f [mwairtay] death
muerto [mwairto] dead
mujer f [mooHair] woman;
wife
multa f fine; parking ticket
mundo m world
muro m wall
muy [mwee] very

nacimiento m [natheem-yento]
birth
nada nothing
nadar to swim
nadie [nad-yay] nobody
naranja f [naranHa] orange
nariz f [nareeth] nose
natación f [natath-yon]
swimming
Navidad f Christmas
necesitar: necesito ...
[netheseeto] I need ...
negocio m [negoth-yo] business
negro black; furious
neumático m [nay-oomateeko]
tyre
ni ... ni ... neither ... nor ...
nieve f [n-yaybay] snow
ningún [neengoon] nobody;
none; not one; no ...
niña f [neen-ya] child

niño m [neen-yo] child
no aparcar no parking
no fumadores no smoking
no funciona out of order
no pisar el césped keep off the grass
noche f [nochay] night
nombre m [nombray] name
nombre de pila first name
norte m [nortay] north
nos us; ourselves
nosotras, nosotros we; us
noticias fpl [noteeth-yass] news
nuestra [nwestra], nuestras, nuestro, nuestros our
nuevo new
nunca never

o or
o ... o ... either ... or ...
objetos perdidos lost property, lost and found
obras fpl roadworks
ocasión f [okass-yon] occasion; opportunity; bargain
de ocasión second hand
oeste m [o-estay] west
oficina f [ofeetheena] office
oír [o-eer] to hear
ojo m [oHo] eye
olvidar to forget
ordenador m computer
oreja f [oray-Ha] ear
oro m gold
os you; to you
otoño m [oton-yo] autumn, (US) fall
otra vez [bayth] again
otro another (one); other

padre m [padray] father
padres mpl parents
pagar to pay
página f [paHeena] page
país m [pa-eess] country
palabra f word
pan m bread
panadería f [panadairee-a] baker's
papel m [papel] paper; rôle
para for; in order to
para que [kay] in order that
parada f stop
parador m hotel restaurant; luxury hotel
parar to stop
parecer [parethair] to seem; to resemble
parecido [paretheedo] similar
pared f [parayd] wall
partido m match
pasado last
pasaje m [pasaHay] plane ticket
pasajero m [pasaHairo] passenger
pasen enter; cross, walk
peaje m [pay-aHay] toll
peatón m [pay-aton] pedestrian
pedir to order; to ask for
película f film, movie
peligro deslizamientos slippery road surface
peligroso dangerous
pelo m [paylo] hair
pelota f ball
peluquería f [pelookairee-a] hairdresser's

pensar to think
pensión completa [komplayta] full board, American plan
peor [pay-or] worse; worst
pequeño (m) [pekayn-yo] small; child
perder [pairdair] to lose; to miss
pero [pairo] but
perro m [pairro] dog
pesado heavy
peso m [payso] weight
pez m [peth] fish
pie m [p-yay] foot
pierna f [p-yairna] leg
pila f battery; pile
piscina f [peestheena] swimming pool
piso m floor; flat, apartment
piso bajo [baHo] ground floor, (US) first floor
plano (m) flat; map
planta sótano basement
plata f silver
plato m plate; dish; course
playa f [pla-ya] beach
plaza f [platha] square; seat
plaza de toros bullring
población f [poblath-yon] village; town; population
pobre [pobray] poor
poco little
pocos few
poder (m) [podair] to be able to; power
poner [ponair] to put
poquito: un poquito [pokeeto] a little bit
por by; through; for

por allí [a-yee] over there
por qué [kay] why
por favor please
porque [porkay] because
portátil [portateel] portable
posada f inn
postal f postcard
precio m [preth-yo] price
precioso [preth-yoso] beautiful; precious
prefijo m [prefeeHo] dialling code, area code
pregunta f question
preguntar to ask
prensa f press; newspapers
primavera f [preemabaira] spring
primero first
principio m [preentheep-yo] beginning
prioridad a la derecha give way/yield to vehicles coming from your right
probar to try
prohibido [pro-eebeedo] prohibited, forbidden; no
prohibido cambiar de sentido no U-turns
pronto soon
pueblo m [pweblo] village; people
puedo [pwaydo] I can
puente m [pwentay] bridge
puerta f [pwairta] door; gate
pues [pwayss] since; so
puro m cigar

que [kay] who; that; which; than

quedarse con to keep
querer [ker**air**] to love; to want
querido [kair**ee**do] dear
¿quién? [k-yen] who?
quizá(s) [k**ee**tha(ss)] maybe

razón f [rath**on**] reason; rate
rea sale
rebajas fpl [reba**H**ass] reductions, sale
recado m message
recibo m [reth**ee**bo] receipt
recién [reth-yen] recently
recién pintado wet paint
reclamaciones fpl [reklamath-**yo**ness] complaints
recorrido m journey
red f network; net
reembolsar [ray-embols**ar**] to refund
regalo m present
reina f [**ray**-eena] queen
Reino Unido m United Kingdom
reír [ray-**eer**] to laugh
repuestos mpl [rep**wes**toss] spare parts
resbaladizo [resbalad**ee**tho] slippery
retrasado late
retraso m delay
retrete m [re**tray**tay] toilets, rest rooms
rey m [ray] king
rico rich
rincón m corner
río m [**ree**-o] river
rojo [**ro**Ho] red

romper to break
ropa f clothes
roto broken
rueda f [**rway**da] wheel

S.A. (Sociedad Anónima) PLC, Inc
saber [sab**air**] to know
sala de espera [esp**air**a] waiting room
saldos sales
salida f exit; departure
salida ciudad take this direction to leave the city
salida de autopista end of motorway/highway; motorway exit
salud f [sal**oo**] health
saludos best wishes
sangre f [**san**gray] blood
sastre m [**sas**tray] tailor
se [say] himself; herself; itself; yourself; themselves; yourselves; oneself
se alquila for hire, to rent
se prohibe ... ... forbidden
se ruega please ...
se ruega no ... please do not ...
se vende for sale
seco dry
seda f silk
seguir [seg**eer**] to follow
según according to
seguro (m) safe; sure; insurance
sello m [**say**-yo] stamp
semana f week
sentido m direction; sense;

meaning

señor [sen-yor] gentleman, man; sir

señora f [sen-yora] lady, woman; madam

señorita f [sen-yoreeta] young lady, young woman; miss

ser [sair] to be

servicio m [sairbeeth-yo] service; toilet

si [see] if

sí [see] yes; oneself; herself; itself; yourself; themselves; yourselves; each other

SIDA m AIDS

siempre [s-yempray] always

siento: lo siento I'm sorry

siglo m century

silla f [see-ya] chair

sin [seen] without

sino but

sin plomo unleaded

sírvase [seerbasay] please

sírvase frío serve cold

sitio m [seet-yo] place

sobre (m) [sobray] envelope; on; above

sois [soyss] you are

sol m sun

solamente [solamentay] only

solo alone

sólo only

somos we are

son they are; you are

sótano m basement

soy [soy] I am

su [soo] his; her; its; their; your

sucio [sooth-yo] dirty

Suiza f [sweetha] Switzerland

sur m south

sus [sooss] his; her; its; their; your

suyo [soo-yo] his; hers; its; theirs; yours

tal such

talla f [ta-ya] size

tal vez [bayth] maybe

tamaño m [taman-yo] size

también [tamb-yen] also

tampoco neither, nor

tan so

tancat closed (in Catalan)

tanto (m) so much; point

tarde (f) [tarday] afternoon; evening; late

tarjeta f [tarнayta] card

taza f [tatha] cup

te [tay] you; yourself

telesilla m [telesee-ya] chairlift

temprano early

tener [tenair] to have

tener que [kay] to have to

ti [tee] you

tía f [tee-a] aunt; bird, woman

tiempo m [t-yempo] time; weather

tienda f [t-yenda] shop, store; tent

tío m [tee-o] uncle; bloke, guy

tirar to pull; to throw; to throw away

tocar to touch; to play

todavía [todabee-a] still; yet

todo all; every; everything

todo seguido [segeedo]

straight ahead
todos everyone
tomar to take
toro m bull
trabajar [trabajar] to work
trabajo m [trabaHo] work
traducir [tradootheer] to translate
traer [tra-air] to bring
tras after
tren m [tren] train
trozo (de) m [trotho (day)] piece (of)
tu [too] your
tú [too] you
tus [tooss] your
tuyo [tooyo] yours

u [oo] or
Ud (usted) [oostay] you (sing)
Uds (ustedes) [oostaydess] you (pl)
un [oon] a
una [oona] a
unas some
uno one; someone
unos some; a few
Usted [oostay] you
Ustedes [oostaydess] you

vale [balay] OK
vaso m glass
Vd (usted) [oostay] you (sing)
Vds (ustedes) you (pl)
vender [bendair] to sell
venir to come
venta f sale
ventana f window
ver [bair] to see; to watch

verdad f [bairda] truth
¿verdad? don't you?; do you?; isn't he?; is he? etc
verde [bairday] green
vez f [bayth] time
viajar [b-yaHar] to travel
viaje m [b-yaHay] journey
vida f life
viejo [b-yayHo] old
vivir to live
volver [bolbair] to come back
volver a hacer algo to do something again
vosotras, vosotros you
vuelo m [bwaylo] flight
vuelta f [bwelta] change
vuestra [bwestra], **vuestras, vuestro, vuestros** your; yours

wáter [batair] toilet, rest room

y [ee] and
ya already
yo I; me

zapatería f [thapatairee-a] shoe shop/store
zona azul [athool] restricted parking area, permit holders only